The Official ECB Guide to
Cricket Grounds

William A. Powell

Happy Birthday
Dad, Have a
lovely '66th',
all my Love
Karla

SUTTON PUBLISHING

in association with the England and Wales Cricket Board

First published in the United Kingdom in 2003 by
Sutton Publishing · Phoenix Mill · Thrupp · Stroud
Gloucestershire · GL5 2BU

British Library Cataloguing in Publication Data

ISBN 0-7509-3084-5

Library of Congress Cataloging in Publication Data applied for

Cover picture:The Grandstand, Lord's, © Graham Morris.
All pictures inside the book were taken by the author unless
otherwise credited.

Dedicated to
Ella Francesca May

While every effort has been made to ensure that the information given in this book
is accurate, the publishers, the author and the England and Wales Cricket Board
do not accept responsibility for any errors or omissions or for any changes in the
details given in this guide or for the consequences of any reliance on the information
provided. The publishers would be grateful if readers would advise them of any
inaccuracies they may encounter so these can be considered for future
editions of the guide.
The inclusion of any place to stay, place to eat, tourist attraction or other
establishment in this guide does not imply an endorsement or recommendation by
the England and Wales Cricket Board, the publisher or the author.
Their details are included for information only. Directions to grounds are for guidance
only and should be used in conjunction with other sources of information.

Typeset in 9/11pt Helvetica
Typesetting and origination by
Sutton Publishing
Printed and bound in England by
J.H. Haynes & Co. Ltd, Sparkford

CONTENTS

ECB

FOREWORD

I WRITE the foreword to this book while watching the 2002 Ashes Test Match at the Adelaide Oval, surely one of the most beautiful international grounds in the world. There are few better pleasures in life than watching top quality cricket in such picturesque and relaxing surroundings!

In the UK we are blessed in having an abundance of wonderful cricket grounds, each of which offers its own set of unique characteristics and charms. Everyone will have their own favourites and I hope readers of this book will find the detailed individual ground guides both informative and useful.

A constant requirement across all grounds, of course, is the need for cricket to offer its customers, both members and the paying public, the services, facilities and quality of 'spectator experience' which they deserve. It is an issue that the ECB, the first-class counties and the MCC have been addressing at first-class county and Test match grounds and this has led to significant improvements at venues all over the country.

In recent years we have witnessed the construction of the large and impressive Radcliffe Road Stand and the new Fox Road Stand at Trent Bridge; at Headingley the old Western Terrace has been torn down and rebuilt, and in the summer of 2002 the new East Stand was opened; the Eric Hollies Stand at Edgbaston was similarly rebuilt, following a highly successful bid for finance from Sport England's 'Safer Sports Grounds Scheme'.

The dedicated work of the MCC continues to ensure Lord's is as popular as ever amongst spectators and players alike, and Surrey CCC is due to embark on a major re-development of The AMP Oval to increase the capacity from 18,500 to 23,000.

All these developments have led to considerable improvements in areas such as spectator comfort, viewing and safety, which are of paramount importance as we strive to continue to attract still larger audiences to both international and county cricket.

Some of the biggest changes have arguably taken place amongst emerging international grounds. Durham's Chester-le-Street not only has a wonderful backdrop in Lumley Castle but also an impressive main stand with excellent facilities and big plans for the future. Hampshire's Rose Bowl, meanwhile, has been perhaps the most exciting single county ground development in the past few years.

Whether it be Canterbury or Worcester, Arundel or Colwyn Bay every ground has its special allure and fascination. I congratulate William Powell on his painstaking work in compiling *The Official ECB Guide to Cricket Grounds* and I wish you an enjoyable read.

David Morgan
Chairman
England and Wales Cricket Board

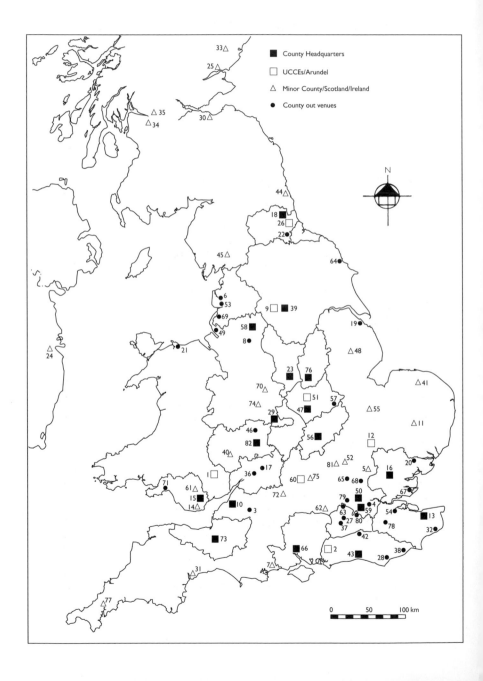

County Headquarters ■
UCCEs/Arundel □
Minor County/Scotland/Ireland △
County out venues ●

LIST OF GROUNDS

THE GROUND PLANS

ALL GROUND plans are diagrammatic and are to an approximate scale of 1:2200. Every attempt has been made to include as much information as possible within the space available.

When defining seating areas, covered seating has taken preference over open seating in those areas where open seating is banked above covered seating, for example at the major Test match grounds. Executive boxes and similar restricted covered areas have also been defined as covered seating.

Toilets situated in separate buildings have been defined on the plans, but additional toilets are to be found within most of the areas of tiered seating and in other permanent buildings. Similarly, the refreshment and restaurant facilities are usually to be found in the existing permanent buildings or in temporary accommodation specially provided on match days.

The areas available to the public and to club members are clearly defined at all the county grounds, but at local club grounds and other venues which are only used on one or a few days each year arrangements may vary from match to match and from year to year.

Special arrangements apply at the seven Test match grounds and the other venues used for one-day internationals and at any other grounds where reserved numbered seat tickets and car park tickets are sold in advance.

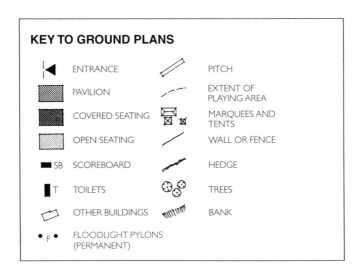

KEY TO GROUND RECORDS AND SCORES

(B&H)	Benson and Hedges Cup Competition (1972–2002)
(C&G)	Cheltenham & Gloucester Trophy (2001–2)
(ECB38)	ECB 38 Counties
(Emir)	Emirates Triangular Tournament (1998)
(F)	Friendly
(GC)	Gillette Cup (1963–80)
(MCCA KO)	Minor Counties CA Knock-out
(NWS)	NatWest Series (2000–2)
(NWT)	NatWest Bank Trophy (1981–2000)
(PT)	Prudential Trophy (1972–82)
(RAC)	Refuge Assurance Cup (1990)
(SL)	Sunday League (incorporating all Sunday League and National Cricket League competitions 1969–2002)
(Tour)	Tour Match
(TT)	Texaco Trophy (1984–98)
(WC)	World Cup Competition (1975, 1979, 1983, 1999)
(WCF)	World Cup Friendly (1999)
*	Not out or unfinished

Statistics for all grounds have been provided by Victor H. Isaacs, Hampshire Cricket Official Scorer and Statistician.

ACKNOWLEDGEMENTS

I AM GRATEFUL to the England and Wales Cricket Board for allowing me to collaborate with them in the production of this fully revised and updated edition of my guide to cricket grounds.

I am indebted to the following who have assisted with this work namely: Tim Lamb, David Morgan, John Read, Richard Kaye, Clare Fathers, John Smedley, James Bailey, David Harker, David East, Nancy Fuller, Mike Fatkin, Tom Richardson, Suzanne Finch, Graham Walker, Paul Millman, Bernard Thomson, Jim Cumbes, Ken Grime, James Whitaker, Kevin Hill, Tracey Mason, Vinny Codrington, Josh Fitch, Victoria Skelton, Daphne Short, Stephen Coverdale, Graham Alsop, David Collier, Lisa Pursehouse, Peter Anderson, Paul Sheldon, Carol Turner, Johnny Grave, Hugh Griffiths, Micky Stewart, Francesca Watson, Dennis Amiss, Keith Cook, Mark Newton, Joan Grundy, Colin Graves, Roger Knight, Stephen Parris, Philip August, Roy New, Kevin Beaumont, Victor Domaine, Peter Gooden, John Pickup, Anita George, Ken Ion, Geoff Evans, John Wood, Ken House, Peter Sykes, Brian Mulholland, Tony North, Stuart Skinner, Richard Jefferson, Alan Stephenson, Peter O'Neill, Andrew Moss, Neville Birch, Stuart Bourne, Toby Pound, Bill Edwards, Colin White, Richard Sula, Robert Barclay, Margaret McCullum, Steve Teasdale, John Wright, Tony Lemons, Chris Wood, Kevin Lyons, Mark Stear, Nikolas and Helen O'Neil, Peter Baverstock, Jamila and Peter W.G. Powell, Vic and Jill Lewis, Graeme Fowler, Dr Guy Jackson, John Roycroft, Brian Curthoys, Sohail Malik, Joshua Malik, Stephanie Lawrence, David J. Robertson, Tracey Stevenson, Gron Jones, Piers Jones, Grenville Holland, Kevin Lyons, Euan McIntyre, Mike Barclay, Gerald Byrne, Dixie and Lynda Harries, Norman de Mesquita, Peter Byrne, Shilpa Patel, Dora Hall-Newman, Jo King, Ted Corbett, Brian Fitzgerald, Victor Isaacs, Paul Bryce, Geoffrey Baker, Michael de Navarro, Alaisdair Baird, Mark and Celia Robertson, Nicola and Vicky Goga, Raman Subba Row, Jennifer Greenhouse, Andrew Hignell, Alex Bannister, John Carr, Kim Flood, Medha Laud, Alan Fordham, Joe Bruce, Mark Huddleston, Kenny Alexander, Chris Lowe, Sarah Dunster, Val Rice, Sarah Moore, Bow Watkinson, Glad Stockdale, Simon Fletcher, Michelle Tilling, Peter Clifford, Jeremy Yates-Round and finally my wife Carol Powell who has supported me in compiling this edition of the book.

INTRODUCTION

THE GROUNDS used regularly for county cricket now number 82 in all and vary from the grandeur of Lord's to the simplest of small club grounds, and from established stadia that can accommodate some 30,000 spectators with facilities of every type to simple local recreation grounds used for cricket (and other sports) with a modest clubhouse, a scoreboard and with space for no more than 1,500 spectators on temporary seats.

Despite the contrasting nature of these grounds, all now provide the opportunity for playing and watching county cricket. This arises in part from the willingness of the county clubs to travel from their home base – the headquarters – and, in the case of Glamorgan, Middlesex and Nottinghamshire to travel into adjoining counties which have no first-class cricket. All this requires dedicated work not only from the county officials but also from the officials and members of the local clubs concerned. This work involves the provision of many hundreds of temporary seats, the erection of tents and marquees for refreshments and hospitality, accommodation for officials (even players sometimes), temporary toilets, first-aid facilities, souvenir shops, press/media areas and the designation of suitable car parks. In this way nearly 60 grounds that otherwise attract only club spectators and have just a single permanent building – a pavilion or clubhouse – and a carefully nurtured cricket square are transformed into venues for first-class county cricket attracting perhaps 5,000 or more spectators on a single day.

In addition to the familiar county cricket grounds (which include the even more familiar seven Test match grounds), first-class cricket is played at a variety of venues including private clubs, recreation grounds, universities, public schools and even on wickets which form part of a factory premises.

Since first compiling a guide to cricket grounds in 1989 I have continued to communicate regularly with all club secretaries and other representatives, and with very few exceptions I have visited each ground personally, mostly while cricket was being played, in order to record in detail its features and to check on the information supplied. Facts have been assembled on the different grounds and their general history and the cricket that has taken place since the inception of each venue. I am particularly grateful to all the clubs who have provided detailed plans of their own grounds and the layout of facilities during a county match. However, improvements and changes are constantly being made at most grounds. At the smaller venues, which may only provide county cricket on a single day per year, the layout of facilities may vary from year to year. This particularly applies to areas restricted to members and sponsors.

Some of the grounds included in this fully revised book will be unfamiliar to many regular cricket followers and it is hoped that this volume will to be an indispensable guide for all those interested in cricket, as my previous ground guides have been. My visits to the grounds included in this guide and my discussions and correspondence with those involved have been extensive in an attempt to be as accurate as possible, but there will still be omissions and no doubt errors. I trust that readers will keep the author informed of any discrepancies and changes so that future editions of the guide may be as thorough and up-to-date as possible. I would like to take this opportunity to thank all those readers who took the trouble to draw my attention to errors in my first two ground guides.

This introduction cannot be concluded without thanking David Morgan, the Chairman of the England & Wales Cricket Board, for kindly writing the foreword and the many people who have assisted me with bringing this information together in an innovative fashion, in particular the members of the First Class Forum, Minor Counties, Scotland, Ireland and other associated organisations. I record in the Acknowledgements all those who have made some contribution.

William A. Powell
Hemel Hempstead, Hertfordshire
April 2003

Marylebone
Cricket Club

Lord's

MARYLEBONE CRICKET CLUB, LORD'S GROUND, ST JOHN'S WOOD ROAD, LONDON NW8 8QN

Pavilion Switchboard	020 7289 1611
Secretariat Fax	020 7289 9100
Library	020 7616 8657
Membership Office	020 7616 8660 **fax** 020 7616 8666
Membership Office Email	membership@mcc.org.uk
Marketing & Events Office	020 7616 8560 **fax** 020 7616 8566
Cricket Office	020 7616 8607 **fax** 020 7616 8604
Laws of Cricket Email	laws@mcc.org.uk
Ticket Office	020 7432 1000 **fax** 020 7616 8700
Ticket Office Email	ticketing@mcc.org.uk
Indoor Cricket School	020 7616 8612 **fax** 020 7616 8616
Lord's Shop	020 7616 8570
Lord's Shop Email	lordsshop@mcc.org.uk
Lord's Museum	020 7616 8658
Sodexho Prestige Catering Office	020 7286 2909
Tours of Lord's Office	020 7616 8595 **fax** 020 7266 3825
Tours of Lord's Office Email	tours@mcc.org.uk
Website	www.lords.org

Founded 1787
Colours red and yellow
Crest the letters 'MCC' entwined as a monogram
Patron HM The Queen
President Sir Timothy Rice
Club Chairman The Rt Hon the Lord Alexander of Weedon QC
Chairman of Finance Oliver Stocken
Chairman of Cricket Ted Dexter
Chairman of Membership Charles Fry
Chairman of Estates Maurice de Rohan
Chairman of Marketing Anthony Wreford
Secretary & Chief Executive Roger Knight
PA to Secretary & Chief Executive Stephanie Lawrence
Deputy Chief Executive David Batts
Head of Cricket Tony Dodemaide
Assistant Secretary (Membership) Colin Maynard
Curator Stephen Green
Head of Communications Iain Wilton
Deputy Head of Communications Laura Garland

Media Liaison Officer Stuart Weatherhead
Estates Manager Stephen Parris
Marketing Manager Jon Robinson
IT Manager Steve Jones
Cricket Office Manager Graeme Rickman
Ticket Office Manager Simon Wakefield
Membership Office Manager Michael Capitelli
Head Coach Clive Radley
Captain appointed on a match-by-match basis
Head Groundsman Michael Hunt
Indoor Cricket School Manager Reg Horne
Club Accountant Simon Gibb
Club Solicitor Holly Roper-Curzon
Manager of Lord's Tours Nik Stewart
Lord's Shop Manager Alan Pryer
Scorer/Statistician David Kendix (International matches only)
Computer Scoreboard Andrew Scarlett
Newsletter members' newsletter
Yearbook/Annual Review free to MCC members only

GROUND

LORD'S CRICKET GROUND, LONDON
NB. In recent years MCC has staged tourists matches at grounds other than at Lord's, namely: Shenley 1996 (MCC v South Africa 'A' and v Pakistan), see Middlesex section for details, Arundel 2001 (MCC v Australia), see Friends of Arundel Castle section for details, and Chesterfield 2002 (MCC v Sri Lanka), see Derbyshire CCC section for details.

OTHER GROUNDS
MCC Young Cricketers play Second XI home matches at several grounds, including High Wycombe CC, London Road, High Wycombe, Buckinghamshire (☎ 01494 522611), Wormsley (see Buckinghamshire section for details), and RAF Sports Ground, Vine Lane, Uxbridge, Middlesex (☎ 01895 237144).

LORD'S

Address Marylebone Cricket Club, Lord's Ground, St John's Wood Road, London NW8 8QN
Prospects of Play ☎ 020 7616 8603

HISTORY OF GROUND AND FACILITIES

MARYLEBONE CRICKET CLUB was founded in 1787 – a fact gathered from a poster for a cricket match in 1837 announcing MCC's golden jubilee. Before then, however, aristocrats and noblemen played their cricket in White Conduit Fields at Islington, London. Like shooting and fox-hunting, cricket was considered a sport for the elite – with plenty of gambling opportunities to boot. (Around £20,000 was bet on a series of games between Old Etonians and England in 1751!)

As London's population grew, so did the nobility's impatience with the crowds who gathered to watch them play. In pursuit of exclusivity, they approached Thomas Lord, a bowler with White Conduit CC, and asked him to set up a new private ground. An ambitious entrepreneur, Lord was encouraged by Lord Winchilsea to lease a ground on Dorset Fields in Marylebone – the site of the modern Dorset Square. He staged his first match – Middlesex (with two players from Berkshire and one from Kent) versus Essex (with two given men) – on 31 May 1787. Thus the Marylebone Cricket Club was formed. A year later, it laid down a Code of Laws, requiring the wickets to be pitched 22 yards apart and detailing how players could be given out. These Laws were adopted throughout the game and today MCC remains the custodian and arbiter of Laws relating to cricket around the world.

After a short stay at Marylebone Bank, Regents Park, between 1811 and 1814, Lord's moved to a new rural ground – previously the site of a duck pond – in St John's Wood. It remains MCC's home. The ground was soon a major success and attracted hordes of players and spectators, forcing Lord to build a pavilion and refreshment stalls. In 1805 the dukes and earls were keen to see their sons play cricket and so hired the ground for an Eton versus Harrow schools cricket match – the start of a world-famous, and ongoing, tradition.

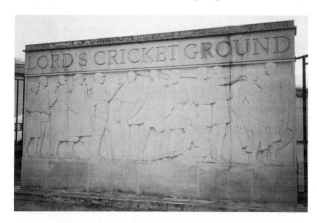

Stone plaque at the corner of St John's Wood Road and Wellington Road behind the MCC Indoor Cricket School.

The Grandstand during Somerset v Yorkshire, C&G Trophy Final, 2002.

In 1825, when Thomas Lord was 70, he sold the ground to a Bank of England director, William Ward, for £5,000. Having provided the Marylebone Cricket Club with a ground for 38 years, Lord retired and then died seven years later, but his name lives on.

The pavilion – housing scorecards, records and trophies – was destroyed in a fire in 1825. Work commenced immediately on a replacement, which opened the following year. At the time, the wicket was 'prepared' before a match by allowing sheep to come in and graze on the grass. However, the club subsequently acquired its first mowing machine and appointed its first groundsman in 1864.

The original MCC colour of sky blue was replaced in Victorian times by the famous red and yellow – now recognised the world over on ties, cricket sweaters and hatbands.

In the 1870s MCC decided it wanted to become involved in county cricket, which was growing in popularity, and, in 1877, it invited Middlesex to adopt Lord's as its county ground – an arrangement which continues after 125 years.

MCC's next step towards establishing itself as cricket's most influential body involved its development of a relationship with Australia, where emigrants had started playing the game competitively. In 1877 James Lillywhite and an England side boarded a steamer and travelled for eight weeks before playing Australia in the first official Test match – although it was not until 26 years later, in 1903, that MCC undertook official responsibility for England's tours 'down under'.

One of MCC's most famous players, Dr W.G. Grace, from Gloucestershire, gave the club even greater recognition through his monumental performances and stature. A painting of him by A.S. Wortley was presented to the club in 1890 and still hangs in the Long Room.

In 1889 the foundation stone was laid for a new pavilion, paid for by a £21,000 loan from William Nicholson, who had made his fortune from distilling gin. A year later it was opened in time for the new season. It is now a listed building and one of the most famous landmarks in world sport.

At the turn of the century, the Board of Control for Test Matches, the Advisory County Cricket Committee and the Imperial Cricket Conference were all set up to cater for the growth in domestic, imperial and other international cricket. These bodies existed until 1968 when there was a major reorganisation of cricket in England.

Since MCC was a private club it could not receive public funds, so it set up a Cricket Council as the governing body of cricket and the Test and County Cricket Board to administer the professional game. It also converted its MCC Cricket Association into the National Cricket Association to look after the recreational game. As a result cricket started to receive financial help from the government. In the 1990s, the structure was changed again with the establishment of the England and Wales Cricket Board (ECB) which took over responsibility for all cricket in England from the TCCB, NCA and Cricket Council.

MCC's role has continued to evolve in response to these changes. Today, its key responsibilities include: ensuring that Lord's remains a ground which is world class, as well as world famous; promoting cricket's Laws and safeguarding its 'spirit'; promoting cricket to young people, for the long-term good of the game; helping to increase cricket's international appeal – not least through its teams' touring programmes; and maintaining its position as the world's most active cricket-playing club.

The Mound Stand seen from inside the NatWest Media Centre.

GROUND RECORDS AND SCORES

FIRST-CLASS MATCHES

Highest innings total for MCC 607 v Cambridge University 1902
Highest innings total against MCC 609 for 8 dec by Cambridge University 1913
Lowest innings total for MCC 27 v Yorkshire 1902
Lowest innings total against MCC 20 by Middlesex 1864
Highest individual innings for MCC 214 E.H. Hendren v Yorkshire 1926
Highest individual innings against MCC 281* W.H. Ponsford for Australians 1934
Highest wicket partnerships for MCC

1st	301 D.L. Amiss & J.M. Brearley	v	Leicestershire	1976
2nd	209 G. Atkinson & A.R. Lewis	v	Yorkshire	1963
3rd	296 W.J. Edrich & E.H. Hendren	v	Surrey	1936
4th	185 M.H. Denness & K.W.R. Fletcher	v	India	1974
5th	201 M.W. Gatting & C.E.B. Rice	v	Rest of the World	1987
6th	200 M.J.K. Smith & J.T. Murray	v	West Indians	1966
7th	169 A.E. Lawton & B.S. Foster	v	South Africans	1907
8th	141 W.B. Franklin & J.C. Hartley	v	Wales	1925
9th	148 E.H. Hendren & A.S. Kennedy	v	Yorkshire	1919
10th	106 D. Bennett & H.W. Tilley	v	Oxford University	1955

Highest wicket partnerships against MCC

1st	211 J.M. Parker & G.M. Turner	for	New Zealanders	1973
2nd	282 J.W. Rutherford & R.N. Harvey	for	Australians	1956
3rd	389 W.H. Ponsford & S.J. McCabe	for	Australians	1934
4th	186 A.V. Avery & T.E. Bailey	for	Essex	1949
5th	198 W. Barber & K.R. Davidson	for	Yorkshire	1934
6th	206 A.R. Border & S.P. O'Donnell	for	Australians	1985
7th	176 F.L.H. Mooney & G.O. Rabone	for	New Zealanders	1949
8th	148 J. Langridge & J.W.A. Stephenson	for	The Rest	1937
9th	113 A. Wood & H. Verity	for	Yorkshire	1938
10th	119* W.H. Ponsford & A.J. Richardson	for	Australians	1926

Best bowling performance in an innings for MCC 9 for 44 A.E.E. Vogler v West Indians 1906
Best bowling performance in an innings against MCC 9 for 62 H. Verity for Yorkshire 1939
Best bowling performance in a match for MCC 13 for 80 W.E. Bowes v The Army 1930
Best bowling performance in a match against MCC 15 for 97 J.C. Laker for Surrey 1954

TEST MATCHES

Highest innings total for England 653 for 4 dec v India 1990
Highest innings total against England 729 for 6 dec by Australia 1930
Lowest innings total for England 53 v Australia 1888
Lowest innings total against England 47 by New Zealand 1958 (lowest 42 for 9 by India 1974)
Highest individual innings for England 333 G.A. Gooch v India 1990
Highest individual innings against England 254 D.G. Bradman for Australia 1930
Highest wicket partnerships for England

1st	268 J.B. Hobbs & H. Sutcliffe	v	South Africa	1924
2nd	221 D.L. Amiss & J.H. Edrich	v	India	1974
3rd	370 W.J. Edrich & D.C.S. Compton	v	South Africa	1947
4th	248 L. Hutton & D.C.S. Compton	v	West Indies	1939
5th	202 M.H. Denness & A.W. Greig	v	India	1974
6th	189 D.C.S. Compton & T.E. Bailey	v	New Zealand	1949
7th	174 M.C. Cowdrey & T.G. Evans	v	West Indies	1957
8th	246 L.E.G. Ames & G.O.B. Allen	v	New Zealand	1931
9th	92 K.W.R. Fletcher & G.G. Arnold	v	New Zealand	1973
10th	83 R. Illingworth & J.A. Snow	v	West Indies	1969

Highest wicket partnerships against England

1st	260 M.A. Taylor & M.J. Slater	for	Australia	1993
2nd	287* C.G. Greenidge & H.A. Gomes	for	West Indies	1984
3rd	211 M.H. Mankad & V.S. Hazare	for	India	1952
4th	221 G.H.S. Trott & E.S. Gregory	for	Australia	1896
5th	216 A.R. Border & G.M. Ritchie	for	Australia	1985
6th	274* G. St A. Sobers & D.A.J. Holford	for	West Indies	1966
7th	155* G. St A. Sobers & B.D. Julien	for	West Indies	1973
8th	130 Hanif Mohammad & Asif Iqbal	for	Pakistan	1967
9th	130 S.R. Waugh & G.F. Lawson	for	Australia	1989
10th	69 H.J.H. Scott & H.F. Boyle	for	Australia	1884
	69 A.A. Mallett & D.K. Lillee	for	Australia	1975

Best bowling performance in an innings for England 8 for 34 I.T. Botham v Pakistan 1978
Best bowling performance in an innings against England 8 for 38 G.D. McGrath for Australia 1997
Best bowling performance in a match for England 15 for 104 H. Verity v Australia 1934
Best bowling performance in a match against England 16 for 137 R.A.L. Massie for Australia 1972
Largest crowd 137,915 England v Australia 1953 (over five days)

ONE-DAY INTERNATIONALS

Highest innings total for England 334 for 4 v India (WC) 1975
Highest innings total against England 326 for 8 by India (NWS) 2002
Highest innings total in non-England ODI 303 for 4 by Australia v Zimbabwe (WC) 1999
Lowest innings total for England 185 v West Indies (PT) 1976
Lowest innings total against England 132 for 3 by India (WC) 1975
Lowest innings total in non-England ODI 132 by Pakistan v Australia (WC) 1999
Highest individual innings for England 137 D.L. Amiss v India (WC) 1975,
137 M.E.Trescothick v Pakistan (NWS) 2001
Highest individual innings against England 138* I.V.A. Richards for West Indies (WC) 1979
Highest individual innings in non-England ODI 132* N.C. Johnson for Zimbabwe v Australia (WC) 1999
Highest wicket partnerships for England

1st	135 G. Boycott & P. Willey	v	West Indies	(PT)	1980
2nd	202 G.A. Gooch & D.I. Gower	v	Australia	(TT)	1985
3rd	213 N.H. Fairbrother & G.A. Hick	v	West Indies	(TT)	1991
4th	170 O.A. Shah & M.E. Trescothick	v	Pakistan	(NWS)	2001
5th	89* M.H. Denness & C.M. Old	v	India	(WC)	1975
6th	36 I.T. Botham & V.J. Marks	v	West Indies	(PT)	1980
7th	77 A.W. Greig & A.P.E. Knott	v	Australia	(PT)	1972
8th	55 R.D. Jackman & D.W. Randall	v	West Indies	(PT)	1976
9th	19 A.R. Caddick & M.E. Trescothick	v	Pakistan	(NWS)	2001
10th	18* G.C. Arnold & J.A. Snow	v	Australia	(PT)	1972

Highest wicket partnerships against England

1st	109 V. Sehwag & S.C. Ganguly	for	India	(NWS)	2002
2nd	138 M.S. Attapattu & R.S. Kaluwitharana	for	Sri Lanka	(Emir)	1998
3rd	134* H.A. Gomes & I.V.A. Richards	for	West Indies	(TT)	1984
4th	103 G.S. Chappell & A.P. Sheahan	for	Australia	(PT)	1972
5th	139 C.L. King & I.V.A. Richards	for	West Indies	(WC)	1979
6th	121 M. Kaif & Yuvraj Singh	for	India	(NWS)	2002
7th	67 P.J.L. Dujon & M.D. Marshall	for	West Indies	(TT)	1988
8th	39 M.A. Holding & I.V.A. Richards	for	West Indies	(PT)	1976
9th	39* Wasim Bari & Zaheer Abbas	for	Pakistan	(WC)	1983
10th	20 I.V.A.Richards & A.M.E.Roberts	for	West Indies	(PT)	1976

Highest wicket partnerships in non-England ODI

1st	79 C.G. Greenidge & D.L. Haynes	for	West Indies v Australia	(WC)	1983
2nd	124 C.G. Greenidge & I.V.A. Richards	for	West Indies v Australia	(WC)	1983
3rd	129 S.R.Waugh & M.E.Waugh	for	Australia v Zimbabwe	(WC)	1999

4th	149 R.B. Kanhai & C.H. Lloyd	for	West Indies v Australia	(WC)	1975
5th	55* T.M.Moody & M.G.Bevan	for	Australia v Zimbabwe	(WC)	1999
6tg	64 R.W. Marsh & G.N. Yallop	for	Australia v West Indies	(WC)	1983
7th	59* N.C.Johnson & H.H.Streak	for	Zimbabwe v Australia	(WC)	1999
8th	41 Rashid Latif & Wasim Akram	for	Pakistan v Australia	(NWS)	2001
9th	8 S.M.H. Kirmani & S. Madan Lal	for	India v West Indies	(WC)	1983
10th	41 D.K. Lillee & J.R. Thomson	for	Australia v West Indies	(WC)	1975

Best bowling performance for England 5 for 44 D. Gough v Australia (TT) 1997
Best bowling performance against England 5 for 34 by M.Muralitharan for Sri Lanka (Emir) 1998
Best bowling performance in non-England ODI 5 for 48 G.J. Gilmour for Australia v West Indies (WC) 1975
Largest crowd 27,835 Australia v Pakistan (WC) 1999

C&G/NWT/GC FINALS

Highest innings total 322 for 5 by Warwickshire v Sussex 1993
Lowest innings total 57 by Essex v Lancashire 1996
Highest individual innings 146 G.Boycott for Yorkshire v Surrey 1965
Highest wicket partnerships

1st	202 G.A. Gooch & B.R. Hardie	for	Essex v Worcestershire	1985
2nd	192 G. Boycott & D.B. Close	for	Yorkshire v Surrey	1965
3rd	198* G.A. Hick & T.M. Moody	for	Worcestershire v Warwickshire	1994
4th	95 D. Lloyd & J. Abrahams	for	Lancashire v Northamptonshire	1976
5th	142 Asif Din & D.A. Reeve	for	Warwickshire v Sussex	1993
6th	103 N.H. Fairbrother & A.N. Hayhurst	for	Lancashire v Sussex	1986
7th	75 R.J. Hadlee & B.N. French	for	Nottinghamshire v Northamptonshire	1987
8th	54 R.A.E. Tindall & A. Long	for	Surrey v Yorkshire	1965
9th	62 Asif Din & G.C. Small	for	Warwickshire v Surrey	1982
10th	22 G.C. Small & R.G.D. Willis	for	Warwickshire v Surrey	1982

Best bowling performance 6 for 18 G.Chapple for Lancashire v Essex 1996

VARSITY MATCHES

Highest innings total 513 for 6 by Oxford University 1996
Lowest innings total 59 by Cambridge University 1923
Highest individual innings 238* Nawab of Pataudi for Oxford University 1934
Highest wicket partnerships

1st	205 A.W. Allen & G.W. Parker	for	Cambridge University	1934
2nd	226 W.G. Keighley & H.A. Pawson	for	Oxford University	1947
3rd	187 Q.J. Hughes & J.P. Pymont	for	Cambridge University	2000
4th	250 C.M. Gupte & C.J. Hollins	for	Oxford University	1994
5th	174 Nawab of Pataudi & H.G.O. Owen-Smith	for	Oxford University	1931
6th	191 M.A. Crawley & S.D. Weale	for	Oxford University	1987
7th	289 G. Goonesena & G.W. Cook	for	Cambridge University	1957
8th	112 H.E. Webb & A.W.H. Mallett	for	Oxford University	1948
9th	97* J.F. Marsh & F.J.V. Hopley	for	Cambridge University	1904
10th	70 C.M. Pitcher & A.R. Whittall	for	Cambridge University	1993

Best bowling performance in an innings 8 for 52 G.J. Toogood for Oxford University 1985
Best bowling performance in a match 13 for 237 I.A.R. Peebles for Oxford University 1930

MINOR COUNTIES C.A. KNOCKOUT FINAL LIMITED-OVERS

Highest innings total 241 for 6 by Staffordshire v Devon 1991
Lowest innings total 188 for 7 by Hertfordshire v Cumberland 1989
Highest individual innings 108* S. Sharp for Cumberland v Hertfordshire 1989
Best bowling performance 4 for 44 D. Halliwell for Cumberland v Hertfordshire 1989

NATIONAL VILLAGE CHAMPIONSHIP FINAL LIMITED-OVERS

Highest innings total 267 for 5 by Goatacre v Dunstall 1990
Lowest innings total 82 for 9 by Longparish v Marchwiel 1980
Highest individual innings 123 K.M. Iles for Goatacre v Dunstall 1990
Best bowling performance 6 for 24 R. Coulson for Cookley v Lindal Moor 1977

For Middlesex CCC records and scores at Lord's Cricket Ground, see Middlesex section.

GROUND INFORMATION

ENTRANCES St John's Wood Road via Grace Gates (players, officials, members and vehicles), St John's Wood Road via Bicentenary Gate (MCC employees and stewards only), St John's Wood Road via East Gate (public), Wellington Road via North Gate (members and vehicles to access Indoor Cricket School and ECB offices), Wellington Road (members and public), Grove End Road (players, officials, vehicles and MCC employees).
MEMBERS' ENCLOSURE Pavilion (members only), Allen Stand (members only upper tier), Warner Stand, Mound Stand (upper – debenture holders only) and Tavern Stand.
MEMBERS' FRIENDS' ENCLOSURES Allen Stand (lower tier), Warner Stand, Mound Stand (upper – debenture holders only) and Tavern Stand.
PUBLIC ENCLOSURE Grand Stand (upper, balcony and lower), Compton Stand (upper and lower), Edrich Stand (upper and lower) and Mound Stand (lower).
COVERED STANDS Pavilion (part), Warner Stand (part), Grand Stand (part), Compton Stand (part), Edrich Stand (part), Mound Stand (part), Tavern Stand (part) and Allen Stand (part).
OPEN STANDS Pavilion (part), Warner Stand (part), Grand Stand (part), Compton Stand (part), Edrich Stand (part), Mound Stand (part), Tavern Stand (part) and Allen Stand (part).
NAME OF ENDS Pavilion End, Nursery End.
GROUND DIMENSIONS 166m × 133m.
REPLAY SCREEN For all televised major matches the screen is located on top of the Edrich Stand.
FIRST AID Point between Warner Stand and Grand Stand and at Nursery End near main toilets.
CODES OF DRESS Members and their guests are expected to maintain an acceptable standard of dress while in the Members' Friends' enclosures. For gentlemen, casual trousers or shorts are acceptable, provided that they are reasonably smart. Jackets are not required, but neat shirts with collars, or polo shirts or sweaters should be worn. Ladies should wear dresses, or skirts, trousers or shorts worn with blouses which may be sleeveless. Garments considered unsuitable for wearing in the Members' Friends' enclosures include the following: cycling shorts or shorts usually worn for playing sport, beach wear, gentlemen's sleeveless shirts or singlet, flip-flop shoes, ripped or badly worn jeans, garments in military camouflage colours and tracksuits. Admittance to the Members' Friends' enclosures will also be refused to anyone wearing dilapidated or offensive garments of any kind. Bare feet, bare torsos or bare midriffs are not permitted under any circumstances. Dress in the Pavilion requires gentlemen to wear ties with tailored coats and acceptable trousers with appropriate shoes. Zip-up golf jackets are not permitted. Coats and ties may be removed on the Pavilion Concourse, and outside balconies, but must be replaced for entry to the Pavilion building. Ladies should wear dresses, or skirts, or trousers worn with blouses. Dresses and blouses may be sleeveless. Religious, traditional or national dress, or service uniform, is permitted. However, the following items of clothing are prohibited: jeans and their close relations, leggings, jodhpur-style trousers, t-shirts, track suits, training shoes, plimsolls, denim clothing and overalls.
BEHAVIOUR The club is keen that standards of behaviour should be maintained and members and spectators are urged to report immediately to the Secretary & Chief Executive any incident, or potential incident, where they feel action should be taken. Bad language is not acceptable at any match and the club will take prompt and strong action should this or any other ground regulation be ignored.
RECIPROCAL ARRANGEMENTS Yes, with Melbourne CC, Sydney Cricket Ground, Hong Kong CC and the Cricket Club of India.
SUPPORTERS' CLUB None.
JUNIORS None.
CORPORATE ENTERTAINING Hospitality suites and private boxes are available at Lord's either on a match, season or debenture period. For further details of MCC Box Scheme contact Marketing Manager ☎ 020 7616 8561 or for County matches contact Hospitality Administrator ☎ 020 7616 8565 or for Conferences contact Events Manager ☎ 020 7616 8563. For major matches other Corporate Hospitality packages are available within the ground from Keith Prowse ☎ 020 8796 1777 or Peter Parfitt Sport ☎ 01423 874874.

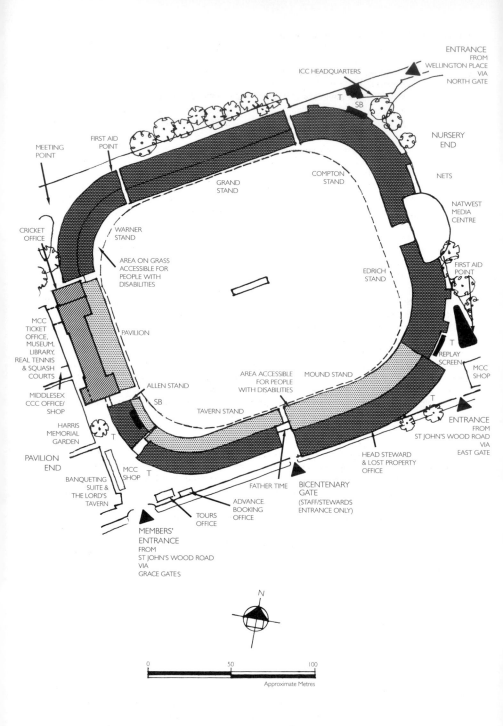

ENTRANCE
FROM
WELLINGTON PLACE
VIA
NORTH GATE

ICC HEADQUARTERS

T   SB

NURSERY
END

NETS

MEETING
POINT

FIRST AID
POINT

GRAND
STAND

COMPTON
STAND

NATWEST
MEDIA
CENTRE

CRICKET
OFFICE

WARNER
STAND

FIRST AID
POINT

AREA ON GRASS
ACCESSIBLE FOR
PEOPLE WITH
DISABILITIES

EDRICH
STAND

MCC
TICKET
OFFICE,
MUSEUM,
LIBRARY,
REAL TENNIS
& SQUASH
COURTS

PAVILION

T

REPLAY
SCREEN

MCC
SHOP

MIDDLESEX
CCC OFFICE/
SHOP

ALLEN STAND

AREA ACCESSIBLE
FOR PEOPLE
WITH DISABILITIES

MOUND STAND

HARRIS
MEMORIAL
GARDEN

SB

T

TAVERN STAND

T

ENTRANCE
FROM
ST JOHN'S WOOD ROAD
VIA
EAST GATE

PAVILION
END

T

MCC
SHOP

HEAD STEWARD
& LOST PROPERTY
OFFICE

BANQUETING
SUITE &
THE LORD'S
TAVERN

FATHER TIME

BICENTENARY
GATE
(STAFF/STEWARDS
ENTRANCE ONLY)

ADVANCE
BOOKING
OFFICE

TOURS
OFFICE

MEMBERS'
ENTRANCE
FROM
ST JOHN'S WOOD ROAD
VIA
GRACE GATES

N

0   50   100
Approximate Metres

FACILITIES FOR VISUALLY IMPAIRED SPECTATORS Yes.

FACILITIES AND ACCESS FOR PEOPLE WITH DISABILITIES INCLUDING WHEELCHAIR ACCESS TO GROUND Yes, via No. 6 Gate in Grove End Road.

DESIGNATED CAR PARK AVAILABLE INSIDE THE GROUND FOR PEOPLE WITH DISABILITIES Yes, by arrangement with MCC at county matches only, not at major matches.

GOOD VIEWING AREAS INSIDE THE GROUND FOR MEMBERS USING WHEELCHAIRS Yes, there is a special small reserved enclosure in front of the Warner Stand for major matches for disabled members and rover ticket holders only. Toilets for the disabled are located in the Mound Stand, Warner Stand and the North Clock Tower.

DESIGNATED VIEWING AREAS FOR PEOPLE USING WHEELCHAIRS Yes, there is a special small reserved enclosure in front of the Warner Stand and in the Mound Stand.

RAMPS TO PROVIDE EASY ACCESS TO BARS & REFRESHMENT OUTLETS FOR PEOPLE USING WHEELCHAIRS Yes, including lifts in the Pavilion and various stands.

FOOD & DRINK FULL RESTAURANT/DINING FACILITIES Members, yes. Public, yes. Members' Dining Room: advance booking required ☎ 020 7616 8652. Warner Stand Restaurant, Pavilion Lounge, Banqueting Suite: advance booking required ☎ 020 7286 2909. Pavilion bars, plus champagne bars and public bars around the ground.

TEMPORARY FOOD/DRINK FACILITIES Members, yes. Public, yes. Lord's Nursery End Food Village offers a number of outlets at major matches otherwise public bars around the ground sell drinks and snacks.

FOOD SUITABLE FOR VEGETARIANS Members, yes. Public, yes.

BARS Members 4, Public 6.

CLUB SHOP Lord's Shop is situated near the East Gate and is open throughout the year. There is a secondary small members' only shop in the Pavilion for major matches only where MCC members' items can be purchased.

CLUB MUSEUM MCC Museum is located to the rear of the Pavilion and is open throughout the year. The collection is the finest in the northern hemisphere and only that at Melbourne CC in Australia is comparable. Tours of Lord's are available and include the Long Room, Dressing Rooms, Media Centre and the MCC Museum for further details contact Lord's Tour ☎ 020 7616 8595.

CRICKET COACHING FACILITIES Yes, contact MCC Indoor Cricket School for full details of Coaching Clinics.

CRICKET NETS Yes, contact MCC Indoor Cricket School for full details of cricket nets and indoor matches.

OTHER SPORTING OR RECREATIONAL FACILITIES ON THE GROUND Real Tennis and squash for MCC members and guests only. Also there are golf, bridge, chess societies which meet throughout the year.

FACILITIES FOR HIRE OR WIDER COMMUNITY USE AT THE GROUND Yes, contact MCC for full details.

WINTER CRICKET EVENTS Functions at Lord's are organised throughout the year. For details and a brochure ☎ Events Office.

CAR PARKING FACILITIES No street parking, though limited areas available on meters and on Sundays. Car parking available for members only during major matches with some local car parking arranged by MCC for members on local school grounds with a park and ride bus service to the ground. Public car parking in central London car parks include NCP at Dorset House, Bilton Towers, Portman Square, Church Street, Bell Street and Acacia Car Park or near Regent's Park Zoo which is now a metered area.

OTHER INFORMATION The ICC and ECB offices are situated at the Nursery End of the ground.

GROUND CAPACITY 30,000.

ANTICIPATED GROUND DEVELOPMENTS New drainage and outfield constructed during winter of 2002/3.

HOW TO GET THERE

 St John's Wood Underground Station (Jubilee Line) 0.5 mile

 LT 6, 13, 16, 46, 82, 98, 113, 139, 189 and 274 pass close to the ground. Also London Country Coaches (Green Line) 719, 757, 768 and 797 from home counties pass near ground. ☎ 020 7222 1234

 There are cycle routes from all parts of London to this area of St John's Wood.

 The ground is currently outside the Central London Congestion Zone. **From north (M1/A1):** from M1, junction 1, follow signs to A5 (Edgware Road), continue on this road towards London, at traffic lights junction with A5205 turn left into St John's Wood Road. **From south (M25/M23):** from M23/M25 junction 7/8 continue north on A23 into London to junction with A203 (Stockwell Road), follow signs to Vauxhall Bridge, cross the Bridge and take A202 (Vauxhall Bridge Road) to Victoria

The Pavilion, Allen Stand and Tavern Stand on the left, and Warner Stand on the right.

Station, bear right on to Wilton Road, follow signs to Hyde Park Corner (A302) (Grosvenor Place), continue up Park Lane to Marble Arch, then take Edgware Road (A5) to St John's Wood, at traffic lights, junction with A5205 turn right into St John's Wood Road. **From east (M25/M11):** from M25 junction 27 continue south on M11 to junction 4 (A406) (North Circular Road), continue west on A406 to Brent Cross, junction with A41 (Hendon Way), continue on A41 to Wellington Road. **From west (M4):** from M4 at Chiswick flyover, turn left on to A406 (Gunnersbury Avenue), at traffic lights turn right on to A4000 (Gunnersbury Lane), continue on A4000 to junction with A40 (Western Avenue), turn right and continue on A40 (Westway) on to A40(M), continue on to Marylebone Road, turn left on to B507 (Lisson Grove), turn right on to A5205 (St John's Wood Road). **From M40:** from M40 continue on A40 (Western Avenue) then as for M4.

London Heathrow Airport ☎ 08700 000123 www.londonheathrowairport.co.uk, London City Airport ☎ 020 7646 0000 www.londoncityairport.co.uk, London Gatwick Airport ☎ 08700 002468 www.londongatwickairport.co.uk

WHERE TO STAY

The Ramada Plaza Hotel (☎ 020 7722 7722) opposite ground plus many other hotels in central or north-west London. For a further selection of places to stay in central/north-west London area visit www.smoothhound.co.uk or www.londontouristboard.com.

WHERE TO EAT

Casa Linga (☎ 020 7722 5959), L'Aventure (☎ 020 7624 6232), The Lord's Tavern (☎ 020 7286 2909), Tino's (☎ 020 7586 6264), Zizzi (☎ 020 7722 7296)

TOURIST INFORMATION London Tourist Information Centre ☎ 020 7760 5630, www.londontouristboard.com

LOCAL RADIO STATIONS Greater London Radio (94.9 MHz FM/1488 kHz MW), Capital Radio/Capital Gold (95.8 MHz FM/1548 kHz MW), LBC (97.3 MHz FM/1152 kHz MW)

LOCAL NEWSPAPERS *Evening Standard, Hampstead & Highgate Express*

Derbyshire

Derby 240803

NORTHANTS v DERBY NJL.

DERBYSHIRE COUNTY CRICKET CLUB, COUNTY CRICKET GROUND, NOTTINGHAM ROAD, DERBY, DERBYSHIRE DE21 6DA

General Enquiries 01332 388101
Commercial 01332 388105
Lund Pavilion 01332 388115
Membership 01332 388106 **fax** 01332 290251
Email post@dccc.org.uk
Website www.dccc.org.uk

Founded 4 November 1870
Colours chocolate, Cambridge blue and amber
Crest rose and imperial crown
National Cricket League Nickname Scorpions
National Cricket League Colours Blue, chocolate and amber
President Sir N. Rudd DL
Chairman G.T. Bowring
Chairman of Cricket Committee L.C. Elliott
Chief Executive Officer J.T. Smedley
Administration Secretary G. Hudson
Hon Treasurer J.M. Nicholas
Club Accountant P. Rose
Commercial Manager K. Stevenson
Commercial Assistant J. Cliff
Shop Manager Mrs P. Taylor
Lund Pavilion Manager A. Evans
IT Manager/Membership Secretary J. Grainger
Club Coach A.R.K. Pierson
Assistant Coach K.M. Krikken

Business Development Manager C.F. Davies
Captain D.G. Cork
Vice Captain M.J. Di Venuto
Groundsman N. Godrich
Scorer 1st XI J.M. Brown
Scorer 2nd XI T. Cottam
Statistician D.J. Baggett
Main Sponsors Banks's, SAPA Profiles Ltd and Rutland Windows & Conservatories
Team Sponsor Rutland Windows & Conservatories (County Championship), Banks's (National Cricket League)
Yearbook £6
Scorecard 50p
National Cricket League Match Programme £1
Newsletter *Out of The Middle* and *DCCC Bulletin* issued with scorecard
Club Shop Derbyshire CCC Shop
Frizzell County Championship Status Division 2
National Cricket League Status Division 2

ACHIEVEMENTS

County Championship Champions 1936
Gillette Cup Finalists 1969
NatWest Trophy Winners 1981
Benson and Hedges Cup Winners 1993, Finalists 1978 and 1988
John Player Sunday League 3rd 1970
Refuge Assurance Sunday League Champions 1990
Refuge Assurance Cup Finalists 1990
Asda Trophy Winners 1982 and 1985
Tilcon Trophy Finalists 1977

COUNTY CRICKET BOARD

Chairman J.F.H. Salisbury
Secretary C.F. Davies
Treasurer R. Milton
Cricket Development Officer H. Dytham
Women & Girls Secretary M. Coates

Address Derbyshire County Cricket Board, County Cricket Ground, Nottingham Road, Derby, Derbyshire DE21 6DA
☎ 01332 388130
Fax 01332 388133

GROUND

Derby (County Cricket Ground, Nottingham Road)
Other grounds used since 1969: Chesterfield (Queen's Park, Boythorpe Avenue), Burton upon Trent (Ind Coope Brewery Ground, Belvedere Road), Burton upon Trent (Allied Brewery Sports Ground), Long Eaton (Trent College, Derby Road), Darley Dale (Station Road), Heanor (Town Ground, Mayfield Road), Checkley (Uttoxeter Road, Checkley), Knypersley (Victoria and Knypersley Social Welfare Centre, Tunstall Road), Leek (Highfield, Macclesfield Road), Ilkeston (Rutland Recreation Ground, West End Drive), Cheadle (Tean Road Sports Ground, Tean Road), Repton (Repton School Ground, Repton) and Buxton (The Park, Park Road)

SECOND XI GROUNDS

In addition to the above-mentioned grounds the following are used for second XI matches:
Denby CC, The Copper Yard, High Bank, Denby Village, Derbyshire ☎ 01332 780646
Dunstall CC, Dunstall Park, near Barton-under-Needwood, Derbyshire ☎ 01283 712346
Glossop CC, The Pavilion, Glossop, Derbyshire ☎ 01457 869755
Ilkeston Rutland CC, Recreation Ground, Oakwell Drive, Ilkeston, Derbyshire ☎ 0115 944 0453
Chesterfield CC, Queen's Park, Boythorpe Avenue, Chesterfield, Derbyshire ☎ 01246 273090
Repton School, The Cricket Pavilion, School Grounds, Willington Road, Repton, Derbyshire ☎ 01283 559200
Sandiacre Town CC, Longmoor Lane, Sandiacre, Derbyshire ☎ 0115 949 7330

The County Cricket Ground from the former Grandstand End looking towards the Scoreboard End.

DERBY

Address County Cricket Ground, Nottingham Road, Derby,
Derbyshire DE21 6DA
Prospects of Play ☎ 01332 383211

HISTORY OF GROUND AND FACILITIES

THE COUNTY CRICKET GROUND occupies part of the former Derby Racecourse and was known as the Racecourse Ground until officials decided that it should be called simply Derbyshire County Cricket Ground.

For racing Derby boasted a straight mile and a grandstand, built in 1911, complete with a copper-domed viewing cupola and stables. These buildings were demolished during the winter of 2001/2. The former straight mile remains to the north of the ground and now provides recreational facilities for the people of the City of Derby. The only remains of the racecourse are the Stewards' Room and some of the stables to the rear of the Lund Pavilion.

The cricket pitch used to be located in the centre of the racecourse but in 1939, when racing ceased, it was moved to its present position. The current square was established in 1955. In 1970, the year of the club's centenary, there was talk of closing the ground altogether because of its poor facilities and pitch. However, it survived and the Lund Pavilion was built in 1982, providing the ground's first 'proper' pavilion. Until then players had used the jockeys' old quarters as changing rooms.

Derby County Football Club played some matches at the Racecourse Ground before moving across the city to the Baseball Ground in 1894. The county cricket ground even staged one FA Cup Final replay and five semi-finals.

The ground was first used by South Derbyshire Cricket Club in 1863, fifteen years after the establishment of the racecourse. It was here that South Derbyshire CC played and defeated the Australian Aborigines, the first touring side, in 1868. Following the formation of Derbyshire County Cricket Club in November 1870 at the Guildhall, the first county match was staged in 1871. Derbyshire county matches were played on the Racecourse Ground between 1884 and 1954.

The County Ground was used for two limited-overs one-day international matches in 1983 between New Zealand and Sri Lanka and then again during the

The Lund Pavilion between the Stewards' Room, which is now used by the scorers, and the club and supporters' buildings.

1999 Cricket World Cup for a match between New Zealand and Pakistan. Derbyshire Scorpions played their first floodlit match against Nottinghamshire Outlaws in June 2000. Floodlit matches were played against Worcestershire Royals in 2001 and Surrey Lions in 2002.

The ground now occupies an area of 17 acres and in 1982 a lease of 125 years was purchased from the owners, Derby City Council, thanks to a generous loan from the local authority. After 1982, in addition to the Lund Pavilion and sponsors' suites, a new scoreboard, the Butterley and the Steetley Stands, the Derbyshire Heatseal Supporters' Club room, Tea Room and Derbyshire County Cricket Club Shop were erected. In 1997 the Butterley Stand was renamed the Don Amott Stand and a permanent steel roof, constructed by Furbuild Developments of Ashbourne, was completed in June 1998.

The ground was for many years called the Charter Land because it was given to the City of Derby by Queen Mary Tudor in her charter of 1554. Once considered one of the least attractive county cricket grounds, it has been much improved in recent years and more improvements are planned. The new road construction has considerably altered the approach to the ground from the large Pentagon Roundabout and from the nearby Sir Frank Whittle Way (A61).

Discussions about developing the County Ground started in 1991. The club sold a portion of land and in 2000 the Virgin Active Leisure Complex was opened on it. The two-storey building includes two indoor swimming pools, a hydrotherapy pool, and a sauna and steam room. Other features include a library with free internet access and a 'Kidsville' area with basketball court, computer games and an area for arts and crafts. The ground floor is used only by members of the Virgin Active Leisure Complex. The complex is sited on the Pentagon Island Roundabout and has its own car parking facilities, totally separate from the county cricket club. The adjacent Days Inn development is expected to be open for business in mid-June 2003.

During 2001/2 the club worked closely with Mike Turner OBE of the ECB (the former Chief Executive/General Manager of Leicestershire County Cricket Club) and the Safer Sports Ground Initiative (SSGI) to obtain 50% funding towards a number of improvements to the whole ground. This was granted in March 2002 with the SSGI providing £25,000 in addition to the £25,000 contributed by the county cricket club. The total of £50,000 has been put to good use on a new concrete stand and steps next to the Tea Bar, 150 new seats in the area near to the Tea Bar, 150 new seats on the concrete bank at the former Grandstand End of the ground, a 2.4 metre high perimeter fence around the entire County Cricket Ground playing area and some temporary fencing to secure the old grandstand site, a new public address system and new security lighting for the administration offices. In 2002 the club also developed an area of improved grassed nets and practice facilities at the Scoreboard End of the ground at a cost of approximately £50,000.

However, the most exciting news revolves around the plans for the Grandstand site, to be developed in conjunction with the Derwent Community Team (DCT) – the local office of the government-funded New Deal in the Community urban Regeneration scheme. If all goes as expected, a new indoor school and community facility will be up and running by late spring 2004.

The club received Stage 1 Sport England approval for around £1.5 million in May 2002. At this point the case officers at Sport England were changing and this held up progress on the original project for an indoor school at the Scoreboard

End of the ground for about two months. Meanwhile, the club continued to negotiate the sale of the Grandstand site with a housing developer. However, contact was maintained with the DCT with regard to its plans for the local area. As a result of this the DCT indicated that it would be able to purchase the Grandstand site, generate funding to complement Sport England money, and construct an indoor cricket school combining commercial and community facilities. This means that the county club funds raised by the sale of land to Virgin and Days Inn, previously ringfenced for the indoor school, could now be allocated to further development and to help secure the long-term future of the club. The club says this also means that it is possible to embark on a joint venture with the local community which will break down many historical barriers, and generate long-term interest from and security with the club's nearest neighbours.

In August 2002 the DCT produced a formal bid for the site. After helpful consultation with Sport England, who agreed that the change of project had much merit, the General Committee agreed to commit to the DCT proposals in early September. The potential housing development for the Grandstand site was put to one side.

Since then, a significant amount of work has been put in by officers and agents of Derbyshire CCC, DCT and Sport England to bring the plan to fruition. As this book goes to print, detailed plans for the proposed building at the Grandstand End have been put forward for planning permission. In addition, the final (Stage 2) Sport England application is being submitted and the DCT funding is near to confirmation. It is envisaged that the £4.2 million project, which will include a significant community sports hall, gymnasium and health café, will commence construction in July 2003. A preferred contractor has been selected after a rigorous interview and consultation process, and it is intended that the grand opening will take place early in the 2004 season. A proportion of the fitting out costs will be met by the club.

As mentioned earlier, the further benefit of this deal to the club is that a large part of the £875,000 raised by the sale of land to Virgin and Days Inn will remain in the bank. This sum is currently ringfenced for ground development and particularly the indoor school, by arrangement with the club's landlord, Derby City Council. However, when the new scheme is realised, this money will not be needed for investment in the indoor school. Discussions are under way with the city council to determine how the funds can best be used to improve the ground and secure the future of Derbyshire CCC. Many ideas have been put forward but the money will be spent with a commercial return in mind – it is highly likely that permanent floodlights will be sought for the start of the 2004 season.

The club has also applied for and been granted a further £30,000 of Safer Sports Grounds funding towards the cost of a new seated stand on the current shop site, replacement seating in various areas and a new concrete path around the perimeter of the ground fencing. This represents 50% of the total cost, and means that in excess of £50,000 additional funding has been generated from this fund. Business Development Manager Colin Davies is responsible for the management of this grant application and has also had considerable input into the indoor school funding packages. The club said: 'The future looks particularly bright for Derbyshire County Cricket Club as we find ourselves in an elevated position among the first-class counties in terms of training facilities. High-quality training and commercial facilities are almost in place – the County Ground will shortly be a venue to match any in the country.'

Other developments have also taken place. The press box which was located in the former Grandstand has been moved to a new box above the Tea Bar which gives an excellent view of the ground. The TV camera/commentary box is positioned at the Scoreboard End when required. A new scoreboard has been erected on the west side opposite the former grandstand. The old scoreboard building is now used as the radio commentary box. A secondary scoreboard was erected in 2000 next to the Lund Pavilion thanks to financial support from the Derbyshire CCSC and is dedicated to the memory of Mrs L. Wilson of Bakewell.

The trees on the west side of the ground were set in National Tree Planting Year in 1973 and were given by Derby Civic Society. The cost of planting was defrayed by Derby County Football Club Limited and Trent Motor Traction Company Limited and this is recorded on a stone tablet near the Stewards' Room. It is possible to park and view the cricket from your car in this area or in front of the bank.

The playing area is large, extending to 152 metres by 167 metres; although the playing area is restricted on the north and west sides by a boundary rope inside the pale fencing which encloses the ground, the boundary can still be as much as 78 metres from the square.

The Derbyshire County Cricket Club Shop is situated next to the Derbyshire CC Supporters' Club headquarters adjacent to the Lund Pavilion. The scorers and the PA announcers now sit in the old Stewards' Room at the Grandstand End of the ground, which affords them a straighter view behind the bowler's arm. The Derbyshire County Cricket Club offices and old indoor cricket school adjoin the entrance and car parking area to the rear of the Lund Pavilion.

This is a large open spacious ground with a capacity of some 9,500. Crowds of about 4,500 are usual for weekend matches although numbers for weekday County Championship matches are lower.

GROUND RECORDS AND SCORES

FIRST-CLASS MATCHES

Highest innings total for county 645 v Hampshire 1898
Highest innings total against county 661 by Nottinghamshire 1901
Lowest innings total for county 26 v Yorkshire 1880
Lowest innings total against county 28 Warwickshire 1937
Highest individual innings for county 238* T.S. Worthington v Sussex 1937
Highest individual innings against county 273* E.G. Hayes for Surrey 1904
Highest wicket partnerships for county

1st	322 H. Storer jun. & J. Bowden	v	Essex	1929
2nd	417 K.J. Barnett & T.W. Tweats	v	Yorkshire	1997
3rd	221 K.J. Barnett & J.E. Morris	v	Northamptonshire	1986
4th	240* M. Azharuddin & P.D. Bowler	v	Lancashire	1991
5th	176 W. Chatterton & G.A. Davidson	v	Hampshire	1898
6th	185 J.G. Wright & S.C. Goldsmith	v	Warwickshire	1988
7th	258 M.P. Dowman & D.G. Cork	v	Durham	2000
8th	124 K.M. Krikken & P.A.J. de Freitas	v	Lancashire	1997
9th	111 E.M. Ashcroft & T. Forrester	v	Nottinghamshire	1902
10th	93 J. Humphries & J. Horsley	v	Lancashire	1914

Highest wicket partnerships against county

1st	309 H.K. Foster & F.L. Bowley	for	Worcestershire	1901
2nd	273 A. Ward & J.T. Tyldesley	for	Lancashire	1901

3rd	338 J.M. Brearley & M.W. Gatting	for	Middlesex	1981
4th	328* C.W.J.Athey & P.Bainbridge	for	Gloucestershire	1985
5th	211 G.H.S. Trott & H. Donnan	for	Australians	1896
6th	372* K.P. Pietersen & J.E. Morris	for	Nottinghamshire	2001
7th	179 F.C. Holland & K.J. Key	for	Surrey	1897
8th	117* L. Townsend & J.D. Bannister	for	Warwickshire	1956
9th	135 H.W. Parks & W.L. Cornford	for	Sussex	1935
10th	109 W. Gunn & R.G. Hardstaff	for	Nottinghamshire	1896

Best bowling performance in an innings for county 9 for 39 G.A. Davidson v Warwickshire 1895
Best bowling performance in an innings against county 10 for 45 R.L. Johnson for Middlesex 1994
Best bowling performance in a match for county 14 for 100 G. Porter v Hampshire 1895
Best bowling performance in a match against county 16 for 101 G. Giffen for Australians 1886
Largest crowd 14,500 v Australians 1948

LIMITED-OVERS MATCHES

Highest innings total for county 365 for 3 v Cornwall (NWT) 1986
Highest innings total against county 329 for 5 by Sussex (NWT) 1997 & 329 for 6 by Nottinghamshire (SL) 1993
Lowest innings total for county 70 v Surrey (SL) 1972
Lowest innings total against county 61 by Sussex (SL) 1978
Highest individual innings for county 173* M.J. Di Venuto v Derbyshire CB (C&G) 2002
Highest individual innings against county 158 R.K. Rao for Sussex (NWT) 1997
Highest wicket partnerships for county

1st	210 P.D. Bowler & C.J. Adams	v	Somerset	(SL)	1993
2nd	286 I.S. Anderson & A. Hill	v	Cornwall	(NWT)	1986
3rd	183 C.J. Adams & K.J. Barnett	v	Northamptonshire	(NWT)	1997
4th	119 K.J. Barnett & B. Roberts	v	Gloucestershire	(B&H)	1991
5th	158* K.J. Barnett & B. Roberts	v	Essex	(SL)	1984
6th	107 C.J. Adams & S.C. Goldsmith	v	Warwickshire	(SL)	1990
7th	92* C.M. Wells & D.G. Cork	v	Lancashire	(B&H)	1994
8th	62 A. Hill & R.W. Taylor	v	Middlesex	(GC)	1978
9th	105 D.G. Moir & R.W. Taylor	v	Kent	(SL)	1984
10th	44 I.D. Blackwell & S.P. Griffiths	v	Glamorgan	(SL)	1999

Highest wicket partnerships against county

1st	148 B.C. Broad & R.T. Robinson	for	Nottinghamshire	(B&H)	1984
2nd	190 D.J. Bicknell & N. Shahid	for	Surrey	(SL)	1995
3rd	165 P.M. Roebuck & R.J. Harden	for	Somerset	(SL)	1987
4th	128 G.D. Lloyd & N.H. Fairbrother	for	Lancashire	(SL)	1997
5th	141 T.E. Jesty & N.E.J. Pocock	for	Hampshire	(GC)	1980
6th	112 R.T. Robinson & K.T. Evans	for	Nottinghamshire	(RAC)	1990
7th	97 A.L. Penberthy & J.N. Snape	for	Northamptonshire	(NWT)	1997
8th	50 D.M. Smith & C.J. Richards	for	Surrey	(B&H)	1979
9th	65 D.E. East & J.K. Lever	for	Essex	(SL)	1982
10th	80* D.L. Bairstow & M. Johnson	for	Yorkshire	(B&H)	1981

Best bowling performance in a match for county 7 for 35 D.E.Malcolm v Northamptonshire (NWT) 1997
Best bowling performance in a match against county 6 for 26 S.R.Lampitt for Worcestershire (B&H) 1994
Largest crowd 7,500 v Essex (SL) 1990

ONE-DAY INTERNATONALS

Highest innings total in ODI 269 for 8 for Pakistan v New Zealand (WC) 1999
Lowest innings total in ODI 181 for New Zealand v Sri Lanka (WC) 1983
Highest individual innings in ODI 73* Inzamam-ul-Haq for Pakistan v New Zealand (WC) 1999
Highest wicket partnerships in ODI

1st	40 Saeed Anwar & Shahid Afridi	for	Pakistan v New Zealand	(WC) 1999
2nd	34 D.S.B.P. Kuruppu & A. Ranatunga	for	Sri Lanka v New Zealand	(WC) 1983

3rd	80 D.S.B.P. Kuruppu & R.L. Dias	for	Sri Lanka v New Zealand	(WC) 1983
4th	36 Ijaz Ahmed & Inzamam-ul-Haq	for	Pakistan v New Zealand	(WC) 1999
5th	41 B.A. Edgar & J.V. Coney	for	New Zealand v Sri Lanka	(WC) 1983
6th	41 Inzamam-ul-Haq & Moin Khan	for	Pakistan v New Zealand	(WC) 1999
7th	83 S.P. Fleming & C.Z. Harris	for	New Zealand v Pakistan	(WC) 1999
8th	45 C.Z. Harris & D.J. Nash	for	New Zealand v Pakistan	(WC) 1999
9th	14* Inzamam-ul-Haq & Saqlain Mushtaq	for	Pakistan v New Zealand	(WC) 1999
10th	65 M.C. Snedden & E.J. Chatfield	for	New Zealand v Sri Lanka	(WC) 1983

Best bowling performance in ODI 5 for 32 A.S. de Mel for Sri Lanka v New Zealand (WC) 1983
Largest crowd 3,074 New Zealand v Pakistan (WC) 1999

GROUND INFORMATION

ENTRANCES Main Gate off Pentagon Island Roundabout (players, officials, press/media, members, public and vehicles) and from (A61) Sir Frank Whittle Way via spine road adjacent to Virgin Active Leisure Complex.
MEMBERS' ENCLOSURE Lund Pavilion.
PUBLIC ENCLOSURE Rest of the ground.
COVERED STANDS Lund Pavilion, Don Amott Stand and Tea Bar.
OPEN STANDS Rest of ground including Grandstand.
GROUND DIMENSIONS 152m × 167m.
NAME OF ENDS Scoreboard End, Former Grandstand End.
REPLAY SCREEN If matches are televised the replay screen is sited at the Grandstand End of the ground.
FIRST AID Adjacent to Club Office.
CODES OF DRESS Spectators are required to dress in an appropriate manner consistent with attending a cricket match. Bare torsos are not acceptable in or in front of the pavilion. Executive Club/Suite users must wear a necktie and jacket.
BEHAVIOUR The club is keen that standards of behaviour should be maintained and members and spectators are urged to report immediately to the CEO any incident, or potential incident, where they feel action should be taken. Bad language is not acceptable at any match and the club will take prompt and strong action should this or any other breach of the ground regulations occur.
RECIPROCAL ARRANGEMENTS Members of Leicestershire, Northamptonshire and Nottinghamshire can gain entry free on production of membership card when Derbyshire are not playing their own county in County Championship matches. Derbyshire members can attend some race meetings at Uttoxeter Racecourse but must book tickets in advance.
SUPPORTERS' CLUB Derbyshire CCSC £5 for DCCC members and £10 for non-DCCC members. Special rates for concessions and husband and wife membership are available.
JUNIORS Junior Derbyshire CCC membership £15 if under 18 and in full-time education.
CORPORATE ENTERTAINING Various packages are available from Commercial Department and include six hospitality boxes in the Lund Pavilion, Executive Suite, Strutt Room, Moss Room and Rutland Room in the Lund Pavilion and marquees by arrangement around the ground. Contact Commercial Department for brochure.
FACILITIES FOR VISUALLY IMPAIRED SPECTATORS Reduced admission, helpers pay full price. Guide dogs allowed by arrangement. Contact club in advance.
FACILITIES AND ACCESS FOR PEOPLE WITH DISABILITIES INCLUDING WHEELCHAIR ACCESS TO GROUND Yes, from Main Entrance.
DESIGNATED CAR PARK AVAILABLE INSIDE THE GROUND FOR PEOPLE WITH DISABILITIES Yes, next to boundary fence at Scoreboard End of the ground with a space for 6 to 8 cars together with ample space outside the perimeter fence of the playing area to the north in front of the Grass Bank. Access to the Grandstand seats is difficult due to lack of concrete ramps.
GOOD VIEWING AREAS INSIDE THE GROUND FOR PEOPLE USING WHEELCHAIRS Yes, particularly on areas of hard standing to the side of the Lund Pavilion and at the Scoreboard End adjacent to the Don Amott Stand. Generally there are no restrictions. Wheelchairs may be a problem on the Grass Bank side if damp. Please request position in advance.
DESIGNATED VIEWING AREAS FOR PEOPLE USING WHEELCHAIRS No.

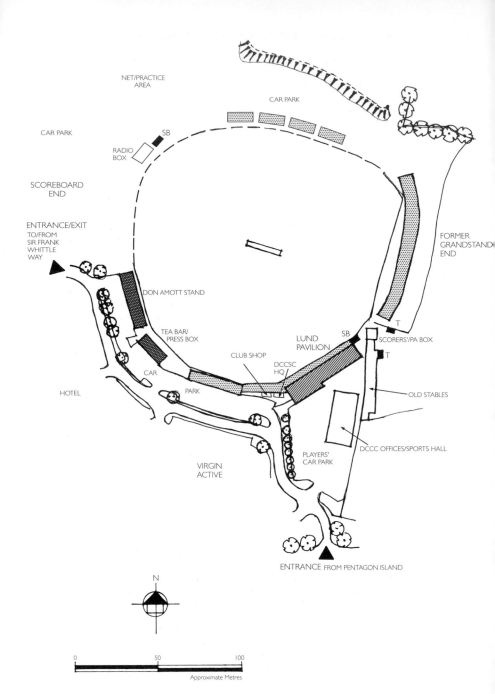

NET/PRACTICE
AREA

CAR PARK

CAR PARK

SB

RADIO
BOX

SCOREBOARD
END

ENTRANCE/EXIT
TO/FROM
SIR FRANK
WHITTLE
WAY

DON AMOTT STAND

FORMER
GRANDSTAND
END

TEA BAR/
PRESS BOX

LUND
PAVILION

SB

CLUB SHOP

SCORERS'/PA BOX

DCCSC
HQ

T

CAR

OLD STABLES

HOTEL

PARK

DCCC OFFICES/SPORTS HALL

PLAYERS'
CAR PARK

VIRGIN
ACTIVE

ENTRANCE FROM PENTAGON ISLAND

N

0   50   100

Approximate Metres

RAMPS TO PROVIDE EASY ACCESS TO BARS & REFRESHMENT OUTLETS FOR PEOPLE USING WHEELCHAIRS Yes, in most areas.

FULL RESTAURANT/DINING FACILITIES Catering by DCCC. Members, yes. Public, limited

TEMPORARY FOOD/DRINK FACILITIES Members, yes. Public, yes.

FOOD SUITABLE FOR VEGETARIANS Members, yes. Public, yes.

BARS Members 2, Public 2.

VARIETIES OF BEER SOLD Banks's.

CHILDREN'S FACILITIES Crèche, no.

CLUB SHOP Yes, Derbyshire CCC Club Shop situated on ground, open match days or orders can be placed via www.dccc.org.uk website.

CLUB MUSEUM No.

CRICKET COACHING FACILITIES Yes, Derbyshire Indoor Cricket School at rear of club offices and outdoor nets.

CRICKET NETS Yes, indoor in Derbyshire Indoor Cricket School and outside to rear of main scoreboard.

OTHER SPORTING OR RECREATIONAL FACILITIES ON THE GROUND Yes, Virgin Active Leisure Complex adjacent to ground. Derby County FC's Pride Park Stadium approximately 20 minutes walk from ground.

FACILITIES FOR HIRE OR WIDER COMMUNITY USE AT THE GROUND Rooms are available for birthday parties, office parties, functions, weddings, funerals, training days, formal dinners and buffets, presentation evenings, exhibitions and conferences. Special rates for DCCC members contact Commercial Department or A. Evans ☎ 01332 388105.

WINTER CRICKET EVENTS Members' Club dinners and lunches are staged in the Lund Pavilion.

CAR PARKING FACILITIES Car parking is available to the rear of the Lund Pavilion for players, officials and press/media. There is also car parking for some members, sponsors and hospitality guests only to the rear of the Stand. Additional car parking is available for members only on the grass to the rear of the main Scoreboard and near the Grass Bank. Valid DCCC membership must be shown. Parking for non-members is £5 per car.

OTHER INFORMATION Indoor sports hall is available for hire to rear of club offices. A second-hand cricket book sales table is available within the Derbyshire CCCSC room near the club shop.

GROUND CAPACITY 9,500.

ANTICIPATED GROUND DEVELOPMENTS A new cricket school/sponsors' boxes to be completed in 2004 sited at the Former Grandstand End. Construction due to commence July 2003.

HOW TO GET THERE

 Derby Midland station 1.25 mile ☎ 08457 484950, www.midlandmainline.co.uk, www.thetrainline.com, www.railtrack.co.uk

 Trent Buses 29 from Derby Midland station to ground, Derby City 42, 43, 44, 45, 46 and 47 from Derby Midland station to bus station, 212 bus passes near ground ☎ 01332 754433 or 292200, 08706 082608, 08705 808080. National Express Coaches ☎ 08705 808080, www.nationalexpress.co.uk

 There are cycle routes from surrounding areas of Derby to this part of the city.

 From north: M1 junction 25, take A52 (west) to Pentagon Roundabout at junction of Nottingham Road and Sir Frank Whittle Way (A61), follow signs to cricket ground, entrance is off Sir Frank Whittle Way. **From south:** as for north. **From east:** from Nottingham take A52 (east), then as for north from M1 junction 25. **From west:** A50, turn left on to A38 (Burton Road) at roundabout stay on A38 (Kingsway) at next roundabout take A52 (east) (Ashbourne Road). Follow A52 to A601 (Ford Street), rejoin A52 at Eastgate. Follow Eastgate to Pentagon roundabout, then as for north.

 East Midlands Airport 01332 852852, www.eastmidlandsairport.co.uk

WHERE TO STAY

Days Inn adjacent to ground opening July 2003 (www.daysinn.com/derby), Best Western Midland Hotel (☎ 01332 345894, www.midland-derby.co.uk), Bonehill Farmhouse (☎ 01332 513553), Chambers House Hotel (☎ 01332 746412), Days Inn Lodge (Derby South) (☎ 0800 0280 400 or 01332 799666, www.daysinn.com), Derby Innkeeper's Lodge (☎ 01332 662504, www.innkeeperslodge.com), Derby Post

The County Cricket Ground looking towards the scoreboard from the Lund Pavilion.

House (☎ 0870 4009023), Express by Holiday Inn (☎ 01332 388000, www.hiexpress.co.uk), Marriott Breadsall Priory Hotel & Country Club (☎ 01332 832235, www.marriotthotels.com), Red Setters Guesthouse (☎ 01332 362770, www.derbycity.com/michael/redset.html), The Georgian House Hotel (☎ 01332 349806, www.thegeorgianhousehotel.co.uk), The Hill House Hotel (☎/fax 01332 361523, www.hillhousehotel.co.uk)

Visit www.visitderby.co.uk or www.smoothhound.co.uk for details of other hotels, guesthouses and bed and breakfasts in and around Derby.

WHERE TO EAT

Darleys on the River (☎ 01332 364987 www.darleys.com), Hotel Restaurant La Gondola (☎ 01332 332895)

TOURIST INFORMATION CENTRE Derby Tourist Information Centre, Assembly Rooms, Market Place, Derby DE1 3AH ☎ 01332 255802, fax 01332 256137, email tourism@derby.gov.uk, vic@derby.gov.uk, www.visitderby.co.uk

LOCAL RADIO STATIONS BBC Radio Derby (104.5 MHz FM/1116 KHz MW), 96 Trent FM/Classic Gold GEM AM (96.2 MHz FM/999 KHz MW)

LOCAL NEWSPAPERS *Derby Evening Telegraph, Derbyshire Times, Derby Trader*

Durham

Chester-le-Street – Riverside
Darlington

DURHAM COUNTY CRICKET CLUB, COUNTY GROUND, RIVERSIDE, CHESTER-LE-STREET, CO. DURHAM DH3 3QR

Telephone	0191 387 1717 **fax** 0191 387 1616
Email	reception.durham@ecb.co.uk
Official site	www.durhamccc.co.uk
Ticket site	www.crickettickets.net
Match day office at out grounds	0191 387 1415
Austin's Bar & Bistro	0191 388 3335
Club Shop	0191 387 2877
Catering	0191 387 1717
Conference & Banqueting	0191 387 4711 **fax** 0191 387 4697
Marketing	0191 387 1717

Founded 1882
Colours maroon, Oxford blue and old gold
Crest coat of arms of County Durham
National Cricket League Nickname Dynamos
National Cricket League Colours Oxford blue, maroon and old gold
Patron A.W. Austin
President M. Pratt MBE
Executive Chairman D.W. Midgley
Board Directors I.M. Howie, R. Jackson, I.D. Mills, B. Thubron, J. Sherrington, T. Moffat MBE, F. Curry, K.W. Gardner MBE
Chief Executive D. Harker
Cricket & Executive Secretary Mrs P. Walton
Director of Cricket G. Cook
County Cashline C. Jobling
Cricket Development N. Brown
Marketing J. Bailey
Membership A. Dovaston
Sponsorship Services L. Mawston
Sponsorship Sales G. Hollins
Women's Cricket Development P. Peel

Captain J.J.B. Lewis
Vice Captain P.D. Collingwood
1st Team Coach M.D. Moxon
2nd Team Coach A.A. Walker
Groundsman D. Measor
1st Team Scorer B. Hunt
2nd Team Scorer D. Graham
Hon Statistician/Historian B. Hunt
Main Sponsors Northern Rock, Costcutter, Sportsnet
Shirt Sponsors Sportsnet www.sportsnet.uk.net
National Cricket League Shirt Sponsors Northern Rock
Newsletter *The Riverside Review*
Scorecards 50p each
National Cricket League Match Programme £2 each
Yearbook £6
Club Shop Durham CCC Shop
Frizzell County Championship Status Division 2
National Cricket League Status Division 2

ACHIEVEMENTS

County Championship Best 8th 1999, 8th Division 1 2000
Minor Counties Championship Champions 1895, 1900, 1901, 1926, 1930, 1976, 1980, 1981 and 1984
Minor Counties Championship Final Winners 1984
Minor Counties English Estates Trophy Competition Winners 1985
Benson and Hedges Cup Initial Season 1992
Gillette Cup 2nd Round 1973

NatWest Series Trophy Quarter-finalists 1992
Cheltenham & Gloucester Trophy Quarter-finalists 2001
Sunday League 7th 1993
National Cricket League Best 9th Division 1 2002 and 2nd Division 2 2001
Britannic Assurance Championship Challenge 1991 Victoria
Tilcon Trophy Finalists 1991
Joshua Tetley Festival Trophy Semi-finalists 1991

DURHAM CRICKET BOARD

Chairman J.D. Robson CBE
Secretary B. Jackson
Treasurer D. Harker
Cricket Development Officer N. Brown
Officer/Youth Coach G. Cook
Women & Girls Secretary P. Peel

Address   Durham County Cricket Club, County Cricket Ground, Riverside, Chester-le-Street, Co
Durham DH3 3QR
☎   0191 387 1717
Fax   0191 387 1616

GROUNDS

Chester-le-Street (County Cricket Ground, Riverside) and Darlington (Feethams Cricket Ground, South
Terrace)
   Other grounds used since 1969: Durham University (Racecourse Ground, Green Lane), Stockton-on-Tees
(Grangefield Road Ground), Hartlepool (Park Drive), Gateshead Fell (Eastwood Gardens, Low Fell), Chester-
le-Street (Ropery Lane), Jesmond (Northumberland CCC Ground, Osborne Avenue, Newcastle-upon-Tyne),
Sunderland (Ashbrooke Cricket Ground), Durham City (Green Lane), South Shields (Westoe Ground, Dean
Road), Bishop Auckland (King's Way), Wearmouth (Carley Hill) and Consett (Blackfyne Ground)

SECOND XI GROUNDS

In addition to the above-mentioned grounds the following will be used for second XI matches:
Norton CC, Station Road, Norton, Stockton-on-Tees, Co. Durham ☎ 01642 554031
Sunderland CC, Ashbrooke, Sunderland. Co. Durham ☎ 0191 528 4536
Felling CC, Heworth Lane, Heworth, Felling, Co. Durham ☎ 0191 469 3645
Philadelphia CC, Bunker Hill, Houghton-le-Spring, Tyne & Wear ☎ 0191 584 1348
Boldon CC, Sunderland Road, East Boldon, Tyne & Wear ☎ 0191 536 4180
Bishop Auckland CC, King's Way, Bishop Auckland ☎ 01388 603371
Chester-le-Street CC, Ropery Lane, Chester-le-Street, Co. Durham ☎ 0191 388 3684
South Northumberland CC, Gosforth, Newcastle-upon-Tyne ☎ 0191 2856716
Stockton-on-Tees CC, The Grangefield Road Ground, Oxbridge Road, Stockton-on-Tees, Cleveland
   ☎ 01642 672835
Hartlepool CC, The Pavilion, Park Drive, Hartlepool, Cleveland ☎ 01429 260875
Tynemouth CC, Preston Avenue, North Shields ☎ 0191 257 6865
Longhirst Hall, Morpeth, Northumberland ☎ 01670 791348
Shildon Railway CC, Hackworth Street, Shildon, Co. Durham ☎ 01388 772068
Durham City CC, The Pavilion, Green Lane, Durham City ☎ 0191 386 9959
Eppleton CC, Church Road, Hetton-le-Hole, Tyne & Wear ☎ 091 526 1271
South Shields CC, Wood Terrace, South Shields ☎ 0191 456 1506
Durham School., Quarryhead Lane, Durham City ☎ 0191 386 9959
Seaton Carew CC, The Pavilion, Hornby Park, Elizabeth Way, Seaton Carew, Hartlepool, Cleveland
   ☎ 01429 260945

CHESTER-LE-STREET RIVERSIDE

Address County Ground, Riverside,
Chester-le-Street, Co Durham DH3 3QR
Prospects of Play ☎ 0191 387 1717

HISTORY OF GROUND AND FACILITIES

DURHAM COUNTY CRICKET CLUB were established on 23 May 1882 and played their first match at Ashbrooke Cricket Ground, Sunderland, on 12 June that year, defeating Northumberland by 4 wickets. Durham were Minor Counties Champions a record-equalling nine times between 1900 and 1984 and became the first minor county to defeat a first-class county in the Gillette Cup in 1973 when they beat Yorkshire. Between 1976 and 1982 Durham played 65 minor county matches without defeat, a record which still stands. In March 1989 the Durham County Cricket Club committee decided to begin procedures to apply to become a first-class cricketing county. Durham were awarded first-class status by the Test and County Cricket Board on 6 December 1991 – the first county to be granted such status for 70 years.

Between 1992 and 1994 Durham led a nomadic existence with no proper home venue, although by this time established players such as Ian Botham, David Graveney, Wayne Larkins, Paul Parker, Geoff Cook, Dean Jones and Simon Hughes were on the playing staff.

In April 1993 Durham County Cricket Club obtained planning approval to create their own ground at Riverside, east of Chester-le-Street, with visions of creating a venue to bring Test and international cricket to the north-east of England. The cricket ground strategic master plan was prepared by Newcastle architects Ainsworth Spark Associates and involved the development of some 6.3 hectares (14.9 acres) of greenfield land. Of the 6.3 hectares, the cricket playing area covers 2.1 hectares (5.2 acres). Work on the outfield and playing surface began in 1993 and this included the construction of a high-quality cricket square in readiness for the beginning of the 1995 season. The work was jointly funded by Chester-le-Street District Council, Durham County Council and Durham County Cricket Club.

The Riverside complex lies in beautiful surroundings. Its centrepiece is, of course, the Riverside Cricket Ground and its fine stands and facilities. Other facilities within the complex include football pitches, an athletics track, a wildlife area, housing, car parking and a town park. Grants were received from the European Regional Development Fund, the Sports Council and the Forestry Commission to enable these facilities to be constructed.

The cricket ground was designed with stands located on its western and southern sides, offering fine views over to the open eastern side towards Lumley Castle and the River Wear. The ground plan allowed space for high-quality facilities with six stand units (five linked) on the western side of the ground and a sixth at the southern end of the playing area. The northern and eastern sides of the ground have areas of tiered tip-up seats which can accommodate 2,000 to 6,000 spectators.

Don Robson Pavilion together with County Stand and executive suites, players' dressing rooms and members' facilities in the main enclosure at Riverside.

The ground was designed during the early 1990s when the planning application was submitted and while this work was being done Durham staged home matches around the county at numerous out venues. For a period the county club's administrative headquarters was in Houghton-le-Spring. The grounds used during 1992, the county's first season in first-class cricket, were: Gateshead Fell Cricket Club, Jesmond in Newcastle-upon-Tyne (home of Northumberland County Cricket Club), Darlington Cricket Club based at Feethams which is still used regularly, Hartlepool Cricket Club, Stockton-on-Tees Cricket Club, Chester-le-Street Cricket Club situated in Ropery Lane (not far from the Riverside complex) and finally the delightful Racecourse Ground at Durham University close to the River Wear. This venue is now being used by Durham UCCE for home matches against counties and for county Second XI fixtures.

Riverside was built in three specific phases between 1995 and 1997. Stage 1 included the enclosure of the ground with walls and landscaping, the provision of permanent administration offices for the county cricket club, and the construction of players' and spectators' facilities in one unit of the western stand. Stage 2 included the provision of further facilities in more units of the western stand, including banqueting and conferencing suites, a souvenir shop, offices and further spectator facilities. Finally, Stage 3 included the completion of the scheme with the construction of the south stand and the final two units of the western stand. The Don Robson Pavilion was opened by HM the Queen on 13 October 1996. In September 1996 the Durham Cricket Academy was formed to nurture young cricketers from County Durham moving into the first-class game. The main scoreboard was built thanks to sponsorship from Callers Pegasus Travel Services. Durham County Cricket Club has used the Riverside County Cricket Ground as its headquarters since 1995.

The main buildings on the western side of the ground are permanent structures and house the following facilities. Ground floor: members' seating, Riverside Health & Gymnasium Club, main reception, shop, membership office, Austin's Bar & Bistro plus toilets including disabled facilities. On Level One: Cricket Office, players' dining room, players' and umpires' rooms, administration offices, members' lounge plus toilets including disabled facilities. On Level Two: Dunelm Lounge, hospitality boxes 0 to 18, Colin Milburn Lounge, Lumley Lounge plus toilets including disabled facilities. The entire building is connected by stairs and lifts in each of the three towers. An induction loop system is installed in the members' lounge for members with hearing difficulties. The seating in front of these stands is mostly open although some areas are partly covered. There is permanent seating at the southern end on the South Terrace and the remainder to the north beyond the main terracing is all of the temporary plastic tip-up variety.

The flat playing area is 155 metres by 145 metres and is defined by a rope and a white fence with some advertising boards. The square can accommodate twenty-two pitches and the ground has ample space for temporary facilities for big matches. The press/media box is situated at the Lumley End. When required the TV camera/commentary box is positioned at the Finchale End directly above and behind the sightscreen.

Durham's first first-class match at Riverside was on 18–22 May 1995 against Warwickshire: the visitors won. Improvements to the ground and facilities have brought high-profile games to Riverside. In May 1999 the World Cup matches between Pakistan and Scotland and Australia and Bangladesh were played here.

View from the main enclosure across the Riverside ground to the main scoreboard with the River Wear and Lumley Castle in the background.

In 2000 Durham County Cricket Club was rewarded by the England and Wales Cricket Board with the first limited-overs one-day internationals in the NatWest Series between West Indies and Zimbabwe and England and West Indies on 15 and 16 June. In 2001 a one-day international match between Australia and Pakistan was due to be played but adverse weather meant it had to be abandoned at 1.55 p.m. without a ball being bowled. The match had sold out, with a 12,000-strong crowd expected.

Other important visitors to the ground have included Lesley Garrett for a concert in aid of the Lord's Taverners on 16 September 2000 and Kate Hoey, then Minister for Sport, who visited Riverside on 15 December 2000. Between 28 and 31 August 2001 England Under-19s hosted West Indies Under-19s in a Test match which was drawn and in August 2002 Riverside hosted England Ladies v New Zealand and Indian Ladies in the NatWest Triangular Tournament. On 4 July 2002 a day/night televised match was played between England and India which also suffered from poor weather during the evening session. In May 2003 the Riverside ground will host the second Test match in the npower series between England and Zimbabwe.

Until the development of The Rose Bowl, Hampshire Cricket's new home in Southampton, this was the newest and most modern cricket ground in the country. It will be counted as the seventh venue to be used by England for home Test matches although strictly speaking it will be the eighth because Sheffield United Football Club's Bramall Lane ground was used for Test matches over 100 years ago and by Yorkshire County Cricket Club until 1973.

Once completed the ground will have a capacity of 20,000. In 2003 the capacity is 15,000, although commonly crowds tend to be between 6,000 and 8,000.

GROUND RECORDS AND SCORES

TEST MATCH RECORDS

None yet established; inaugural Test match in 2003.

FIRST-CLASS MATCHES

Highest innings total for county 485 for 3 v Durham UCCE 2001
Highest innings total against county 516 for 6 for Leicestershire 1996
Lowest innings total for county 74 v Yorkshire 1998
Lowest innings total against county 67 for Durham UCCE 2001
Highest individual innings for county 190 P.D. Collingwood v Sri Lankans 2002
Highest individual innings against county 200* D.J. Cullinan for South Africans 1998
Highest wicket partnerships for county

1st	130 J.J.B. Lewis & J.E. Morris	v	Glamorgan	1998
2nd	258 J.J.B. Lewis & M.L. Love	v	Nottinghamshire	2001
3rd	142 J.J.B. Lewis & P.D. Collingwood	v	Durham UCCE	2002
4th	204 J.J.B. Lewis & J. Boiling	v	Derbyshire	1997
5th	170 P.D. Collingwood & M.P. Speight	v	Nottinghamshire	1999
6th	148 S.M. Katich & I.D. Hunter	v	Leicestershire	2000
7th	127 D.R. Law & J.E. Brinkley	v	Hampshire	2001
8th	130 P.D. Collingwood & P. Mustard	v	Sri Lankans	2002
9th	93 N.J. Speak & N. Killeen	v	Kent	2000
10th	53 A. Pratt & N.G. Hatch	v	Sussex	2001

Highest wicket partnerships against county

1st	206 N.V. Knight & M.A. Wagh	for	Warwickshire	1997
2nd	151 S.L. Campbell & B.C. Lara	for	West Indians	1995
3rd	248 O.A. Shah & S.P. Fleming	for	Middlesex	2001
4th	218 M.E. Waugh & A. Habib	for	Essex	2002
5th	121 P.A. Cottey & M.J. Powell	for	Glamorgan	1998
6th	284 P.V. Simmons & P.A. Nixon	for	Leicestershire	1996
7th	175 W.K. Hegg & I.D. Austin	for	Lancashire	1996
8th	125 R.J. Turner & M.P.L. Bulbeck	for	Somerset	1999
9th	99 G.A. Hick & M.J. Rawnsley	for	Worcestershire	2001
10th	110 C.E.W. Silverwood & R.D. Stemp	for	Yorkshire	1996

Best bowling performance in an innings for county 7 for 51 S.J.E. Brown v Lancashire 2000
Best bowling performance in an innings against county 8 for 69 A.R. Caddick for Somerset 1995
Best bowling performance in a match for county 11 for 192 S.J.E. Brown v Warwickshire 1995
Best bowling performance in a match against county 11 for 105 M.S. Kasprowicz for Glamorgan 2002
Largest crowd 6,500 v Warwickshire 1995

LIMITED OVERS MATCHES

Highest innings total for county 326 for 4 v Herefordshire (NWT) 1995
Highest innings total against county 344 for 4 for Leicestershire (SL) 1996
Lowest innings total for county 91 v Hampshire (NWT) 2000
Lowest innings total against county 107 for Derbyshire (B&H) 2000
Highest individual innings for county 125 S. Hutton v Herefordshire (NWT) 1995
Highest individual innings against county 125 D.I. Stevens for Leicestershire (SL) 2002
Highest wicket partnerships for county

1st	255 M.A. Roseberry & S. Hutton	v	Herefordshire	(NWT)	1995
2nd	120 N. Peng & M.L. Love	v	Hampshire	(C&G)	2001
3rd	166 M.L. Love & P.D. Collingwood	v	Hampshire	(SL)	2001
4th	140* P.D. Collingwood & J.J.B. Lewis	v	Leicestershire	(B&H)	2001
5th	115 J.A. Daley & J.J.B. Lewis	v	Middlesex	(SL)	1999
6th	83 M.P. Speight & M.J. Foster	v	Scotland	(B&H)	1998
7th	48* M.A. Gough & A. Pratt	v	Lancashire	(SL)	2001
8th	58* M.A. Gough & G.D. Bridge	v	Lancashire	(B&H)	2002
9th	50* M.M. Betts & N. Killeen	v	Worcestershire	(B&H)	1998
10th	45* N. Killeen & N.G. Hatch	v	Yorkshire	(SL)	2002

Highest wicket partnerships against county

1st	170 S.P. James & M.P. Maynard	for	Glamorgan	(SL)	1998
2nd	109 B.G. Lockie & D.R. Lockhart	for	Scotland	(B&H)	1998
3rd	221 A. Habib & V.J. Wells	for	Leicestershire	(B&H)	1997
4th	121* S.C. Ecclestone & M.N. Lathwell	for	Somerset	(SL)	1997
5th	140* D.L. Maddy & A. Habib	for	Leicestershire	(SL)	1996
6th	109 K.D. James & A.N. Aymes	for	Hampshire	(SL)	1995
7th	65* D.A. Leatherdale & S.R. Lampitt	for	Worcestershire	(SL)	1997
8th	38* J.S. Foster & R.S. Clinton	for	Essex	(SL)	2001
9th	25 M.J. Marvell & M.J. Saggers	for	Minor Counties	(B&H)	1996
10th	48 R.K. Illingworth & A. Sheriyar	for	Worcestershire	(B&H)	1998

Best bowling performance in a match for county 6 for 30 S.J.E. Brown v Northamptonshire (B&H) 1997
Best bowling performance in a match against county 6 for 27 P.J. Franks for Nottinghamshire (SL) 2000
Largest crowd 4,750 v Lancashire (SL) 1997

ONE-DAY INTERNATIONALS

Highest innings total for England in ODI 171 for 0 v West Indies (NWS) 2000
Highest innings against England in ODI 285 for 4 by India (NWS) 2002
Highest innings total in non-England ODI 290 for 4 for Zimbabwe v West Indies (NWS) 2000
Lowest innings total for England in ODI 171 for 0 v West Indies (NWS) 2000
Lowest innings against England in ODI 169 for 8 by West Indies (NWS) 2000

Lowest innings total in non-England ODI 167 for Scotland v Pakistan (WC) 1999
Highest individual innings for England ODI 87* M.E. Trescothick v West Indies (NWS) 2000
Highest individual innings against England ODI 105* S.R. Tendulkar for India (NWS) 2002
Highest individual innings in non-England ODI 112* M.W. Goodwin for Zimbabwe v West Indies (NWS) 2000
Highest wicket partnerships for England in ODI

1st	171* M.E. Trescothick & A.J. Stewart	v	West Indies	(NWS)	2000
2nd	23* N. Hussain & N.V. Knight	v	India	(NWS)	2002
3rd to 10th	yet to be established				

Highest Wicket Partnerships against England in ODI

1st	6 S.L. Campbell & W.W. Hinds	for	West Indies	(NWS)	2000
2nd	48 D. Mongia & V. Sehwag	for	India	(NWS)	2002
3rd	4 D. Mongia & S.R. Tendulkar	for	India	(NWS)	2002
4th	169 S.R. Tendulkar & R. Dravid	for	India	(NWS)	2002
5th	64* S.R. Tendulkar & Yuvraj Singh	for	India	(NWS)	2002
6th	30 R.D. Jacobs & R.L. Powell	for	West Indies	(NWS)	2000
7th	28 R.D. Jacobs & F.A. Rose	for	West Indies	(NWS)	2000
8th	6 N.A.M. McLean & F.A. Rose	for	West Indies	(NWS)	2000
9th	1* N.A.M. McLean & M. Dillon	for	West Indies	(NWS)	2000
10th	yet to be established				

Highest wicket partnerships in non-England ODI

1st	98 A.C. Gilchrist & M.E. Waugh	for	Australia v Bangladesh	(WC)	1999
2nd	173 S.L. Campbell & B.C. Lara	for	West Indies v Zimbabwe	(WC)	1999
3rd	24 M.W. Goodwin & A.D.R. Campbell	for	Zimbabwe v West Indies	(WC)	1999
4th	70* T.M. Moody & R.T. Ponting	for	Australia v Bangladesh	(WC)	1999
5th	186* M.W. Goodwin & G.W. Flower	for	Zimbabwe v West Indies	(WC)	1999
6th	103 Yousuf Youhana & Moin Khan	for	Pakistan v Scotland	(WC)	1999
7th	66* Yousuf Youhana & Wasim Akram	for	Pakistan v Scotland	(WC)	1999
8th	35* Minhajul Abedin & Enamul Haque	for	Bangladesh v Australia	(WC)	1999
9th	11 G.M. Hamilton & Asim Butt	for	Scotland v Pakistan	(WC)	1999
10th	7 G.M. Hamilton & N.R. Dyer	for	Scotland v Pakistan	(WC)	1999

Best bowling performance for England ODI 3 for 27 A.D. Mullally v West Indies (NWS) 2000
Best bowling performance against England ODI 1 for 31 Z. Khan for India (NWS) 2002
Best bowling performance in non-England ODI 3 for 11 Shoaib Akhtar for Pakistan v Scotland 1999
Largest crowd 7,061 Australia v Bangladesh (WC) 1999

GROUND INFORMATION

ENTRANCES From Main Entrance to Riverside from Ropery Lane (players, officials, members, public and vehicles) thence through gates 1 to 6 to the west and north sides of the Riverside Ground.
MEMBERS' ENCLOSURE Don Robson Pavilion, County Stand and defined members' enclosure.
PUBLIC ENCLOSURE Rest of the ground.
COVERED STANDS Don Robson Pavilion (part) and County Stand (part).
OPEN STANDS Don Robson Pavilion (part), County Stand (part) and rest of ground to include other permanent and temporary stands.
NAME OF ENDS Lumley End, Finchale End.
GROUND DIMENSIONS 155m × 145m.
REPLAY SCREEN If matches are televised the replay screen is sited on the east side of the ground.
FIRST AID Situated in main enclosure.
CODES OF DRESS Consistent with the prestige of being a member of a County Cricket Club, members are requested to dress in an appropriate manner.
BEHAVIOUR The Board is most concerned that standards of behaviour must be maintained at all matches involving Durham. Bad language is not acceptable at any cricket match and the Board will take the strongest possible action against transgressors.
RECIPROCAL ARRANGEMENTS Durham CCC members can gain access to Newcastle Racecourse for certain

race meetings. 10% off Durham CCC membership is offered to members of Northumberland CCC and Cumberland CCC.

SUPPORTERS' CLUB Dunelm Cricket Society. Details from Gillian Edger ☎ 020 7514 1915.

JUNIORS Young & Junior Lions membership is available to under-11s for £15 and Junior membership for over-12s to under-17s £25 per year. Contact Membership Secretary ☎ 0191 387 1717 ext 2872 for further information.

CORPORATE ENTERTAINING Durham CCC Conference & Banqueting Department offers corporate entertainment in the Boardroom, Finchale Lounge, Lumley Lounge, Colin Milburn Lounge, Dunelm Lounge, Riverside Suite or in one of 20 Executive Boxes. These are available to hire on a season or match by match basis. Contact Conference & Banqueting Department ☎ 0191 387 4711 fax 0191 387 4697 for further details and a copy of the brochure.

FACILITIES FOR VISUALLY IMPAIRED SPECTATORS No reduced admission. Guide dogs are allowed. No advance warning necessary to attend matches.

FACILITIES AND ACCESS FOR PEOPLE WITH DISABILITIES INCLUDING WHEELCHAIR ACCESS TO GROUND Yes, from Ropery Lane via entrance Gate 1.

DESIGNATED CAR PARK AVAILABLE INSIDE THE GROUND FOR PEOPLE WITH DISABILITIES Yes, near Gate 1.

DESIGNATED VIEWING AREAS FOR PEOPLE USING WHEELCHAIRS Yes, there are 31 wheelchair bays situated in front of the western stands including the Don Robson Pavilion and County Stand.

RAMPS TO PROVIDE EASY ACCESS TO BARS & REFRESHMENT OUTLETS FOR PEOPLE USING WHEELCHAIRS Yes, all buildings can be accessed by ramp and some have a lift.

FULL RESTAURANT/DINING FACILITIES Members, yes. Public, yes. A full restaurant is available in Austin's Bar & Bistro which was awarded AA Rosette in June 1999. Pre-booking is essential at weekends. Austin's is open to non-members 7 days per week. Opening hours Monday–Saturday 10.00 a.m.–11.00 p.m., Sunday 12 noon–10.30 p.m. Reservations recommended when cricket is being played ☎ 0191 388 3335.

TEMPORARY FOOD/DRINK FACILITIES Members, yes. Public, yes.

FOOD SUITABLE FOR VEGETARIANS Members, yes. Public, yes.

BARS Members 2, Public 1.

VARIETIES OF BEER SOLD Newcastle Brown Ale.

CHILDREN'S FACILITIES Crèche, no. Play area, no.

CLUB SHOP Yes, Durham CCC Club Shop available within Don Robson Pavilion Stand ☎ 0191 387 2877.

CLUB MUSEUM Yes, Durham Cricket & Sports Museum is situated in the building at the southern, Finchale End of the ground.

CRICKET COACHING FACILITIES Yes, contact Durham CCC for details for facilities in the summer and winter months.

CRICKET NETS Yes, contact Durham CCC for details for facilities in the summer and winter months.

OTHER SPORTING OR RECREATIONAL FACILITIES ON THE GROUND Yes, gymnasium beneath Don Robson Pavilion and Western Stands. Sports complex close by at Finchale End of ground including athletics track and football pitches.

FACILITIES FOR HIRE OR WIDER COMMUNITY USE AT THE GROUND Durham CCC Conference & Banqueting Department offers corporate entertainment in the Boardroom, Finchale Lounge, Lumley Lounge, Colin Milburn Lounge, Dunelm Lounge, Riverside Suite or in one of 20 Executive Boxes. Rooms are available for functions, weddings, exhibitions, Christmas lunches, conferences and business and private entertainment. These are available to hire on a season or match by match basis or out of season. Contact Conference & Banqueting Department ☎ 0191 387 4711 Fax 0191 387 4697 for further details and a copy of the brochure.

WINTER CRICKET EVENTS Members' Club dinners and lunches are staged in the winter months. Also The Cricket Society North-East Branch and the Dunelm Cricket Society hold regular meetings in the weekday evenings. Contact Durham CCC, The Cricket Society North-East or Dunelm Cricket Society for details.

CAR PARKING FACILITIES Ample car parking adjoining Riverside Complex for players, officials, press/media, members and the general public. Riverside is easily accessible from junction 63 off the A1(M) by car and there is plenty of car parking available close to the ground at a cost of £3 per day on match days.

OTHER INFORMATION The Brick Wall behind the sightscreen at the northern Lumley End of the ground has some commemorative plaques in place near gate 5.

GROUND CAPACITY 15,000.

ANTICIPATED GROUND DEVELOPMENTS A new hotel complex to the north of the County Stand close to Gates 2 and 3.

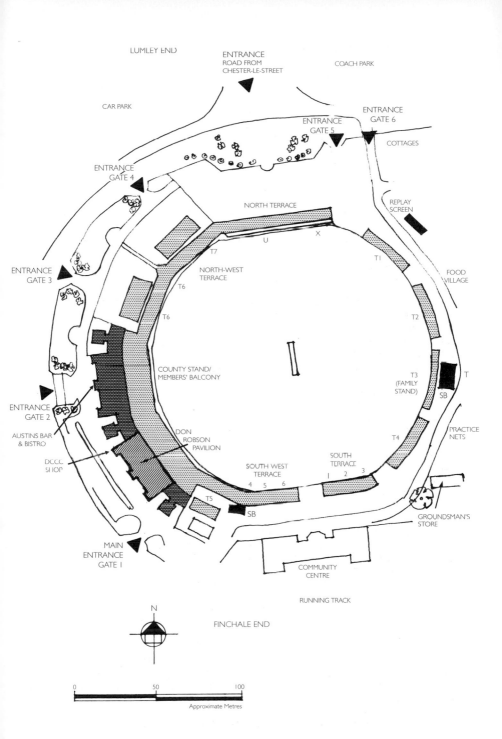

LUMLEY END

ENTRANCE
ROAD FROM
CHESTER-LE-STREET

COACH PARK

CAR PARK

ENTRANCE
GATE 5

ENTRANCE
GATE 6

COTTAGES

ENTRANCE
GATE 4

REPLAY
SCREEN

NORTH TERRACE

U   X

T7   T1

FOOD
VILLAGE

ENTRANCE
GATE 3

NORTH-WEST
TERRACE

T6

T6   T2

COUNTY STAND/
MEMBERS' BALCONY

T3
(FAMILY
STAND)

T

SB

ENTRANCE
GATE 2

AUSTINS BAR
& BISTRO

T4

PRACTICE
NETS

DON
ROBSON
PAVILION

DCCC
SHOP

SOUTH
TERRACE

SOUTH WEST
TERRACE

4   5   6   1   2   3

T5

SB

GROUNDSMAN'S
STORE

MAIN
ENTRANCE
GATE 1

COMMUNITY
CENTRE

N

RUNNING TRACK

FINCHALE END

0   50   100

Approximate Metres

HOW TO GET THERE

 Chester-le-Street station 1 mile. From the railway station walk straight down the road and over the mini-roundabout. At the junction (Lambton Arms on the left), turn right up the main street. Go straight over the mini-roundabout and at the next roundabout turn left down Ropery Lane – keep on the right hand side of the road. You will pass Chester-le-Street CC on the left behind the wall. At the next roundabout cross over the road and the Riverside ground is in front of you. ☎ Enquiries and reservations 08457 225225, 0870 602 3322 or 0191 387 1387, fax 0191 387 3386, email customerservices.ns@ems.rail.co.uk. Web www.gner.co.uk, www.northern-spirit.co.uk, www.railtrack.com, www.thetrainline.co.uk, www.chester-le-track.co.uk

 X1, X2, X46, X69, 722, 723, 724, 734, 737, 775 and 778 Go-Ahead Northern, Go-North East, Tees & District, United, OK Travel, Primrose Coaches and Gardiners Coaches travel through Chester-le-Street 1.0 mile from ground. Bus Information Line ☎ 0845 6060 260 or 0191 386 4411 ext 3337 or National Express Coaches ☎ 08705 808080 www.nationalexpress.co.uk

 There are cycle routes from surrounding areas of Chester-le-Street to this part of the town. A cycle path is located close to the ground and can be accessed from both Durham and Washington.

 From north: from A1(M) Junction 63 take A167. Follow A167 to roundabout with B1284 (Ropery Lane). Follow Ropery Lane for signs to Durham County Cricket Club, Riverside. **From south**: A1(M) Junction 63 and then as for from north. **From east**: from B1284, Woodstone Village, Houghton le Spring stay on B1284 (Lumley New Road). At roundabout take the second exit. At roundabout take the first exit. At roundabout take the second exit and follow signs for Riverside. **From west**: from B6313, Hett Hills, Chester le Street stay on B6313 to roundabout with A167 (Park Road). Exit roundabout on to B1284 then as for from north.

 Newcastle Airport ☎ 0191 286 0966 or Teesside Airport ☎ 01950 460 654

WHERE TO STAY

Beamish Park (☎ 01207 281260), Eslington Villa Hotel (☎ 0191 487 6017), Seaham Hall Hotel (☎ 0191 516 1400), Kings Lodge Hotel (☎ 0191 370 9977), Holiday Inn Washington (☎ 0870 400 9084), Lumley Castle Hotel (☎ 0191 389 1111), Lambton Arms Hotel (☎ 0191 388 3265), The Lambton Worm (☎ 0191 388 3386), The Cookson Public House (☎ 0191 389 2044), The Old Manse (☎ 0191 410 2486), Waldridge Hall Farm (☎ 0191 388 4210), Bees Cottage (☎ 0191 384 5775), Dun Cow Inn (☎ 01740 20894), Chilton Lodge (☎ 0191 385 2694), Peterlee Lodge (☎ 0191 586 2161), Rainton Lodge (☎ 0191 512 0540)

For other places to stay in Chester-le-Street, Durham or Washington area ☎ 0191 384 3720, 0191 375 3046, 0191 384 3720 or visit www.smoothhound.co.uk, www.visitnorthumbria.com, www.durham.gov.uk.

WHERE TO EAT

Barn Again Bistro (☎ 0191 230 3338), Bistro 21 (☎ 0191 384 4354), Café 21 (☎ 0191 222 0755), Dragon House (☎ 0191 232 0868), Forsters Restaurant (☎ 0191 519 0929), Fisherman's Lodge (☎ 0191 281 3281), Francesca's (☎ 0191 281 6586), Lord Crewe Arms (☎ 01434 675251), The Rose Tree (☎ 0191 386 8512), Lisann's Restaurant (☎ 0191 383 0352), King Neptune (☎ 0191 261 6657), Leela's (☎ 0191 230 1261), Pani's (☎ 0191 232 4366 www.pani.net), Paradiso (☎ 0191 221 1240 www.paradiso.co.uk), Sachins (☎ 0191 261 9035), Shaheens Indian Bistro (☎ 0191 386 0960), Tasca (☎ 0191 230 4006), Valley Junction 397 (☎ 0191 281 6397), Vujon (☎ 0191 221 0601)

TOURIST INFORMATION CENTRE Durham Tourist Information Centre, Market Place, Durham, County Durham ☎ 0191 384 3720 www.durham.gov.uk

OTHER USEFUL INFORMATION

Newcastle United Football Club ☎ 0191 201 8400 email admin@nufc.co.uk www.nufc.co.uk
Sunderland Football Club ☎ 0191 551 5000 www.safc.com

Northumbria Tourist Board ☎ 0191 375 3046 www.visitnorthumbria.com
Hotel Booking Line with GNER Trains ☎ 01904 671111

LOCAL RADIO STATIONS BBC Radio Newcastle (96.0 MHz FM/1458 KHz MW), BBC Radio Cleveland
(95.0 MHz FM/1548 KHz MW), TFM Radio (96.6 MHz FM/1170 KHz MW).

LOCAL NEWSPAPERS *The Northern Echo, Evening Gazette, Hartlepool Mail , The Journal, The Evening
Chronicle, Sunderland Echo*

DARLINGTON

Address Darlington Cricket and Athletic Club, Feethams Cricket Ground,
South Terrace, Darlington, Co Durham DL1 5JD
Prospects of Play ☎ 01325 250044

HISTORY OF GROUND AND FACILITIES

DARLINGTON CRICKET CLUB, established *circa* 1827, originally played on a
ground in Park Street but hosted their last fixture there in October 1866. The club
then moved to 10 rented acres south of Feethams, the house where a Mr J.
Pease lived. Late in 1866 a new cricket ground was levelled and the turf was
transferred from the Park Street ground.

The first Durham County Cricket Club Minor County Championship match to
be staged at Feethams took place on 24 and 25 June 1895 against Cheshire
and the last match was against Staffordshire on 18 and 19 July 1990. No Minor
County Championship match was staged at Darlington in 1991 but in 1992 the
ground hosted first-class matches with Somerset who were soundly beaten by 8
wickets on 2, 3 and 4 June. On 30 August the Sunday League fixture with arch
rivals and neighbours Yorkshire was abandoned as a washout.

The Darlington Cricket and Athletic Club arranged some important matches
during their early years, including in 1870 a three-day match between an All
England XI and twenty-two local players. In 1896 Darlington CC joined the North
Yorkshire and South Durham Cricket League, since renamed the Girobank North
Yorkshire & South Durham Cricket League, and won in their first season.

In 1897 the club were told by their landlord that the ground was to be sold, but
were given first option to purchase it. After much effort the ground was
purchased for the sum of £4,000 at a meeting in the Mechanics' Hall and in 1903
it was transferred to a trust which is still in existence

Darlington Cricket Club currently field three XIs throughout the season and
play in the Kerridge, Banks, Saunders, Austin, Mathew Oswald, Smith Print,
Haith, Robinson, James Bell, Ken Walsh, Thirds and Grainden county cup
knock-out competitions on a regular basis.

The brick cricket pavilion was constructed in 1903 by Mr T. Boyd, then
principal building contractor in Darlington, at an estimated cost of £900 after the
previous structure was demolished. The architect was Mr Fred W. Brookes and
the pavilion was opened on 12 May 1906 by Mr E.D. Walker JP. The pavilion was
used by athletes, cricketers and footballers for changing and also by members.
The three large club rooms could accommodate up to 320 people.

Darlington Cricket Club Pavilion.

The Arthur Sanders pavilion enclosure was officially opened by Leslie Crowther, then President of Lord's Taverners, on 2 June 1992 and construction of the groundsman's store and tea bar was funded by the Foundation for Sports & Arts and was built by T. Weatherald Limited in 1993.

The ground was once shared with the 'Quakers', Darlington Football Club, who were formed in 1883 and turned professional in 1908. The cricket ground and football ground are now separated by the football stand at the Feethams End although the grounds are situated within the same complex and have the same entrance. The only player to have represented Darlington cricket and football clubs (1950–6) to a high standard is Harry M. Clark who also represented Sheffield Wednesday and Hartlepool football clubs (261 league matches scoring 63 goals).

Many famous players have played at Feethams Cricket Ground including Dr W.G. Grace, Learie Constantine, Len Hutton, Hedley Verity and Vivian Richards. In 1901 the touring South Africans played Durham and won by 446 runs thanks to 151 by A.V.C. Blisset and match bowling figures of 9 for 126 by J.H. Sinclair. On 10 July 1907 Dr W.G. Grace played for a North Yorkshire and South Durham League XI against a North Durham XI and scored 51 runs. A copy of this scorecard is on display in the pavilion together with a number of photographs and items of cricket memorabilia relating to Feethams Ground and Darlington Cricket Club.

On 17–19 September 1909 Sir E.D. Walker's XI played Mr J. Bucknell's XI and included in these teams were W. Rhodes, S. Haigh, E. Drake, G. Hirst, E. Tyldesley and D. Denton.

In 1923 the West Indians tourists played Durham County Cricket Club on the ground winning by 180 runs and in 1991 the West Indians again visited

Feethams when a two-day match was staged by the Minor Counties Cricket Association. A number of limited-overs matches have been staged at Darlington and these have included Gillette Cup/NatWest Trophy matches hosted by Durham CCC against Hertfordshire (1964), Northamptonshire (1984), Middlesex (1987 and 1989), Somerset (1988) and Glamorgan (1991). Darlington also hosted one Benson and Hedges Cup zonal group match for Minor Counties against Northamptonshire in 1988 when the visitors won by 44 runs. Durham's NatWest Trophy 1st round tie against Glamorgan in 1991 produced 630 runs in the match.

In 1991 Darlington Borough Council contributed £20,000 towards improving the facilities at Feethams Cricket Ground to enable first-class cricket to be staged here during 1992–5 while Durham County Cricket Club's new County Headquarters Ground at Riverside in Chester-le-Street was being developed. In 2002 the only first-class match played here was against Derbyshire in the Frizzell County Championship.

Players to have represented Darlington Cricket Club and played first-class or minor county cricket include: Andy Fothergill, John Lister, Simon Daniels, Peter Barnes, John Johnston, Steve Malone, Neil Riddell, Simon Davis and Paul Romaines.

The ground capacity is 5,000 with fixed permanent seating for 900. Approximately 2,200 folding temporary seats are installed for county matches. A radio commentary position is situated on the pavilion balcony. The press box is sited in a temporary box on the bank to the west of the playing area. When required, the TV camera/commentary box is positioned at the Football Ground End directly above and behind the sightscreen.

In 2003 Darlington will host the Durham Cricket Board v Glamorgan Cheltenham & Gloucester Trophy third round match.

The Feethams Ground lies on the southern edge of the town centre.

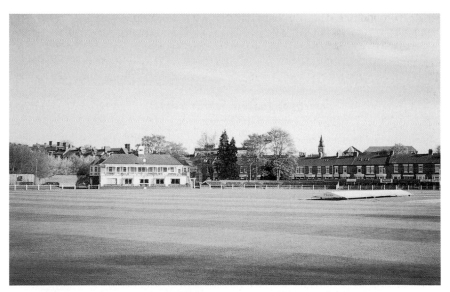

Feethams Cricket Ground seen from Football Ground End.

GROUND RECORDS AND SCORES

FIRST-CLASS MATCHES

Highest innings total for county 459 for 9 dec v Derbyshire 2000
Highest innings total against county 538 for 6 dec for Surrey 1994
Lowest innings total for county 134 v Leicestershire 1998
Lowest innings total against county 132 by Kent 1997
Highest individual innings for county 159 P.W.G. Parker v Warwickshire 1993
Highest individual innings against county 190 D.J. Bicknell for Surrey 1994
Highest wicket partnerships for county

1st	202 G. Fowler & W. Larkins	v	Warwickshire	1993
2nd	69 J.I. Longley & J.E. Morris	v	Worcestershire	1995
3rd	157 S.M. Katich & P.D. Collingwood	v	Derbyshire	2000
4th	119 D.A. Blenkiron & M. Prabhakar	v	Worcestershire	1995
5th	185 P.W.G. Parker & J.A. Daley	v	Warwickshire	1993
6th	57 N.J. Speak & J.A. Daley	v	Leicestershire	1998
7th	87 J.I. Longley & C.W. Scott	v	Surrey	1994
8th	110 J.J.B. Lewis & J. Boiling	v	Kent	1997
9th	88 C.W. Scott & D.A. Graveney	v	Surrey	1994
10th	44* S.J.E. Brown & S.J. Harmison	v	Derbyshire	2000

Highest wicket partnerships against county

1st	98 D.J. Bicknell & A.W. Smith	for	Surrey	1994
2nd	95 D.J. Bicknell & G.P. Thorpe	for	Surrey	1994
3rd	101 M.P. Dowman & S.P. Titchard	for	Derbyshire	2000
4th	222 D.J. Bicknell & A.D. Brown	for	Surrey	1994
5th	209 D.L. Maddy & A. Habib	for	Leicestershire	1998
6th	76 D.P. Ostler & N.M.K. Smith	for	Warwickshire	1993
7th	48 N.M.K. Smith & P.A. Smith	for	Warwickshire	1993
8th	80 S.P. Titchard & T.A. Munton	for	Derbyshire	2000
9th	28 A. Habib & A.D. Mullally	for	Leicestershire	1998
10th	29 A.D. Mullally & M.T. Brimson	for	Leicestershire	1998

Best bowling performance in an innings for county 7 for 29 M.M. Betts v Kent 1997
Best bowling performance in an innings against county 7 for 49 P.V. Simmons for Leicestershire 1998
Best bowling performance in a match for county 10 for 88 M.M. Betts v Derbyshire 2000
Best bowling performance in a match against county 10 for 125 A.P. Igglesden for Kent 1993
Largest crowd 5,000 v South Africans 1901 and v West Indians 1923

LIMITED-OVERS MATCHES

Highest innings total for county 305 for 9 v Glamorgan (NWT) 1991
Highest innings total against county 345 for 2 by Glamorgan (NWT) 1991
Lowest innings total for county 125 v Kent (SL) 1997
Lowest innings total against county 63 by Hertfordshire (GC) 1963
Highest individual innings for county 109 J.D. Glendenen v Glamorgan (NWT) 1991
Highest individual innings against county 151* M.P. Maynard for Glamorgan (NWT) 1991
Highest wicket partnerships for county

1st	91* I.T. Botham & W. Larkins	v	Kent	(SL)	1993
2nd	77 J.E. Morris & N.J. Speak	v	Leicestershire	(SL)	1998
3rd	92 J.E. Morris & P. Bainbridge	v	Derbyshire	(NWT)	1994
4th	72 J.D. Glendenen & P. Bainbridge	v	Glamorgan	(NWT)	1991
5th	103 J.D. Glendenen & D.A. Blenkiron	v	Glamorgan	(NWT)	1991
6th	48 M.P. Speight & M.J. Symington	v	Derbyshire	(SL)	2000
7th	107 A.C. Cummins & C.W. Scott	v	Surrey	(SL)	1994
8th	32 D.G.C. Ligertwood & J. Boiling	v	Worcestershire	(SL)	1995
9th	17 D.A. Graveney & A. Walker	v	Derbyshire	(NWT)	1994
10th	26 M.J. Saggers & N. Killeen	v	Leicestershire	(SL)	1998

Highest wicket partnerships against county

1st	96 P.M. Roebuck & J.J.E. Hardy	for	Somerset	(NWT)	1988
2nd	93 D.L. Haynes & M.W. Gatting	for	Middlesex	(NWT)	1989
3rd	259* H. Morris & M.P. Maynard	for	Glamorgan	(NWT)	1991
4th	109 T.J.G. O'Gorman & M. Azharuddin	for	Derbyshire	(NWT)	1984
5th	54 Asif Din & R.G. Twose	for	Warwickshire	(SL)	1993
6th	56 A.W. Smith & G.J. Kersey	for	Surrey	(SL)	1994
7th	20 P.R. Downton & A.R.C. Fraser	for	Middlesex	(NWT)	1989
8th	39 W. Larkins & D. Ripley	for	Northamptonshire	(NWT)	1984
9th	13 I.J. Sutcliffe & D.J. Millns	for	Leicestershire	(SL)	1998
10th	10 C.V.L. Marques & J. Iberson	for	Hertfordshire	(GC)	1964

Best bowling performance in a match for county 4 for 13 S.H. Young v Hertfordshire (GC) 1963
Best bowling performance in a match against county 5 for 43 D.G. Cork for Derbyshire (NWT) 1994
Largest crowd 5,000 v Middlesex (NWT) 1987 and MCCA v West Indies 1990

GROUND INFORMATION

ENTRANCES South Terrace (players, officials, press/media and vehicles) South Terrace – via Main Gate (members, public and vehicles). From former Darlington Football Club Ground – via car park (members and public).

MEMBERS' ENCLOSURE Pavilion, Pavilion Terrace, South Terrace enclosure and defined members' enclosure including temporary raised plastic seating.

MEMBERS' ZONE Pavilion, Pavilion Terrace, South Terrace enclosure and defined members' enclosure including temporary raised plastic seating.

PUBLIC ENCLOSURE Rest of the ground.

COVERED STANDS Pavilion and Tea Bar.

OPEN STANDS Pavilion Terrace, South Terrace enclosure, East Side Benches and temporary raised plastic seating areas and ground level seating surrounding the playing area.

NAME OF ENDS Football Ground End, South Terrace End.

GROUND DIMENSIONS 124m × 133m.

REPLAY SCREEN If televised matches are played the replay screen is sited by the groundsman's house at the South Terrace End of the ground.

FIRST AID Situated in Pavilion and in temporary caravan.

CODES OF DRESS Consistent with the prestige of being a member of a County Cricket Club, members are requested to dress in an appropriate manner.

BEHAVIOUR The Board is most concerned that standards of behaviour must be maintained at all matches involving Durham. Bad language is not acceptable at any cricket match and the Board will take the strongest possible action against transgressors.

RECIPROCAL ARRANGEMENTS Durham CCC Members can gain access to Newcastle Racecourse for certain race meetings. 10% off Durham CCC membership is offered to members of Northumberland CCC and Cumberland CCC.

SUPPORTERS' CLUB Dunelm Cricket Society. Details from Gillian Edger ☎ 020 7514 1915.

JUNIORS Young & Junior Lions membership is available to under-11s for £15 and Junior membership for over-12s to under-27s costs £25 per year. Contact Membership Secretary ☎ 0191 387 1717 ext 2872 for further information.

CORPORATE ENTERTAINING Durham CCC Marketing Department offers corporate entertainment in the temporary marquees. These are available to hire on a match by match basis. Contact Marketing Department ☎ 0191 387 4711 Fax 0191 387 4697 for further details and a copy of the brochure.

FACILITIES FOR VISUALLY IMPAIRED SPECTATORS No reduced admission. Guide dogs are allowed. No advance warning necessary to attend matches.

FACILITIES AND ACCESS FOR PEOPLE WITH DISABILITIES INCLUDING WHEELCHAIR ACCESS TO GROUND Yes, from South Terrace.

DESIGNATED CAR PARK AVAILABLE INSIDE THE GROUND FOR PEOPLE WITH DISABILITIES Yes, there is a car parking area set aside to the side of the pavilion.

GOOD VIEWING AREAS INSIDE THE GROUND FOR PEOPLE USING WHEELCHAIRS Yes, special area situated to the left of the pavilion.

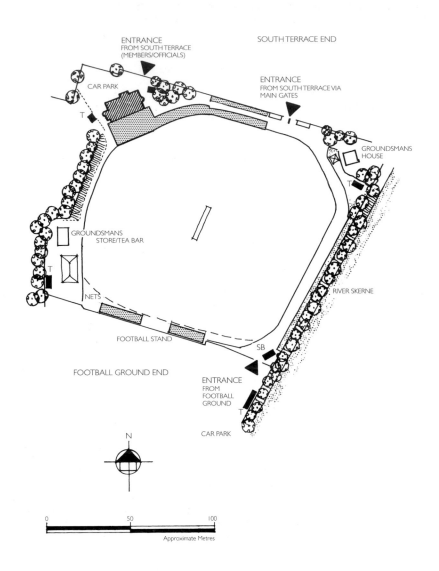

ENTRANCE
FROM SOUTH TERRACE
(MEMBERS/OFFICIALS)

SOUTH TERRACE END

CAR PARK

ENTRANCE
FROM SOUTH TERRACE VIA
MAIN GATES

T

GROUNDSMANS
HOUSE

T

GROUNDSMANS
STORE/TEA BAR

RIVER SKERNE

T

NETS

FOOTBALL STAND

SB

FOOTBALL GROUND END

ENTRANCE
FROM
FOOTBALL
GROUND

T

CAR PARK

N

0   50   100
Approximate Metres

RAMPS TO PROVIDE EASY ACCESS TO BARS & REFRESHMENT OUTLETS FOR PEOPLE USING WHEELCHAIRS Yes, buildings can be accessed by ramp.
FOOD & DRINK FULL RESTAURANT/DINING FACILITIES Members, yes, in main Pavilion Lounge. Public, no.
TEMPORARY FOOD/DRINK FACILITIES Members, yes. Public, yes.
FOOD SUITABLE FOR VEGETARIANS Members, yes. Public, yes.
BARS Members 3, Public 2.
VARIETIES OF BEER SOLD Newcastle Brown Ale.
CHILDREN'S FACILITIES Crèche, no. Play area, no.

CLUB SHOP Yes, Durham CCC Souvenir Shop is situated in a tent at the South Terrace End of the ground.
CLUB MUSEUM No, but there are some old cricket pictures and items of cricket interest in the pavilion which relate to Darlington Cricket Club.
CRICKET COACHING FACILITIES Yes, contact Darlington CC.
CRICKET NETS Yes, contact Darlington CC.
OTHER SPORTING OR RECREATIONAL FACILITIES ON THE GROUND Yes, hockey.
FACILITIES FOR HIRE OR WIDER COMMUNITY USE AT THE GROUND Rooms are available for functions, weddings, exhibitions, Christmas lunches, conferences and business and private entertainment. Contact Darlington CC.
WINTER CRICKET EVENTS Darlington CC hold dinners and functions during the winter months.
CAR PARKING FACILITIES Limited car parking within the ground to the rear of the pavilion for 120 cars and at the Football Ground End for 400+ cars. Otherwise use town centre car parks or street parking to south-west of town centre a short distance walk away from the ground.
OTHER INFORMATION Ground adjacent to Darlington Football Club's Feethams Ground. Even though the football club have a new stadium in the town, this ground is still to be used for Division 3 matches.
GROUND CAPACITY 5,000.
ANTICIPATED GROUND DEVELOPMENTS None currently planned.

HOW TO GET THERE

 Darlington 0.25 mile. ☎ 08457 484950, 0870 602 3322 email customerservices.ns@ems.rail.co.uk www.gner.co.uk, www.northern-spirit.co.uk, www.railtrack.com or www.thetrainline.co.uk

 Darlington Transport Company bus 2 links Darlington station with ground, also Darlington Transport Company and United buses 1, 1A, 3A, 3B, 4, 4A, 5, 6, 6A, 7, 11A, X13, X14, X35, X50, X51, X70, 68, 68A, 722 and 723 link Darlington bus station with surrounding areas, bus station 0.25 mile from ground. ☎ 01325 488777, 01325 468771 or Bus Information Line ☎ 0191 386 4411 ext 2337, 0845 6060 260 or National Express Coaches ☎ 08705 808080 www.nationalexpress.co.uk

 There are cycle routes from surrounding areas of Darlington to this part of the town.

 From north: A1(M) Junction 59 take A167. Follow A167 around Darlington town centre following signs for Northallerton to reach A167 (Victoria Road). Follow A167 (Victoria Road) across the next roundabout. Then bear left on to Feethams South. Turn right on to South Terrace. Turn left to Feethams Ground. **From south**: A1(M) Junction 57 on to the A66(M). At roundabout take A66 (Bridge Road). At roundabout take A167 (Grange Road). At roundabout take A167 (Victoria Road). Follow A167 (Victoria Road) across the next roundabout. Then as from north. **From east**: A67, at roundabout take B6280 and follow it to junction with A167. At roundabout take the first exit on to A167 (St Cuthberts Way). At roundabout take second exit on to A167 (Victoria Road). Follow A167 (Victoria Road) across the next roundabout. Then as from north. **From west**: from A67, High Coniscliffe. At roundabout take B6280 (Coniscliffe Road) and follow it to junction with A167. At roundabout take second junction on to A167 (Victoria Road). Follow A167 (Victoria Road) across the next roundabout. Then as from north.

 Newcastle Airport ☎ 0191 286 0966 Teesside Airport ☎ 01950 460 654

WHERE TO STAY

Aberlady Guest House (☎ 01325 461449), The Devonport (☎ 01325 332255), Blackwell Grange Moat House (☎ 01325 380888), Coachman Hotel (☎ 01325 286116), The Greenbank Hotel (☎ 01325 462624), Kings Head Swallow Hotel (☎ 01325 380222), Headlam Hall Hotel (☎ 01325 730238)
For further small hotels and guest houses in the Darlington area ☎ 0191 384 3720, 0191 375 3046, 0191 384 3720 or visit www.smoothhound.co.uk, www.darlington.gov.uk.

The pavilion at Darlington in 1992 during the Durham v Hampshire County Championship match.

WHERE TO EAT

There is a huge variety of restaurants and eateries in central Darlington 5 minutes' walk from the ground.

TOURIST INFORMATION CENTRE Darlington Tourist Information, 13 Horsemarket, Darlington, Co. Durham DL1 5PW ☎ 01325 388666, fax 01325 388667, www.darlington.gov.uk

OTHER USEFUL TELEPHONE NUMBERS AND ADDRESSES

Darlington Football Club ☎ 01325 240240 www.darlington-fc.net
Middlesbrough Football Club ☎ 01642 877700 www.mfc.co.uk
Hartlepool United Football Club ☎ 01429 272584
Northumbria Tourist Board ☎ 0191 375 3046 www.visitnorthumbria.com
Hotel Booking Line with GNER Trains ☎ 01904 671111

LOCAL RADIO STATIONS BBC Radio Newcastle (96.0 MHz FM/1458 KHz MW), BBC Radio Cleveland (95.0 MHz FM/1548 KHz MW), TFM Radio (96.6 MHz FM/1170 KHz MW).

LOCAL NEWSPAPERS *The Northern Echo, Evening Gazette, Hartlepool Mail, Darlington and Stockton Times, Darlington Journal*

Essex

Chelmsford ×2
Colchester
Southend-on-Sea

ESSEX COUNTY CRICKET CLUB, COUNTY CRICKET GROUND, NEW WRITTLE STREET, CHELMSFORD CM2 0PG

General Enquiries	01245 252420 **fax** 01245 254030
Membership	01245 254010
Essex Junior Eagles	01245 254010
Morrant Essex Club Shop	01245 254020
Cricket School	01245 254028
Ticket Office	01245 254010
Commercial/Corporate	01245 254001
Cricket Operations	01245 254018
Catering (Alexanders Catering)	01245 491114
Boundary Club	01245 284929
Prospects of Play	0871 871 6166 (recorded message)
Website	www.essexcricket.org.uk
Email	administration.essex@ecb.co.uk

Founded 14 January 1876
Colours blue, gold and red
Crest three scimitars above scroll bearing *Essex* underneath
National Cricket League Nickname Eagles
National Cricket League Colours yellow, red and blue
President D.J. Insole CBE, MA
Chairman N.R.A. Hilliard
Vice Chairman J.F. Barker
Chairman of Cricket G.J. Saville
Treasurer K. Brown
Solicitor B.M. Crawford
Chairman Cricket Committee G.J. Saville
Chief Executive Officer D.E. East
Cricket Operations Manager A.W. Lilley
Commercial Manager D. Comley
Finance Manager C. Griffiths
Administration Manager Mrs N. Fuller
Membership Secretary/PA to CEO Ms K. Garwood
Commercial Administrator Ms E.C. Rowley
Sales Executive T. Harding
Head Coach G.A. Gooch OBE
Assistant Coach J.H. Childs

Club Captain N. Hussain OBE
Team Captain R.C. Irani
Ground Manager G. Childs
Head Groundsman S. Kerrison
Club Shop Manager Mrs C. Proctor
Physiotherapist J. Davis
Essex Boundary Club M. Rowley
Scorer 1st XI D. Norris
Scorer 2nd XI A. Choat
Historian A.F. Debenham
Statistician B. Heald
Main Sponsor Panacea IT Infrastructure Services Provider
Training Wear Sponsor First Great Eastern Railway
National Cricket League Shirt Sponsor Shepherd Neame Master Brewers
Yearbook £10
Scorecard 50p
Newsletter Essex CCC Newsletter (free to members)
Club Shop Essex club shop is run by Morrant Group Limited
Frizzell County Championship Status Division 1
National Cricket League Status Division 1

ACHIEVEMENTS

County Championship Champions 1979, 1983, 1984, 1986, 1991, 1992; Champions Division 2 2002
NatWest Trophy Winners 1985, 1997, Finalists 1996

Benson and Hedges Cup Winners 1979, 1998, Finalists 1980, 1983, 1985, 1989 and 2001
Sunday League Winners 1981, 1984, 1985
Refuge Assurance Cup Winners 1989
Ward Building Products Four Counties Trophy Winners 1988

COUNTY CRICKET BOARD

Chairman D.L. Acfield
Chief Executive D.E. East
Secretary G. Jelley
Treasurer Ms J. Cole
Cricket Operations Manager A.W. Lilley
Cricket Development Officers M. Boyers, G. Jelley, R. Hayne

Address   County Cricket Ground, New Writtle Street, Chelmsford, Essex CM2 OPG
☎   01245 254015
Fax   01245 254021

GROUNDS

Chelmsford (County Cricket Ground, New Writtle Street), Colchester (Castle Park, Sportsway off Catchpool Road) and Southend-on-Sea (Southchurch Park)
  Other grounds used since 1969: Colchester (Garrison 'A' Ground, Napier Road), Brentwood (Old County Ground, Shenfield Road), Harlow (Sportscentre, Hammarskjold Road), Leyton (Leyton High Road Youth Sports Ground, High Road), Westcliff-on-Sea (Chalkwell Park), Purfleet (Thames Board Mills Sports Ground) and Ilford (Valentine's Park, Cranbrook Road)

SECOND XI GROUNDS

In addition to the above mentioned grounds the following are used for Second XI matches:
Aveley CC, Cricket Ground, Aveley (no ☎ on ground)
Billericay CC, Rutters Field, Blunts Wall Road, Billericay ☎ 01277 655202
Bishop's Stortford CC, Cricket Field Lane, Bishop's Stortford ☎ 01279 654463 (see Hertfordshire section for details)
Brentwood CC, Old County Ground, Shenfield Road, Brentwood ☎ 01277 212580
Coggeshall CC, Hare Field, Coggeshall Hamlet, Kelvedon Road, Coggeshall ☎ 01376 562988
Felsted School, Felsted, near Dunmow (no ☎ on ground)
Halstead CC, Star Stile, Colne Engaine, Halsted (off A131 Sudbury Road) ☎ 01787 479009
Leigh-on-Sea CC, Chalkwell Park, London Road, Leigh-on-Sea ☎ 01702 76603
Maldon CC, The Promenade, Maldon High Street, Maldon (no ☎ on ground)
Newbury Park CC, Newbury Park Sports Ground, Ford Sports & Social Club, Aldborough, Near Ilford ☎ 0208 590 3797
Old Brentwoods CC, Ashwells Road, off Ongar Road, Bentley, Brentwood ☎ 01277 374070
Orsett & Thurrock CC, School Lane, Orsett ☎ 01375 891746
Romford CC, Gidea Park, Romford ☎ 01708 760855
Saffron Walden CC, Anglo American Playing Fields, Little Walden Road, Saffron Walden ☎ 01799 522683
Wickford CC, Patmore Memorial Ground, Runwell Road, Wickford ☎ 01268 763023

CHELMSFORD

Address County Cricket Ground, New Writtle Street, Chelmsford CM2 OPG
Prospects of Play ☎ 01245 254049

HISTORY OF GROUND AND FACILITIES

THE COUNTY CRICKET GROUND has been the headquarters of Essex cricket since 1967 and most of the county club's home matches are staged here. The ground was used previously by Essex CCC between 1926 and 1939, 1946 and 1948, and 1950 and 1956 when Chelmsford CC rented it annually from the Wenley Trust. In those days the county headquarters was at Leyton, a venue which has not staged first-class cricket since 1977. The first first-class match to be staged at New Writtle Street was on 20, 22 and 23 June 1925 when Essex played Oxford University.

Other matches held in Chelmsford by Essex CCC were staged at the RHP Sports and Social Club in Rainsford Road, formerly the Hoffman's Athletic Ground, in 1959 and 1961. The first match was with Lancashire in 1951 and the last was with South Africa Fezela in 1961.

The County Cricket Ground is located barely half a mile from where the rivers Can and Chelmer meet. The River Can flows alongside the ground at the rear of the pavilion and Tom Pearce Stand. In February 1964, assisted by a loan, Essex were able to purchase the ground for £15,000. Much development has taken place since then; about £750,000 was spent on building the pavilion, which was completed in 1970, and other stands. The inside of the pavilion was refurbished during the late 1990s with funds from the Essex Boundary Supporters' Club. At the same time the pavilion was enlarged to the rear to include improved toilets on the ground floor, enlarged players' and officials' accommodation and the extension of ECCC's administration offices on the first floor.

Essex first staged a County Championship match here in 1926 against Somerset, at a time when most home matches were still being staged at Leyton. It

The weathervane on top of the Tom Pearce Stand at the River End of the County Cricket Ground.

is a compact ground for a county headquarters, but much has been made of the limited space available. The ground slopes slightly from south-east to north-west and the installation of a new improved drainage system in 1982 means it is one of the best-drained grounds on the county circuit. Previously the ground was liable to flood because of the proximity of the River Can and the high water table. The cricket field was for some time used as an emergency helicopter pad for the nearby hospital, until the casualty department was moved elsewhere in the town. Memorial Gates were installed in 1990 at the New Writtle Street main entrance to the ground and the popular seats in the public enclosure on the former hospital side of the ground were also partially covered.

Chelmsford City Football Club's ground was once situated close by but was built on during the late 1990s. This area now accommodates a new housing estate, the Falcon Bowls Club and the Esporta Fitness Centre.

There are two scoreboards on the ground – the main box is on the east side and a smaller secondary board is situated at high level next to Morrant Essex Club Shop, but if the replay screen is used this scoreboard is hidden. The ground was without a permanent scoreboard until 1981 when an attractive building including a groundsman's store was built. This has recently been refurbished with improved numbering and an electronic information board.

The press box and media point are now situated on the top of the River Stand. The TV camera and commentary point is situated high above the sightscreen at the River End of the ground.

The playing area, which is defined by advertisement boards, is about 132 metres by 128 metres but is reduced on the north side in front of the Tom Pearce Stand because of the proximity of the River Can.

Many memorable performances have taken place at Chelmsford, including Graham Gooch's 275 against Kent in 1988 and Surrey's lowest innings of 14 in 1983. In 2002 S.S. Das, the Indian opening batsman, scored 250 in the tourists' match against Essex, which was the highest individual innings on the ground against Essex, surpassing the 244 made by the great Wally Hammond for Gloucestershire in 1928.

In 1991 the ground was used for the first time for one of the Bull Test matches between Young England and Young Australia and later in the season hosted the inaugural and only Britannic Assurance Challenge between Essex, the 1991 County Champions, and Victoria, the Australian Sheffield Shield Winners of 1990/1. During the 1999 World Cup warm-up matches were staged by Essex against England and Bangladesh.

The ground has hosted international cricket on three occasions. First in 1983 when a Prudential Cup match was staged between Australia and India and then again in 1999 during the World Cup when the ground hosted matches between South Africa and Zimbabwe and Bangladesh and New Zealand.

The executive boxes, main pavilion and corporate dining marquees, County Cricket Ground.

Middlesex CCC have used Chelmsford twice for home matches: once in the County Championship against Somerset in 1977 because Lord's was being prepared for the Gillette Cup final (between Middlesex and Glamorgan) and then against Essex at home, although playing away, in the Norwich Union League in 2000.

In 2002 the club was granted permission by the local authority to install permanent floodlighting at Chelmsford.

GROUND RECORDS AND SCORES

FIRST-CLASS MATCHES

Highest innings total for county 761 for 6 dec v Leicestershire 1990
Highest innings total against county 686 by Lancashire 1996
Lowest innings total for county 65 v Worcestershire 1947, 1973
Lowest innings total against county 14 by Surrey 1983
Highest individual innings for county 275 G.A. Gooch v Kent 1988
Highest individual innings against county 250 S.S. Das for Indians 2002
Highest wicket partnerships for county

1st	316 G.A. Gooch & P.J. Prichard	v	Kent	1994
2nd	403 G.A. Gooch & P.J. Prichard	v	Leicestershire	1990
3rd	239 P.J. Prichard & M.E. Waugh	v	Kent	1990
4th	290 Salim Malik & N. Hussain	v	Derbyshire	1993
5th	275 S.G. Law & D.D.J. Robinson	v	Somerset	1999
6th	204 D.D.J. Robinson & S.D. Peters	v	New Zealanders	1999
7th	169 D.R. Pringle & M.A.Garnham	v	Derbyshire	1991
8th	149 N. Hussain & D.E. East	v	Leicestershire	1988
9th	126* K.W.R. Fletcher & J.K. Lever	v	Gloucestershire	1970
10th	110 J.R. Sheffield & T.H. Wade	v	Warwickshire	1929

Highest wicket partnerships against county

1st	279 C.F. Walters & H.H.I. Gibbons	for	Worcestershire	1934
2nd	217 G.F.J. Liebenberg & D.J. Cullinan	for	South Africans	1998
3rd	239 K.S. Duleepsinghji & H.W. Parks	for	Sussex	1931
4th	358 S.P. Titchard & G.D. Lloyd	for	Lancashire	1996
5th	268 M.W. Gatting & J.E. Emburey	for	Middlesex	1983
6th	256* C.J. Tavare & A.P.E. Knott	for	Kent	1982
7th	222 C.S. Cowdrey & S.A. Marsh	for	Kent	1988
8th	164 M.W.Alleyne & I.D. Fisher	for	Gloucestershire	2002
9th	142 D.A. Leatherdale & R.K. Illingworth	for	Worcestershire	1993
10th	118 R.J.L. Hammond & J.H.G. Deighton	for	Combined Services	1950

Best bowling performance in an innings for county 9 for 59 M.S. Nichols v Hampshire 1927
Best bowling performance in an innings against county 8 for 75 I.D.K. Salisbury for Sussex 1996
Best bowling performance in a match for county 13 for 117 J.K. Lever v Leicestershire 1979
Best bowling performance in a match against county 14 for 117 A.A. Walker for Durham 1995
Largest crowd 9,500 v West Indians 1991

LIMITED-OVERS MATCHES

Highest innings total for county 388 for 7 v Scotland (B&H) 1992
Highest innings total against county 318 for 8 by Lancashire (NWT) 1992
Lowest innings total for county 61 v Lancashire (B&H) 1992
Lowest innings total against county 58 by Somerset (SL) 1977
Highest individual innings for county 144 G.A. Gooch v Hampshire (NWT) 1990

Highest individual innings against county 157* M.G. Bevan for Sussex (B&H) 2000

Highest wicket partnerships for county

1st	223 G.A. Gooch & A.W. Lilley	v	Oxford & Cambridge Universities	(B&H)	1979
2nd	167 S.G. Law & N. Hussain	v	Sussex	(SL)	1996
3rd	179 G.A. Gooch & K.S. McEwan	v	Scotland	(NWT)	1984
4th	136* R.C. Irani & A.P. Grayson	v	Worcestershire	(NWT)	1997
5th	121 S.G. Law & R.C. Irani	v	Durham	(NWT)	1996
6th	105 R.C. Irani & P.J. Prichard	v	Durham	(NWT)	1996
7th	92 B.E.A. Edmeades & S. Turner	v	Nottinghamshire	(SL)	1969
8th	109 R.E. East & N. Smith	v	Northamptonshire	(B&H)	1977
9th	67 S. Turner & R.E. East	v	Gloucestershire	(GC)	1973
10th	52* A.P. Cowan & P.M. Such	v	Nottinghamshire	(SL)	1998

Highest wicket partnerships against county

1st	173 V.P. Terry & C.L. Smith	for	Hampshire	(NWT)	1990
2nd	174 H. Morris & M.P. Maynard	for	Glamorgan	(SL)	1996
3rd	271 C.J. Adams & M.P. Bevan	for	Sussex	(B&H)	2000
4th	179 J.P. Crawley & A. Flintoff	for	Lancashire	(SL)	1999
5th	185* B.M. McMillan & Asif Din	for	Warwickshire	(SL)	1986
6th	128* A. McGrath & G.M. Fellows	for	Yorkshire	(C&G)	2002
7th	91 C.H. Lloyd & J. Simmons	for	Lancashire	(GC)	1971
8th	80 G.R. Cass & J.D. Inchmore	for	Worcestershire	(SL)	1975
9th	48 N.V. Radford & G.R. Dilley	for	Worcestershire	(NWT)	1987
10th	50 D.J.S. Taylor & H.R. Moseley	for	Somerset	(B&H)	1981

Best bowling performance in a match for county 6 for 49 G.R. Napier v Worcestershire (SL) 2001
Best bowling performance in a match against county 6 for 16 P.J. Hacker for Nottinghamshire (SL) 1980
Largest crowd 9,500 v Worcestershire (BHC) 1991

ONE-DAY INTERNATIONALS

Highest innings total in ODI 247 by India v Australia (WC) 1983
Lowest innings total in ODI 116 by Bangladesh v New Zealand (WC) 1999
Highest individual innings in ODI 76 N.C. Johnson for Zimbabwe v South Africa (WC) 1999
Highest wicket partnerships

1st	65 N.C. Johnson & G.W. Flower	for	Zimbabwe v South Africa	(WC)	1999
2nd	66 N.C. Johnson & M.W. Goodwin	for	Zimbabwe v South Africa	(WC)	1999
3rd	45 M.J. Horne & S.P. Fleming	for	New Zealand v Bangladesh	(WC)	1999
4th	53 Yashpal Sharma & S.M. Patil	for	India v Australia	(WC)	1983
5th	39 Yashpal Sharma & N. Kapil Dev	for	India v Australia	(WC)	1983
6th	28 G.J. Whittall & S.V. Carlisle	for	Zimbabwe v South Africa	(WC)	1999
7th	66 D.J. Cullinan & S.M. Pollock	for	South Africa v Zimbabwe	(WC)	1999
8th	43 S.M. Pollock & L. Klusener	for	South Africa v Zimbabwe	(WC)	1999
9th	17 S. Madan Lal & S.M.H. Kirmani	for	India v Australia	(WC)	1983
10th	35 L. Klusener & A.A. Donald	for	South Africa v Zimbabwe	(WC)	1999

Best bowling performance in ODI 4 for 20 S. Madan Lal for India v Australia (WC) 1983
Largest crowd 4,696 South Africa v Zimbabwe (WC) 1999

GROUND INFORMATION

ENTRANCES New Writtle Street through main gate (players, officials, press/media, members, public and vehicles), Parkway through river gate (members only).
MEMBERS' ENCLOSURE Pavilion, Pavilion Terrace, Tom Pearce Stand Upper/Lower, River End Stand Upper and Hayes Close End (part).
PUBLIC ENCLOSURE Rest of the ground including part covered stand opposite pavilion.
COVERED STANDS Pavilion (part), Tom Pearce Stand Lower, River Stand (part) and popular side opposite Pavilion (part).

OPEN STANDS Pavilion (part), Pavilion Terrace, Tom Pearce Stand Upper, River Stand Upper, River End Stand, popular side (part) and Hayes Close End (part).

NAME OF ENDS Hayes Close End, River End.

GROUND DIMENSIONS 132m × 128m.

REPLAY SCREEN If televised matches are staged at the ground the replay screen is sited near Morrant Essex CCC Shop.

FIRST AID Adjacent to rear of Spinners Bar at River End of the ground.

CODES OF DRESS Spectators are required to dress in an appropriate manner consistent with attending a cricket match. Bare torsos are not acceptable in, or in front of the pavilion. Executive Club/Suite users must wear smart casual clothing.

BEHAVIOUR The club is keen that standards of behaviour should be maintained and members and spectators are urged to report immediately to the CEO any incident, or potential incident, where they feel action should be taken. Bad language is not acceptable at any match and the club will take prompt and strong action should this or any other ground regulation be ignored.

RECIPROCAL ARRANGEMENTS Members of Hampshire, Kent and Sussex can gain entry free on production of membership card when Essex is not playing their own county.

SUPPORTERS' CLUB The Boundary Club £12 (ECCC members), £18 (non-ECCC members). Special rates for concessions and husband and wife membership are available.

JUNIORS Junior Eagles membership £5.

CORPORATE ENTERTAINING Various packages are available. Executive box hire and marquees are available at Chelmsford for 20 plus guests. Corporate Brochure is available from Commercial Department at the club.

FACILITIES FOR VISUALLY IMPAIRED SPECTATORS No reduced admission. Guide dogs allowed by arrangement with club in advance.

FACILITIES AND ACCESS FOR PEOPLE WITH DISABILITIES INCLUDING WHEELCHAIR ACCESS TO GROUND Yes, from New Writtle Street.

DESIGNATED CAR PARK AVAILABLE INSIDE THE GROUND FOR PEOPLE WITH DISABILITIES Yes, to the rear of the pavilion. If space is available within ground there is space for vehicles adjacent to the entrance gate at the Hayes Close End of the ground next to the Executive Boxes.

GOOD VIEWING AREAS INSIDE THE GROUND FOR PEOPLE USING WHEELCHAIRS Yes, particularly on areas of hard standing to the side of the pavilion and at both the River End and Hayes Close Ends of the ground. Generally there are no restrictions. Wheelchairs may be a problem on the popular side. Please request position in advance.

RAMPS TO PROVIDE EASY ACCESS TO BARS & REFRESHMENT OUTLETS FOR PEOPLE USING WHEELCHAIRS Yes.

FOOD & DRINK FULL RESTAURANT/DINING FACILITIES Members, yes. Public, no.

TEMPORARY FOOD/DRINK FACILITIES Members, yes. Public, yes.

FOOD SUITABLE FOR VEGETARIANS Members, yes. Public, yes.

BARS Members 2, Public 1.

VARIETIES OF BEER SOLD Shepherd Neame.

CHILDREN'S FACILITIES Crèche, no. Bouncy castle, yes, when available, for floodlit matches.

CLUB SHOP Yes, Morrant Essex Club Shop and Cricket Equipment Shop.

CLUB MUSEUM No, but currently being considered.

CRICKET COACHING FACILITIES Yes, Essex Indoor Cricket School at rear of pavilion.

CRICKET NETS Yes, indoor in Essex Indoor Cricket School and outside on outfield near main scoreboard.

OTHER SPORTING OR RECREATIONAL FACILITIES ON THE GROUND Yes, Esporta Health & Fitness Club (☎ 01245 396060) is located next to the ground on the former Chelmsford Football Club Ground as is the Falcon Bowls and Indoor Bowls Club (☎ 01255 677383).

FACILITIES FOR HIRE OR WIDER COMMUNITY USE AT THE GROUND Rooms are available for functions, wedding receptions, exhibitions and conferences and possible use of playing area.

WINTER CRICKET EVENTS Members' club dinners and lunches are staged in the Executive Suite which is also used by the Essex Cricket Society. Membership is £12 per annum. For further information ☎ 01245 420706. Meetings are held once a month between September and March.

CAR PARKING FACILITIES Car parking is available to the rear of the pavilion for players, officials and press/media. There is also very limited car parking for some members, sponsors and hospitality guests only to the rear of the Essex CCC Indoor Cricket School. Additional car parking is available for members only on production of valid ECCC Membership Ticket in Meteor Way Car Park only. This car park is available for all home matches. The car park in Meteor Way opens at 9 a.m. on each day of operation and is locked 30 minutes after close of play. Leaving vehicles there overnight is not recommended. Alternative car parking for members/public is available

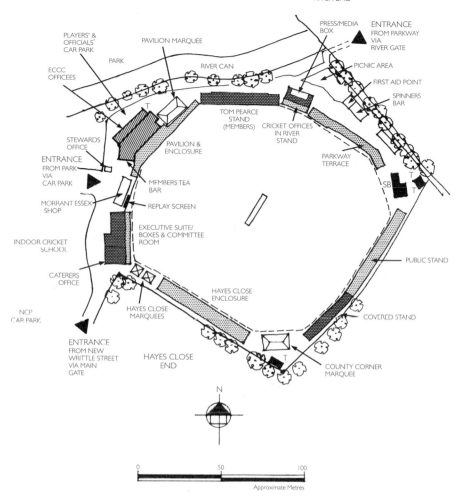

adjoining the members' entrance gate in New Writtle Street where an NCP car park is available (175 spaces). It is heavily used by commuters on weekdays but is largely available at weekends – 1-minute walk from main entrance in New Writtle Street. Car parking for the public at various short and long stay car parks in the town centre. There is little or no street parking available within walking distance of the ground.

OTHER INFORMATION Groups of school children, the disabled and disadvantaged can usually gain entry to ground only for Championship matches if requested in advance, contact club for details. A second-hand cricket book stall run by Donald Scott of Brackley is available near the Members' Gate and rear of Morrant Essex Club Shop at some matches.

GROUND CAPACITY 6,000.

ANTICIPATED GROUND DEVELOPMENTS None presently planned.

HOW TO GET THERE

 Chelmsford station 0.5 miles ☎ 08459 505000, 020 7247 5488, www.yourtrain.co.uk

 From surrounding areas to Chelmsford Bus Station, thence 0.5 mile walk ☎ 0345 000333, www.arriva.co.uk

There are cycle routes from surrounding areas of Chelmsford to this part of the town.

 From north: from A130 (Essex Regiment Way) exit roundabout on to A138 (Chelmer Valley Road) and follow A138 to junction with B1007, take B1007 (New London Road), turn right into New Writtle Street. **From south:** from B1002 take A1016, at roundabout take A414 (London Road), at roundabout take B1007 (Moulsham Street then New London Road), turn left into New Writtle Street. **From east:** from A130 (Southend Road) take A1114 (Southend Road), continue on A414, take A138 (Parkway), turn left on to B1007 (New London Road), turn right on to New Writtle Street. **From west:** follow A414 into Chlemsford (Ongar Road, London Road), take B1007 (Moulsham Street then New London Road, turn left on to New Writtle Street.

 Stansted Airport ☎ 08700 000303, Southend Airport ☎ 01702 340201

WHERE TO STAY

Atlantic Hotel (☎ 01245 268168 www.atlantichotel.co.uk), Beechcroft Hotel (☎ 01245 352462),County Hotel (☎ 01245 455700 www.countyhotel-essex.co.uk), Miami Hotel (☎ 01245 264848 www.miamihotel.co.uk), Rothmans (☎ 01245 473837), Snows Hotel (☎ 01245 352004 www.snowshotel.com), South Lodge Hotel (☎ 01245 264564), Youngs Riverside Inn (☎ 01245 266881)
　　Also visit www.smouthhound.co.uk for details of other places to stay in and around Chelmsford.

WHERE TO EAT

The Courtyard, 12 Baddow Road, Chelmsford (☎ 01245 355557),The Green Man Pub, Howe Street, near Great Waltham, Chelmsford (free park & ride to County Cricket Ground) (☎ 01245 360203 www.pickapub.co.uk), The Orange Tree Pub, 6 Lower Anchor Street, Chelmsford (☎ 01245 262664), The United Brethren Pub, New Writtle Street, Chelmsford (☎ 01245 265165)

TOURIST INFORMATION Chelmsford Tourist Information Centre, E Block, County Hall, Market Road, Chelmsford, Essex CM1 1GG ☎e 01245 283 400

LOCAL RADIO STATIONS BBC London Live (94.9 MHz FM/1458 KHz MW), BBC Essex (93.5/103.5 MHz FM/765/729/1530 KHz MW), Essex FM/Breeze Radio (96.3 MHz FM/1431 KHz MW), Ten17 (101.7 MHz FM)

LOCAL NEWSPAPERS *Evening Echo, Evening Standard, Essex Chronicle, Chelmsford Weekly News, Yellow Advertiser*

COLCHESTER

Address Colchester and East Essex Cricket Club, Castle Park (Lower), Sportsway, off Catchpool Road, Colchester
Prospects of Play ☎ 01206 769071

HISTORY OF GROUND AND FACILITIES

THE CASTLE PARK CRICKET GROUND is the home of the Colchester and East Essex Cricket Club, which was founded in 1862. The ground is located off Catchpool Road very close to the River Colne, which flows around its southern end. Castle Park is the second ground to be used by Essex CCC in Colchester. The Military Garrison 'A' Ground was used from 1924 to 1931, and again in 1958 because of flooding at Castle Park. Limited-overs John Player League matches were staged at the Garrison 'A' Ground between 1969 and 1973; the first match was against Hampshire and the last was with Somerset.

The first first-class match staged at Castle Park was on 18, 19 and 20 June 1914 when Essex hosted Worcestershire in a County Championship match. The championship match with Derbyshire in 1966 was to have been played at Castle Park, but after the first two days were washed out, the final day's play was transferred to the Garrison Ground. The following year *Wisden* remarked: 'though seventeen wickets fell for 246 runs, not even a first innings decision could be reached'.

Castle Park is susceptible to flooding due to the high water table. The ground is near the Castle Mound from which parkland slopes away to the rich meadows of the valley and the cricket field. Castle Park also suffers during poor weather and this is well recorded in the club's history. In 1958 on the third day of a championship match with Leicestershire the ground was totally submerged, chairs and boundary boards floated across the playing area and the Colchester secretary had to wear waders to get about.

The River Colne forms the southern boundary of the ground. Adjoining the river in the south-west corner of the ground is the pavilion, the only permanent building which was constructed in 1909 ready for the 1910 season. It is some 50 metres from the playing area. All other facilities are temporary.

The playing area is approximately circular in shape being 132 metres by 128 metres and is defined by advertising boards. The scoreboard is the temporary travelling scorebox used by the county club for all matches away from Chelmsford. During the Colchester Cricket Festival Week spectators are close enough to feel involved rather than detached in remote stands, but the lack of covered seating means the ground can be unpleasant if the weather is poor.

After Essex's first County Championship match with Worcestershire in 1914 games were staged annually at Castle Park although there was later a break of some years. Essex returned in the period 1934–9 and then in 1946. Today Essex take one championship match and two limited-overs matches to the ground, usually in August for the cricket festival. Since 2000 one limited-overs National Cricket League match has been played here under floodlights. Essex Eagles games were played here against Surrey Lions in 2000, Middlesex Crusaders in 2001 and Gloucestershire Gladiators in 2002.

Castle Park holds one unique cricket record: it is the only ground on which a player has scored a double century in each innings of a match. Arthur Fagg achieved this feat for Kent in 1938. Castle Park was also a favourite ground of Essex President Doug Insole CBE MA, who scored his only double century against Yorkshire there in 1949. More recently Ken McEwan in four consecutive seasons scored over 500 runs on the ground including 181 and 189 in one week. Ground records have also included centuries before lunch by Gordon Barker and Arthur Fagg, a career-best bowling performance by Peter Smith against Middlesex in 1947 and an aggregate of 600 runs in a John Player Sunday League match with Warwickshire in 1982.

GROUND RECORDS AND SCORES

FIRST-CLASS MATCHES

Highest innings total for county 662 for 7 dec v Hampshire 1995
Highest innings total against county 564 by Gloucestershire 1998
Lowest innings total for county 44 v Northamptonshire 1986

Lowest innings total against county 56 by Sussex 1957
Highest individual innings for county 219* D.J. Insole v Yorkshire 1949
Highest individual innings against county 244 A.E. Fagg for Kent 1938
Highest wicket partnerships for county

1st	194* G.A. Gooch & D.D.J. Robinson	v	Gloucestershire	1996
2nd	246 J.P. Stephenson & P.J. Prichard	v	Yorkshire	1991
3rd	333 R.M. Taylor & J. O'Connor	v	Northamptonshire	1937
4th	287 G.A. Gooch & N. Hussain	v	Northamptonshire	1991
5th	190* K.W.R. Fletcher & B.R. Hardie	v	Derbyshire	1980
6th	178 T.E. Bailey & R. Smith	v	Lancashire	1951
7th	131 T.E. Bailey & R. Smith	v	Middlesex	1952
8th	152 F.H. Vigar & R. Smith	v	Derbyshire	1948
9th	131 T.N. Pearce & R. Smith	v	Kent	1938
10th	97 R.N.S. Hobbs & K.C. Preston	v	Warwickshire	1963

Highest wicket partnerships against county

1st	283 A.E. Fagg & P.R. Sunnucks	for	Kent	1938
2nd	189 J.H. Parks & A. Melville	for	Sussex	1934
3rd	220* M.A. Atherton & N.H. Fairbrother	for	Lancashire	1990
4th	144 J.A. Daley & D.C. Boon	for	Durham	1999
5th	170 I.J. Sutcliffe & B.F. Smith	for	Leicestershire	1997
6th	132 D.C.S. Compton & J.H.A. Hulme	for	Middlesex	1936
7th	141 V.W.C. Jupp & G.B. Street	for	Sussex	1921
8th	139 B.F. Smith & D.J. Millns	for	Leicestershire	1997
9th	113 W.K. Hegg & D.P. Hughes	for	Lancashire	1990
10th	58 J.N. Snape & B.W. Gannon	for	Gloucestershire	2000

Best bowling performance in an innings for county 9 for 77 T.P.B. Smith v Middlesex 1947
Best bowling performance in an innings against county 8 for 41 C.T. Spencer for Leicestershire 1959
Best bowling performance in a match for county 16 for 215 T.P.B. Smith v Middlesex 1947
Best bowling performance in a match against county 14 for 94 C.T. Spencer for Leicestershire 1959
Largest crowd 8,000 v Middlesex 1947

LIMITED-OVERS MATCHES

Highest innings total for county 299 for 4 v Warwickshire (SL) 1982
Highest innings total against county 301 for 6 by Warwickshire (SL) 1982
Lowest innings total for county 117 v Warwickshire (SL) 1999
Lowest innings total against county 97 by Gloucestershire (SL) 2002
Highest individual innings for county 156* K.S. McEwan v Warwickshire (SL) 1982
Highest individual innings against county 114 D.R. Turner for Hampshire (SL) 1984
Highest wicket partnerships for county

1st	161 N. Hussain & S.G. Law	v	Surrey	(SL)	2000
2nd	214 J.P. Stephenson & M.E. Waugh	v	Lancashire	(SL)	1990
3rd	64 B.R. Hardie & D.R. Pringle	v	Northamptonshire	(SL)	1986
4th	82 Salim Malik & N. Shahid	v	Middlesex	(SL)	1993
5th	110 M.E. Waugh & N. Hussain	v	Nottinghamshire	(SL)	1988
6th	58* K.S. McEwan & K.R. Pont	v	Worcestershire	(SL)	1980
7th	36 N. Phillip & S. Turner	v	Gloucestershire	(SL)	1983
8th	73 D.R. Pringle & N.A. Foster	v	Worcestershire	(SL)	1989
9th	34* D.R. Law & J.E. Bishop	v	Hampshire	(SL)	2000
10th	8* R.E. East & J.K. Lever	v	Surrey	(GC)	1978

Highest wicket partnerships against county

1st	135 K.D. Smith & T.A. Lloyd	for	Warwickshire	(SL)	1982
2nd	75 M.A. Atherton & G.D. Lloyd	for	Lancashire	(SL)	1990
3rd	98* A.I. Kallicharran & G.W. Humpage	for	Warwickshire	(SL)	1978
4th	105 D.M. Ward & A.J. Hollioake	for	Surrey	(SL)	1994
5th	94 G.W. Humpage & Asif Din	for	Warwickshire	(SL)	1982
6th	69 D.L. Maddy & J.M. Dakin	for	Leicestershire	(SL)	1997

7th	40 T.M.B. Bailey & C.G. Greenidge	for	Northamptonshire	(SL)	2002
8th	31 S.N.V. Waterton & N.G.B. Cook	for	Northamptonshire	(SL)	1986
9th	30* T.M.B. Bailey & M.S. Panesar	for	Northamptonshire	(SL)	2002
10th	19 M.P. Bicknell & Saqlain Mushtaq	for	Surrey	(SL)	2000

Best bowling performance in a match for county 6 for 33 T.D. Topley v Nottinghamshire (SL) 1988
Best bowling performance in a match against county 4 for 22 D.P. Hughes for Lancashire (SL) 1975
Largest crowd 9,000 v Worcestershire (SL) 1989

GROUND INFORMATION

ENTRANCES Sportsway – off Catchpool Road (players, officials, members, public and vehicles), King's Meadow (members), Castle Park grounds – via footbridge (members and public).

MEMBERS' ENCLOSURE Pavilion and defined members' enclosure at Castle Park End of the ground including tiered plastic seating areas.

SPONSORS' ZONE Tents and marquees to the west of the playing area.

PUBLIC ENCLOSURE Rest of the ground.

COVERED STANDS Pavilion (part).

OPEN STANDS Temporary plastic raised and ground level seating surrounding the playing area.

NAME OF ENDS Sportsway End, Castle Park End.

GROUND DIMENSIONS 132m × 128m.

REPLAY SCREEN If televised matches are staged at the ground the replay screen is sited at the Castle Park End of the ground.

FIRST AID Tent situated at Sportsway End near entrance to ground.

CODES OF DRESS Spectators are required to dress in an appropriate manner consistent with attending a cricket match. Bare torsos are not acceptable in or in front of the pavilion. Executive Club/Suite users must wear smart casual clothing.

BEHAVIOUR The club is keen that standards of behaviour should be maintained and members and spectators are urged to report immediately to the CEO any incident, or potential incident, where they feel action should be taken. Bad language is not acceptable at any match and the club will take prompt and strong action should this or any other ground regulation be ignored.

RECIPROCAL ARRANGEMENTS Members of Hampshire, Kent and Sussex can gain entry free on production of membership card when Essex is not playing their own county.

SUPPORTERS' CLUB The Boundary Club £12 (ECCC members), £18 (non-ECCC members). Special rates for concessions and husband and wife membership are available. Marquee may be available for members during Colchester Festival at Castle Park.

JUNIORS Junior Eagles membership £5.

CORPORATE ENTERTAINING Various packages available from MBE to Corporate Hospitality bookings. Marquees are situated to western side of playing area and are available at Colchester for 20 plus guests. Corporate brochure is available from Commercial Department at the club.

VISUALLY IMPAIRED SPECTATORS No reduced admission. Guide dogs allowed by arrangement with club in advance.

FACILITIES AND ACCESS FOR PEOPLE WITH DISABILITIES INCLUDING WHEELCHAIR ACCESS TO GROUND Yes, from Catchpool Road/Sportsway junction entrance to ground.

DESIGNATED CAR PARK AVAILABLE INSIDE THE GROUND FOR PEOPLE WITH DISABILITIES Yes, in King's Meadow Field to the west of the ground. If space is available within ground there is room for a couple of vehicles near to the temporary raised seating area at the Sportsway End of the ground. This must be requested in advance.

GOOD VIEWING AREAS INSIDE THE GROUND FOR PEOPLE USING WHEELCHAIRS Yes. Generally there are no restrictions, but there is no concrete hardstanding close to the playing area so wheelchairs may be a problem when weather is poor. Please request position in advance.

DESIGNATED VIEWING AREAS FOR PEOPLE USING WHEELCHAIRS Yes, at both the Castle Park End and Sportsway End of the ground by the sightscreen.

RAMPS TO PROVIDE EASY ACCESS TO BARS & REFRESHMENT OUTLETS FOR PEOPLE USING WHEELCHAIRS Yes, in front of pavilion and by sightscreen at Sportsway End of the ground.

FOOD & DRINK FULL RESTAURANT/DINING FACILITIES Members, yes. Public, no.

TEMPORARY FOOD/DRINK FACILITIES Members, yes. Public, yes.

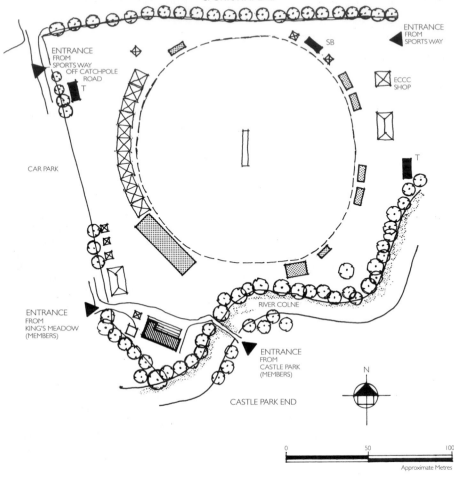

SPORTSWAY END

ENTRANCE FROM SPORTS WAY

ENTRANCE FROM SPORTS WAY OFF CATCHPOLE ROAD

ECCC SHOP

SB

CAR PARK

RIVER COLNE

ENTRANCE FROM KING'S MEADOW (MEMBERS)

ENTRANCE FROM CASTLE PARK (MEMBERS)

CASTLE PARK END

N

0   50   100

Approximate Metres

FOOD SUITABLE FOR VEGETARIANS Members, yes. Public, yes.

BARS Members 1, Public 1.

VARIETIES OF BEER SOLD Shepherd Neame.

CHILDREN'S FACILITIES Crèche, no. Playground and swings nearby in Castle Park.

CLUB SHOP Yes, Morrant Essex Club Shop in marquee.

CLUB MUSEUM No, other than pictures and memorabilia relating to Colchester and East Essex CC in the pavilion.

CRICKET COACHING FACILITIES Contact Colchester & East Essex CC.

CRICKET NETS Contact Colchester & East Essex CC.

OTHER SPORTING OR RECREATIONAL FACILITIES ON THE GROUND Yes, ground used by Colchester Hockey Club and sited close to Leisure World complex. ☎ 01206 282010, www.colchesterleisureworld.com.

FACILITIES FOR HIRE OR WIDER COMMUNITY USE AT THE GROUND None.

WINTER CRICKET EVENTS None, other than related to Colchester & East Essex CC.

CAR PARKING FACILITIES Car parking is available in King's Meadow to the west of the ground off Sportsway for 1,000+ cars. Members of ECCC free, others £5 per car.

OTHER INFORMATION Castle Park is a wonderful oasis of horticultural splendour in the Roman town. Within Castle Park's 9.3 hectares there are Sensory Gardens, Hollytrees Museum where you can find out about life in Colchester over the last 300 years, Pitch & Putt, the oldest Roman Wall in Britain and a well-appointed café near the Victorian bandstand. At some matches a second-hand cricket book stall is run by Donald Scott of Brackley.

GROUND CAPACITY 6,000.

ANTICIPATED GROUND DEVELOPMENTS None presently planned.

HOW TO GET THERE

 Colchester North or Colchester Town stations 0.75 miles ☎ 08459 505000, 020 7247 5488, www.yourtrain.co.uk

 First Eastern National and Arriva Colchester from surrounding areas to Colchester Bus Station off High Street, thence 0.75 miles walk to ground. Some buses from the north do pass closer to the ground. ☎ 01206 544449 (Arriva Colchester), www.arriva.co.uk, ☎ 01206 366911 (First Eastern National), 0345 000333, National Express Coaches ☎ 08705 808080, www.nationalexpresscoaches.co.uk

 There are cycle routes from surrounding areas of Colchester to this part of the town.

 From north: from A134 (Bury St Edmunds) continue on A134 (Nayland Road) (south) towards Colchester, at roundabout take second exit on to North Station Road, at next roundabout take A133 (Cowdray Avenue), turn right on to Catchpool Road. **From south:** from B1025 (West Mersea) stay on B1025 (Mersea Road) towards Colchester, at roundabout take A134 (Southway), continue on A134 to junction with (A133), take A133 (Colne Bank Avenue then Cowdray Avenue), turn right into Catchpool Road. **From east:** from A120 take A1232 (Old Ipswich Road), continue to junction with A133 (Cowdray Avenue), then as for south. **From west:** from A12, stay on A12 (London Road) (east), at Tollgate roundabout take exit for Colchester town centre (A1124), continue on this road to junction with A133, take A133 (Colne Bank Avenue, then Cowdray Avenue), turn right into Catchpool Road.

 Stansted Airport ☎ 08700 000303, Southend Airport ☎ 01702 340201

WHERE TO STAY

Athelstan House Guesthouse (☎ 01206 548652), Birds Farm (☎ 01206 823838), Butterfly Hotel (☎ 01206 230900 www.butterflyhotels.co.uk), Five Lakes Hotel Golf & Country Club (☎ 01621 868888 www.fivelakes.co.uk), Holiday Inn (☎ 0870 400 9020 www.holiday-inn.com/colchester), Maison Talbooth (☎ 01206 322367 www.talbooth.com), Milsoms (☎ 01206 322795), Nutcrackers Guesthouse (☎ 01206 543085), Peveril Hotel (☎ 01206 574001), Red Lion Hotel (☎ 01206 577986 www.brook-hotels.fsnet.co.uk), Tall Trees Guesthouse (☎ 01206 576650), The Marks Tey Hotel (☎ 01206 210001 www.marksteyhotel.co.uk), The Old Manse B&B (☎ 01206 545154 www.doveuk.com/oldmanse), The Rose & Crown Hotel (☎ 01206 866677 www.rose-and-crown.com), The Stoke by Nayland Club Hotel (☎ 01206 262836 www.stokebynaylandclub.co.uk), Wivenhoe House Hotel (☎ 01206 863666 www.wivenhoehousehotel.co.uk)
    Also visit www.smoothhound.co.uk for details of other places to stay in and around Colchester.

WHERE TO EAT

The Lemon Tree (☎ 01206 767337 www.the-lemon-tree.com), Le Talbooth (☎ 01206 323150, www.talbooth.com), Maison Talbooth (☎ 01206 322367), Milsoms (☎ 01206 322795)

OTHER USEFUL INFORMATION

www.colchesterwhatson.org

TOURIST INFORMATION Colchester Tourist Information Centre, 1 Queen Street, Colchester, Essex CO1 2PG ☎ 01206 282920

LOCAL RADIO STATIONS BBC London Live (94.9 MHz FM/1458 KHz MW), BBC Essex (93.5/103.5 MHz FM/765/729/1530 KHz MW), Essex FM/Breeze Radio (96.3 MHz FM/1431 KHz MW), Ten17 (101.7 MHz FM), Radio Orwell (97.1 MHz FM/1170 KHz MW)

LOCAL NEWSPAPERS *Colchester Leader, Essex County Standard, Colchester Evening Gazette, Yellow Advertiser*

SOUTHEND-ON-SEA

Address Southend-on-Sea Cricket Club, The Pavilion,
Southchurch Park, Northumberland Crescent, Southend-on-Sea
Prospects of play ☎ 01702 615195

HISTORY OF GROUND AND FACILITIES

SOUTHEND-ON-SEA has two cricket grounds, both of which have been used for first-class matches by the county club: Southchurch Park and Chalkwell Park at Westcliff-on-Sea. Southchurch Park is more frequently used because it can accommodate larger crowds and has plenty of space surrounding the playing area. However, in 1989 the wicket at Southchurch Park was the first to be reported to the TCCB at Lord's as unfit for first-class cricket by the umpires during the Yorkshire championship match. This cost the home side 24 points and dashed their hopes of winning the championship.

Essex paid their first visit to Southchurch Park in 1906 when the visitors were Leicestershire; a copy of the scorecard of this first match is on display in the pavilion. Essex have played at Southchurch Park each season since 1914 except for 1959, 1962, 1965 and 1967. Since 1977 all matches staged by the county at Southend have been played at Southchurch Park.

Southchurch Park is owned and maintained by the local council. It was in the ownership of the monks of Christ Church Canterbury from AD 823 and it was on the Southchurch foreshore that the cultivation of oysters is said to have begun.

Southchurch Park is the home of the Old Southendian and Southchurch Cricket Club who are members of the Shepherd Neame Essex Cricket League, the premier Essex league. They field four teams on Saturdays, two on Sundays and youth teams too. The club were established in 1874 and have played here since 1895.

The pavilion was built in 1929. The clubhouse was used by the Westcliff Hockey club (now folded) until 1997 and this building is now the base for the Old Southendian and Southchurch Cricket Club. Hockey has not been played here since 1997.

Apparently, anecdotal evidence suggests that the pavilion was used by Bradman's visiting Australians in 1948 and it is envisaged that the old Southendian and Southchurch Cricket Club will create a montage of information about this match on one of the walls of the clubhouse in the near future.

The ground is situated north of the boating lake and the two pavilions are on the north side of the lake. The playing area is usually 170 metres by 123 metres and defined by advertising boards. This is a well-maintained, tree-enclosed recreation ground and a good view of the cricket may be obtained from all areas.

The ground is sufficiently large to allow two club games to be played simultaneously. There are three separate cricket squares, of which the central one is exclusively used by the county for matches during the Southend Festival Week, which usually takes place annually in July. Essex now play one championship match and one limited-overs match at Southchurch Park.

The most recent piece of history made on the ground was in 1983 when Essex scored 310 for 5 against Glamorgan with Graham Gooch hitting 176. Don Bradman scored 187 in 125 minutes here in 1948.

GROUND RECORDS AND SCORES

FIRST-CLASS MATCHES

Highest innings total for county 503 v Hampshire 1936
Highest innings total against county 721 by Australians 1948
Lowest innings total for county 56 v West Indians 1963
Lowest innings total against county 43 by Kent 1925
Highest individual innings for county 205 M.S. Nichols v Hampshire 1936
Highest individual innings against county 255* H. Sutcliffe for Yorkshire 1924
Highest wicket partnerships for county

1st	214 G.A. Gooch & J.P. Stephenson	v	Worcestershire	1986
2nd	221 D.R. Wilcox & M.S. Nichols	v	Hampshire	1936
3rd	209 M.S. Nichols & J. O'Connor	v	Kent	1936
4th	239* D.J. Insole & T.E. Bailey	v	Nottinghamshire	1955
5th	158 B.R. Hardie & K.W.R. Fletcher	v	Somerset	1985
6th	181 H.P. Crabtree & D.R. Wilcox	v	South Africans	1947
7th	131 T.N. Pearce & T.P.B. Smith	v	Australians	1948
8th	263 D.R. Wilcox & R.M. Taylor	v	Warwickshire	1946
9th	160 D.R. Wilcox & R. Smith	v	Yorkshire	1947
10th	53 J.E. Bishop & A.R. Clarke	v	Worcestershire	2002

Highest wicket partnerships against county

1st	243 N.F.M. Popplewell & P.M. Roebuck	for	Somerset	1985
2nd	314 H. Sutcliffe & E. Oldroyd	for	Yorkshire	1924
3rd	204 H.S. Squires & B. Constable	for	Surrey	1949
4th	227 M.J. Powell & M.P. Maynard	for	Glamorgan	2000
5th	251 D.M. Smith & P. Moores	for	Sussex	1992
6th	166 S.J.E. Loxton & R.A. Saggers	for	Australians	1948
7th	150 C. Hallows & R.K. Tyldesley	for	Lancashire	1923
8th	99 C. Hallows & C.H. Parkin	for	Lancashire	1923
9th	72 W.H. Livsey & F.A. Gross	for	Hampshire	1926
10th	75 C.R.M. Atkinson & K.D. Biddulph	for	Somerset	1950

Best bowling performance in an innings for county 9 for 117 T.P.B. Smith v Nottinghamshire 1948
Best bowling performance in an innings against county 10 for 53 A.P. Freeman for Kent 1930
Best bowling performance in a match for county 12 for 131 G.M. Louden v Derbyshire 1920
Best bowling performance in a match against county 16 for 94 A.P. Freeman for Kent 1930
Largest crowd 16,000 v Australians 1948

LIMITED-OVERS MATCHES

Highest innings total for county 310 for 5 v Glamorgan (SL) 1983
Highest innings total against county 285 by Glamorgan (SL) 2000
Lowest innings total for county 120 v Hampshire (SL) 1999
Lowest innings total against county 153 for 6 by Lancashire (SL) 1981
Highest individual innings for county 176 G.A. Gooch v Glamorgan (SL) 1983
Highest individual innings against county 110* A.P. Wells for Sussex (SL) 1992
Highest wicket partnerships for county

1st	203 D.D.J. Robinson & S.G. Law	v	Surrey	(SL)	1996
2nd	126 G.A. Gooch & M.E. Waugh	v	Yorkshire	(SL)	1989
3rd	103* M.E. Waugh & P.J. Prichard	v	Sussex	(SL)	1992
4th	117 S.G. Law & D.R. Law	v	Kent	(SL)	1998
5th	101* K.W.R. Fletcher & N. Phillip	v	Glamorgan	(SL)	1984
6th	74* S.D. Peters & J.S. Foster	v	Glamorgan	(SL)	2000
7th	51* R.C. Irani & M.C. Ilott	v	Somerset	(SL)	1995
8th	39 A. Habib & J.D. Middlebrook	v	Hampshire	(SL)	2002
9th	17* K.R. Pont & N. Smith	v	Middlesex	(SL)	1977
10th	22 N. Smith & J.K. Lever	v	Surrey	(SL)	1978

Highest wicket partnerships against county

1st	108 G.D. Mendis & P.J. Graves	for	Sussex	(SL)	1979
2nd	93 M. Newell & P. Johnson	for	Nottinghamshire	(SL)	1990
3rd	124 S.P. James & M.P. Maynard	for	Glamorgan	(SL)	2000
4th	101 R.J. Harden & A.N. Hayhurst	for	Somerset	(SL)	1995
5th	76 P.A. Cottey & O.D. Gibson	for	Glamorgan	(SL)	1994
6th	77 A.P. Wells & P. Moores	for	Sussex	(SL)	1992
7th	47* A.P. Wells & A.C.S. Pigott	for	Sussex	(SL)	1992
8th	37* A.C.S. Pigott & A. Long	for	Sussex	(SL)	1979
9th	67 M.W.W. Selvey & J.E. Emburey	for	Middlesex	(SL)	1977
10th	20 M.J. Walker & A.P. Igglesden	for	Kent	(SL)	1998

Best bowling performance in a match for county 5 for 41 D.R. Pringle v Gloucestershire (SL) 1985
Best bowling performance in a match against county 5 for 19 J.F. Steele for Leicestershire (GC) 1977
Largest crowd 5,000 v Glamorgan (SL) 1983

GROUND INFORMATION

ENTRANCES Kensington Road (members, public and vehicles), Northumberland Crescent (players, officials, members, public and vehicles).

MEMBERS' ENCLOSURE Pavilion and defined members' enclosure between players' pavilion and members' pavilion at Boating Lake End of the ground, together with temporary raised plastic seating and ground level seating surrounding the playing area.

SPONSORS' ZONE From members' zone to Northumberland Crescent entrance to ground to the east of the playing area.

PUBLIC ENCLOSURE Northumberland Crescent, grass terraced area and the rest of the ground.

COVERED STANDS Players' and members' pavilions together with small covered temporary members stand.

OPEN STANDS Temporary raised plastic seating and ground level seating surrounding the playing area.

NAME OF ENDS Northumberland Crescent End, Boating Lake End.

GROUND DIMENSIONS 170m × 123m.

REPLAY SCREEN If televised matches are staged at the ground the replay screen is sited at the Northumberland Crescent End of the ground.

FIRST AID Tent at Boating Lake End of ground.

CODES OF DRESS Spectators are required to dress in an appropriate manner consistent with attending a cricket match. Bare torsos are not acceptable in, or in front of the pavilion. Executive Club/Suite users must wear smart casual clothing.

BEHAVIOUR The club is keen that standards of behaviour should be maintained and members and spectators are urged to report immediately to the CEO any incident, or potential incident, where they feel action should be taken. Bad language is not acceptable at any match and the club will take prompt and strong action should this or any other ground regulation be ignored.

RECIPROCAL ARRANGEMENTS Members of Hampshire, Kent and Sussex can gain entry free on production of membership card when Essex is not playing their own county.

SUPPORTERS' CLUB The Boundary Club £12 (ECCC members), £18 (non-ECCC members). Special rates for concessions and husband and wife membership are available. Marquee is available during Southend Festival at Southchurch Park.

JUNIORS Junior Eagles membership £5.

CORPORATE ENTERTAINING Various packages available from MBE to Corporate Hospitality bookings. Marquees are available at Southend-on-Sea for 20 plus guests. Corporate Brochure is available from Commercial Department at the club.

FACILITIES FOR VISUALLY IMPAIRED SPECTATORS No reduced admission. Guide dogs allowed if arranged in advance with club.

FACILITIES AND ACCESS FOR PEOPLE WITH DISABILITIES INCLUDING WHEELCHAIR ACCESS TO GROUND Yes, from Kensington Road and Northumberland Crescent end of the ground.

DESIGNATED CAR PARK AVAILABLE INSIDE THE GROUND FOR PEOPLE WITH DISABILITIES Yes, to the east of the ground. If space is available within ground there is space for several vehicles near the temporary scoreboard at the Northumberland Crescent End of the ground if arranged in advance.

GOOD VIEWING AREAS INSIDE THE GROUND FOR PEOPLE USING WHEELCHAIRS Yes. Generally there are no

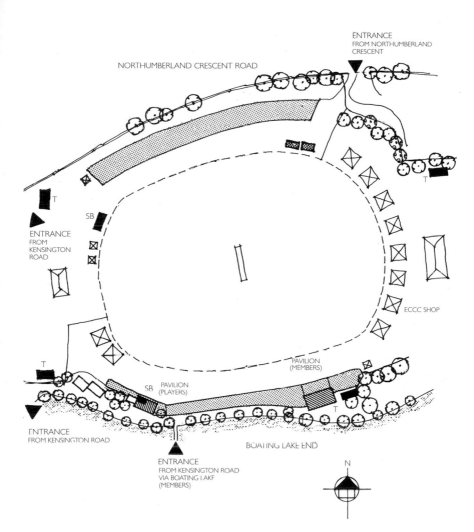

NORTHUMBERLAND CRESCENT ROAD

ENTRANCE
FROM NORTHUMBERLAND
CRESCENT

ENTRANCE
FROM
KENSINGTON
ROAD

SB

T

ECCC SHOP

PAVILION
(MEMBERS)

SB

PAVILION
(PLAYERS)

T

ENTRANCE
FROM KENSINGTON ROAD

BOATING LAKE END

ENTRANCE
FROM KENSINGTON ROAD
VIA BOATING LAKE
(MEMBERS)

N

0   50   100
Approximate Metres

restrictions. Close to the sightscreen or in front of the pavilion or to the left of the pavilion on the hard standing at the Boating Lake End is best. Please request position in advance.

DESIGNATED VIEWING AREAS FOR PEOPLE USING WHEELCHAIRS Yes, at both the Boating Lake End near pavilion and at the Northumberland Crescent End near the temporary scoreboard.

RAMPS TO PROVIDE EASY ACCESS TO BARS & REFRESHMENT OUTLETS FOR PEOPLE USING WHEELCHAIRS No.

FOOD & DRINK FULL RESTAURANT/DINING FACILITIES Members, yes. Public, no.

TEMPORARY FOOD/DRINK FACILITIES Members, yes. Public, yes.

FOOD SUITABLE FOR VEGETARIANS Members, yes. Public, yes.

BARS Members 1, Public 1.

VARIETIES OF BEER SOLD Shepherd Neame.

CHILDREN'S FACILITIES Crèche, no. Playground and swings nearby in Southchurch Park.

CLUB SHOP Yes, Morrant Essex Club Shop in marquee on Kensington Road side of the ground.

CLUB MUSEUM No, other than pictures and memorabilia relating to Southend-on-Sea CC in the pavilion.

CRICKET COACHING FACILITIES Contact Southend-on-Sea CC.

CRICKET NETS Contact Southend-on-Sea CC.

OTHER SPORTING OR RECREATIONAL FACILITIES ON THE GROUND Southend-on-Sea Hockey Club and nearby athletics track.

FACILITIES FOR HIRE OR WIDER COMMUNITY USE AT THE GROUND None.

WINTER CRICKET EVENTS None, other than related to Southend-on-Sea CC.

CAR PARKING FACILITIES Car parking is available to the east of the playing area for players, officials and members only, free on production of a valid ECCC membership ticket. Alternative car parking can be found at Lifstan Road car park (£2) and in neighbouring residential streets, the seafront or town centre multi-storey car parking a short distance walk away from the ground.

OTHER INFORMATION Southchurch Park is a public park situated next to an athletics track and a large boating lake. It is a five-minute walk away from the seafront and plenty of guesthouses and bed & breakfast hotels. A second-hand cricket book stall run by Donald Scott of Brackley close to the members' entrance in Kensington Road is available at some matches.

GROUND CAPACITY 8,000.

ANTICIPATED GROUND DEVELOPMENTS None presently planned.

HOW TO GET THERE

 Southend East station 0.5 mile ☎ 08459 505000, 020 7247 5488, www.yourtrain.co.uk

 Eastern National No. 20 Shoeburyness-Hullbridge passes Southend Central and Victoria station, ☎ 01702 430534. Nos. 7, 8, 67 and 68 pass close to the ground. Southend Public Transport ☎ 01702 434444, Thamesway Buses 01268 525251

 There are cycle routes to this area of the town.

 From north: from Chelmsford (A130) continue to junction with A127 (Southend Arterial Road), turn left and continue on A127 to junction with A13 (Queensway), turn left and continue on A13 (Southchurch Road), turn right on to Chase Road, then left on to Ambleside Drive, turn right on to Kensington Road. **From south:** from M25 junction 30 bear right (north) on to A13, continue on A13 towards Southend, at junction with A130 turn left (north) and continue to junction with A127, then proceed as for north. **From east:** from Poynters Lane, Shoeburyness, stay on Poynters Lane, bear left on to B1017 (Poynters Lane), at roundabout take third exit on to A13 (Bournes Green Chase), continue on this road (Southchurch Boulevard) to junction with Chase Road, turn left into Chase Road, then as for north. **From west:** from M25 junction 29 take A127 (Southend Arterial Road) and continue to junction with A13 (Queensway), then as for north.

 Stansted ☎ 08700 000303, Southend ☎ 01702 340201, London City ☎ 020 7646 0000

WHERE TO STAY

Airport Moat House (☎ 01702 546344), Argyle Hotel (☎ 01702 339483), Balmoral Hotel (☎ 01702 342947), Retreat Guest House (☎ 01702 348217 www.retreatguesthouse.co.uk), Welbeck Hotel (☎ 01702 347736). There are many other seaside hotels and guesthouses in the area.

WHERE TO EAT

Many restaurants in central Southend-on-Sea and in Westcliff-on-Sea.

TOURIST INFORMATION Southend-on-Sea Tourist Information Centre, 19 High Street, Southend-on-Sea, Essex SS1 1JE ☎ 01702 215120

LOCAL RADIO STATIONS BBC London Live (94.9 MHz FM/1458 KHz MW), BBC Essex (93.5/103.5 MHz FM/765/729/1530 KHz MW), Essex FM/Breeze Radio (96.3 MHz FM/1431 KHz MW), Ten17 (101.7 MHz FM)

LOCAL NEWSPAPERS *Evening Echo*, *Evening Standard*, *Yellow Advertiser*, *Southend Standard*, *Southend District News*

Glamorgan

**Cardiff – Sophia Gardens
Colwyn Bay
Swansea**

GLAMORGAN COUNTY CRICKET CLUB, SOPHIA GARDENS, CARDIFF CF11 9XR

General enquiries	029 2040 9380, **fax** 029 2040 9390
Membership Department	029 2040 9380
Marketing	029 2041 9381/9340
Pavilion Restaurant and Catering Office	029 2041 9350/9353
Astoria Cricket Shop	029 2040 9398
Indoor Cricket School	029 2041 9309/9308
Email	glam@ecb.co.uk
Website	www.glamorgancricket.com

Founded 6 July 1888
Colours blue and gold
Crest daffodil
National Cricket League Nickname Dragons
National Cricket League Colours red, black and white
Patron HRH The Prince of Wales KG KT PC GCB
President A.R. Lewis
Chairman G. Elias QC
Deputy Chairman H.D. Davies
Trustees G. Craven, G.W. Jones, A.R. Lewis and F.D. Morgan
Hon Treasurer R.N. Weston
Hon Life Vice Presidents Rt Hon The Lord Griffiths MC, Rt Hon N. Kinnock, Sir A. Cox CBE, P.B. Clift and R.P. Russell
Chairman of Cricket Committee P.J.E. Needham
Chief Executive Officer M.J. Fatkin
PA to CEO/Cricket Secretary Mrs C. Watkin
Commercial Director A.K. Ball
Financial Controller P.T. Pullin
Accounts Assistant A.P. Jenkins
Membership Secretary Mrs J.R. Pockett
Business Development Executive Miss A. Cheshire
Marketing Assistant Mrs S.E. Harfleet
Indoor Cricket Centre Manager P.L. Ingram
Indoor Cricket Centre Assistant R.V. Almond
Catering Manager A. Quilter

Physiotherapist E. Mustafa MCSP
Grounds Supervisor L.A. Smith
Ground Staff A.J. Noyes, M. Cusack and R. James
Club Shop Manager (franchise to Astoria Cricket Shop of Wales) J. Sylvester
Club Coach J. Derrick
Academy Director Welsh Cricket Academy S.L. Watkin
Captain S.P. James
Vice Captain R.D.B. Croft
2nd XI Captain A.D. Shaw
Scorer 1st XI G.N. Lewis
Scorer 2nd XI B. Jones
Hon Librarian N. Francis
Hon Statistician Dr A.K. Hignell
Hon Medical Consultants Dr R. Evans and J.A. Fairclough
Main Sponsors S.A. Brain & Company Limited
Shirt Sponsors S.A. Brain & Company Limited (County Championship) and Powerade (National Cricket League)
Yearbook £5
Scorecard 50p
National Cricket League Programme & Scorecard £1.50
Newsletter/Magazine *Glamorgan Matters*
Frizzell County Championship Status Division 2
National Cricket League Status Division 1

ACHIEVEMENTS

County Championship Champions 1948, 1969 and 1997
Gillette Cup Finalists 1977
NatWest Trophy Semi-finalists 1993, 1995 and 1997
Benson and Hedges Cup Finalists 2000, Semi-finalists 1988

Sunday League Champions 1993
Norwich Union National League Champions Division 1 2002, Champions Division 2 2001
Tilcon Trophy Winners 1980, Finalists 1987
Severn Trophy Finalists 1987

CRICKET BOARD OF WALES

Chairman H.D. Davies
Secretary M.J. Fatkin
Treasurer G.C. Crimp
Director of Cricket M. Frost
Cricket Development Officer (Cardiff) G. Paulsen
Cricket Development Officer (North Wales) J. Huband
Cricket Development Officer (Mid Wales) P. Brett
Cricket Development Officer (South East Wales) S. Watkins
Cricket Development Officer (West Wales) J. Cartwright
Women & Girls Cricket Chair Miss J. Collins

Address Cricket Board of Wales, Sophia Gardens, Cardiff CF11 9XR
☎ 029 2041 9336
Fax 029 2040 9390
Email cbw@ecb.co.uk
Website www.glamorgancricket.com

GROUNDS

Cardiff (Sophia Gardens), Colwyn Bay (Penrhyn Avenue, Rhos-on-Sea) and Swansea (St Helen's Ground, Bryn Road).

Other grounds used since 1969: Newport (Athletic Club Sports Ground, Rodney Parade), Llandudno (The Oval, Gloddaeth Avenue), BP Llandarcy (BP Oil Llandarcy Refinery Limited Sports Ground, Crymlyn Bog), Neath (The Gnoll, Dyfed Road), Ebbw Vale (Eugene Cross Park, New Church Road), Abergavenny (Pen-y-Pound, Avenue Road), Pentyrch & Old Monktonians (Parc-y-Dwrlyn, Penuel Road, Pentyrch), Merthyr Tydfil (Hoover Sports Ground, Merthyr Road), Llanelli (Stradey Park, Denham Avenue), Pontypridd (Ynysangharad Park, Ynysybwl Road) and Aberystwyth (University College of Wales Sports Ground, Llanbadarn Road).

SECOND XI GROUNDS

Abergavenny CC, Pen-y-Pound, Avenue Road, Abergavenny ☎ 01873 852350 (see Cardiff UCCE section for details)
Ammanford CC, Ammanford Park, Ammanford ☎ 01269 594988
Gowerton CC, Cricket Ground, Gowerton ☎ 01792 538329
Neath CC, The Gnoll, Dyfed Road, Neath ☎ 01639 643719
Newport CC, Spytty Park, Newport ☎ 01633 281236
Panteg CC, Panteg House, Panteg ☎ 01495 763605
Pontarddulais CC, Pontarddulais Park, Pontarddulais ☎ 01792 882556
Sully Centurians CC, Burham Avenue, Sully, Vale of Glamorgan ☎ 01446 734762
Usk CC Cricket Ground, Maryport Street, Usk ☎ 01291 673754

Premier Members' seating with suites and lounges to the rear and a secondary scoreboard at Sophia Gardens, Cardiff.

CARDIFF

Address Sophia Gardens, Cardiff CF11 9XR
Prospects of Play ☎ 029 2040 9380

HISTORY OF GROUND AND FACILITIES

GLAMORGAN'S DREAM of having a ground of their own was only realised in 1995, more than seven decades after the county's entry into first-class cricket. In 1921 when Glamorgan made their debut in the first-class game the club owned just a small office in High Street, Cardiff, and played their home matches at a variety of grounds. This way of life helped to fly the flag, but was far from ideal. However, all attempts to find a permanent home ground proved abortive until 24 November 1995 when GCCC acquired a new 125-year lease on Sophia Gardens from the previous leaseholders, Cardiff Athletic Club. This was already familiar territory because matches had long been played at Sophia Gardens – the first first-class game staged here by GCCC was against the Indian touring team on 24–26 May 1967 and the first championship match with Northamptonshire followed shortly after.

The ground is located close to the River Taff and takes its name from Sophia, the second wife of the second Marquess of Bute. It was originally part of the Bute Estate which stretched north from the city along both banks of the River Taff and close to Cardiff Castle. Once literally an area of gardens, which opened in 1858, this was a haven for the people of the city to promenade and listen to bands during the summer. A bowling green, a bandstand and a large recreation field were set out. The latter is currently the site of the cricket current ground but it has had a very colourful history. For example, in September 1891 it hosted Buffalo Bill's Wild West Show and in June 1899 Barnum and Bailey's travelling circus and menagerie staged shows here.

The area was passed to the City Corporation in 1947 by the fifth Marquess of Bute and the Sophia Gardens Pavilion was opened in April 1951. It was the venue for concerts by Cliff Richard and Danny Kaye, among others, and hosted boxing and wrestling events during the 1958 Commonwealth Games. Soon after the games the city planners considered ideas to develop the gardens' Gala Field and the adjoining Pontcanna Fields to the north. Various plans were submitted for a racecourse and a multi-purpose recreation complex, including a skating rink, bowling alley and a ballroom. Glamorgan County Cricket Club also put in a bid to acquire Gala Field in order to create a new cricket ground and solve the problems caused by the lack of space at Cardiff Arms Park, a mile away to the south, which was the base for various sections of the Cardiff Athletic Club, including cricket. However, this scheme was rejected.

Then in 1963 a new plan was devised for the redevelopment of Cardiff Arms Park and the acquisition of Gala Field for sports including cricket and tennis. In 1964 the City Corporation gave its approval, and Cardiff Athletic Club secured a 99-year lease on the Sophia Gardens area. In 1964/65 work began on laying out a new wicket at the former Gala Field. The project to turn Cardiff Arms Park into the national stadium was also under way. In August 1966 Cardiff Cricket Club staged their first ever game on the Sophia Gardens ground, and on the 13, 15 and 16 of the same month Glamorgan staged their final county match at the Arms Park, against Somerset.

The new pavilion was built by E. Taylor and Company of Treforest at a cost of £25,000 and a £3,500 scoreboard was installed, the latter thanks to a donation from a London Welsh sportsman, Sir Edward Lewis. In 1967 Cardiff Cricket Club held a cricket week to celebrate the centenary of the club and the opening of the new ground. Matches were played with a number of sides including MCC, the Glamorgan Nomads and the Forty 'XL' Club. The Forty side included Wilfred Wooller, Harold Gimblett, Dick Spooner, Bob Broadbent and Bob Appleyard.

Some 10.5 acres of the Gala Field were used for cricket. The rest of the 23 acres was occupied in 1970–1 when the City Corporation offered land to the Sports Council for the Welsh Institute of Sport. The land to the north of the cricket playing area was also used by

Wilfred Wooller (1912–97) Memorial Gates which form the main entrance to Sophia Gardens.

Cardiff Rugby Football Club's Second XV, and this was also the home of Cardiff Tennis Club. In 1985 Glamorgan CCC moved their offices from 6 High Street to the south-western corner of the ground.

Sophia Gardens has witnessed some notable matches despite its relatively short history in first-class cricket. For example, in 1969 Glamorgan won the County Championship here, beating Worcestershire by 147 runs. Some 16,000 people attended this match, still a record attendance for the ground. Then in 1976 Glamorgan deprived Somerset of the John Player Sunday League in front of 11,500 spectators; this was probably the largest crowd for a limited-overs match at the ground (although the total is unofficial). The evenly-fought contest culminated in a nail-biting finish as Graham Burgess was run out off the final ball to leave Glamorgan the victors by one run. On 6 July 1987 the Welsh county celebrated their centenary year by staging a match with Gloucestershire for the Severn Trophy in the presence of HRH Prince Charles and Princess Diana. The ground has also been the venue for Glamorgan's quarter-and semi-finals contests in one-day competitions, including the 1995 NatWest games with Middlesex and Warwickshire. The Middlesex match was watched by a crowd of around 7,000 and the Warwickshire game by 9,500.

On 24 June 2002 England hosted Wales here in the first international one-day match between the two nations. Wales won by 8 wickets. It is hoped that matches between the two teams will become regular fixtures.

The ground capacity is now set at up to 12,000. In 1999 a crowd of 6,400 watched the World Cup match between Australia and New Zealand and in 2001 the one-day international NatWest Series tie between Australia and Pakistan attracted a record full-house crowd of 10,000.

Press/media box, River Taff End plastic tip-up seating, the main scoreboard and groundsman's facilities at Sophia Gardens.

Wilfred Wooller once said Sophia Gardens has 'a quite delightful rural setting' but the weather is not always kind to cricket in this part of the world and some have described it in other ways. In 1985 Glamorgan lost so many days to poor weather that members suggested the ground's name should be changed to Sophia Lakes because of the pools forming on the outfield.

There was a plan to move GCCC to Cardiff Docklands but after much discussion the idea was rejected. The club purchased Sophia Gardens outright in the winter of 1995/6 and since then a strategic master plan costing some £9m has got under way. The first of the developments included the new National Cricket Centre, together with the Cathedral Suite, Premier Lounge, Jones, Riches, Lewis, Watkins and Parkhouse suites, Premier Members' seating, the shop, administration offices, new outdoor nets and two new scoreboards. This first phase of the project (designed by Cardiff-based architectural practice HLN) began in 1998/9 and was complete in time for the 1999 Cricket World Cup, which saw GCCC host the eventual winners Australia. Other developments include the reconstruction of the River Stand at the Taff End of the ground. This concrete stand with blue plastic seats has new toilets and includes toilet facilities for disabled people. The new groundsman's store includes a scoreboard and food kiosk. The media/press box, also at the River Taff End, has been refurbished, as have the former club offices which are now executive boxes named the Clay, Clift, Wooller and Shepherd suites.

At the Cathedral Road End there are ample open terraces and behind them hockey pitches and tennis courts. The Wilfred Wooller Memorial Gates at this end of the ground were opened on 29 June 2001 ahead of the County Championship match with Northamptonshire.

To the north-west of the playing area is the new Glamorgan County Cricket Club headquarters together with the Indoor Cricket School, sponsors' lounges, Gold Members' seating, hospitality and catering outlets, restaurant, library and club offices and reception area. The library is extensive and there is also an excellent collection of cricket memorabilia which was donated by the Harries family in memory of Ronald Harries of Welwyn Garden City, Hertfordshire, who was without any doubt Glamorgan's number one supporter. On the ground floor of this new building is the Astoria Cricket Shop of Wales which sells Glamorgan County Cricket Club souvenirs and cricket equipment.

Phase two of the redevelopment programme will comprise a new pavilion, media facilities and players' dressing rooms at the Cathedral Road End and phase three a covered grandstand, containing 24 corporate hospitality boxes, on the site of the current pavilion which will be demolished once the new pavilion has been built.

Sophia Gardens is one of the most improved county cricket grounds in the country. It is a ground worthy of a capital city. In recognition of this the ECB arranged two one-day international fixtures here in 1999 and 2001, and South Africa are scheduled to meet Zimbabwe here in the 2003 NatWest Series.

GROUND RECORDS AND SCORES

FIRST-CLASS MATCHES

Highest innings total for county 597 for 8 dec v Durham 1997
Highest innings total against county 701 for 9 dec by Surrey 2001
Lowest innings total for county 31 v Middlesex 1997
Lowest innings total against county 52 by Hampshire 1968
Highest individual innings for county 233* H. Morris v Warwickshire 1997
Highest individual innings against county 313* S.J. Cook for Somerset 1990
Highest wicket partnerships for county

1st	240 J.A. Hopkins & A.L. Jones	v	Gloucestershire	1984
2nd	252 M.P. Maynard & D.L. Hemp	v	Northamptonshire	2002
3rd	284 J.P. Maher & M.J. Powell	v	Essex	2001
4th	425* A. Dale & I.V.A. Richards	v	Middlesex	1993
5th	174 P.D. Swart & M.J. Llewellyn	v	Northamptonshire	1978
6th	159 M.P. Maynard & M.J. Cann	v	Gloucestershire	1989
7th	135 M.P. Maynard & A.D. Shaw	v	Essex	2000
8th	116* R.C. Ontong & J. Derrick	v	Kent	1988
9th	105 R.C. Ontong & M.A. Nash	v	Essex	1978
10th	93 G.C. Holmes & E.A. Moseley	v	Lancashire	1981

Highest wicket partnerships against county

1st	362 M.D. Moxon & M.P. Vaughan	for	Yorkshire	1996
2nd	260 R.G. Lumb & K. Sharp	for	Yorkshire	1984
3rd	285* S.J. Cook & C.J. Tavare	for	Somerset	1990
4th	251 N.J. Speak & G.D. Lloyd	for	Lancashire	1996
5th	320 Abdur Razzaq & E.C. Joyce	for	Middlesex	2002
6th	222* A.P. Wells & A.I.C. Dodemaide	for	Sussex	1991
7th	128 G.J. Parsons & A.C. Storie	for	Warwickshire	1987
8th	147* R.C. Irani & T.J. Mason	for	Essex	2000
9th	155 S.J. Storey & R.D. Jackman	for	Surrey	1973
10th	144 A. Sidebottom & A. Robinson	for	Yorkshire	1977

Best bowling performance in an innings for county 8 for 63 A.W. Allin v Sussex 1976
Best bowling performance in an innings against county 9 for 57 P.I. Pocock for Surrey 1979
Best bowling performance in a match for county 13 for 127 R.C. Ontong v Nottinghamshire 1986
Best bowling performance in a match against county 13 for 102 D.L. Underwood for Kent 1979
Largest crowd 16,000 v Worcestershire 1969

LIMITED-OVERS MATCHES

Highest innings total for county 373 for 7 v Bedfordshire (NWT) 1998
Highest innings total against county 330 for 4 by Somerset (GC) 1978
Lowest innings total for county 76 v Middlesex (SL) 1975
Lowest innings total against county 69 by Hampshire (B&H) 2000
Highest individual innings for county 154* H. Morris v Staffordshire (NWT) 1989
Highest individual innings against county 145 P.W. Denning for Somerset (GC) 1978
Highest wicket partnerships for county

1st	192* S.P. James & H. Morris	v	Dorset	(NWT)	1995
2nd	172 S.P. James & A. Dale	v	Middlesex	(SL)	1993
3rd	187 J.A. Hopkins & M.P. Maynard	v	Nottinghamshire	(SL)	1989
4th	119 M.P. Maynard & P.A. Cottey	v	Essex	(SL)	1994
5th	134 A. Jones & G. Richards	v	Gloucestershire	(SL)	1977
6th	136 M.P. Maynard & O.D. Gibson	v	Warwickshire	(SL)	1996
7th	76 A.E. Cordle & J.W. Solanky	v	Leicestershire	(SL)	1974
8th	102 R.C. Ontong & J. Derrick	v	Kent	(B&H)	1985
9th	52 Waqar Younis & S.L. Watkin	v	Middlesex	(B&H)	1998
10th	45 M.J. Powell & O.T. Parkin	v	Somerset	(SL)	2002

Highest wicket partnerships for county

1st	213 M.D. Moxon & A.A. Metcalfe	for	Yorkshire	(B&H)	1991
2nd	166 T.S. Curtis & G.A. Hick	for	Worcestershire	(SL)	1992
3rd	128 P.W.G. Parker & A.P. Wells	for	Sussex	(NWT)	1990
4th	149 R.D.V. Knight & P.J. Graves	for	Sussex	(SL)	1976
5th	132 V.J. Wells & A. Habib	for	Leicestershire	(SL)	1998
6th	113 R.J. Turner & A.N. Hayhurst	for	Somerset	(B&H)	1996
7th	67 R.L. Johnson & M.A. Feltham	for	Middlesex	(NWT)	1995
	67 D.P. Ostler & G. Welch	for	Warwickshire	(B&H)	1996
8th	73 N. Shahid & M.C. Ilott	for	Essex	(NWT)	1994
9th	65 C.W.J. Athey & S. Oldham	for	Yorkshire	(SL)	1977
10th	38 R.G. Williams & J.C.J. Dye	for	Northamptonshire	(SL)	1976

Best bowling performance in a match for county 6 for 20 R.D.B. Croft v Worcestershire (SL) 1994 and S.D. Thomas v Combined Universities (B&H) 1995
Best bowling performance in a match against county 6 for 20 T.E. Jesty for Hampshire (SL) 1975
Largest crowd 9,500 v Warwickshire (NWT) 1995

ONE-DAY INTERNATIONALS

Highest innings total in ODI 258 for 3 by Australia v Pakistan (NWS) 2001
Lowest innings total in ODI 213 for 8 by Australia v New Zealand (WC) 1999
Highest individual innings in ODI 91* Yousuf Youhana for Pakistan v Australia (NWS) 2001
Highest wicket partnerships in ODI

1st	20 A.C. Gilchrist & M.E. Waugh	for	Australia v Pakistan	(NWS)	2001
2nd	92 R.T. Ponting & M.E. Waugh	for	Australia v Pakistan	(NWS)	2001
3rd	94 D.S. Lehmann & R.T. Ponting	for	Australia v New Zealand	(NWS)	2001
4th	116* M.G. Bevan & S.R. Waugh	for	Australia v Pakistan	(NWS)	2001
5th	148 C.L. Cairns & R.G. Twose	for	New Zealand v Australia	(WC)	1999
6th	17* A.C. Parore & R.G. Twose	for	New Zealand v Australia	(WC)	1999
7th	124 Rashid Latif & Yousuf Youhana	for	Pakistan v Australia	(NWS)	2001
8th	32 Waqar Younis & Yousuf Youhana	for	Pakistan v Australia	(NWS)	2001
9th	13 Saqlain Mushtaq & Yousuf Youhana	for	Pakistan v Australia	(NWS)	2001
10th	3 Shoaib Mohammad & Yousuf Youhana	for	Pakistan v Australia	(NWS)	2001

Best bowling performance in ODI 4 for 37 G.I. Allott for New Zealand v Australia (WC) 1999
Largest crowd 10,000 Australia v Pakistan (NWS) 2001

GROUND INFORMATION

ENTRANCES Cathedral Road through Wilfred Wooller Gates (members and the public as pedestrians, players' and officials' cars only), North Gate (members, public, press/media, Gold and Premier Club members and cars) and Taff Gate (members and public pedestrians only).

MEMBERS' ENCLOSURE Non-defined areas, although Premier Members (Block J) and Vice President Members (Block C) have their own areas. Main bar in the pavilion is for members only.

PUBLIC ENCLOSURE Rest of the ground.

COVERED STANDS National Cricket Centre and Premier Block J seats.

OPEN STANDS Blocks A, B in Taff Stand; C Vice Presidents; D, E, and F Pavilion; G and H and Cathedral Road End; and K on former rugby ground between National Cricket Centre and new groundsman's store and main scoreboard.

ENDS Cathedral Road End and River Taff End.

GROUND DIMENSIONS 142m × 146m.

REPLAY SCREEN If televised matches are staged the replay screen is sited at the north side of the ground between the two main scoreboards.

FIRST AID Situated behind Clay, Clift, Wooller and Shepherd suites near South Gate. Other facilities to north of ground on major match days.

CODES OF DRESS Spectators are required to dress in an appropriate manner consistent with attending a cricket match. Bare torsos are not acceptable in or in front of the pavilion.

BEHAVIOUR The club is keen that standards of behaviour should be maintained and members and spectators are urged to report immediately to the CEO any incident, or potential incident, where they feel action should be taken. Bad language is not acceptable at any match and the club will take prompt and strong action should this or any other ground regulation be ignored.

RECIPROCAL ARRANGEMENTS Members of Gloucestershire, Somerset and Worcestershire can gain free entry to championship matches on production of their membership card when Glamorgan are not playing their own county.

SUPPORTERS' CLUB There is an official supporters' club but The St Helen's Balconiers is the main body which organises trips for home and away matches. Details from John Williams ☎ 01792 414671. Other organisations include the Sophians; details from the club.

JUNIORS Glamorgan Short Legs (Junior) membership is available to under-16s for £10 per year. Contact membership secretary ☎ 029 2040 9380, for further information.

CORPORATE ENTERTAINING GCCC offers corporate entertainment in the Cathedral, Jones, Riches, Lewis, Watkins, Parkhouse, Clay, Clift, Shepherd and Wooller suites. These are available to hire on a season or match-by-match basis and marquee options are available. Contact the marketing department on ☎ 029 2041 9381 for further details and a copy of the brochure.

FACILITIES FOR VISUALLY IMPAIRED SPECTATORS No reduction. Guide dogs are allowed. Contact club in advance.

FACILITIES AND ACCESS FOR PEOPLE WITH DISABILITIES INCLUDING WHEELCHAIR ACCESS TO GROUND Yes, from South Gate and North Gate.

DESIGNATED CAR PARK AVAILABLE INSIDE THE GROUND FOR PEOPLE WITH DISABILITIES Yes, by arrangement.

GOOD VIEWING AREAS INSIDE THE GROUND FOR PEOPLE USING WHEELCHAIRS Yes, there is a special area at both the River Taff and Cathedral Road Ends of the ground. Seating is also available within the National Cricket Centre where a lift is provided to gain access to upper floors.

DESIGNATED VIEWING AREAS FOR PEOPLE USING WHEELCHAIRS Yes.

RAMPS TO PROVIDE ACCESS TO BARS & REFRESHMENT OUTLETS FOR PEOPLE USING WHEELCHAIRS Yes, some buildings can be accessed by ramp but others have a lift.

FULL RESTAURANT/DINING FACILITIES Members, yes. Public, yes. A full restaurant is available in the Cathedral Suite in the National Cricket Centre Restaurant situated at the Cathedral Road End of the ground. Catering is provided by the club ☎ 029 2041 9350.

TEMPORARY FOOD/DRINK FACILITIES Members, yes. Public, yes.

FOOD SUITABLE FOR VEGETARIANS Members, yes. Public, yes.

BARS Members 4, Public 2.

VARIETIES OF BEER SOLD Brains.

CHILDREN'S FACILITIES Crèche, no. Play area, no.

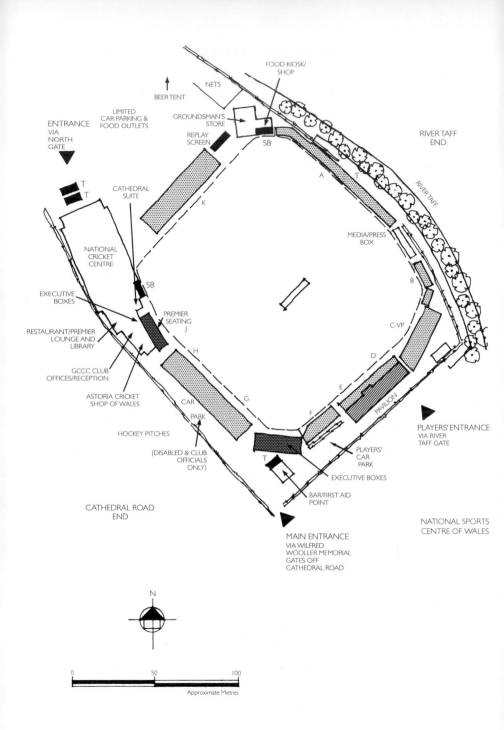

BEER TENT

ENTRANCE
VIA
NORTH
GATE

LIMITED
CAR PARKING &
FOOD OUTLETS

NETS

FOOD KIOSK/
SHOP

GROUNDSMAN'S
STORE

REPLAY
SCREEN

SB

RIVER TAFF
END

RIVER TAFF

CATHEDRAL
SUITE

A

T

K

NATIONAL
CRICKET
CENTRE

MEDIA/PRESS
BOX

EXECUTIVE
BOXES

SB

B

RESTAURANT/PREMIER
LOUNGE AND
LIBRARY

PREMIER
SEATING
J

C-VP

GCCC CLUB
OFFICES/RECEPTION

H

D

ASTORIA CRICKET
SHOP OF WALES

CAR
PARK

G

E

PAVILION

HOCKEY PITCHES

F

PLAYERS' ENTRANCE
VIA RIVER
TAFF GATE

(DISABLED & CLUB
OFFICIALS
ONLY)

T

PLAYERS'
CAR
PARK

EXECUTIVE BOXES

CATHEDRAL ROAD
END

BAR/FIRST AID
POINT

NATIONAL SPORTS
CENTRE OF WALES

MAIN ENTRANCE
VIA WILFRED
WOOLLER MEMORIAL
GATES OFF
CATHEDRAL ROAD

N

0   50   100
Approximate Metres

CLUB SHOP Yes, franchise to Astoria Sports and called the Cricket Shop of Wales ☎ 029 2040 9398, fax 029 2040 9399.

CLUB MUSEUM Yes, Glamorgan CCC, but limited. (There are plans to include a new one in a future phase of ground development.) Museum is located in the National Cricket Centre complex on the first floor and includes a fine library and the collection of the late Ronald Harries.

CRICKET COACHING FACILITIES Yes, Glamorgan CCC's National Cricket Centre provides coaching and is open throughout the year. Contact the National Cricket Centre for details.

CRICKET NETS Yes, contact the National Cricket Centre for details.

OTHER SPORTING OR RECREATIONAL FACILITIES ON THE GROUND No, other than links with Welsh Institute of Sport and Sports Council for Wales for some shared use during major events.

FACILITIES FOR HIRE OR WIDER COMMUNITY USE AT THE GROUND Rooms are available for functions, weddings, exhibitions, Christmas lunches, conferences and business and private entertainment. Rugby union and football hospitality is available for Wales international matches which are staged at the Millennium Stadium. Packages include programme, pre-match refreshments, lunch and a complimentary gift. Contact the marketing department on ☎ 029 2040 9381 for further details and a copy of the brochure.

WINTER CRICKET EVENTS Members' Club dinners and lunches are staged in the winter months, as well as Christmas parties. Contact Glamorgan CCC office for details.

CAR PARKING Spaces are available on the ground through the North Gate for sponsors, Premier Club members, some members and press/media, and to the rear of the pavilion (accessed through the South Gate) for players, officials and disabled drivers. Other parking is available (at a reasonable daily charge) within Sophia Gardens to the south of the Welsh Institute of Sport accessed off Cathedral Road and there are some spaces on North Road on the other side of Bute Park north of Cardiff Castle with a link to the ground via a bridge over the River Taff.

OTHER INFORMATION All permanent seats on the ground are blue and all temporary seats are green.

GROUND CAPACITY 12,000.

HOW TO GET THERE

Cardiff Central 1 mile. National rail enquiries ☎ 08457 484950, www.thetrainline.com, www.railtrack.co.uk. Regional companies: www.alphaline.co.uk, www.centraltrains.co.uk, www.midlandmainline.com, www.walesandwest.co.uk.

Cardiff Bus services 21, 25, 32, 33, 62, 62C and 65C from Cardiff Central Bus Station and also buses 21, 25 and 33 from city centre pass close to ground ☎ 029 2039 6521. Bus Information Line ☎ 0870 608 2608 or National Express Coaches ☎ 08705 808080, www.nationalexpress.co.uk. Arriva Cymru ☎ 01248 750444, www.arriva.co.uk. Stagecoach Red & White ☎ 01633 266336, www.stagecoachgroup.com. First Cymru ☎ 01792 580580, www.firstgroup.com. Travel Line provides services from surrounding areas to Cardiff, ☎ 08706 082608.

There are cycle routes from central and surrounding areas of Cardiff to this part of the city.

From north: A470 (Northern Avenue), continue on A4161 (North Road then Kingsway Ffordd Y Brenin), bear left on to A4161 (Duke Street), continue on A4161 (Castle Street and Cowbridge Road), bear right on to A4119 (Cathedral Road), turn right on to Sophia Close for Sophia Gardens. **From south:** A4232 (Grangetown Link), B4267 (Leckwith Road), bear right on to A4161 (Wellington Street), continue on A4161 (Cowbridge Road), turn left on to A4119 (Cathedral Road), turn right on to Sophia Close for Sophia Gardens. **From east:** M4 Exit 29, bear left on to A48(M), bear left on to A48 (Mill Lane), turn left on to A4119 (Cardiff Road), bear left on to A4119 (Pen-Hill Road), bear right on to A4119 (Cathedral Road), turn left on to Sophia Close for Sophia Gardens. **From west:** M4 Exit 33, at the roundabout take A4232 and follow directions as from the south.

Cardiff International Airport ☎ 01446 711111, www.cial.co.uk

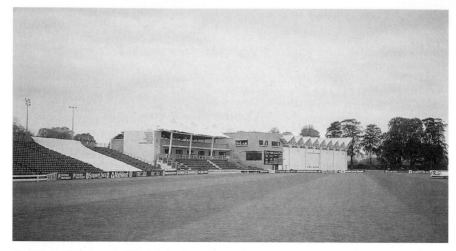

The National Cricket Centre for Wales including the county club's offices, Astoria Sports shop, nets, Premier Members' seating, suites and lounges. It was built on the site of the old main scoreboard.

WHERE TO STAY

Angel Hotel (☎ 029 2064 9200), Austins Hotel (☎ 029 2037 7148, www.hotelcardiff.com), Cardiff Moat House Hotel (☎ 029 2058 9988), Churchills Hotel (☎ 029 2040 1300, www.churchillshotel.co.uk), Copthorne (☎ 029 2059 9100), Hanover International Hotel (☎ 029 2047 5000), Hilton Hotel (☎ 029 2064 6300), Holiday Inn City (☎ 0870 400 8140), Holiday Inn North (☎ 0870 400 8141), Jurys Hotel (☎ 029 2034 1441), Marriott Hotel Cardiff (☎ 029 2039 9944), Sandringham Hotel (☎ 029 2023 216), St David's Hotel & Spa (☎ 029 2045 4045, www.rfhotels.com), St Mellons Hotel (☎ 01633 680355), The Big Sleep (☎ 029 2063 6363, www.thebigsleephotel.com), The Town House Hotel (☎ 029 2023 9399, www.thetownhousecardiff.co.uk), Thistle Hotel (☎ 0870 333 9157), Vale of Glamorgan Hotel (☎ 01443 667800)

For further small hotels and guest houses in and around Cardiff ☎ 01437 765 777 or visit www.smoothhound.co.uk or www.breakoutworld.com.

WHERE TO EAT

Armless Dragon (☎ 029 2038 2357), Celtic Cauldron (☎ 029 2082 2083), Chikako's (☎ 029 2066 5279), Happy Gathering (☎ 029 2039 7531), Izakaya (☎ 029 2049 2939), King Balti (☎ 029 2048 2890), La Brasserie (☎ 029 2037 2164, www.le-monde.co.uk/brasserie.html), La Cassoulet (☎ 029 2022 1905), Le Gallois (☎ 029 2034 1264, www.legallois.co.uk), Le Monde (☎ 029 2038 7376, www.le-monde.co.uk) Noble House (☎ 029 2038 8430), Riverside Cantonese (☎ 029 2037 2163), The Greenhouse Café (☎ 029 2039 7531), Tides Restaurant at St David's Hotel & Spa (☎ 029 2031 3018, www.rfhotels.com), Woods Brasserie (☎ 029 2049 2400), Y Mochyn Du (☎ 029 2037 1599)

OTHER USEFUL INFORMATION

Cardiff City Football Club ☎ 029 2022 1001, www.cardiffcity.co.uk
The Welsh Institute of Sport ☎ 029 2030 0500, email wis@scw.co.uk
Cardiff Rugby Club ☎ 029 2030 2000, fax 029 2030 2001, www.cardiffrfc.com
The Millennium Stadium Tours ☎ 029 2082 2228, www.cardiff-stadium.co.uk
Cardiff & Glamorgan Heritage Coast ☎ 029 2022 7281, email enquiries@cardifftic.co.uk

LOCAL RADIO STATIONS BBC Radio Wales (882 KHz MW), Red Dragon FM/Capital Radio (97.4 MHz FM/1359 KHz MW), Real Radio (105–106 FM)

LOCAL NEWSPAPERS *South Wales Echo, Wales on Sunday, The Western Mail*

COLWYN BAY

Address Colwyn Bay Cricket Club, The Pavilion, Penrhyn Avenue,
Rhos-on-Sea, Colwyn Bay, Clwyd, North Wales LL28 4LR
Prospects of Play ☎ 01492 544103 or 01492 545082

HISTORY OF GROUND AND FACILITIES

WILFRED WOOLLER was brought up in Rhos-on-Sea and brought county cricket
to North Wales. In 1947 Glamorgan County Cricket Club visited Colwyn Bay at
the instigation of Wilfred Wooller and Geoff Gadd when matches were staged
with a North Wales XI and a Lancashire League XI which included Learie
Constantine, George Tribe, Cec Pepper and Charlie Hallows.

Wilfred Wooller's grandfather had built the original pavilion which was opened
by Lord Colwyn in May 1924, the year Colwyn Bay CC was founded. The ground
at Penrhyn Avenue was laid on the bed of the old River Conway, although locals
say the area was probably a swamp or large ditch. The ground is square in
shape and little has changed since 1924 other than the introduction of some
banking at the southern end which allows for some deckchairs on the terrace.
Ground improvements in 1950 cost £4,000 and in 1969 the old pavilion was
demolished and a new one built. The pavilion is located to the south-east of the
playing area with the main entrance to the ground off Penrhyn Avenue. The
pavilion was built by voluntary subscriptions in recognition of those members
who gave service to their country in the Second World War and was opened by
HRH The Duke of Gloucester on 8 June 1960. Some cricket memorabilia and
photographs of old Colwyn Bay Cricket Club teams and some well-known
players who have appeared at the ground are displayed on the walls of the bar
and members' room. These include Sir Learie Constantine, the three Ws –
Worrell, Weekes and Walcott, Godfrey Evans, Wes Hall, George Headley and
Sydney Barnes, who lived in the town, played for the club and acted as a coach
in the nets in the 1920s. The pavilion has excellent facilities and a glance at the
records board will show that the club have supported many charity fund-raising
events including making a donation of £15,000 to the Prisoners of War Fund and
the Liverpool Air Raid Disaster Fund. The Colwyn Bay Cricket Club have staged
benefit matches for a number of players including: Haydn Davies, Willie Jones,
Allan Watkins, Cyril Washbrook, Richard Pollard, Winston Place and Jack Ikin.

The venue has been used by Glamorgan for 17 first-class matches (15 in the
County Championship) and 13 limited-overs matches in the Sunday League. The
first Glamorgan first-class fixture was played here on 27, 29 and 30 August 1966
when Derbyshire were the visitors for a County Championship match.

After 1966 further matches were staged with Worcestershire in 1967,
Cambridge University and Oxford University in 1968, Leicestershire in 1969,
Pakistani Eaglets in 1970, Gloucestershire in 1971 and Sussex in 1974. In 1972
and 1973 John Player Sunday League matches were staged against
Worcestershire and Yorkshire.

A County Championship match was played here in 1974 against Sussex but it
was not until 1990 that the county again travelled 180 miles from their Cardiff
headquarters to stage cricket at this ground when Lancashire were the visitors

for a three-day championship match and a Refuge Assurance Sunday League match over a May Bank Holiday weekend.

In 1991 a County Championship match against Nottinghamshire was scheduled to be played here but this was switched back to Cardiff. In 1992 Colwyn Bay again hosted Lancashire and since 1995 it has been a regular home venue for Glamorgan, usually in late August for one County Championship and one National Cricket League fixture.

In 1929 Wales played the touring South Africans at Colwyn Bay and in 1930 Wales played the Minor Counties Cricket Association here. Other teams have also played Minor County Championship matches at the ground. Between 1930 and 1935 Denbighshire County Cricket Club, long since disbanded, used the ground. During 1955 the Colwyn Bay Cricket Festival was introduced and the following teams were represented: Glamorgan County Cricket Club, North Wales XI, Sir Learie Constantine's XI, R.W.V. Robins' XI, Vinoo Mankad's Indian XI and R.H. Moore's XI. During one match Frank Worrell scored 194 which is still the highest individual score on the ground. It took just 112 minutes and included five 6s and thirty 4s. Funds for improvements to the pavilion came from the proceeds of these various matches.

In 1984 the League Cricket Conference staged a two-day match with the West Indian touring team. The West Indians scored 401 and 275 for 2 declared and the Conference XI replied with 136 and 76 for 8. Former West Indian captain Richie Richardson top scored with 149*.

Colwyn Bay Cricket Club play in the North Wales Competition and field two XIs throughout the season together with a number of colts teams. The ground is shared with Colwyn Bay Hockey Club and the adjoining field, which is used for car parking and refreshments during county matches, is used by Rhos United Football Club during the winter. Penrhyn Avenue was used by Minor Counties Wales 14 times between 1988 and 2000 for Minor Counties Championship matches with Shropshire in 1988, 1992 and 2000, Oxfordshire in 1989, Wiltshire in 1990, Buckinghamshire in 1991, Cheshire in 1993 and 1999, Dorset in 1994, Herefordshire in 1995, Devon in 1996 and 1998 and finally Nottinghamshire in the NatWest Trophy in 1998.

The ground is owned by the club and permanent facilities include the pavilion/clubhouse which contains changing rooms, toilets, two bars, refreshment areas, a games room and on the first floor a balcony and groundsman's flat. Other facilities include the large tea pavilion and a two-storey scoreboard. The scoreboard is located in the northern corner of the ground and next to this are the press and scorers' tents. On the bank opposite the John Smiths tea pavilion and HSBC Suite are new outdoor cricket nets, refreshment marquees and temporary toilets.

The TV camera/commentary box is located at the top of the bank at the Embankment/Town End, sometimes known as the Victor Wilde Drive End. The playing area is square in shape and falls slightly towards the Penrhyn Avenue End of the ground. The dimensions of the playing area are 115 metres by 107 metres and the boundary is defined by a rope and some advertising boards. In general the playing area is tight against the boundary walls and fences so during play it can become difficult to walk around it. To the south of the ground the boundary is the bottom of the embankment. Victor Wilde Drive End affords the best views, especially if you sit at the top next to the palisade fence.

GROUND RECORDS AND SCORES

FIRST-CLASS MATCHES

Highest innings total for county 718 for 3 dec v Sussex 2000
Highest innings total against county 530 by Middlesex 1995
Lowest innings total for county 183 v Derbyshire 1966
Lowest innings total against county 118 by Derbyshire 1966
Highest individual innings for county 309* S.P. James v Sussex 2000
Highest individual innings against county 171 J.E.R. Gallian for Nottinghamshire 2002
Highest wicket partnerships for county

1st	374 M.T.G. Elliott & S.P. James	v	Sussex	2000
2nd	216 S.P. James & J.H. Kallis	v	Nottinghamshire	1999
3rd	281 S.P. James & M.J. Powell	v	Nottinghamshire	1999
4th	217 S.P. James & A.D. Dale	v	Nottinghamshire	2002
5th	96 S.P. James & R.D.B. Croft	v	Nottinghamshire	1997
6th	135 L.W. Hill & J.A. Hopkins	v	Gloucestershire	1971
7th	75 M.J. Powell & D.A. Cosker	v	Lancashire	1998
8th	95 A. Dale & D.A. Cosker	v	Lancashire	2001
9th	66 C.P. Metson & S.L. Watkin	v	Lancashire	1990
10th	29 C.P. Metson & S. Bastien	v	Lancashire	1992

Highest wicket partnerships against county

1st	172 J.E.R. Gallian & G.E. Welton	for	Nottinghamshire	2002
2nd	19 J.C. Pooley & M.R. Ramprakash	for	Middlesex	1995
3rd	15 J.P. Crawley & M.J. Chilton	for	Lancashire	1998
4th	129 W. Larkins & P. Bainbridge	for	Durham	1993
5th	209 J.D. Carr & K.R. Brown	for	Middlesex	1995
6th	232 C.J. Adams & U.B.A. Rashid	for	Sussex	2000
7th	13 U. Afzaal & A.G. Wharf	for	Nottinghamshire	1999
8th	104 N.H. Fairbrother & G. Chapple	for	Lancashire	2001
9th	80* C.M. Tolley & J.E. Hindson	for	Nottinghamshire	1997
10th	59 P.J. Franks & R.D. Stemp	for	Nottinghamshire	1999

Best bowling performance in an innings for county 9 for 49 A.E. Cordle v Leicestershire 1969
Best bowling performance in an innings against county 7 for 47 D.C. Morgan for Derbyshire 1966
Best bowling performance in a match for county 13 for 110 A.E. Cordle v Leicestershire 1969
Best bowling performance in a match against county 9 for 82 D.C. Morgan for Derbyshire 1966
Largest crowd 6,000 v Derbyshire 1966

LIMITED-OVERS MATCHES

Highest innings total for county 271 for 6 v Durham (SL) 1993
Highest innings total against county 246 for 6 by Lancashire (SL) 1990
Lowest innings total for county 147 v Nottinghamshire (SL) 1999
Lowest innings total against county 105 by Durham (SL) 1993
Highest individual innings for county 100 M.P. Maynard v Lancashire (SL) 1990 and 100 H. Morris v Middlesex (SL) 1995
Highest individual innings against county 104* G. Boycott for Yorkshire (SL) 1973
Highest wicket partnerships for county

1st	94 S.P. James & H. Morris	v	Durham	(SL)	1993
2nd	142 S.P. James & J.H. Kallis	v	Nottinghamshire	(SL)	1997
3rd	143 M.P. Maynard & I.V.A. Richards	v	Lancashire	(SL)	1990
4th	54 M.P. Maynard & M.J. Powell	v	Nottinghamshire	(SL)	2000
5th	100* H. Morris & P.A. Cottey	v	Lancashire	(SL)	1992
6th	54* S.P. James & M.A. Wallace	v	Nottinghamshire	(SL)	2002
7th	27 M.J. Powell & A.W. Evans	v	Nottinghamshire	(SL)	1997
8th	14 S.D. Thomas & A.P. Davies	v	Lancashire	(SL)	2001
9th	3 M.J. Powell & S.D. Thomas	v	Nottinghamshire	(SL)	1997

	3 S.D. Thomas & D.A. Cosker	v	Lancashire	(SL)	2001
10th	3 S.D. Thomas & O.T. Parkin	v	Nottinghamshire	(SL)	1997

Highest wicket partnerships against county

1st	98 G. Boycott & J.H. Hampshire	for	Yorkshire	(SL)	1973
2nd	46 G. Chapple & A. Flintoff	for	Lancashire	(SL)	2001
3rd	95* D.J. Bicknell & P. Johnson	for	Nottinghamshire	(SL)	2000
4th	129 N.J. Astle & M.P. Dowman	for	Nottinghamshire	(SL)	1997
5th	93 G.D. Lloyd & W.K. Hegg	for	Lancashire	(SL)	2001
6th	74 D.E.R. Stewart & G.R. Cass	for	Worcestershire	(SL)	1969
7th	71 W.K. Hegg & I.D. Austin	for	Lancashire	(SL)	1994
8th	36* S.J. Randall & P.J. Franks	for	Nottinghamshire	(SL)	2002
9th	26 P. Bainbridge & D.A. Graveney	for	Durham	(SL)	1993
10th	22 D.A. Graveney & S.P. Hughes	for	Durham	(SL)	1993

Best bowling performance in a match for county 6 for 22 A. Dale v Durham (SL) 1993

Best bowling performance in a match against county 4 for 45 A.R. Oram for Nottinghamshire (SL) 1997

Largest crowd 5,500 v Lancashire (SL) 1990

GROUND INFORMATION

ENTRANCES Penrhyn Avenue (players, officials, members and vehicles), Church Road – car park (members, public and vehicles).

MEMBERS' ENCLOSURE Pavilion, clubhouse and defined members enclosure between John Smiths Tea Pavilion/HSBC Suite and scoreboard at the Penrhyn Avenue End of the ground.

PUBLIC ENCLOSURE Rest of the ground.

COVERED STANDS Pavilion, Tea Pavilion and temporary covered stands if brought in.

OPEN STANDS Rest of the ground including temporary raised plastic seats, ground-level seats/benches surrounding the playing area and deckchairs on the embankment at the Town End of the ground.

NAME OF ENDS Penrhyn Avenue End, Victor Wilde Drive End.

GROUND DIMENSIONS 115m × 107m.

REPLAY SCREEN If televised matches are staged at the ground the replay screen is sited at the Embankment End.

FIRST AID Tent behind John Smiths Tea Pavilion.

CODES OF DRESS Spectators are required to dress in an appropriate manner consistent with attending a cricket match. Bare torsos are not acceptable in or in front of the pavilion. Executive Club/Suite users must wear a necktie and jacket.

BEHAVIOUR The club is keen that standards of behaviour should be maintained and members and spectators are urged to report immediately to the CEO or a Colwyn Bay official any incident, or potential incident, where they feel action should be taken. Bad language is not acceptable at any match and the club will take prompt and strong action should this or any other ground regulation be ignored.

RECIPROCAL ARRANGEMENTS Members of Gloucestershire, Somerset and Worcestershire can gain entry free for championship matches on production of membership card when Glamorgan are not playing their own county.

SUPPORTERS' CLUB Trips organised by The St Helen's Balconiers. Details from John Williams ☎ 01792 414671.

JUNIORS As Cardiff.

CORPORATE ENTERTAINING Glamorgan CCC offer corporate entertainment in the temporary marquees and occasionally in Tea Pavilion and HSBC Suite. These are available for hire on a match-by-match basis. Contact Marketing Department ☎ 029 2040 9381 for further details and a copy of the brochure.

FACILITIES FOR VISUALLY IMPAIRED SPECTATORS No reduction. Guide dogs are allowed. Contact club in advance.

FACILITIES AND ACCESS FOR PEOPLE WITH DISABILITIES INCLUDING WHEELCHAIR ACCESS TO GROUND Yes, from Penrhyn Avenue Entrance.

DESIGNATED CAR PARK AVAILABLE INSIDE THE GROUND FOR PEOPLE WITH DISABILITIES Yes, there is a special area provided on the hard standing path between the main scoreboard and pavilion at the Penrhyn Avenue End of the ground, close to pedestrian entrance.

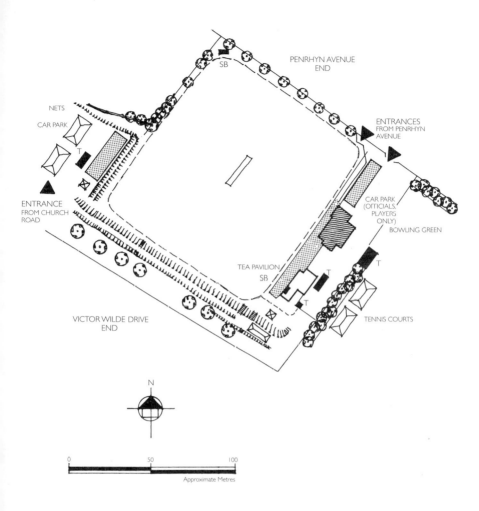

PENRHYN AVENUE END

NETS

CAR PARK

ENTRANCES FROM PENRHYN AVENUE

ENTRANCE FROM CHURCH ROAD

CAR PARK (OFFICIALS, PLAYERS ONLY)

BOWLING GREEN

TEA PAVILION SB

VICTOR WILDE DRIVE END

TENNIS COURTS

N

0   50   100
Approximate Metres

GOOD VIEWING AREAS INSIDE THE GROUND FOR PEOPLE USING WHEELCHAIRS Yes, there is a special area near the sightscreen at the Penrhyn Avenue End of the ground.

RAMPS TO PROVIDE EASY ACCESS TO BARS & REFRESHMENT OUTLETS FOR PEOPLE USING WHEELCHAIRS Yes, to gain entry into pavilion/clubhouse.

FOOD & DRINK FULL RESTAURANT/DINING FACILITIES Members, no. Public, no.

TEMPORARY FOOD/DRINK FACILITIES Members, yes. Public, yes.

FOOD SUITABLE FOR VEGETARIANS Members, no. Public, no.

BARS Members 1, Public 1.

VARIETIES OF BEER SOLD John Smiths.

CHILDREN'S FACILITIES Crèche, no. Play area, no.

CLUB SHOP Yes, Astoria Sports as the Cricket Shop of Wales have a temporary outlet on the ground selling Glamorgan CCC souvenirs.

CLUB MUSEUM No.

CRICKET COACHING FACILITIES Yes, contact Colwyn Bay CC for details.

CRICKET NETS Yes, contact Colwyn Bay CC for details.

OTHER SPORTING OR RECREATIONAL FACILITIES ON THE GROUND Yes, hockey and bowls.

FACILITIES FOR HIRE OR WIDER COMMUNITY USE AT THE GROUND HSBC Suite is available for functions, weddings, exhibitions, Christmas lunches, conferences and business and private entertainment. Contact Colwyn Bay CC for further details.

WINTER CRICKET EVENTS Members' Club dinners and lunches are organised in the winter months. Contact Colwyn Bay CC for details.

CAR PARKING FACILITIES Car parking is available at the rear of the pavilion for players and officials and in an adjoining field off Church Road to the south-west of the playing area for members and the public. Alternatively street parking is available within the local neighbourhood.

OTHER INFORMATION All permanent seats on the ground are blue and all temporary seats are green. The majority of seating is temporary and only 2,000 seats are provided so spectators would be advised to bring their own to popular matches.

GROUND CAPACITY 4,500.

ANTICIPATED GROUND DEVELOPMENTS None currently planned.

HOW TO GET THERE

 Colwyn Bay station, 1.5 miles, is served by Alphaline and Virgin Trains services on the Manchester Piccadilly, Crewe and Chester routes to and from Holyhead. ☎ 08457 484950, 0121 643 4444, 0870 900 0766 or Reservations ☎ 0870 000 6060, 0870 900 0773, 08457 000125 www.alphaline.co.uk, www.centraltrains.co.uk, www.thetrainline.com, www.railtrack.co.uk

 Crosville North Wales Bus service M16 passes ground and links Colwyn Bay station with Rhos-on-Sea. Bus Information Line 0870 608 2608. National Express Coaches ☎ 08705 808080, www.nationalexpress.co.uk. Arriva Cymru ☎ 01248 750444, www.arriva.co.uk, Stagecoach Red & White ☎ 01633 266336 www.stagecoachgroup.com, and First Cymru ☎ 01792 580580 www.firstgroup.com, Travel Line ☎ 08706 082608 all provide services from surrounding areas to Colwyn Bay.

 There are cycle routes from Colwyn Bay and surrounding areas to Rhos-on-Sea.

 From A55 westbound: from A55 take B5113 (Princes Drive). Turn right on to B5113 (Egerton Road). Turn right on to A547 (Conway Road). Bear right on to B5115 (Brompton Avenue). Continue on B5115 (Llandudno Road). Bear right on to Church Road. Turn right on to Penrhyn Avenue. Turn right for Colwyn Bay CC. **From A55 eastbound:** take B5115 (Brompton Avenue). Continue on B5115 (Llandudno Road). Bear right on to Church Road. Turn right on to Penrhyn Avenue. Turn right for Colwyn Bay CC.

 Liverpool John Lennon Airport ☎ 0151 288 4000 www.liverpooljohnlennonairport.com Airportxpress 500 Bus ☎ 0151 236 7676 Easyjet ☎ 0870 6000 000 www.easyjet.com Euroceltic ☎ 0870 0400 100 www.euroceltic.com

WHERE TO STAY

Hotel Seventy Degrees (☎ 01492 534626), The Cedar Tree (☎ 01492 545867), Norfolk House Hotel (☎ 01492 531757), Marine Hotel (☎ 01492 530295), St Tudno Hotel (☎ 01492 874411 www.st-tudno.co.uk) For further small hotels and guest houses in the Colwyn Bay and Rhos-on-Sea area ☎ 01492 530478, fax 01472 534789, email enquiries@breakoutworld.com, www.smoothhound.co.uk, www.breakoutworld.com.

WHERE TO EAT

La Dolce Vita (☎ 01492 541145), Garden Room Restaurant (☎ 01492 874411), Groes Inn (☎ 01492 650545), Bodysgallen Hall (☎ 01492 584466 www.bodysgallen.com), Queens Head (☎ 01492 546570), Richards Restaurant (☎ 01492 877924), St Tudno Hotel (☎ 01492 874411 www.st-tudno.co.uk), Sandbach Teashop (☎ 01492 876522)

TOURIST INFORMATION Colwyn Bay Tourist Information Centre, 40 Station Road, Colwyn Bay, North Wales LL29 8BU ☎ 01492 530478 fax 01492 534789 email info@visitwales.com www.visitwales.com

Wales Tourist Board ☎ 0800 328 1000 www.visitwales.co.uk
Wales Travel Flexipass ☎ 0870 900 0773 www.flexipass.com
Conway County Borough Council ☎ 01492 575361 or 01492 575387 fax 01452 513664 email tourism@conway.gov.uk www.colwyn-bay-tourism.co.uk
Tourist Information Colwyn Bay ☎ 01492 876413 email llandudno.tic@virgin.net

LOCAL RADIO STATIONS BBC Radio Wales (882 KHz MW), Radio City Ltd/Magic 1548 (96.7 MHz/FM/1548 KHz MW)

LOCAL NEWSPAPERS *Evening Leader, Western Mail, Liverpool Echo, Daily Post, North Wales Weekly News, North Wales Pioneer*

SWANSEA

Address Swansea Cricket and Football Club, The Pavilion, St Helen's Cricket Ground, Bryn Road, Swansea, West Glamorgan, Wales SA2 0AR
Prospects of Play ☎ 01792 424242

HISTORY OF GROUND AND FACILITIES

THE SECOND MAJOR GROUND at which Glamorgan County Cricket Club play is at St Helen's, Swansea, the home of the Swansea Cricket and Football Club. The ground is located to the west of the city centre off the Mumbles Road and is enclosed by Bryn Road, Gorse Lane and Mumbles Road. Both rugby union and cricket are played here and most of the terracing facilities are permanent and available for viewing both games. The pavilion was built in 1927 and has had various extensions, additions and refurbishment. The most recent was in 1980 when a new eastern wing was constructed.

The ground takes its name from a medieval convent dedicated to St Helen that was built by an order of Augustinian nuns on the foreshore of Swansea Bay. During the sixteenth century the land and the convent passed to the Herbert family, who in turn sold it to Colonel Llewellyn Morgan, who was a major landowner in the city.

By the eighteenth century Swansea was a thriving port and the area along the shore of Swansea Bay developed into a popular and desirable residential area. The gentlemen used the foreshore for their healthy recreation and there are records from the 1780s of ball games being staged on Crumlin Burrows to the east of the Tawe as well as to the west on the sands near the convent. A notice in the *Hereford Journal* for May 1785 suggests that a formal club had been formed: 'gentlemen subscribers are desired to meet at the bathing house early to appoint a steward for the day and a treasurer for the season'. It seems likely that the members of this early club just played among themselves, similar to the modern-day membership of a golf club.

By the early nineteenth century, fixtures were secured with teams from Neath, Llanelli and Merthyr, and the club secured the use of part of a field near the former convent. The departure of leading players and an outbreak of cholera in

Swansea Cricket and Football Club Pavilion. (*Nikolas O'Neil*)

the 1840s presented a few temporary barriers to the growth of cricket in Swansea but the expansion of the transport network in South Wales and a further increase in trade at the port of Swansea both acted as catalysts.

In 1850 a Swansea Cricket Club was established and the first match was with Llanelli Cricket Club. The club's finances steadily became healthier, allowing them to hire decent professionals, such as Henry Grace and Alfred Pocock, and by the 1860s Swansea Cricket Club had became one of the top sides in South Wales. One of the leading members was Mr J.T.D. Llewellyn, the influential squire of Penllegaer. The Old Etonian and Oxford-educated industrialist had a wide range of sporting contacts in South Wales and London, and as a result Swansea CC secured fixtures against the MCC. With quite an extensive and impressive fixture list, the only worry for the club was the often poor nature of the wicket. Its rough state led to the dropping of the MCC game, but even so, Llewellyn was able to arrange other exhibition matches. In 1866 a XXII of Swansea challenged the United All England Eleven, and in July 1868 a game was staged against the Australian Aborigines touring team. The success of these special fixtures led to plans being set in motion for the club to acquire a larger recreation ground as a decent and proper home for the various sporting teams representing Swansea.

In 1872 an approach was made to Colonel Morgan regarding the sandbanks lining the foreshore, and by the end of the year an agreement was reached for the creation of a new sports field. The sandbanks were levelled, turned and rolled at a cost of £2,000 and during the summer of 1873 Swansea Cricket Club played their first games at their new permanent home. The ground was known as New Cricket Field, St Helen's, and was used for athletics as well as cricket. During the winter rugby football was also staged at St Helen's. Llewellyn continued to give his support to the club, and helped to finance the building of a pavilion and dressing room to serve both the summer and winter games. Through his efforts, St Helen's became one of the best equipped grounds in

South Wales, and an indication of this was the staging of a three-day game between a XXII of Swansea and District against a United South of England XI in May 1876, followed in 1878 by a two-day game between the South Wales Cricket Club and the Australian tourists.

In 1874 Swansea Rugby Football Club and Swansea Cricket Club amalgamated to form the Swansea Cricket and Football Club and the club still has that name.

The western expansion of the industrial town and the popularity of the seafront with residents and visitors alike meant that the Colonel's land was viewed as a prime area for building. With land near the docks and town centre becoming increasingly congested, Swansea Town Council passed a resolution in 1879 to acquire the sports field for building purposes. The leading members of the Cricket and Football Club voiced their vehement opposition, while Llewellyn offered to donate £500 to preserve the field for recreational pursuits. The strong club pressure and Llewellyn's gentle persuasion forced the council to agree that St Helen's should remain as a sports ground.

Mr J.T.D. Llewellyn was also the catalyst behind the formation of Glamorgan County Cricket Club in 1888, and through his influence the St Helen's ground staged some of the county's home games. Glamorgan paid their first visit to Swansea in June 1890 for a match with the MCC, and the ground's first inter-county fixture took place in August 1891 against Devon, although the weather badly interfered with the contest.

Since the early 1880s there had been a small groundsman's cottage in the south-west corner of the ground, and by the turn of the century it was the home of Billy Bancroft, the Swansea and Glamorgan cricket professional and international rugby player who acted as St Helen's first caretaker-cum-groundsman.

Llewellyn oversaw a number of other improvements to the St Helen's complex in the early twentieth century, including a £1,200 donation towards the laying of grass banking around the ground, the construction of decent seating and the erection of a perimeter wall. After the First World War, a new cricket pavilion was built on Bryn Road, while a rugby grandstand was erected along the Mumbles Road in the 1920s. By this time Glamorgan had become a first-class side, and on May 28, 30 and 31 1921 St Helen's staged its first County Championship match as Glamorgan played Leicestershire. The visitors won by 20 runs. It wasn't until the end of July that Glamorgan were able to celebrate their first victory at Swansea, defeating Worcestershire by an innings and 53 runs.

But victories were few and far between at Swansea in these early years, as visiting players often cruelly exposed the fragility of Glamorgan's batting and bowling attack. By the late 1920s the county had secured the services of several professional bowlers who could utilise the slow, sandy wicket, and in 1927 Jack Mercer and Frank Ryan bowled Nottinghamshire out for 61 to stop the visitors from winning the championship. Indeed, there are stories of the visiting players sitting in front of the dressing rooms and on the top of the steps leading up the grass bank from the pitch, with tears streaming down their cheeks as they saw the title slip from their grasp.

The two-storey pavilion was extended during the winter of 1926/7. On the lower floors were the changing rooms, umpires' room and groundsman's store, while on the upper floor was a bar, colonnade and veranda. In 1939 this impressive building and the ground became the property of the Swansea Town Corporation, which has owned it ever since.

The ground had been staging Welsh Rugby internationals since December 1882, but by the end of the Second World War, there were doubts over the future of Welsh games at St Helen's. In a bid to keep the internationals, the Corporation made further ground improvements: the grass banking was replaced with tiered concrete terraces.

During the war the ground was used as a military training camp. Afterwards much building took place, including a new rugby grandstand, new terracing and pavilion facilities. Other events staged at the ground have included hockey, rugby league football, jazz concerts and a programme in the 'It's a Knock-out' BBC TV series.

In 1959 the Memorial Gates were installed opposite the Cricketers Inn in memory of past players who have represented Swansea Cricket and Football Clubs. The gates were donated by the Swansea and District RSC.

From the players' pavilion there used to be 67 steps down to the field. This could be a very long walk back for a batsman who had been dismissed first ball for a duck. Since building developments in the 1980s the distance has been reduced to 45 steps!

In 1964 140-feet high floodlight pylons were installed and they dominate the ground in each corner. Since the ground is used for both rugby and cricket, there are scoreboards for both games.

International touring sides have until recent years usually played Glamorgan at Swansea and the county has defeated all Test nations here except West Indies and Sri Lanka. More recently, this fixture has reverted to Sophia Gardens, the Glamorgan County Club headquarters. Two international matches have been staged at St Helen's: in 1973 a Prudential Trophy match between England and New Zealand and in 1983 a Prudential Cup match between Pakistan and Sri Lanka.

Many of Glamorgan's finest hours have come at Swansea including in 1927 a victory over Nottinghamshire by an innings and 81 runs which deprived Nottinghamshire of the championship and in 1964 a victory over the Australians by 36 runs. The attendance at the latter match was 50,000, which remains a record crowd. Crowds for recent matches have usually reached 5,000 to 6,000. However, 10,000 attended the England versus New Zealand Prudential Trophy match in 1973.

Three of the most significant cricket records took place here. In 1968, while batting for Nottinghamshire, Gary Sobers hit Malcolm Nash for 36 runs in a single six-ball over. (Frank Hayes of Lancashire hit 34 off one over from the same bowler in 1977.) Clive Lloyd hit 201 for the West Indians in two hours in 1976 and equalled Gilbert Jessop's record for the fastest ever double century in first-class cricket. In 1990 Tom Moody playing for Warwickshire scored the fastest century in first-class cricket, reaching his hundred off 36 balls in only 26 minutes to break the record of 37 minutes held jointly by P.G.H. Fender and S. O'Shaughnessy. Tom Moody hit seven 6s and eleven 4s but the bowling was tossed up by Matthew Maynard and Tony Cottey to obtain an early declaration.

The last Welsh Rugby Union international match was staged at St Helen's in 1954, but it is still the home of a first-class side – Swansea RFC have established themselves as one of the top teams in Welsh club rugby. During the last 15 years they have developed the facilities for playing and hosting club rugby. Considerable extensions have been made to the pavilion, with sponsors' boxes and a large VIP lounge being added. New seating areas have been built and the steep concrete terraces together with the scoreboard on the eastern side of the ground were demolished during the winter of 1995/6.

Glamorgan County Cricket Club have staged 524 matches in all competitions on this ground with 329 first-class matches and 129 limited-overs matches in all, the first of which was in the Gillette Cup against Warwickshire in 1966. Between 1988 and 1996 Glamorgan introduced an annual floodlit match with an International XI which took place in early August. The ground is also used by Wales for Minor County Championship matches and these have included games against Devon in 1989, Berkshire in 1991, Wiltshire in 1993 and 1999, Oxfordshire in 1997 and 2001, Cornwall in 1998 and Leicestershire (NatWest Trophy) in 2001. A Glamorgan Second XI fixture was staged with Lancashire in 1949 and on 14 July 1996 the ground hosted a match between Wales Minor Counties and the South African 'A' team. Today only a single first-class match is hosted during the season plus a single limited-overs match, which usually tends to be with the same opponents, subject to league status, though in 2003 the ground also staged Glamorgan's three-day fixture against India 'A'.

The scorers' box and press box are high above the terracing close to the main pavilion. The TV camera/commentary box is positioned directly behind and above the sightscreen at the Sea End on a gantry. The rugby pitch has been used for sponsors' marquees and during the festival period can be heavily tented.

The playing area is 130 metres by 118 metres and is defined by a rope and advertising boards. The ground is dominated by the large floodlight pylons and huge areas of terracing.

Should play be interrupted by rain or bad light then a visit to the Cricketers' Hotel opposite the ground may be of value. There are plenty of items of cricket interest on the walls and meals have even been served on place mats made from old scorecards! Some photographs and historic items of cricket and rugby memorabilia can be viewed in the St Helen's Lounge.

The ground is delightful when the sun is out but tends to be a rather cold place to watch cricket when it is windy or wet.

GROUND RECORDS AND SCORES

FIRST-CLASS MATCHES

Highest innings total for county 547 for 6 dec v Northamptonshire 1933
Highest innings total against county 554 for 4 dec by West Indians 1976
Lowest innings total for county 36 v Hampshire 1922
Lowest innings total against county 40 by Somerset 1968
Highest individual innings for county 233 M.J.L. Turnbull v Worcestershire 1937
Highest individual innings against county 257 A.H. Bakewell for Northamptonshire 1933
Highest wicket partnerships for county

1st	330 R.C. Fredericks & A. Jones	v	Northamptonshire	1972
2nd	206 D.E. Davies & T.L. Brierley	v	Nottinghamshire	1939
3rd	223 H. Morris & M.P. Maynard	v	Gloucestershire	1997
4th	194 A.H. Dyson & D. Davies	v	Gloucestershire	1929
5th	199* Javed Miandad & G.C. Holmes	v	Leicestershire	1984
6th	195 F.B. Pinch & G.C. Cording	v	Worcestershire	1921
7th	211 P.A. Cottey & O.D. Gibson	v	Leicestershire	1996
8th	166 G. Richards & M.A. Nash	v	Leicestershire	1978
9th	203* J.J. Hills & J.C. Clay	v	Worcestershire	1929
10th	143 T. Davies & S.A.B. Daniels	v	Gloucestershire	1982

Highest wicket partnerships against county

1st	223 B.C. Carris & P.A. Gibb	for	Cambridge University	1938
2nd	301 P.J. Sharpe & D.E.V. Padgett	for	Yorkshire	1970
3rd	242 S.J. Cook & C.J. Tavare	for	Somerset	1991
4th	287 C.H. Lloyd & L.G. Rowe	for	West Indians	1976
5th	335 B.F. Butcher & C.H. Lloyd	for	West Indians	1969
6th	276 M.J. Leyland & E. Robinson	for	Yorkshire	1926
7th	138* D.J. Humphreys & R.K. Illingworth	for	Worcestershire	1984
8th	151 C.J. Richards & S.T. Clarke	for	Surrey	1981
9th	130 J.E. Walsh & P. Corrall	for	Leicestershire	1949
10th	122 S. Turner & D.L. Acfield	for	Essex	1974

Best bowling performance in an innings for county 9 for 43 J.S. Pressdee v Yorkshire 1965
Best bowling performance in an innings against county 9 for 60 H. Verity for Yorkshire 1930
Best bowling performance in a match for county 17 for 212 J.C. Clay v Worcestershire 1937
Best bowling performance in a match against county 15 for 52 V.W.C. Jupp for Northamptonshire 1925
Largest crowd 50,000 v Australians 1948

LIMITED-OVERS MATCHES

Highest innings total for county 344 for 5 v Lincolnshire (NWT) 1994
Highest innings total against county 294 for 5 by Hampshire (NWT) 1983
Lowest innings total for county 42 v Derbyshire (SL) 1979
Lowest innings total against county 76 by Minor Counties (B&H) 1985
Highest individual innings for county 162* I.V.A. Richards v Oxfordshire (NWT) 1993
Highest individual innings against county 132 J.J. Whitaker for Leicestershire (SL) 1984

Highest wicket partnerships for county

1st	176* A. Jones & J.A. Hopkins	v	Minor Counties	(B&H)	1980
2nd	204 S.P. James & A. Dale	v	Lincolnshire	(NWT)	1994
3rd	176 H. Morris & I.V.A. Richards	v	Dorset	(NWT)	1990
4th	121 A.R. Lewis & M.J. Llewellyn	v	Hampshire	(B&H)	1973
5th	129 A.R. Lewis & E.W. Jones	v	Hertfordshire	(GC)	1969
6th	105 S.P. James & A.D. Shaw	v	Gloucestershire	(SL)	1997
7th	102 E.W. Jones & M.A. Nash	v	Hampshire	(B&H)	1976
8th	88 B.A. Davis & M.A. Nash	v	Kent	(SL)	1970
9th	87 M.A. Nash & A.E. Cordle	v	Lincolnshire	(GC)	1974
10th	41 J.W. Solanky & D.L. Williams	v	Kent	(SL)	1973

Highest wicket partnerships against county

1st	157 D.L. Haynes & S.F.A.F. Bacchus	for	West Indians	(Tour)	1980
2nd	152 M.A. Roseberry & M. Prabhakar	for	Durham	(SL)	1995
3rd	157 D.R. Turner & T.E. Jesty	for	Hampshire	(SL)	1977
4th	178 J.J. Whitaker & P. Willey	for	Leicestershire	(SL)	1984
5th	105 A.J. Moles & D.P. Ostler	for	Warwickshire	(SL)	1990
6th	70 M.P. Speight & P. Moores	for	Sussex	(SL)	1991
7th	71 S.A. Marsh & M.A. Ealham	for	Kent	(SL)	1992
8th	63* R. Illingworth & P. Booth	for	Leicestershire	(GC)	1977
9th	30 S.J. O'Shaughnessy & P.J.W. Allott	for	Lancashire	(SL)	1986
10th	30 R.K. Illingworth & C.M. Tolley	for	Worcestershire	(SL)	1993

Best bowling performance in a match for county 7 for 16 S.D. Thomas v Surrey (SL) 1998
Best bowling performance in a match against county 6 for 26 A.J. Murphy for Surrey (NWT) 1994
Largest crowd 6,000 v Leicestershire (GC) 1977

ONE-DAY INTERNATIONALS

Highest innings total in ODI for England 159 for 3 v New Zealand (PT) 1973
Highest innings total in ODI against England 158 by New Zealand (PT) 1973
Highest innings total in non-England ODI 338 for 5 for Pakistan v Sri Lanka (WC) 1983
Lowest innings total in ODI for England 159 for 3 v New Zealand (PT) 1973

Lowest innings total in ODI against England 158 by New Zealand v England (PT) 1973
Lowest innings total in non-England ODI 288 for 9 by Sri Lanka v Pakistan (WC) 1983
Highest individual innings in ODI for England 100 D.L. Amiss v New Zealand (PT) 1973
Highest individual innings in ODI against England 55 V. Pollard for New Zealand (PT) 1973
Highest individual innings in non-England ODI 82 Zaheer Abbas & Mohsin Khan for Pakistan v Sri Lanka (WC) 1983
Highest wicket partnerships in ODI for England

1st	96 D.L. Amiss & G. Boycott	v	New Zealand	(PT)	1973
2nd	1 D.L. Amiss & G.R.J. Roope	v	New Zealand	(PT)	1973
3rd	38 D.L. Amiss & F.C. Hayes	v	New Zealand	(PT)	1973
4th	24* K.W.R. Fletcher & F.C. Hayes	v	New Zealand	(PT)	1973

5th to 10th yet to be established.

Highest wicket partnerships in ODI against England

1st	4 R.E. Redmond & G.M. Turner	for	New Zealand	(PT)	1973
2nd	5 B.E. Congdon & G.M. Turner	for	New Zealand	(PT)	1973
3rd	5 B.F. Hastings & G.M. Turner	for	New Zealand	(PT)	1973
4th	1 M.G. Burgess & G.M. Turner	for	New Zealand	(PT)	1973
5th	55 V. Pollard & G.M. Turner	for	New Zealand	(PT)	1973
6th	11 V. Pollard & K.J. Wadsworth	for	New Zealand	(PT)	1973
7th	27 V. Pollard & B.R. Taylor	for	New Zealand	(PT)	1973
8th	25 R.J. Hadlee & B.R. Taylor	for	New Zealand	(PT)	1973
9th	11 R.O. Collinge & R.J. Hadlee	for	New Zealand	(PT)	1973
10th	14 R.J. Hadlee & H.J. Howarth	for	New Zealand	(PT)	1973

Highest wicket partnerships in non-England ODI

1st	88 Mohsin Khan & Mudassar Nazar	for	Pakistan v Sri Lanka	(WC)	1983
2nd	68 Mohsin Khan & Zaheer Abbas	for	Pakistan v Sri Lanka	(WC)	1983
3rd	73 Javed Miandad & Zaheer Abbas	for	Pakistan v Sri Lanka	(WC)	1983
4th	96 Imran Khan & Javed Miandad	for	Pakistan v Sri Lanka	(WC)	1983
5th	7 Ijaz Faqih & Imran Khan	for	Pakistan v Sri Lanka	(WC)	1983
6th	14 D.S. de Silva & D.S.B.P. Kuruppu	for	Sri Lanka v Pakistan	(WC)	1983
7th	23 A.L.F. de Mel & D.S. de Silva	for	Sri Lanka v Pakistan	(WC)	1983
8th	54 R.G. de Alwis & D.S. de Silva	for	Sri Lanka v Pakistan	(WC)	1983
9th	28 R.G. de Alwis & R.J. Ratnayake	for	Sri Lanka v Pakistan	(WC)	1983
10th	26* H.G. de Alwis & V.B. John	for	Sri Lanka v Pakistan	(WC)	1983

Best bowling performance in ODI for England on ground 4 for 32 J.A. Snow v New Zealand (PT) 1973
Best bowling performance in ODI against England on ground 1 for 32 B.E. Congdon for New Zealand (PT) 1973
Best bowling performance on ground in non-England ODI on ground 3 for 40 Sarfraz Nawaz for Pakistan v Sri Lanka (WC) 1973
Largest crowd 10,000 England v New Zealand (PT) 1973

GROUND INFORMATION

ENTRANCES Bryn Road (players, officials and members) Mumbles Road (members and public) Swansea Rugby Ground – via Mumbles Road (members and public).
MEMBERS' ENCLOSURE Pavilion, clubhouse, St Helen's Lounge and defined members' terrace enclosure at Pavilion End of the ground.
PUBLIC ENCLOSURE Rest of the ground.
COVERED AREAS Pavilion, clubhouse, St Helen's Lounge and Main Rugby Stand.
OPEN STANDS Pavilion terrace enclosure together with all permanent tiered terraces and seating surrounding the playing area.
NAME OF ENDS Pavilion End, Mumbles Road End.
GROUND DIMENSIONS 130m × 118m.
REPLAY SCREEN If televised matches are played at the ground the replay screen is sited on the rugby ground.
FIRST AID Situated in rugby grandstand.

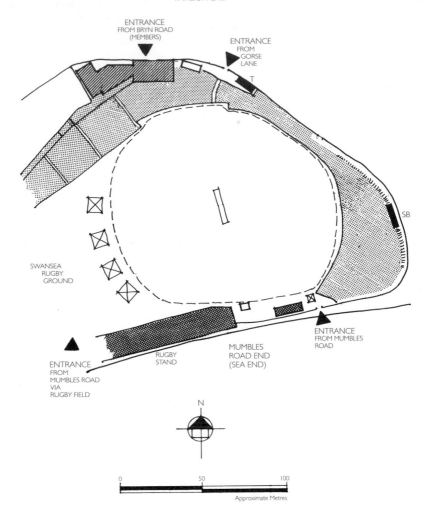

CODES OF DRESS Spectators are required to dress in an appropriate manner consistent with attending a cricket match. Bare torsos are not acceptable in, or in front of the pavilion. Executive Club/Suite users must wear a necktie and jacket.

BEHAVIOUR The club is keen that standards of behaviour should be maintained and members and spectators are urged to report immediately to the CEO or ground safety officer any incident, or potential incident, where they feel action should be taken. Bad language is not acceptable at any match and the club will take prompt and strong action should this or any other ground regulation be ignored.

RECIPROCAL ARRANGEMENTS Members of Gloucestershire, Somerset and Worcestershire can gain entry to Championship matches free on production of membership card when Glamorgan is not playing their own county.

SUPPORTERS' CLUB There is an official supporters' club but the body organising trips to matches is called The St Helen's Balconiers. They also raise funds to help keep county cricket in Swansea and have a bar on the ground at the Mumbles Road end. Details from John Williams ☎ 01792 414671.

JUNIORS As Cardiff.

CORPORATE ENTERTAINING There is a facility for corporate entertainment in the suites in the Swansea Cricket and Rugby Pavilion. These are available to hire on a match by match basis. Contact Marketing Department ☎ 029 2040 9381 for further details or Swansea Rugby Club.

FACILITIES FOR VISUALLY IMPAIRED SPECTATORS No reduction. Guide dogs are allowed. Contact club in advance.

FACILITIES AND ACCESS FOR PEOPLE WITH DISABILITIES INCLUDING WHEELCHAIR ACCESS TO GROUND Yes, from Mumbles Road Gate.

DESIGNATED CAR PARK AVAILABLE INSIDE THE GROUND FOR PEOPLE WITH DISABILITIES No.

GOOD VIEWING AREAS INSIDE THE GROUND FOR PEOPLE USING WHEELCHAIRS Yes, special area, request suitable position. Pavilion enclosure not recommended due to steep steps. Ideal position at Sea End near sightscreen.

RAMPS TO PROVIDE EASY ACCESS TO BARS & REFRESHMENT OUTLETS FOR PEOPLE USING WHEELCHAIRS Yes.

FOOD & DRINK FULL RESTAURANT/DINING FACILITIES Members Yes. Public No. A full restaurant is available in the Swansea Cricket & Football Club Pavilion. Catering is provided by Swansea Rugby Club. Also a full bar, tea bar and food facility at the Balconiers' Bar at the Mumbles Road end.

TEMPORARY FOOD/DRINK FACILITIES Members, yes. Public, yes.

FOOD SUITABLE FOR VEGETARIANS Members, yes. Public, yes.

BARS Members 2, Public 1.

VARIETIES OF BEER SOLD Brains, Carling, Fosters.

CHILDREN'S FACILITIES Crèche, no. Play Area, no.

CLUB SHOP Yes, franchise to Astoria Sports is the Cricket Shop of Wales situated in a temporary facility on the ground.

CLUB MUSEUM No, but there are plenty of photographs in the Swansea Cricket and Football Club Pavilion.

CRICKET COACHING FACILITIES No.

CRICKET NETS No.

OTHER SPORTING OR RECREATIONAL FACILITIES ON THE GROUND Yes, rugby union.

FACILITIES FOR HIRE OR WIDER COMMUNITY USE AT THE GROUND Rooms are available for functions, weddings, exhibitions, Christmas lunches, conferences and business and private entertainment. Contact Swansea Cricket & Football Club for further details and a copy of the brochure.

WINTER CRICKET EVENTS No.

CAR PARKING FACILITIES Car parking is available within the ground for players and officials only. Car parking for members and the public is available outside the ground in neighbouring streets Bryn Road, King Edward Road, St Helen's Avenue and the Mumbles car park which is sited on the seafront.

OTHER INFORMATION The ground is situated a minute's walk from the beach front and Swansea Bay.

GROUND CAPACITY 3,500.

ANTICIPATED GROUND DEVELOPMENTS None currently planned.

HOW TO GET THERE

 Swansea station 1.5 miles. ☎ 08457 484950, 08457 125678, 0870 900 0766, reservations 0870 000 6060, 0870 900 0773, 08457 000125, email customerservices@wwtrains.co.uk, www.alphaline.co.uk, www.centraltrains.co.uk, www.greatwesterntrains.co.uk, www.walesandwest.co.uk, www.thetrainline.com, www.railtrack.co.uk

 South Wales Transport 1, 2, 3 and 14 from Swansea bus station 0.75 mile from Swansea station – numerous services linking rail station with bus station pass ground, also South Wales Transport to Mumbles, Sketty, Ostermouth and Brynmill pass close to ground. For further details of times of travel contact Bus Information Line ☎ 01792 485511, 0870 608 2608, www.southwalestransport.co.uk. Also National Express coaches and Stagecoach South Wales services terminate at the central bus station in the City Centre. You can then walk three quarters of a mile to the ground, or catch one of many services run by South Wales Transport as above. National Express Coaches ☎ 08705 808080, www.nationalexpress.co.uk, Arriva Cymru ☎ 01248 750444, www.arriva.co.uk, Stagecoach Red & White ☎ 01633 266336, www.stagecoachgroup.com, First Cymru ☎ 01792 580580, www.firstgroup.com or Travel Line ☎ 08706 082608 provide services from surrounding areas to Swansea

 From north and west: At M4 Junction 47 take A483. At roundabout take A483. Turn right on to A4216 (Station Road then Cockett Road then Vivian Road). Turn left on to A4118 (Gower Road then

Sketty Road). Turn right on to Bernard Street. Turn left on to Marlborough Road. Turn right on to Finsbury Terrace. Continue into Gorse Lane for St Helen's Cricket Ground. **From south and east:** At M4 Junction 42 take A483. At roundabout take A483 (Fabian Way). Continue west on A4067 (Quay Parade and then Victoria Road). Bear left on to A4067 (Oystermouth Road). Bear right on to A4067 (Mumbles Road). Turn right on to local road. Turn right on to A4067 (Mumbles Road). Bear left on to Gorse Lane for St Helen's Cricket Ground.

 Cardiff International Airport ☎ 01446 711111, www.cial.co.uk

WHERE TO STAY

Morgans Hotel (☎ 01792 459050 www.dermotts.org.uk), Patricks (☎ 01792 360199, www.patricks-restaurant.co.uk), Dragon Hotel (☎ 01792 651074), Beaumont Hotel (☎ 01792 343044), Dolphin Hotel (☎ 01792 350011), Mumbles Hotel (☎ 01792 367147), Tenby House Guesthouse (☎ 01792 360795), The Guesthouse (back of ground) (☎ 01792 466947)

For a further selection of small hotels and guest houses in Swansea area ☎ 01437 765 777 email enquiries@breakoutworld.com, www.smoothhound.co.uk, www.breakoutworld.com.

WHERE TO EAT

La Brasseria (☎ 01792 469683), Dermotts at Morgans Hotel (☎ 01792 459050 www.dermotts.org.uk), Moghul Brasserie (☎ 01792 475131), Opium Den (☎ 01792 456160), Patricks (☎ 01792 360199 www.patricks-restaurant.co.uk)

TOURIST INFORMATION Swansea Tourist Information Centre, PO Box 59, Singleton Street, Swansea SA1 3QG. ☎/fax 01792 468321 or Wales Tourist Board, PO Box 1, Cardiff CF24 2XN ☎ 08701 211251 email info@visitwales.com www.visitwales.com

OTHER USEFUL INFORMATION

Swansea Rugby Football Club ☎ 01792 424242
Swansea City Football Club ☎ 01792 633400, www.swanseacity.net
The Welsh Institute of Sport ☎ 029 2030 0500 email wis@scw.co.uk, www.sports-council-wales.co.uk
The Millennium Stadium Tours ☎ 029 2082 2228, www.cardiff-stadium.co.uk
Wales Tourist Board ☎ 0800 328 1000, www.visitwales.co.uk
Wales Travel Flexipass ☎ 0870 9000773, www.flexipass.com

LOCAL RADIO STATIONS BBC Radio Wales (882 KHz MW), BBC Radio Cymru (93.1 MHz FM/882 KHz MW), Red Dragon FM/Capital Radio (97.4 MHz FM/1359 KHz MW), Swansea Sound (96.4 MHz FM/1170 KHz MW)

LOCAL NEWSPAPERS *South Wales Echo, Wales on Sunday, The Western Mail, South Wales Evening Post*

Gloucestershire

Bristol × |
Cheltenham – Cheltenham College
Gloucester – King's School

GLOUCESTERSHIRE COUNTY CRICKET CLUB, THE ROYAL & SUN ALLIANCE COUNTY GROUND, NEVIL ROAD, BISHOPSTON, BRISTOL BS7 9EJ

General Enquiries and Marketing	0117 910 8000
Match Information	0117 910 8040
Ticket Sales and Information Bookings	0117 910 8010
Club Shop	0117 910 8020
Lindley Catering	0117 910 8032 (Bristol)
Conference Bookings	0117 910 8025
Gold Bond	0117 910 8016
All departments except Catering fax	0117 924 1193
Catering Office	0117 942 3027
Email	enquiries.glos@ecb.co.uk
Website	www.gloucestershire.cricinfo.com

Founded 1871
Colours blue, gold, brown, silver, green and red
Crest Coat of Arms of the City and County of Bristol
National Cricket League Nickname Gladiators
National Cricket League Colours dark blue and white trim
Patron The Lord Vestey
President G.F. Collis
Chairman A.H. Haines
Vice Chairman R. Parsons
Hon Treasurer J.R. Harris OBE
Chief Executive Officer T. Richardson
Executive Assistant J Lobb
Chairman Cricket Committee A.S. Brown
Ground Operations Manager P. Hall
Finance Manager B. Cooke
Finance Officer P. Huntley
Membership Secretary P. Holloway
Sales Manager J. Fletcher
Events Organiser A. Pope
Director of Cricket J.G. Bracewell
Director of Development & Operations A.W. Stovold

Academy Director & 2nd XI Coach A.J. Wright
Coaching Administrator L. Allen
Captain M.W. Alleyne
Physiotherapists Kinetic Fitness Spinal and Sports Physiotherapy Centre
Scorer 1st XI K.T. Gerrish
Scorer 2nd XI E. Jones
Head Groundsman S. Williams
Shop Manager M. Weston
Catering Manager I. Patterson
Statistician K.T. Gerrish
Hon Curator/Librarian and Historian K.T. Gerrish
Yearbook £6
Scorecard 50p
National Cricket League Programme & Scorecard £2 *The Gladiator*
Magazine/Newsletter *No Boundaries* (free to members)
Frizzell County Championship Status Division 2
National Cricket League Status Division 1

ACHIEVEMENTS

County Championship Champions 1874, 1876, 1877, Joint Champions 1873
Gillette Cup Winners 1973
NatWest Bank Trophy Winners 1999, 2000
Benson and Hedges Cup Winners 1977, 1999, 2000, Finalists 2001
John Player Sunday League 6th 1969, 1973, 1977
Refuge Assurance Sunday League 2nd 1988

Norwich Union National League Winners Division 1 2000, Winners Division 2 2002
Refuge Assurance Cup Semi-finalists 1988
Tilcon Trophy Winners 1987, Finalists 1979, 1982
Ward Four Counties Knockout Competition Semi-finalists 1988
Severn Trophy Winners 1987
Seeboard Trophy Finalists 1991

GLOUCESTERSHIRE CRICKET BOARD

Chairman T. Crouch
Secretary D. Howell
Treasurer K. Booker
Cricket Development Officer/Women & Girls Secretary M.J. Bailey

Address Gloucestershire Cricket Board, The Royal and Sun Alliance County Ground, Nevil Road,
Bishopston, Bristol BS7 9EJ
☎ 0117 910 8000
Fax 0117 924 1193

GROUNDS
Bristol (The Royal & Sun Alliance County Ground, Nevil Road), Cheltenham (College Ground, Thirlestaine
Road) and Gloucester (King's School, Archdeacon Meadow)
Other grounds used since 1969: Gloucester (Winget Sports Ground, Tuffley Avenue), Cheltenham Town
(Victoria Ground, Prince's Street), Cheltenham Dowty Arle Court (Dowty Arle Court CC, Sir George Dowty PLC
Sports Ground), Lydney (Recreational Trust Ground, Swan Road), Swindon (County Ground, County Road),
Moreton-in-Marsh (Moreton Cricket Ground, Batsford Road), Trowbridge (Trowbridge CC County Cricket
Ground, Timbrell Street), Stroud (Eriniod Ground) and Tewkesbury (Swilgate)

SECOND XI GROUNDS
In addition to the above, the following ground is used for Second XI matches:
Bristol University Sports Centre, Coombe Lane, Coombe Dingle, Bristol BS9 2BC ☎ 0117 962 6718
Hatherley & Reddings CC, North Park, Shurdington Road, Cheltenham ☎ 01242 862608

Tablet on the Grace Gates at Nevil Road,
Bristol.

BRISTOL

Address The Royal & Sun Alliance County Ground, Nevil Road, Bishopston,
Bristol BS7 9EJ
Prospects of Play ☎ 0117 910 8040

HISTORY OF GROUND AND FACILITIES

THE ROYAL AND SUN ALLIANCE County Cricket Ground (previously known as the Phoenix Assurance Company Ground) is in Ashley Down in the north of the city. The observant visitor will notice that the surrounding roads bear the names of other first-class and minor counties. The county's previous home ground was Clifton College.

The present ground, which was first used by Gloucestershire County Cricket Club in 1899 against Lancashire, was laid out to W.G. Grace's specification. Later, in 1916, it was sold to the Fry's Chocolate company to get the county club out of debt and became known as Fry's Ground. The county club repurchased the ground in 1932 after forming the Gloucestershire County Cricket Club Company Limited.

Since W.G. Grace first contemplated the development of the ground a century ago, many changes have taken place, but there still remains a sense of spaciousness about the area. The ground now has indoor cricket nets, squash and tennis courts, and football pitches during the winter months.

GCCC have played on three other grounds in the city, at Clifton College from 1871 to 1932, Durdham Down 1870 and Greenbank from 1922 to 1928. Clifton was the last to be used when a match was staged with All India in August 1932.

From 1840 until the 1870s the land on which the ground now stands was used by Muller's orphanage. The orphanage building still exists today but now forms

The pavilion and Cricket Centre at the County Cricket Ground, Bristol.

part of the City of Bristol College campus. The main entrance to the ground from Nevil Road is through the Grace Gates. A tablet on the gates was erected on the centenary of W.G.'s birth, 18 July 1948. John Arlott wrote: 'in the public mind W.G. was Gloucestershire'; he scored many of his centuries at Bristol.

The pavilion, built in the 1880s, was refurbished between October 1991 and July 1992. While the work was in progress a number of matches were played at Dowty Arle Court, Cheltenham. Other ground improvements made at Bristol during the mid-1990s include a new indoor cricket school, together with the replacement of wooden seats with white plastic tip-up seats.

Other changes have been made in recent years. The Jessop Tavern, which used to house the press box, was built in 1958 but was demolished in 1998/9 and reconstructed along with the new, architecturally splendid Jessop Stand in 1999 ready for the Cricket World Cup. The Diana Princess of Wales Education Centre is below it. The main scoreboard is nearby; it was constructed in 1971 and refurbished in 1998. The Jessop Stand was designed by a local architect, Peter Smith, and although much smaller is similar to the New Mound Stand at Lord's. It cost £750,000 and was part funded by the Princess Diana Memorial Fund because the late Princess was once a patron of the club and the Foundation for Sport and the Arts.

The Mound Stand was built during the 1960s along with the Grace Room and Hammond Room, which now form the main restaurant for members at the pavilion end. The press/media room is located at the Pavilion End of the Mound Stand close to the Indoor Cricket School.

The playing area is 154 metres by 156 metres and is defined by rope and advertising boards completely surrounding the perimeter. The ground capacity is 8,000 and around 3,500 permanent seats are provided but further seating is installed for popular matches. The TV camera/commentary box is positioned behind the sightscreen at the Ashley Down End.

The ground is surrounded by housing and to the south are the City of Bristol College campus buildings, built of similar stone to the Pavilion. Many photographs of old county teams and former players, together with some history of the Gloucestershire County Cricket Club, can be found in the Pavilion and bar areas.

Nevil Road has seen some fascinating and important matches. In August 1930 Gloucestershire tied with the Australian tourists and the city erupted with excitement. Gloucestershire were dismissed for 72 in their first innings but in their second Wally Hammond scored 89 before Tom Goddard and Charlie Parker tied up the match, including Bradman and all.

Ground records include highest individual innings by Wally Hammond and Michael Hussey for Northamptonshire together with best bowling performances by E.G. Dennett, Tom Goddard, F.A. Tarrant and F.H. Parris. The ground has been used for limited-overs international fixtures since 1983 with further matches staged in the 1999 Cricket World Cup and in the NatWest Series. The club hopes to install permanent floodlighting at Bristol in the near future.

With Grace and Jessop, Dipper and Hammond, Sinfield and Barnett, Crapp and Emmett, Goddard and Parker, Graveney and Allen, Zaheer Abbas and Proctor, Russell, Walsh and Harvey on the role of honour, few grounds have a record to compare with Bristol's for nurturing some of the best players in the game.

GROUND RECORDS AND SCORES

FIRST-CLASS MATCHES

Highest innings total for county 643 for 5 dec v Nottinghamshire 1946
Highest innings total against county 774 for 7 dec by Australians 1948
Lowest innings total for county 22 v Somerset 1920
Lowest innings total against county 25 by Somerset 1947
Highest individual innings for county 302* W.R. Hammond v Glamorgan 1934
Highest individual innings against county 310* M.E.K. Hussey for Northamptonshire 2002
Highest wicket partnerships for county

1st	362 A.J. Wright & G.D. Hodgson	v	Nottinghamshire	1995
2nd	236 W. Troup & C.L. Townsend	v	Somerset	1898
3rd	306 M.G.N. Windows & C.G. Taylor	v	Nottinghamshire	2001
4th	233 W. Troup & C.L. Townsend	v	Nottinghamshire	1898
5th	242 W.R. Hammond & B.O. Allen	v	Somerset	1946
6th	226* W.R. Hammond & G.M. Emmett	v	Nottinghamshire	1946
7th	229 K.M. Curran & R.C. Russell	v	Somerset	1990
8th	239 W.R. Hammond & A.E. Wilson	v	Lancashire	1938
9th	239 W.G. Grace & S.A.P. Kitcat	v	Sussex	1896
10th	131 W.R. Gouldsworthy & J.G.W.T. Bessant	v	Somerset	1923

Highest wicket partnerships against county

1st	391 A. Shrewsbury & A.O. Jones	for	Nottinghamshire	1899
2nd	316 J.L. Hopgood & G.E. Tyldesley	for	Lancashire	1934
3rd	270 R.C. on tong & Javed Miandad	for	Glamorgan	1981
4th	262 D.L. Amiss & A.I. Kallicharran	for	Warwickshire	1979
5th	222 P.A. Slocombe & B.C. Rose	for	Somerset	1982
6th	318 M.E.K. Hussey & G.P. Swann	for	Northamptonshire	2002
7th	185 E. Wainwright & G.H. Hirst	for	Yorkshire	1897
8th	159 D.S. de Silva & A.L.F. de Mel	for	Sri Lankans	1981
9th	176 R. Moorhouse & G.H. Hirst	for	Yorkshire	1894
10th	147 E.M. Sprot & A.E. Fielder	for	Hampshire	1911

Best bowling performance in an innings for county 10 for 40 E.G. Dennett v Essex 1906
Best bowling performance in an innings against county 9 for 41 F.A. Tarrant for Middlesex 1907
Best bowling performance in a match for county 17 for 106 T.W.J. Goddard v Kent 1939
Best bowling performance in a match against county 15 for 98 F. Parris for Sussex 1894
Largest crowd 15,000 v Australians 1930 and 1948

LIMITED-OVERS MATCHES

Highest innings total for county 351 for 2 v Scotland (NWT) 1997
Highest innings total against county 349 for 6 by Lancashire (NWT) 1984
Lowest innings total for county 49 v Middlesex (SL) 1978
Lowest innings total against county 68 for Cheshire (NWT) 1992
Highest individual innings for county 177 A.J. Wright v Scotland (NWT) 1997
Highest individual innings against county 142* J.P. Maher for Glamorgan (B&H) 2001
Highest wicket partnerships for county

1st	311 A.J. Wright & N.J. Trainor	v	Scotland	(NWT)	1997
2nd	171 A.W. Stovold & C.W.J. Athey	v	Nottinghamshire	(B&H)	1987
3rd	169 R.J. Cunliffe & S. Young	v	Surrey	(B&H)	1997
4th	207 R.C. Russell & A.J. Wright	v	British Universities	(B&H)	1998
5th	127* A.J. Wright & M.J. Church	v	Hampshire	(B&H)	1998
6th	113 R.J. Cunliffe & M.W. Alleyne	v	Hampshire	(B&H)	1996
7th	108* C.W.J. Athey & J.W. Lloyds	v	Warwickshire	(B&H)	1990
8th	52 M.W. Alleyne & C.A. Walsh	v	Hertfordshire	(NWT)	1993
	52 R.C. Williams & C.A. Walsh	v	Glamorgan	(SL)	1994
9th	45* K.M. Curran & D.V. Lawrence	v	Scotland	(B&H)	1985

10th	33 R.C. Russell & C.A. Walsh	v	Surrey	(NWT)	1998

Highest wicket partnerships against county

1st	197* T.S. Curtis & T.M. Moody	for	Worcestershire	(SL)	1991
2nd	194 M.W. Gatting & M.R. Ramprakash	for	Middlesex	(SL)	1991
3rd	146 R.J. Boyd-Moss & R.J. Bailey	for	Northamptonshire	(SL)	1984
4th	157* C.H. Lloyd & J. Abrahams	for	Lancashire	(SL)	1983
5th	156 A.J. Stewart & A.J. Hollioake	for	Surrey	(NWT)	1998
6th	123 S.A. Selwood & M.P. Dowman	for	Derbyshire	(SL)	2002
7th	91 A.W. Evans & O.D. Gibson	for	Glamorgan	(SL)	1996
8th	61 M.E. Trescothick & D.A. Reeve	for	Somerset	(B&H)	1998
9th	68 P.A. Neale & N. Gifford	for	Worcestershire	(SL)	1980
10th	61 J.M. Rice & A.M.E. Roberts	for	Hampshire	(B&H)	1975

Best bowling performance in a match for county 6 for 20 D.V. Lawrence v Combined Universities (B&H) 1991
Best bowling performance in a match against county 6 for 33 E.J. Barlow for Derbyshire (B&H) 1978
Largest crowd 7,500 v Nottinghamshire (NWT) 1987

ONE-DAY INTERNATIONALS

Highest innings total for England in ODI 268 for 4 v Australia (NWS) 2001
Highest innings total against England in ODI 272 for 5 by Australia (NWS) 2001
Highest innings total in non-England ODI 329 for 2 for India v Kenya (WC) 1999
Lowest innings total for England in ODI 268 for 4 v Australia (NWS) 2001
Lowest innings total against England in ODI 272 for 5 by Australia (NWS) 2001
Lowest innings total in non-England ODI 202 by West Indies v Pakistan (WC) 1999
Highest individual innings for England in ODI 84 N.V. Knight v Australia (NWS) 2001
Highest individual innings against England in ODI 102 R.T. Ponting for Australia (NWS) 2001
Highest individual innings in non-England ODI 140* S.R. Tendulkar for India v Kenya (WC) 1999

Highest wicket partnerships for England in ODI

1st	13 M.E. Trescothick & A.D. Brown	v	Australia	(NWS)	2001
2nd	124 N.V. Knight & M.E. Trescothick	v	Australia	(NWS)	2001
3rd	52 N.V. Knight & A.J. Stewart	v	Australia	(NWS)	2001
4th	9 N.V. Knight & O.A. Shah	v	Australia	(NWS)	2001
5th	70* O.A. Shah & B.C. Hollioake	v	Australia	(NWS)	2001

6th to 10th yet to be established

Highest wicket partnerships against England in ODI

1st	12 A.C. Gilchrist & M.E. Waugh	for	Australia	(NWS)	2001
2nd	89 M.E.Waugh & R.T.Ponting	for	Australia	(NWS)	2001
3rd	97 R.T.Ponting & D.R.Martyn	for	Australia	(NWS)	2001
4th	13 R.T.Ponting & A.Symonds	for	Australia	(NWS)	2001
5th	19 A.Symonds & S.R.Waugh	for	Australia	(NWS)	2001
6th	42* S.R.Waugh & I.J.Harvey	for	Australia	(NWS)	2001

7th to 10th yet to be established

Highest wicket partnerships in non-England ODI

1st	89 G.M. Turner & J.G. Wright	for	New Zealand v Sri Lanka	(WC)	1983
2nd	85 M.S. Atapattu & K.C. Sangakkara	for	Sri Lanka v India	(NWS)	2002
3rd	237* R.S. Dravid & S.R. Tendulkar	for	India v Kenya	(WC)	1999
4th	71 R.S. Madugalle & L.R.D. Mendis	for	Sri Lanka v New Zealand	(WC)	1983
5th	73* G.W. Flower & N.C. Johnson	for	Zimbabwe v West Indies	(NWS)	2000
6th	74 M. Kaif & S.R. Tendulkar	for	India v Sri Lanka	(NWS)	2002
7th	74 Azhar Mahmood & Wasim Akram	for	Pakistan v West Indies	(WC)	1999
8th	19 K.L.T. Arthurton & S. Chandapaul	for	West Indies v Pakistan	(WC)	1999
9th	34 S.Chanderpaul & M. Dillon	for	West Indies v Pakistan	(WC)	1999
10th	8 C.R.D. Fernando & W.P.U.J.C. Vaas	for	Sri Lanka v India	(NWS)	2002

Best bowling performance for England in ODI 2 for 44 D. Gough v Australia (NWS) 2001
Best bowling performance against England in ODI 2 for 55 G.D. McGrath for Australia (NWS) 2001
Best bowling performance in non-England ODI 5 for 25 R.J. Hadlee for New Zealand v Sri Lanka (WC) 1983
Largest crowd 15,000 England v Australia (NWS) 2001

GROUND INFORMATION

ENTRANCES Nevil Road – via Grace Gates (players, officials, press/media, members, public and vehicles), Ashley Down Road via College Gates (members, public and vehicles).

MEMBERS' ENCLOSURE Pavilion and defined area at Pavilion End of the ground.

PUBLIC ENCLOSURE Rest of the ground.

COVERED STANDS Mound Stand (part), Jessop Stand.

OPEN STANDS Hammond Roof, Mound Stand (part), Office Stand.

NAME OF ENDS Pavilion End, Ashley Down End.

GROUND DIMENSIONS 154m × 156m.

REPLAY SCREEN If televised matches are staged at the ground the replay screen is sited at the Ashley Down End of the ground.

FIRST AID Room available near Press Box in Mound Stand at Pavilion End of the ground.

CODES OF DRESS The club does not lay down strict standards of dress in the enclosure but expects 'smart-casual' dress to be worn, especially in the pavilion.

BEHAVIOUR The club is keen that standards of behaviour should be maintained and members and spectators are urged to report immediately to any steward any incident, or potential incident, where they feel action should be taken. Bad language is not acceptable at any match and the club will take prompt and strong action should this or any other ground regulation be ignored. Obstructing passageways, singing indecent songs, using indecent language, making unnecessary noise by means including persistent chanting, use of radios without an ear-piece, use of mobile telephones, possession of and/or waving of banners is not permitted.

RECIPROCAL ARRANGEMENTS Members of Glamorgan, Somerset and Worcestershire can gain entry free to County Championship matches on production of membership card when Gloucestershire is not playing their own county.

SUPPORTERS' CLUB Gloucester Exiles produce newsletter: *Outside Edge*. Contact Gloucestershire Exiles, Flat 6, 4 Square Court, 405 Nelson Road, Hounslow, Middlesex TW3 3UN for details.

JUNIORS Junior Gladiator Membership for under-16s £12 per annum. Contact 0117 910 8017 for details.

CORPORATE ENTERTAINMENT Facilities are available in Grace Room, President's Suite, Merchant Investors Suite, Proctor Suite, Players Lounge, Diana Princess of Wales Education Centre, and Phoenix Lounge plus Jessop Stand Boxes and temporary marquees when applicable. Contact Marketing Department for details and a brochure.

FACILITIES FOR VISUALLY IMPAIRED SPECTATORS No reduced admission, guide dogs allowed.

FACILITIES AND ACCESS FOR PEOPLE WITH DISABILITIES INCLUDING WHEELCHAIR ACCESS TO GROUND Yes, access via Grace Gates and College Gates.

DESIGNATED CAR PARK AVAILABLE INSIDE THE GROUND FOR PEOPLE WITH DISABILITIES Yes, to rear of Mound Stand and near reception, shop and offices.

GOOD VIEWING AREAS INSIDE THE GROUND FOR PEOPLE USING WHEELCHAIRS Yes, in front of Jessop Stand and near reception, shop and offices.

DESIGNATED VIEWING AREAS FOR PEOPLE USING WHEELCHAIRS Yes, Jessop Stand Concourse.

RAMPS TO PROVIDE EASY ACCESS TO BARS & REFRESHMENT OUTLETS FOR PEOPLE USING WHEELCHAIRS Yes.

FOOD & DRINK FULL RESTAURANT/DINING FACILITIES The Hammond Bar is the main members' bar. Lindley Catering Limited serve a variety of snacks and meals at lunch and tea. The Grace Room is the members' dining area and lunch and tea can be booked in advance ☎ 0117 910 8013. The Jessop Bar is a public facility and offers meals, snacks and bar facilities.

TEMPORARY FOOD/DRINK FACILITIES Members, yes. Public, no.

FOOD SUITABLE FOR VEGETARIANS Members, yes. Public, yes.

BARS Members 2, Public 1.

VARIETIES OF BEER Coors, Grolsch, Carling, Bass, Worthington Creamflow.

CHILDREN'S FACILITIES Crèche, no. Children's play area, no.

CLUB SHOP The Cricket Shop at The County Ground, Bristol is one of the best on the county circuit selling a wide range of items including books, clothing, leisure merchandise, ties, gifts and equipment. Open Monday to Friday 9 a.m. to 5 p.m. and Saturday 9 a.m. to 1 p.m. and open all day on match days.

CLUB MUSEUM Yes, in pavilion.

CRICKET COACHING FACILITIES Yes, contact Gloucestershire CCC for details.

CRICKET NETS Yes, contact Gloucestershire CCC for details.

OTHER SPORTING OR RECREATIONAL FACILITIES ON THE GROUND Yes, contact Gloucestershire CCC for details.

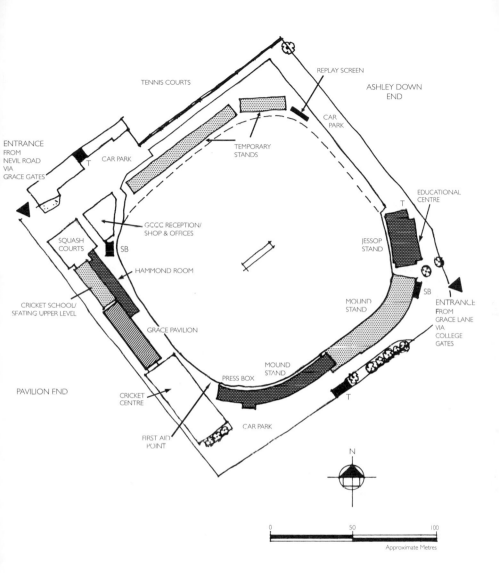

TENNIS COURTS

REPLAY SCREEN

ASHLEY DOWN
END

CAR
PARK

ENTRANCE
FROM
NEVIL ROAD
VIA
GRACE GATES

T

CAR PARK

TEMPORARY
STANDS

EDUCATIONAL
CENTRE

T

GCCC RECEPTION/
SHOP & OFFICES

JESSOP
STAND

SQUASH
COURTS

SB

HAMMOND ROOM

SB

MOUND
STAND

ENTRANCE
FROM
GRACE LANE
VIA
COLLEGE
GATES

CRICKET SCHOOL/
SEATING UPPER LEVEL

GRACE PAVILION

PAVILION END

CRICKET
CENTRE

PRESS BOX

MOUND
STAND

T

FIRST AID
POINT

CAR PARK

N

0   50   100

Approximate Metres

FACILITIES FOR HIRE OR WIDER COMMUNITY USE AT THE GROUND Yes, contact Gloucestershire CCC for details.
WINTER CRICKET EVENTS Members' dinners and meetings staged by the Gloucestershire Cricket Lovers'
Society monthly between October and March.
CAR PARKING FACILITIES Car parking is available within the ground to the rear of the new sports complex and
Mound Stand, together with an area to the north of the playing area from where cricket can be viewed from
cars and at the Ashley Down End of the ground and within City of Bristol College. Street parking is also
available within the neighbouring streets surrounding the ground.
OTHER INFORMATION There is a second-hand cricket book outlet in the shop which is run by Ken Faulkner of
Wokingham, Berkshire.
GROUND CAPACITY 8,000 – county matches, 15,000 – international matches with additional temporary seating
installed.
ANTICIPATED GROUND DEVELOPMENTS None.

HOW TO GET THERE

 Montpelier station 0.75 mile, Bristol Temple Meads station 2.5 miles, Bristol Parkway 5 miles. ☎ 08457 484950, www.greatwestern.co.uk

 City Line 8, 9 and 78 from Bristol Temple Meads station approach road, 72 or 73 from Bristol Parkway station, 72, 73, 74, 75, 76, 77 from Travel Inn (by bus station) in the city centre pass close to the ground. ☎ 0117 955 5111, 0117 926 0767

 There are cycle routes from surrounding areas of Bristol to this part of the city.

 From north: from M5 junction 16 take A38 (Gloucester Road), continue on A38 and turn left on to Nevil Road **From south:** take A37 to junction with A4, continue on A4 towards Bristol city centre, follow signs to A38 (north) (North Street), continue on A38 (Gloucester Road) and turn right on to Nevil Road **From east:** leave M4 at junction 19, turn left on to M32, continue to junction 3, turn left on to B4051 (Lower Ashley Road), continue on B4051 (Ashley Road), turn right on to B4052 (Sussex Place), continue on this road to Ashley Down Road, turn left on to Kennington Avenue, then turn left on to Nevil Road **From west:** from M5 junction 9 take A369 (Martcombe Road), turn left (east) on to B3129 (Bridge Road), continue on B3129 towards Bristol city centre, turn right on to Queens Road (A4018), follow signs to A38 (Gloucester Road), turn left on to A38, then as for south.

 Bristol Airport ☎ 0870 1212 747

WHERE TO STAY

Bristol Marriott Hotel City Centre (☎ 0117 929 4281), Hilton Bristol (☎ 01454 201144), Holiday Inn Bristol (☎ 0117 976 9988), Jury's Bristol Hotel (☎ 0117 923 0333), Thistle Hotel (☎ 0117 333 9130)
    For a further selection of places to stay in the Bristol area visit www.bristol.org.uk or www.smoothhound.co.uk.

WHERE TO EAT

Bell's Diner (☎ 0117 924 0357), Browns (☎ 0117 930 4777), Glass Boat (☎ 0117 929 0704), Harveys (☎ 0117 927 5034), Red Snapper (☎ 0117 973 7999), Tico Tico (☎ 0117 923 8700)

TOURIST INFORMATION Bristol Tourist Information Centre, St Nicholas Church, St Nicholas Street, Bristol BS1 1UE ☎ 0117 926 0767 www.tourism.bristol.gov.uk

LOCAL RADIO STATIONS BBC Radio Bristol (95.5 MHz FM/1548 KHz MW), GWR (96.3 MHz FM/1260 KHz MW), Galaxy (101 FM/97.2 FM)

LOCAL NEWSPAPERS *Bristol Evening Post, Western Daily Press, Bristol Journal, Bristol Observer, Green 'Un*

CHELTENHAM COLLEGE

Address Cheltenham College, College Sports Ground,
Thirlestaine Road, Cheltenham
Prospects of Play ☎ 01242 522000

HISTORY OF GROUND AND FACILITIES

GLOUCESTERSHIRE COUNTY CRICKET CLUB have staged a cricket festival at the Cheltenham College Ground since 1872. This usually takes place in July after the college term has ended. The initial match was with Surrey in July 1872.

Today Gloucestershire take three championship matches and two limited-overs Sunday league matches to the College ground for the annual festival which is always well supported.

The first visits to Cheltenham College were organised by James Lillywhite, the former Sussex player. He died in 1882 and never knew the full success of the venture he had initiated. The festival is the longest on the county circuit and spans 11 to 12 consecutive cricket days – weather and fixtures permitting!

The county have visited two other grounds in the town and in 1991 played for the first time at Dowty Arle Court Cricket Club, west of the town centre.

In 1969 the first limited-overs match was staged at Cheltenham College and after good attendances a second was added in 1975. The ground has seen many achievements over the years including 318* and match figures of 17 for 89 from Dr W.G. Grace. The county collapsed to 17 all out against the Australian touring team in 1896 thanks to some fine bowling by the visitors – Trumble 6 for 8 and M'Kibbin 4 for 7. Other achievements include notable performances by Jessop, born in Cheltenham, who hit 51 in 18 minutes against Yorkshire in 1895 and Hammond who, in 1928 in his first match on the famous ground, scored 139 and 143 and while fielding took ten catches against Surrey. Tom Goddard and Charlie Parker, two great county bowlers, have both enjoyed matches here, especially after rain and before wickets were covered.

Three overseas players have fond memories of Cheltenham College: Mike Proctor the South African all-rounder who in 1979 against Yorkshire repeated his own record of three lbws in a hat trick, the previous being against Essex in 1972; Zaheer Abbas of Pakistan who scored 205 and 108, both undefeated, against Sussex in 1977; and finally New Zealander Glenn Turner who scored 181 for

Gymnasium which serves as the cricket pavilion at Cheltenham College. (*Paul Bryce*)

neighbours Worcestershire in 1974 during their championship-winning season. Matches with touring teams have been staged here rather than at Bristol.

The main permanent building used by the county is the college gymnasium with its twin steeples of yellow brick and its trellised balcony. This is used as a pavilion and stands on the Thirlestaine Road side of the ground. Other buildings on this side of the playing area are smaller pavilions for school cricket, used during term time only. The college chapel overlooks the ground and was built in 1893. It is possibly the most significant feature of the College Ground and appears in many photographs. The scoreboard is in front of the gymnasium. The playing area is 120 metres by 150 metres and is defined by advertising boards and a rope around part of the playing area. When required the TV camera/commentary box is positioned on a gantry at the College Lawn End. The school buildings provide a beautiful backcloth to the cricket festival on this extremely pleasant out ground.

GROUND RECORDS AND SCORES

FIRST-CLASS MATCHES

Highest innings total for county 608 for 7 dec v Sussex 1934
Highest innings total against county 607 for 6 dec by Kent 1910
Lowest innings total for county 17 v Australians 1896
Lowest innings total against county 27 by Surrey 1874
Highest individual innings for county 318* W.G. Grace v Yorkshire 1876
Highest individual innings against county 229 J.E. Morris for Derbyshire 1993
Highest wicket partnerships for county

1st	169 G.M. Emmett & B.O. Allen	v	Essex	1949
2nd	251 C.J. Barnett & W.R. Hammond	v	Sussex	1934
3rd	269 B.O. Allen & W.R. Hammond	v	Worcestershire	1937
4th	190 W.W.F. Pullen & E.M. Grace	v	Middlesex	1884
5th	261 W.G. Grace & W.O. Moberly	v	Yorkshire	1876
6th	245 P. Bainbridge & M.W. Alleyne	v	Lancashire	1989
7th	131 F.J. Seabrook & W.L. Neale	v	Leicestershire	1933
8th	127 M.W. Alleyne & C.A. Walsh	v	Kent	1994
9th	129 H.V. Page & W.O. Vizard	v	Nottinghamshire	1883
10th	130 M.C.J. Ball & J. Lewis	v	Worcestershire	1999

Highest wicket partnerships against county

1st	221 B.C. Broad & R.T. Robinson	for	Nottinghamshire	1986
2nd	218 W. Bardsley & C.G. Macartney	for	Australians	1921
3rd	224 G. Boycott & K. Sharp	for	Yorkshire	1983
4th	192 N.J. Speak & D.C. Boon	for	Durham	1999
5th	302* J.E. Morris & D.G. Cork	for	Derbyshire	1993
6th	206 J. O'Connor & J.H.W.T. Douglas	for	Essex	1923
7th	134* J.R. Mason & F.H. Huish	for	Kent	1910
8th	134 Intikhab Alam & R.P. Baker	for	Surrey	1977
9th	120 J. Langridge & M.W. Tate	for	Sussex	1934
10th	157 W.E. Astill & W.H. Marlow	for	Leicestershire	1933

Best bowling performance in an innings for county 10 for 113 T.W.J. Goddard v Worcestershire 1937
Best bowling performance in an innings against county 10 for 66 A.A. Mailey for Australians 1921
Best bowling performance in a match for county 17 for 89 W.G. Grace v Nottinghamshire 1877
Best bowling performance in a match against county 15 for 184 W.H. Lockwood for Surrey 1899
Largest crowd 15,000 v Middlesex 1947

LIMITED-OVERS MATCHES

Highest innings total for county 344 for 6 v Northamptonshire (SL) 2001
Highest innings total against county 303 for 7 by Essex (SL) 1995
Lowest innings total for county 99 v Derbyshire (SL) 1993
Lowest innings total against county 85 by Warwickshire (SL) 1973
Highest individual innings for county 117 M.G.N. Windows v Northamptonshire (SL) 2001
Highest individual innings against county 105* G.A. Gooch for Essex (NWT) 1992
Highest wicket partnerships for county

1st	151 Sadiq Mohammad & A.W. Stovold	v	Kent	(SL)	1977
2nd	112 A.W. Stovold & K.M. Curran	v	Leicestershire	(SL)	1987
3rd	171 C.M. Spearman & M.G.N. Windows	v	Hampshire	(SL)	2002
4th	155 M.G.N. Windows & C.G. Taylor	v	Northamptonshire	(SL)	2001
5th	133 R.J. Cunliffe & R.C. Russell	v	Yorkshire	(SL)	1999
6th	91* R.C. Russell & M.W. Alleyne	v	Kent	(SL)	2000
7th	47 R.C. Russell & M.W. Alleyne	v	Yorkshire	(SL)	1988
8th	73* C.G. Taylor & M.C.J. Ball	v	Worcestershire	(SL)	2000
9th	70 M.W. Cawdron & R.C.J. Williams	v	Essex	(SL)	1995
10th	37* J.N. Snape & A.M. Smith	v	Hampshire	(SL)	2002

Highest wicket partnerships against county

1st	90 P.V. Simmons & V.J. Wells	for	Leicestershire	(SL)	1996
2nd	131 M.D. Moxon & R.J. Blakey	for	Yorkshire	(SL)	1990
3rd	158* C.J. Richards & M.A. Lynch	for	Surrey	(SL)	1988
4th	143 A. Habib & G.I. Macmillan	for	Leicestershire	(SL)	1996
5th	157 J.D. Ratcliffe & J.A. Knott	for	Surrey	(SL)	1998
6th	82 K.J. Barnett & K.M. Krikken	for	Derbyshire	(SL)	1997
7th	94* S.C. Goldsmith & K.J. Barnett	for	Derbyshire	(SL)	1991
8th	89 W.S. Kendall & S.D. Udal	for	Hampshire	(SL)	2002
9th	27* T.L. Penney & G.C. Small	for	Warwickshire	(SL)	1996
10th	28 I.D.K. Salisbury & A.G. Robson	for	Sussex	(SL)	1992

Best bowling performance in a match for county 5 for 20 J.H. Shackleton v Surrey (SL) 1977
Best bowling performance in a match against county 4 for 14 S.J. Base for Derbyshire (SL) 1993
Largest crowd 6,750 v Essex (SL) 1975

GROUND INFORMATION

ENTRANCES Thirlestaine Road (players, officials, members, public and vehicles), Sandford Road (members and public).
MEMBERS' ENCLOSURE Gymnasium (used as a pavilion by players and members) and defined members' enclosure to the south of the playing area.
PUBLIC ENCLOSURE Rest of the ground.
COVERED STANDS None.
OPEN STANDS Temporary ground level and tiered plastic seating surrounding the playing area.
NAME OF ENDS Chapel End, College Lawn End.
GROUND DIMENSIONS 120m × 150m.
FIRST AID First aid post in tent at Chapel End of the ground.
CODES OF DRESS The club does not lay down strict standards of dress in the enclosure but expects 'smart-casual' dress to be worn especially in the pavilion.
BEHAVIOUR The club is keen that standards of behaviour should be maintained and members and spectators are urged to report immediately to any steward any incident, or potential incident, where they feel action should be taken. Bad language is not acceptable at any match and the club will take prompt and strong action should this or any other ground regulation be ignored. Obstructing passageways, singing indecent songs, using indecent language, making unnecessary noise by means including persistent chanting, use of radios without an ear-piece, use of mobile telephones, possession of and/or waving of banners is not permitted.
RECIPROCAL ARRANGEMENTS Members of Glamorgan, Somerset and Worcestershire can gain entry free to County Championship matches on production of membership card when Gloucestershire is not playing their own county.

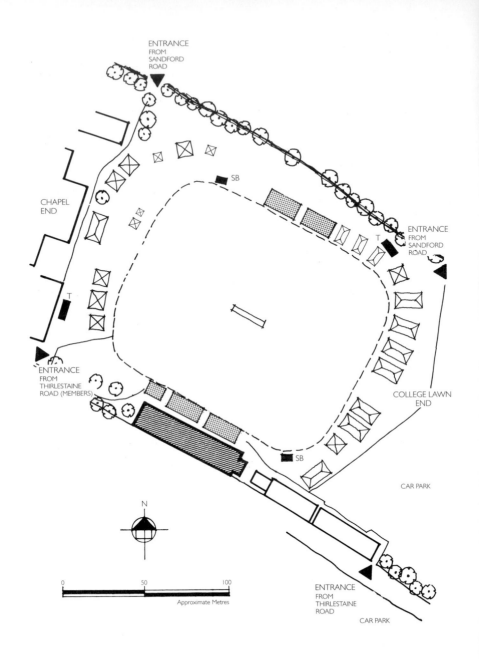

ENTRANCE
FROM
SANDFORD
ROAD

SB

CHAPEL
END

T

ENTRANCE
FROM
SANDFORD
ROAD

T

ENTRANCE
FROM
THIRLESTAINE
ROAD (MEMBERS)

COLLEGE LAWN
END

SB

CAR PARK

N

0   50   100

Approximate Metres

ENTRANCE
FROM
THIRLESTAINE
ROAD

CAR PARK

SUPPORTERS' CLUB Gloucester Exiles produce newsletter: *Outside Edge*. Contact Gloucestershire Exiles, Flat 6, 4 Square Court, 405 Nelson Road, Hounslow, Middlesex TW3 3UN for details.

JUNIORS Junior Gladiator Membership for under-16s £12 per annum. Contact ☎ 0117 910 8017 for details.

CORPORATE ENTERTAINMENT Facilities are available in various temporary marquees at the College Lawn End of the ground. Contact Marketing Department for details and a brochure.

FACILITIES FOR VISUALLY IMPAIRED SPECTATORS No reduced admission, guide dogs allowed.

FACILITIES AND ACCESS FOR PEOPLE WITH DISABILITIES INCLUDING WHEELCHAIR ACCESS TO GROUND Yes, access via chapel entrance in Sandford Road and via members' entrance in Thirlestaine Road.

DESIGNATED CAR PARK AVAILABLE INSIDE THE GROUND FOR PEOPLE WITH DISABILITIES Yes, to rear of corporate marquees at College Lawn End of the ground.

GOOD VIEWING AREAS INSIDE THE GROUND FOR PEOPLE USING WHEELCHAIRS Yes.

DESIGNATED VIEWING AREAS FOR PEOPLE USING WHEELCHAIRS No.

RAMPS TO PROVIDE EASY ACCESS TO BARS & REFRESHMENT OUTLETS FOR PEOPLE USING WHEELCHAIRS No.

FOOD & DRINK FULL RESTAURANT/DINING FACILITIES Contact Catering Department at Cheltenham in advance. Otherwise temporary facilities are available in marquees and around the ground for members and the general public.

TEMPORARY FOOD/DRINK FACILITIES Members, yes. Public, yes.

FOOD SUITABLE FOR VEGETARIANS Members, yes. Public, yes.

BARS Members 1, Public 3.

VARIETIES OF BEER Coors, Grolsch, Carling, Bass, Worthington Creamflow.

CHILDREN'S FACILITIES Crèche, no. Children's play area, no. Look out for C&G Game Zone on Sandford Road side of the ground and Gladiators' marquee close by.

CLUB SHOP Gloucestershire CCC Mobile Cricket Shop in cabin at Chapel End of ground.

CLUB MUSEUM No.

CRICKET COACHING FACILITIES No.

CRICKET NETS No.

OTHER SPORTING OR RECREATIONAL FACILITIES ON THE GROUND No.

FACILITIES FOR HIRE OR WIDER COMMUNITY USE AT THE GROUND No.

WINTER CRICKET EVENTS No.

CAR PARKING FACILITIES Car parking is available in the ground at the College Lawn End for players, officials and members, through the entrance to the south of the ground, which is also used by spectators. Car parking at £5 per car for non-car park pass holders is also available within easy walking distance.

OTHER INFORMATION Second-hand cricket book dealers from Wokingham and Malvern usually attend matches. Dealers with paintings and cigarette and trade cards also have stalls as well as Gloucester RFC.

GROUND CAPACITY 5,000.

ANTICIPATED GROUND DEVELOPMENTS None planned.

HOW TO GET THERE

 Cheltenham Spa station 1 mile ☎ 08457 484950, www.thamestrains.co.uk or www.greatwesterntrains.co.uk

 Cheltenham and District L from town centre. There is a bus link from Cheltenham Spa station to the town centre, ☎ 01242 522021.

 There are cycle routes to this area of the town.

 From north and west from M5 junction 11 take A40 (east) towards Cheltenham, continue on A40 (Gloucester Road then Lansdown Road), at island filling station turn right on to Andover Road. Go over traffic lights into Suffolk Road. Go over traffic lights into Thirlestaine Road. **From south:** from Cirencester (A435) continue to junction with A40, turn left on to A40 and continue on this road to Cheltenham College **From east:** follow A40 towards Cheltenham town centre, College is on this road.

WHERE TO STAY

Clarence Court Hotel (☎ 01242 580411 Hotel Kandinsky (☎ 01242 527788), The Carlton Hotel (☎ 01242 514453), The George Hotel (☎ 01242 235751),The Queens Hotel (☎ 0870 400 8107), The Thistle (☎ 01242 232691)

For a further selection of places to stay in the Cheltenham area visit www.visitcheltenham.com or www.smoothhound.co.uk.

WHERE TO EAT

Champignon Sauvage (☎ 01242 573449), Daffodil (☎ 01242 700055), Mayflower (☎ 01242 522426), Le Petit Blanc (☎ 01242 266800), Ruby (☎ 01242 250909), Storyteller (☎ 01242 250343)

TOURIST INFORMATION Cheltenham Tourist Information, 77 Promenade, Cheltenham, Gloucestershire GL50 1PP ☎ 01242 522878, www.cheltenham.gov.uk

LOCAL RADIO STATIONS BBC Radio Gloucestershire (104.7 MHz FM/865 KHz MW), Severn Sound (102.4 MHz FM/774 KHz MW)

LOCAL NEWSPAPERS *Gloucestershire Echo*

GLOUCESTER
King's School

13 06 04
GLOSV. NCCC
(45 OVERS) **Address** The Pavilion, King's School, Archdeacon Meadow,
WITH RAYMOND) St Oswald's Road, Gloucester
NCCC WON . **Prospects of Play** ☎ 01452 308381

HISTORY OF GROUND AND FACILITIES

KING'S SCHOOL GROUND at Archdeacon Meadow is located close to Gloucester city centre and is sited between St Oswald's Road and the railway line, which runs to the north of the playing area. The area was known by locals as Tabby Pitt's Pool during the 1880s when it used to flood regularly. King's School is the third ground to be used for county cricket in the city, the previous venues being the Spa Ground where 56 matches were played between 1882 and 1923 and Tuffley Park which hosted 182 matches between 1923 and 1992 until problems with the wicket resulted in the ground being deleted from the fixture list at the end of the 1992 season.

In 1993 Gloucestershire played their first match at King's School. This is a new ground which was until some 20 years ago a rubbish tip and it is believed that below the wicket there are two rusty double-decker buses and parts of several old army tanks. The ground was developed with the assistance of Bernard Flack, then groundsman at Edgbaston. In 1981 George Balmer joined the school as grounds-man and since then the ground has gone from strength to strength to such an extent that in 1988 Peter Lacey, the headmaster, approached the county club to stage a Second XI match at the ground.

In 1993 the first Gloucester King's School Festival match was staged between Gloucestershire and Worcestershire in the County Championship. Since then a single championship and a single National Cricket League match have been staged at the ground annually. Entertainment on the ground during Festival Week is limited but the Headmaster's Marquee takes pride of place opposite the pavilion.

The entrance to the ground is from St Oswald's Road and the only permanent buildings are the pavilion and scoreboard. Crowds tend to number between 2,500 and 3,500.

Gloucestershire v
Worcestershire at
King's School, 1992.

GROUND RECORDS AND SCORES

FIRST-CLASS MATCHES

Highest innings total for county 417 v Durham 2001
Highest innings total against county 568 by Zimbabweans 2000
Lowest innings total for county 101 v Worcestershire 1993
Lowest innings total against county 130 by Worcestershire 1995
Highest individual innings for county 132 M.W. Alleyne v Durham 2001
Highest individual innings against county 194 M.W. Goodwin for Zimbabweans 2000
Highest wicket partnerships for county

1st	111 A.J. Wright & N.J. Trainor	v	Surrey	1996
2nd	71 G.D. Hodgson & M.A. Lynch	v	Worcestershire	1995
	71 T.H.C. Hancock & A.J. Wright	v	Yorkshire	1998
3rd	114 A.J. Wright & M.W. Alleyne	v	Yorkshire	1998
4th	154 C.G. Taylor & M.W. Alleyne	v	Durham	2001
5th	125 A.J. Wright & R.I. Dawson	v	Surrey	1994
6th	117 T.H.C. Hancock & R.C. Russell	v	Surrey	1996
7th	207 R.C. Russell & I.D. Fisher	v	Essex	2002
8th	158 M.W. Alleyne & M.C.J. Ball	v	Essex	2002
9th	114 R.C. Russell & A.M. Smith	v	Yorkshire	1998
10th	36 J.N. Snape & B.W. Gannon	v	Essex	1999

Highest wicket partnerships against county

1st	121 D.J. Bicknell & A.J. Stewart	for	Surrey	1994
2nd	180 D.D.J. Robinson & A. Habib	for	Essex	2002
3rd	190* A. Flower & G.W. Flower	for	Zimbabweans	2000
4th	139 S.G. Law & R.C. Irani	for	Essex	1999
5th	108 P.J. Prichard & A.P. Grayson	for	Essex	1999
6th	60 M.J. Wood & R.J. Blakey	for	Yorkshire	1998
7th	91* D.M. Ward & G.J. Kersey	for	Surrey	1996
8th	60 J.P. Stephenson & Z.K. Sharif	for	Essex	2002
9th	80 P.A. Strang & B.C. Strang	for	Zimbabweans	2000
10th	54 A.P. Cowan & M.C. Ilott	for	Essex	2002

Best bowling performance in an innings for county 8 for 95 J. Lewis v Zimbabweans 2000
Best bowling performance in an innings against county 8 for 55 C. White for Yorkshire 1998
Best bowling performance in a match for county 10 for 125 A.M. Smith v Worcestershire 1995
Best bowling performance in a match against county 9 for 62 R.K. Illingworth for Worcestershire 1993
Largest crowd 3,500 v Worcestershire 1993

LIMITED-OVERS MATCHES

Highest innings total for county 206 v Yorkshire (SL) 1998
Highest innings total against county 225 for 3 by Worcestershire (SL) 1995
Lowest innings total for county 66 v Surrey (SL) 1996
Lowest innings total against county 138 by Worcestershire (SL) 1999
Highest individual innings for county 88 M.W. Alleyne v Yorkshire (SL) 1998
Highest individual innings against county 82* T.S. Curtis for Worcestershire (SL) 1995
Highest wicket partnerships for county

1st	52 K.J. Barnett & R.I. Dawson	v	Worcestershire	(SL)	1999
2nd	46 A.J. Wright & M.A. Lynch	v	Worcestershire	(SL)	1995
3rd	48 M.W. Alleyne & A.J. Wright	v	Yorkshire	(SL)	1998
4th	39 M.W. Alleyne & M.J. Church	v	Yorkshire	(SL)	1998
5th	39 M.W. Alleyne & J.N. Snape	v	Warwickshire	(SL)	2001
6th	52 T.H.C. Hancock & M.C.J. Ball	v	Yorkshire	(SL)	1998
7th	54 M.W. Alleyne & M.A. Hardinges	v	Essex	(SL)	2002
8th	48 R.C. Russell & M.C.J. Ball	v	Worcestershire	(SL)	1995
9th	46 M.W. Alleyne & M.J. Cawdron	v	Warwickshire	(SL)	2001
10th	18* M.J. Cawdron & J.M.M. Averis	v	Warwickshire	(SL)	2001

Highest wicket partnerships against county

1st	97 P.J. Prichard & S.G. Law	for	Essex	(SL)	1997
2nd	110 T.S. Curtis & T.M. Moody	for	Worcestershire	(SL)	1995
3rd	115 D.R. Brown & D.P. Ostler	for	Warwickshire	(SL)	2001
4th	83 D.J. Bicknell & N. Shahid	for	Surrey	(SL)	1996
5th	116 A. Flower & M.L. Pettini	for	Essex	(SL)	2002
6th	32* J.D. Ratcliffe & B.C. Hollioake	for	Surrey	(SL)	1996
7th	34 B. Parker & R.J. Blakey	for	Yorkshire	(SL)	1998
8th	8 J.P. Stephenson & T.J. Phillips	for	Essex	(SL)	2002
9th	3 S.R. Lampitt & M.J. Rawnsley	for	Worcestershire	(SL)	1999
10th	9 S.R. Lampitt & A. Sheriyar	for	Worcestershire	(SL)	1999

Best bowling performance for county 4 for 29 A.M. Smith v Yorkshire (SL) 1998
Best bowling performance against county 5 for 57 N.V. Radford for Worcestershire (SL) 1995
Largest crowd 4,500 v Worcestershire (SL) 1993

GROUND INFORMATION

ENTRANCES St Oswald's Road (players, officials, members, public and vehicles).
MEMBERS' ENCLOSURE Pavilion and defined members' enclosure.
PUBLIC ENCLOSURE Rest of the ground.
COVERED STANDS Pavilion.
OPEN STANDS Temporary ground level seating surrounding the playing area.
NAME OF ENDS Pavilion End, Tennis Courts End.
GROUND DIMENSIONS 130m × 125m.
FIRST AID First aid post in tent at Pavilion End.
CODES OF DRESS The club does not lay down strict standards of dress in the enclosure but expects 'smart-casual' dress to be worn especially in the pavilion.
BEHAVIOUR The club is keen that standards of behaviour should be maintained and members and spectators are urged to report immediately to any steward any incident, or potential incident, where they feel action should be taken. Bad language is not acceptable at any match and the club will take prompt and strong action should this or any other ground regulation be ignored. Obstructing passageways, singing indecent songs, using indecent language, making unnecessary noise by means including persistent chanting, use of radios without an ear-piece, use of mobile telephones, possession of and/or waving of banners is not permitted.
RECIPROCAL ARRANGEMENTS Members of Glamorgan, Somerset and Worcestershire can gain entry free for County Championship matches on production of membership card when Gloucestershire is not playing their own county.

SUPPORTERS' CLUB Gloucester Exiles produce newsletter: *Outside Edge*. Contact Gloucestershire Exiles, Flat 6, 4 Square Court, 405 Nelson Road, Hounslow, Middlesex TW3 3UN for details.

JUNIORS Junior Gladiator Membership for under-16s £10 per annum. Contact ☎ 0117 910 8017 for details.

CORPORATE ENTERTAINMENT Facilities are available in various temporary marquees on the railway line side of the ground. Contact Marketing Department for details and a brochure.

FACILITIES FOR VISUALLY IMPAIRED SPECTATORS No reduced admission, guide dogs allowed.

FACILITIES AND ACCESS FOR PEOPLE WITH DISABILITIES INCLUDING WHEELCHAIR ACCESS TO GROUND Yes, access via St Oswald's Road entrance to rear of pavilion.

DESIGNATED CAR PARK AVAILABLE INSIDE THE GROUND FOR PEOPLE WITH DISABILITIES Yes, to rear corporate marquees at Pavilion End of the ground.

GOOD VIEWING AREAS INSIDE THE GROUND FOR PEOPLE USING WHEELCHAIRS Yes.

DESIGNATED VIEWING AREAS FOR PEOPLE USING WHEELCHAIRS No.

RAMPS TO PROVIDE EASY ACCESS TO BARS & REFRESHMENT OUTLETS FOR PEOPLE USING WHEELCHAIRS No.

FOOD & DRINK FULL RESTAURANT/DINING FACILITIES Members, yes. Public, no.

TEMPORARY FOOD/DRINK FACILITIES Members, yes. Public, yes.

FOOD SUITABLE FOR VEGETARIANS Members, yes. Public, yes.

BARS Members 1, Public 1.

VARIETIES OF BEER Coors, Grolsch, Carling, Bass, Worthington Creamflow.

CHILDREN'S FACILITIES Crèche, no. Children's play area, no.

CLUB SHOP Gloucestershire CCC mobile cricket shop in cabin at St Oswald's Road side of ground.

CLUB MUSEUM No.

CRICKET COACHING FACILITIES No.

CRICKET NETS No.

OTHER SPORTING OR RECREATIONAL FACILITIES ON THE GROUND Squash, tennis courts, pitch & putt golf, leisure centre.

WINTER CRICKET EVENTS No.

CAR PARKING FACILITIES Car parking is available in the ground at the Pavilion End for players, officials and members, through the main entrance to the rear of the pavilion off St Oswald's Road, which is also used by spectators. Car parking is also available a short walk away from the ground in Lower Westgate Street (NCP) and in Oxleas.

OTHER INFORMATION Second-hand cricket book dealers from Wokingham and Malvern usually have stalls at matches.

GROUND CAPACITY 3,500.

ANTICIPATED GROUND DEVELOPMENTS None planned.

HOW TO GET THERE

  Gloucester Central station 0.5 mile ☎ 08457 484950, www.greatwesterntrains.co.uk

  Stagecoach buses from city centre pass outside the ground ☎ 01452 527516

  There are cycle routes from surrounding areas to this part of the city.

  From north, south and east from M5 junction 11 take A40 (west), at roundabout turn right on to A40, at roundabout turn left on to A38 (Tewkesbury Road), at roundabout turn right on to St Oswald's Road. **From west:** from A40, take the A417) (Over Causeway) and continue to St Oswald's Road.

WHERE TO STAY

Bowden Hall (☎ 01452 64121), Crest Hotel (☎ 01452 63311), Fleece Hotel (☎ 01452 22762), New County Hotel (☎ 01452 24977)

For other places to stay in the Gloucester area visit www.gloucester.org.uk or www.smoothhound.co.uk.

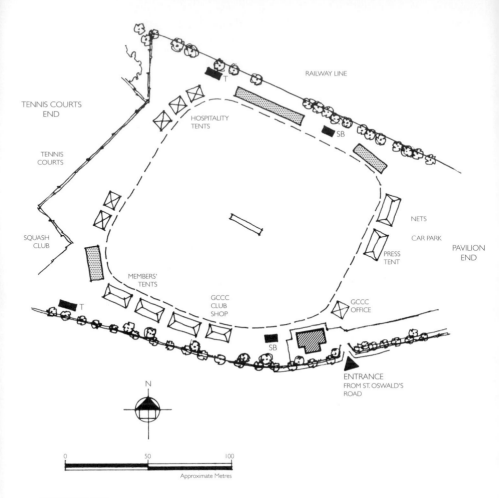

WHERE TO EAT

Corse Lawn (☎ 01452 780771)

TOURIST INFORMATION Gloucester Tourist Information Centre, St Michael's Tower, The Cross, Gloucester, Gloucestershire GL1 1PD ☎ 01452 421188, www.gloucester.gov.uk

LOCAL RADIO STATIONS BBC Radio Gloucestershire (104.7 MHz FM/865 KHz MW), Severn Sound (102.4 MHz FM/774 KHz MW), BBC Radio Hereford and Worcester (94.7 MHz FM).

LOCAL NEWSPAPERS *Gloucester Citizen, Gloucestershire Echo*

HAMPSHIRE
CRICKET

Hampshire

HAMPSHIRE
HAWKS

Southampton – The Rose Bowl × 2

HAMPSHIRE CRICKET, THE ROSE BOWL, BOTLEY ROAD, WEST END, SOUTHAMPTON SO30 3XH

In February 2002 the structure of Hampshire County Cricket Club changed. The organisation and operation of the 150-acre development is now controlled by Rose Bowl plc with all cricket matters being operated under the name of Hampshire Cricket.

ROSE BOWL plc

Executive Chairman R.G. Bransgrove
Non-Executive Directors M.C.J. Nicholas, F. Janmohamed, J.J. Hamer
Executive Directors N.S. Pike, T.M. Tremlett
Company Secretary M.H. Le Bas

HAMPSHIRE CRICKET

Main Switchboard 023 8047 2002 **fax** 023 8047 2122
Email enquiries@rosebowlplc.com
Web www.hampshire.cricinfo.com, www.rosebowlplc.com

Founded 12 August 1863
Colours blue, gold and white
Crest Tudor rose and crown
National Cricket League Nickname Hawks
National Cricket League Colours black
Patron W.J. Weld
President A.C.D. Ingleby-Mackenzie
Trustees C.N. Laine, M.H. Le Bas
Chairman (members' committee) R.J. Treherne
Managing Director N.S. Pike
Director of Cricket T.M. Tremlett
Financial Controller L. Hayes ACIB
Commercial & Marketing Director S. White
Membership & Ticketing Manager J. Smithers

Cricket Manager V.P. Terry
2nd XI Coach/Academy Director T.C. Middleton
Captain To be appointed
Vice Captain W.S. Kendall
Physiotherapists P. Farhart, D. Newman
Scorer 1st XI V.H. Isaacs
Scorer 2nd XI A.E. Weld
Head Groundsman N. Gray
Statistician V.H. Isaacs
Hon Curator and Historian D. Allen
Yearbook £8.50
Scorecard 50p
Frizzell County Championship Status Division 2
National Cricket League Status Division 2

ACHIEVEMENTS

County Championship Champions 1961 and 1973
Gillette Cup Semi-finalists 1966, 1976
NatWest Trophy Winners 1991, Semi-finalists 1983, 1985, 1987, 1988, 1989, 1990, 1998 and 2000
Benson and Hedges Cup Winners 1988, 1992, Semi-finalists 1975, 1977
John Player Sunday League Champions 1975, 1978, 1986

Fenner Trophy Winners 1975, 1976, 1977, Joint Winners 1980
Tilcon Trophy Winners 1976
Asda Cricket Challenge Trophy Winners 1984, 1986
Ward Four Counties Knockout Competition Winners 1990
Joshua Tetley Festival Trophy Joint Winners 1992

HAMPSHIRE CRICKET BOARD

Chairman J. Levick
Secretary C. Savage
Treasurer G. Thomas
Cricket Development Manager N. Rider
Cricket Development Officer (District & Clubs) A. Rowe
Cricket Development Officer (Performance) R.J. Maru
Cricket Development Officer (Schools) A. Hobday
Cricket Development Officer (Women & Girls) C. Slaney

Address   Hampshire Cricket Board, The Rose Bowl, Botley Road, West End, Southampton, Hants
SO30 3XH
☏   023 8046 5816 **Fax** 023 8047 5618

GROUND

Southampton (The Rose Bowl, West End)
   Other grounds used since 1969 are: Southampton (County Cricket Ground, Northlands Road),
Bournemouth (Dean Park, Cavendish Road), Basingstoke (May's Bounty, Bounty Road) and Portsmouth
(United Services Officers' Sports Ground, Burnaby Road)

SECOND XI GROUNDS

Southampton (The Rose Bowl, West End)
Basingstoke & North Hants CC, May's Bounty, Bounty Road, Basingstoke ☏ 01256 473646
Bournemouth Sports Club, Chapel Gate Ground, Kinson Park, Near Hurn Airport, East Parley, Bournemouth
   ☏ 01202 581933
United Services Portsmouth CC, United Services Officers' Sports Ground, Burnaby Road, Portsmouth
   ☏ 023 9252 2351

Main pavilion, together with committee and sponsors' marquees and press tent at The Rose Bowl.

SOUTHAMPTON

Address The Rose Bowl, Botley Road, West End, Southampton,
Hants SO30 3XH
Prospects of Play ☎ 023 8047 2022

HISTORY OF GROUND AND FACILITIES

THE ROSE BOWL is Hampshire County Cricket Club's fourth headquarters ground
in its 139-year history (previous headquarters being the Antelope Ground,
Daniel Day's Itchen Ground and the County Cricket Ground in Northlands Road).
It is one of the most exciting and ambitious projects undertaken in the south of
England for many years and is establishing a blueprint for the development of
cricket grounds and leisure facilities.

Situated in 61 hectares adjacent to the M27 motorway, the site is owned by
The Queen's College, Oxford. It was leased to Hampshire County Cricket Club in
1996 for the development of a state-of-the-art county cricket ground with
additional leisure, sporting and community facilities.

Following a successful application to the National Lottery (which provided
funding of £7.2 million) and the sale of the club's Northlands Road ground, home
to Hampshire since 1885, construction of the main infrastructure began in March
1997. The golf clubhouse and nursery pavilion followed in 1998. The following
year work began on the three-storey pavilion, the Cricket Academy and the
Atrium Bar. While the Cricket Academy and the Atrium Bar were in use during
the 2001 season, the pavilion was not ready until the start of the 2002 season.

The top balcony of the main pavilion at The Rose Bowl.

Rear of main pavilion.

Designed by the award-winning architects Michael Hopkins & Partners (who were also responsible for the Mound Stand at Lord's), the first-class cricket ground had an initial capacity of 6,000 which has now been extended to 9,000 fixed seats situated on terraces overlooking the playing area. An increase capacity, for one-day internationals or even Test Matches, can easily be accommodated with additional tiered seating on the berm surrounding the ground.

The design of The Rose Bowl resembles a circular amphitheatre with the first-class playing area in the middle surrounded by terraced seating that leads up to a flat circular area housing the facilities listed below plus a boulevard avenue attractively bordered by London plane trees.

The feature building on the site is the spectacular three-storey pavilion with its highly distinctive canopied roof. Curved to give all spectators a magnificent view of both the cricket and the surrounding southern Hampshire countryside, this state-of-the-art steel and glass building decorated with club memorabilia houses a Lord's-style Long Room used by the Executive Club, hospitality suites, bars and catering facilities as well as superb facilities for players and officials. This is the first cricket ground in the UK to provide jacuzzis in the players' dressing rooms! The Membership Office is situated on the ground floor of the pavilion. Attractively connecting the pavilion to the large indoor Cricket Academy, which has been sympathetically built into the hillside, is a glass-roofed Atrium Bar. From here, in a clockwise direction from the pavilion, are: the Hampshire Cricket Offices, media/press and scorers' marquee, covered stand (100 seats), toilets, the Hampshire shop, covered stand (100 seats), food and bar outlet, main electronic scoreboard, sightscreen, toilets, a secondary smaller electronic scoreboard, the committee marquee, hospitality boxes and an area with facilities for disabled people.

The design offers a totally fresh approach to watching cricket on the county circuit and for the seasoned cricket watcher a warm day's play at The Rose Bowl could make you think you were in Sharjah or Karachi. Further covered seating is planned for the future.

Other sporting facilities at The Rose Bowl include a nursery ground and clubhouse, the cricket academy, Connors health and fitness centre (containing the very latest equipment, squash courts, aerobic studio, sauna, steam rooms, solarium) and The County Golf Club with its nine-hole/18-tee golf course. Planning permission has already been granted for a £3m state-of-the-art, 20-acre golf driving range plus clubhouse, bar and shop. A hotel complex on land adjacent to the site was completed in the summer of 2003.

The very first cricket matches at The Rose Bowl took place in 2000 when the 2nd XI played on both the Main and the Nursery Grounds. The inaugural first-team match took place on 2 May 2001 when Hampshire hosted Essex in the Benson and Hedges Cup zonal round. One week later the first-class season began with a match against Worcestershire. Later that year the highlight of the summer and this first Rose Bowl season proved to be the Tour Match against the powerful Australians played out in sweltering heat. The impressive crowd of 5,800 who watched the first day and the first session of the match will need no reminder of Hampshire's success as they totally outplayed their illustrious visitors, bowling them out for just 97 with Alan Mullally taking 5 for 18. Other memorable moments of the first two years were the two highly successful floodlit matches (against Sussex and Lancashire).

Despite considerable praise and admiration expressed for The Rose Bowl's design and innovation, the development of the £24 million pound project suffered

Main entrance from Marshall Drive.

Marshall Drive was named in memory of Malcolm and Roy Marshall, both of Hampshire and West Indies.

from financial difficulties and in October 2000 it became clear that the club did not have sufficient funds to complete its plans. A Hampshire businessman and cricket enthusiast, Rod Bransgrove, took over as Chairman of the club at that time, undertaking to procure the funds necessary to complete this fine development. This led to the establishment of Rose Bowl plc, the renaming of the club as 'Hampshire Cricket' and the subsequently successful share issue in 2002.

In August 2002 the England and Wales Cricket Board confirmed that The Rose Bowl was to be awarded a NatWest Series one-day international match in 2003 between South Africa and Zimbabwe. This will be the first occasion that the ground will host a one-day international and only the fourth one-day international ever to be staged in Southampton. The Rose Bowl was also awarded the opening televised match to launch the ECB Twenty20 Cup Competition in June 2003.

The ground has only one entrance from Botley Road via Marshall Drive, which was named in memory of those two great Hampshire and West Indian cricketers who played for the county, Roy Marshall and Malcolm Marshall. Both will always be remembered for their whole-hearted contributions, Roy as a stylish opening batsman and Malcolm as one of the world's all-time greatest fast bowlers. From the main entrance, vehicle parking is clearly marked, as are directions to all additional facilities such as The County Golf Club. Access into the main cricket ground (for the pavilion, Cricket Academy, health and fitness club etc.) may be made either through the West Gate or the East Gate.

GROUND RECORDS AND SCORES

FIRST-CLASS MATCHES

Highest innings total for county 437 v Surrey 2001
Highest innings total against county 500 for 7 dec by Sussex 2002
Lowest innings total for county 123 v Indians 2002
Lowest innings total against county 97 by Australians 2001
Highest individual innings for county 166 D.A. Kenway v Nottinghamshire 2001
Highest individual innings against county 195 M.W. Goodwin for Sussex 2001
Highest wicket partnerships for county

1st	97 N.C. Johnson & J.S. Laney	v	Somerset	2002
2nd	83 G.W. White & W.S. Kendall	v	Sussex	2001
3rd	147 D.A. Kenway & R.A. Smith	v	Gloucestershire	2001
4th	182 R.A. Smith & N.C. Johnson	v	Australians	2001
5th	76 R.A. Smith & W.S. Kendall	v	Yorkshire	2002
	76 J.D. Francis & N. Pothas	v	Surrey	2002
6th	83 A.D. Mascarenhas & A.N. Aymes	v	Nottinghamshire	2001
7th	142 J.P. Stephenson & A.D. Mascarenhas	v	Worcestershire	2001
8th	130 AN Aymes & S.D. Udal	v	Derbyshire	2001
9th	95 S.D. Udal & A.C. Morris	v	Sussex	2001
10th	43 J.R.C. Hamblin & A.D. Mullally	v	Kent	2002

Highest wicket partnerships against county

1st	162* R.R. Montgomerie & M.H. Yardy	for	Sussex	2001
	(M.W.Goodwin retired hurt at 17–0, full partnership 197.)			
2nd	197 I.J. Ward & N. Shahid	for	Surrey	2002
3rd	239 I.J. Ward & G.P. Thorpe	for	Surrey	2002
4th	177 M.J. Powell & I.R. Bell	for	Warwickshire	2001
5th	149 V.J. Wells & D.I. Stevens	for	Leicestershire	2002
6th	119 D.R. Hewson & J.N. Snape	for	Gloucestershire	2001
7th	89 P.A. Nixon & M.M. Patel	for	Kent	2002
8th	81 R.J. Bailey & A.D. Edwards	for	Derbyshire	2001
9th	44 J.N. Gillespie & A.A. Nofke	for	Australians	2001
10th	135 C.M.W. Read & R.D .Stemp	for	Nottinghamshire	2001

Best bowling performance in an innings for county 8 for 90 A.D. Mullally v Warwickshire 2001
Best bowling performance in an innings against county 6 for 23 J.M. Anderson for Lancashire 2002
Best bowling performance in a match for county 9 for 47 A.D. Mascarenhas v Middlesex 2001
Best bowling performance in a match against county 9 for 50 J.M. Anderson for Lancashire 2002
Largest crowd 5,800 v Australians 2001

LIMITED-OVERS MATCHES

Highest innings total for county 289 for 4 v Northamptonshire 2002
Highest innings total against county 285 for 6 by Northamptonshire 2002
Lowest innings total for county 115 v Kent 2002
Lowest innings total against county 110 by Sussex 2002
Highest individual innings for county 110* W.S. Kendall v Middlesex 2002
Highest individual innings against county 102* B. Zuiderent for Sussex 2001
Highest wicket partnerships for county

1st	78 N.C. Johnson & D.A. Kenway	v	Sussex	(SL)	2002
2nd	98 N.C. Johnson & J.P. Crawley	v	Northamptonshire	(SL)	2002
3rd	76 N.C. Johnson & J.D. Francis	v	Northamptonshire	(SL)	2002
4th	132 J.D. Francis & W.S. Kendall	v	Essex	(SL)	2002
5th	103 W.S. Kendall & S.D. Udal	v	Middlesex	(SL)	2002
6th	62* N. Pothas & A.D. Mascarenhas	v	Gloucestershire	(SL)	2002
7th	44 N. Pothas & W.S. Kendall	v	Surrey	(SL)	2002
8th	28 S.D. Udal & C.T. Tremlett	v	Derbyshire	(SL)	2001

	28 J.D. Francis & S.D. Udal	v	Middlesex	(SL)	2001
9th	29 S.D. Udal & A.N. Aymes	v	Surrey	(B&H)	2001
10th	39 L.R. Prittipaul & C.T. Tremlett	v	Essex	(SL)	2001

Highest wicket partnerships against county

1st	85 D.D.J. Robinson & W.I. Jefferson	for	Essex	(SL)	2002
2nd	144 M.W. Goodwin & B. Zuiderent	for	Sussex	(B&H)	2001
3rd	151 A. Flintoff & J.P. Crawley	for	Lancashire	(SL)	2001
4th	77 C.M. Spearman & M.W. Alleyne	for	Gloucestershire	(SL)	2002
5th	89 E.C. Joyce & J.W.M. Dalrymple	for	Middlesex	(SL)	2002
6th	83 J.S. Foster & A.P. Cowan	for	Essex	(SL)	2001
7th	46 W.J. House & M.J.G. Davis	for	Sussex	(SL)	2001
8th	61 S.J. Cook & P.N. Weekes	for	Middlesex	(B&H)	2002
9th	24* J.M. Golding & M.J. Saggers	for	Kent	(B&H)	2002
10th	11 N.C. Phillips & N.G. Hatch	for	Durham	(SL)	2001

Best bowling performance in a match for county 5 for 27 A.D. Mascarenhas v Gloucestershire (SL) 2002
Best bowling performance in a match against county 4 for 18 A.P. Davies for Glamorgan (SL) 2001
Largest crowd 5,400 v Lancashire (SL) 2002

ONE-DAY INTERNATIONALS

(None yet established; inaugural one-day international in 2003. These records are for the former County Cricket Ground, Northlands Road, Southampton)
Highest innings total in ODI 275 for 8 for Sri Lanka v Kenya (WC) 1999
Lowest innings total in ODI 156 by New Zealand v West Indies (WC) 1999
Highest individual innings in ODI 84 D.L. Houghton for Zimbabwe v Australia (WC) 1983
Highest wicket partnerships in ODI

1st	72 S.T. Jayasuriya & R.S. Mahanama	for	Sri Lanka v Kenya	(WC)	1999
2nd	78 K.J. Hughes & G.M. Wood	for	Australia v Zimbabwe	(WC)	1983
3rd	72 R.D. Jacobs & B.C. Lara	for	West Indies v New Zealand	(WC)	1999
4th	104 M.S. Atapattu & A. Ranatunga	for	Sri Lanka v Kenya	(WC)	1999
5th	69 A.R. Border & G.N. Yallop	for	Australia v Zimbabwe	(WC)	1983
6th	161 M.O. Odumbe & A. Vadher	for	Kenya v Sri Lanka	(WC)	1999
7th	50 C.Z. Harris & A.C. Parore	for	New Zealand v West Indies	(WC)	1999
8th	64 D.P.M. Jayawardene & W.P.U.J.C. Vaas	for	Sri Lanka v Kenya	(WC)	1999
9th	25 C.Z. Harris & G.R. Larsen	for	New Zealand v West Indies	(WC)	1999
10th	27 V.R. Hogg & A.J. Traicos	for	Zimbabwe v Australia	(WC)	1983

Best bowling performance in ODI 4 for 46 M. Dillon for West Indies v New Zealand (WC) 1999
Largest crowd 5,000 New Zealand v West Indies (WC) 1999

GROUND INFORMATION

The ground remains under development and facilities will change in the years ahead.
ENTRANCE Via Marshall Drive from Botley Road (B3035).
MEMBERS' ENCLOSURE Pavilion and the defined members' seating located at Pavilion End of the ground
PUBLIC ENCLOSURE Rest of the ground.
COVERED STANDS Pavilion plus two stands with limited seating on the west side of the ground.
OPEN STANDS Plastic tip-up seating in terraced layers surrounds the entire playing area.
MEMBERSHIP Annual membership details are available from the Membership and Ticketing Office.
NAME OF ENDS Pavilion End, Northern End.
GROUND DIMENSIONS 180m × 185m.
REPLAY SCREEN If matches are televised the replay screen is sited close to the West Gate.
FIRST AID Ground Control Office.
CODES OF DRESS Spectators are required to dress in an appropriate manner consistent with attending a cricket match. Bare torsos are not acceptable in or in front of the pavilion.
BEHAVIOUR The club is keen that standards of behaviour should be maintained and members and spectators are urged to report immediately to the Managing Director any incident, or potential incident, where they feel action should be taken. Strong action will be taken for any breach of the ground regulations.

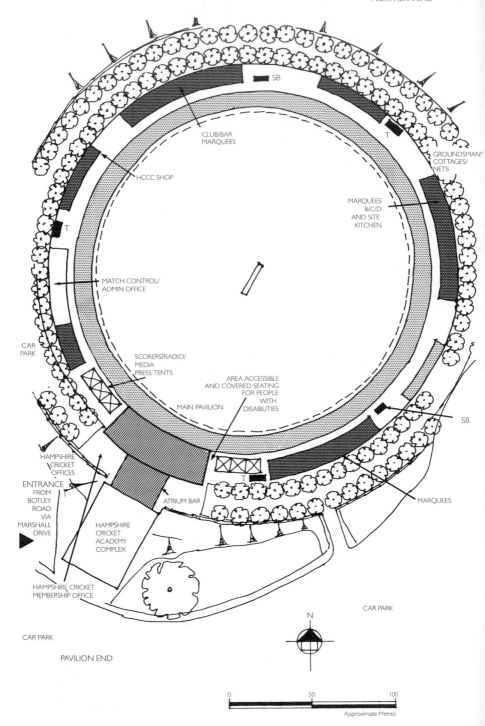

NORTHERN END

SB

CLUB/BAR
MARQUEES

GROUNDSMAN'
COTTAGES/
NETS

T

HCCC SHOP

MARQUEES
B/C/D
AND SITE
KITCHEN

T

MATCH CONTROL/
ADMIN OFFICE

CAR
PARK

SCORERS/RADIO/
MEDIA
PRESS TENTS

AREA ACCESSIBLE
AND COVERED SEATING
FOR PEOPLE
WITH
DISABILITIES

SB

MAIN PAVILION

HAMPSHIRE
CRICKET
OFFICES

T

MARQUEES

ENTRANCE
FROM
BOTLEY
ROAD
VIA
MARSHALL
DRIVE

ATRIUM BAR

HAMPSHIRE
CRICKET
ACADEMY
COMPLEX

HAMPSHIRE CRICKET
MEMBERSHIP OFFICE

CAR PARK

N

CAR PARK

PAVILION END

0   50   100

Approximate Metres

RECIPROCAL ARRANGEMENTS For championship matches members of Essex, Kent and Sussex can gain free entry on production of their membership card (excluding their own county v Hampshire match).

CORPORATE ENTERTAINING The club offers a variety of corporate hospitality including The Executive Club (currently located in the Long Room on the first floor of the main pavilion with a fine view of the cricket) plus hospitality boxes and executive marquees which are available to hire on a season or match-by-match basis. Contact Marketing Department on ☎ 023 8047 2009 for further details and a copy of the brochure.

FACILITIES AND ACCESS FOR PEOPLE WITH DISABILITIES INCLUDING WHEELCHAIR ACCESS TO GROUND Yes, through East Gate.

DESIGNATED CAR PARK AVAILABLE INSIDE GROUND FOR PEOPLE WITH DISABILITIES Yes, near to the East Gate.

DESIGNATED VIEWING AREAS FOR PEOPLE USING WHEELCHAIRS Yes.

RAMPS TO PROVIDE ACCESS TO BARS & REFRESHMENT OUTLETS FOR PEOPLE USING WHEELCHAIRS Yes, all buildings, bars and refreshment areas may be accessed by ramp. There is a lift in the pavilion.

FULL RESTAURANT/DINING FACILITIES Members, yes. Public, yes.

FRANCHISE FOOD/DRINK OUTLETS Members, yes. Public, yes.

VEGETARIAN OPTIONS Members, yes. Public Yes.

BARS Currently Members 2, Public 2.

CHILDREN'S FACILITIES Crèche, no. Play area, planned.

CLUB SHOP The Hampshire Shop is currently situated in temporary facilities to the west side of the ground.

CLUB MUSEUM There is an extensive collection of pictures and memorabilia displayed in the pavilion and Atrium Bar.

CRICKET COACHING FACILITIES The club offers extensive coaching programmes for all ages and abilities using a state-of-the-art, six-lane indoor cricket academy, a nursery ground with its own pavilion plus three outdoor net areas.

CRICKET NETS See above.

OTHER SPORTING OR RECREATIONAL FACILITIES ON THE GROUND Connors health and fitness centre. The County Golf Club with nine-hole/18-tee golf course.

FACILITIES FOR HIRE OR WIDER COMMUNITY USE AT THE GROUND Throughout the year (excluding match days) extensive indoor and outdoor facilities are available for events and functions including weddings, exhibitions, shows and conferences. Contact ☎ 023 8047 2002 for further details of availability, prices and menus.

CAR PARKING Ample car parking spaces are available at The Rose Bowl for most matches. Season tickets and daily parking are available. Occasionally, (e.g. for one-day internationals) a park and ride scheme is operated by the club.

GROUND CAPACITY 9,000 (excluding the installation of temporary stands/seating).

ANTICIPATED GROUND DEVELOPMENTS Current plans include further permanent seating; new administration offices; a permanent club shop; golf driving range and clubhouse; additional hospitality facilities. A 130 bed-room Express by Holiday Inn hotel is being constructed on land adjacent to the site and will open in July 2003.

HOW TO GET THERE

 Hedge End Station (Eastleigh/Portsmouth line via Fareham) is less than 10 minutes by taxi from the ground. There is no direct bus service to the station but on certain days the club operates its own shuttle bus. Southampton Airport/Parkway Station (London Waterloo/Bournemouth line via Basingstoke (connections to Oxford), Winchester and Southampton Central (connections to Salisbury and the West) is 10 minutes by taxi from the ground. There is a direct bus service supplemented on certain days by the club's shuttle bus. ☎ 023 8021 3600, 0845 6000 0650, 08457 484950, www.swtrains.co.uk, www.thetrainline.com, www.railtrack.co.uk

 On certain days (mainly one-day matches) in 2002 the club operated its own shuttle bus from Hedge End and Southampton Airport/Parkway stations. At the end of certain Sunday matches, a shuttle bus also ran to Southampton city centre to cover a gap in the public services. A public service runs from Southampton city centre to The Rose Bowl (First Bus service 8A on Monday to Saturday and 4E on Sunday) and the journey takes 30 minutes. Buses run every 20 minutes Monday to Friday, half-hourly on Saturdays and hourly on Sundays. Solent Blue Line service, Nos 29 or 29A, operate a service from Southampton Airport/Parkway station to The Rose Bowl with a journey time of 12 minutes. This service runs every 30 minutes Monday to Saturday and hourly on Sundays. It is also possible to travel by bus directly from Eastleigh, Hamble, Winchester and

Woolston as well as Petersfield (n.b. not on Sundays). ☎ 023 8059 5974/ 023 8061 8233 or Travel Line 0870 6082608/023 8022 4554. Web www.soton.ac.uk/-unilink, www.solent.blue.com, www.firstsoton.co.uk

 There are cycle routes from surrounding areas of Southampton to West End.

 The Rose Bowl is situated in West End, a short way from the M27 Junction 7.
From north: from M3 junction 14, take M27 (east) to junction 7. At roundabout take A334 (Charles Watts Way), follow this to roundabout and take B3035 (Botley Road) **From south & east:** from M27 junction 7 follow as for north **From west:** from M27 junction 7 follow as for north.

 Southampton Airport ☎ 023 8062 9600, www.southamptonairport.co.uk
Bournemouth Airport ☎ 01202 364000, www.bournemouthairport.co.uk

WHERE TO STAY

Express by Holiday Inn (at ground from July 2003, www.hiexpress.com/southampton), Ibis Accor Hotel (☎ 023 8063 4463 www.ibis.co.uk), Botley Grange Hotel (☎ 01489 787700, www.botleygrangehotel.co.uk), The Concorde Club & Hotel (☎ 023 8065 1478), De Vere Grand Harbour Hotel (☎ 023 8063 3033), Post House/Crest, Eastleigh (☎ 0870 400 9075), Solent Hotel, Whiteley (☎ 01489 880000), 40 Downscroft Gardens, Southampton (☎ 01489 784726, email victor.isaacs@btconnect.com), Primrose Cottage, Southampton (☎ 023 8046 6348, www.primrose.cottage.co.uk), Twin Oaks Guesthouse (☎ 01489 690054), 9 Holly Gardens, Southampton (☎ 023 8047 7832), Oakmount House, Southampton (☎ 023 8047 1240, www.oakmounthotelco.uk), 5 Haselfoot Gardens, Southampton (☎ 023 8046 3277), Marriott Meon Valley (☎ 01329 833455, fax 01329 834411)
For further small hotels and guest houses in the Southampton area visit www.smoothhound.co.uk.

TOURIST INFORMATION Southampton Tourist Information Centre, 9 Civic Centre Road, Southampton, Hampshire S014 7LP ☎ 023 8022 1106 fax 023 8063 1437 email tourist@southampton.gov.uk, www.southampton.gov.uk
Eastleigh Tourist Information Centre, The Point, Eastleigh ☎ 023 8064 1261

LOCAL RADIO STATIONS BBC Radio Solent (96.1 MHz FM / 999/1359 KHz MW), Ocean Radio/Power (103.2 MHz FM/1170 KHz MW)

LOCAL NEWSPAPERS *The Southern Daily Echo, The News, Hampshire Chronicle*

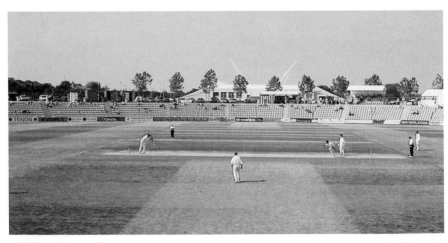

Cricket at The Rose Bowl viewed from the secondary scoreboard during Hampshire v Yorkshire County Championship match in 2002.

Kent

Canterbury
Beckenham
Folkestone
Maidstone
Tunbridge Wells

KENT COUNTY CRICKET CLUB, ST LAWRENCE CRICKET GROUND, OLD DOVER ROAD, CANTERBURY, KENT CT1 3NZ

Telephone 01227 456886, **fax** 01227 762168
Catering 01227 762000
Email kent@ecb.co.uk
Website www.kccc.com

Founded Formation of present club 6 December 1870
Colours maroon and white
Crest white horse on red background
National Cricket League Nickname Spitfires
National Cricket League Colours light blue, maroon and white
Patron HRH The Duke of Kent KG
President R.H.B. Neame, CBE, DL
Vice Presidents D.E. Beney, E. Crush MC
Chairman C.F. Openshaw
Chairman Cricket Committee M.H. Denness
Hon Treasurer A.A. Dunning DL, DCL
Chief Executive Officer P.E. Millman
Operations Manager B. St C. Thomson
Director of Cricket I.J. Brayshaw
Youth Director Coach C. Stone
Second XI Coach S.C. Willis
Head of Marketing J.H. Fordham FCIB
Finance Manager M.A. Fowle BA, ACA
Business Development Manager B.W. Luckhurst
Commercial Executive Mrs J. Owens

Membership & Customer Services Manager Mrs J.Y. Symes
PA to CEO Mrs C. Dunne
Accountant R. Green
Office Manager Mrs J. Cryer
Receptionist Mrs N. Watkins
Groundsman M. Grantham
Captain D.P. Fulton
Vice Captain M.A. Ealham
Scorer 1st XI J. Foley
Scorer 2nd XI C.A. Booth
Hon Medical Adviser R.E.C. Collins FRCS
Hon Curator/Historian D.J. Robertson
Hon Statistician H.R. Milton
Sponsors Shepherd Neame Limited
www.shepherdneame.co.uk
Yearbook £5 (free to Kent members)
Scorecard 50p
National Cricket League Programme £2
Newsletter *Kent County Cricket Club Newsletter*
Frizzell County Championship Status Division 1
National Cricket League Status Division 1

ACHIEVEMENTS

County Championship Champions 1906, 1909, 1910, 1913, 1970, 1978, Joint Champions 1977
Gillette Cup Winners 1967, 1974 Finalists 1971
NatWest Bank Trophy Finalists 1983, 1984
Benson and Hedges Cup Winners 1973, 1976, 1978 Finalists 1977, 1986, 1992, 1995, 1997
John Player Sunday League Champions 1972, 1973, 1976

Axa Equity & Law Sunday League Champions 1995
Norwich Union National League Champions 2001
Fenner Trophy Winners 1971, 1973
Tilcon Trophy Finalists 1980
Seeboard Trophy Winners 1990, 1993 Finalists 1989

KENT CRICKET BOARD

Chairman C. Swadkin
Secretary P. Millman
Chairman of Finance R. Fagg
Cricket Development Officer D. Sear
Development Secretary C. Gould
Accounts Administrator Miss T. Dibble
Women & Girls Secretary M. Lane (Women), D. Collins (Girls)

Address Kent County Cricket Board, St Lawrence Cricket Ground, Old Dover Road, Canterbury, Kent CT1 3NZ
☎ 01227 456886
Fax 01227 762168

GROUNDS

Canterbury (St Lawrence Cricket Ground, Old Dover Road), Tunbridge Wells (Nevill Cricket Ground, Warwick Park), Folkestone (Folkestone Sports Ground, Cheriton Road), Beckenham (Kent County Cricket Ground, Worsley Bridge Road) and Maidstone (Mote Park, Willow Way)

Other grounds used since 1969: Blackheath (Rectory Field, Charlton Road), Dartford (Hesketh Park, Pilgrims Way), Dover (Crabble Athletic Ground, Lewisham Road) and Gravesend (Bat & Ball Ground, Wrotham Road)

SECOND XI GROUNDS

In addition to the above-mentioned grounds the following are used for Second XI matches:
Sibton Park CC, Longage Hill, Lyminge, Near Folkestone, Kent ☎ 01303 863251
Sutton Valence School, School Ground, North Street, Sutton Valence, near Maidstone, Kent ME17 3HN ☎ 01622 842281
Tonbridge School, School Grounds, High Street, Tonbridge, Kent TN9 1JP ☎ 01732 365555

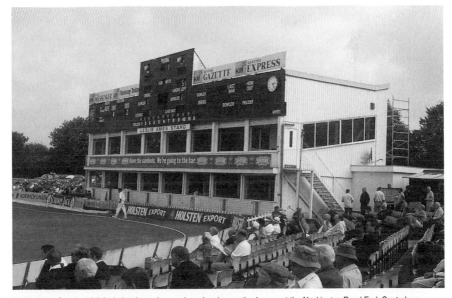

Leslie Ames Stand, which includes the main scoreboard and executive boxes, at the Nackington Road End, Canterbury.

CANTERBURY

Address St Lawrence Cricket Ground, Old Dover Road,
Canterbury, Kent CT1 3NZ
Prospects of Play ☎ 01227 456886 (Extension 237)

HISTORY OF GROUND AND FACILITIES

THE ST LAWRENCE CRICKET GROUND in Old Dover Road was opened in 1847 and was known at that time as the Beverley or East Kent cricket ground. This name came from the previous ground, which was leased from the Beverley Club between 1841 and 1846 and was situated beyond the cavalry barracks. This ground has since been developed for housing close to Vauxhall Lakes and the nearby gravel quarry workings. The present name comes from the site of the St Lawrence hospital founded in 1137. The St Lawrence Ground is one of two in the county owned by Kent CCC. The other venue is the new Kent County Cricket Ground at Beckenham, the former Lloyds Bank Sports Ground, in Worsley Bridge Road.

The ground originally formed part of the Winter's Farm Estate, Nackington. It was bought from the landlord, Earl Sondes, for the sum of £4,500 in 1896. In addition to the games staged by Kent County Cricket Club the ground has also been used by the Beverley Cricket Club, The St Lawrence & Highland Court Cricket Club, formerly the St Lawrence Cricket Club (established in 1864 with the specific purpose of making greater use of the ground) and 'F' Division of the Kent Police. The first match of importance staged on the ground was in early August 1847 when Kent played England and won by 3 wickets.

Frank Woolley Stand, Stuart Chiesman Pavilion, Pavilion Annexe and secondary scoreboard viewed from the Nackington Road End.

Canterbury Cricket Week is usually staged in early August. The first was organised back in 1842, the first at the St Lawrence Ground taking place in 1847. From the early twentieth century Canterbury Week included two championship matches and in recent years has also hosted a limited-overs match. Since the introduction of four-day championship games only a single championship match and a limited-overs match have been played.

The War Memorial on the Old Dover Road side of the ground near the main public entrance.

The pavilion was built in 1900 at a cost of £2,638 and was refurbished, enlarged and renamed the Stuart Chiesman Pavilion in 1970 as a result of the Club Centenary Appeal. Adjacent to the pavilion is the Annexe, built in 1908/9 at a cost of £1,696. The Iron Stand was constructed in 1897 and was renamed the Leslie Ames Stand in 1973. It now accommodates private executive boxes and an enlarged scoreboard. The concrete stand was built during the winter of 1926/7 at a cost of £5,918 and was named the Frank Woolley Stand in 1973. The Colin Cowdrey Stand was built in 1986 and cost £600,000. This stand has three levels: on the ground floor are the Kent CCC Eleventh Man souvenir shop and a cricket equipment sports shop. On the first floor is the Cornwallis Room (which affords views of the cricket), a members' bar and restaurant. The second floor houses the Harris Room, a suite for members. Most of the funds to build the Colin Cowdrey Stand came from the Kent CCC Project '85 appeal.

In the winter of 1990/1 the Howard Levett Kent Indoor Cricket School was demolished. During the winter of 1991/2 the Ames Levett Indoor Cricket School was constructed; it includes cricket nets, changing facilities, a restaurant for use during county matches, and the 'Seventies Room', which records Kent's achievements in that decade. The school also houses Lucky's Bar marking the achievements of former Kent and England opening batsman Brian Luckhurst who was the school's first manager.

Depending on where the wicket is pitched, a lime tree may be within the playing area on the Old Dover Road side of the ground. It is believed to have been cleared three times by hits from West Indians Learie Constantine in 1928 and Carl Hooper in 1992, and Jim Smith of Middlesex in 1939. In 2001/2 the lime tree was pollarded to encourage growth of small branches around the top of the trunk which will improve its appearance and shape. The lime tree is in good health and now only the lower branches require pruning.

In 1999 Canterbury staged two World Cup warm-up matches, Kent v England and Kent v South Africa, and then a match in the Cricket World Cup when England played Kenya and beat them by 9 wickets. In 2000 West Indies played Zimbabwe in the NatWest One-Day International Series; Zimbabwe won. In 2003 the ground will be used again for the NatWest One-Day International Series for a match between South Africa and Zimbabwe.

There is a small but improved museum in the Chiesman Pavilion which houses a display of Colin Cowdrey's blazers and cricket memorabilia together with other items including balls, bats, trophies, china and some fine pictures. The TV camera and commentary box is at the Nackington Road End and the radio commentary box is on the top floor of the pavilion.

The playing area is 150 metres by 135 metres and is defined by a rope and advertising boards. On the Old Dover Road side of the ground, close to the roped off area for press car parking, is the memorial to Colin Blythe and other former Kent CCC players who fell in the two world wars.

Crowds at Canterbury commonly reach 4,000 to 5,000. The capacity is set at 15,000. The club has an annual open day during the early part of the season which has been rather successful in recent years.

Ground records have included 344 by W.G. Grace for MCC in 1876 which was followed in matches against Nottinghamshire and Yorkshire with 177 and 318* respectively, a record 839 in three consecutive innings which still stands today. His younger brother E.M. took 10 for 69 and scored 192* for MCC against the Gentlemen of Kent in 1862 in a 12-a-side match.

GROUND RECORDS AND SCORES

FIRST-CLASS MATCHES

Highest innings total for county 616 for 7 dec v Somerset 1996
Highest innings total against county 676 by Australians 1921
Lowest innings total for county 46 v Surrey 1862
Lowest innings total against county 37 by Philadelphians 1908
Highest individual innings for county 275* M.J. Walker v Somerset 1996
Highest individual innings against county 344 W.G. Grace for MCC 1876
Highest wicket partnerships for county

1st	300 N.R. Taylor & M.R. Benson	v	Derbyshire	1991
2nd	366 S.G. Hinks & N.R. Taylor	v	Middlesex	1990
3rd	283 H.T.W. Hardinge & F.E. Woolley	v	South Africans	1924
4th	251 C.J. Tavare & A.G.E. Ealham	v	Worcestershire	1979
5th	277 F.E. Woolley & L.E.G. Ames	v	New Zealanders	1931
6th	235 G.R. Cowdrey & S.A. Marsh	v	Yorkshire	1992
7th	180 F.G.H. Chalk & B.H. Valentine	v	Hampshire	1937
8th	146 P.A. Strang & S.A. Marsh	v	Leicestershire	1997
9th	120 W.J. Fairservice & C. Blythe	v	Lancashire	1905
10th	125 P.A. Nixon & D.D. Masters	v	Hampshire	2000

Highest wicket partnerships against county

1st	307 Saeed Anwar & Saleem Elahi	for	Pakistanis	2001
2nd	260 D.J. Bicknell & G.P. Thorpe	for	Surrey	1995
3rd	413 D.J. Bicknell & D.M. Ward	for	Surrey	1990
4th	266 K.D. Walters & G.S. Chappell	for	Australians	1972
5th	252 A.J. Stewart & M.A. Lynch	for	Surrey	1985
6th	337 R.R. Montgomerie & D.J. Capel	for	Northamptonshire	1995
7th	270 C.P. Mead & J.P. Parker	for	Hampshire	1926
8th	149 P. Whitticase & P.A.J. de Freitas	for	Leicestershire	1986
9th	111 J.G. Dixon & F.H. Gillingham	for	Essex	1919
10th	116 C.I.J. Smith & I.A.R. Peebles	for	Middlesex	1939

Best bowling performance in an innings for county 9 for 35 J. Jackson v England 1858
Best bowling performance in an innings against county 10 for 92 W.G. Grace for MCC in a 12-a-side match 1873

Best bowling performance In a match for county 15 for 94 A.P. Freeman v Somerset 1931
Best bowling performance in a match against county 15 for 147 W.G. Grace for MCC in a 12-a-side match 1873
Largest crowd 23,000 v Australians 1948

LIMITED-OVERS MATCHES

Highest innings total for county 359 for 4 v Dorset (NWT) 1989
Highest innings total against county 304 for 8 by Warwickshire (B&H) 1997
Lowest innings total for county 73 v Middlesex (B&H) 1979
Lowest innings total against county 76 by Northamptonshire (SL) 2000
Highest individual innings for county 136* C.J. Tavare v Gloucestershire (SL) 1978
Highest individual innings against county 146 G.S. Clinton for Surrey (NWT) 1985
Highest wicket partnerships for county

1st	229 T.R. Ward & M.R. Benson	v	Surrey	(B&H)	1995
2nd	241 T.R. Ward & P.A. de Silva	v	Surrey	(SL)	1995
3rd	208 C.L. Hooper & A.P. Wells	v	Durham	(SL)	1998
4th	146 C.S. Cowdrey & A.G.E. Ealham	v	Sussex	(B&H)	1977
	146 C.J. Tavare & A.G.E. Ealham	v	Glamorgan	(SL)	1980
5th	127 A.G.E. Ealham & J.N. Shepherd	v	Middlesex	(SL)	1971
	127 C.S. Cowdrey & G.R. Cowdrey	v	Surrey	(B&H)	1986
6th	122 M.A. Ealham & N.J. Llong	v	British Universities	(B&H)	1997
7th	67 A.P.E. Knott & G.W. Johnson	v	Hampshire	(B&H)	1982
8th	93 N.R. Taylor & R.M. Ellison	v	Hampshire	(SL)	1988
9th	44 R.P. Davis & M.J. M.CCague	v	Derbyshire	(B&H)	1992
10th	31* M.M. Patel & J.B.deC. Thompson	v	Glamorgan	(B&H)	1996

Highest wicket partnerships against county

1st	241 S.M. Gavaskar & B.C. Rose	for	Somerset	(B&H)	1980
2nd	176 G. Cook & R.J. Bailey	for	Northamptonshire	(SL)	1989
3rd	154 R.C. Ontong & Javed Miandad	for	Glamorgan	(SL)	1982
4th	114 C.T. Radley & R.O. Butcher	for	Middlesex	(B&H)	1983
5th	220* CC Lewis & P.A. Nixon	for	Leicestershire	(SL)	1999
6th	110 A.J. Hollioake & G.J. Kersey	for	Surrey	(SL)	1993
7th	89 N. Shahid & M.P. Bicknell	for	Surrey	(B&H)	1995
8th	93 D. Ripley & J.P. Taylor	for	Northamptonshire	(C&G)	2001
9th	55 R.D. Jackman & G. Monkhouse	for	Surrey	(B&H)	1982
10th	43 N.M.K. Smith & M.A. Sheikh	for	Warwickshire	(C&G)	2002

Best bowling performance in a match for county 6 for 41 T.N. Wren v Somerset (B&H) 1995
Best bowling performance in a match against county 6 for 18 D. Wilson for Yorkshire (SL) 1969
Largest crowd 12,000 v Somerset (GC) 1974

ONE-DAY INTERNATIONALS

Highest innings total for England in ODI 204 for 1 v Kenya (WC) 1999
Highest innings total against England in ODI 203 by Kenya (WC) 1999
Highest innings total in non-England ODI 256 for 4 by Zimbabwe v West Indies (NWS) 2000
Lowest innings total for England in ODI 204 for 1 v Kenya (WC) 1999
Lowest innings total against England in ODI 203 by Kenya (WC) 1999
Lowest innings total in non-England ODI 186 for 8 West Indies v Zimbabwe (NWS) 2000
Highest individual innings for England in ODI 88* N. Hussain v Kenya (WC) 1999
Highest individual innings against England in ODI 71 S.O. Tikolo for Kenya (WC) 1999
Highest individual innings in non-England ODI 83 G.J. Whittall for Zimbabwe v West Indies (NWS) 2000
Highest wicket partnerships for England in ODI

1st	45 N. Hussain & A.J. Stewart	v	Kenya	(WC)	1999
2nd	159* N. Hussain & G.A. Hick	v	Kenya	(WC)	1999

3rd to 10th yet to be established.

Highest wicket partnerships against England in ODI

1st	7 K.O. Otieno & R.D. Shah	for	Kenya	(WC)	1999
2nd	100 R.D. Shah & S.O. Tikolo	for	Kenya	(WC)	1999
3rd	8 S.O. Tikolo & M.O. Odumbe	for	Kenya	(WC)	1999
4th	15 S.O. Tikolo & H.S. Modi	for	Kenya	(WC)	1999
5th	12 S.O. Tikolo & A.V. Vadher	for	Kenya	(WC)	1999
6th	8 S.O. Tikolo & T.M. Odoyo	for	Kenya	(WC)	1999
7th	31 T.M. Odoyo & A.Y. Karim	for	Kenya	(WC)	1999
8th	5 T.M. Odoyo & A.O. Suji	for	Kenya	(WC)	1999
9th	16 T.M. Odoyo & M. Sheikh	for	Kenya	(WC)	1999
10th	1 T.M. Odoyo & M.A. Suji	for	Kenya	(WC)	1999

Highest wicket partnerships in non-England ODI

1st	89 N.C. Johnson & G.J. Whittall	for	Zimbabwe v West Indies	(NWS)	2000
2nd	29 G.J. Whittall & M.W. Goodwin	for	Zimbabwe v West Indies	(NWS)	2000
3rd	96 A.D.R. Campbell & G.J. Whittall	for	Zimbabwe v West Indies	(NWS)	2000
4th	17 J.C. Adams & B.C. Lara	for	West Indies v Zimbabwe	(NWS)	2000
5th	27* A.D.R. Campbell & A. Flower	for	Zimbabwe v West Indies	(NWS)	2000
6th	17 R.D. Jacobs & R.L. Powell	for	West Indies v Zimbabwe	(NWS)	2000
7th	46 R.D. Jacobs & F.A. Rose	for	West Indies v Zimbabwe	(NWS)	2000
8th	54 R.D. Jacobs & N.A.M. McLean	for	West Indies v Zimbabwe	(NWS)	2000
9th	29* N.A.M. McLean & M. Dillon	for	West Indies v Zimbabwe	(NWS)	2000

Best bowling performance for England in ODI 4 for 34 D. Gough v Kenya (WC) 1999

Best bowling performance against England in ODI 1 for 65 T. Odoyo for Kenya (WC) 1999

Best bowling performance in non-England ODI 2 for 16 N.C. Johnson for Zimbabwe v West Indies (NWS) 2000

Largest crowd 9,643 England v Kenya (WC) 1999

GROUND INFORMATION

ENTRANCES Two in Old Dover Road (players, officials, members, public and vehicle entrance) with separate pedestrian entrance nearby, Nackington Road (members, public and vehicles) and Forstal Oast House Gate (pedestrians only).

MEMBERS' ENCLOSURE Pavilion, Pavilion Annexe, Frank Woolley Stand and Cowdrey Stand (ground and first floor only).

PUBLIC ENCLOSURE Rest of the ground. At certain matches members of the public can pay a transfer charge at the ticket office for day entry to the members' enclosure. There are approximately 6,500 permanent seats and temporary ones are installed for popular matches. Spectators can bring their own seats if they wish to sit on the grass near the lime tree boundary at the Nackington Road End.

COVERED STANDS Chiesman Pavilion (part), Pavilion Annexe, Frank Woolley Stand (part), Cowdrey Stand (part) and Leslie Ames Stand (Executive Suites).

OPEN STANDS Frank Woolley Stand (part), Colin Cowdrey Stand (part) together with permanent ground-level and tiered plastic seating surrounding the playing area.

NAME OF ENDS Pavilion End, Nackington Road End.

GROUND DIMENSIONS 150m × 135m.

REPLAY SCREEN If matches are televised the replay screen is sited near the Leslie Ames Stand at the Nackington Road End of the ground.

FIRST AID Adjacent to Club Office at the top of The Drive.

CODES OF DRESS Spectators are required to dress in an appropriate manner consistent with attending a cricket match. Bare torsos are not acceptable in or in front of the pavilion. Harris Room users must wear a necktie and jacket.

BEHAVIOUR The club is keen that standards of behaviour should be maintained and members and spectators are urged to report without delay to the KCCC office any incident, or potential incident, where they feel action should be taken. Bad language is not acceptable at any match and the club will take prompt and strong action should this or any other ground regulation be ignored.

RECIPROCAL ARRANGEMENTS Members of Essex, Hampshire and Sussex can gain entry free on production of membership card when Kent is not playing their own county.

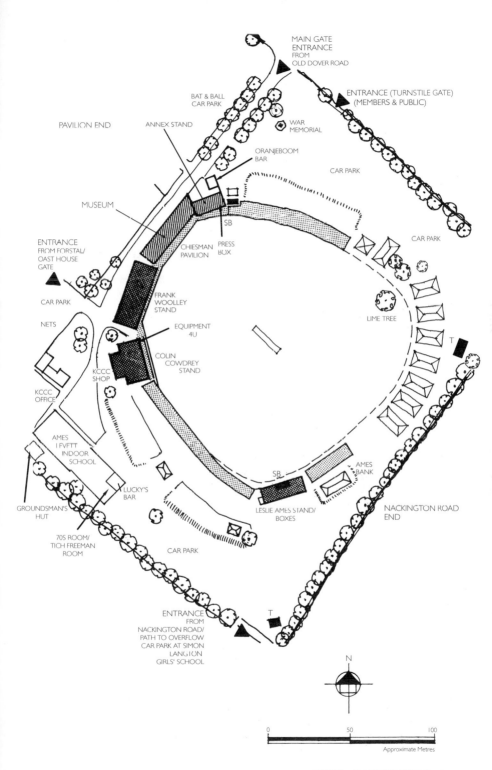

MAIN GATE
ENTRANCE
FROM
OLD DOVER ROAD

ENTRANCE (TURNSTILE GATE)
(MEMBERS & PUBLIC)

BAT & BALL
CAR PARK

PAVILION END

ANNEX STAND

WAR
MEMORIAL

ORANJEBOOM
BAR

CAR PARK

MUSEUM

CAR PARK

SB

CHIESMAN
PAVILION

PRESS
BOX

ENTRANCE
FROM FORSTAL/
OAST HOUSE
GATE

CAR PARK

FRANK
WOOLLEY
STAND

NETS

EQUIPMENT
4U

LIME TREE

COLIN
COWDREY
STAND

KCCC
SHOP

T

KCCC
OFFICE

AMES
LEVETT
INDOOR
SCHOOL

SB

AMES
BANK

LUCKY'S
BAR

NACKINGTON ROAD
END

GROUNDSMAN'S
HUT

LESLIE AMES STAND/
BOXES

70S ROOM/
TICH FREEMAN
ROOM

CAR PARK

ENTRANCE
FROM
NACKINGTON ROAD/
PATH TO OVERFLOW
CAR PARK AT SIMON
LANGTON
GIRLS' SCHOOL

T

N

0   50   100

Approximate Metres

SUPPORTERS' CLUB £10 per person per annum. Special rates for concessions and husband and wife membership are available. ☎ 01732 354067 for details.

JUNIORS Kent Kit Kat Kids membership is available to under-18s (£8 country), (£15 full membership). Contact Membership & Customer Services Manager for full details.

CORPORATE ENTERTAINING Function room and other entertainment facilities at Ames Levett Sports Centre. Also marquees, 14 executive boxes in Leslie Ames Stand and conference and banqueting facilities available at matches. Contact Marketing Manager for details.

FACILITIES FOR VISUALLY IMPAIRED SPECTATORS Free entry for helper. Guide dogs allowed. Please give club office advance warning as early as possible.

FACILITIES AND ACCESS FOR PEOPLE WITH DISABILITIES INCLUDING WHEELCHAIR ACCESS TO GROUND ☎ main office for details.

DESIGNATED CAR PARK AVAILABLE INSIDE THE GROUND FOR PEOPLE WITH DISABILITIES ☎ main office for details.

GOOD VIEWING AREAS INSIDE THE GROUND FOR PEOPLE USING WHEELCHAIRS Yes, particularly on areas of hard standing in front of the Frank Woolley Stand.

DESIGNATED VIEWING AREAS FOR PEOPLE USING WHEELCHAIRS Yes, in front of Frank Woolley Stand, lower section at Colin Cowdrey Stand end beneath the Committee Room balcony.

RAMPS TO PROVIDE EASY ACCESS TO BARS & REFRESHMENT OUTLETS FOR PEOPLE USING WHEELCHAIRS Yes, lift in Colin Cowdrey Stand.

FOOD & DRINK FULL RESTAURANT/DINING FACILITIES Restaurant service in Colin Cowdrey Stand. Members, yes. Public, yes. Catering by Morton's Fork Limited ☎ 01227 762000. Restaurant service is also available in the 'Seventies Room' of the Sports Centre.

TEMPORARY FOOD/DRINK FACILITIES Members, yes. Public, yes.

FOOD SUITABLE FOR VEGETARIANS Members, yes. Public, yes.

BARS Members 3, Public 2.

VARIETIES OF BEER SOLD Shepherd Neame.

CHILDREN'S FACILITIES Crèche on occasions. Free coaching on Sundays of National Cricket League matches. Annual open day usually in May.

CLUB SHOP Yes, Kent CCC Eleventh Wicket, the official club shop, and a secondary cricket equipment shop situated in lower Colin Cowdrey Stand.

CLUB MUSEUM No, although in the pavilion and other areas there are cabinets displaying memorabilia including the Lord Cowdrey Collection and there is a Library in the Colin Cowdrey Stand available to club members by arrangement .

CRICKET COACHING FACILITIES Yes, Ames Levett Indoor Cricket School at top of The Drive.

CRICKET NETS Yes, indoor in Ames Levett Indoor Cricket School.

OTHER SPORTING OR RECREATIONAL FACILITIES ON THE GROUND Yes, Ames Levett Sports Centre including squash courts, indoor football, indoor cricket ☎ 01227 784996.

FACILITIES FOR HIRE OR WIDER COMMUNITY USE AT THE GROUND Rooms are available for functions, weddings, exhibitions and conferences.

WINTER CRICKET EVENTS None.

CAR PARKING FACILITIES Ample car parking is available at most matches for members with car park passes and the public at a cost of £10 per car although this depends on weather conditions. During Canterbury Cricket Week and Cheltenham & Gloucester quarter and semi-finals space may be limited to members only. There is an overflow car park off the Old Dover Road in the nearby school field. There is also limited street parking surrounding the ground and in city centre car parks approximately 15 minutes walk from the ground. Cricket can be viewed from your own car on the ring to the south but space is limited. Cars may also be parked on the eastern elevated area but windscreen must be covered to reduce reflective glare. It is recommended that spectators use the four park and ride car parks on the edge of the city and travel to the ground by bus.

OTHER INFORMATION Groups of school children, the disabled and disadvantaged are usually allowed into the ground at reduced rates but must be requested in advance. Contact club for details. At all matches there is a second-hand book stall located near the rear of secondary scoreboard run by David Summerfield of Alfriston.

GROUND CAPACITY 15,000.

ANTICIPATED GROUND DEVELOPMENTS Kent County Cricket Club has issued a vision statement and produced a strategic plan for the ground to 2010 which includes new hospitality boxes, press/media box and scoreboard at the Nackington Road End together with hotel development on the Old Dover Road side of the ground. Also included in the vision are new grass practice nets on the Old Dover Road side of the ground and on the

Hospital side a redevelopment of the cricket school with new nets, hard surface outside lighting, classroom and camera systems plus all-weather floodlit practice pitches.

HOW TO GET THERE

 Canterbury East station 1 mile, Canterbury West station 1.5 miles. ☎ 08457 484950, 0870 603 0405, www.connex.co.uk

 Stagecoach East Kent Buses 15, 16 and 17 from Canterbury bus station to Folkestone pass ground, also 339 from city centre; C1, C2 and C5 link Canterbury rail stations with the bus station. ☎ 01843 581333, 08702 433711, Travel line 0870 608 2608, Kent Council Transport Information Service 0800 696996, Bus Information 01227 472082, www.stagecoachgroup.com. Canterbury Park & Ride available from Dover Road, Wincheap or Sturry Road £1.50 per day ☎ 01227 862000.

 There are cycle routes from surrounding areas of Canterbury to this part of the city.

 From north: from M20 junction 7 turn left on to A249, at M2 junction 5 (Sittingbourne) bear right on to M2, at junction 7 (Boughton Street) turn right on to A2, follow this to junction with A2050, turn left and follow signs to cricket ground. **From south:** from M20 junction 13 bear right on to A20, follow this road to junction with A260, bear left and continue to junction with A2 (north), continue to junction with A2050 then as for north. **From east:** from A257, turn left on to A2050, then as for north. **From west:** from M20 junction 11 (Stanford) turn left on to B2068, continue to junction with A2050 then as for north.

 Kent International Airport ☎ 01843 825063

WHERE TO STAY

Blazing Donkey Country Hotel (☎ 01304 617362), Cathedral Gate Hotel (☎ 01227 464381), Chaucer Lodge ☎/Fax 01227 www.thechaucerlodge.co.uk), County Hotel (☎ 01227 766266), Ebury Hotel (☎ 01227 768433 www.ebury-hotel.com), Ersham Lodge (☎ 01227 455482 www.ersham-lodge.co.uk), Express by Holiday Inn (☎ 01227 865000), Falstaff Hotel (☎ 01227 462138 www.corushotels.com/falstaff), Slatters Hotel (☎ 01227 463271), St Lawrence Guesthouse (☎ 01227 451336), The Abbot's Fireside Hotel (☎ 01303 840265 www.abbotsfireside.co.uk), The Bow Window (☎ 01227 721264 www.bowwindowinn.co.uk), The Canterbury Hotel (☎ 01227 450551 www.canterbury-hotel-apartments.co.uk), The Chaucer (☎ 01227 464427 www.thechaucerhotel.co.uk), The Old Coach House (☎ 01227 831218), Victoria Hotel (☎ 01227 459333)
    Contact Canterbury Accommodation Booking Service ☎ 01227 780063, www.canterbury.co.uk or www.smoothhound.co.uk for details of other places to stay in and around Canterbury.

WHERE TO EAT

Augustines (☎ 01227 453063), Crab & Winkle Seafood Restaurant (☎ 01227 779377), Café des Amis (☎ 01227 464390), Dunkerleys (☎ 01304 375016), Kudos 52 (☎ 01227 761126), Skippers (☎ 01227 830788), The Abbot's Fireside Restaurant (☎ 01303 840265), Whitstable Oyster Fishery Company (☎ 01227 276856)

TOURIST INFORMATION Canterbury Tourist Information Centre, 34 St Margaret's Street, Canterbury, CT1 2TG ☎ 01227 766567, www.canterbury.co.uk

LOCAL RADIO STATIONS BBC Radio Kent (774 MW), Invicta FM/Capital Gold (103.1 MHz FM/1242 KHz MW)

LOCAL NEWSPAPERS *Kent Messenger, Medway Today, Kentish Gazette, Kent and Sussex Courier*

BECKENHAM

Address Kent County Cricket Ground, The Pavilion, Worsley Bridge Road,
Beckenham, Kent BR3 1RU
Prospects of Play ☎ 020 8650 8444

HISTORY OF GROUND AND FACILITIES

IN 2003 THE CRICKET GROUND in Beckenham, south-east London, became the
first new ground to be used by Kent for 49 years.

The 25-acre ground dates back to 17 July 1918 when Lloyds Bank acquired
7 acres of land to establish a sports club on the site. It was named the Lloyds
Bank Sports Club Ground but the club did not move there to play matches until
1922.

The original Lloyds Bank Sports Club pavilion was built in 1925 and during the
Second World War was taken over by the local fire service. The square was
maintained but the outfield was used for garaging fire engines and also for
allotments. Cricket was played here until 1940 but did not commence again until
1946. After the Second World War Memorial Gates were erected at the Copers
Cope Road entrance to the ground and were dedicated to those members of the
club who fell during the conflict. Between 1979 and 1983 Kent County Cricket
Club used the ground for Second XI and Under-25 matches. It was known then
as the Cornhill Insurance Sports Ground.

The ground was also used by Lloyds Bank for soccer, rugby, hockey, tennis,
netball, rounders and softball. The site included three football pitches, two rugby
pitches, three hockey pitches, two netball courts and fourteen tennis courts (six
hard and eight grass). In the original pavilion, which was demolished during the
winter of 2001/2 to make way for retirement homes, there were thirty rooms
which included seven dining rooms, a billiard room, table tennis rooms and
badminton courts in the main hall.

The ground was acquired by Leander Sports Club, Kent County Cricket Club,
Bromley Council and Wates Homes in 1999/2000, since when the venue has
been under joint venture ownership. A new cricket pavilion, designed by Paul
Davis & Partners of London, includes Kent County Cricket Club's Centre Office,
a bar and lounge area on the ground floor with dressing rooms, showers, toilets
and an umpires' room on the upper level with a players' viewing balcony. This
building is currently the only permanent structure on the ground and is situated
on the Worsley Bridge Road side. To the south is Crystal Palace Football Club's
training ground and to the south-west of the playing area are the remains of
former Lloyds Bank Sports Club pavilion.

Entrance to the ground is from Worsley Bridge Road although there are likely
to be further entrances in Copers Cope Road once a retirement homes
development project has been completed. A small scoreboard is situated near
the pavilion. No permanent seating is provided. Temporary seats are installed but
it is advisable to bring your own to popular matches.

Kent Cricket is not new to Beckenham, as matches have been staged by the
county club at a number of venues in addition to the former Lloyds Bank Sports
Ground. These include 14 matches at Beckenham Cricket Club's Foxgrove

The pavilion.

Ground, which was first used between 22 and 24 July 1886 when Kent hosted Surrey and last used between 3 and 5 August 1905. The county have also visited the Midland Bank Sports Ground (now HSBC Cricket Club), Lennard Road, New Beckenham, which was used for a John Player League match with Lancashire on 10 May 1970. Other venues used in Beckenham for Second XI fixtures by Kent have included London Transport Sports Ground, Langley Park, Hawksbrook Lane between 1960 and 1964 and the National Westminster Bank Sports Ground, also in Copers Cope Road, between 1976 and 1978.

The ground was used for first-class cricket by Kent on 9–11 June 1954 when Gloucestershire were the visitors for a County Championship match. The match lasted two days and was drawn because the final day was washed out; Kent won on the first innings. A Second XI match was staged here with Somerset between 21 and 23 August 2002.

GROUND RECORDS AND SCORES

FIRST-CLASS MATCHES

Highest innings total for county 160 v Gloucestershire 1954
Highest innings total against county 110 by Gloucestershire 1954
Lowest innings total for county 34 for 3 v Gloucestershire 1954
Lowest innings total against county 110 by Gloucestershire 1954
Highest individual innings for county 48 R.C. Wilson v Gloucestershire 1954
Highest individual innings against county 26 D.M. Young for Gloucestershire 1954
Highest wicket partnerships for county

1st	8 A.E. Fagg & A.H. Phebey	v	Gloucestershire	1954
2nd	37 A.E. Fagg & R.C. Wilson	v	Gloucestershire	1954
3rd	25 R.C. Wilson & J. Pettiford	v	Gloucestershire	1954
4th	17 R.C. Wilson & P. Hearn	v	Gloucestershire	1954
5th	11 R.C. Wilson & A.C. Shirreff	v	Gloucestershire	1954
6th	3 R.C. Wilson & M.D. Fenner	v	Gloucestershire	1954
7th	12 R.C. Wilson & E.G. Witherden	v	Gloucestershire	1954
8th	2 R.C. Wilson & R.R. Dovey	v	Gloucestershire	1954
9th	27 R.R. Dovey & D.V.P. Wright	v	Gloucestershire	1954
10th	18 D.V.P. Wright & J.C.T. Page	v	Gloucestershire	1954

Highest wicket partnerships against county

1st	23 G.M. Emmett & C.A. Milton	for	Gloucestershire	1954
2nd	1 G.M. Emmett & T.W. Graveney	for	Gloucestershire	1954
3rd	25 T.W. Graveney & D.M. Young	for	Gloucestershire	1954
4th	2 D.M. Young & A.E. Wilson	for	Gloucestershire	1954
5th	17 D.M. Young & G.E. Lambert	for	Gloucestershire	1954
6th	5 A.E. Wilson & G.E. Lambert	for	Gloucestershire	1954
7th	8 J. Mortimore & G.E. Lambert	for	Gloucestershire	1954
8th	17 J.V.C. Griffiths & C. Cook	for	Gloucestershire	1954
9th	12 C. Cook & B.D. Wells	for	Gloucestershire	1954
10th	0 B.D. Wells & F.P. McHugh	for	Gloucestershire	1954

Best bowling performance in an innings for county 6 for 55 A.C. Shirreff v Gloucestershire 1954
Best bowling performance in an innings against county 5 for 56 C. Cook for Gloucestershire 1954
Best bowling performance in a match for county 6 for 55 A.C. Shirreff v Gloucestershire 1954
Best bowling performance in a match against county 5 for 29 F.P. McHugh for Gloucestershire 1954
Largest crowd 2,874 v Gloucestershire 1954

LIMITED-OVERS MATCHES

No limited-overs matches played to date.

GROUND INFORMATION

ENTRANCES Worsley Bridge Road (players, officials, members, pedestrians), Copers Cope Road (pedestrians and vehicles) and North Gate (pedestrians and vehicles).
MEMBERS' ENCLOSURE Pavilion.
PUBLIC ENCLOSURE Rest of the ground.
COVERED STANDS Pavilion (part).
OPEN STANDS Pavilion (part), together with temporary ground-level and tiered plastic seating surrounding the playing area.
NAME OF ENDS Crystal Palace End, North End.
GROUND DIMENSIONS 160m × 155m.
REPLAY SCREEN If televised matches are staged at the ground the replay screen is likely to be staged on the Copers Cope Road side of the ground.
FIRST AID In the pavilion.
CODES OF DRESS Spectators are required to dress in an appropriate manner consistent with attending a cricket match. Bare torsos are not acceptable in or in front of the pavilion.
BEHAVIOUR The club is keen that standards of behaviour should be maintained and members and spectators are urged to report immediately to the temporary Kent CCC office any incident, or potential incident, where they feel action should be taken. Bad language is not acceptable at any match and the club will take prompt and strong action should this or any other ground regulation be ignored.
RECIPROCAL ARRANGEMENTS Members of Essex, Hampshire and Sussex can gain entry free on production of membership card when Kent is not playing their own county.
SUPPORTERS' CLUB £10 per person per annum. Special rates for concessions and husband and wife membership are available. ☎ 01732 354067 for details.
JUNIORS Kent Kit Kat Kids membership is available to under-18s (£8 country), (£15 full membership). Contact Membership & Customer Services Manager for full details.
CORPORATE ENTERTAINING Marquees with various facilities are available for hire available at matches. Contact Marketing Manager for details.
FACILITIES FOR VISUALLY IMPAIRED SPECTATORS Free entry for helper. Guide dogs allowed. Please give club office advance warning as early as possible.
FACILITIES AND ACCESS FOR PEOPLE WITH DISABILITIES INCLUDING WHEELCHAIR ACCESS TO GROUND Yes, from all entrances.
DESIGNATED CAR PARK AVAILABLE INSIDE THE GROUND FOR PEOPLE WITH DISABILITIES Yes.
GOOD VIEWING AREAS INSIDE THE GROUND FOR PEOPLE USING WHEELCHAIRS Yes.
DESIGNATED VIEWING AREAS FOR PEOPLE USING WHEELCHAIRS Yes, in front of the pavilion.
RAMPS TO PROVIDE EASY ACCESS TO BARS & REFRESHMENT OUTLETS FOR PEOPLE USING WHEELCHAIRS Yes.

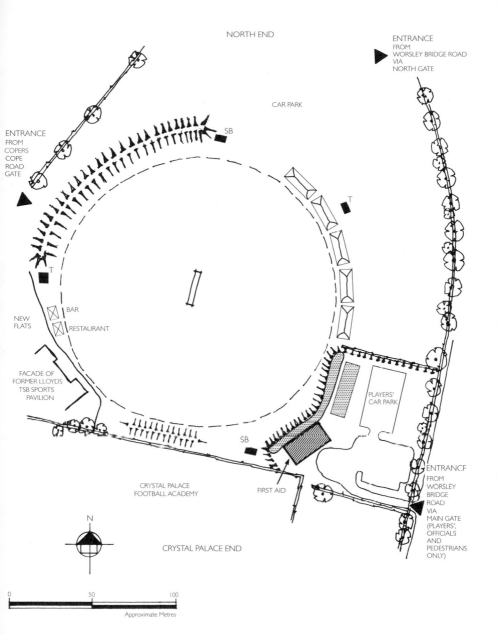

NORTH END

ENTRANCE FROM WORSLEY BRIDGE ROAD VIA NORTH GATE

CAR PARK

SB

T

ENTRANCE FROM COPERS COPE ROAD GATE

T

NEW FLATS

BAR

RESTAURANT

FACADE OF FORMER LLOYDS TSB SPORTS PAVILION

PLAYERS' CAR PARK

SB

ENTRANCE FROM WORSLEY BRIDGE ROAD VIA MAIN GATE (PLAYERS', OFFICIALS AND PEDESTRIANS ONLY)

CRYSTAL PALACE FOOTBALL ACADEMY

FIRST AID

N

CRYSTAL PALACE END

0   50   100

Approximate Metres

FOOD & DRINK FULL RESTAURANT/DINING FACILITIES Members, no. Public, yes. Sandwiches and snack meals, catering provided by Morton's Fork Limited in marquee. ☎ 01227 762000.

TEMPORARY FOOD/DRINK FACILITIES Members, yes. Public, yes.

FOOD SUITABLE FOR VEGETARIANS Members, yes. Public, yes.

BARS Members 1, Public 1.

VARIETIES OF BEER SOLD Shepherd Neame.

CHILDREN'S FACILITIES Crèche, no. Bouncy castle, yes, when available, for floodlit matches.

CLUB SHOP Yes, Kent CCC Eleventh Wicket club shop is situated in a temporary marquee when Kent CCC matches are staged at the ground.

CLUB MUSEUM No, although there are pictures of Kent players on the walls of the staircase in the pavilion and in the main entrance there is a collection of pictures, scorecard and signatures of the match and players that took part in the first-class match on the former Lloyds Bank Sports Ground in 1954.

CRICKET COACHING FACILITIES Yes. Contact Centre Manager or Kent CCC.

CRICKET NETS Yes, outdoor by arrangement Centre Manager or contact Kent CCC.

OTHER SPORTING OR RECREATIONAL FACILITIES ON THE GROUND Yes, hockey and football.

FACILITIES FOR HIRE OR WIDER COMMUNITY USE AT THE GROUND Rooms are available for functions, weddings, exhibitions and conferences. Contact Marketing Department at Kent CCC.

WINTER CRICKET EVENTS No.

CAR PARKING FACILITIES Car parking is available at the northern end of the ground and is accessed from Copers Cope Road and Worsley Bridge Road for players, officials, members, press/media only. Ample car parking is available at most matches, free for KCCC members with car park passes and for the public at a cost of £10 per car although this depends on weather conditions. There is also limited street parking surrounding the ground. Cricket can be viewed from cars from the ring to the eastern side of the playing area but space is limited.

OTHER INFORMATION Groups of school children, the disabled and disadvantaged can usually gain entry to ground for championship matches if requested in advance. Contact club for details. There is also a second-hand cricket book stall run by David Summerfield of Alfriston.

GROUND CAPACITY 8,000.

ANTICIPATED GROUND DEVELOPMENTS New scoreboard together with seating and grassed banking areas.

HOW TO GET THERE

 Lower Sydenham or Beckenham Junction stations. ☎ 08457 484950, 0870 603 0405, www.connex.co.uk

 LRT 351, 252 and 356 pass ground with stops in Worsley Bridge Road. ☎ 020 7222 1234

 There are ample cycle paths and routes from surrounding areas of Beckenham to the ground.

 From north: from Central London take A201, at Elephant and Castle take A2 (Old Kent Road), continue to New Cross Gate and take right turn (Lewisham Way) on to A20, continue through Lewisham to junction with A21 and turn right on to A21 (Lewisham High Street), continue on A21 towards Bromley, turn right on to A2015 (Beckenham Hill Road), turn right on to Stumps Hill, turn right on to Worsley Bridge Road. **From south:** from M23/M25 Junction 7 follow A23 (Brighton Road) to junction with A235, bear right (Brighton Road), at Croydon turn east on A232, at Shirley turn left on to A215 (Shirley Road), bear right on to A222 (Addiscombe Road), then right again on to A214, bear left on to A222, continue on this road (Croydon Road) to roundabout, take second exit (A2015) (Rectory Road), turn right on to Stumps Hill, turn right into Worsley Bridge Road. **From east:** from M25 junction 3 follow A20 (London), turn left on to A205 (South Circular Road), at Lewisham turn left on to A21, then as for north. **From west:** from A308 (Kingston-upon-Thames) take A3 towards London, at junction with A205 (South Circular Road) turn right and follow South Circular Road to Lewisham, at junction with A21 turn right, then as for north.

 London City Airport ☎ 020 7646 0000

WHERE TO STAY

Visit www.smoothhound.co.uk for details of hotels, guesthouses and bed and breakfasts in and around Beckenham and Bromley.

WHERE TO EAT

Contact www.harden.com for suitable locations near ground.

TOURIST INFORMATION Bromley Tourist Information Centre, www.bromley.gov.uk

LOCAL RADIO STATIONS BBC Radio London Live 94.9 FM, BBC Radio Kent (774 MW), Invicta FM/Capital Gold (103.1 MHz FM/1242 KHz MW), LBC 1152AM

LOCAL NEWSPAPERS *Kent Messenger, Evening Standard*

FOLKESTONE

Address Folkestone Cricket Club, The Pavilion, Cheriton Road, Cheriton, Folkestone, Kent CT19 5JU
Prospects of Play ☎ 01303 253366

HISTORY OF GROUND AND FACILITIES

FOLKESTONE CRICKET CLUB was established in 1856. The first matches staged by Kent County Cricket Club in the town took place in 1862 and 1863 at the Sandgate Hill ground, the original home of the Folkestone Cricket Club. At the turn of the century the club was searching for a new ground in the town centre and chose a site close to the North Downs that was originally a part of the Earl of Radnor's Broad Mead Farm in the Cheriton district. The ground was levelled and prepared under the supervision of Alec Hearne, a former Kent player, for the inaugural match in 1905 when a local side played a Kent Club and Ground XI. Lord Harris said in his after-dinner speech at a reception given at the conclusion of the match that regular first-class cricket should be staged on the ground.

The initial first-class match on the Cheriton Road ground was staged twenty years later in September 1925 when the Gentlemen took on the Players. After this match Kent County Cricket Club played the MCC and thus began the Folkestone Festival week. First-class matches were played periodically from 1926 and from 1961 the Folkestone week became an annual feature in late August. Kent stopped using the ground in 1991 when the last match there was staged with Essex. In late August 2001 and early September 2002 the ground hosted a four-day cricket festival comprising teams from a Kent Select XI, Belgium, France and the Netherlands competing in the European Cricket Challenge. The competition evolved from the desire of Shepway Borough Council to bring first-class cricket back to Folkestone.

The present pavilion and stands were built in 1926 supported by a donation of £1,000 from the Earl of Radnor. The buildings were designed by a local architect, R. Pope. The ground extends to 30 acres and includes Folkestone Invicta Football Club, tennis courts and bowling greens. The Cheriton Road ground is located very close to the Folkestone Channel Tunnel terminal; the marshalling yard can be seen from the ground and regular high-speed trains can also be heard. Folkestone

Main entrance turnstile at Cheriton Road.

Cricket Club play in the Forester Kent County League and field two XIs throughout the season.

The main scoreboard is to the north-east of the ground and also has a store for the groundsman's equipment. The TV camera and commentary box position is directly above and behind the sightscreen at the Cheriton Road End. The radio commentary box is situated on the roof of the pavilion adjoining the press box. The playing area is 134 metres by 170 metres and is defined by a rope and advertising boards. The ground capacity is 8,000; 4,000 seats are provided but spectators are advised to bring their own to popular matches.

Major performances on the ground have included double centuries from Leslie Ames and Herbert Sutcliffe. Fred Ridgway, playing for Kent against Derbyshire in 1951, took 4 wickets in 4 balls.

GROUND RECORDS AND SCORES

FIRST-CLASS MATCHES

Highest innings total for county 592 for 5 dec v Gloucestershire 1933
Highest innings total against county 544 by Essex 1991
Lowest innings total for county 61 v Essex 1929
Lowest innings total against county 65 by Warwickshire 1986
(nb: lowest first-class score on ground 55 for MCC v South 1933)
Highest individual innings for county 295 L.E.G. Ames v Gloucestershire 1933
Highest individual innings against county 230 H. Sutcliffe for Yorkshire 1931
Highest wicket partnerships for county

1st	178 N.R. Taylor & M.R. Benson	v	Nottinghamshire	1983
2nd	228 H.T.W. Hardinge & F.E. Woolley	v	Hampshire	1929
3rd	259 L.E.G. Ames & L.J. Todd	v	Gloucestershire	1933
4th	180 L.E.G. Ames & I.S. Akers-Douglas	v	Essex	1929
5th	218 L.E.G. Ames & B.H. Valentine	v	Gloucestershire	1933
6th	164 J.N. Shepherd & A.G.E. Ealham	v	Northamptonshire	1968
7th	130 S.C. Willis & J.B.deC. Thompson	v	Cambridge University	1995
8th	109 A.G.E. Ealham & J.N. Shepherd	v	Yorkshire	1977
9th	158 A.G.E. Ealham & A. Brown	v	Glamorgan	1968
10th	62 C.S. Cowdrey & D.L. Underwood	v	Hampshire	1985

Highest wicket partnerships against county

1st	166 A. Jones & R.C. Fredericks	for	Glamorgan	1971
2nd	258 H. Sutcliffe & E. Oldroyd	for	Yorkshire	1931
3rd	212 W.J. Stewart & M.J.K. Smith	for	Warwickshire	1962
4th	260 C.E.B. Rice & P. Johnson	for	Nottinghamshire	1984
5th	150 Salim Malik & N. Hussain	for	Essex	1991
6th	136 R.H. Bettington & F.T. Mann	for	MCC	1928
7th	91 P.B. Clift & J.F. Steele	for	Leicestershire	1983
8th	136 J.M. Sims & B.L. Munce	for	Middlesex	1934
9th	70 E. Robinson & G.G. Macauley	for	Yorkshire	1931
10th	84 A. Wharton & J.D. Stone	for	Lancashire	1949

Best bowling performance in an innings for county 9 for 61 A.P. Freeman v Warwickshire 1932
Best bowling performance in an innings against county 8 for 32 R.G. Marlar for Cambridge University 1953
Best bowling performance in a match for county 17 for 92 A.P. Freeman v Warwickshire 1932
Best bowling performance in a match against county 13 for 90 R.G. Marlar for Cambridge University 1953
Largest crowd 5,000 v Gloucestershire 1933

LIMITED-OVERS MATCHES

Highest innings total for county 281 for 5 v Warwickshire (SL) 1983
Highest innings total against county 225 for 4 by Middlesex (SL) 1990
Lowest innings total for county 84 v Gloucestershire (SL) 1969
Lowest innings total against county 118 by Derbyshire (SL) 1976
Highest individual innings for county 122* C.J. Tavare v Warwickshire (SL) 1983
Highest individual innings against county 86 R.T. Robinson for Nottinghamshire (SL) 1984
Highest wicket partnerships for county

1st	83 M.H. Denness & D. Nicholls	v	Leicestershire	(SL)	1971
2nd	119 B.W. Luckhurst & M.H. Denness	v	Middlesex	(SL)	1975
3rd	170 C.J. Tavare & D.G. Aslett	v	Warwickshire	(SL)	1983
4th	40 D.G. Aslett & C.S. Cowdrey	v	Nottinghamshire	(SL)	1984
5th	85 S.E. Leary & A.G.E. Ealham	v	Worcestershire	(SL)	1970
6th	77* C.J. Tavare & R.M. Ellison	v	Worcestershire	(SL)	1988
7th	41 A.P.E. Knott & J.N. Shepherd	v	Warwickshire	(SL)	1974
8th	36 J.N. Shepherd & R.W. Hills	v	Derbyshire	(SL)	1976
9th	19 R.W. Hills & D.L. Underwood	v	Leicestershire	(SL)	1978
10th	12 J.N. Graham & J.C.J. Dye	v	Gloucestershire	(SL)	1969

Highest wicket partnerships against county

1st	122 D.L. Haynes & M.A. Roseberry	by	Middlesex	(SL)	1990
2nd	82 R.T. Robinson & C.E.B. Rice	by	Nottinghamshire	(SL)	1984
3rd	46 T.A. Lloyd & G.W. Humpage	by	Warwickshire	(SL)	1983
	46 M.A. Roseberry & K.R. Brown	by	Middlesex	(SL)	1990
4th	110* D.A. Leatherdale & P.A. Neale	by	Worcestershire	(SL)	1988
5th	68 R.B. Kanhai & D.L. Murray	by	Warwickshire	(SL)	1974
6th	54 N. Hussain & N. Shahid	by	Essex	(SL)	1991
7th	54 J.T. Murray & K.V. Jones	by	Middlesex	(SL)	1972
8th	23 C.J. Richards & R.D. Jackman	by	Surrey	(SL)	1981
9th	46* D.L. Murray & D.J. Brown	by	Warwickshire	(SL)	1974
10th	16 J.P. Agnew & P.M. Such	by	Leicestershire	(SL)	1989

Best bowling performance in a match for county 4 for 9 L. Potter v Derbyshire (SL) 1985
Best bowling performance in a match against county 5 for 60 J.A. Jameson for Warwickshire (SL) 1974
Largest crowd 7,500 v Derbyshire (SL) 1976

GROUND INFORMATION

ENTRANCES Cheriton Road (players, officials, members, public and vehicles), Cornwallis Avenue (members, public and vehicles).
MEMBERS' ENCLOSURE Pavilion, Pavilion Terrace and West Stand (part).
PUBLIC ENCLOSURE West Stand (part) and rest of the ground.
COVERED STANDS Pavilion (part), West Stand and South Stand.
OPEN STANDS Pavilion (part) together with temporary ground-level seating surrounding the playing area.
NAME OF ENDS Cheriton Road End, North Downs End.
GROUND DIMENSIONS 134m × 170m.
REPLAY SCREEN If televised matches are staged at the ground the replay screen is sited to the South Downs End of the ground.
FIRST AID In pavilion.
CODES OF DRESS Spectators are required to dress in an appropriate manner consistent with attending a cricket match. Bare torsos are not acceptable in or in front of the pavilion.
BEHAVIOUR The club is keen that standards of behaviour should be maintained and members and spectators are urged to report immediately to the temporary KCCC office any incident, or potential incident, where they feel action should be taken. Bad language is not acceptable at any match and the club will take prompt and strong action should this or any other ground regulation be ignored.
RECIPROCAL ARRANGEMENTS Members of Essex, Hampshire and Sussex can gain entry free on production of membership card when Kent is not playing their own county.

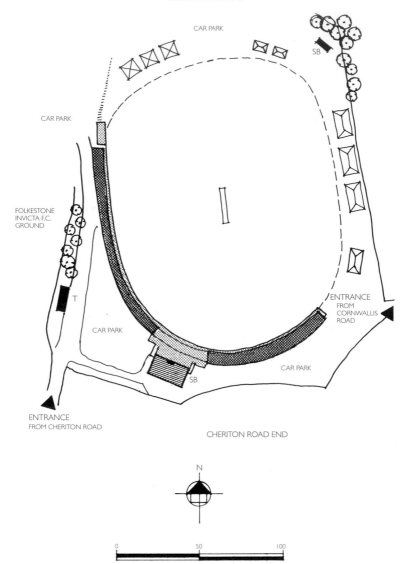

NORTH DOWNS END

CAR PARK

SB

CAR PARK

FOLKESTONE
INVICTA F.C.
GROUND

T

CAR PARK

ENTRANCE
FROM
CORNWALLIS
ROAD

CAR PARK

SB

ENTRANCE
FROM CHERITON ROAD

CHERITON ROAD END

N

0   50   100

Approximate Metres

SUPPORTERS' CLUB £10 per person per annum. Special rates for concessions and husband and wife membership are available. ☎ 01732 354067 for details.

JUNIORS Kent Kit Kat Kids membership is available to under-18s (£8 country and £15 full membership). Contact Membership & Customer Services Manager for full details.

CORPORATE ENTERTAINING Marquees are available for hire at matches with various facilities. Contact Marketing Manager for details.

FACILITIES FOR VISUALLY IMPAIRED SPECTATORS Free entry for helper. Guide dogs allowed. Please give club office advance warning as early as possible.

FACILITIES AND ACCESS FOR PEOPLE WITH DISABILITIES INCLUDING WHEELCHAIR ACCESS TO GROUND Yes, from Cheriton Road.

DESIGNATED CAR PARK AVAILABLE INSIDE THE GROUND FOR PEOPLE WITH DISABILITIES Yes, at North Downs End of the ground by the sightscreen.

GOOD VIEWING AREAS INSIDE THE GROUND FOR PEOPLE USING WHEELCHAIRS Yes, particularly on areas of hard standing to the side of the pavilion. Wheelchairs may be a problem on the West Stand as the steps are rather steep.

DESIGNATED VIEWING AREAS FOR PEOPLE USING WHEELCHAIRS Yes, at North Downs End of ground near sightscreen, request suitable position.

RAMPS TO PROVIDE EASY ACCESS TO BARS & REFRESHMENT OUTLETS FOR PEOPLE USING WHEELCHAIRS No.

FOOD & DRINK FULL RESTAURANT/DINING FACILITIES Members, no. Public, no. Sandwiches and snacks, catering provided by Morton's Fork Limited. ☎ 01227 762000.

TEMPORARY FOOD/DRINK FACILITIES Members, yes. Public, yes.

FOOD SUITABLE FOR VEGETARIANS Members, yes. Public, yes.

BARS Members 1, Public 1.

VARIETIES OF BEER SOLD Shepherd Neame.

CHILDREN'S FACILITIES None.

CLUB SHOP Yes, Kent CCC Eleventh Wicket club shop in marquee is available during Kent CCC matches.

CLUB MUSEUM No.

CRICKET COACHING FACILITIES Yes, contact Folkestone CC.

CRICKET NETS No.

OTHER SPORTING OR RECREATIONAL FACILITIES ON THE GROUND Folkestone Invicta FC ground is adjacent. The ground is also used for hockey and both Folkestone men's and ladies' clubs use the recreation area facilities during the winter months.

FACILITIES FOR HIRE OR WIDER COMMUNITY USE AT THE GROUND Rooms are available for hire. Contact Folkestone CC.

WINTER CRICKET EVENTS No.

CAR PARKING FACILITIES Car parking for members is available on the hockey ground but spectators can also watch cricket from their cars at the North Downs End of the ground. Car parking at the southern end of the ground is entered from Cheriton Road or from Cornwallis Road. Car parking is also available on Sundays at the nearby Safeway supermarket.

OTHER INFORMATION At some matches a second-hand cricket book stall is run by David Summerfield of Alfriston.

GROUND CAPACITY 8,000.

ANTICIPATED GROUND DEVELOPMENTS None planned.

HOW TO GET THERE

Folkestone Central and Folkestone West stations 0.5 mile, and Folkestone station 0.75 mile. ☎ 08457 484950, 0870 603 0405, www.connex.co.uk

From surrounding areas to bus station, thence 1 mile. Stagecoach East Kent Buses F1, F3, F6 and F9 link bus station and Folkestone Central station with ground. ☎ 01843 581333, 08702 433711, Travel Line ☎ 0870 608 2608, Kent Council Transport Information Service ☎ 0800 696996, Bus Information ☎ 01227 472082, www.stagecoachgroup.com

There are cycle routes from surrounding areas of Folkestone to this part of the town.

From north: from Canterbury, take A2050 to junction with A2, continue on A2 to junction with A260, follow A260 to Folkestone, continue on A2034 (Cheriton Road) to ground. **From south:** from A259, at Seabrook turn left on to B2063, turn right on to B2064. Follow Cheriton Road for ground. **From east:** from A20/M20 junction 13 take A20 (Cherry Garden Avenue), turn left on to A2034 (Cheriton Road), then as for north. **From west:** from M20 junction 12, take A20, then as for east.

Kent International Airport ☎ 01843 825063, Lydd Airport ☎ 01797 322411

Burlington Hotel (☎ 01303 255301), Clifton Hotel (☎ 01303 241231), Kentmere Guesthouse (☎/Fax 01303 259661), Langhorne Garden Hotel (☎ 01303 257233), Sandgate Hotel (☎ 01303 220444), Wards Hotel & Restaurant (☎ 01303 245166)
    Also visit www.smoothhound.co.uk for details of other places to stay in and around Folkestone.

WHERE TO EAT

La Terrasse (☎ 01303 220444), Wards Restaurant (☎ 01303 245166)

TOURIST INFORMATION Folkestone Tourist Information Centre ☎ 01303 258594

LOCAL RADIO STATIONS BBC Radio Kent (774 MW), Invicta FM/Capital Gold (103.1 MHz FM/1242 KHz MW)

LOCAL NEWSPAPERS *Kent Messenger, Medway Today, Folkestone & Dover People, Folkestone, Hythe & Romney Marsh Herald*

MAIDSTONE

Address The Mote Cricket Club, The Pavilion, Mote Park, Willow Way, Maidstone, Kent ME15 7RN
Prospects of Play ☎ 01622 754159 or 754545

HISTORY OF GROUND AND FACILITIES

MOTE PARK is probably one of the loveliest grounds in the south of England. It is located in Mote Park within the 558-acre Mote Estate to the east of the town centre. The estate dates back to the thirteenth century and situated within the park is Mote House, a late eighteenth-century building which is now a Cheshire Home.

Mote Cricket Club was formed in 1857 and is one of the oldest in the county. Sir Marcus Samuel, later the first Viscount Bearsted, the last private owner of the Mote Estate, was responsible for levelling the playing area in 1908 and it is now on three terraces. At that time the wicket was moved 90 degrees to its present layout.

The main pavilion was constructed in the winter of 1909/10 and is little changed. The smaller pavilion known as the Tabernacle, one of cricket's architectural curiosities, was originally Viscount Bearsted's private cricket pavilion from which he viewed matches. The Tabernacle is used as an office by Kent County Cricket Club staff during the County Festival Week. After the first Viscount's death, the second Viscount sold the estate in 1928 to its present owners, Maidstone Borough Council, but the cricket ground was reserved and presented to the Mote Cricket Club after the sale.

The first Kent County Cricket Club match staged at Mote Park was in June 1859 when an MCC team were the visitors. Kent came again in 1861 and 1862 for matches with Surrey and Cambridgeshire, but it was not until 1870 that the county club began to play regularly at Maidstone. A cricket festival week was granted in 1907 and has been a permanent feature since 1910. Since the introduction of four-day championship cricket one championship match and one limited-overs match have been played here. Matches with touring sides have occasionally been staged at Mote Park rather than at Canterbury, the county club headquarters, and these have included fixtures with the Australians in 1890, Philadelphians in 1897 and South Africans in 1912.

Mote Cricket Club play in the Forester Kent Cricket League and field four XIs on a Saturday and three XIs on a Sunday throughout the summer. The club also have one mid-week team and a Colts section.

The ground is on three levels and the cricket pitch is a flat, circular area. The playing area is 136 metres by 135 metres and is defined by a rope and some advertising boards. The pavilion, which is one of the most attractive at a county out-ground, is situated on the west side of the ground together with the Mote Squash Club and permanent raised seating. There is also a members' enclosure between the pavilion and the Tabernacle. Close to the Tabernacle is a small area for sponsors' tents and a small secondary scoreboard is located under the trees.

The TV camera position and commentary box are situated directly above and behind the sightscreen at the southern end. The radio commentary box is within the pavilion area. The scorers' box is in the roof of the pavilion and the press box is situated on the first floor of the pavilion. The ground capacity is 8,000 and seating is provided for roughly 85% of that number.

Ground performances have included double centuries from Percy Chapman against Lancashire and from Graeme Fowler for Lancashire. 'Tich' Freeman, David Halfyard and Derek Underwood have all enjoyed fine bowling spells here for the home county. Maidstone is also the home of Lashings Cricket Club.

Pavilion and squash club at Mote Park.

GROUND RECORDS AND SCORES

FIRST-CLASS MATCHES

Highest innings total for county 580 for 6 dec v Essex 1947
Highest innings total against county 546 for 9 dec by Derbyshire 1995
Lowest innings total for county 38 v Lancashire 1881
Lowest innings total against county 31 by Hampshire 1967
Highest individual innings for county 260 A.P.F. Chapman v Lancashire 1927
Highest individual innings against county 226 G. Fowler for Lancashire 1984
Highest wicket partnerships for county

1st	251 L.J. Todd & A.E. Fagg	v	Leicestershire	1949
2nd	273 L.J. Todd & L.E.G. Ames	v	Essex	1947
3rd	268 M.R. Benson & G.R. Cowdrey	v	Essex	1990
4th	368 P.A. de Silva & G.R. Cowdrey	v	Derbyshire	1995
5th	241 M.H. Denness & M.C. Cowdrey	v	Somerset	1973
6th	284 A.P.F. Chapman & G.B. Legge	v	Lancashire	1927
7th	151* A.L. Dixon & D.G. Ufton	v	Gloucestershire	1960
8th	124 H.P. Dinwiddy & A.E. Watt	v	Leicestershire	1933
9th	107 M.W. Fleming & M.M. Patel	v	Yorkshire	1994
10th	103 J. Seymour & A. Fielder	v	Worcestershire	1904

Highest wicket partnerships against county

1st	236 A.J. Wright & I.P. Butcher	for	Gloucestershire	1989
2nd	282 D. Brookes & L. Livingston	for	Northamptonshire	1954
3rd	168 M.A. Atherton & T.E. Jesty	for	Lancashire	1990
4th	224 C.J. Adams & C.M. Wells	for	Derbyshire	1995
5th	156 J.R. Reid & B. Sinclair	for	New Zealanders	1965
6th	206* J.S. Pressdee & A. Rees	for	Glamorgan	1964
7th	250 H.E. Dollery & J.S. Ord	for	Warwickshire	1953
8th	122 T.N. Pearce & T.P.B. Smith	for	Essex	1947
9th	87 A.J.H. Luard & F.G. Roberts	for	Gloucestershire	1893
10th	62 R.W.V. Robins & L.H. Gray	for	Middlesex	1938

Best bowling performance in an innings for county 10 for 131 A.P. Freeman v Lancashire 1929
Best bowling performance in an innings against county 9 for 108 T.P.B. Smith for Essex 1948
Best bowling performance in a match for county 15 for 117 D.J. Halfyard v Worcestershire 1959
Best bowling performance in a match against county 15 for 123 F.G. Roberts for Gloucestershire 1897
Largest crowd 8,000 v Essex 1948

LIMITED-OVERS MATCHES

Highest innings total for county 338 for 6 v Somerset (B&H) 1996
Highest innings total against county 297 for 7 for Kent (SL) 2000
Lowest innings total for county 86 v Somerset (SL) 1978
Lowest innings total against county 65 by Warwickshire (SL) 1979
Highest individual innings for county 112 M.A. Ealham v Derbyshire (SL) 1995
Highest individual innings against county 121 G.D. Mendis for Sussex (SL) 1982
Highest wicket partnerships for county

1st	133 B.W. Luckhurst & G.W. Johnson	v	Leicestershire	(SL)	1974
2nd	147 M.R. Benson & N.R. Taylor	v	Glamorgan	(SL)	1991
3rd	150 Asif Iqbal & M.H. Denness	v	Gloucestershire	(SL)	1976
4th	91 Asif Iqbal & A.G.E. Ealham	v	Sussex	(SL)	1977
5th	112 C.J. Tavare & J.N. Shepherd	v	Lancashire	(SL)	1979
6th	90 A.P.E. Knott & G.W. Johnson	v	Somerset	(SL)	1982
7th	84* C.J. Tavare & G.W. Johnson	v	Northamptonshire	(SL)	1985
8th	61 S.C. Goldsmith & C. Penn	v	Hampshire	(SL)	1987
9th	31 R.M. Ellison & R.P. Davis	v	Lancashire	(SL)	1990
10th	33 C. Penn & K.B.S. Jarvis	v	Sussex	(SL)	1992

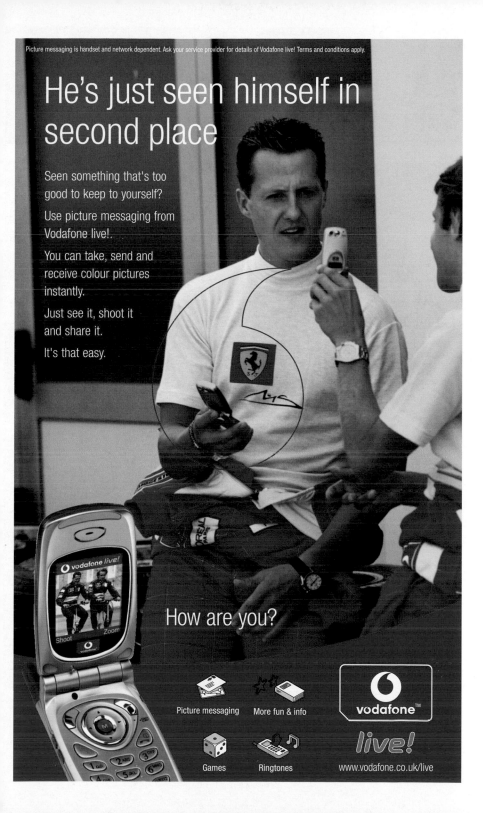

are you npowered?

npower Test Matches 2003

(Test Match: 5-day International)

ECB

England v Zimbabwe

Thu 22 - Mon 26 May	1st Test	England v Zimbabwe	Lord's	4
Thu 5 - Mon 9 June	2nd Test	England v Zimbabwe	Durham	SKY

England v South Africa

Thu 24 - Mon 28 July	1st Test	England v South Africa	Edgbaston	4
Thu 31 July - Mon 4 Aug	2nd Test	England v South Africa	Lord's	4
Thu 14 - Mon 18 Aug	3rd Test	England v South Africa	Trent Bridge	4
Thu 21 - Mon 25 Aug	4th Test	England v South Africa	Headingley	4
Thu 4 - Mon 8 September	5th Test	England v South Africa	AMP Oval	4

4 Televised by Channel 4.   **SKY** Televised by Sky Sports

npower Women's Test Series

(Test Match: 3-day International)

England Women v South Africa Women

7-10 Aug	1st Test	England v South Africa	Shenley Cricket Ground, Herts
20-23 Aug	2nd Test	England v South Africa	Taunton

ENGLAND AND WALES CRICKET BOARD
Developing cricket from playground to Test arena

www.ecb.co.uk

How to Buy a Ticket

ECB

International Matches

npower Test Matches: Five day international match. White clothing.

The NatWest Challenge: One day international match, 50 overs each side. Three match series (one match under lights). Coloured clothing.

The NatWest Series: One day international match, 50 overs each side. 10 match series (two matches under lights). Coloured clothing.

ECB International Ticketline 08705 33 88 33

County Matches

To buy match tickets to any of the following ECB competitions, please call the grounds directly. Telephone numbers are listed below.

Frizzell County Championship: Four day county competition. Two divisions of nine counties. White clothing.

Cheltenham & Gloucester Trophy (C&G Trophy): One day knockout domestic competition. 50 overs each side. Includes 18 first class counties, qualifying county boards, 20 minor counties, Holland, Denmark, Ireland and Scotland. White Clothing.

National Cricket League (NCL): One day county competition, 45 overs each side. Two divisions of nine counties plus Scotland. A number of matches are played under lights. Coloured Clothing.

Twenty20 Cup: Two hours forty-five minutes, 20 overs a side county competition. Three regions of six counties. Culminates in two semi-finals and a final on the same day. Coloured clothing.

County Ticketline Contacts

Derbyshire	01332 383211	Middlesex (via MCC)	020 7432 1066
Durham	0191 387 5151	Northamptonshire	01604 514455
Essex	01245 254 030	Nottinghamshire	0870 168 8888
Glamorgan	029 2040 9380	Scotland	0131 313 7423
Gloucestershire	0117 910 8010	Somerset	01823 272946
Hampshire	023 8047 2002	Surrey	020 7582 7764
Kent	01227 456886 (ext.232)	Sussex	01273 827100
Lancashire	0161 282 4040	Warwickshire	0121 446 5506
Leicestershire	0116 283 2128	Worcestershire	01905 748 474
		Yorkshire	0113 278 7394

ENGLAND AND WALES CRICKET BOARD
Developing cricket from playground to Test arena

www.ecb.co.uk

The NatWest Challenge & The NatWest Series 2003

(50 overs each side, coloured clothing)

ECB

The NatWest Challenge	Tue 17 June	**England v Pakistan**	Old Trafford ◐	SKY
	Fri 20 June	**England v Pakistan**	AMP Oval	SKY
⚡NatWest	Sun 22 June	**England v Pakistan**	Lord's	SKY

The NatWest Series	Thu 26 June	**England v Zimbabwe**	Trent Bridge	SKY
	Sat 28 June	**England v South Africa**	AMP Oval	SKY
⚡NatWest	Sun 29 June	**Zimbabwe v South Africa**	Canterbury	SKY
	Tue 1 July	**England v Zimbabwe**	Headingley	SKY
	Thu 3 July	**England v South Africa**	Old Trafford ◐	SKY
	Sat 5 July	**Zimbabwe v South Africa**	Cardiff	SKY
	Sun 6 July	**England v Zimbabwe**	Bristol	SKY
	Tue 8 July	**England v South Africa**	Edgbaston ◐	SKY
	Thu 10 July	**Zimbabwe v South Africa**	Rose Bowl	SKY
	Sat 12 July	**Final**	Lord's	SKY

SKY Televised by Sky Sports ◐ Floodlit match

The NatWest Women's Series

(50 overs per side:1-day International)

England Women v South Africa Women

13 Aug	1st ODI	**England v South Africa**	Chelmsford
16 Aug	2nd ODI	**England v South Africa**	Bristol
17 Aug	3rd ODI	**England v South Africa**	Cardiff

ENGLAND AND WALES CRICKET BOARD
Developing cricket from playground to Test arena

www.ecb.co.uk

Frizzell County Championship 2003

(4-day matches)

ECB

FRIZZELL County Championship	Essex	Kent	Lancs	Leic	Middx	Notts	Surrey	Sussex	Warks
HOME TEAMS								**FIRST DIVISION**	
Essex	•	27/6	2/7	23/7	18/4	3/9	21/5	20/8	11/9
Kent	30/7	•	30/5	23/4	14/5	9/7	4/9	4/6	17/9
Lancashire	14/5	15/7	•	4/6	21/8	23/4	26/8	10/9	23/7
Leicestershire	30/4	10/9	30/7	•	21/5	27/6	21/8	15/7	2/7
Middlesex	4/6	13/8	9/5	9/7	•	10/9	27/6	23/4	15/7
Nottinghamshire	30/5	20/8	17/9	26/8	30/7	•	9/5	25/7	18/4
Surrey	17/9	2/7	18/4	14/5	23/7	13/8	•	30/5	30/4
Sussex	9/7	30/4	14/8	17/9	5/9	21/5	30/7	•	27/6
Warwickshire	23/4	21/5	3/9	14/8	26/8	4/6	9/7	9/5	•

	Derbys	Durham	Glam	Glouc	Hants	North	Somer	Worc	Yorks
HOME TEAMS								**SECOND DIVISION**	
Derbyshire	•	24/7	18/4	9/7	17/9	20/8	30/4	30/5	2/7
Durham	21/5	•	17/9	30/4	20/8	9/7	30/7	14/5	15/7
Glamorgan	4/6	13/8	•	9/5	23/4	10/9	9/7	27/6	25/8
Gloucestershire	3/9	10/9	19/8	•	14/5	4/6	18/4	23/7	30/7
Hampshire	13/8	4/6	15/7	27/6	•	31/7	21/5	3/9	30/4
N'thamptonshire	27/6	3/9	30/5	23/4	2/7	•	23/7	17/9	14/5
Somerset	10/9	23/4	14/5	2/7	26/8	14/8	•	4/6	27/6
Worcestershire	15/7	2/7	31/7	21/5	18/4	30/4	20/8	•	12/9
Yorkshire	9/5	30/5	21/5	17/9	23/7	18/4	3/9	13/8	•

(4-day matches commencing from indicated date).

Frizzell Women's County Championship

Sat 26 July - Wed 30 July   University Grounds, Cambridge

ENGLAND AND WALES CRICKET BOARD
Developing cricket from playground to Test arena

www.ecb.co.uk

ECB National Cricket League 2003

(1-day matches, 45 overs per side)

ECB

ECB NATIONAL CRICKET LEAGUE

HOME TEAMS	Essex	Glam	Glouc	Kent	Leic	Surrey	Warks	Worc	Yorks
FIRST DIVISION									
Essex	•	5/8	17/7	10/5	27/7	27/4	15/6	28/8	10/9
Glamorgan	13/7	•	18/5	5/5	2/9	14/9	10/8	8/6	24/8
Gloucestershire	7/9	27/7	•	27/8	5/5	25/5	8/6	27/4	3/8
Kent	3/8	6/7	15/6	•	27/4	3/9	21/9	11/8	8/6
Leicestershire	10/8	4/5	1/6	14/9	•	20/8	3/8	13/7	18/5
Surrey	8/6	17/8	5/8	18/5	21/9	•	4/5	27/7	6/7
Warwickshire	18/5	22/6	31/8	24/8	13/8	13/7	•	9/9	27/4
Worcestershire	21/9	29/7	24/8	25/5	15/6	5/5	6/7	•	7/9
Yorkshire	5/5	25/5	21/9	27/7	22/6	31/8	6/8	17/8	•

HOME TEAMS	Derbys	Durham	Hants	Lancs	Middx	North	Notts	Scot	Somer	Sussex
SECOND DIVISION										
Derbyshire	•	31/8	21/9	15/6	3/8	24/8	23/7	7/9	4/5	10/8
Durham	25/5	•	24/8	5/5	21/9	13/7	5/8	4/5	3/8	26/8
Hampshire	17/8	8/6	•	7/9	5/5	30/7	13/7	4/8	25/5	4/5
Lancashire	4/8	22/6	18/5	•	19/8	27/4	8/6	25/5	28/7	14/9
Middlesex	27/4	10/8	14/9	6/7	•	25/5	17/8	17/6	13/7	8/6
N'thamptonshire	18/5	7/9	6/7	21/9	27/7	•	4/5	6/8	12/8	15/6
Nottinghamshire	5/5	15/6	21/7	3/8	22/6	31/8	•	14/9	7/9	24/8
Scotland	20/5	7/7	1/6	9/7	19/5	26/8	6/7	•	9/5	28/8
Somerset	14/9	27/4	10/8	1/9	5/8	8/6	18/5	15/6	•	6/7
Sussex	13/7	22/7	5/8	13/8	3/9	5/5	25/5	3/8	21/9	•

☾ Floodlit match. **SKY** Sky Sports televised matches shown in yellow. Visit **www.ecb.co.uk** for full fixtures list.

ECB Women's Super Fours

Sat 17 May	The Braves v Super Strikers	The V Team v Knight Riders	Venue tbc
Sun 25 May	The Braves v Knight Riders	Super Strikers v The V Team	Taunton
Mon 26 May	Super Strikers v Knight Riders	The Braves v The V Team	Taunton
Sun 1 June	Super Strikers v Knight Riders	The Braves v The V Team	Reading CC
Sat 14 June	The Braves v Knight Riders	Super Strikers v The V Team	Venue tbc
Sun 15 June	The V Team v Knight Riders	The Braves v Super Strikers	Venue tbc

ENGLAND AND WALES CRICKET BOARD
Developing cricket from playground to Test arena
www.ecb.co.uk

Highest wicket partnerships against county

1st	139* W. Larkins & R.J. Bailey	for	Northamptonshire	(SL)	1985
2nd	172 D. Byas & D.S. Lehmann	for	Yorkshire	(SL)	1998
3rd	90 D.L. Amiss & J.A. Jameson	for	Warwickshire	(SL)	1969
4th	91* C.L. Smith & K.D. James	for	Hampshire	(SL)	1987
5th	157 A. Singh & G. Welch	for	Warwickshire	(SL)	1999
6th	80 A.P. Grayson & P.J. Hartley	for	Yorkshire	(SL)	1994
7th	55 C.J. Adams & C.M. Wells	for	Derbyshire	(SL)	1995
8th	44* K.A. Parsons & G.D. Rose	for	Somerset	(SL)	2000
9th	31 G.D. Clough & G.J. Smith	for	Nottinghamshire	(SL)	2001
10th	48* A.N. Hayhurst & K.J. Shine	for	Somerset	(B&H)	1996

Best bowling performance in a match for county 5 for 19 D.L. Underwood v Gloucestershire (SL) 1972
Best bowling performance in a match against county 4 for 23 A.W. Greig for Sussex (SL) 1977
Largest crowd 14,000 v Leicestershire (SL) 1974

GROUND INFORMATION

ENTRANCES Willow Way (players, officials, members, public and vehicles), Mote Avenue (members, public and vehicles).

MEMBERS' ENCLOSURE Pavilion, Mote Squash Club and defined members' enclosure between raised temporary stand next to the Squash Club building and the Tabernacle.

PUBLIC ENCLOSURE Rest of the ground.

COVERED STANDS Pavilion (part).

OPEN STANDS Pavilion (part) together with permanent and temporary raised seating at bank level and ground-level seating surrounding the playing area.

NAME OF ENDS Top End, Lower End.

GROUND DIMENSIONS 136m × 135m.

REPLAY SCREEN If matches are televised the replay screen is sited at the Top End of the ground.

FIRST AID In the pavilion.

CODES OF DRESS Spectators are required to dress in an appropriate manner consistent with attending a cricket match. Bare torsos are not acceptable in, or in front of the pavilion.

BEHAVIOUR The club is keen that standards of behaviour should be maintained and members and spectators are urged to report immediately to the temporary Kent CCC office any incident, or potential incident, where they feel action should be taken. Bad language is not acceptable at any match and the club will take prompt and strong action should this or any other ground regulation be ignored.

RECIPROCAL ARRANGEMENTS Members of Essex, Hampshire and Sussex can gain entry free on production of membership card when Kent is not playing their own county.

SUPPORTERS' CLUB £10 per person per annum. Special rates for concessions and husband and wife membership are available. ☎ 01732 354067 for details.

JUNIORS Kent Kit Kat Kids membership is available to under-18s (£8 country), (£15 full membership). Contact Membership & Customer Services Manager for full details.

CORPORATE ENTERTAINING Marquees are available for hire at matches with various facilities. Contact Marketing Manager for details.

FACILITIES FOR VISUALLY IMPAIRED SPECTATORS Free entry for helper. Guide dogs allowed. Please give club office advance warning as early as possible.

FACILITIES AND ACCESS FOR PEOPLE WITH DISABILITIES INCLUDING WHEELCHAIR ACCESS TO GROUND Yes, from Willow Way.

DESIGNATED CAR PARK AVAILABLE INSIDE THE GROUND FOR PEOPLE WITH DISABILITIES Yes, at Top End of the ground by the sightscreen.

GOOD VIEWING AREAS INSIDE THE GROUND FOR PEOPLE USING WHEELCHAIRS Yes, particularly on areas of hard standing to the side of the pavilion. Wheelchairs may be a problem on the grassed banks around the playing area as the ground is situated in a natural bowl.

RAMPS TO PROVIDE EASY ACCESS TO BARS & REFRESHMENT OUTLETS FOR PEOPLE USING WHEELCHAIRS Yes.

FOOD & DRINK FULL RESTAURANT/DINING FACILITIES Members, no. Public, no. Sandwiches and snack meals, catering provided by Morton's Fork Limited ☎ 01227 762000.

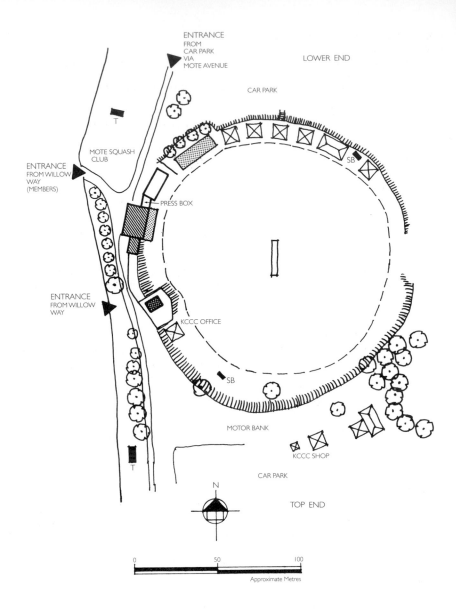

ENTRANCE
FROM
CAR PARK
VIA
MOTE AVENUE

LOWER END

CAR PARK

MOTE SQUASH
CLUB

ENTRANCE
FROM WILLOW
WAY
(MEMBERS)

SB

PRESS BOX

ENTRANCE
FROM WILLOW
WAY

KCCC OFFICE

SB

MOTOR BANK

KCCC SHOP

CAR PARK

N

TOP END

T

T

0   50   100
Approximate Metres

FOOD & DRINK FULL RESTAURANT/DINING FACILITIES Members, no. Public, no. Sandwiches and snack meals, catering provided by Morton's Fork Limited ☎ 01227 762000.
TEMPORARY FOOD/DRINK FACILITIES Members, yes. Public, yes.
FOOD SUITABLE FOR VEGETARIANS Members, yes. Public, yes.
BARS Members 1, Public 1.
VARIETIES OF BEER SOLD Shepherd Neame.
CHILDREN'S FACILITIES None.
CLUB SHOP Yes, Kent CCC Eleventh Wicket club shop in marquee at Kent CCC matches.
CLUB MUSEUM No.

CRICKET COACHING FACILITIES Yes, contact The Mote CC.

CRICKET NETS No.

OTHER SPORTING OR RECREATIONAL FACILITIES ON THE GROUND Maidstone RFC ground is adjacent at southern end of the ground.

FACILITIES FOR HIRE OR WIDER COMMUNITY USE AT THE GROUND Rooms are available for hire. Contact The Mote CC.

WINTER CRICKET EVENTS No.

CAR PARKING FACILITIES Car parking is free for members with car park passes otherwise it is £10 per car. There is car parking is at the Lower End for 1,000 cars and at the Top End of the ground for 250 cars.

OTHER INFORMATION At all matches a second-hand cricket book stall run by David Summerfield of Alfriston is located at the top of the bank.

GROUND CAPACITY 8,000.

ANTICIPATED GROUND DEVELOPMENTS None planned.

HOW TO GET THERE

 Maidstone East station 1 mile, Maidstone West station 1.25 miles ☎ 08457 484950, www.connex.co.uk

 Boro' Line 85 from High Street and Chequers Centre 0.25 mile from both rail stations. Routes 5 and 12 pass the ground. ☎ 01622 690060 or Kent Council Transport Information ☎ 0800 696996

 There are cycle routes from surrounding areas of Maidstone to this part of the town.

 From north: from M2 junction 3 turn right on to A229, continue on this road through Maidstone town centre (Upper Stone Street), turn left on to Waterloo Street, turn right on to St Philips Avenue then turn left into Lower Road, turn left at junction with Willow Way for Mote CC. **From south:** from A229 continue north towards Maidstone (Linton Hill), turn right on to Park Way, at roundabout take first exit (West Park Road), then right on to Upper Road and into Willow Way. **From east:** from M20 junction 7 take A249, continue to A20 (Andrew Broughton Way), turn right on to Square Hill Road, at roundabout turn on to Mote Avenue, turn right into Willow Way. **From west:** from M25 junction 5 take M26, at junction 2A take A20 (east) towards Maidstone and continue to Maidstone town centre, then as for north.

 Kent International Airport ☎ 01843 825063

WHERE TO STAY

Jarvis Great Danes (☎/Fax 01622 631163), King Street Hotel (☎ 01622 663266), Langley Oast (☎/Fax 01622 863523), Larkfield Hotel (☎ 01732 846858), Lime Tree Hotel (☎ 01622 859509), Ringlestone Inn & Farmhouse Hotel (☎ 01622 859900), Royal Star Hotel (☎ 01622 755721), The Woolhouse (☎ 01622 820778), Wynngarth Farmhouse (☎ 01622 812616)

Also visit www.smoothhound.co.uk for details of other places to stay in and around Maidstone.

WHERE TO EAT

Bottle House (☎ 01892 870306), Lashings Restaurant & Bar (☎ 01622 755030), Lime Tree Restaurant (☎ 01622 859509)

TOURIST INFORMATION Maidstone Tourist Information Centre, The Gatehouse, Palace Gardens, Mill Street, Maidstone, Kent. ME15 6YE ☎ 01622 602169, www.maidstone.gov.uk

LOCAL RADIO STATIONS BBC Radio Kent (774 MW), Invicta FM/Capital Gold (103.1 MHz FM/1242 KHz MW)

LOCAL NEWSPAPERS *Kent Messenger, Medway Today, Kentish Gazette, Kent and Sussex Courier, East Kent Mercury, Maidstone Borough News*

TUNBRIDGE WELLS

Address Tunbridge Wells Cricket Club, The Pavilion, Nevill Cricket Ground,
Nevill Gate, Warwick Park, Tunbridge Wells, Kent TN2 5ES
Prospects of Play ☎ 01892 520846

HISTORY OF GROUND AND FACILITIES

THE NEVILL CRICKET GROUND is the home of Tunbridge Wells Cricket Club,
established in 1762, and Blue Mantles Cricket Club, established in 1895.
Tunbridge Wells Cricket Club played at the Higher Common Ground in Fir Tree
Road between 1786 and 1884 until their move to Nevill Gate in 1895. Kent
County Cricket Club also played on the Common from 1845 to 1884. The area is
now protected by the Conservators of Tunbridge Wells Common exclusively for
cricket and hockey.

Nevill Gate Cricket Ground was acquired by the Tunbridge Wells Cricket,
Football and Athletic Club on a lease of 99 years from the Eridge Park Estate of
the Marquess of Abergavenny (family name Nevill). Work began on the ground in
1896 and since then it has been used for football, cycle racing, athletics, archery,
hockey, cricket and lawn tennis. Tennis courts border the ground on one side and
a tournament is staged annually, usually in August. The ground was opened in

Pavilion and Blue Mantles Stand.

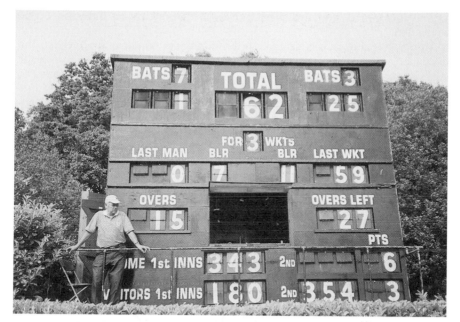

The main scoreboard at the Railway End.

1898 by the Marquess of Abergavenny and the first Kent County Cricket Club match was in 1901 when Lancashire were the visitors. The present pavilion and additional buildings were constructed in 1903 at a cost of £1,200 but in 1913 it suffered extensive fire damage during a suffragettes' campaign and was rebuilt shortly afterwards. After the First World War the ground became a picketing area for the cavalry; several hundred horses tethered over the playing area did little to improve the wicket and the outfield! The ground is now owned and maintained by Tunbridge Wells Borough Council which took control in 1946.

The Nevill Ground is probably one of the most beautiful on the county circuit especially during Tunbridge Wells's Cricket Festival, which is usually staged in early June when the giant purple blooms of the rhododendrons curving around the playing arena form a superb setting.

Tunbridge Wells Cricket Club play in the Forester Kent Cricket League and field three XIs most weekends throughout the season. The Blue Mantles Cricket Club play friendly matches throughout the season on weekdays and matches have been staged with MCC and other established clubs in the past.

In 1983 an international match was held at the ground when the Prudential World Cup fixture between India and Zimbabwe followed the traditional Kent v Sussex County Championship match during the Festival. Kapil Dev hit a super 175* in that match, the highest individual innings in the history of the competition until Vivian Richards' innings in Karachi during the 1987 Reliance World Cup. That record has since been superseded and is now held by South African Gary Kirsten who achieved 188* versus United Arab Emirates at Rawalpindi in 1996.

The Tunbridge Wells Cricket Festival now consists of one championship match and one limited-overs match. A celebrity match is also occasionally staged with county players during this week. Crowds usually reach between 3,000 and 4,000.

The main scoreboard is situated in the north-east corner of the ground. The secondary small scoreboard and scorers' rooms are situated on the roof of the main pavilion with the small press box. The playing area, which is 138 metres by 135 metres, is flat and is defined by a rope and advertising boards.

Players who have represented Tunbridge Wells Cricket Club and played first-class cricket include Mike Willard of Cambridge University, Peter Hearn and Bob Woolmer, both of Kent. Ground records at the Nevill Ground have included double hundreds from James Seymour and Wally Hammond and fine bowling from 'Tich' Freeman, V.W.C. Jupp and A.E. Lewis. Limited-overs centuries have been scored by Peter Richardson and Ken Suttle. Colin Blythe once bowled 12 overs here against Sussex and gave only one run away in an hour.

GROUND RECORDS AND SCORES

FIRST-CLASS MATCHES

Highest innings total for county 519 for 6 dec v Warwickshire 1928
Highest innings total against county 563 by Gloucestershire 1934
Lowest innings total for county 58 v Leicestershire 1938
Lowest innings total against county 25 by Worcestershire 1960
Highest individual innings for county 214 J. Seymour v Essex 1914
Highest individual innings against coun 290 W.R. Hammond for Gloucestershire 1934
Highest wicket partnerships for county

1st	243 C.J. Burnup & E.W. Dillon	v	Hampshire	1902
2nd	262 H.T.W. Hardinge & F.E. Woolley	v	Warwickshire	1928
3rd	220 F.E. Woolley & B.H. Valentine	v	Sussex	1938
4th	220 J. Seymour & D.W. Jennings	v	Essex	1914
5th	254 E. Humphreys & A.P. Day	v	Lancashire	1910
6th	233 R. Mayes & W. Murray-Wood	v	Sussex	1952
7th	194 L.E.G. Ames & T.A. Pearce	v	Northamptonshire	1932
8th	120 L.E.G. Ames & T.A. Pearce	v	Middlesex	1932
9th	161 B.R. Edrich & F. Ridgway	v	Sussex	1949
10th	77 M.A. Ealham & B.J. Trott	v	Sussex	2002

Highest wicket partnerships against county

1st	238 A. Dale & H. Morris	for	Glamorgan	1995
2nd	193 J.H. Parsons & L.T.A. Bates	for	Warwickshire	1926
3rd	294 J.M. Parks & Jas. Langridge	for	Sussex	1951
4th	285 B.C. Broad & D.W. Randall	for	Nottinghamshire	1990
5th	200 G. Cox & H.T. Bartlett	for	Sussex	1949
6th	204 P.A. Perrin & C.P. McGahey	for	Essex	1906
7th	195 W.R. Hammond & C.C.R. Dacre	for	Gloucestershire	1934
8th	183 T.E. Bailey & C. Griffiths	for	Essex	1952
9th	136* N.M. McVicker & G.D. McKenzie	for	Leicestershire	1975
10th	77 R. Appleyard & M.J. Cowan	for	Yorkshire	1957

Best bowling performance in an innings for county 8 for 38 A.P. Freeman v Northamptonshire 1932
Best bowling performance in an innings against county 10 for 127 V.W.C. Jupp for Northamptonshire 1932
Best bowling performance in a match for county 16 for 82 A.P. Freeman v Northamptonshire 1932
Best bowling performance in a match against county 14 for 141 A.E. Lewis for Somerset 1910
Largest crowd 7,000 v Sussex 1946

LIMITED-OVERS MATCHES

Highest innings total for county 242 v Sussex (GC) 1963
Highest innings total against county 314 for 7 by Sussex (GC) 1963
Lowest innings total for county 99 v Nottinghamshire (SL) 1996
Lowest innings total against county 120 by Surrey (SL) 1970
Highest individual innings for county 127 P.E. Richardson v Sussex (GC) 1963
Highest individual innings against county 104 K.G. Suttle for Sussex (GC) 1963
Highest wicket partnerships for county

1st	82 M.V. Fleming & R.W.T. Key	v	Nottinghamshire	(SL)	2002
2nd	77 M.R. Benson & C.L. Hooper	v	Sussex	(SL)	1994
3rd	147 C.L. Hooper & N.R. Taylor	v	Gloucestershire	(SL)	1993
4th	50 D.J. Cullinan & M.J. Walker	v	Somerset	(SL)	2001
5th	82 G.R. Cowdrey & N.J. Llong	v	Sussex	(SL)	1996
6th	65 N.J. Llong & M.J. Walker	v	Sussex	(SL)	1996
7th	69 M.H. Denness & R.A. Woolmer	v	Surrey	(SL)	1970
8th	49 T.R. Ward & P.A. Strang	v	Warwickshire	(SL)	1997
9th	22 A.Brown & D.L. Underwood	v	Sussex	(GC)	1963
10th	25 D.L. Underwood & J.C.J. Dye	v	Sussex	(GC)	1963

Highest wicket partnerships against county

1st	68 D.M. Smith & K. Greenfield	by	Sussex	(SL)	1994
2nd	80 T.H.C. Hancock & K.J. Barnett	by	Gloucestershire	(SL)	2000
3rd	100 K.G. Suttle & E.R. Dexter	by	Sussex	(GC)	1963
4th	90 K.G. Suttle & J.M. Parks	by	Sussex	(GC)	1963
5th	53 P.A. Cottey & A. Dale	by	Glamorgan	(SL)	1995
6th	66 N.J. Lenham & D.R. Law	by	Sussex	(SL)	1996
7th	21 D.R. Law & V.C. Drakes	by	Sussex	(SL)	1996
8th	44* G.C. Cooper & F.R. Pountain	by	Sussex	(GC)	1963
9th	44 G.D. Clough & A.J. Harris	by	Nottinghamshire	(SL)	2002
10th	6 R.C. Russell & A.M. Babington	by	Gloucestershire	(SL)	1993

Best bowling performance in a match for county 4 for 14 R.A. Woolmer v Sussex (B&H) 1972
Best bowling performance in a match against county 6 for 49 S.R. Barwick for Glamorgan (SL) 1995
Largest crowd 6,000 v Sussex (GC) 1963

ONE-DAY INTERNATIONALS

Highest innings total in ODI 266 for 8 by India v Zimbabwe (WC) 1983
Lowest innings total for in ODI 235 by Zimbabwe v India (WC) 1983
Highest individual innings in ODI 175* N. Kapil Dev for India v Zimbabwe (WC) 1983
Highest wicket partnerships in ODI

1st	44 R.D. Brown & G.A. Paterson	for	Zimbabwe v India	(WC)	1983
2nd	6 K. Srikkanth & M. Amarnath	for	India v Zimbabwe	(WC)	1983
3rd	13 R.D. Brown & A.J. Pycroft	for	Zimbabwe v India	(WC)	1983
4th	25 R.D. Brown & D.L. Houghton	for	Zimbabwe v India	(WC)	1983
5th	17 D.L. Houghton & D.A.G. Fletcher	for	Zimbabwe v India	(WC)	1983
6th	60 N. Kapil Dev & R.M.H. Binny	for	India v Zimbabwe	(WC)	1983
7th	55 K.M. Curran & I.P. Butchart	for	Zimbabwe v India	(WC)	1983
8th	62 N. Kapil Dev & S. Madan Lal	for	India v Zimbabwe	(WC)	1983
9th	126* N. Kapil Dev & S.M.H. Kirmani	for	India v Zimbabwe	(WC)	1983
10th	5 P.W.E. Rawson & A.J. Traicos	for	Zimbabwe v India	(WC)	1983

Best bowling performance in ODI 3 for 42 S. Madan Lal for India v Zimbabwe (WC) 1983
Largest crowd 6,000 India v Zimbabwe 1983 (WC)

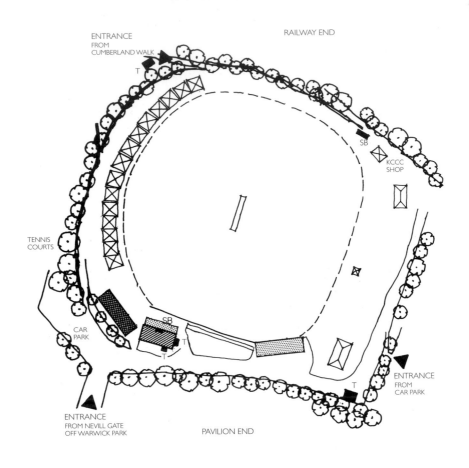

ENTRANCE
FROM
CUMBERLAND WALK

RAILWAY END

T

SB

KCCC
SHOP

TENNIS
COURTS

CAR
PARK

SB

T

T

ENTRANCE
FROM
CAR PARK

T

ENTRANCE
FROM NEVILL GATE
OFF WARWICK PARK

PAVILION END

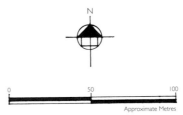

N

0   50   100

Approximate Metres

GROUND INFORMATION

ENTRANCES Nevill Gate – via Warwick Park (players, officials, members, public and vehicles), car park – via path off Warwick Park (members and public), Cumberland Walk (members and public).
MEMBERS' ENCLOSURE Pavilion together with defined members' enclosure at the Pavilion End of the ground.
PUBLIC ENCLOSURE Rest of the ground.
COVERED STANDS Pavilion (part) and Blue Mantles Stand.

OPEN STANDS Pavilion (part) together with temporary raised plastic and ground-level seating surrounding the playing area.

NAME OF ENDS Pavilion End, Railway End.

GROUND DIMENSIONS 138m × 135m.

REPLAY SCREEN If televised matches are staged at the ground the replay screen is sited the Railway End of the ground.

FIRST AID At rear of the pavilion.

CODES OF DRESS Spectators are required to dress in an appropriate manner consistent with attending a cricket match. Bare torsos are not acceptable in or in front of the pavilion.

BEHAVIOUR The club is keen that standards of behaviour should be maintained and members and spectators are urged to report immediately to the temporary Kent CCC office any incident, or potential incident, where they feel action should be taken. Bad language is not acceptable at any match and the club will take prompt and strong action should this or any other breach of the ground regulations be ignored.

RECIPROCAL ARRANGEMENTS Members of Essex, Hampshire and Sussex can gain entry free on production of membership card when Kent is not playing their own county.

SUPPORTERS' CLUB £10 per person per annum. Special rates for concessions and husband and wife membership are available. Supporters' marquee is situated to the west of the playing area. ☎ 01732 354067 for details.

JUNIORS Kent Kit Kat Kids membership is available to under-18s (£8 country), (£15 full membership). Contact Membership & Customer Services Manager for full details.

CORPORATE ENTERTAINING Marquees with various facilities are available for hire at matches. Contact Marketing Manager for details.

FACILITIES FOR VISUALLY IMPAIRED SPECTATORS Free entry for helper. Guide dogs allowed. Please give club office advance warning as early as possible.

FACILITIES AND ACCESS FOR PEOPLE WITH DISABILITIES INCLUDING WHEELCHAIR ACCESS TO GROUND Yes, from Nevill Gate.

DESIGNATED CAR PARK AVAILABLE INSIDE THE GROUND FOR PEOPLE WITH DISABILITIES Yes, at Pavilion End of the ground by the sightscreen.

GOOD VIEWING AREAS INSIDE THE GROUND FOR PEOPLE USING WHEELCHAIRS Yes, particularly on areas of hard standing to the side of the pavilion. Wheelchairs may be a problem on the grassed areas around the playing area if the ground is damp.

DESIGNATED VIEWING AREAS FOR PEOPLE USING WHEELCHAIRS Defined area available close to main pavilion, otherwise request suitable position.

RAMPS TO PROVIDE EASY ACCESS TO BARS & REFRESHMENT OUTLETS FOR PEOPLE USING WHEELCHAIRS Yes.

FOOD & DRINK FULL RESTAURANT/DINING FACILITIES Members, no. Public, no. Sandwiches and snack meals, catering provided by Morton's Fork Limited. ☎ 01227 762000.

TEMPORARY FOOD/DRINK FACILITIES Members, yes. Public, yes.

FOOD SUITABLE FOR VEGETARIANS Members, yes. Public, yes.

BARS Members 1, Public 1.

VARIETIES OF BEER SOLD Shepherd Neame.

CHILDREN'S FACILITIES None.

CLUB SHOP Yes, Kent CCC Eleventh Wicket club shop in marquee at Railway End near scoreboard at Kent CCC matches.

CLUB MUSEUM No.

CRICKET COACHING FACILITIES Yes, contact Tunbridge Wells CC.

CRICKET NETS Yes, contact Tunbridge Wells CC.

OTHER SPORTING OR RECREATIONAL FACILITIES ON THE GROUND Tennis, both hard and grass courts.

FACILITIES FOR HIRE OR WIDER COMMUNITY USE AT THE GROUND Rooms are available for hire. Contact Tunbridge Wells CC.

WINTER CRICKET EVENTS No.

CAR PARKING FACILITIES Car parking is available within the ground for players, officials, press/media and some members near the hard tennis courts. There is also a four-acre field available for parking adjoining the ground. Parking in the field is free for KCCC members with car park passes, otherwise the charge is £10 per car. Some parking may be available in nearby streets although when Festival Week is in progress there may be some restrictions.

OTHER INFORMATION A second-hand cricket book stall at the top of the bank to the east of the playing area is run by David Summerfield of Alfriston.
GROUND CAPACITY 5,500.
ANTICIPATED GROUND DEVELOPMENTS None planned.

HOW TO GET THERE

 Tunbridge Wells station 0.75 mile. ☎ 08457 484950, www.connex.co.uk

 From surrounding areas to Frant Road End routes 252, 254, 256, 280, 283 and 791, also via Hawkenbury End route 285 buses stop at Forest Road thence walk to ground. ☎ 01622 690060, Kent Council Transport Information ☎ 0800 696996

 There are cycle routes from surrounding areas of Tunbridge Wells to this part of the town.

 From north: from M25 junction 5 take A21, continue on A21 to junction with A26 (Quarry Hill Road), at roundabout continue on A26 (Mount Ephraim), bear left on to A267, turn left into Warwick Park and turn left into Nevill Gate. **From south:** from A267, continue on A267 towards Tunbridge Wells town centre (Frant Road), turn right into Roedean Road, bear right on to Warwick Park, turn left into Nevill Gate. **From east:** from A229 (Cranbrook) turn left on to A262, at junction with A21 bear right, continue to junction with A264, turn left towards Tunbridge Wells town centre (Pembury Road), turn left on to Halls Hole Road, continue on Halls Grove Road, turn left on to Forest Road, bear left on to Nelson Road, bear right on to Napier Road, bear left on to Forest Road, bear right into Warwick Park, turn right on to Nevill Gate. **From west:** from A264 Crawley stay on A264, turn right on to A26 (London Road), bear left on to A267, turn left on to Warwick Park and turn left into Nevill Gate.

 Lydd Airport ☎ 01797 322411

WHERE TO STAY

Calverley Hotel (☎ 01892 536801), Dare Hill Hotel & Golf Club (☎ 01580 200112), Ramada Jarvis Tunbridge Wells (☎/Fax 01892 823567), Royal Wells Inn (☎ 01892 511188), Russell Hotel (☎ 01892 544833), Spa Hotel (☎ 01892 520331), The Old Parsonage Hotel (☎/Fax 01892 750773), The Swan Hotel (☎/Fax 01892 541450)
  Also visit www.smoothhound.co.uk for details of other hotels, guesthouses and bed and breakfasts in and around Tunbridge Wells area.

WHERE TO EAT

Bottle House (☎ 01892 870306), Hotel du Vin et Bistro (☎ 01892 526455), Signor Franco (☎ 01892 549199)

TOURIST INFORMATION Tunbridge Wells Tourist Information Centre, The Old Fish Market, The Pantiles, Tunbridge Wells, Kent TN2 5TN ☎ 01892 515675

LOCAL RADIO STATIONS BBC Radio Kent (774 MW), Invicta FM/Capital Gold (103.1 MHz FM/1242 KHz MW)

LOCAL NEWSPAPERS *Kent Messenger, Medway Today, Kent and Sussex Courier*

Lancashire County
Cricket Club

Lancashire

**Old Trafford
Blackpool
Liverpool
Lytham
Southport**

LANCASHIRE COUNTY CRICKET CLUB, OLD TRAFFORD CRICKET GROUND, TALBOT ROAD, OLD TRAFFORD, MANCHESTER M16 0PX

Main Switchboard & General Enquiries	0161 282 4000
Ticket & Membership Office	0161 282 4040 **fax** 0161 873 8353
Conference & Banqueting Office	0161 282 4020 **fax** 0161 282 4030
Old Trafford Lodge	0161 874 3333 **fax** 0161 874 3399
Email	lodge@lccc.co.uk
Sales & Marketing Department	0161 282 4020 **fax** 0161 282 4030
Email	hospitality@lccc.co.uk
Cricket Development Office	0161 282 4187/4188 **fax** 0161 282 4151
The Cricket Centre	0161 282 4039/4037 **fax** 0161 282 4151
Development Association	0161 282 4053 **fax** 0161 282 5540
All other Departments fax	0161 282 4100
Email	enquiries@lccc.co.uk
Website	www.lccc.co.uk, www.lancashirecricket.net

Founded 12 January 1864
Colours red, green and blue
Crest red rose
National Cricket League Nickname Lightning
National Cricket League Colours red with blue and white trim
Patron HM The Queen
President Sir Denis Landau
Chairman J. Simmons MBE
Vice Chairman M.J. Birnie
Chief Executive Officer J. Cumbes
Cricket Manager M. Watkinson
Coach/2nd XI Captain G. Yates
Captain W.K. Hegg
Academy Director J. Stanworth
Groundsman P. Marron
Cricket Centre Manager T. Holt
Stadium Manager D. Arrowsmith
Finance Controller M. Leng-Smith
Sales & Marketing Manager G. Durbin
Catering & Lodge General Manager G. Greig

PA Announcer M. Proctor
Scorer 1st XI A. West
Scorer 2nd XI D. White
Hon Treasurer D. Hodgkiss
Hon Curator K.A. Hayhurst
Hon Librarian B. Watkins
Hon Statistician Reverend M.G. Lorimer
Club Sponsors LBM Solutions
Shirt Sponsors LBM Solutions
Official Kit Suppliers Exito
Magazine *Lancashire Spin* £1.50 (Free to members issued spring, summer and winter)
Yearbook £10
Scorecard 50p
National Cricket League Match Official Programme & Scorecard £1.80
Club Shop Lancashire Cricket Store ☎ 0161 282 4050 **fax** 0161 282 4030, www.lccc.co.uk
Frizzell County Championship Status Division 1
National Cricket League Status Division 2

ACHIEVEMENTS

County Championship Champions 1881, 1897, 1904, 1926, 1927, 1928, 1930, 1934, Joint Champions 1879, 1882, 1889, 1950
Gillette Cup Winners 1970, 1971, 1972, 1975 Finalists 1974, 1976
NatWest Trophy Winners 1990, 1996, 1998 Finalists 1986
Benson and Hedges Cup Winners 1984, 1990, 1995, 1996 Finalists 1991, 1993
John Player Sunday League Champions 1969, 1970
Refuge Assurance Sunday League Champions 1989

Norwich Union National League Champions 1998, 1999
Refuge Assurance Cup Winners 1988 Finalists 1991
Fenner Trophy Finalists 1971, 1972
Asda Trophy Winners 1983 Finalists 1982, 1985, 1987
Ward Four Counties Knockout Competition Semi-finalists 1988
Lambert & Butler Cup (TCCB 7-a-side Floodlit Competition) Winners 1981
Minor Counties Champions 1907, 1934, 1937, 1948, 1949, 1960, 1964

LANCASHIRE CRICKET BOARD

Chairman Dr T. Crook
Director A.N. Hayhurst
Secretary N. Girvin
Warburton Cricket Community Co-ordinator D. Hudson
Cricket Development Officers R. Singh, B. Denning, J. Brindle

Address Lancashire Cricket Board, Old Trafford Cricket Ground, Talbot Road, Old Trafford,
Manchester M16 OPX
☎ 0161 282 4029
Fax 0161 282 4151
Newsletter *LCB News*
Website www.lancashirecricket.co.uk

GROUNDS

Manchester (Old Trafford Cricket Ground, Talbot Road), Blackpool (Stanley Park, West Park Drive), Liverpool (Aigburth Cricket Ground, Aigburth Road), Lytham (Church Road, Lytham) and Southport (Trafalgar Road, Birkdale).

No other grounds have been used since 1969.

SECOND XI GROUNDS

In addition to the above the following grounds are used for Second XI matches:
Grappenhall CC, Broad Lane, Grappenhall ☎ 01925 263497
Middleton CC, Rochdale Road, Middleton ☎ 0161 643 3595
Nelson CC, Lower Parrock Road, Nelson ☎ 01282 614810
Northern CC, Moor Park, Great Crosby, Liverpool L23 2SX ☎ 0151 924 1594
Wigan CC, Bull Hey, Parsons Walk, Wigan WN1 1RU ☎ 01942 241581

Warwick Road End seen from the top of the Washbrook and Statham Stand during the England v Sri Lanka Test match in 2002.

OLD TRAFFORD

Address Old Trafford Cricket Ground, Talbot Road, Manchester M16 0PX
Prospects of Play ☎ 0161 282 4000 – wait for options and then press 4 on your key pad. Prospects of play will be available from two hours prior to the scheduled start, and updated if and when appropriate.

HISTORY OF GROUND AND FACILITIES

OLD TRAFFORD has been the home of cricket in Manchester since 1857 when the new ground was opened. Lancashire County Cricket Club play almost all of their matches at Old Trafford, and Test matches and one-day international fixtures are also regularly staged here.

Old Trafford is the third ground in Manchester to be used for cricket. The first was at Moss Lane, Moss Side, but it closed in 1847 and play moved to Chester Road, Stretford, where matches were staged from 1848 to 1854 by the Manchester Cricket Club. After the move to Old Trafford, the former Stretford ground became the White City Stadium which featured greyhound racing, athletics and later stock car racing.

Old Trafford is situated a short distance west of Chester Road. The first match staged here was between Manchester Cricket Club and its neighbours and arch rivals Liverpool CC. The inaugural first-class match was between England and Another England XI in 1860. Lancashire County Cricket Club was formed in 1864 and the first Lancashire match was staged with Middlesex in 1865. The first Test match was held in 1884 when England played Australia.

Main entrance.

The 18-acre ground was owned by Sir Thomas de Trafford until 1898 when Manchester Cricket Club purchased it from the de Trafford Estate for £24,082. The original pavilion had been built four years earlier in 1894. It was used as a hospital during the First World War and was bombed during the Second World War.

The ground was also used by Manchester Cricket Club, since disbanded, and the Lancashire Second XI and the Club and Ground XIs. Part of the ground at the Stretford End was sold to a DIY store and garden centre during the 1960s. The nearby government office towers are named after famous former Lancashire cricketers: Statham, MacLaren, Duckworth and Washbrook.

Most of the buildings are located on the Talbot Road side of the ground. All the seating is permanent and the majority is now of the white plastic tip-

LCCC bell on the ground floor of the pavilion near the players' entrance.

up variety. In 1982 a ground development appeal raised £200,000 and in 1984 a further £47,000 was raised from a Test Centenary Appeal. Much development took place using this money, including some executive boxes and press/commentary facilities. Other additions have included a Lancashire Cricket Museum and a members' library in the Pavilion. There are plenty of items of cricket interest in the Pavilion, which was designed by Mr T. Muirhead, the architect who designed the pavilion at The Oval. The 1984 season saw the Centenary of Test Cricket at Old Trafford and in 1989 Lancashire celebrated their 125th anniversary.

The press box is known as the Sir Neville Cardus Gallery and was opened by John Arlott OBE on the eve of the first Cornhill Test Match between England and Pakistan on 3 June 1987.

During the late 1990s further development took place including the construction of the Washbrook and Statham Stand opposite the pavilion, the demolition of the former H Stand and the construction of a new indoor cricket school.

Probably the most innovative development was the building of the Old Trafford Lodge, a 68-room travel lodge. One side of this building, which is adjacent to the field of play, doubles up as executive boxes when cricket matches and pop concerts are being staged. During the winter of 1999/2000 the club upgraded the main scoreboard at the Warwick Road End, laid some new wickets in the cricket square and improved car parking facilities. In spring 2001 the club obtained planning permission for eight permanent floodlight pylons. During the winter of 2001/2 the entire playing area was improved with a new £100,000 state-of-the-art drainage system which was installed ready for the beginning of the 2002 season.

Having first staged concerts at Old Trafford in 1992, Lancashire have been cramming in the crowds for pop idols as well as cricketers. Between 10 and 13 July 2002 the four-day 'Move' concerts sponsored by Virgin Trains were staged at Old Trafford with crowds of 15,000 attending. Artists included David Bowie, Green Day, Paul Weller and Manchester group New Order. Later in 2002 Old Trafford welcomed the Queen's Jubilee Baton Relay ahead of the opening day of the Commonwealth Games in Manchester. Following the success of earlier concerts, the Lancashire Club also arranged appearances by Manchester band Oasis on 14 and 15 September 2002 at Old Trafford; 50,000 attended each day.

Eagle-eyed cricket watchers at Old Trafford will have noticed that the clock face on the pavilion's West Turret was replaced in 2002. The Long Room in the pavilion has also been redecorated. During the winter of 2002/3 the pavilion roof was replaced and the players' dressing rooms rebuilt at a cost of around £900,000.

The current ground capacity is set at 19,512 for international matches and this is achieved regularly for Test matches, one-day internationals and important Lancashire limited-overs matches. The ground has staged all major county competitions as well as all forms of Test and one-day international cricket. The best crowd of recent years was 22,022 for the World Cup Semi-final match between Pakistan and New Zealand in 1999.

Ground performances have included scores of over 300 or more from Frank Watson and Bobby Simpson. Bowling achievements include Jim Laker's 19 Australian wickets in 1956.

The 1991 Refuge Assurance Cup Final was staged at Old Trafford with Worcestershire beating Lancashire for the second time in a major final in the same season. Old Trafford has also hosted many floodlit matches in the National Cricket League and NatWest one-day internationals series. Lancashire staged a match against Lashings Cricket Club on 18 August 2002 and Lashings won by 2 wickets using the Duckworth-Lewis method of scoring.

The playing area is flat and defined by a rope and advertising boards mounted on a white metal fence. It is 143 metres by 149 metres and is approximately circular in shape. Should poor weather end a match early or provide a lengthy break in play a visit to the Manchester United Football Club museum is recommended as it is only a short walk from the ground.

GROUND RECORDS AND SCORES

FIRST-CLASS MATCHES

Highest innings total for county 676 for 7 v Hampshire 1911
Highest innings total against county 597 by London county 1903
Lowest innings total for county 25 v Derbyshire 1871
Lowest innings total against county 24 by Sussex 1890
Highest individual innings for county 312 J.E.R. Gallian v Derbyshire 1996
Highest individual innings against county 282* A. Sandham for Surrey 1928
Highest wicket partnerships for county

1st	350* C. Washbrook & W. Place	v	Sussex	1947
2nd	371 F.B. Watson & G.E. Tyldesley	v	Surrey	1928
3rd	279 J.W.H. Makepeace & G.E. Tyldesley	v	Nottinghamshire	1926
4th	255 H. Pilling & D. Bailey	v	Kent	1969

5th	237 J.P. Crawley & W.K. Hegg	v	Northamptonshire	1995
6th	278 J. Iddon & H.R.W. Butterworth	v	Sussex	1932
7th	245 A.H. Hornby & J. Sharp	v	Leicestershire	1912
8th	158 J. Lyon & R.M. Ratcliffe	v	Warwickshire	1979
9th	138 C. Washbrook & E. Price	v	Middlesex	1946
10th	146 G. Chapple & P.J. Martin	v	Durham	1997

Highest wicket partnerships against county

1st	318 W.W. Keeton & R.T. Simpson	for	Nottinghamshire	1949
2nd	321* J.G. Wright & P.N. Kirsten	for	Derbyshire	1980
3rd	330 A.E. Dipper & W.R. Hammond	for	Gloucestershire	1925
4th	308 G.A. Davidson & W. Storer	for	Derbyshire	1896
5th	221 C.J. Burnup & T.N. Perkins	for	Kent	1900
6th	229 D.B. D'Oliveira & S.J. Rhodes	for	Worcestershire	1990
7th	159 J.C. Hubble & C.S. Hurst	for	Kent	1922
8th	198 K.M. Krikken & D.G. Cork	for	Derbyshire	1996
9th	162 W. Rhodes & S. Haigh	for	Yorkshire	1904
10th	172 A. Needham & R.D. Jackman	for	Surrey	1982

Best bowling performance in an innings for county 10 for 55 J. Briggs v Worcestershire 1900
Best bowling performance in an innings against county 10 for 79 A.P. Freeman for Kent 1931
Best bowling performance in a match for county 17 for 137 W. Brearley v Somerset 1905
Best bowling performance in a match against county 16 for 65 G. Giffen for Australians 1886
Largest crowd 78,617 v Yorkshire 1926

LIMITED-OVERS MATCHES

Highest innings total for county 372 for 5 v Gloucestershire (NWT) 1990
Highest innings total against county 314 for 5 by Worcestershire (B&H) 1980
Lowest innings total for county 76 v Somerset (SL) 1972
Lowest innings total against county 68 by Glamorgan (B&H) 1973
Highest individual innings for county 136 G. Fowler v Sussex (B&H) 1991
Highest individual innings against county 162* C.G. Greenidge for Hampshire (SL) 1983

Highest wicket partnerships for county

1st	107 M.A. Atherton & S.P. Titchard	v	Worcestershire	(NWT)	1995
2nd	250 J.E.R. Gallian & J.P. Crawley	v	Nottinghamshire	(B&H)	1995
3rd	227 D. Lloyd & F.C. Hayes	v	Minor Counties (N)	(B&H)	1973
4th	234* D. Lloyd & C.H. Lloyd	v	Gloucestershire	(GC)	1978
5th	114 C.H. Lloyd & D.P. Hughes	v	Surrey	(GC)	1977
6th	104 C.H. Lloyd & M. Watkinson	v	Worcestershire	(NWT)	1985
7th	130 D.P. Hughes & A.N. Hayhurst	v	Kent	(SL)	1987
8th	66 W.K. Hegg & G. Yates	v	Yorkshire	(B&H)	1996
9th	46 J. Dyson & P. Lever	v	Essex	(GC)	1963
10th	82 G. Chapple & P.J. Martin	v	Worcestershire	(SL)	1996

Highest Wicket Partnerships against County

1st	176 D.L. Haynes & M.A. Roseberry	for	Middlesex	(SL)	1990
2nd	191 G.M. Turner & P.A. Neale	for	Worcestershire	(B&H)	1980
3rd	175 W.J. Cronje & J.J. Whitaker	for	Leicestershire	(B&H)	1995
4th	122 A.J. Hollioake & I.J. Ward	for	Surrey	(SL)	1998
5th	99* P.W. Romaines & M.W. Alleyne	for	Gloucestershire	(SL)	1988
6th	167* M.G. Bevan & R.J. Blakey	for	Yorkshire	(B&H)	1996
7th	82* S.M. Pollock & D.R. Brown	for	Warwickshire	(B&H)	1996
8th	112 A.L. Penberthy & J.E. Emburey	for	Northamptonshire	(NWT)	1996
9th	80 S.A. Marsh & T.A. Merrick	for	Kent	(B&H)	1991
10th	45 A.T. Castell & D.W. White	for	Hampshire	(GC)	1970

Best bowling performance in a match for county 6 for 10 C.E.H. Croft v Scotland (B&H) 1982
Best bowling performance in a match against county 8 for 26 K.D. Boyce for Essex (SL) 1971
Largest crowd 33,000 v Yorkshire (SL) 1970

TEST MATCHES

Highest innings total for England 627 for 9 dec v Australia 1934
Highest innings total against England 658 for 8 dec by Australia 1964
Lowest innings total for England 71 v West Indies 1976
Lowest innings total against England 58 by India 1952
Highest individual innings for England 256 K.F. Barrington v Australia 1964
Highest individual innings against England 311 R.B. Simpson for Australia 1964
Highest wicket partnerships for England

1st	225 G.A. Gooch & M.A. Atherton	v	India	1990
2nd	134 A.E. Fagg & W.R. Hammond	v	India	1936
3rd	267 G.P. Thorpe & M.P. Vaughan	v	Pakistan	2001
4th	176 M.E. Trescothick & A.J. Stewart	v	West Indies	2000
5th	191 E.H. Hendren & M. Leyland	v	Australia	1934
6th	169 I.T. Botham & G. Miller	v	India	1982
7th	142 R.C. Russell & J.E. Emburey	v	Australia	1989
8th	168 R. Illingworth & P. Lever	v	India	1971
9th	95 G.O.B. Allen & H. Verity	v	Australia	1934
10th	60 R.A. Smith & D.E. Malcolm	v	India	1990

Highest wicket partnerships against England

1st	203 V.M. Merchant & Mushtaq Ali	for	India	1936
2nd	200 I. Barrow & G.A. Headley	for	West Indies	1933
3rd	176 D.J. Cullinan & G. Kirsten	for	South Africa	1998
4th	189 S.V. Manjrekar & M. Azharuddin	for	India	1990
5th	219 R.B. Simpson & B.C. Booth	for	Australia	1964
6th	180*S.R.Waugh & I.A. Healy	for	Australia	1993
7th	160 S.R. Tendulkar & M. Prabhakar	for	India	1990
8th	97 S.M. Patil & S. Madan Lal	for	India	1982
9th	104 R.W. Marsh & J.W. Gleeson	for	Australia	1972
10th	98 A.K. Davidson & G.D. McKenzie	for	Australia	1961

Best bowling performance in an innings for England 10 for 53 J.C. Laker v Australia 1956
Best bowling performance in an innings against England 8 for 31 F. Laver for Australia 1909
Best bowling performance in a match for England 19 for 90 J.C. Laker v Australia 1956
Best bowling performance in a match against England 11 for 157 L. Gibbs for West Indies 1963

ONE-DAY INTERNATIONALS

Highest innings total for England in ODI 295 for 8 v Pakistan (PT) 1982
Highest innings total against England in ODI 284 for 5 by New Zealand (TT) 1986
Highest innings total in non-England ODI 262 for 8 by India v New Zealand (WC) 1983
Lowest innings total for England in ODI 86 v Australia (NWS) 2001
Lowest innings total against England in ODI 45 by Canada (WC) 1979
Lowest innings total in non-England ODI 86 by Sri Lanka v West Indies (WC) 1975
Highest individual innings for England in ODI 142* C.W.J. Athey v New Zealand (TT) 1986
Highest individual innings against England in ODI 189* I.V.A. Richards for West Indies (TT) 1984
Highest individual innings in non-England ODI 114* G.M. Turner for New Zealand v India (WC) 1975
Highest wicket partnerships for England in ODI

1st	193 C.W.J. Athey & G.A. Gooch	v	New Zealand	(TT)	1986
2nd	125 D.L. Amiss & K.W.R. Fletcher	v	Australia	(PT)	1972
3rd	115 D.I. Gower & A.J. Lamb	v	India	(TT)	1986
4th	127 N.H. Fairbrother & G.A. Hick	v	Australia	(TT)	1993
5th	96* G.A. Hick & R.A. Smith	v	Pakistan	(TT)	1992
6th	41 CC Lewis & R.J. Rhodes	v	South Africa	(TT)	1994
7th	54 G. Miller & D.R. Pringle	v	Pakistan	(PT)	1982
8th	41 D.W. Randall & R.W. Taylor	v	New Zealand	(WC)	1979
9th	47 N.A. Foster & A.J. Lamb	v	West Indies	(TT)	1984
10th	17 A.R. Caddick & A.D. Mullally	v	Australia	(NWS)	2001

Highest wicket partnerships against England in ODI

1st	82 Aamir Sohail & Saeed Anwar	for	Pakistan	(TT)	1996
2nd	108 M.A. Taylor & M.E. Waugh	for	Australia	(TT)	1993
3rd	99 Aamir Sohail & Inzamum-ul-Haq	for	Pakistan	(TT)	1992
4th	121 C.L. Hooper & I.V.A. Richards	for	West Indies	(TT)	1991
5th	113 J.J. Crowe & M.D. Crowe	for	New Zealand	(TT)	1986
6th	104 N. Kapil Dev & R.J. Shastri	for	India	(TT)	1986
7th	51 R.W. Marsh & K.J. O'Keeffe	for	Australia	(PT)	1977
8th	59 E.A.E. Baptiste & I.V.A. Richards	for	West Indies	(TT)	1984
9th	19 B.P. Bracewell & B.L. Cairns	for	New Zealand	(PT)	1978
	19 U.D.U. Chandana & D.N.T. Zoysa	for	Sri Lanka	(NWS)	2002
10th	106* M.A. Holding & I.V.A. Richards	for	West Indies	(TT)	1984

Highest wicket partnerships in non-England ODI

1st	194 Saeed Anwar & W. Wasti	for	Pakistan v New Zealand	(WC)	1999
2nd	96 R.L. Dias & S.R.D.E.S. Wettimuny	for	Sri Lanka v India	(WC)	1979
3rd	43 D.B. Vengsarkar & G.R. Vishwanath	for	India v Sri Lanka	(WC)	1979
4th	94 S.P. Fleming & R.G. Twose	for	New Zeland v Pakistan	(WC)	1999
5th	60 M. Azharuddin & R.R. Singh	for	India v Pakistan	(NWS)	1999
6th	73 R.M.H. Binny & Yashpal Sharma	for	India v West Indies	(WC)	1983
7th	55 S. Abid Ali & S. Madan Lal	for	India v New Zealand	(WC)	1975
8th	30* C.L. Cairns & D.J. Nash	for	New Zealand v Pakistan	(WC)	1999
9th	60 S. Abid Ali & S. Venkataraghavan	for	India v New Zealand	(WC)	1975
10th	71 J. Garner & A.M.E. Roberts	for	West Indies v India	(WC)	1983

Best bowling performance for England in ODI 4 for 8 C.M. Old v Canada (WC) 1979
Best bowling performance against England in ODI 4 for 26 G.F. Lawson for Australia (TT) 1985
Best bowling performance in non-England ODI 5 for 14 G.D. McGrath for Australia v West Indies (WC) 1999
Largest crowd 22,002 New Zealand v Pakistan (WC) 1999

GROUND INFORMATION

ENTRANCES Warwick Road (members and public), Talbot Road via Car Park A (players, officials, media/press, members, public and vehicles), Great Stone Road (members, public and vehicles).

MEMBERS' ENCLOSURE Pavilion, Ladies' Pavilion and defined permanent enclosure in front of these two buildings.

PUBLIC ENCLOSURE Warwick Road End terraced seating enclosure A, B & C (Eddie Paynter Stand), D and E (A.N. Hornby Stand), F (Washbrook and Statham Stand Upper/Lower), terraced seating enclosure G, J and K.

COVERED STANDS Pavilion (part) and Washbrook and Statham Stand Lower (part).

OPEN STANDS Pavilion (part), Pavilion enclosure, Stands A, B and C (Eddie Paynter Stand), D and E (A.N. Hornby Strand), F (Washbrook and Statham Stand Upper), terraced seating enclosure G, J and K, Board of Control Stand and Ladies' Pavilion enclosure.

NAME OF ENDS Stretford End, Warwick Road End.

GROUND DIMENSIONS 143m × 149m.

REPLAY SCREEN If floodlit matches are televised the replay screen is sited at the Warwick Road End near the main scoreboard.

FIRST AID First Aid Room is located on the ground floor of the Executive Suite at the Stretford End of the ground.

BEHAVIOUR The Lancashire Committee is most concerned that standards of behaviour should be maintained and improved at all grounds, particularly those within Lancashire. Members and subscribers are requested to report to the Ground Authorities any incident or potential incident where they feel action should be taken. Bad language is not acceptable at any cricket match and the Lancashire Committee will take the strongest action. Dress standards are consistent with the prestige of being a member of a major county cricket club; members are required to dress in an appropriate manner. The minimum requirement for adult entry into the Members' Enclosure for members, subscribers and guests is neat casual dress.

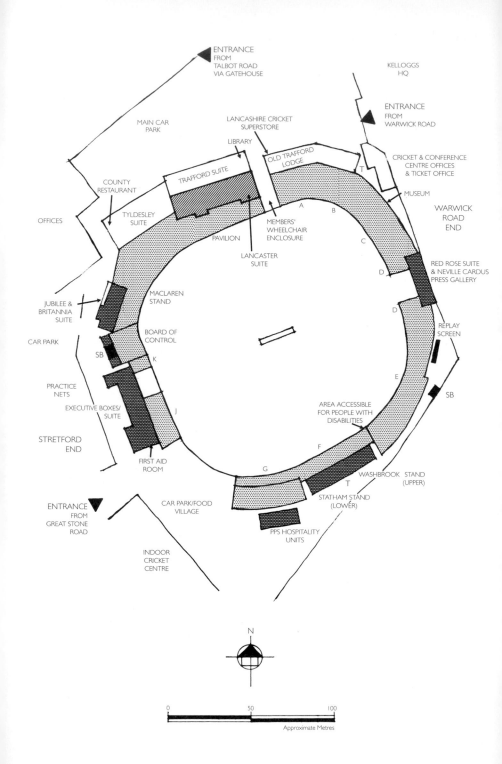

ENTRANCE
FROM
TALBOT ROAD
VIA GATEHOUSE

KELLOGGS
HQ

ENTRANCE
FROM
WARWICK ROAD

MAIN CAR
PARK

LANCASHIRE CRICKET
SUPERSTORE

LIBRARY

OLD TRAFFORD
LODGE

CRICKET & CONFERENCE
CENTRE OFFICES
& TICKET OFFICE

TRAFFORD SUITE

T

COUNTY
RESTAURANT

MUSEUM

WARWICK
ROAD
END

TYLDESLEY
SUITE

A

OFFICES

PAVILION

MEMBERS'
WHEELCHAIR
ENCLOSURE

B

C

RED ROSE SUITE
& NEVILLE CARDUS
PRESS GALLERY

LANCASTER
SUITE

D

JUBILEE &
BRITANNIA
SUITE

MACLAREN
STAND

D

REPLAY
SCREEN

CAR PARK

BOARD OF
CONTROL

SB

K

E

SB

PRACTICE
NETS

EXECUTIVE BOXES/
SUITE

J

STRETFORD
END

AREA ACCESSIBLE
FOR PEOPLE WITH
DISABILITIES

FIRST AID
ROOM

F

G

ENTRANCE
FROM
GREAT STONE
ROAD

CAR PARK/FOOD
VILLAGE

WASHBROOK   STAND
(UPPER)

T

STATHAM STAND
(LOWER)

INDOOR
CRICKET
CENTRE

PPS HOSPITALITY
UNITS

N

0   50   100
Approximate Metres

RECIPROCAL ARRANGEMENTS Lancashire County Cricket Club members have arrangements to use the facilities at the WACA Ground at Perth and vice versa.

SUPPORTERS' CLUB Unofficial travel club. No supporters' club.

JUNIORS Annual membership for Lancashire County Cricket Club Juniors who are under 18 on 1 February is £10.

CORPORATE ENTERTAINING Old Trafford has facilities for dinners, lunches, conferences, civil ceremonies and wedding receptions, exhibitions, business meetings/events, health and safety training, dinner dances and parties, property auctions, sporting dinners, Christmas, work and birthday parties and presentation evenings. The Executive suites and boxes are available for matches and on non-match days by arrangement. These include: Red Rose Suite, Lancaster Suite, Private Executive Boxes, County/Tyldesley Suite and the Indoor Cricket Centre. Contact the Conference and Banqueting Office for further information and a copy of the brochure.

FACILITIES FOR VISUALLY IMPAIRED SPECTATORS Free entry, also for helper, no guide dogs allowed.

FACILITIES AND ACCESS FOR PEOPLE WITH DISABILITIES INCLUDING WHEELCHAIR ACCESS TO GROUND Yes, through main entrance in Talbot Road. Toilet for use by disabled beneath Block A and Washbrook and Statham Stand F.

DESIGNATED CAR PARK AVAILABLE INSIDE THE GROUND FOR PEOPLE WITH DISABILITIES Yes – in either Car Park A or B entered from Talbot Road. Regretfully, due to limited space, only members with LCCC disabled parking passes are allowed to park in the disabled car parking bays in Car Park A. Club stewards will only be too happy to assist any wheelchair users upon request. It helps us to assist you if you notify the club well in advance when you will be attending the ground.

GOOD VIEWING AREAS INSIDE THE GROUND FOR PEOPLE USING WHEELCHAIRS Yes, Washbrook and Statham F Stand enclosure for wheelchairs and for members in the members' special wheelchair enclosure adjoining pavilion. Viewing facilities for wheelchair users and their families are available in front of the members' enclosure, and in front of Stand F (Washbrook and Statham Stand). Toilets for wheelchair users are situated at the rear of these viewing areas.

DESIGNATED VIEWING AREAS FOR PEOPLE USING WHEELCHAIRS Yes.

RAMPS TO PROVIDE EASY ACCESS TO BARS & REFRESHMENT OUTLETS Yes.

FOOD AND DRINK FULL RESTAURANT/DINING FACILITIES Members, yes. Public, yes. Members' Suite: (members and guests only) full bar facilities available throughout the match and for one hour after the close of play, hot and cold snacks, tea and coffee are served. Tyldesley Suite: (members and non-members) full bar facilities available throughout the match, bar snacks available at lunch time. (The suite may be closed on certain Saturdays after 2 p.m.) During major matches, a lunch and tea package will be available to members and their guests. Forms are available from the Conference & Banqueting Sales Office. Early booking is advised. Jubilee Suite: (members, subscribers and guests) full bar facilities available throughout the match with a limited range of cold snacks, tea and coffee served from 10 a.m. The County Restaurant: (members and non-members) is open from 12 noon to 3 p.m. Monday to Friday, on selected match days and before all Manchester United home matches. Table d'hôte menu and bar facilities are available. Advance booking is strongly advised at the weekends and for football matches. LCCC Members using the restaurant will be charged a special booking rate. Bookings can be made in advance by ☎ 0161 282 4020. For further information contact the Conference and Catering Office on ☎ 0161 282 4020.

TEMPORARY FOOD/DRINK FACILITIES Yes, in various outlets around the ground.

FOOD SUITABLE FOR VEGETARIANS Members, yes. Public, yes.

BARS Members 3, Public 6.

VARIETIES OF BEER SOLD Thwaites Smooth Beer.

CLUB SHOP Yes, Lancashire County Cricket Club Superstore beneath A block and at various smaller booths around the ground on Test and one-day international match days. Superstore is open Monday to Friday 9 a.m. to 5 p.m. plus match days and in December only on Saturdays 9 a.m. to 4 p.m. Visit www.lccc.co.uk to order online. A second-hand bookstall is open at Lancashire matches and is organised by Janet Haines and Mark Langwieser.

CLUB MUSEUM Yes, open on match days only with free entry. The collection traces the history of the club back to 1864. Bats used by W.G. Grace, C.B. Fry, G.L. Jessop, G.O.B. Allen and D.C.S. Compton are on view as well as the bat with which Lancashire's greatest, Archie MacLaren, achieved his 424 for Lancashire v Somerset at Taunton in 1895. Other items include letters, cups, trophies, medals, blazers, caps, photographs and a whole host of other smaller items of cricket memorabilia.

CLUB LIBRARY Collection of some 3,000 cricket books is available for members and journalists for research purposes. The library is situated in the pavilion next to the Committee Room. Some books can be loaned out only to LCCC members. Contact Mr B. Watkins, Librarian c/o Club Office, for further details and opening hours on non-match days.

CRICKET COACHING FACILITIES Yes, available in the Cricket Centre but not available on match days.

CRICKET NETS Indoor cricket nets available in Cricket Centre and some grass nets at the Stretford End of the ground within the outside practice area.

OTHER SPORTING OR RECREATIONAL FACILITIES ON THE GROUND None.

FACILITIES FOR HIRE OR WIDER COMMUNITY USE AT THE GROUND Conference, exhibition and banqueting facilities for up to 450 people available throughout the year.

WINTER CRICKET EVENTS Members' club dinners and lunches are staged in the pavilion which is also used by the Lancashire and Cheshire Cricket Society. Membership is £12 per annum which includes a £4 joining fee. For further information contact Lancashire and Cheshire Cricket Society, 114 Norwood Road, Stretford, Manchester M32 8PP. Meetings are held once twice a month between September and March annually.

CAR PARKING FACILITIES Reserved permits: there is currently a waiting list and only renewal applications can be accepted. Reserved permits admit to the main car park A for all cricket matches only. Permits for LCCC matches only: for County Championship and National Cricket League matches, parking will be available on the Practice Ground, car park B. Additional space will also be available at Trafford Town Hall for matches played on Sundays only. Permits for LCCC and International matches only: as above, but note international match parking arrangements are not usually finalised until near to the date of the matches. Disabled permits: there is currently a waiting list for these and only renewals can be accepted. Additional car parking is available at Stretford Sports Centre, B&Q Store and Manchester United FC car park for major matches. Charges range from approximately £5 to £8 per car per day. Please note that the car parks at Stretford Sports Centre, B&Q and Manchester United are not managed by LCCC.

OTHER INFORMATION Regrading of terraced seating at Warwick Road End on Stand D plus work to drainage system on the field was successfully carried out in readiness for beginning of the 2002 season.

GROUND CAPACITY 19,512.

ANTICIPATED GROUND DEVELOPMENTS None presently planned.

HOW TO GET THERE

Old Trafford (MetroLink Tram GMTR) MetroLink from Manchester Piccadilly station is adjacent to ground, ☎ 0161 228 7811, 0161 205 2000, 08457 484950, www.GMPTE.com. Virgin Trains Reservations ☎ 08457 222 333, www.virgin.com/trains or www.railtrack.co.uk

Buses 112, 113, 115 and 720 from Manchester Piccadilly to ground, also 17 and 115 to Talbot Road, 52 and 53 to Trafford Bar and 114, 252, 253, 254, 255, 256, 257, 263 and 264 to Chester Road thence walk to ground. Manchester Bus Information ☎ 0161 228 7811, Bus Information Line ☎ 0870 608 2608, National Express Coaches ☎ 0990 808080, www.gobycoach.com

There are cycle routes from central and surrounding areas of Manchester to this part of Old Trafford.

Ground is 2.5 miles south-west of the city centre on the east side of A56 in Old Trafford close to Manchester United football ground. **From north:** from M62 junction 18 take M60 (south-west), follow this to junction 12, signposted Trafford Park, exit on to M602 (Salford), at junction 3 take A5063 (Salford Quays/Trafford Park), follow signs to Old Trafford Cricket Ground towards Chorlton (White City Way), to junction with A5067 (Talbot Road). **From south:** at M6 junction 19 take A556, following signs to M56/Manchester, at end of M56 road becomes A5103, keep on this and then take M60 (south) towards Stretford, at junction 7 take A56 and follow signs to Old Trafford Cricket Ground. **From east:** from M62: at junction 18 road becomes M60 (Ring Road north), follow this to junction 12, then as for north. **From west:** from M62 (east) follow signs to Manchester, at junction 12 take M602, then as for north.

Manchester Airport Information ☎ 0161 489 3000 www.manchesterairport.co.uk, Airport Rail Link ☎ 08457 484950

WHERE TO STAY

Old Trafford Lodge (☎ 0161 874 3333 www.lccc.co.uk/lodge), Campanile Hotel (☎ 0161 833 1845 www.campanile.co.uk), Copthorne Hotel (☎ 0161 873 7321 www.millenniumhotels.com), Cresta Court Hotel (☎ 0161 927 7272 www.cresta-court.co.uk), Crowne Plaza The Midland (☎ 0161 236 3333 www.manchester-themidland.crowneplaza.com), Golden Tulip (☎ 0161 873 8899 www.goldentulipmanchester.co.uk), Jurys Inn (☎ 0161 953 8888 www.jurysdoyle.com), Le Meridien Palace (☎ 0161 288 1111 www.lemeridien.com), Le Meridien Victoria and Albert (☎ 0161 838 4130 www.lemeridien.com), Lowry Hotel (☎ 0161 827 4000 www.roccofortehotels.com), Malmaison Hotel (☎ 0161 278 1000 www.malmaison.com), Renaissance Hotel (☎ 0161 831 6000 www.renaissancehotels.com), Somerset Atrium (☎ 0870 870 9394 www.the-ascott.com), Travel Inn Metro (☎ 0870 238 3315 www.travelinn.co.uk)

WHERE TO EAT

Cachumba (☎ 0161 445 2479), Darbar (☎ 0161 224 4392), Didsbury Brasserie (☎ 0161 438 0064), East Chinese Restaurant (☎ 0161 236 1188), Great Kathmandu (☎ 0161 434 6413), Green's (☎ 0161 434 4259), The Greenhouse (☎ 0161 224 0730 www.thegreenhouserest.freeuk.com), Lead Station (☎ 0161 881 5559), The Lime Tree (☎ 0161 445 1217 www.thelimetree.com), The Lowry (☎ 0161 876 2121 www.thelowry.com), Metropolitan (☎ 0161 374 9559), The Nose (☎ 0161 445 3653), Palmiro (☎ 0161 860 7330 www.palmiro.net), Rhodes & Co (☎ 0161 868 1900), Shezan (☎ 0161 224 3116)

TOURIST INFORMATION Manchester Visitor Information Centre and Gift Shop, Town Hall Extension, Lloyd Street, St. Peters Square, Manchester ☎ 0161 234 3157 www.destinationmanchester.com, Manchester Online www.manchesteronline.co.uk

OTHER USEFUL INFORMATION

British Airways Reservations UK ☎ 0845 773 3377
Manchester United FC ☎ 0161 868 8000
Manchester City FC ☎ 0161 232 3000
Road Travel Airtax ☎ 0161 499 9000
Road Travel Mantax ☎ 0161 230 3333
The Lowry box office 0161 876 2000 www.thelowry.com

LOCAL RADIO STATIONS BBC Radio Greater Manchester Radio (GMR) (95.1 MHz FM/ KHz MW) Key 103/Magic 1152 (103 MHz FM/1152 KHz MW) BBC Radio Lancashire (104.5 MHz FM/1557 KHz MW)

LOCAL NEWSPAPERS *Manchester Evening News, Sunday Sports Pink*

BLACKPOOL

Address Blackpool Cricket Club, Stanley Park, West Park Drive,
Blackpool FY3 9GQ
Prospects of Play ☎ 01253 393347, or 0161 282 4000 – wait
for options, then press 4

HISTORY OF GROUND AND FACILITIES

BLACKPOOL CRICKET CLUB was founded in 1888 and plays in the Northern Cricket League. Cricket has been played in Blackpool since 1890 when there was a ground close to the Royal Palace Gardens, although the first mention of cricket on the Fylde Coast was at Rossall School and at Poulton in 1879.

Blackpool Cricket Club's present ground is rather a long walk from the seafront and most holiday residential areas. The ground at Stanley Park, formerly Whitegate Park, was donated to the club in 1924 by Sir Lindsay Parkinson who required that it should be owned by Trustees comprising one member of the Blackpool Cricket Club and either himself or another member of his family. Another condition was that the club should erect a stand for spectators; the present pavilion was built in 1925 to satisfy this condition. The ground covers an area of 5 acres and is enclosed within the park. It has a character of its own although refurbishment is long overdue. In 1957 an additional stand was built costing £6,000 as well as a scoreboard and groundsman's store.

Blackpool Cricket Club have staged late summer festivals comprising a county match followed by a match against the current touring side and then club games. The club have hosted four games against the Indian, South African and the West Indian touring sides. In 1961, when the Australians were unable to attend, a match was staged between XIs from the North and the South. The main Blackpool Cricket Festival was abandoned in 1961 and Lancashire stopped playing matches at Stanley Park in 1978. Not until ten years later did county cricket return with a Refuge Assurance Sunday League match against Middlesex. Lancashire tend to play fixtures at Stanley Park in August annually so as to attract the holiday crowds. In 2002 a County Championship fixture was played against Somerset and the Norwich Union National League match with Derbyshire was staged here on 14 July 2002. The latter was moved to Blackpool because a pop concert was being staged at Old Trafford.

The first first-class match at Blackpool was held in 1905 when the North played the South. Lancashire County Cricket Club first staged a match on the present ground in 1904 against an England XI but in order to prolong the match the Laws of cricket were not adhered to in the later stages of the game and the match was ruled not to be first-class. Many benefit matches have been staged on the ground including one for Geoffrey Boycott and Ian Botham in 1984.

Blackpool Cricket Club have a great tradition of having cricket professionals with Test match status. These have included Ted McDonald, Stewie Dempster, Harold Larwood, Bill Alley, Rohan Kanhai, Hanif Mohammad, Cammie Smith, Jim Parks (Sen), Pankaj Roy, Mushtaq Mohammad, Mahinder Singh and Jack Simmons. Bernard Reidy, who represented Lancashire and Cumberland, played regularly for the club after his first-class career ended.

Many of the permanent buildings on the ground have been dedicated to officials. These include members' seating adjoining the pavilion 'dedicated to Winnie and Fred Dawson for their lifetime work for the club', the scoreboard 'thanks to donations from Mr W.B. Corry' in 1954 and in 1979 in 'memory of past chairman Mr J. Holden – funds raised by ladies committee'.

Ground performances have included double hundreds from Mike Atherton and Peter Kirsten, the latter while playing for Derbyshire. Best bowling performances include those of Bob Berry, Tommy Mitchell, Cecil Parkin and Graeme Welch. In the limited-overs game Neil Fairbrother's 100* against Glamorgan in 1989 was achieved in 86 minutes from just 71 balls including four 6s and seven 4s.

The main scoreboard is sited to the north-east of the playing area and to the north there is a car parking area as well as the groundsman's store and some additional seating. The ground is completely enclosed by a wall and trees on all four sides. The playing area is flat, measures 131 metres by 126 metres and is defined by a rope and some advertising boards. The TV camera/commentary box is situated at the Nursery End of the ground directly above and behind the sightscreen on a gantry. Ground attendance is usually in the region of 5,500 to 6,000. Seats are provided for around 75% of these places but spectators are advised to bring their own to popular matches.

Some historic photographs of Blackpool Cricket Club can be seen in the pavilion bar and lounge area.

GROUND RECORDS AND SCORES

FIRST-CLASS MATCHES

Highest innings total for county 589 v Derbyshire 1994
Highest innings total against county 490 for 8 dec by Derbyshire 1994
Lowest innings total for county 62 v Kent 1956
Lowest innings total against county 39 by Hampshire 1967
Highest individual innings for county 268* M.A. Atherton v Glamorgan 1999
Highest individual innings against county 204* P.N. Kirsten for Derbyshire 1981
Highest wicket partnerships for county

1st	265 D. Lloyd & B. Wood	v	Sussex	1970
2nd	153 D.M. Green & H. Pilling	v	Warwickshire	1965
3rd	237 G.E. Tyldesley & J. Iddon	v	Worcestershire	1929
4th	113 D.M. Green & P.T. Marner	v	Warwickshire	1959
5th	156 J.T. Ikin & N.D. Howard	v	Glamorgan	1950
6th	178 W.K. Hegg & I.D. Austin	v	Derbyshire	1992
7th	135 K.J. Grieves & G. Clayton	v	India	1959
8th	77 I.D. Austin & G. Yates	v	Warwickshire	1997
9th	107 A. Wharton & M.J. Hilton	v	Gloucestershire	1951
10th	83 G. Yates & G. Chapple	v	Derbyshire	1994

Highest wicket partnerships against county

1st	225 T.S. Curtis & P. Bent	for	Worcestershire	1991
2nd	159 W.J. Stewart & A. Townsend	for	Warwickshire	1959
3rd	141 W.J. Stewart & M.J.K. Smith	for	Warwickshire	1959
4th	199 D.J. Insole & T.E. Bailey	for	Essex	1960
5th	152 P.N. Kirsten & K.J. Barnett	for	Derbyshire	1981
6th	113 C.G. Borde & A.G. Kripal Singh	for	Indians	1959
7th	106 M.L. Jaisimha & A.G. Kripal Singh	for	Indians	1959
8th	93 B.L. Reynolds & M.E. Scott	for	Northamptonshire	1968
9th	107 A.F. Giles & T. Frost	for	Warwickshire	1997
10th	98* R.W. Tolchard & K. Higgs	for	Leicestershire	1975

Best bowling performance in an innings for county 10 for 102 R. Berry v Worcestershire 1953
Best bowling performance in an innings against county 8 for 38 T.B. Mitchell for Derbyshire 1933
Best bowling performance in a match for county 15 for 95 C.H. Parkin v Glamorgan 1923
Best bowling performance in a match against county 11 for 140 G. Welch for Warwickshire 1997
Largest crowd 13,782 v Glamorgan 1950

LIMITED-OVERS MATCHES

Highest innings total for county 244 for 5 v Glamorgan (SL) 1989
Highest innings total against county 155 by Middlesex (SL) 1988
Lowest innings total for county 198 for 8 by Durham (SL) 2001
Lowest innings total against county 110 by Glamorgan (SL) 1989
Highest individual innings for county 100* N.H. Fairbrother v Glamorgan (SL) 1989
Highest individual innings against county 73* G.F.Shephard for Warwickshire CB (C&G) 2001

Highest wicket partnerships for county

1st	146 D. Lloyd & F.M. Engineer	v	Sussex	(SL)	1976
2nd	78 G.D. Mendis & T.E. Jesty	v	Middlesex	(SL)	1988
3rd	136 A. Flintoff & N.H. Fairbrother	v	Durham	(C&G)	2001
4th	65 G.D. Mendis & M. Watkinson	v	Middlesex	(SL)	1988
5th	43 D. Byas & R.C. Driver	v	Derbyshire	(SL)	2002
6th	50* N.H. Fairbrother & Wasim Akram	v	Glamorgan	(SL)	1989
7th	55 D. Byas & G. Yates	v	Derbyshire	(SL)	2002
8th	6 G. Yates & K.W. Hogg	v	Derbyshire	(SL)	2002
9th	23 K.W. Hogg & J. Wood	v	Derbyshire	(SL)	2002
10th	4* J. Wood & P.J. Martin	v	Derbyshire	(SL)	2002

Highest wicket partnerships against county

1st	22 N. Peng & D.R. Law	for	Durham	(C&G)	2001
2nd	26 D.R. Law & M.L. Love	for	Durham	(C&G)	2001
3rd	82 J.A. Snow & Javed Miandad	for	Sussex	(SL)	1986
4th	40 S.D. Stubbings & D.G. Cork	for	Derbyshire	(SL)	2002
5th	27 S.D. Stubbings & S.A. Selwood	for	Derbyshire	(SL)	2002
6th	41 P.D. Collingwood & M.A. Gough	for	Durham	(C&G)	2001
7th	68 J.E. Emburey & P.R. Downton	for	Middlesex	(SL)	1988
8th	34 S.A. Selwood & J.I.D. Kerr	for	Derbyshire	(SL)	2002
9th	86 G.F. Shephard & S. Platt	for	Warwickshire CB	(C&G)	2001
10th	24 S.P. Hughes & N.G. Cowans	for	Middlesex	(SL)	1988

Best bowling performance in a match for county 4 for 17 M. Watkinson v Middlesex (SL) 1988
Best bowling performance in a match against county 3 for 43 S.P. Hughes for Middlesex (SL) 1988
Largest crowd 12,000 v Sussex (SL) 1976

GROUND INFORMATION

ENTRANCES West Park Drive (players, officials, members, public and vehicles).
MEMBERS' ENCLOSURE Pavilion and defined members enclosure to the west of the playing area.
PUBLIC ENCLOSURE Rest of the ground.
COVERED STANDS Pavilion and Ladies' Pavilion.
OPEN STANDS Permanent tiered seating and temporary ground level surrounding the playing area.
NAME OF ENDS Pavilion End, Nursery End.
GROUND DIMENSIONS 131m × 126m.
REPLAY SCREEN If televised matches are staged at the ground the replay screen is sited at the Nursery End of the ground.
FIRST AID First Aid Room in the pavilion and in a tent at the Nursery End of the ground.
BEHAVIOUR The Lancashire Committee is most concerned that standards of behaviour should be maintained and improved at all grounds, particularly those within Lancashire. Members and subscribers are requested to report to the Ground Authorities any incident or potential incident where they feel action should be taken. Bad language is not acceptable at any cricket match and the Lancashire Committee will take the strongest action. Dress standards are consistent with the prestige of being a member of a major county cricket club; members are required to dress in an appropriate manner. The minimum requirement for adult entry into the Members' Enclosure for members, subscribers and guests is neat casual dress.
RECIPROCAL ARRANGEMENTS Lancashire County Cricket Club members have arrangements to use the facilities at the WACA Ground at Perth and vice versa.
SUPPORTERS' CLUB Unofficial travel club. No supporters' club.
JUNIORS Annual membership for Lancashire County Cricket Club Juniors who are under 18 on 1 February is £10.
CORPORATE ENTERTAINING Marquees are available. Contact the Conference and Banqueting Office for further information and a copy of the brochure.
FACILITIES FOR VISUALLY IMPAIRED SPECTATORS Free entry, also for helper. No guide dogs allowed.
FACILITIES AND ACCESS FOR PEOPLE WITH DISABILITIES INCLUDING WHEELCHAIR ACCESS TO GROUND Yes, through main gates off West Park Drive.

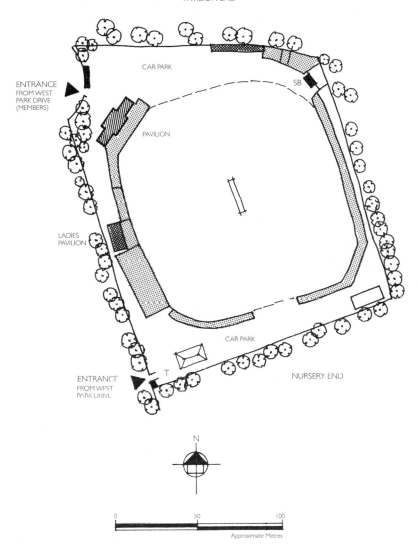

PAVILION END

CAR PARK

ENTRANCE
FROM WEST
PARK DRIVE
(MEMBERS)

SB

PAVILION

LADIES
PAVILION

CAR PARK

NURSERY END

ENTRANCE
FROM WEST
PARK DRIVE

T

N

0   50   100

Approximate Metres

DESIGNATED CAR PARK AVAILABLE INSIDE THE GROUND FOR PEOPLE WITH DISABILITIES Yes, to rear of the pavilion but contact Blackpool CC in advance.
GOOD VIEWING AREAS INSIDE THE GROUND FOR PEOPLE USING WHEELCHAIRS Yes, at Pavilion End of the ground by sightscreen.
DESIGNATED VIEWING AREAS FOR PEOPLE USING WHEELCHAIRS Yes.
RAMPS TO PROVIDE EASY ACCESS TO BARS AND REFRESHMENT OUTLETS Yes, but avoid banked area.
FOOD AND DRINK FULL RESTAURANT/DINING FACILITIES Members, yes. Public, yes. A good lunch can be obtained in the Pavilion Bar for about £5 per head. For further information contact Blackpool CC.
TEMPORARY FOOD/DRINK FACILITIES Yes, in various outlets around the ground.
FOOD SUITABLE FOR VEGETARIANS Members, yes. Public, yes.

BARS Members 1, Public 3.

VARIETIES OF BEER SOLD Thwaites Smooth Beer, Long Smartish, Boddingtons and Bass.

CLUB SHOP Lancashire County Cricket Club has a souvenir shop at matches. Visit www.lccc.co.uk to order online.

CLUB MUSEUM No, although there are pictures in the pavilion relating to Blackpool CC.

CLUB LIBRARY No.

CRICKET COACHING FACILITIES Yes, for members of Blackpool CC.

CRICKET NETS Yes, for members of Blackpool CC.

OTHER SPORTING OR RECREATIONAL FACILITIES ON THE GROUND There are facilities for putting and tennis within the park. Adjacent to ground in Stanley Park is an athletics track and rugby facilities.

FACILITIES FOR HIRE OR WIDER COMMUNITY USE AT THE GROUND Yes, ground is used for Youth and Junior cricket competitions.

WINTER CRICKET EVENTS Members' club dinners and lunches are staged in the pavilion which is also used by the Fylde Coast Cricket Society, membership of which is £10 per annum. Meetings are held once a month between September and March.

CAR PARKING FACILITIES Car parking is available within the ground on top of the bank at the Nursery End of the ground where cricket can be viewed from cars and to the rear of the pavilion for LCCC Members only with appropriate car park passes but numbers are strictly limited. When space is available for the public car parking is £3. Further car parking is available in Stanley Park at £3 per car and surrounding streets where restrictions have not been implemented because of the cricket.

OTHER INFORMATION Look out for a book written by local sportswriter Gerry Wolstenholme titled from *Peak to Pool* documenting matches between Lancashire and Derbyshire.

GROUND CAPACITY 6,000.

ANTICIPATED GROUND DEVELOPMENTS None presently planned.

HOW TO GET THERE

Blackpool North station 1 mile, Blackpool South station 0.75 mile. ☎ 08457 484950, Virgin Trains Rail Ticket Reservations ☎ 08457 222333, www.virgin.com/trains, www.railtrack.co.uk

Blackpool Transport 16 and 26 from Talbot Square adjacent to Blackpool North station to within 0.25 mile of ground, 21 and 44b from Abingdon Street to Stanley Park. ☎ 01253 473000, National Express Coaches ☎ 0990 808080, www.gobycoach.com

There are cycle routes from central Blackpool, the seafront and other parts of the town.

The ground is 1 mile inland from the coast and Stanley Park is well signposted. From M6 junction 32 take M55 (west), at junction 4 take A583 for North Shore (Preston New Road), turn right on to Gorse Road, turn left on to West Park Drive.

Blackpool Airport ☎ 01253 343434

WHERE TO STAY

Elgin Hotel (☎ 01253 351433 www.elginhotel.com), Hotel Sheraton (☎ 01253 352723 Freephone 0800 317295 www.hotelsheraton.co.uk), Liberty's Hotel (☎ 01253 291155 www.libertyshotel.com), Palm Beach Hotel (☎ 01253 400328 www.palmbeachhotel.co.uk), Queens Hotel (☎ 01253 342015 www.thequeenshotelblackpool.co.uk) , The Claremont Hotel (☎ 0845 458 4222 www.choice-hotels.co.uk), The Cliffs Hotel (☎ 0845 458 4222 www.choice-hotels.co.uk), The Royal York Hotel (☎ 01253 752424 www.royalyorkblackpool.co.uk), The Savoy and Clifton Hotels (☎ 01253 621481 www.savoyhotelblackpool.com), The Viking Hotel (☎ 0845 458 4222 www.choice-hotels.co.uk)

For a further selection of small hotels and guest houses in Blackpool contact Blackpool Hotel and Guest House Association Limited, 87a Coronation Street, Blackpool, Lancashire FY1 4PD ☎ 01253 621891, www.blackpool-stay.co.uk or www.smoothhound.co.uk.

September Brasserie (☎ 01253 623282)
There are numerous other eateries on the seafront catering for all tastes.

TOURIST INFORMATION Blackpool Tourist Information Centre, 1 Clifton Street, Blackpool, Lancashire FY1 1LY
☎ 01253 478222, www.blackpooltourism.com. Blackpool Guide Information ☎ 0870 444 5566 or
0870 444 5588

OTHER USEFUL INFORMATION

Blackpool Tower ☎ 01253 622242, www.blackpooltower.co.uk
Blackpool Zoo ☎ 01253 830830,
Blackpool Football Club ☎ 01253 405331, www.blackpoolfc.co.uk
Blackpool Pleasure Beach ☎ 0870 444 5566, www.blackpoolpleasurebeach.co.uk
Blackpool Sea Life Centre ☎ 01253 622445
Blackpool Sandcastle ☎ 01253 343602
Blackpool Show Booking Line ☎ 01253 292029
Blackpool Model Village ☎ 01253 763827
Grundy Art Gallery ☎ 01253 478170
Tussaud's Waxworks ☎ 01253 625953
Three Piers ☎ 01253 292029
Winter Gardens ☎ 01253 292029

LOCAL RADIO STATIONS BBC Radio Lancashire (104.5 MHz FM/1557 KHz MW), Red Rose Radio (97.3 MHz
FM/999 KHz MW)

LOCAL NEWSPAPERS *The Blackpool Gazette, Lancashire Evening Post, Lancashire Evening Telegraph, West
Lancashire Gazette*

LIVERPOOL

Address Liverpool Cricket Club, The Pavilion, Aigburth Road,
Grassendale, Liverpool L19 3QF
Prospects of Play ☎ 0151 427 2930, 0161 282 4000 –
wait for options, press 4

HISTORY OF GROUND AND FACILITIES

AIGBURTH CRICKET GROUND is barely 5 miles from the Liver Building and has
been the home of the Liverpool Cricket Club since 1881.

The club was founded in 1807, the year the Mosslake Cricket Society was
formed. Before that, cricket had been played at the Mersey Bowmen's Archery
Ground. Today's Liverpool Cricket Club emerged from the Mosslake Society and
moved to Wavertree Road in the Edge Hill district of the city in 1829. This ground
staged games between 1859 and 1872 including important and first-class
matches between the Gentlemen of the North and Gentlemen of the South from
11–13 August 1859 – the Gentlemen of the South won by 85 runs. Another
match between the North and the South was played from 27–29 August 1863 –
the North won by 84 runs. On 23, 24 and 25 August 1866 Lancashire staged the
first first-class match at Wavertree Road when Surrey were the visitors, Surrey

winning by 3 wickets. In 1872 a first-class match between North and South was staged, the South winning by an innings and 20 runs.

Liverpool Cricket Club moved three more times and by 1877 was without a ground. The Earl of Sefton rescued the club with an offer of a temporary ground at Croxteth Park. Liverpool CC then moved to Aigburth in 1881.

The ground is located on the corner of Aigburth Road and Riversdale Road which leads down towards the River Mersey. The pavilion was constructed in 1880 by the building contractor Cubitts. It is located at the Aigburth Road End and is rather grand for an out ground. When it was built Liverpool was a thriving port and club members were generous in their support.

The first Lancashire County Cricket Club match was staged here in 1881 when Cambridge University were the visitors. Since then first-class matches have been staged regularly. In 2002 Kent played out a splendid championship match winning on the last day by 6 wickets having been set a target of 360. Aigburth tends to be used for one County Championship fixture a year although it occasionally misses out in favour of Blackpool, Lytham or Southport. Liverpool. is the county's oldest home venue for matches outside of Old Trafford.

Lancashire have occasionally played one or two limited-overs matches at Aigburth in the early part of the season. These have included one-day matches with the touring sides and Benson and Hedges zonal matches. In 2001 Lancashire played three Benson and Hedges Cup matches at Aigburth during the early part of the season and in 2002 West Indies 'A' visited.

Many famous players have represented Liverpool and Lancashire including A.G. Steel, D.Q. Steel, E.C. Hornby, R.E. Barlow and J. White. Many tour matches have been staged at Aigburth since the 1882 Australians visited the ground. Other tourists have been the South Africans, West Indians, Canadians, Philadelphians, The Germantown Cricket Club from Philadelphia who played against the Gentlemen of Liverpool, and the Parsees.

Liverpool Cricket Club were among the founder members of the Youngers Liverpool and District Competition and field four XIs throughout the season. The club now plays in the Chelmere Homes Liverpool and District Competition.

During Lancashire's long association with Liverpool Cricket Club there have been many memorable performances on the Aigburth ground. In 1903 J.T. Tyldesley scored 248 and 29 years later Wally Hammond scored 264 for Gloucestershire – still the highest individual innings at Aigburth.

The extensive Liverpool Cricket Club pavilion would be a credit to any county ground and provides first-class facilities for players and members. The Pavilion balcony, high above the playing area and directly behind the sightscreen at the Pavilion End, is used as the radio commentary box and TV camera/commentary box.

The main scoreboard is situated in the south corner of the ground and to the north-west is the covered stand with seats, groundsman's stores, toilets, bar and refreshment facilities. There is a small press box at ground level within this stand. The official scorers sit nearby on this side, below the level of the playing area, which makes it difficult for them to view the play. The flat playing area is 142 metres by 138 metres and is defined by a rope and advertising boards. Around 4,000 seats are provided; the ground capacity is 5,000.

GROUND RECORDS AND SCORES

FIRST-CLASS MATCHES

Highest innings total for county 502 for 9 dec v Leicestershire 1929
Highest innings total against county 514 by Gloucestershire 1932
Lowest innings total for county 28 v Australians 1896
Lowest innings total against county 22 by Glamorgan 1924
Highest individual innings for county 248 J.T. Tyldesley v Worcestershire 1903
Highest individual innings against county 264 W.R. Hammond for Gloucestershire 1932
Highest wicket partnerships for county

1st	368 A.C. MacLaren & R.H. Spooner	v	Gloucestershire	1903
2nd	290 B. Wood & H. Pilling	v	Glamorgan	1976
3rd	184 F.C. Hayes & D. Lloyd	v	Nottinghamshire	1981
4th	242 J.T. Tyldesley & A.H. Hornby	v	Worcestershire	1903
5th	175 N.D. Howard & J.T. Ikin	v	Northamptonshire	1948
6th	198 J. Iddon & G. Duckworth	v	Leicestershire	1929
7th	103 J. Hallows & J. Sharp	v	Hampshire	1901
8th	121 L.O.S. Poidevin & W.R. Cuttell	v	Somerset	1906
9th	109 G. Chapple & P.J. Martin	v	Kent	2002
10th	173 J. Briggs & R. Pilling	v	Surrey	1885

Highest wicket partnerships against county

1st	200 K.J. Barnett & P.D. Bowler	for	Derbyshire	1990
2nd	210 S.P. James & A. Dale	for	Glamorgan	1997
3rd	229 D.W. Randall & C.E.B. Rice	for	Nottinghamshire	1981
4th	227 F.M.M. Worrell & K.B. Trestrail	for	West Indians	1950
5th	167 H.K. Foster & G. Gaukrodger	for	Worcestershire	1903
6th	116 W.C.L. Creese & G.S. Boyes	for	Hampshire	1936
7th	195* W. Wooller & W.E. Jones	for	Glamorgan	1947
8th	124 W.E. Astill & G. Geary	for	Leicestershire	1929
9th	200 G.W. Cook & C.S. Smith	for	Cambridge University	1957
10th	113 J.G. Greig & C. Robson	for	Hampshire	1901

Best bowling performance in an innings for county 9 for 35 H. Dean v Warwickshire 1909
Best bowling performance in an innings against county 9 for 33 A.S. Kennedy for Hampshire 1920
Best bowling performance in a match for county 17 for 91 H. Dean v Yorkshire 1913
Best bowling performance in a match against county 16 for 69 T.G. Wass for Nottinghamshire 1906
Largest crowd 15,164 v Northamptonshire 1948

LIMITED-OVERS MATCHES

Highest innings total for county 257 for 7 v Derbyshire (B&H) 1988
Highest innings total against county 297 for 6 by West Indians (Tour) 1984
Lowest innings total for county 139 v Durham (B&H) 2001
Lowest innings total against county 117 by Derbyshire (B&H) 2001
Highest individual innings for county 94 G. Fowler v West Indians (Tour) 1984
Highest individual innings against county 186* C.G. Greenidge for West Indians (Tour) 1984
Highest wicket partnerships for county

1st	121* M.A. Atherton & M.J. Chilton	v	Derbyshire	(B&H)	2001
2nd	128 D. Lloyd & H. Pilling	v	Gloucestershire	(B&H)	1978
3rd	88 H. Pilling & C.H. Lloyd	v	Northamptonshire	(SL)	1970
4th	93 H. Pilling & F.C. Hayes	v	Leicestershire	(B&H)	1977
5th	86 C.H. Lloyd & N.H. Fairbrother	v	Nottinghamshire	(B&H)	1986
6th	50 M. Watkinson & A.N. Hayhurst	v	Derbyshire	(B&H)	1988
7th	26 C.H. Lloyd & M. Watkinson	v	Nottinghamshire	(B&H)	1986
8th	85 C. Maynard & J. Simmons	v	West Indians	(Tour)	1984
9th	25* J. Simmons & P.J.W. Allott	v	Nottinghamshire	(B&H)	1986
10th	1* P.J. Martin & M. Muralitharan	v	Yorkshire	(B&H)	2001

Highest wicket partnerships against county

1st	140 K.J. Barnett & P.D. Bowler	for	Derbyshire	(B&H)	1988
2nd	59 R.M. Prideaux & A. Lightfoot	for	Northamptonshire	(SL)	1970
3rd	229 C.G. Greenidge & H.A. Gomes	for	West Indians	(Tour)	1984
4th	64 R.G.A. Headley & G. Miller	for	Derbyshire	(B&H)	1975
5th	28 J.J.B. Lewis & N.J. Speak	for	Durham	(B&H)	2001
6th	98 C.E.B. Rice & J.D. Birch	for	Nottinghamshire	(B&H)	1986
7th	72 J. Birkenshaw & P.B. Clift	for	Leicestershire	(B&H)	1977
8th	13 K.M. Krikken & T.M. Smith	for	Derbyshire	(B&H)	2001
9th	15 B.S. Crump & L.A. Johnson	for	Northamptonshire	(SL)	1970
10th	8 L.A. Johnson & Sarfraz Nawaz	for	Northamptonshire	(SL)	1970

Best bowling performance in a match for county 5 for 23 P. Lever v Northamptonshire (SL) 1970
Best bowling performance in a match against county 4 for 53 R.J. Hadlee for Nottinghamshire (B&H) 1986
Largest crowd 7,633 v West Indians (Tour) 1984

GROUND INFORMATION

ENTRANCES Aigburth Road (players, officials and vehicles, members, press/media), Riversdale Road (members, public and vehicles).

MEMBERS' ENCLOSURE Pavilion, Ladies' Pavilion/Restaurant and defined members' enclosure.

PUBLIC ENCLOSURE Rest of the ground.

COVERED STANDS Pavilion, Pavilion balcony/terrace (part) and Ladies' Pavilion.

OPEN STANDS Pavilion balcony/terrace (part) together with temporary raised plastic seating areas and ground level seating surrounding the playing area.

NAME OF ENDS Aigburth Road End and River End.

GROUND DIMENSIONS 142m × 138m.

REPLAY SCREEN If televised matches are staged at the ground the replay screen is sited at the Mersey End of the ground.

FIRST AID First Aid Room in the pavilion and in a tent at the River End of the ground.

BEHAVIOUR The Lancashire Committee is most concerned that standards of behaviour should be maintained and improved at all grounds, particularly those within Lancashire. Members and subscribers are requested to report to the ground authorities any incident or potential incident where they feel action should be taken. Bad language is not acceptable at any cricket match and the Lancashire Committee will take the strongest action. Dress standards are consistent with the prestige of being a member of a major county cricket club; members are required to dress in an appropriate manner. The minimum requirement for adult entry into the Members' Enclosure for members, subscribers and guests is neat casual dress.

RECIPROCAL ARRANGEMENTS Lancashire County Cricket Club members have arrangements to use the facilities at the WACA Ground at Perth and vice versa.

SUPPORTERS' CLUB Unofficial travel club. No supporters' club.

JUNIORS Annual membership for Lancashire County Cricket Club Juniors aged under 18 on 1 February is £10.

CORPORATE ENTERTAINING Marquees are available. Contact the Conference and Banqueting Office for further information and a copy of the brochure.

FACILITIES FOR VISUALLY IMPAIRED SPECTATORS Free entry, also for helper. No guide dogs allowed.

FACILITIES AND ACCESS FOR PEOPLE WITH DISABILITIES INCLUDING WHEELCHAIR ACCESS TO GROUND Yes, through main gates off Aigburth Road.

DESIGNATED CAR PARK AVAILABLE INSIDE THE GROUND FOR PEOPLE WITH DISABILITIES Yes, situated at Mersey End of the ground but contact Liverpool CC in advance.

GOOD VIEWING AREAS INSIDE THE GROUND FOR PEOPLE USING WHEELCHAIRS Yes, at Pavilion End and Mersey End of the ground by sightscreens.

DESIGNATED VIEWING AREAS FOR PEOPLE USING WHEELCHAIRS Yes, at Pavilion End and Mersey Ends of the ground by sightscreen and in special small area sited on Riversdale Road side of the ground.

RAMPS TO PROVIDE EASY ACCESS TO BARS & REFRESHMENT OUTLETS Yes, but access to the pavilion is poor.

FOOD AND DRINK FULL RESTAURANT/DINING FACILITIES Members, yes. Public, no. Pavilion Bar sells snacks and drinks. Restaurant service available in Ladies Pavilion numbers limited. For further information contact Liverpool CC.

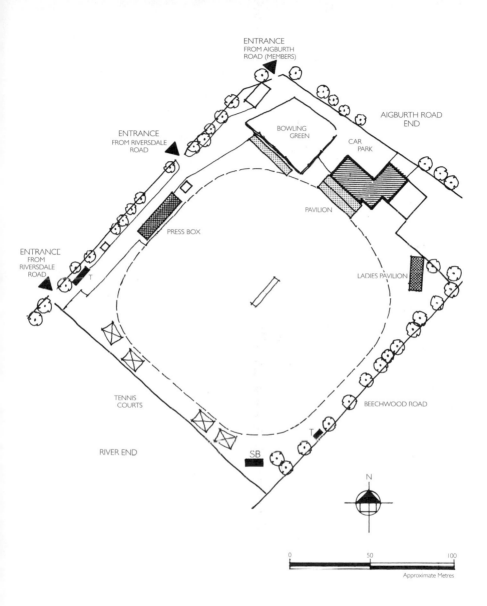

ENTRANCE
FROM AIGBURTH
ROAD (MEMBERS)

AIGBURTH ROAD
END

BOWLING
GREEN

CAR
PARK

ENTRANCE
FROM RIVERSDALE
ROAD

PAVILION

PRESS BOX

ENTRANCE
FROM
RIVERSDALE
ROAD

LADIES PAVILION

T

TENNIS
COURTS

BEECHWOOD ROAD

T

RIVER END

SB

N

0   50   100

Approximate Metres

TEMPORARY FOOD/DRINK FACILITIES Yes, in various outlets around the ground.
FOOD SUITABLE FOR VEGETARIANS Members, yes. Public, yes.
BARS Members 2, Public 1.
VARIETIES OF BEER SOLD Thwaites Smooth Beer, three real ales, Boddingtons and Bass.
CLUB SHOP Lancashire County Cricket Club has a mobile souvenir shop at matches. Visit www.lccc.co.uk to order online.
CLUB MUSEUM No, although there are pictures in the pavilion relating to Liverpool CC and Aigburth.
CLUB LIBRARY No.
CRICKET COACHING FACILITIES Yes, summer only, for members of Liverpool CC.
CRICKET NETS Yes, summer only, for members of Liverpool CC.

OTHER SPORTING OR RECREATIONAL FACILITIES ON THE GROUND Rugby union, football, bowls, squash, tennis and hockey.

FACILITIES FOR HIRE OR WIDER COMMUNITY USE AT THE GROUND Yes, ground is used for Youth and Junior cricket competitions.

WINTER CRICKET EVENTS Members' club dinners and lunches are staged in the pavilion which is also used by the Merseyside Cricket Society. Membership is £10 per annum. Meetings are held once a month between September and March.

CAR PARKING FACILITIES Car parking is available from 9 a.m. within the ground for players and officials only, but members may park on the lower ground adjoining the Mersey Rail railway line, off Riversdale Road and Beechwood Road. Free for LCCC car park pass holders otherwise £3 (cash only). Alternatively street parking is also available in neighbouring streets a short distance walk away from the ground.

OTHER INFORMATION Sir Donald Bradman rated Aigburth as one of his six favourite grounds. Other Lancashire greats such as Cyril Washbrook also enjoyed playing at Liverpool.

GROUND CAPACITY 5,000.

ANTICIPATED GROUND DEVELOPMENTS None presently planned.

HOW TO GET THERE

 Aigburth station 0.5 mile or Cressington station 4 miles (both accessed from Liverpool Lime Street station), ☎ 0151 236 7676, 0870 608 2608, 08457 484950, Virgin Trains Rail Ticket Reservations 08457 222333, www.virgin.com/trains, www.railtrack.co.uk

 Merseybus 20, 26, 32, 82, Crosville X5 and H25 from Liverpool Lime Street station pass ground. Bus Information Line/Mersey Travel Information ☎ 0151 236 7676, National Express Coaches ☎ 0990 808080, www.gobycoach.com, www.nationalexpress.co.uk

 There are cycle routes from central and surrounding areas of Liverpool to this part of Aigburth.

 AA signs are usually erected from the end of the M62. **From north, south and east:** from M62 junction 6 take A5300 (Knowsley Expressway), bear left on to A562 Speke Road, continue on A561 (Speke Boulevard, Speke Road), turn right on to A561 Garston Way, continue on A561 Aigburth Road for Liverpool CC. **From west:** from M53 Kingsway follow signs to Mersey Tunnel, turn left on to A59 (Scotland Road), at roundabout take the first exit on to A5040 (Old Haymarket), bear on to A5038 (St Johns Lane), turn left on to A5038 (St Georges Place), turn right on to Lime Street, turn right on to Renshaw Street, continue on Berry Street, then Duke Street and then Great George Street, take A561 (St James Place, park Place, Park Road), turn left on to Dingle Lane, turn right on to The Elms, turn left on to Aigburth Road, turn right on to Aigburth Hall Avenue, turn left on to Riversdale Road for Liverpool CC.

FERRIES Norse Merchant ☎ 0870 600 4321 www.norsemerchant.com, Seacat ☎ 08705 523523, www.seacat.co.uk, Isle of Man Steam Packet ☎ 08705 523 523 www.steam-packet.com

 Liverpool John Lennon Airport ☎ 0151 288 4000 www.liverpooljohnlennonairport.com, Airportxpress 500 Bus ☎ 0151 236 7676, Easyjet ☎ 0870 6000 000 www.easyjet.com, Euroceltic ☎ 08700 400 100 www.euroceltic.com

WHERE TO STAY

Aplin House Guest Accommodation (☎ 0151 427 5047), Britannia Adelphi Hotel (☎ 0151 709 7200 www.britanniahotels.com), Crowne Plaza (☎ 0845 601 1125 www.crowneplaza.com), Express by Holiday Inn (☎ 0845 601 1125 www.hiexpress.co.uk), Holiday Inn City Centre (☎ 0845 601 1125 www.holidayinn-liverpool.co.uk), Innkeepers Lodge (☎ 0151 494 1032), Marriott City Centre (☎ 0845 601 1125 www.marriotthotels.com/lpllp), Marriott Liverpool South (☎ 0845 601 1125 www.marriotthotels.com/lplms), Moat House (☎ 0845 601 1125 www.moathousehotels.com), The Gladstone (☎ 0845 601 1125), Thistle Hotel (☎ 0845 601 1125 www.thistlehotels.com)

For a further selection of places to stay in Liverpool contact Accommodation Hotline ☎ 0845 601 1125 (local call rate) www.smoothhound.co.uk.

WHERE TO EAT

L'Alouette (☎ 0151 727 2142), Becher's Brook (☎ 0151 707 0005), Gulshan (☎ 0151 427 2273 www.gulshan-liverpool.com), Left Bank (☎ 0151 734 5040 www.leftbankfrenchrestaurant.co.uk), Number 7 Café (☎ 0151 709 9633), St. Petersburg (☎ 0151 709 6676 www.st-petersburg.virtualave.net), Tai Pan (☎ 0151 207 3888), Yuet Ben (☎ 0151 709 5772), Ziba (☎ 0151 708 8870)

TOURIST INFORMATION Merseyside Welcome Centre, Clayton Square Shopping Centre, Liverpool L1 1QR ☎ 0151 709 3631 Fax 0151 708 0204 www.visitliverpool.com, www.liverpool.gov.uk, Liverpool Tourist Information Line ☎ 0906 680 6886 (25p per minute), North West Tourist Board v 01942 821222, England's Northwest Information Line ☎ 0845 600 6040, City Sightseeing Tours ☎ 0151 933 2324, Liverpool Ducks (sightseeing tours in amphibious vehicle) ☎ 0151 708 7799.

OTHER USEFUL INFORMATION

Aintree Racecourse ☎ 0151 522 2929, www.aintree.co.uk
Liverpool Playhouse ☎ 0151 709 4776
Maritime Museum ☎ 0151 478 4499, www.merseysidemaritimemuseum.org.uk
The Beatles Story ☎ 0151 709 1963
Liverpool Football Club Museum ☎ 0151 260 6677, www.liverpoolfc.tv
Everton Football Club Tour ☎ 0151 330 2277, www.evertonfc.com
St Helens Rugby League ☎ 0870 746 9900, www.saints.uk.com
Widnes Rugby League ☎ 0151 510 6000
Tate Liverpool Gallery ☎ 0151 702 7400, www.tate.org.uk/liverpool
Liverpool Philharmonic Hall ☎ 0151 709 3789

LOCAL RADIO STATIONS BBC Radio Merseyside (95.8 MHz FM/1485 KHz MW), Radio City/Magic 1548 (96.7 MHz FM/1548 KHz MW)

LOCAL NEWSPAPERS *Liverpool Daily Post, Liverpool Echo, Liverpool Star*

LYTHAM

Address Lytham Cricket Club, Lytham Cricket and Sports Club, The Pavilion, Church Road, Lytham FY8 5DQ
Prospects of Play ☎ 01253 734137

HISTORY OF GROUND AND FACILITIES

LYTHAM CRICKET CLUB was founded in 1855 by the Squire of Lytham, John de Vere Clifton, and cricket matches were staged near Lytham Hall for the people of the town and those who worked on the estate. Lytham Hall was designed by the distinguished eighteenth-century architect Mr T. Carr of York. The original cricket ground was located close to the hall to the north of the railway line. The present ground is south of the railway line and is home to the Lytham Cricket and Sports Club. It is on an 11.25-acre site surrounded by trees. The facilities are shared with the Lytham Hockey Club, Lytham Tennis Club and Clifton Casuals Football Club. Lytham Cricket Club play in the Manchester Association Cricket League and also have teams represented in the Liverpool and District Competition. ~ords say that three Lytham cricketers played for Lancashire although research may well reveal more. Those known are Robert Dewhurst, (1872–5), Joseph Eccles (1886–9) and Richard Sutcliffe (1978). The venue should not be confused with Lytham St Anne's CC.

Lancashire County Cricket Club made their first visit to Church Road in 1985 for a County Championship fixture with Northamptonshire which was affected by rain. Lancashire teams had visited the ground previously for Second XI matches with Northumberland, Cheshire and Glamorgan. Benefit matches were also staged at Lytham for John Sullivan, Keith Goodwin, Peter Lee, David Lloyd, Jack Simmons and Clive Lloyd. Since 1985 visits have been made by Glamorgan, Sussex, Nottinghamshire, Essex, Northamptonshire and Surrey. A match was not staged in 1990 because several wickets within the square were being re-laid.

The only permanent buildings on the ground are the Pavilion and clubhouse located close to the parish hall and St Cuthbert's Church. The interesting old scoreboard, which is a listed building, is located under the trees near the tennis courts. A smaller secondary scoreboard is opposite. The clubhouse has a number of photographs and items of cricket interest including an aerial photograph of the first County Championship match staged in 1985.

Performances at Lytham have included one notable achievement from a number 10 batsman: in 1985 against Northamptonshire David Makinson, who later represented Cumberland County Cricket Club, hit seven 6s off Richard Williams in his innings of 58*. Lytham has also seen some fine bowling performances from Mike Watkinson and Jack Simmons, Dermot Reeve for Sussex, and Rodney Ontong for Glamorgan.

The main scoreboard during the Lancashire v Sussex match in 1987.

The ground capacity is 5,000 and 2,500 seats are provided. The playing area is 136 metres by 131 metres and is defined by a rope and some advertising boards. A Lancashire County Cricket Club mobile shop may be sited at the Church Road End. A radio commentary position is located in the clubhouse and if required a TV camera/commentary position would be located at the Church Road End.

GROUND RECORDS AND SCORES

FIRST-CLASS MATCHES

Highest innings total for county 381 v Essex 1989
Highest innings total against county 450 for 6 dec by Northamptonshire 1991
Lowest innings total for county 95 v Essex 1989
Lowest innings total against county 96 by Sussex 1987
Highest individual innings for county 172 J.P. Crawley v Surrey 1992
Highest individual innings against county 171 J.P. Stephenson for Essex 1989
Highest wicket partnerships for county

1st	75 J.P. Crawley & M.A. Atherton	v	Worcestershire	1998
2nd	161 J.P. Crawley & N.J. Speak	v	Surrey	1992
3rd	152 J.P. Crawley & N.H. Fairbrother	v	Surrey	1992
4th	58 J. Abrahams & S.J. O'Shaughnessy	v	Glamorgan	1986
5th	104 N.H. Fairbrother & R.C. Irani	v	Kent	1993
6th	98 S.P. Titchard & M. Watkinson	v	Sussex	1995
7th	77 W.K. Hegg & I.D. Austin	v	Worcestershire	1998
8th	21 P.J.W. Allott & J. Simmons	v	Sussex	1987
	21 P.A.J. de Freitas & I.D. Austin	v	Essex	1989
9th	79 P.A.J. de Freitas & J.D. Fitton	v	Essex	1989
10th	72 D.J. Makinson & B.P. Patterson	v	Northamptonshire	1985

Highest wicket partnerships against county

1st	120 G.A. Gooch & J.P. Stephenson	for	Essex	1989
2nd	114 D.J. Bicknell & G.P. Thorpe	for	Surrey	1992
3rd	236 N.A. Stanley & A.J. Lamb	for	Northamptonshire	1991
4th	162 J.P. Stephenson & N. Hussain	for	Essex	1989
5th	96 A.J. Lamb & K.M. Curran	for	Northamptonshire	1991
6th	87 A.D. Brown & M.P. Bicknell	for	Surrey	1992
	87 C.L. Hooper & S.A. Marsh	for	Kent	1993
7th	156 C.L. Hooper & M.A. Ealham	for	Kent	1993
8th	88 A.P. Wells & I.D.K. Salisbury	for	Sussex	1995
9th	27 P.A.W. Heseltine & A.C.S. Pigott	for	Sussex	1995
10th	24 R.J. Chapman & R.K. Illingworth	for	Worcestershire	1998

Best bowling performance in an innings for county 7 for 25 M. Watkinson v Sussex 1987
Best bowling performance in an innings against county 7 for 37 D.A. Reeve for Sussex 1987
Best bowling performance in a match for county 10 for 145 J. Simmons v Glamorgan 1986
Best bowling performance in a match against county 12 for 182 M.M. Patel for Kent 1993
Largest crowd 6,750 v Sussex 1987

GROUND INFORMATION

ENTRANCES Church Road (players, officials, members, public and vehicles), Upper Westby Street (members, public and vehicles).
MEMBERS' ENCLOSURE Pavilion (players and officials only), clubhouse (members only) together with defined members' enclosure to the west and south of the playing area.
PUBLIC ENCLOSURE Rest of the ground.

COVERED STANDS Pavilion/clubhouse.

OPEN STANDS Temporary raised plastic seating, permanent tiered timber seating and temporary ground-level seating surrounding the playing area.

NAME OF ENDS Church Road End, Railway End.

GROUND DIMENSIONS 136m × 131m.

REPLAY SCREEN If televised matches are staged at the ground the replay screen is sited at the Church Road End of the ground.

FIRST AID First Aid Room is located in the Members' Pavilion.

BEHAVIOUR The Lancashire Committee is most concerned that standards of behaviour should be maintained and improved at all grounds, particularly those within Lancashire. Members and subscribers are requested to report to the Ground Authorities any incident or potential incident where they feel action should be taken. Bad language is not acceptable at any cricket match and the Lancashire Committee will take the strongest action. Dress standards are consistent with the prestige of being a member of a major county cricket club; members are required to dress in an appropriate manner. The minimum requirement for adult entry into the Members' Enclosure for members, subscribers and guests is neat casual dress.

RECIPROCAL ARRANGEMENTS Lancashire County Cricket Club members have arrangements to use the facilities at the WACA Ground at Perth and vice versa.

SUPPORTERS' CLUB Unofficial travel club. No supporters' club.

JUNIORS Annual membership for Lancashire County Cricket Club Juniors aged under 18 on 1 February is £10.

CORPORATE ENTERTAINING Marquees are available. Contact the Conference and Banqueting Office for further information and a copy of the brochure.

FACILITIES FOR VISUALLY IMPAIRED SPECTATORS Free entry, also for helper. No guide dogs allowed.

FACILITIES AND ACCESS FOR PEOPLE WITH DISABILITIES INCLUDING WHEELCHAIR ACCESS TO GROUND Yes, through main gates off Church Road.

DESIGNATED CAR PARK AVAILABLE INSIDE THE GROUND FOR PEOPLE WITH DISABILITIES Yes, situated at Church Road End of the ground but contact Lytham CC in advance.

GOOD VIEWING AREAS INSIDE THE GROUND FOR PEOPLE USING WHEELCHAIRS Yes, at Church Road End of the ground by sightscreen.

DESIGNATED VIEWING AREAS FOR PEOPLE USING WHEELCHAIRS No.

RAMPS TO PROVIDE EASY ACCESS TO BARS & REFRESHMENT OUTLETS Yes, to clubhouse.

FOOD AND DRINK FULL RESTAURANT/DINING FACILITIES Members, yes. Public, no. Clubhouse/pavilion bar sells snacks and drinks. Restaurant service is available in a marquee for members only, numbers limited. For further information contact Lytham CC.

TEMPORARY FOOD/DRINK FACILITIES Yes, in various outlets around the ground.

FOOD SUITABLE FOR VEGETARIANS Members, yes. Public, yes.

BARS Members 2, Public 2.

VARIETIES OF BEER SOLD Thwaites Smooth Beer, three real ales, Boddingtons and Bass.

CLUB SHOP Lancashire County Cricket Club has a mobile souvenir shop at matches. Visit www.lccc.co.uk to order online.

CLUB MUSEUM No, although there are pictures in the pavilion relating to Lytham CC.

CLUB LIBRARY No.

CRICKET COACHING FACILITIES Yes, summer and part winter only, for members of Lytham CC.

CRICKET NETS Yes, summer and part winter only, for members of Lytham CC.

OTHER SPORTING OR RECREATIONAL FACILITIES ON THE GROUND Tennis, football and hockey.

FACILITIES FOR HIRE OR WIDER COMMUNITY USE AT THE GROUND Functions and sports facilities are available within the clubhouse for hire. Contact Lytham CC.

WINTER CRICKET EVENTS Members' club dinners and lunches are staged in the pavilion which is also used by the Fylde Coast Cricket Society. Membership is £10 per annum. Meetings are held once a month between September and March.

CAR PARKING FACILITIES Car parking is available within the ground for players and officials only, entrance from Church Road and for members only to the east of the playing area entered from Upper Westby Street. Parking is also available in nearby car parks or on the seafront.

GROUND CAPACITY 5,000.

OTHER INFORMATION Ground is situated a short walk away from the seafront at Lytham and not far from Royal Lytham St Anne's Golf Club.

ANTICIPATED GROUND DEVELOPMENTS None presently planned.

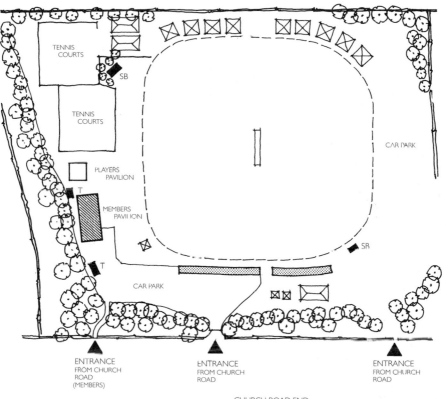

RAILWAY END

RAILWAY LINE

TENNIS COURTS

SB

TENNIS COURTS

CAR PARK

PLAYERS PAVILION

T

MEMBERS PAVILION

SB

T

CAR PARK

ENTRANCE FROM CHURCH ROAD (MEMBERS)

ENTRANCE FROM CHURCH ROAD

ENTRANCE FROM CHURCH ROAD

CHURCH ROAD END

N

| 0 | 50 | 100 |

Approximate Metres

HOW TO GET THERE

 Lytham station 0.5 mile connects with Blackpool and Preston. ☎ 08457 484950, Virgin Trains Rail Ticket Reservations ☎ 08457 222 333, www.virgin.com/trains, www.railtrack.co.uk

 From surrounding areas to Lytham town centre, thence 0.5 mile walk. Bus 11 and 11A to Lytham, 167 St Anne's to Preston and 193 St Anne's to Kirkham pass outside the ground in Church Road. National Express Coaches ☎ 0990 808080, www.gobycoach.com

There are cycle routes to this part of Lytham.

 From M6 junction 32 take M55, at end of M55 take A583 (Preston New Road), turn right on to Whitehill Road, turn left on to Wild Lane, continue on North Houses Lane, turn on to B5261 (Heyhouses Lane), continue on Blackpool Road then Church Road for Lytham CC.

 Blackpool Airport ☎ 01253 343434

WHERE TO STAY

Chadwick Hotel (☎ 01253 720061), Clifton Arms Hotel (☎ 01253 739898), Dalmeny Hotel (☎ 01253 712236), Glendower Hotel (☎ 01253 723241), The Grand Hotel (☎ 01253 721288 www.the-grand.co.uk), Lindum Hotel (☎ 01253 721534), Premier Lodge (☎ 0870 700 1424 www.premierlodge.co.uk), St Ives Hotel (☎ 01253 720011), Strathmore Hotel (☎ 01253 725478)

For a further selection of places to stay in Lytham St Anne's or Blackpool contact Blackpool Hotel and Guest House Association Limited, 87a Coronation Street, Blackpool, Lancashire FY1 4PD, ☎ 01253 621891, www.blackpool-stay.co.uk or www.smoothhound.co.uk.

WHERE TO EAT

September Brasserie (☎ 01253 623282)

There are numerous other eateries on the seafront catering for all tastes.

TOURIST INFORMATION Lytham St Anne's Tourist Information Centre, 290 Clifton Drive South, Lytham St Anne's, Lancashire FY8 1LH ☎ 01253 725610

OTHER USEFUL INFORMATION

Blackpool Tower ☎ 01253 622242, www.blackpooltower.co.uk
Blackpool Zoo ☎ 01253 830830
Blackpool Football Club ☎ 01253 405331, www.blackpoolfc.co.uk
Blackpool Pleasure Beach ☎ 0870 444 5566, www.blackpoolpleasurebeach.co.uk
Blackpool Sea Life Centre ☎ 01253 622445
Blackpool Sandcastle ☎ 01253 343602
Blackpool Show Booking Line ☎ 01253 292029
Blackpool Model Village ☎ 01253 763827
Grundy Art Gallery ☎ 01253 478170
Tussaud's Waxworks ☎ 01253 625953
Three Piers ☎ 01253 292029
Winter Gardens ☎ 01253 292029

LOCAL RADIO STATIONS BBC Radio Lancashire (104.5 MHz FM/1557 KHz MW), Red Rose Radio (97.3 MHz FM/999 KHz MW)

LOCAL NEWSPAPERS *The Blackpool Gazette, Lancashire Evening Post, Lancashire Evening Telegraph, West Lancashire Gazette*

SOUTHPORT

Address Southport and Birkdale Cricket Club, The Pavilion,
Trafalgar Road, Birkdale, Southport PR8 2HF
Prospects of Play ☎ 01704 569951, 0161 282 4000 –
wait for options, then press 4

HISTORY OF GROUND AND FACILITIES

THE TRAFALGAR ROAD CRICKET GROUND is the home of Southport and Birkdale
Cricket Club which was founded in 1859. Originally the ground was largely an
area of waste and sand hills to the south of the Southport to Liverpool railway
line but in 1850 much development took place in the area thanks to Mr J.
Aughton, an enterprising builder from Preston. The ground was purchased in
1884, with agreement from the Weld-Blundell family and the Birkdale Park Land
Company, and the Birkdale Cricket Ground Company was established. The
pavilion was built in 1881 at a cost of about £300. Birkdale Cricket Club was
founded in 1874 and merged with the Southport Cricket Club in 1901.

The Pavilion was rebuilt in 1965 at a cost of £28,000 and was opened by Lord
Derby. A County Championship match with Derbyshire was staged in the same
season and Lancashire disposed of the visitors in two days, which perhaps was
just as well as it rained heavily on the third day. The Ladies' Pavilion and a
bowling green were constructed in 1958.

The ground was used in 1957 by the Minor Counties Cricket Association. It
has also been used by Southport Hockey Club, Lancashire County Police and
the Australian Ladies' Cricket Team as well as for schoolgirls' hockey matches.

The first Lancashire County Cricket Club visit to the ground for a first-class
game was in 1959 when Worcestershire were the visitors for a County
Championship match, although a Brian Statham benefit match had been played
there previously. Since then championship cricket has been played every other
year, usually in June, although in recent years Southport has tended to be used
in a rotational way with Lytham Cricket Club. In 1967, due to waterlogged areas
on the outfield at Old Trafford the tour match with the Indians was switched from
Manchester to Southport and a crowd of 6,000 attended.

In 1969 the first limited-overs match was staged with Glamorgan in the John
Player Sunday League. Other limited-overs matches have followed, the most
recent being a Benson and Hedges Cup zonal group match with Scotland in
1991. The 1969 Glamorgan match was televised and some 10,500 spectators
attended. This is still a record attendance for a match on the ground. These days
the capacity is 5,000 and crowds of 4,500 to 5,000 are achieved for County
Championship matches.

Southport and Birkdale Cricket Club play in the Liverpool and District Cricket
Competition and in recent years have spent considerable sums on a new
scoreboard and tiered terracing, which accommodates 2,000 spectators. The
railway embankment runs along the far side of the ground. The ground is tree-
lined and rather confined compared with other Lancashire venues.

The radio commentary box and TV camera/commentary box positions are at the Harrod Drive End. The playing area is 121 metres by 126 metres and is defined by a rope and some advertising boards.

The Birkdale area is known more for golf than cricket and Royal Birkdale Golf Club is only a short distance away.

GROUND RECORDS AND SCORES

FIRST-CLASS MATCHES

Highest innings total for county 521 v Somerset 1994
Highest innings total against county 523 for 4 by Warwickshire 1982
Lowest innings total for county 70 v Essex 1978 and v Northamptonshire 1984
Lowest innings total against county 80 by Derbyshire 1965
Highest individual innings for county 281* J.P. Crawley v Somerset 1994
Highest individual innings against county 254 G.W. Humpage for Warwickshire 1982
Highest wicket partnerships for county

1st	226* G. Fowler & D. Lloyd	v	Warwickshire	1982
2nd	149 C.H. Lloyd & D. Lloyd	v	Worcestershire	1979
3rd	163 G.D. Mendis & N.H. Fairbrother	v	Nottinghamshire	1990
4th	166 J.P. Crawley & N.J. Speak	v	Somerset	1994
5th	107 J.P. Crawley & M. Watkinson	v	Warwickshire	1999
6th	123 K.J. Grieves & B.J. Booth	v	Worcestershire	1959
7th	123* J.D. Bond & D.P. Hughes	v	Northamptonshire	1971
8th	65 N.V. Radford & M.F. Malone	v	Northamptonshire	1980
9th	76 M. Watkinson & I. Folley	v	Surrey	1985
10th	122 J.P. Crawley & A.A. Barnett	v	Somerset	1994

Highest wicket partnerships against county

1st	200 B.A. Richards & C.G. Greenidge	for	Hampshire	1973
2nd	152 P.D. Atkins & A.J. Stewart	for	Surrey	1988
3rd	201 R.J. Boyd-Moss & D.J. Wild	for	Northamptonshire	1984
	201 G. Cook & R.J. Bailey	for	Northamptonshire	1989
4th	470 A.I. Kallicharran & G.W. Humpage	for	Warwickshire	1982
5th	145* M.J. Smedley & G. St. A. Sobers	for	Nottinghamshire	1968
6th	145 G.I. Burgess & K.E. Palmer	for	Somerset	1966
7th	117 B.P. Julian & G.J. Kersey	for	Surrey	1996
8th	121* S. Turner & R.E. East	for	Essex	1972
9th	55 R.J. Turner & Mushtaq Ahmed	for	Somerset	1994
10th	46 R.M. Pearson & J.E. Benjamin	for	Surrey	1996

Best bowling performance in an innings for county 8 for 30 Wasim Akram v Somerset 1994
Best bowling performance in an innings against county 7 for 56 K.E. Palmer for Somerset 1966
Best bowling performance in a match for county 13 for 147 Wasim Akram v Nottinghamshire 1986
Best bowling performance in a match against county 10 for 175 E.E. Hemmings for Nottinghamshire 1986
Largest crowd 4,500 v Worcestershire 1959

LIMITED-OVERS MATCHES

Highest innings total for county 195 for 2 v Essex (SL) 1974
Highest innings total against county 218 for 6 by Warwickshire (B&H) 1979
Lowest innings total for county 162 for 9 v Derbyshire (B&H) 1976
Lowest innings total against county 110 by Derbyshire (B&H) 1976
Highest individual innings for county 101 D. Lloyd v Essex (SL) 1974
Highest individual innings against county 71 I.L. Philip for Scotland (B&H) 1987
Highest wicket partnerships for county

1st	169 B. Wood & D. Lloyd	v	Essex	(SL)	1974

2nd	41 B. Wood & H. Pilling	v	Warwickshire	(B&H)	1979
3rd	50 D.W. Varey & S.J. O'Shaughnessy	v	Scotland	(B&H)	1987
4th	77* S.J. O'Shaughnessy & J. Abrahams	v	Scotland	(B&H)	1987
5th	15 D. Lloyd & F.M. Engineer	v	Derbyshire	(B&H)	1976
6th	42 D. Lloyd & D.P. Hughes	v	Derbyshire	(B&H)	1976
7th	28 D. Lloyd & J. Simmons	v	Derbyshire	(B&H)	1976
8th	5 J. Simmons & R.M. Ratcliffe	v	Derbyshire	(B&H)	1976
9th	20 R.M. Ratcliffe & P. Lever	v	Derbyshire	(B&H)	1976
10th	2* P. Lever & P.G. Lee	v	Derbyshire	(B&H)	1976

Highest wicket partnerships for county

1st	53 I.L. Philip & K. Scott	for	Scotland	(B&H)	1987
2nd	85 I.L. Philip & R.G. Swan	for	Scotland	(B&H)	1987
3rd	11 K.W.R. Fletcher & K.S. McEwan	for	Essex	(SL)	1974
4th	44 Majid Khan & B.A. Davis	for	Glamorgan	(SL)	1969
	44 K.S. McEwan & R.M.O. Cooke	for	Essex	(SL)	1974
5th	48 J. Whitehouse & G.W. Humpage	for	Warwickshire	(B&H)	1979
6th	32 K.S. McEwan & G.A. Gooch	for	Essex	(SL)	1974
7th	47* G.W. Humpage & A.M. Ferreira	for	Warwickshire	(B&H)	1979
8th	29 R.W. Taylor & P.E. Russell	for	Derbyshire	(B&H)	1976
9th	12 D.L. Snodgrass & J.E. Ker	for	Scotland	(B&H)	1987
10th	21 P.E. Russell & M. Hendrick	for	Derbyshire	(B&H)	1976

Best bowling performance in a match for county 5 for 12 B. Wood v Derbyshire (B&H) 1976
Best bowling performance in a match against county 5 for 30 M. Hendrick for Derbyshire (B&H) 1976
Largest crowd 10,500 v Glamorgan (SL) 1969

GROUND INFORMATION

ENTRANCES Trafalgar Road (players, officials, members, public and vehicles).
MEMBERS' ENCLOSURE Pavilion, Ladies' Pavilion and defined members' enclosure.
PUBLIC ENCLOSURE Rest of the ground.
COVERED STANDS Pavilion, Ladies' Pavilion and Late-Cut Bar.
OPEN STANDS Permanent raised tiered seating in front of the scoreboard together with temporary raised plastic seating and ground level seating surrounding the playing area.
NAME OF ENDS Grosvenor Road End, Harrod Drive End.
GROUND DIMENSIONS 121m × 126m.
REPLAY SCREEN If televised matches are staged at the ground the replay screen is sited at the Grosvenor Road End of the ground.
FIRST AID First Aid Room is located in the Members' Pavilion.
BEHAVIOUR The Lancashire Committee is most concerned that standards of behaviour should be maintained and improved at all grounds, particularly those within Lancashire. Members and subscribers are requested to report to the Ground Authorities any incident or potential incident where they feel action should be taken. Bad language is not acceptable at any cricket match and the Lancashire Committee will take the strongest action. Dress standards are consistent with the prestige of being a member of a major county cricket club; members are required to dress in an appropriate manner. The minimum requirement for adult entry into the Members' Enclosure for members, subscribers and guests is neat casual dress.
RECIPROCAL ARRANGEMENTS Lancashire County Cricket Club members have arrangements to use the facilities at the WACA Ground at Perth and vice versa.
SUPPORTERS' CLUB Unofficial travel club. No supporters' club.
JUNIORS Annual membership for Lancashire County Cricket Club Juniors aged under 18 on 1 February is £10.
CORPORATE ENTERTAINING Marquees are available. Contact the Conference and Banqueting Office for further information and a copy of the brochure.
FACILITIES FOR VISUALLY IMPAIRED SPECTATORS Free entry, also for helper. No guide dogs allowed.
FACILITIES AND ACCESS FOR PEOPLE WITH DISABILITIES INCLUDING WHEELCHAIR ACCESS TO GROUND Yes, through entrance from Trafalgar Road at rear of the pavilion.

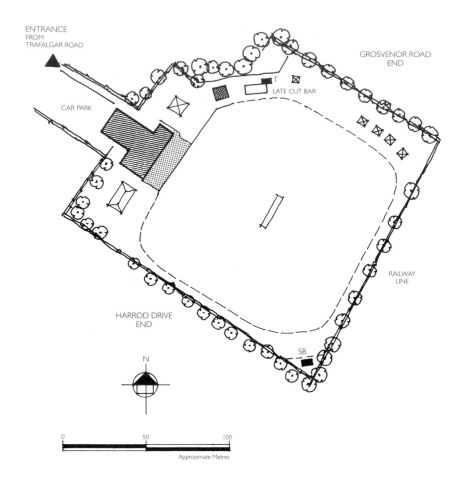

ENTRANCE
FROM
TRAFALGAR ROAD

GROSVENOR ROAD
END

LATE CUT BAR

CAR PARK

RAILWAY
LINE

HARROD DRIVE
END

N

0   50   100

Approximate Metres

DESIGNATED CAR PARK AVAILABLE INSIDE THE GROUND FOR PEOPLE WITH DISABILITIES Yes, situated at
Grosvenor Road End of the ground space for 3 to 5 cars but contact Southport and Birkdale CC in advance.
GOOD VIEWING AREAS INSIDE THE GROUND FOR PEOPLE USING WHEELCHAIRS Yes, at Grosvenor Road End of
the ground by sightscreen and on hard standing in front of the pavilion.
DESIGNATED VIEWING AREAS FOR PEOPLE USING WHEELCHAIRS Yes.
RAMPS TO PROVIDE EASY ACCESS TO BARS AND REFRESHMENT OUTLETS Yes, to the pavilion.
FOOD AND DRINK FULL RESTAURANT/DINING FACILITIES Members, yes. Public, yes. Clubhouse/pavilion bar
which sells snacks and drinks. Restaurant service is available in a marquee for members only, numbers
limited. Refreshments can also be obtained from the 'Late Cut' Bar. For further information contact Southport
and Birkdale CC.
TEMPORARY FOOD/DRINK FACILITIES Yes, in various outlets around the ground.
FOOD SUITABLE FOR VEGETARIANS Members, yes. Public, no.
BARS Members 2, Public 2.
VARIETIES OF BEER SOLD Thwaites Smooth Beer, three real ales, Boddingtons and Bass.
CLUB SHOP Lancashire County Cricket Club has a mobile souvenir shop at matches. Visit www.lccc.co.uk to
order online.
CLUB MUSEUM No, although there are pictures in the pavilion relating to Southport and Birkdale CC.
CLUB LIBRARY No.

CRICKET COACHING FACILITIES Yes, summer and winter only, for members of Southport and Birkdale CC.
CRICKET NETS Yes, summer and winter only, for members of Southport and Birkdale CC.
OTHER SPORTING OR RECREATIONAL FACILITIES ON THE GROUND Tennis, squash, racketball and hockey.
FACILITIES FOR HIRE OR WIDER COMMUNITY USE AT THE GROUND Conference and function facilities available for hire. Contact Southport and Birkdale CC.
WINTER CRICKET EVENTS Members' club dinners and lunches are staged in the pavilion which is also used by the West Lancashire Cricket Society. Membership is £10. Meetings are held once a month between September and March.
CAR PARKING FACILITIES Car parking for Players and Officials and some members is available by the main entrance at the rear of the pavilion off Trafalgar Road and space is also available neighbouring streets and in the large car park at Royal Birkdale Golf Club situated off the main A565 road some 10 minutes' walk from the ground.
OTHER INFORMATION Ground is situated a short walk away from the beach at Southport and is not very far from Royal Birkdale Golf Club.
GROUND CAPACITY 5,000.
ANTICIPATED GROUND DEVELOPMENTS None presently planned.

HOW TO GET THERE

 Birkdale Merseyrail station 0.5 mile or Hillside Merseyrail station 0.5 mile. Both link with Liverpool Lime Street or Southport stations. ☎ 0151 236 7676, 0870 608 2608 (local call rate), 08457 484950, Virgin Trains Rail Ticket Reservations 08457 222333, www.virgin.com/trains or www.railtrack.co.uk

 Merseybus 16, 105, 284 from Southport Monument to within 0.25 mile of the ground, also 10 and 17 from surrounding area pass ground. Bus Information Line/Mersey Travel Information ☎ 0151 236 7676, National Express Coaches ☎ 0990 808080, www.gobycoach.com, www.nationalexpress.co.uk

 There are cycle routes from the seafront and surrounding areas to this part of the seaside resort.

 From north: from M6 junction 28 take right turn B5256 (Leyland Way), at junction with A49 turn right (Wigan Road), turn right on to B5248 (Heald House Road), follow Church Road, then Towngate, Fox Lane, Leyland Lane, Slater Lane, Mill Street, Dunkirk Lane, Cocker Bar Road and North Road to junction with B5247, turn right (Carr House Lane), at roundabout take A59 (south) to junction with A565 (Southport New Road), follow A565 into Southport (Preston New Road, Park Crescent, Lord Street), at Lord Street turn left into Gainsborough Road for the ground. From south and east: from M6 junction 26, exit roundabout on to M58, at M58 junction 3 exit roundabout on to A570 (Rainford Road), follow A570 to junction with B5243, turn left (Jacksmere Lane), continue on B5243 (Heathey Lane, Birkdale Cop) turn left on to Moss Road, turn left on to Guildford Road, turn right on to Kew Road and continue to junction with A5267, turn left (Eastbourne Road), follow Crescent Road and Grosvenor Road, turn left on to Trafalgar Road to ground. Alternative route from south via Liverpool: from M57 junction 7 turn left on to A5036 (Dunnings Bridge Road), then take A5207 (Copy Lane), continue on A5207 to junction with A565 (Formby bypass), continue on A565, at Liverpool Avenue junction with Gainsborough Road turn right into Gainsborough Road.

 Liverpool John Lennon Airport ☎ 0151 288 4000, Blackpool Airport ☎ 01253 343434

WHERE TO STAY

Alhambra Hotel (☎ 01704 534485 www.alhambrahotel.co.uk), Crimond Hotel (☎ 01704 536456 www.crimondhotel.com), Dukes Folly Hotel (☎ 01704 533355 www.dukesfolly.co.uk), Prince of Wales Hotel (☎ 01704 536688), Scarisbrook Hotel (☎ 01704 543000 www.sarisbrook.com), The Bold Hotel (☎ 01704 532578 www.boldhotel.com), The Royal Clifton Hotel (☎ 01704 533771 www.royalclifton.co.uk), Tree Tops Country House (☎ 01704 572430)
    For further details of places to stay contact Accommodation Hotline ☎ 0845 601 1125, 0151 934 2432, email accommodation@visitsouthport.com.

The pavilion at Trafalgar Road, home of Southport & Birkdale Cricket Club.

WHERE TO EAT

Hesketh Arms (☎ 01704 509548), L'Auberge Bistro (☎ 01704 530671), Warehouse Brasserie (☎ 01704 544662)

TOURIST INFORMATION Southport Tourist Information Centre, 112 Lord Street, Southport, Lancashire PR8 1NY ☎ 01704 533333, Fax 01704 500175, email info@visitsouthport.com, www.visitsouthport.com

OTHER USEFUL INFORMATION

Pleasure Land ☎ 08702 200204, www.pleasureland.uk.com
Southport and Lytham Golf ☎ 0151 934 2453, www.golf-england.co.uk
Southport Coastline ☎ 01704 570173, www.merseyside/com/sefton_coast
Southport Events ☎ 01704 395511, www.visitsouthport.com
Southport Pier ☎ 01704 531710, www.southportpier.org
Southport Weekender ☎ 01207 549 223, www.southportweekender.co.uk

LOCAL RADIO STATIONS BBC Radio Merseyside (95.8 MHz FM/1485 KHz MW), BBC Radio Lancashire (104.5 MHz FM/1557 KHz MW), Red Rose Radio (97.3 MHz FM/999 KHz MW)

LOCAL NEWSPAPERS *Liverpool Daily Post, Liverpool Echo, Liverpool Star, Southport Visitor*

Leicestershire

Leicester
Oakham School

LEICESTERSHIRE COUNTY CRICKET CLUB, COUNTY GROUND, GRACE ROAD, LEICESTER LE2 8AD

General Enquiries	0116 283 2128 **fax** 0116 244 0363
Catering Department	0116 245 2429
Ticket Office	0116 283 2128
Membership Department	0116 283 2128
Hospitality and Conference Sales	0116 245 2412 or 0116 245 2451
Pavilion Restaurant and Catering Office	0116 245 2429
Indoor Cricket School	0116 245 2448
Email	leicestershirecc@ukonline.co.uk
Website	www.leicestershireccc.com

Founded 25 March 1879

Colours dark green and scarlet

Crest red running fox

National Cricket League Nickname Foxes

National Cricket League Colours scarlet, green, white and yellow

Patrons The Lord Lieutenant of Leicestershire, The High Sheriff of Leicestershire, The Chairman of Leicestershire County Council, The Rt Revd the Lord Bishop of Leicester, The Right Worshipful The Lord Mayor of Leicester

President B.A.F. Smith, DL

Hon Treasurer R. Goadby

Hon Secretary J.J. Stone

Hon Life President T.L. Bennett

General Manager K.P. Hill

PA to General Manager M.A. Holt

Sales and Marketing Manager T. Stevenson

Membership Secretary P. Hancock

Head Coach P. Whitticase

Coaching Consultant J. Birkenshaw

Captain P.A.J. DeFreitas

Physiotherapist C. Mortimer

Scorer 1st XI G.A. York

Scorer 2nd XI D. Ayriss

Cricket Development Manager A. Woods

Head Groundsmen A. Ward and A. Whiteman

Club Shop Friends of Grace Road

Hon Archivist & Historian S. Michael

Hon Curator J. Barlow

Statistician D.A. Lambert

Sponsors Kirby & West Dairy

Yearbook £10

Scorecard 50p

National Cricket League Programme & Scorecard £2

Frizzell County Championship Status Division 1

National Cricket League Status Division 1

ACHIEVEMENTS

County Championship Champions 1975, 1996 and 1998

Gillette Cup Semi-finalists 1977

NatWest Bank Trophy Finalists 1992, Semi-finalists 1987

Cheltenham & Gloucester Trophy Finalists 2001

Benson and Hedges Cup Winners 1972, 1975, 1985, Finalists 1974

John Player Sunday League Champions 1974 and 1977

Norwich Union National League Runners-up Division 1   2001

Fenner Trophy Winners 1979

Tilcon Trophy Winners 1984 and 1986

Ward Four Counties Knockout Competition Semi-finalists 1989

Lambert & Butler (TCCB 7-a-side Floodlit Competition) Finalists 1981

COUNTY CRICKET BOARD

Chairman J. Sinnott
Secretary/Cricket Development Manager/Women & Girls Cricket Development Officer A. Woods
Treasurer J. Steer
Excellence Coach R.M. Cobb

Address Leicestershire & Rutland Cricket Board, County Ground, Grace Road, Leicester LE2 8AD
☎ 0116 244 2198
Fax 0116 244 2198

GROUNDS

Leicester (County Cricket Ground, Grace Road) and Oakham (Oakham School, Doncaster Close)
    Other grounds used since 1969 are: Coalville (Snibston Colliery Ground, Owen Street) Loughborough (Park Road, Loughborough), Hinckley (Coventry Road) and Hinckley (Hinckley Town CC, Leicester Road)

SECOND XI GROUNDS

Hinckley Town CC, The Pavilion, Leicester Road, Hinckley, Leicestershire ☎ 01455 615336
Oakham School, The Pavilion, Doncaster Close, Station Road, Oakham, Rutland ☎ 01572 722487

Bennett End Stand, media complex, executive boxes and secondary computerised scoreboard viewed from the top of the pavilion, Grace Road, Leicester.

LEICESTER

Address County Ground, Grace Road, Leicester, Leicestershire LE2 8AD
Prospects of Play ☎ 0116 283 2128

HISTORY OF GROUND AND FACILITIES

CRICKET IN LEICESTER is said to have begun in about 1780 at Saint Margaret's Pasture, between the River Soar and the canal, but it was not until 1877 that the Leicestershire Cricket Ground Company purchased some 16 acres of land bordered by Grace, Milligan and Hawkesbury Roads. The ground takes its name from Grace Road, not Dr W.G. Grace.

The greater part of the 16 acres was laid out and prepared for cricket and the first match took place in April 1878. The first Leicestershire first-class match was with Yorkshire in 1894 and the first county match in 1895. Leicestershire County Cricket Club used the ground from 1879 but after five years of County Championship cricket it was thought in 1901 that a more accessible ground was needed closer to the city. The county club moved to Aylestone Road and in the same year the company sold most of its land.

County cricket continued at the Aylestone Road ground until 1939, but during the Second World War the ground used by the military and was damaged. It was also partly used for industrial developments. Improvements in public transport suggested a return to Grace Road and the county club moved back to the ground they had left forty-six years earlier. At this time the land was owned by the local education authority and was the sports ground of the City of Leicester School. LCCC brought with them from Aylestone Road the old pavilion known as the Meet and a heavy roller.

In 1966 the Grace Road ground was finally purchased by the club and later years have seen considerable development with the erection of a new pavilion, dressing rooms and an indoor cricket school at the Pavilion End. The latter has since been superseded by a new Indoor Cricket School at the Bennett End, formerly known as the Hawkesbury Road End.

Situated some two miles due south of the city, the ground is rather inaccessible as it is in a residential area. However, it is perhaps one of the best equipped grounds on the county circuit and is the second largest playing area in the world.

The pavilion was opened on 25 June 1966 by the Lord Bishop of Leicester, the Right Reverend R.R. Williams DD, and the Pavilion Suite was opened by The Lord Lieutenant of Leicestershire, Colonel R.A. St G. Martin OBE, JP, on 7 July 1979.

In 1993 the new Indoor Cricket School was constructed at the Bennett End, opposite the pavilion and this building includes, on the ground floor, the Bennett End Bar, Indoor Cricket School with changing rooms, toilet facilities and the offices of the Leicestershire & Rutland Cricket Board. On the first floor is the Championship Lounge, Media Centre and four hospitality boxes.

A white boundary fence runs all round the perimeter of the playing area, which measures 151 metres by 133 metres. The pitch runs in a north–south direction. The main scoreboard is at the Bennett End. In 1987 a memorial clock tower surmounted by a running fox weathervane was added to the building, as a result of a bequest in the will of Cecily Williams, widow of the late Bishop of Leicester. The main TV camera position is on the top of the Pavilion roof as is the radio commentary box. It is possible to view the cricket from a limited area of the car park, but the reflection of the sun off windscreens can cause problems for players in the afternoon; spectators may be asked to cover windscreens.

Grace Road has staged several limited-overs one-day internationals in the World Cup. A Prudential Cup match was staged in 1983 between India and Zimbabwe and then in 1999 the ground hosted matches between India and Zimbabwe and Scotland and the West Indies. In 1991 a Young England v Young Australians Test match was staged at Grace Road. In 1999 LCCC

Scoreboard on the Milligan Road side of the ground.

hosted the India team ahead of the World Cup and played two World Cup warmup matches against India on 7 May and Sri Lanka on 11 May. Grace Road has also been used for Young England and Under-19 Test Matches in recent years.

GROUND RECORDS AND SCORES

FIRST-CLASS MATCHES

Highest innings total for county 638 for 8 dec v Worcestershire 1996
Highest innings total against county 694 for 6 by Australians 1956
Lowest innings total for county 28 v Australians 1899
Lowest innings total against county 24 by Glamorgan 1971
Highest individual innings for county 261 P.V. Simmons v Northamptonshire 1994
Highest individual innings against county 281* K.R. Miller for Australians 1956
Highest wicket partnerships for county

1st	390 B. Dudleston & J.F. Steele	v	Derbyshire	1979
2nd	289* J.C. Balderstone & D.I. Gower	v	Essex	1981
3rd	305 J.C. Balderstone & B.F. Davison	v	Nottinghamshire	1974
4th	290* P. Willey & T.J. Boon	v	Warwickshire	1984
5th	320 J.J. Whitaker & A. Habib	v	Worcestershire	1996
6th	253 P.V. Simmons & P.A. Nixon	v	Northamptonshire	1994
7th	187 V.J. Wells & D.J. Millns	v	Essex	1996
8th	164 M.R. Hallam & C.T. Spencer	v	Essex	1964
9th	119 P.A. Nixon & A.R.K. Pierson	v	Lancashire	1993
10th	228 R. Illingworth & K. Higgs	v	Northamptonshire	1977

Highest wicket partnerships against county

1st	299 B. Wood & D. Lloyd	for	Lancashire	1972
2nd	324* M.C. Carew & R.C. Fredericks	for	West Indians	1969
3rd	340* F.M.M. Worrell & E. de C. Weekes	for	West Indians	1950
4th	299 W.M. Wallace & M.P. Donnelly	for	New Zealanders	1949

5th	329 F. Mitchell & E. Wainwright	for	Yorkshire	1899
6th	259 D. Brookes & E. Davis	for	Northamptonshire	1947
7th	177 E.J. Diver & A.S. Glover	for	Warwickshire	1897
8th	172 I.V.A. Richards & I.T. Botham	for	Somerset	1983
9th	181 A. Bacher & J.T. Botten	for	South Africans	1965
10th	109* M.P. Bicknell & I.D.K. Salisbury	for	Surrey	2001

Best bowling performance in an innings for county 9 for 29 J. Cotton v Indians 1967
Best bowling performance in an innings against county 9 for 68 G.G. Walker for Derbyshire 1895
Best bowling performance in a match for county 15 for 136 A. Woodcock v Nottinghamshire 1894
Best bowling performance in a match against county 15 for 108 J.B. Statham for Lancashire 1964
Largest crowd 16,000 v Australians 1948

LIMITED-OVERS MATCHES

Highest innings total for county 406 for 5 v Berkshire (NWT) 1996
Highest innings total against county 326 for 9 by Hampshire (NWT) 1987
Lowest innings total for county 36 v Sussex (SL) 1973
Lowest innings total against county 62 by Northamptonshire (GC) 1974/by Middlesex (SL) 1998
Highest individual innings for county 201 V.J.Wells v Berkshire (NWT) 1996
Highest individual innings against county 158 Zaheer Abbas for Gloucestershire (NWT) 1983
Highest wicket partnerships for county

1st	228 P.V. Simmons & V.J. Wells	v	Kent	(SL)	1996
2nd	241 P.V. Simmons & V.J. Wells	v	Middlesex	(SL)	1994
3rd	209 P. Willey & D.I. Gower	v	Ireland	(NWT)	1986
4th	131* R.W. Tolchard & J.C. Balderstone	v	Lancashire	(SL)	1974
5th	153 J.M. Dakin & D.L. Maddy	v	Durham	(B&H)	1996
6th	102 M.G. Bevan & N.D. Burns	v	Warwickshire	(SL)	2002
7th	112* B.F. Smith & G.J. Parsons	v	Derbyshire	(SL)	1993
8th	116* N.D. Burns & P.A.J. de Freitas	v	Northamptonshire	(SL)	2001
9th	78 V.J. Wells & G.J. Parsons	v	Lancashire	(SL)	1993
10th	47 J. Ormond & C.C. Lewis	v	Durham	(B&H)	2000

Highest wicket partnerships against county

1st	201 J.H. Hampshire & C.W.J. Athey	for	Yorkshire	(SL)	1978
2nd	187 A.R. Butcher & R.D.V. Knight	for	Surrey	(SL)	1983
3rd	169* N.J. Speak & N.H. Fairbrother	for	Lancashire	(B&H)	1996
4th	161 P.A. Cottey & D.L. Hemp	for	Glamorgan	(NWT)	1995
5th	190 R.J. Blakey & M.J. Foster	for	Yorkshire	(SL)	1993
6th	123 D.A. Reeve & T.L. Penney	for	Warwickshire	(NWT)	1994
7th	129* D. Byas & D. Gough	for	Yorkshire	(SL)	1991
8th	62 M.J. DiVenuto & T.M. Smith	for	Derbyshire	(B&H)	2001
	62 G.O. Jones & J.M. Golding	for	Kent	(SL)	2002
9th	62* G.D. Bridge & A.M. Davies	for	Durham	(B&H)	2002
10th	69 J. Simmons & C.D. Matthews	for	Lancashire	(B&H)	1988

Best bowling performance in a match for county 6 for 17 K. Higgs v Glamorgan (SL) 1973
Best bowling performance in a match against county 6 for 22 M.K. Bore for Nottinghamshire (B&H) 1980
Largest crowd 8,000 v Northamptonshire (NWT) 1987

ONE-DAY INTERNATIONALS

Highest innings total in ODI 252 for 9 by Zimbabwe v India (WC) 1999
Lowest innings total in ODI 68 by Scotland v West Indies (WC) 1999
Highest individual innings in ODI 68* A. Flower for Zimbabwe v India (WC) 1999
Highest wicket partnerships in ODI

1st	21 S. Chanderpaul & P.V. Simmons	for	West Indies v Scotland	(WC)	1999
2nd	42 J.G. Heron & G.A. Paterson	for	Zimbabwe v India	(WC)	1983
3rd	69 M. Amarnath & S.M. Patil	for	India v Zimbabwe	(WC)	1983
4th	99 A.D. Jadeja & S. Ramesh	for	India v Zimbabwe	(WC)	1999

5th	60 A.D.R. Campbell & A. Flower	for Zimbabwe v India	(WC)	1999
6th	9* N. Kapil Dev & Yashpal Sharma	for India v Zimbabwe	(WC)	1983
7th	44 N.R. Mongia & R.R. Singh	for India v Zimbabwe	(WC)	1999
8th	29 A. Flower & H.H. Streak	for Zimbabwe v India	(WC)	1999
9th	20 Asim Butt & G.M. Hamilton	for Scotland v West Indies	(WC)	1999
10th	7 I.P. Butchart & A.J. Traicos	for Zimbabwe v India	(WC)	1983

Best bowling performance in ODI 3 for 7 C.A. Walsh for West Indies v Scotland (WC) 1999
Largest crowd 4,005 India v Zimbabwe (WC) 1999

GROUND INFORMATION

ENTRANCES Park Hill Drive (players and officials cars only, also members and public as pedestrians), Curzon Road (members, public, press/media and all vehicles) and Milligan Road (players and officials and cars only also match day Executive Club entrance only).

MEMBERS' ENCLOSURE Defined area between the Meet and the George Geary Stand in front of the pavilion and including the top of the pavilion in the Butler Stand, Fernie Suite and Quorn Suite.

PUBLIC ENCLOSURE Rest of the ground.

COVERED STANDS The Meet, Pavilion and George Geary Stand.

OPEN STANDS All permanent seating surrounding the playing area plus the Indoor Cricket School seats at the Bennett End of the ground.

NAME OF ENDS Pavilion End, Bennett End.

GROUND DIMENSIONS 151m × 133m.

REPLAY SCREEN If televised matches are staged at the ground the replay screen is sited at the Bennett End.

FIRST AID Situated behind The Meet and in the Indoor Cricket School.

CODES OF DRESS Spectators are required to dress in an appropriate manner consistent with attending a cricket match. Bare torsos are not acceptable in, or in front of the pavilion. Executive Club/Suite users must wear a necktie and jacket.

BEHAVIOUR The club is keen that standards of behaviour should be maintained and members and spectators are urged to report immediately to the General Manager any incident, or potential incident, where they feel action should be taken. Bad language is not acceptable at any match and the club will take prompt and strong action should this or any other ground regulation be ignored.

RECIPROCAL ARRANGEMENTS Members of Derbyshire, Northamptonshire and Nottinghamshire can gain entry free on production of membership card when Leicestershire are not playing their own county.

SUPPORTERS' CLUB Friends of Grace Road membership £5 per year. Details from Friends of Grace Road, 11 Sherborne Avenue, Wigston Magna, Leicester LE18 2GP.

JUNIORS Charlie Fox membership for under-13s £5 per year, junior membership (over-13s to under-18s) £10.50 per year. Contact Membership Secretary (☎ 0116 283 2128) for further information.

CORPORATE ENTERTAINING Leicestershire CCC offers corporate hospitality, which is available for all home games involving Leicestershire's 1st XI. Packages are available to suit a range of budgets and suites can accommodate from 2 to 60 guests. For further details contact the Sales Office (☎ 0116 245 2412).

FACILITIES FOR VISUALLY IMPAIRED SPECTATORS Guide dogs are allowed. Contact Club in advance.

FACILITIES AND ACCESS FOR PEOPLE WITH DISABILITIES INCLUDING WHEELCHAIR ACCESS TO GROUND From Park Hill Drive or Curzon Road entrances to the ground.

DESIGNATED CAR PARK AVAILABLE INSIDE THE GROUND FOR PEOPLE WITH DISABILITIES In car park at Bennett End of the ground.

GOOD VIEWING AREAS INSIDE THE GROUND FOR PEOPLE USING WHEELCHAIRS Yes, there is a special area at the Bennett End and at the Pavilion End of the ground, and a further position adjacent to the main scoreboard. A suitable position should be requested with steward on arrival. A limited amount of space is set aside for cars with disabled stickers at the Bennett End of the ground from where cricket can be viewed from your vehicle. A disabled toilet is situated within the Indoor Cricket School at the Bennett End of the ground.

RAMPS TO PROVIDE EASY ACCESS TO BARS & REFRESHMENT OUTLETS FOR PEOPLE USING WHEELCHAIRS Yes, some buildings can be accessed by ramp but others have small steps and stewards will assist if necessary. There are toilet facilities for people with disabilities in the Indoor School, The Meet and the pavilion via the Charles Palmer Suite Restaurant.

FOOD & DRINK FULL RESTAURANT/DINING FACILITIES Members, yes. Public, yes. The Pavilion Restaurant is

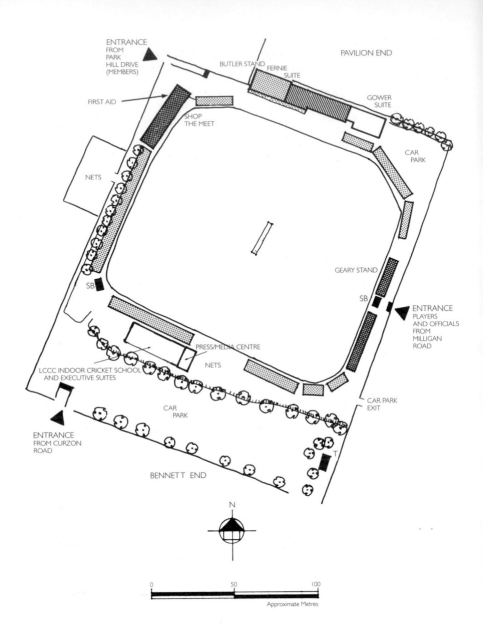

ENTRANCE
FROM
PARK
HILL DRIVE
(MEMBERS)

PAVILION END

BUTLER STAND

FERNIE
SUITE

FIRST AID

GOWER
SUITE

SHOP
THE MEET

CAR
PARK

NETS

GEARY STAND

SB

SB

ENTRANCE
PLAYERS
AND OFFICIALS
FROM
MILLIGAN
ROAD

PRESS/MEDIA CENTRE

LCCC INDOOR CRICKET SCHOOL
AND EXECUTIVE SUITES

NETS

CAR PARK
EXIT

ENTRANCE
FROM CURZON
ROAD

CAR
PARK

T

BENNETT END

N

0   50   100

Approximate Metres

situated in the Charles Palmer Suite and the recently refurbished Fox Bar, and in the Meet Upper there is a restaurant and bar.

TEMPORARY FOOD/DRINK FACILITIES Members, yes. Public, yes.

FOOD SUITABLE FOR VEGETARIANS Members, yes. Public, yes.

BARS Members 4, Public 2.

VARIETIES OF BEER SOLD Worthington and Guinness.

CHILDRENS FACILITIES Crèche, no. Play area, no.

CLUB SHOP Yes, the Friends of Grace Road Shop is located on the ground floor of the Meet bar and Restaurant Stand.

CLUB MUSEUM The Leicestershire CCC Museum is located in the Charles Palmer Suite within the pavilion complex. The museum displays a collection of many photographs as well as other items of cricket memorabilia including caps, ties and chinaware. There are more photographs and plaques in the adjoining room and on the first floor of the Meet charting the history of the running fox county.

CRICKET COACHING FACILITIES Leicestershire CCC's Indoor Cricket School provides coaching and is open for coaching throughout the year. Contact the Indoor Cricket School for details.

CRICKET NETS Leicestershire CCC's Indoor Cricket School is open for nets throughout the year. Contact the Indoor Cricket School for details.

OTHER SPORTING OR RECREATIONAL FACILITIES ON THE GROUND No.

FACILITIES FOR HIRE OR WIDER COMMUNITY USE AT THE GROUND Rooms are available for functions, weddings, exhibitions, Christmas lunches, conferences and business and private entertainment. Contact Hospitality and Conference Sales Department (☎ 0116 245 2451) for further details and a copy of the brochure.

WINTER CRICKET EVENTS Members' club dinners and lunches are staged in the pavilion. Contact Leicestershire CCC Club Office for details.

CAR PARKING FACILITIES There is a large car park at the Bennett End of the ground, which is entered from Curzon Road and can accommodate 300 cars. Otherwise street parking close to ground is available, although car parking in roads immediately adjacent to the ground is restricted when major matches are being played.

OTHER INFORMATION Ted Kirwan of Grace Books and Cards based in Oadby, Leicestershire, has a table with a selection of old cricket books and other items of cricket memorabilia for sale near the Park Hill Drive entrance to the ground at most Sunday matches only. There is no entrance to the ground from Grace Road itself.

GROUND CAPACITY 6,500.

ANTICIPATED GROUND DEVELOPMENTS None.

HOW TO GET THERE

 Leicester Midland station 2 miles, South Wigston station 2.25 miles ☎ 08457 484950, 08457 125678, www.midlandmainline.com, www.thetrainline.com, www.railtrack.co.uk

 Midland Fox Buses 26, 37, 37A, 38, 38A, 47, 48, 48A, 68, 73 and 76 from Belvoir Street (0.25 miles from Leicester station) to Aylestone Road (A426), thence 5 minutes walk to ground, also Leicester Corporation Bus 23 from city centre to Aylestone Road (A426), thence 5 minutes walk to ground. Midland Fox Travel Line ☎ 0116 251 1411 or St Margaret's bus station ☎ 0870 608 2608

 There are cycle routes throughout the area.

 From north: from M1 junction 21 bear left (east) on to A5460, then take A563 (east) towards Aylestone, at junction with A426 turn left (Lutterworth Road), continue on A426 (Aylestone Road), turn right on to Duncan Road, then second left on to Curzon Road. **From south:** from M1 junction 21 take third exit on to A5460, then as for north. **From east:** stay on A47 west (Uppingham Road), continue on A47 to roundabout, take second exit (A594, St George's Way), continue on A594 (Waterloo Way), follow on to Welford Road, follow signs to A426 (Aylestone Road), turn left on to Duncan Road, then second left on to Curzon Road. **From west:** from M69, Leicester, to M1 junction 21, then as for north.

 East Midlands Airport ☎ 01332 852852 www.eastmidlandsairport.co.uk, Birmingham International Airport ☎ 0121 767 5511 www.birminghaminternationalairport.co.uk

WHERE TO STAY

Burlington Hotel (☎ 0116 270 5112), Corus Time Out Hotel (☎ 0116 278 7898 www.corushotels.co.uk/timeout), Days Inn Welcome Break (☎ 0116 239 0534 www.daysinn.com), Gables Hotel (☎ 0116 270 6969 www.thegables.co.uk), Hilton Hotel (☎ 0116 263 0066 www.leicester.hilton.co.uk), Holiday Inn Leicester (☎ 0116 253 1161 www.leicester.holiday-inn.com), Holiday Inn Leicester West (☎ 0116 263 9206 www.leicester.holiday-inn.com), Horse & Hounds Premier Lodge (☎ 0870 700 1418 www.premierlodge.com), Ibis (☎ 0116 248 7200), Leicester Stage Hotel (☎ 0116 288 6161 www.stagehotel.co.uk), Ramada Jarvis Hotel (☎ 0116 255 5599 www.jarvis.co.uk), Spindle Lodge Hotel

(☎ 0116 233 8801 www.smoothhound.co.uk/hotels/spindle.html), The Belmont Hotel (☎ 0116 254 4773 www.belmonthotel.co.uk), The Regency Hotel (☎ 0116 270 9634 www.the-regency-hotel.com)
    For a further selection of places to stay in the Leicester area ☎ 0116 299 8888 or visit www.smoothhound.co.uk or www.discoverleicester.com.

WHERE TO EAT

Bobby's (☎ 0116 266 0106 www.bobbys.co.uk), The Case (☎ 0116 251 7675 www.thecase.co.uk), Curry Fever (☎ 0116 266 2941), Friends Tandoori (☎ 0116 266 8809), Covatis Italian (☎ 0116 251 8251), Opera House (☎ 0116 223 6666), Sharmilee Indian Vegetarian Restaurant (☎ 0116 261 0503 www.sharmilee.co.uk), Shimla Pinks (☎ 0116 247 1471), Stones (☎ 0116 291 0004), The Tiffin (☎ 0116 247 0420 www.the-tiffin.co.uk), Watsons (☎ 0116 222 7770)

TOURIST INFORMATION Leicester Tourist Information Centre, 7–9 Every Street, Town Hall Square, Leicester, Leicestershire LE1 6AG. ☎ 0116 299 8888, 0116 265 7039, 0116 265 7302, 0116 265 7038, 0116 265 7333, www.leicester.gov.uk, www.discoverleicester.com, www.leicestershire.gov.uk

OTHER USEFUL INFORMATION

De Montfort Hall Box Office ☎ 0116 233 3111, www.demontforthall.co.uk
City Museum and Art Gallery ☎ 0116 254 0595
Leicester City Football Club ☎ 0116 291 5000, www.lcfc.co.uk
Leicester City New Football Stadium Tours ☎ 0116 222 8692 (admission free)
Leicester Tigers Rugby Football Club ☎ 0116 254 1607, 08701 283430, www.leicestertigers.com
Leicester Racecourse ☎ 0116 271 6515
National Space Centre ☎ 0870 607 7223, www.spacecentre.co.uk
Leicester Local Travel Line ☎ 0870 608 2608

LOCAL RADIO STATIONS BBC Radio Leicester (95.1 MHz FM/837 KHz MW), Leicester Sound (105.4 MHz FM/1260 KHz MW)

LOCAL NEWSPAPER *Leicester Mercury*

OAKHAM SCHOOL

Address Oakham School, The Pavilion, Doncaster Close, Station Road,
Oakham, Rutland LE15 6DT
Prospects of Play ☎ 01572 722487

HISTORY OF GROUND AND FACILITIES

RUTLAND'S MOTTO 'MULTUM IN PARVO' means 'much in little' and those who visit Doncaster Close, the cricket ground of Oakham School, will find the place rather tranquil compared with the concrete buildings and conurbation of Leicestershire County Cricket Club's headquarters and main ground at Leicester.

    Oakham and the surrounding Rutland countryside have a unique place in the history of cricket. Some 2 miles from the county town of Rutland, the smallest county in England, sited close to the village of Burley was the mansion of Burley-on-the-Hill, which was the seat of the Finch family for many years. George Finch was the Ninth Earl of Winchilsea and he is regarded as the chief founder of the Marylebone Cricket Club in 1787. Finch arranged matches during the 1790s in the park at Burley-on-the-Hill and some of the most famous cricketers of the time played for him. In 1854 an All England team visited Uppingham and in 1881 Finch began staging matches between the MCC and Rutland. These matches were staged at the Lime Kilns Ground just off Brooke Road, Oakham, which is still the home of Oakham Town Cricket Club. Leicestershire County Cricket Club used this ground for Second XI matches in 1924, from 1958 to 1967 and again in 1969. The Pavilion was built between 1938 and 1940 and was opened in May 1940 by the Earl of Ancaster. It is known as the J.M. Bradshaw Pavilion – he was a cousin of J.C. Bradshaw and he died suddenly on 5 December 1938 aged 31. In 1954 a combined Leicestershire and Rutland XI played the Canadian Touring team at Oakham Town CC.

Oakham School is a fully co-educational boarding and day school which includes cricket amongst the sports on offer. The Master-in-Charge of Cricket is Frank C. Hayes, the former Lancashire and England batsman, who is supported by the Cricket Professional, David S. Steele, the former Northamptonshire, Derbyshire, Leicestershire and England batsman.

The Doncaster Close ground is the only ground in the county of Rutland which has been used to stage first-class cricket. In 1907 the MCC staged two matches here and it has also been used by the Gentlemen of Leicestershire for annual cricket weeks.

In 1935 the first first-class match was staged when Leicestershire played Kent, who were defeated by an innings. In the following year Derbyshire were the visitors and they were the victors. Derbyshire were in fact County Champions ahead of the match at Oakham School. In 1937 Warwickshire visited and then in 1938 Kent came back to Doncaster Close.

The original thatched pavilion was destroyed by fire in 1972, the same year that the Sports Hall was constructed at the Station Road End of the ground. The present pavilion was built in 1902–3 and was opened on 4 July 1903 by Old

The Wharton Pavilion.

Oakhamian Mr C.R. Jacobs, who was then President of the Rugby Football Union. It is named in memory of Sir Anthony Wharton CBE TD DL, (Old Oakhamian, 1917–80), who was a Trustee of Oakham School from 1959 to 1980 and was himself a former President of the Rugby Football Union. The new pavilion is built in brick and was cleverly converted from the former gymnasium. The conversion of this building from a gymnasium was made possible by the generosity of Mrs Pauline Bayles and Mrs Ruth Marrin, sisters of Sir Anthony, and by his friends and the many Old Oakhamians and parents who subscribed to the Quarter Centenary Appeal Fund.

The Stumps Bar in the Wharton Pavilion was opened by Northamptonshire and England batsman Allan Lamb on 15 April 1999 and in a cabinet on one wall is a set of 12 World Cup signed cricket bats from that year's competition.

The only two Old Oakhamians to have played first-class matches on the ground are A.P.F. 'Percy' Chapman, captain of Kent in 1935 who scored 47 runs and had played for the School XI in 1914 scoring 279 runs and taking 8 wickets, and J.A.S. Taylor for Leicestershire in 1937, scoring 22 runs and taking 0 for 10, who played 47 matches for the School XI from 1931 to 1935 during which time he amassed 1,866 runs, bagged 58 wickets and held 27 catches. On the walls of the pavilion are photographs of nearly every School 1st XI cricket team from 1891 onwards.

Oakham School's Doncaster Close ground is a welcome addition to the county circuit and further matches are planned at this attractive and well-organised school venue. The only other school venues presently being used for first-class cricket are King's School Gloucester, Cheltenham College, Millfield School and Whitgift School.

Five first-class matches were staged on the ground between 1935 and 2000 and two limited-overs matches were held in 2001 and 2002. On 4 to 6 July 1999 an ECB XI played Sri Lanka 'A' touring team, in 2000 a NatWest Under-19 Test was staged between England and Sri Lanka and in 2001 a NatWest Under-19 Test was staged between England and the West Indies. Also in 1999, ahead of the Cricket World Cup, India, who were being hosted by Leicestershire County Cricket Club at Grace Road, staged a match on 28 April against the Loughborough Students team. India amassed 291 for 4 with Mohammed Azharuddin 66 and Sachin Tendulkar 64. The Students were 98 all out. Robin Singh 2 for 6 and Ajay Jadeja 2 for 7 were the pick of the bowlers

In 2002 the Sir Henry Grierson Trophy was awarded to Oakham School by the XL Forty Club at their annual dinner at the Savoy Hotel, London.

GROUND RECORDS AND SCORES

FIRST-CLASS MATCHES

Highest innings total for county 343 v Warwickshire 1937
Highest innings total against county 519 by Kent 1938
Lowest innings total for county 121 v Derbyshire 1936
Lowest innings total against county 56 by Kent 1935
Highest individual innings for county 125 N.F. Armstrong v Warwickshire 1937
Highest individual innings against county 295* A.D. Brown for Surrey 2000

Highest wicket partnerships for county

1st	180 G.L. Berry & C.S. Dempster	v	Kent	1938
2nd	57 G.L. Berry & N.F. Armstrong	v	Kent	1935
3rd	103 N.F. Armstrong & G.S. Watson	v	Warwickshire	1937
4th	69 G.L. Berry & F.T. Prentice	v	Kent	1935
5th	38 N.F. Armstrong & G. Lester	v	Warwickshire	1937
6th	95 F.T. Prentice & P.R. Cherrington	v	Kent	1938
7th	31 D.I. Stevens & P.A.J. de Freitas	v	Surrey	2000
8th	55 P.A.J. de Freitas & N.D. Burns	v	Surrey	2000
9th	26 G. Geary & H.A. Smith	v	Kent	1935
10th	36 G.O. Dawkes & W.H. Flamson	v	Kent	1938

Highest wicket partnerships against county

1st	84 W.A. Hill & J. Buckingham	for	Warwickshire	1937
2nd	209 T.S. Worthington & D. Smith	for	Derbyshire	1936
3rd	101 A.E. Fagg & B.H. Valentine	for	Kent	1938
4th	135 B.H. Valentine & F.G.H. Chalk	for	Kent	1938
5th	38 B.H. Valentine & L.J. Todd	for	Kent	1938
6th	100 B.H. Valentine & C.H. Todd	for	Kent	1938
7th	120 R.E.S. Wyatt & P. Cranmer	for	Warwickshire	1937
8th	141 A.D. Brown & A.J. Tudor	for	Surrey	2000
9th	33 A.D. Brown & I.D.K. Salisbury	for	Surrey	2000
10th	141 A.D. Brown & Saqlain Mushtaq	for	Surrey	2000

Best bowling performance in an innings for county 6 for 141 W.H. Flamson v Warwickshire 1937
Best bowling performance in an innings against county 8 for 123 A.P. Freeman for Kent 1935
Best bowling performance in a match for county 8 for 121 H.A. Smith v Kent 1935
Best bowling performance in a match against county 11 for 106 F.E. Woolley for Kent 1938
Largest crowd 4,000 v Kent 1938

LIMITED-OVERS MATCHES

Highest innings total for county 207 for 4 v Nottinghamshire 2001
Highest innings total against county 204 by Nottinghamshire 2001
Highest individual innings for county 67* D.J. Marsh v Nottinghamshire 2001
Highest individual innings against county 75 P. Johnson for Nottinghamshire 2001

Highest wicket partnerships for county

1st	70 V.J. Wells & J.M. Dakin	v	Nottinghamshire	2001
2nd	31 J.M. Dakin & T.R. Ward	v	Nottinghamshire	2001
3rd	0 J.M. Dakin & D.J. Marsh	v	Nottinghamshire	2001
4th	96 D.J. Marsh & B.F. Smith	v	Nottinghamshire	2001
5th	10* D.J. Marsh & D.L. Maddy	v	Nottinghamshire	2001

6th to 10th yet to be established.

Highest wicket partnerships against county

1st	15 D.J. Bicknell & G.E. Welton	for	Nottinghamshire	2001
2nd	2 G.E. Welton & G.S. Blewett	for	Nottinghamshire	2001
3rd	57 G.E. Welton & U. Afzaal	for	Nottinghamshire	2001
4th	44 U. Afzaal & P. Johnson	for	Nottinghamshire	2001
5th	52 P. Johnson & K.P. Pietersen	for	Nottinghamshire	2001
6th	29 P. Johnson & C.M.W. Read	for	Nottinghamshire	2001
7th	1 P. Johnson & P.J. Franks	for	Nottinghamshire	2001
8th	3 P.J. Franks & A.J. Harris	for	Nottinghamshire	2001
9th	0 P.J. Franks & R.D. Stemp	for	Nottinghamshire	2001
10th	1 P.J. Franks & G.J. Smith	for	Nottinghamshire	2001

Best bowling performance in a match for county 4 for 44 D.J. Marsh v Nottinghamshire 2001
Best bowling performance in a match against county 2 for 26 P.J. Franks for Nottinghamshire 2001
Largest crowd 3,000 v Nottinghamshire (SL) 2001

GROUND INFORMATION

ENTRANCES Station Road (players and officials cars only plus members and public, pedestrians only). Members and public via pedestrian entrance (west) from car park off Kilburn Road and also from Buchanans Drive through School for match officials only.

MEMBERS' ENCLOSURE Pavilion and defined members' area which is roped off.

PUBLIC ENCLOSURE Rest of the ground.

COVERED STANDS Pavilion (part).

OPEN STANDS All temporary seating surrounding the playing area.

GROUND DIMENSIONS 128m × 135m.

NAME OF ENDS Nursery End, Sports Hall End.

REPLAY SCREEN If televised matches are staged at the ground the replay screen is sited by the Doncaster Close End of the ground.

FIRST AID In the pavilion and in sports hall.

CODES OF DRESS Spectators are required to dress in an appropriate manner consistent with attending a cricket match. Bare torsos are not acceptable in, or in front of the pavilion. Executive Club/Suite users must wear a necktie and jacket.

BEHAVIOUR The club is keen that standards of behaviour should be maintained and members and spectators are urged to report immediately to the General Manager any incident, or potential incident, where they feel action should be taken. Bad language is not acceptable at any match and the club will take prompt and strong action should this or any other ground regulation be ignored.

RECIPROCAL ARRANGEMENTS Members of Derbyshire, Northamptonshire and Nottinghamshire can gain entry free on production of membership card when Leicestershire are not playing their own county.

SUPPORTERS' CLUB Friends of Grace Road membership £5 per year. Details from Friends of Grace Road, 11 Sherborne Avenue, Wigston Magna, Leicester, LE18 2GP.

JUNIORS Charlie Fox membership for under-13s £5 per year, junior membership (over-13s to under-18s) £10.50 per year. Contact Membership Secretary (☎ 0116 283 2128) for further information.

CORPORATE ENTERTAINING Leicestershire CCC offers corporate hospitality, which is available for all home games involving Leicestershire's 1st XI. Packages are available to suit a range of budgets and suites can accommodate from 2 to 60 guests. For further details contact the Sales Office (☎ 0116 245 2412) for further information and a brochure.

FACILITIES FOR VISUALLY IMPAIRED SPECTATORS Guide dogs are allowed. Contact club in advance.

FACILITIES AND ACCESS FOR PEOPLE WITH DISABILITIES Yes, from Kilburn Road via Pedestrian Entrance (West).

DESIGNATED CAR PARK AVAILABLE INSIDE THE GROUND FOR PEOPLE WITH DISABILITIES Yes, in Kilburn Road car park.

GOOD VIEWING AREAS INSIDE THE GROUND FOR PEOPLE USING WHEELCHAIRS No special area. A suitable position should be requested with steward on arrival. A limited amount of space is set aside for cars with disabled stickers at the Doncaster Close End of the ground by the sightscreen, from where cricket can be viewed from vehicle.

RAMPS TO PROVIDE EASY ACCESS TO BARS & REFRESHMENT OUTLETS FOR PEOPLE USING WHEELCHAIRS Yes, some buildings can be accessed by ramp but others have small steps and stewards will assist if necessary.

FOOD & DRINK FULL RESTAURANT/DINING FACILITIES Executive members, yes. Members, yes. Public, yes.

TEMPORARY FOOD/DRINK FACILITIES Members, yes. Public, yes.

FOOD SUITABLE FOR VEGETARIANS Members, yes. Public, yes.

BARS Members 1, Public 1.

VARIETIES OF BEER SOLD Worthington, Guinness.

CHILDREN'S FACILITIES Crèche, no. Play area, no.

CLUB SHOP The Friends of Grace Road Shop have a table in a small tent.

CLUB MUSEUM No, but there are plenty of cricket photographs and pictures relating to previous Leicestershire CCC matches at the School Ground plus other important matches in the pavilion and on the walls within the entrance to the Sports Hall. Look out for some famous old boys amongst them including A.P.F. Chapman.

CRICKET COACHING FACILITIES Yes, contact Oakham School for full details.

CRICKET NETS Yes, contact Oakham School for full details.

OTHER SPORTING OR RECREATIONAL FACILITIES ON THE GROUND Swimming pool, sports hall, Fives courts, tennis courts and rugby and football pitches close by.

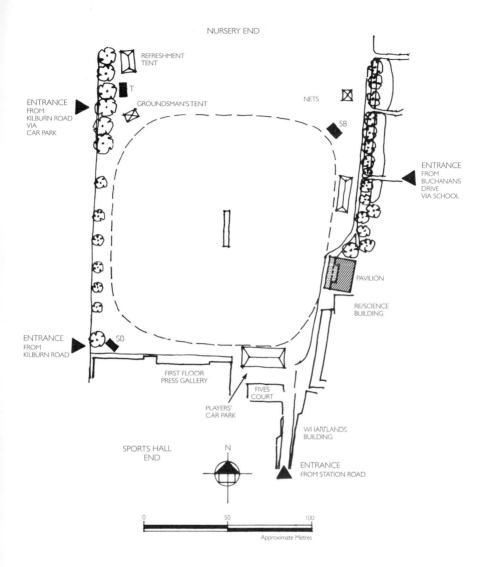

NURSERY END

REFRESHMENT
TENT

T

GROUNDSMAN'S TENT

NETS

ENTRANCE
FROM
KILBURN ROAD
VIA
CAR PARK

SB

ENTRANCE
FROM
BUCHANANS
DRIVE
VIA SCHOOL

PAVILION

RE/SCIENCE
BUILDING

ENTRANCE
FROM
KILBURN ROAD

SB

FIRST FLOOR
PRESS GALLERY

FIVES
COURT

PLAYERS'
CAR PARK

WHARFLANDS
BUILDING

SPORTS HALL
END

N

ENTRANCE
FROM STATION ROAD

0   50   100
Approximate Metres

FACILITIES FOR HIRE OR WIDER COMMUNITY USE AT THE GROUND Contact Oakham School for full details.
WINTER CRICKET EVENTS None.
CAR PARKING FACILITIES Car parking is available for 300 cars with the School Grounds at £4 per car and is accessed via Kilburn Road on the Farside Playing Fields.
OTHER INFORMATION Ted Kirwan of Grace Books and Cards based in Oadby, Leicestershire, sometimes has a table with a selection of old cricket books and other items of cricket memorabilia for sale at matches.
GROUND CAPACITY 4,000.
ANTICIPATED GROUND DEVELOPMENTS None currently planned.

HOW TO GET THERE

Oakham station is 0.25 miles from the ground and is on the line between Birmingham New Street and Stansted Airport, Cambridge and Norwich. ☎ 08457 484950, 0121 643 4444 or Reservations ☎ 0870 000 6060, www.centraltrains.com, www.thetrainline.com, www.railtrack.co.uk

CrossCounty Service operated by Arriva Fox County, which serves Leicestershire and Rutland. Bus 747, from Leicester St. Margaret's Bus Station to Uppingham North Street East passes through Oakham. For information contact Busline ☎ 0116 251 1411, Travel Line 0870 608 2608, National Express ☎ 0900 808080, www.gobycoach.com, www.nationalexpress.com

 There are cycle routes to this area of the town. There is also a 25 mile off road cycle route around nearby Rutland Water.

 From north: from M1 junction 24 take A6 (south), at junction with A6006 follow A6006 towards Melton Mowbray, follow signs to A606 (Oakham), in Oakham turn left on to B668 (Station Road), turn left on to Kilburn Road. **From south:** from A14 at Kettering turn off at junction 7 and follow A43 (east), turn left on to A6003 (Rockingham Road, Uppingham Road) and continue to Oakham, turn left on to A606 (Catmos Street), turn right on to B668 (Burley Road), turn left on to Station Road, turn right on to Kilburn Road. **From east:** from A1(M) junction 17 (Peterborough) continue on A1 to junction with A606, turn left (west) on to A606 (Empingham Road), continue on this road into Oakham, turn right on to B668 (Burley Road), turn left on to Station Road, turn right on to Kilburn Road. **From west:** from Leicester take A47 (Uppingham Road), continue on this road to roundabout at junction with A6003, take second exit (north) and continue into Oakham, turn left on to A606 (Catmos Street), turn right on to B668 (Burley Road), turn left on to Station Road, turn right on to Kilburn Road.

 Stansted Airport ☎ 08700 000303 www.stanstedairport.co.uk, Birmingham International Airport ☎ 0121 767 5511 www.birminghaminternationalairport.co.uk

WHERE TO STAY

Barnsdale Hall Hotel and Country Club (☎ 01572 757901 www.barnsdalehotel.co.uk), Clifton House Guesthouse (☎ 01572 722362), Grove Guesthouse (☎ 01572 722814),Lord Nelsons House Hotel (☎ 01572 723199 www.nelsons-house.com), Manton Lodge Farm (☎ 01572 737269), Milburn Hotel (☎ 01572 723330 www.rutnet.co.uk/milburnhotel), The Admiral Hornblower (☎ 01572 723004 www.hornblowerhotel.co.uk), The Old Wisteria Hotel (☎ 01572 722844), Whipper-In Hotel (☎ 01572 756971 www.brook-hotels.co.uk)
   For a further selection of places to stay in the Oakham area contact ☎ 01572 724329 www.smoothhound.co.uk or www.rutnet.co.uk.

WHERE TO EAT

Admiral Hornblower Restaurant & Bar (☎ 01572 723004), Fox & Hounds (☎ 01572 812403), Hambleton Hall (☎ 01572 756991), Lord Nelsons House Restaurant (☎ 01572 723199), The Old Wisteria Restaurant (☎ 01572 722844), Whipper-In Restaurant (☎ 01572 756971)

TOURIST INFORMATION Oakham Tourist Information Centre, Flores House, High Street, Oakham, Rutland LE15 8PX. ☎ 01572 724329 www.rutnet.co.uk

OTHER USEFUL INFORMATION

Oakham School ☎ 01572 758758, www.oakham.org.uk
Rutland Water Tourist Information Centre ☎ 01572 653026, www.rutlandwater.net

LOCAL RADIO STATIONS BBC Radio Leicester (95.1 MHz FM/837 KHz MW), Leicester Sound (105.4 MHz FM/1260 KHz MW)

LOCAL NEWSPAPERS *Leicester Mercury, Rutland Times*

Middlesex

**Lord's
Richmond
Shenley
Southgate
Uxbridge**

MIDDLESEX COUNTY CRICKET CLUB, LORD'S CRICKET GROUND, ST JOHNS WOOD ROAD, LONDON NW8 8QN

Telephone	020 7289 1300
fax	020 7289 5831
Email	middx@middlesexccc.com
Website	www.middlesexccc.com
Middlesex Cricket Academy	East End Road, Finchley, London N3 2TA
Telephone	020 8346 8020
Fax	020 8349 1241

Founded 2 February 1864

Colours blue

Crest three Seaxes

National Cricket League Nickname Crusaders

National Cricket League Colours dark blue with white and red trim

Patron HRH The Prince Philip, Duke of Edinburgh KG, KT

President R.A. Gale

Vice Presidents M.P. Murray, R. Gerard OBE, KStJ, D. Bennett

Chairman P.H. Edmonds

Chairman Cricket Committee D. Bennett

Hon Treasurer G.W. Norris

Secretary V.J. Codrington

PA to Secretary Miss V.L. Skelton

Assistant Secretary J.E. Fitch

Membership Secretary Mrs D.M. Short

Merchandise Shop Manager E.C.P. Howes

Head Coach J.E. Emburey

Assistant Coach J.C. Pooley

Youth Coach P.A. Knappett

Captain A.J. Strauss

Vice Captain O.A. Shah

Scorer 1st XI M.J. Smith

Scorer 2nd XI A.P. Jones

Physiotherapist B. Spencer

Groundsmen M. Hunt (Lord's), A. Atkinson (Shenley) and S. Martin (Southgate)

Middlesex Academy Manager Mrs J. Cruder

Sponsors Northern Rock

Yearbook £10 (free to Middlesex members)

Scorecard 30p or 50p depending on fixture

Match Programme £1.70 (£1.20 to members) issued for all home matches

Magazine *The Crusader* Middlesex County Cricket Club Official Magazine (free to Middlesex members)

Frizzell County Championship Status Division 1

National Cricket League Status Division 2

ACHIEVEMENTS

County Championship Champions 1866, 1903, 1920, 1921, 1947, 1976, 1980, 1982, 1985, 1990, 1993; Joint Champions 1949, 1977

Gillette Cup Winners 1977, 1980, Finalists 1975

NatWest Trophy Winners 1984, 1988, Finalists 1989

Benson and Hedges Cup Winners 1983, 1986, Finalists 1975

John Player Sunday League 2nd 1982

Refuge Assurance Sunday League 3rd 1988

Sunday League Champions 1992

Norwich Union National League Best 4th Division 2 2000

Refuge Assurance Cup Winners 1990

MIDDLESEX CRICKET BOARD

Chairman A.E Moss
Secretary P.H. Painton
Treasurer J.A. Hamblin
Administration & Development Secretary D.R. Holland
Youth & Coaching Development Officer P.A. Knappett
Community Cricket Officer G.C. West (Middlesex Academy)
Women & Girls Development Officer Miss L. Poole (Middlesex Academy)
Development Projects Executive Mrs P. Chambers (Middlesex Academy)

Address Middlesex Cricket Board, Lord's Cricket Ground, St John's Wood Road,
London NW8 8QN
☎ 020 7266 1650
Fax 020 7289 5831
Email david.holland@middlesexccc.com
Website www.middlesexccc.com

GROUNDS

London (Lord's Cricket Ground, St John's Wood Road), Richmond (Old Deer Park, Kew Road), Shenley (Denis Compton Oval, Shenley), Southgate (The Walker Cricket Ground, Waterfall Road) and Uxbridge (Gatting Way, Park Road)
Other grounds used since 1969: Enfield (Lincoln Road, Enfield) and Watford Town (Woodside, Garston)

SECOND XI GROUNDS

In addition to the above mentioned grounds the following are used for Second XI matches:
Ealing CC, Corfton Road, Ealing, London W5 ☎ 020 8997 1858
Finchley CC, adjoining Middlesex Cricket Academy, East End Road, Finchley, London N3 ☎ 020 8346 1822
Harrow CC, Wood End Road, Harrow, Middlesex ☎ 020 8422 0932
Merchant Taylor's School, Sandy Lodge Lane, Moor Park, Northwood, Middlesex, no ☎ on ground
RAF Sports Ground, Vine Lane, Uxbridge, Middlesex ☎ 01895 237144
Winchmore Hill CC, The Paulin Ground, Ford's Grove, Winchmore Hill, London N21 ☎ 020 8360 1271

The Warner Stand, Lord's.

LORD'S

For a history of the ground together with ground information, where to stay and how to get there please refer to the Marylebone Cricket Club section of this guide.

GROUND RECORDS AND SCORES

FIRST-CLASS MATCHES FOR MIDDLESEX

Highest innings total for county 612 for 8 dec v Nottinghamshire 1921
Highest innings total against county 665 by West Indians 1939
Lowest innings total for county 20 v MCC 1864
Lowest innings total against county 35 by Somerset 1899
Highest individual innings for county 277* E.H. Hendren v Kent 1922
Highest individual innings against county 316* J.B. Hobbs for Surrey 1926
Highest wicket partnerships for county

1st	367* G.D. Barlow & W.N. Slack	v	Kent	1981
2nd	380 F.A. Tarrant & J.W. Hearne	v	Lancashire	1914
3rd	424* W.J. Edrich & D.C.S. Compton	v	Somerset	1948
4th	325 J.W. Hearne & E.H. Hendren	v	Hampshire	1919
5th	217 M.R. Ramprakash & K.R. Brown	v	Surrey	1995
6th	270 J.D. Carr & P.N. Weekes	v	Gloucestershire	1994
7th	264 J.D. Carr & P.N. Weekes	v	Somerset	1994
8th	182* M.H.C. Doll & H.R. Murrell	v	Nottinghamshire	1913
9th	142 R. Routledge & J.M. Sims	v	Surrey	1951
10th	230 R.W. Nicholls & W. Roche	v	Kent	1899

Highest wicket partnerships against county

1st	266 N. Kilner & E.J. Smith	for	Warwickshire	1927
2nd	258 T.S. Curtis & G.A. Hick	for	Worcestershire	1987
3rd	301 H. Sutcliffe & M. Leyland	for	Yorkshire	1939
4th	316 D.J. Bicknell & K.P. Pietersen	for	Nottinghamshire	2002
5th	288 A.D. Brown & I.D.K. Salisbury	for	Surrey	1999
6th	226* V.S. Hazare & V.H. Mankad	for	Indians	1946
7th	199 K.P. Pietersen & P.J. Franks	for	Nottinghamshire	2001
8th	192 W.L. Neale & A.E. Wilson	for	Gloucestershire	1938
	192 T.L. Penney & K.J. Piper	for	Warwickshire	1992
9th	123 W.A.Flint & H.Larwood	for	Nottinghamshire	1927
10th	132 V.A. Valentine & H.C. Griffith	for	West Indians	1933

Best bowling performance in an innings for county 10 for 40 G.O.B. Allen v Lancashire 1929
Best bowling performance in an innings against county 9 for 38 R.C. Robertson-Glasgow for Somerset 1924
Best bowling performance in a match for county 15 for 47 F.A. Tarrant v Hampshire 1913
Best bowling performance in a match against county 15 for 68 F.W. Tate for Sussex 1902
Largest crowd 15,000 v Derbyshire 1947

LIMITED-OVERS MATCHES

Highest innings total for county 290 for 6 v Worcestershire (SL) 1990
Highest innings total against county 322 for 4 by Somerset (B&H) 1996
Lowest innings total for county 72 v Northamptonshire (SL) 2002
Lowest innings total against county 59 by Somerset (GC) 1977
Highest individual innings for county 158 G.D. Barlow v Lancashire (NWT) 1984
Highest individual innings against county 151* M.P. Maynard for Glamorgan (B&H) 1996

Highest wicket partnerships for county

1st	167 M.A. Roseberry & J.C. Pooley	v	Derbyshire	(SL)	1991
2nd	223 M.J. Smith & C.T. Radley	v	Hampshire	(GC)	1977
3rd	165 M.R. Ramprakash & J.D. Carr	v	Nottinghamshire	(SL)	1993
4th	185* M.R. Ramprakash & M.W. Gatting	v	Hampshire	(SL)	1993
5th	120 K.R. Brown & P.N. Weekes	v	Sussex	(B&H)	1998
6th	119 K.R. Brown & D.J. Nash	v	British Universities	(B&H)	1995
7th	132 K.R. Brown & N.F. Williams	v	Somerset	(SL)	1988
8th	112 D.C. Nash & A.A. Noffke	v	Sussex	(B&H)	2002
9th	73 D.C. Nash & A.R.C. Fraser	v	Northamptonshire	(SL)	1999
10th	45 W.W. Daniel & R.J. Maru	v	Kent	(SL)	1980

Highest wicket partnerships against county

1st	167 M.D. Moxon & A.A. Metcalfe	for	Yorkshire	(SL)	1991
2nd	188 M.N. Lathwell & S.C. Ecclestone	for	Somerset	(B&H)	1996
3rd	153* C.E.B. Rice & P. Johnson	for	Nottinghamshire	(SL)	1986
4th	141 S.R. Waugh & R.J. Bartlett	for	Somerset	(SL)	1988
	141 G.W. White & A.N. Aymes	for	Hampshire	(NWT)	1998
5th	105 C.W.J. Athey & K.M. Curran	for	Gloucestershire	(SL)	1985
6th	104 I.T. Botham & N.F.M. Popplewell	for	Somerset	(NWT)	1983
7th	91 G.J. Saville & R.N.S. Hobbs	for	Essex	(B&H)	1972
8th	105 W.K. Hegg & I.D. Austin	for	Lancashire	(SL)	1991
9th	88 S.N. Hartley & A. Ramage	for	Yorkshire	(SL)	1982
10th	39* A.A. Khan & M.A. Robinson	for	Sussex	(SL)	1997

Best bowling performance in a match for county 7 for 22 J.R. Thomson v Hampshire (B&H) 1981
Best bowling performance in a match against county 6 for 33 V.A. Holder for Worcestershire (SL) 1972
Largest crowd 15,000 v Somerset (NWT) 1983

RICHMOND

Address Richmond Cricket Club, The Pavilion, Old Deer Park,
187 Kew Road, Richmond, Surrey, TW9 2AZ
Prospects of Play ☎ 020 8332 6696

HISTORY OF GROUND AND FACILITIES

RICHMOND CRICKET CLUB are based at Old Deer Park, Richmond, and belong to the Middlesex County Cricket League even though Richmond is in Surrey. The ground is next to Kew Gardens. The club currently field four league sides on a Saturday and two or three on a Sunday. The 1st, 2nd and 3rd XIs play in the Middlesex County Cricket League, of which the 1st XI were champions in 1998. The Gentlemen's XI (4th team) are also members of a Saturday league. The club are also active in cup cricket at a national and local level, and Sunday cricket is given an important role with a full fixture list until October.

Richmond Cricket Club aspire to have the leading colts section in south-west London. There are currently 150 colts (between the ages of 5 and 16) playing recreational and competitive cricket for Richmond. A number represent Middlesex in their own age groups.

Richmond have impressive practice facilities including four artificial nets and a ˙ne in the middle. In 2002 Ben Hutton from Middlesex assisted with coaching

The Old Deer Park with cricket in progress between Middlesex and Nottinghamshire in the Norwich Union National League, 2000. Kew Gardens and the London Welsh RFC stand are in the background.

during weekly practice sessions. Middlesex commitments permitting, he also turned out for Richmond Cricket Club 1st XI on Saturdays.

The ground is in Old Deer Park and the facilities are shared with the London Welsh Rugby Football Club who use it for matches in the winter months.

As early as the nineteenth century a gate charge was made to enter the ground: 6d for a person on foot, 1s or 2s 6d for a horseman and a rich man in his carriage had to pay from 2s 6d to 5s.

Many former and current Test and county cricketers have played for Richmond Cricket Club and as a result it has been one of the strongest in the Greater London area for many years. They include G.L. Jessop (Gloucestershire), G.A. Faulkner (South Africa), H.L. Dales, C.D. Gray, C. Goldie and B. Hutton (Middlesex), H.S. Squires (Surrey), B.L. Bisgood (Somerset), T.B. Reddick (Nottinghamshire), G.R. Langdale and P. Vaulkhard (Derbyshire). Chris Goldie, the former Cambridge University, Middlesex and Hampshire wicket-keeper, is a member of Richmond Cricket Club and is also a committee member of the county club.

Middlesex CCC have staged two National Cricket League fixtures at Old Deer Park – against Nottinghamshire in 2000 and then with Sussex in 2001. The ground has also been used by Surrey CCC for 2nd XI matches. In 2003 Middlesex return to Richmond for a National Cricket League match with Scotland and for a Twenty20 match with Kent.

GROUND RECORDS

LIMITED-OVERS MATCHES

Highest innings total for county 148 for 3 v Nottinghamshire (SL) 2000
Highest innings total against county 125 for 7 by Nottinghamshire (SL) 2000

Lowest innings total for county 109 v Sussex (SL) 2001
Lowest innings total against county 110 for 2 by Sussex (SL) 2001
Highest individual innings for county 53* M.R. Ramprakash v Nottinghamshire (SL) 2000
Highest individual innings against county 43 J.E.R. Gallian for Nottinghamshire (SL) 2000
Highest wicket partnerships for county

1st	34 A.J. Strauss & D. Alleyne	v	Nottinghamshire	(SL)	2000
2nd	36 D. Alleyne & J.L. Langer	v	Nottinghamshire	(SL)	2000
3rd	35 O.A. Shah & E.C. Joyce	v	Sussex	(SL)	2001
4th	75* M.R. Ramprakash & E.C. Joyce	v	Nottinghamshire	(SL)	2000
5th	11 O.A. Shah & C.B. Keegan	v	Sussex	(SL)	2001
6th	9 O.A. Shah & S.P. Fleming	v	Sussex	(SL)	2001
7th	0 O.A. Shah & D.C. Nash	v	Sussex	(SL)	2001
8th	10 D.C. Nash & S.J. Cook	v	Sussex	(SL)	2001
9th	6 S.J. Cook & A.J. Coleman	v	Sussex	(SL)	2001
10th	1 A.J. Coleman & T.F. Bloomfield	v	Sussex	(SL)	2001

Highest wicket partnerships against county

1st	46 R.R. Montgomerie & J.R. Carpenter	for	Sussex	(SL)	2001
2nd	21 R.R. Montgomerie & M.J.G. Davis	for	Sussex	(SL)	2001
3rd	43* R.R. Montgomerie & M.W. Goodwin	for	Sussex	(SL)	2001
4th	50 J.E.R. Gallian & U. Afzaal	for	Nottinghamshire	(SL)	2000
5th	18 U. Afzaal & M.N. Bowen	for	Nottinghamshire	(SL)	2000
6th	9 U. Afzaal & C.M.W. Read	for	Nottinghamshire	(SL)	2000
7th	0 U. Afzaal & C.M. Tolley	for	Nottinghamshire	(SL)	2000
8th	6* C.M. Tolley & P.R. Reiffel	for	Nottinghamshire	(SL)	2000

9th and 10th yet to be established.
Best bowling performance in a match for county 3 for 26 R.L. Johnson v Nottinghamshire (SL) 2000
Best bowling performance in a match against county 4 for 24 M.J.G. Davis for Sussex (SL) 2001
Largest crowd 3,500 v Nottinghamshire 2000

GROUND INFORMATION

ENTRANCES Kew Road (players, officials, press/media, members, public and vehicles).
MEMBERS' ENCLOSURE Pavilion and defined members' area in front of pavilion.
PUBLIC ENCLOSURE Rest of the ground.
COVERED STANDS Pavilion.
OPEN STANDS Rest of ground.
NAME OF ENDS Pavilion End, Town End.
GROUND DIMENSIONS 153m × 140m.
REPLAY SCREEN If televised matches are staged at the ground the replay screen is sited on the rugby ground side.
FIRST AID In the pavilion.
CODES OF DRESS Spectators are required to dress in an appropriate manner consistent with attending a cricket match. Bare torsos are not acceptable in, or in front of the pavilion. Executive Club/Suite users must wear a necktie and jacket.
BEHAVIOUR The club is keen that standards of behaviour should be maintained and members and spectators are urged to report immediately to the CEO any incident, or potential incident, where they feel action should be taken. Bad language is not acceptable at any match and the club will take prompt and strong action should this or any other ground regulation be ignored.
RECIPROCAL ARRANGEMENTS Members of Richmond CC can use the pavilion when Middlesex is playing on the ground.
SUPPORTERS' CLUB Seaxe Club £10 per annum, contact Middlesex CCC for details.
JUNIORS Junior Crusader Kids £10 per annum. Contact Membership Department for details.
CORPORATE ENTERTAINING Contact Middlesex CCC for details of corporate hospitality in marquees on ground.
FACILITIES FOR VISUALLY IMPAIRED SPECTATORS No reduction. Guide dogs are allowed. Contact club in advance.

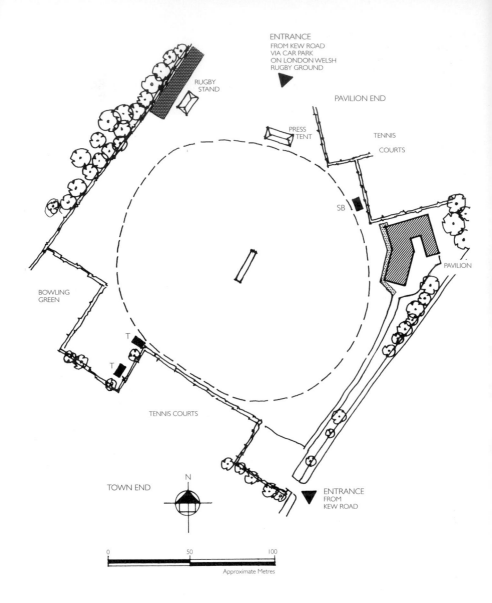

ENTRANCE
FROM KEW ROAD
VIA CAR PARK
ON LONDON WELSH
RUGBY GROUND

RUGBY
STAND

PAVILION END

PRESS
TENT

TENNIS

COURTS

SB

PAVILION

BOWLING
GREEN

T

T

TENNIS COURTS

TOWN END

N

ENTRANCE
FROM
KEW ROAD

0   50   100

Approximate Metres

FACILITIES AND ACCESS FOR PEOPLE WITH DISABILITIES INCLUDING WHEELCHAIR ACCESS TO GROUND Yes, from Kew Road entrance.

DESIGNATED CAR PARK AVAILABLE INSIDE THE GROUND FOR PEOPLE WITH DISABILITIES Yes, there is a car parking area set aside on the rugby ground.

GOOD VIEWING AREAS INSIDE THE GROUND FOR PEOPLE USING WHEELCHAIRS Yes, generally around the whole boundary although because of the steps it is difficult to get into the pavilion.

DESIGNATED VIEWING AREAS FOR PEOPLE USING WHEELCHAIRS Yes.

RAMPS TO PROVIDE EASY ACCESS TO BARS & REFRESHMENT OUTLETS FOR PEOPLE USING WHEELCHAIRS No.

FOOD & DRINK FULL RESTAURANT/DINING FACILITIES Members, yes. Public, yes. Food can be purchased from the outlet in the pavilion lounge area.

TEMPORARY FOOD/DRINK FACILITIES Members, yes. Public, yes.

FOOD SUITABLE FOR VEGETARIANS Members, yes. Public, yes.
BARS Members 1, Public 1.
VARIETIES OF BEER SOLD Various brands available.
CHILDREN'S FACILITIES Crèche, no. Play area, no.
CLUB SHOP Middlesex CCC have a mobile shop on the ground sited in the pavilion bar area.
CLUB MUSEUM No.
CRICKET COACHING FACILITIES Yes, contact Richmond CC.
CRICKET NETS Yes, contact Richmond CC.
OTHER SPORTING OR RECREATIONAL FACILITIES ON THE GROUND Rugby union, hockey and squash.
FACILITIES FOR HIRE OR WIDER COMMUNITY USE AT THE GROUND Rooms are available for functions, weddings, exhibitions, Christmas lunches, conferences and business and private entertainment. Contact Richmond CC for details.
WINTER CRICKET EVENTS No.
CAR PARKING FACILITIES Car parking is available within the ground through the Kew Road car park entrance gate.
GROUND CAPACITY 5,000.
ANTICIPATED GROUND DEVELOPMENTS None currently planned.

HOW TO GET THERE

Richmond Underground station (District Line) 0.75 mile ☎ 0845 330 9875, Richmond station 0.75 mile ☎ 08457 484950, www.railtrack.com, www.thetrainline.co.uk

 Buses from Chiswick to Richmond pass Kew Gardens near the ground ☎ 020 7222 1234.

 There are cycle routes from Richmond and surrounding areas.

 From north: from M1 junction 1 at Brent Cross take A406 west (North Circular Road), continue on A406 to Chiswick Flyover roundabout, take fourth exit on to Chiswick High Road (A205), follow this road into Kew Bridge Road (A315), at Kew Green take right fork into Kew Road (A307), Old Deer Park is on the right hand side. **From south:** from end of M3 continue on A316 through Twickenham (Chertsey Road), cross Twickenham Bridge and at traffic lights take left turn on to Kew Road (A307), Old Deer Park is on the left hand side. **From east:** from Hammersmith Flyover (A4) continue on Great West Road to Hogarth Roundabout, take first exit (A316) (Burlington Lane), continue on A316 to Richmond Circus junction, follow signs to A307 (Kew Road), Old Deer Park is on the left hand side. **From west:** from M4 junction 2 follow A4 (Great West Road) to Chiswick Flyover roundabout, then as for north.

 London Heathrow Airport ☎ 08700 000123

WHERE TO STAY

Chelwood House (☎ 020 8876 8733), Melbury Hotel (☎ 020 8876 3930), Pro Kew Gardens (☎ 020 8876 3354), Quinns Hotel (☎ 020 8940 5444)
 For further places to stay in the Richmond area visit www.smoothhound.co.uk.

WHERE TO EAT

Burnt Chair (☎ 020 8940 9488 www.burntchair.com), Canyon (☎ 020 8948 2944 www.canyonfood.co.uk).
 Other restaurants can be found in Kew Road, 3 minutes' walk from the ground.

TOURIST INFORMATION Richmond Tourist Information Centre www.richmond.gov.uk

LOCAL RADIO STATIONS Greater London Radio (94.9 MHz FM/1458 KHz MW), Capital Radio (95.8 MHz FM/1548 KHz MW,) LBC (97.3 MHz FM/1152 KHz MW).

LOCAL NEWSPAPERS *Evening Standard*

250503. MX v NORTHANTS NUL. NORTHANTS WON 3 BALLS TO SPARE. MET JOHN MACKIE FIRST TIME I MET HIM FOR 30 YR. OFFICIAL VICTORY BY 8 WKTS

SHENLEY

Address Shenley Cricket Centre, The Pavilion, The Denis Compton Oval,
Radlett Lane, Shenley, Hertfordshire WD7 9DW
Prospects of Play ☎ 01923 859022

HISTORY OF GROUND AND FACILITIES

CECIL RAPHAEL, cousin of John E. Raphael (Oxford University CC and Surrey CCC), purchased the house and 45-acre estate of Porters Park, Shenley, in about 1902. One of the first things he did was to develop a cricket ground south-west of the main house, Porters Mansion. Contrary to the often repeated statement that the cricket ground was based on the plan of the Kennington Oval, it is in fact circular and approximately 160 metres in diameter. Cecil Raphael also developed the cricket pavilion. It was extended to the rear during the mid-1990s by the Shenley Park Trustees. There is photographic evidence that John E. Raphael played cricket on the ground at Shenley as a member of his cousin's country house staff team.

In recent years the Shenley Park Trust has suggested that Dr W.G. Grace was responsible for the design of the ground. However, established cricket historians who have written extensively on Grace have produced no evidence that he was concerned with the design of this cricket ground. However, both Cecil and John E. Raphael were members of the Marylebone Cricket Club and it is possible that W.G. was asked for a little advice. Cecil Raphael sold the Porters Park estate in 1928 to Middlesex County Council for the development of what became Shenley Hospital.

The ground was named the Denis Compton Oval in 1996 after an opening ceremony by Middlesex and England batsman D.C.S. Compton, who was invited by the then cricket centre co-ordinator Eric (W.E.) Russell. In 1996 the first first-class three-day match was staged in Hertfordshire when an MCC side took on the touring South Africa 'A' team. During the same summer a one-day match was held between an MCC XI and the Pakistan touring team. Both matches were well attended (some 2,000 to 3,000 each day). Around 90 days of cricket are usually on offer at the ground each season. These include first-class matches, England Women's Test matches, Minor Counties fixtures with Hertfordshire County Cricket Club, club, village, youth, schoolboy and regional matches.

During the summer of 2002 Middlesex County Cricket Club ventured into this part of Hertfordshire, some 14 miles from Lord's, to play two matches. They played a first-class three-day match with the touring Sri Lankans between 11 and 13 May and in a Norwich Union National League one-day match the Middlesex Crusaders took on Lancashire Lightning.

Middlesex CCC have staged first-class and limited-overs fixtures outside their county boundary before. The first was way back in 1870 when the CCC played two home matches at Kennington Oval against Surrey (the visitors, although playing at home) because the Lille Bridge Ground at West Brompton was unfit. The second occasion was in 1939 when the County Championship fixture with Nottinghamshire was staged at Kennington Oval as Lord's Cricket Ground was required for the annual Eton v Harrow school match. In 1977 Middlesex staged

Members' enclosure (in front of the pavilion and marquee).

their home Schweppes County Championship fixture with Somerset at the County Cricket Ground, New Writtle Street, Chelmsford, because Lord's was being prepared for the Gillette Cup Final. Four years later in 1981 Middlesex ventured to Hertfordshire and to Woodside in Garston, Watford, for the first and only time for a limited-overs fixture with the Sri Lanka touring team before they attained Test status in 1984. Sri Lanka totalled 211 (49.2 overs) with Duleep Mendis scoring 64. Middlesex responded with 209 for 9 (50 overs) with Keith Tomlins scoring 58 and D.S. de Silva returning figures of 4 for 28. Sri Lanka won by just 2 runs. In 2000 Middlesex played a home Norwich Union League Division 2 fixture with Essex (the visitors, although playing on home soil) at Chelmsford.

The permanent buildings at Shenley include the main pavilion which has been altered and improved in recent years. The pavilion terrace offers bench seating for members and the covered part is used for the press, scorers and commentary points. On the first floor are the players' dressing rooms, balconies overlooking the ground, a large dining room with balcony overlooking the nursery ground and the ECB Pitch Inspector's Office.

The scoreboard situated on the Porters Park Golf Club side of the ground was built in 1990 and was improved in the late 1990s with the introduction of electronic numbering.

Chris Wood, the England and Wales Cricket Board's Pitches Administrator, was the groundsman at Shenley before he took over the Test and first-class grounds position from the legendary Harry Brind in 1999. Brind had trained Wood at the beginning of his career at Kennington Oval.

The cricket centre is managed by Bob Jones and is leased by a Sri Lankan businessman who himself played minor county cricket for Suffolk CCC.

The Shenley Park Trust is open to the public and there is a lovely walk of about four miles around the cricket ground and surrounding area. Shenley

Village Cricket Club uses the Nursery Ground to the rear of the main pavilion throughout the season.

On Sunday 28 July 2002 the Bunbury XI, established by David English, took on the Vic Lewis Cricket Club in aid of Paul Weekes' Benefit Year at Shenley and to celebrate 50 Golden Years of Vic Lewis' Charity Cricket XI, 1952–2002. The Middlesex team played for the Vic Lewis XI and won the match by 6 wickets in an exciting finish with Jamie Dalrymple hitting the winning runs off the last ball of the game.

GROUND RECORDS AND SCORES

FIRST-CLASS MATCHES

Highest innings total for county 274 v Sri Lankans 2002
Highest innings total against county 281 for 4 by Sri Lankans 2002
Lowest innings total for county 274 v Sri Lankans 2002
Lowest innings total against county 186 by Sri Lankans 2002
Highest individual innings for county 93 E.C. Joyce v Sri Lankans 2002
Highest individual innings against county 125* D.P.M.D. Jayawardene for Sri Lankans 2002
Highest wicket partnerships for county

1st	6 A.J. Strauss & S.G. Koenig	v	Sri Lankans	2002
2nd	8 A.J. Strauss & R.M.S. Weston	v	Sri Lankans	2002
3rd	31 A.J. Strauss & O.A. Shah	v	Sri Lankans	2002
4th	114 O.A. Shah & E.C. Joyce	v	Sri Lankans	2002
5th	0 E.C. Joyce & B.L. Hutton	v	Sri Lankans	2002
6th	5 E.C. Joyce & P.N. Weekes	v	Sri Lankans	2002
7th	61 E.C. Joyce & D. Alleyne	v	Sri Lankans	2002
8th	19 D. Alleyne & A.W. Laraman	v	Sri Lankans	2002
9th	28 A.W. Laraman & T.A. Hunt	v	Sri Lankans	2002
10th	2 A.W. Laraman & T.F. Bloomfield	v	Sri Lankans	2002

Highest wicket partnerships against county

1st	81 M.S. Atapattu & S.T. Jayasuriya	for	Sri Lankans	2002
2nd	21 S.T. Jayasuriya & K.C. Sangakkara	for	Sri Lankans	2002
3rd	17 S.T. Jayasuriya & D.P.M.D. Jayawardene	for	Sri Lankans	2002
4th	35 D.P.M.D. Jayawardene & P.A. de Silva	for	Sri Lankans	2002
5th	179* D.P.M.D. Jaywardene & H.P. Tillakaratne	for	Sri Lankans	2002
6th	9 H.P. Tillakaratne & R.P. Arnold	for	Sri Lankans	2002
7th	0 H.P. Tillakaratne & U.D.U. Chandana	for	Sri Lankans	2002
8th	13 H.P. Tillakaratne & K.E.A. Upashantha	for	Sri Lankans	2002
9th	25 K.E.A. Upashantha & T.C.B. Fernando	for	Sri Lankans	2002
10th	25 T.C.B. Fernando & P.D.R.L. Perera	for	Sri Lankans	2002

Best bowling performance in an innings for county 4 for 37 B.L. Hutton v Sri Lankans 2002
Best bowling performance in an innings against county 4 for 72 T.C.B. Fernando for Sri Lankans 2002
Best bowling performance in a match for county 4 for 80 B.L. Hutton v Sri Lankans 2002
Best bowling performance in a match against county 4 for 72 T.C.B. Fernando for Sri Lankans 2002
Largest crowd 2,950 v Sri Lankans 2002

LIMITED-OVERS MATCHES

Highest innings total for county 198 for 5 v Lancashire (SL) 2002
Highest innings total against county 199 for 4 by Lancashire (SL) 2002
Lowest innings total for county 198 for 5 v Lancashire (SL) 2002
Lowest innings total against county 199 for 4 by Lancashire (SL) 2002
Highest individual innings for county 86* N.R.D. Compton v Lancashire (SL) 2002
Highest individual innings against county 84* M.J. Chilton for Lancashire (SL) 2002

Highest wicket partnerships for county

1st	12 R.M.S. Weston & S.G. Koenig	v	Lancashire	(SL)	2002
2nd	12 R.M.S. Weston & P.N. Weekes	v	Lancashire	(SL)	2002
3rd	4 R.M.S. Weston & N.R.D. Compton	v	Lancashire	(SL)	2002
4th	13 N.R.D. Compton & E.C. Joyce	v	Lancashire	(SL)	2002
5th	15 N.R.D. Compton & J.W.M. Dalrymple	v	Lancashire	(SL)	2002
6th	142* N.R.D. Compton & B.L. Hutton	v	Lancashire	(SL)	2002

7th to 10th yet to be established.

Highest wicket partnerships against county

1st	18 D. Byas & M.J. Chilton	for	Lancashire	(SL)	2002
2nd	14 M.J. Chilton & S.G. Law	for	Lancashire	(SL)	2002
3rd	99 M.J. Chilton & C.P. Schofield	for	Lancashire	(SL)	2002
4th	48 M.J. Chilton & A.J. Swann	for	Lancashire	(SL)	2002
5th	20* M.J. Chilton & T.M. Rees	for	Lancashire	(SL)	2002

6th to 10th yet to be established

Best bowling performance in a match for county 2 for 27 T.F. Bloomfield v Lancashire (SL) 2002
Best bowling performance in a match against county 2 for 41 J.M. Anderson for Lancs (SL) 2002
Largest crowd 3,275 v Lancashire (SL) 2002

GROUND INFORMATION

ENTRANCES Radlett Lane through main gate (players, officials, media, members and public and all vehicles).
MEMBERS' ENCLOSURE Pavilion and defined members' area including marquee.
PUBLIC ENCLOSURE Rest of the ground.
COVERED STANDS Pavilion (part).
OPEN STANDS Pavilion (part) and rest of the ground.
NAME OF ENDS Pavilion End, Cornfield End.
GROUND DIMENSIONS 155m × 145m.
REPLAY SCREEN If televised matches are staged at the ground the replay screen is sited to the right of the scoreboard.
FIRST AID Situated in the pavilion.
CODES OF DRESS Spectators are required to dress in an appropriate manner consistent with attending a cricket match. Bare torsos are not acceptable in, or in front of the pavilion. Executive Club/Suite users must wear a necktie and jacket.
BEHAVIOUR The club is keen that standards of behaviour should be maintained and members and spectators are urged to report immediately to the CEO any incident, or potential incident, where they feel action should be taken. Bad language is not acceptable at any match and the club will take prompt and strong action should this or any other ground regulation be ignored.
RECIPROCAL ARRANGEMENTS Members of Shenley Cricket Centre can gain entry free on production of membership card when Middlesex or MCC is playing on the ground.
SUPPORTERS' CLUB Seaxe Club £10 per annum, contact Middlesex CCC for details.
JUNIORS Junior Crusader Kids £10 per annum, contact Membership Department for details.
CORPORATE ENTERTAINING Shenley Cricket Centre has a marquee on the ground at the Pavilion End of the ground where food and bar facilities are available for corporate guests. Contact Marketing Shenley Cricket Centre ☎ 01923 859022 for further details and a copy of the brochure.
FACILITIES FOR VISUALLY IMPAIRED SPECTATORS No reduction. Guide dogs are allowed. Contact Shenley Cricket Centre in advance.
FACILITIES AND ACCESS FOR PEOPLE WITH DISABILITIES INCLUDING WHEELCHAIR ACCESS TO GROUND Yes, from Radlett Lane.
DESIGNATED CAR PARK AVAILABLE INSIDE THE GROUND FOR PEOPLE WITH DISABILITIES Yes, there is a car parking area set aside near the pavilion.
GOOD VIEWING AREAS INSIDE THE GROUND FOR PEOPLE USING WHEELCHAIRS Yes, there is a special area on the hard standing near the pavilion.
DESIGNATED VIEWING AREAS FOR PEOPLE USING WHEELCHAIRS Yes.

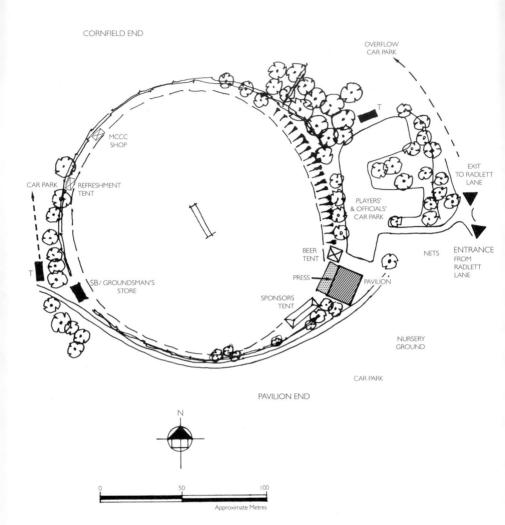

CORNFIELD END

OVERFLOW
CAR PARK

T

MCCC
SHOP

EXIT
TO RADLETT
LANE

CAR PARK   REFRESHMENT
TENT

PLAYERS'
& OFFICIALS'
CAR PARK

BEER
TENT

NETS   ENTRANCE
FROM
RADLETT
LANE

T

SB / GROUNDSMAN'S
STORE

PRESS   PAVILION

SPONSORS
TENT

NURSERY
GROUND

CAR PARK

PAVILION END

N

| 0 | 50 | 100 |
Approximate Metres

RAMPS TO PROVIDE EASY ACCESS TO BARS & REFRESHMENT OUTLETS FOR PEOPLE USING WHEELCHAIRS Yes, the pavilion can be accessed by a ramp.
FOOD & DRINK FULL RESTAURANT/DINING FACILITIES Members, yes. Public, no. A restaurant is in the Marquee situated at the Pavilion Road End of the ground. Catering is provided by Peter Rowden Event Catering ☎ 01189 476568 or 01923 859022.
TEMPORARY FOOD/DRINK FACILITIES Members, yes. Public, yes.
FOOD SUITABLE FOR VEGETARIANS Members, yes. Public, yes.
BARS Members 1, Public 1.
VARIETIES OF BEER SOLD Greene King.
CHILDREN'S FACILITIES Crèche, no. Play area, no. There is a play area close to the wild flower orchard at the top end of Radlett Lane.
CLUB SHOP Yes, Middlesex CCC have a small outlet situated in a small tent at the Cornfield End of the ground.

CLUB MUSEUM No, but there are a number of items of cricket interest in the pavilion including a list of centuries scored by Denis Compton during his distinguished cricket career.
CRICKET COACHING FACILITIES Yes, contact Shenley Cricket Centre for full details ☎ 01923 859022.
CRICKET NETS Yes, contact Shenley Cricket Centre for full details ☎ 01923 859022.
OTHER SPORTING OR RECREATIONAL FACILITIES ON THE GROUND Pro-celebrity golf days and gala dinners. Contact Shenley Cricket Centre for full details ☎ 01923 859022.
FACILITIES FOR HIRE OR WIDER COMMUNITY USE AT THE GROUND Rooms are available for functions, weddings, exhibitions, Christmas lunches, conferences and business and private entertainment. Contact Commercial Department Shenley Cricket Centre ☎ 01923 859022 for further details and a copy of the brochure.
WINTER CRICKET EVENTS Contact Shenley Cricket Centre for details ☎ 01923 859022.
CAR PARKING FACILITIES Car parking is available on the Nursery Ground, entry from Radlett Lane, and in adjoining fields to the rear of the main scoreboard. Cost: £5 per car.
OTHER INFORMATION The ground is the only venue in Hertfordshire to have staged a first-class match and was opened by Lord Cowdrey of Tonbridge, CBE, and later, when renamed, by Denis Compton.
GROUND CAPACITY 6,000.
ANTICIPATED GROUND DEVELOPMENTS None currently planned.

HOW TO GET THERE

Radlett station 1.5 mile ☎ 08457 484950, www.thameslink.co.uk, www.thetrainline.com, www.railtrack.co.uk

Arriva the Shires & Essex Buses pass ground. Timetable information ☎ 0870 608 2608. Also during major matches a shuttle bus 'Shenley Shuttle' operates between Radlett railway station and the Black Lion Public House to and from the ground in Radlett Lane.

There are cycle routes from St Albans, Radlett and Borehamwood and surrounding areas to this area of Shenley.

From north: from M1 junction 7 continue (east) on M10, at roundabout (junction 1) take A414, bear right on to B5378 and follow it along Shenley Lane, Shenleybury and Black Lion Hill, turn right on to Radlett Lane. **From south:** from A5183 at Elstree, continue on A5183 (Watling Street), turn right on to Shenley Hill, turn right on to Shenley Road and follow it to Radlett Lane. **From east:** from M25 junction 22 take A1081, at roundabout B556 (Bell Lane), continue on Bell Lane, turn right at second roundabout B5378 (Shenleybury), continue on this road to roundabout at Black Lion Hill, bear right on to Radlett Lane. **From west:** from M25 junction 22, then as for east.

London Heathrow Airport ☎ 08700 000123, London Luton Airport ☎ 01582 405100

WHERE TO STAY

Avalon Hotel (☎ 01727 857858), Comfort Hotel (☎ 01727 848849), Quality Hotel (☎ 01727 857858), Thistle Hotel (☎ 0870 333 9144)
    Forfurther hotels and guest houses to stay in St Albans, Radlett or Borehamwood visit www.smoothhound.co.uk.

WHERE TO EAT

La Gondola (☎ 01727 822015 www.lagondola.co.uk), White House, King William IV, The Queen Adelaide and The Black Lion, together with restaurants in Radlett, are within 1 mile of the ground.

TOURIST INFORMATION St Albans Tourist Information Centre www.stalbans.gov.uk

LOCAL RADIO STATIONS Greater London Radio (94.9 MHz FM/1458 KHz MW), BBC 3 Counties Radio (95.5 MHz FM/1161 KHz MW), Capital Radio (95.8 MHz FM/1548 KHz MW), LBC (97.3 MHz FM/1152 KHz MW)

LOCAL NEWSPAPERS *Watford Observer, Welwyn & Hatfield Times, Hertfordshire Advertiser, Evening Standard*

SOUTHGATE

Address Southgate Cricket Club, The Walker Cricket Ground Trust, The Pavilion, The Waterfall Cricket Ground, Waterfall Road, Southgate, London N14 7JZ
Prospects of Play ☎ 020 8886 8381

HISTORY OF GROUND AND FACILITIES

THE WALKER CRICKET GROUND is the home of Southgate Cricket Club, founded in 1855.

Southgate CC has two picturesque cricket grounds together with a full-time groundsman, catering and bar staff. Many famous cricket personalities have been associated with the club including Sir Cyril Hawker and T.N. 'Tom' Pearce. The latter represented Cambridge University, MCC, Essex and entered his own team, T.N. Pearce's XI, in the Scarborough Cricket Festival annually.

The Walkers, probably the most famous Middlesex cricketing family, played at Waterfall Road. They lived close by at Cannon Hill and all seven brothers represented the local club. John Walker founded Southgate Cricket Club in 1855 and was responsible for levelling and returfing the ground. The Walker family raised a team called 'Middlesex' to play Kent at Southgate in 1859. They were also responsible for founding Middlesex CCC in 1863/4 and producing a county team which first played at Lord's in 1877. Another brother, Vyell Walker, took ten wickets in an innings in three separate matches during his career. Vyell was elected president of Middlesex CCC in 1891 and he also was a member of the MCC committee.

The ground was originally called Chapel Fields and many of the early matches staged here involving United All England teams, MCC and Southgate Cricket Club attracted crowds of 10,000 or more. It was given the name 'The Walker Cricket Ground' by a Deed of Trust on 19 December 1907; the document was signed by R.D. Walker who was the last surviving of the seven brothers.

Southgate Cricket Club currently field four XIs on both Saturday and Sunday, together with a mid-week team. The club were founder members of the Middlesex County Cricket League in 1972 and have won the league trophy twice, in 1976 and 1977. Southgate play some of the best amateur cricket in the county and regularly reach the quarter-final stages of the National Club Championship. The club won the John Haig Trophy at Lord's in 1977, beating Bowdon Cricket Club from Cheshire.

In 1991, for the first time in the history of Sunday League cricket, Middlesex staged two home matches away from Lord's at Southgate against Leicestershire and Worcestershire.

The only permanent buildings on the ground are the pavilion/clubhouse, electronic scoreboard, groundsman's house, known as The Walker Cottage, and store. There is also a thriving squash club with six courts. The ground has an artificial pitch within the square and some grass cricket nets.

The playing area is 145 metres by 125 metres and falls away towards the Church End to the south. The TV camera/commentary box position would be situated at the Adelaide End if required.

Inside the pavilion there are two old cricket bats used by the Walker brothers

Christ Church in Waterfall Road provides a backcloth to Middlesex's regular cricket festivals at the delightful John Walker Cricket Ground.

together with a report entitled 'Cricket in the time of the Walkers'. There are also a number of team photographs and a large display recording the 1977 John Haig Cup Final with Bowdon. Other Southgate cricket memorabilia is also on show. The library in the pavilion is run by the Administrative Director of the Walker Cricket Ground Trust, Christopher Sexton.

The ground facilities are shared with Southgate Adelaide CC (1870), Southgate Hockey Club (1886), Southgate Adelaide Hockey Club (1926), Squash Rackets Club (1975), Oakwood Netball Club (1958), 6th Southgate Scout Group (1918), The Walker Association (1975) and The Weld Lawn Tennis Club (1924). Southgate Hockey Club has counted Richard Dodds and Sean Kerly among its members. Both represented Great Britain.

Players to have represented Southgate CC and Middlesex County Cricket Club include Alan Fairbairn, Wilf Slack and spin bowler Phil Tufnell.

GROUND RECORDS AND SCORES

FIRST-CLASS MATCHES

Highest innings total for county 543 v Derbyshire 2001
Highest innings total against county 441 by Essex 2002
Lowest innings total for county 71 v Kent 1859
Lowest innings total against county 47 by Kent 1859
Highest individual innings for county 241 M.W. Gatting v Essex 1998
Highest individual innings against county 182* K.J. Barnett for Gloucestershire 2002, R.C. Irani for Essex 2002

Highest wicket partnerships for county

1st	372 M.W. Gatting & J.L. Langer	v	Essex	1998
2nd	161 S.G. Koenig & B.L. Hutton	v	Essex	2002
3rd	85 A.J. Strauss & M.R. Ramprakash	v	Worcestershire	2000
4th	292 O.A. Shah & B.L. Hutton	v	Derbyshire	2001
5th	63 O.A. Shah & S.J. Cook	v	Derbyshire	2001
6th	157 R.M.S. Weston & D.C. Nash	v	Essex	2002
7th	78 P.N. Weekes & D.C. Nash	v	Essex	2002
8th	50 D.C. Nash & S.J. Cook	v	Essex	2002
9th	74 A.R.C. Fraser & R.L. Johnson	v	Glamorgan	2000
10th	71 D.C. Nash & P.C.R. Tufnell	v	Essex	2002

Highest wicket partnerships against county

1st	76 C.M. Spearman & K.J. Barnett	for	Gloucestershire	2002
2nd	74 M.T.G. Elliott & M.J. Powell	for	Glamorgan	2000
3rd	97 A.P. Grayson & S.G. Law	for	Essex	1998
4th	167 D.D.J. Robinson & R.C. Irani	for	Essex	2002
5th	84 S.G. Law & R.C. Irani	for	Essex	1998
6th	44 R.C. Irani & J.M. Dakin	for	Essex	2002
7th	104 R.C. Irani & D.R. Law	for	Essex	1998
8th	114 A.N. Aymes & S.D. Udal	for	Hampshire	2001
9th	70 R.C. Irani & T.J. Phillips	for	Essex	2002
10th	43 A.C. Morris & C.T. Tremlett	for	Hampshire	2001

Best bowling performance in an innings for county 7 for 133 Abdur Razzaq v Essex 2002
Best bowling performance in an innings against county 6 for 64 V.C. Drakes for Nottinghamshire 1999
Best bowling performance in a match for county 10 for 133 P.C.R Tufnell v Derbyshire 2001
Best bowling performance in a match against county 11 for 50 G. Wigzell for Kent 1859
Largest crowd 10,000 v Kent 1859

LIMITED-OVERS MATCHES

Highest innings total for county 255 for 9 v Kent (SL) 1991
Highest innings total against county 276 for 6 by Kent (SL) 1991
Lowest innings total for county 114 v Derbyshire (SL) 1999
Lowest innings total against county 58 by Somerset (NWT) 2000
Highest individual innings for county 102* P.N. Weekes v South Africa (WCF) 1999
Highest individual innings against county 93 M.W. Alleyne for Gloucestershire (SL) 2002, 93 M.V. Boucher for South Africa (WCF) 1999
Highest wicket partnerships for county

1st	43* A.J. Strauss & M.A. Roseberry	v	Somerset	(NWT)	2000
	43 M.W. Gatting & M.A. Roseberry	v	Kent	(SL)	1991
2nd	83 M.A. Roseberry & M.R. Ramprakash	v	Kent	(SL)	1991
3rd	83 M.R. Ramprakash & P.N. Weekes	v	Somerset	(NWT)	2000
4th	55 E.C. Joyce & O.A. Shah	v	Surrey	(SL)	2002
5th	65 J.L. Langer & P.N. Weekes	v	Somerset	(SL)	1999
6th	35 O.A. Shah & J.W.M. Dalrymple	v	Surrey	(SL)	2002
7th	124* R.M.S. Weston & D.C. Nash	v	Derbyshire	(SL)	2001
8th	49 K.P. Dutch & A.G.J. Fraser	v	Durham	(NWT)	1998
9th	66* K.P. Dutch & R.L. Johnson	v	Durham	(NWT)	1998
10th	19 O.A. Shah & T.F. Bloomfield	v	Essex	(SL)	2001

Highest wicket partnerships against county

1st	144 J. Cox & J.I.D. Kerr	for	Somerset	(SL)	1999
2nd	135 M.R. Benson & N.R. Taylor	for	Kent	(SL)	1991
3rd	121* M.R. Ramprakash & R. Clarke	for	Surrey	(SL)	2002
4th	61 S.M. Katich & P.D. Collingwood	for	Durham	(SL)	2000
5th	114 M.W. Alleyne & A.P.R. Gidman	for	Gloucestershire	(SL)	2002
6th	24 J.S. Foster & A.P. Cowan	for	Essex	(SL)	2001
7th	35 N.J. Speak & M.M. Betts	for	Durham	(NWT)	1998

8th	35 N.R.C. Dumelow & R.K. Illingworth	for	Derbyshire	(SL)	2001
9th	9 S.M. Katich & I.D. Hunter	for	Durham	(SL)	2000
10th	37* S.M. Katich & N. Killeen	for	Durham	(SL)	2000

Best bowling performance in a match for county 5 for 17 C.B. Keegan v Hampshire (SL) 2001
Best bowling performance in a match against county 5 for 14 A.P. Cowan for Essex (SL) 2001
Largest crowd 4,500 v Gloucestershire (SL) 2002

GROUND INFORMATION

ENTRANCES Waterfall Road (players, officials, press/media, members, public and vehicles). There is also an entrance for members and the public from the car park adjoining the tennis courts to the south-east of the playing area.
MEMBERS' ENCLOSURE Pavilion and defined members' area in front of pavilion.
PUBLIC ENCLOSURE Rest of the ground.
COVERED STANDS Pavilion.
OPEN STANDS Rest of ground.
NAME OF ENDS Waterfall Road End, Adelaide End.
GROUND DIMENSIONS 145m × 125m.
REPLAY SCREEN If televised matches are staged at the ground the replay screen is sited to the right of the scoreboard on tennis courts.
FIRST AID Situated in tent.
CODES OF DRESS Spectators are required to dress in an appropriate manner consistent with attending a cricket match. Bare torsos are not acceptable in, or in front of the pavilion. Executive Club/Suite users must wear a necktie and jacket.
BEHAVIOUR The club is keen that standards of behaviour should be maintained and members and spectators are urged to report immediately to the CEO any incident, or potential incident, where they feel action should be taken. Bad language is not acceptable at any match and the club will take prompt and strong action should this or any other ground regulation be ignored.
RECIPROCAL ARRANGEMENTS Members of Southgate CC can use the pavilion when Middlesex is playing on the ground.
DESIGNATED VIEWING AREAS FOR PEOPLE USING WHEELCHAIRS Yes.
RAMPS TO PROVIDE EASY ACCESS TO BARS & REFRESHMENT OUTLETS FOR PEOPLE USING WHEELCHAIRS No.
FOOD & DRINK FULL RESTAURANT/DINING FACILITIES Members, yes. Public, yes. A members' restaurant is available in a marquee otherwise food can be purchased from the outlet in the pavilion lounge area.
TEMPORARY FOOD/DRINK FACILITIES Members, yes. Public, yes.
FOOD SUITABLE FOR VEGETARIANS Members, yes. Public, yes.
BARS Members 1, Public 1.
SUPPORTERS' CLUB Seaxe Club £10 per annum, contact Middlesex CCC for details.
JUNIORS Junior Crusader Kids £10 per annum. Contact Membership Department for details.
CORPORATE ENTERTAINING Contact Middlesex CCC for details of corporate hospitality in marquees on ground.
FACILITIES FOR VISUALLY IMPAIRED SPECTATORS No reduction. Guide dogs are allowed. Contact club in advance.
FACILITIES AND ACCESS FOR PEOPLE WITH DISABILITIES INCLUDING WHEELCHAIR ACCESS TO GROUND Yes, from Waterfall Road entrance.
DESIGNATED CAR PARK AVAILABLE INSIDE THE GROUND FOR PEOPLE WITH DISABILITIES Yes, there is a car parking area set aside near rear of marquees at Adelaide End of the ground and near main entrance in Waterfall Road.
GOOD VIEWING AREAS INSIDE THE GROUND FOR PEOPLE USING WHEELCHAIRS Yes, generally around the whole boundary although because of the steps it is difficult to get into the pavilion.
VARIETIES OF BEER SOLD Various brands available.
CHILDREN'S FACILITIES Crèche, no. Play area, no.
CLUB SHOP Middlesex CCC have a mobile shop on the ground sited in a tent at the Adelaide End of the ground.
CLUB MUSEUM No.
CRICKET COACHING FACILITIES Yes, contact Southgate CC.
CRICKET NETS Yes, contact Southgate CC.
OTHER SPORTING OR RECREATIONAL FACILITIES ON THE GROUND Football, squash, hockey and tennis.

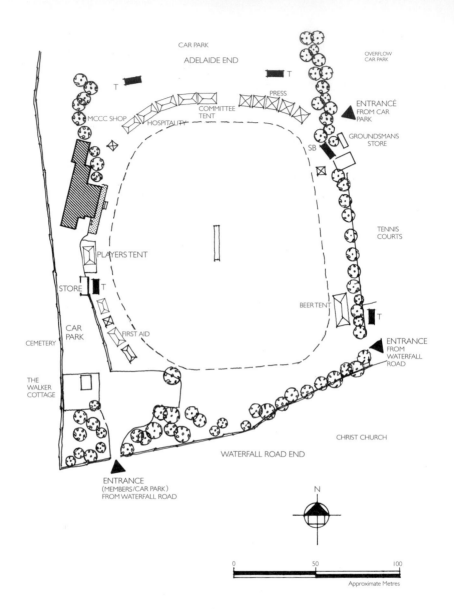

CAR PARK

ADELAIDE END

OVERFLOW
CAR PARK

T

T

PRESS

COMMITTEE
TENT

MCCC SHOP

HOSPITALITY

ENTRANCE
FROM CAR
PARK

GROUNDSMANS
STORE

SB

TENNIS
COURTS

PLAYERS TENT

STORE

T

CAR
PARK

FIRST AID

CEMETERY

BEER TENT

T

ENTRANCE
FROM
WATERFALL
ROAD

THE
WALKER
COTTAGE

CHRIST CHURCH

WATERFALL ROAD END

ENTRANCE
(MEMBERS/CAR PARK)
FROM WATERFALL ROAD

N

0   50   100

Approximate Metres

FACILITIES FOR HIRE OR WIDER COMMUNITY USE AT THE GROUND Rooms are available for functions, weddings, exhibitions, Christmas lunches, conferences and business and private entertainment. Contact Chris Sexton at Southgate CC for details.

WINTER CRICKET EVENTS No.

CAR PARKING FACILITIES Car parking is available via the Waterfall Road entrance gate. Car parking is also available to the north of the ground and in two further adjoining fields.

OTHER INFORMATION The Walker brothers, founders of Southgate Cricket Club, are buried in the graveyard of Christ Church in Waterfall Road. Secondhand book dealer Donald Scott of Brackley has a stall at some matches.

GROUND CAPACITY 6,000.

ANTICIPATED GROUND DEVELOPMENTS None currently planned.

Southgate Underground station (Piccadilly Line) 0.75 mile ☎ 0845 330 9875. New Southgate station 1 mile ☎ 08457 484950, www.railtrack.com, www.thetrainline.co.uk

 Buses W6, 121 and 299 pass near the ground ☎ 020 7222 1234

 There are cycle routes from Southgate and surrounding areas.

 From north: from M1 junction 2 (Fiveways Corner) take A1 towards London (Great North Way), bear left at junction with A406 (North Circular Road), continue on A406 to crossroads with A109, turn left on to A109 (Station Road), turn right on to A1003 (Barnet Road), at Betstyle Circus continue on A1003 (Waterfall Road), Southgate Cricket Club is on the left hand side. **From south:** from Bounds Green Road (A109) continue to North Circular Road (A406), then as for north. **From east:** from M25 junction 25 take A10 towards London (Great Cambridge Road), continue on A10 to junction with A406, follow signs to A111 (Hedge Lane), continue on A111 (Bourne Hill), turn left on to Amberley Road, bear right on to The Mall, at junction with Cannon Hill (A1004) cross on to A1003 (The Green), continue into Waterfall Road. **From west:** from M25 junction 25, then as for east.

 London Heathrow Airport ☎ 08700 000123, London Luton Airport ☎ 01582 405100

WHERE TO STAY

Innkeepers Lodge (☎ 0870 243 0500)
For further places to stay in the Southgate area visit www.smoothhound.co.uk.

WHERE TO EAT

There are restaurants in Southgate High Street and Broadway 15 minutes walk from the ground.

TOURIST INFORMATION Southgate Tourist Information Centre www.southgate.gov.uk

LOCAL RADIO STATIONS Greater London Radio (94.9 MHz FM/1458 KHz MW), Capital Radio (95.8 MHz FM/1548 KHz MW), LBC (97.3 MHz FM/1152 KHz MW).

LOCAL NEWSPAPER *Evening Standard*

UXBRIDGE

Address Uxbridge Cricket Club, The Pavilion, Gatting Way, Park Road,
Uxbridge, Middlesex
Prospects of Play ☎ 01895 237571

HISTORY OF GROUND AND FACILITIES

UXBRIDGE CRICKET CLUB, founded in 1789, claims to be the oldest club in Middlesex. Its ground at Park Road was only inaugurated in 1971, but cricket in the Uxbridge district is said to date from about 1730; the previous grounds used were the Moor, Uxbridge Common (opposite the present ground) and from 1858 the site in Cricketfield Road. The latter was vacated after 112 years' use at the end of the 1970 season in order to make way for the construction of the new Uxbridge Civic Centre.

The club's current ground is part of a large sports complex providing facilities for squash, football, tennis and bowls as well as a swimming pool and a dry ski slope, all with ample car parking adjoining. The pavilion, which was constructed during the winter of 1970/1, has been extended to include squash courts and an additional members' bar which is used as a players' dining area. The County Bar and viewing area were opened in 1981 by Phil Edmonds.

As late as a month before the first club match in 1971 the outfield was still desolate, resembling a paddy field. The first match was staged on 11 July 1971 when Colin Smith's XI played Uxbridge CC. At that match Freddie Brown, then President of MCC, said with considerable foresight that county cricket would be staged on the ground. Two first-class groundsmen assisted with the square in the club's early years: Ted Swannell from Lord's and Chris Hawkins from Old Trafford. In 1991 groundsman Richard Ayling, who is now at Merchant Taylors' School, Northwood, was presented with the TCCB runners-up award for the best out ground of the season by Donald Carr OBE.

Middlesex County Cricket Club were approached to play a match at Uxbridge in 1979 by Club President, Tom Try, and staged a one-day Prudential Cup warm-up match with the West Indies touring side. This match lasted only 49 minutes before the heavens opened and the match was washed out. Middlesex were not perturbed and returned to play their first first-class game at Uxbridge in August 1980 against Derbyshire who were defeated by 10 wickets. The venue was chosen primarily to free Lord's Cricket Ground to allow preparations to be made for the Centenary Test Match between England and Australia and the eighteenth and last Gillette Cup Final which Middlesex won, beating neighbours Surrey.

Middlesex staged 33 first-class matches at Uxbridge between 1980 and 1998 as part of the Uxbridge Cricket Festival. Seven limited-overs matches have been held at Uxbridge: in the NatWest Trophy with Cumberland in 1985, Nottingham-shire in 1987 and 1989, Surrey in 1990, Durham in 1992, Northamptonshire in 1994 and Gloucestershire in 1997. In 1983 a Benson and Hedges Cup zonal match with Glamorgan was abandoned without a ball being bowled.

Uxbridge CC field four XIs and one midweek XI throughout the season. Among players to have represented Uxbridge and Middlesex are B.J.T. Bosanquet, Norman Cowans and Roland Butcher. The club now play in the Middlesex County Cricket League, having formerly been founder members of the Thames Valley League. Uxbridge CC emerged as one of the leading club teams in Middlesex thanks to the sterling efforts of A.W.P. 'Tony' Fleming, known to many as the former Grounds Manager at Lord's.

The pavilion houses photographs and memorabilia of Uxbridge CC. In 1989 the club celebrated their bicentenary and many functions took place during the season including a club tour of Australia and Bangkok.

Although Park Road is one of the main access roads from Uxbridge town centre to the M40 motorway, the ground is screened from the traffic by high hedges. The ground is approximately level and the playing area is near circular at 124 metres by 122 metres.

The pavilion/clubhouse, a good modern complex, is situated in the north-east corner of the ground furthest from the entrance, while the scoreboard is in the north-west corner. These are the only two permanent buildings on the ground other than a groundsman's store. The TV camera/commentary position is located directly above and behind the sightscreen at the Gatting Way end of the ground on a gantry.

In 1991 an exhibition match between India and Pakistan attracted a crowd of 6,500 and had to be abandoned when the crowd invaded the pitch.

GROUND RECORDS AND SCORES

FIRST-CLASS MATCHES

Highest innings total for county 567 for 8 dec v Northamptonshire 1998
Highest innings total against county 627 for 6 dec for Worcestershire 1998
Lowest innings total for county 118 v Lancashire 1997
Lowest innings total against county 121 by Hampshire 1983
Highest individual innings for county 206* D.L.Haynes v Kent 1989
Highest individual innings against county 168 G.A.Hick for Worcestershire 1992
Highest wicket partnerships for county

1st	361 I.J.F. Hutchinson & D.L. Haynes	v	Kent	1989
2nd	197 P.N. Weekes & M.R. Ramprakash	v	Somerset	1996
3rd	319* D.L. Haynes & M.W. Gatting	v	Essex	1989
4th	197 M.W. Gatting & C.T. Radley	v	Surrey	1981
5th	289 C.T. Radley & P.R. Downton	v	Northamptonshire	1985
6th	100 M.R. Ramprakash & M.W. Gatting	v	Somerset	1988
7th	124 P.R. Downton & G.D. Rose	v	Warwickshire	1986
8th	94 N.F. Williams & C.P. Metson	v	Gloucestershire	1984
9th	74 C.P. Metson & S.P. Hughes	v	Gloucestershire	1984
10th	36 J.E. Emburey & P.C.R. Tufnell	v	Sussex	1987

Highest wicket partnerships against county

1st	129 S.J. Cook & P.M. Roebuck	for	Somerset	1990
2nd	133 V.S. Solanki & G.A. Hick	for	Worcestershire	1998
3rd	185 V.J. Wells & W.J. Cronje	for	Leicestershire	1995
4th	222 G.A. Hick & T.M. Moody	for	Worcestershire	1998
5th	119* S.R. Tendulkar & R.J. Blakey	for	Yorkshire	1992
6th	191 T.M. Moody & D.A. Leatherdale	for	Worcestershire	1998
7th	127 P.C.L. Holloway & R.J. Turner	for	Somerset	1996
8th	96 G. Miller & T.D. Topley	for	Essex	1989
9th	75 P.A. Neale & R.M. Ellcock	for	Worcestershire	1984
10th	83 G.A. Hick & R.D. Stemp	for	Worcestershire	1992

Best bowling performance in an innings for county 6 for 48 P.H. Edmonds v Hampshire 1982
Best bowling performance in an innings against county 8 for 32 P.J. Martin for Lancashire 1997
Best bowling performance in a match for county 10 for 59 V.A.P. van der Bijl v Derbyshire 1980
Best bowling performance in a match against county 13 for 79 P.J. Martin for Lancashire 1997
Largest crowd 3,500 v Gloucestershire 1986

LIMITED-OVERS MATCHES

Highest innings total for county 291 for 5 v Surrey (NWT) 1990
Highest innings total against county 288 for 8 by Surrey (NWT) 1990
Lowest innings total for county 197 v Lancashire (SL) 1997
Lowest innings total against county 135 by Essex (SL) 1994
Highest individual innings for county 104 M.R. Ramprakash v Surrey (NWT) 1990
Highest individual innings against county 129* A.J. Lamb for Northamptonshire (NWT) 1994
Highest wicket partnerships for county

1st	78 D.L. Haynes & M.A. Roseberry	v	Northamptonshire	(NWT)	1994
2nd	94 M.A. Roseberry & M.R. Ramprakash	v	Surrey	(NWT)	1990
3rd	126 M.R. Ramprakash & K.R. Brown	v	Surrey	(NWT)	1990
4th	107 M.R. Ramprakash & J.D. Carr	v	Yorkshire	(SL)	1992
5th	117 M.R. Ramprakash & M.W. Gatting	v	Northamptonshire	(SL)	1995

6th	98 M.R. Ramprakash & P.E. Wellings	v	Somerset	(SL)	1996
7th	32* J.C. Pooley & K.P. Dutch	v	Gloucestershire	(NWT)	1997
8th	22 D.C. Nash & K.P. Dutch	v	Essex	(SL)	1998
9th	30 J.C. Pooley & A.R.C. Fraser	v	Lancashire	(SL)	1997
10th	14 A. Needham & W.W. Daniel	v	Nottinghamshire	(NWT)	1997

Highest wicket partnerships against county

1st	130 B.C. Broad & R.T. Robinson	by	Nottinghamshire	(NWT)	1987
2nd	95 G.S. Clinton & A.J. Stewart	by	Surrey	(NWT)	1990
3rd	163 R.J. Bailey & A.J. Lamb	by	Northamptonshire	(NWT)	1994
4th	123 P.W.G. Parker & I.T. Botham	by	Durham	(NWT)	1992
5th	116 M.A. Lynch & M.W. Alleyne	by	Gloucestershire	(NWT)	1997
6th	59 M.A. Lynch & R.C. Russell	by	Gloucestershire	(NWT)	1997
7th	79 R.J. Harden & G.D. Rose	by	Somerset	(SL)	1996
8th	53 K.T. Medlycott & C.K. Bullen	by	Surrey	(NWT)	1990
9th	34 J.D.R. Benson & C.W. Wilkinson	by	Leicestershire	(SL)	1991
10th	11* C.W. Wilkinson & J.N. Maguire	by	Leicestershire	(SL)	1991

Best bowling performance in a match for county 5 for 32 R.S. Yeabsley v Essex (SL) 1994
Best bowling performance in a match against county 4 for 41 S.P. Hughes for Durham (NWT) 1992
Largest crowd 5,750 v Nottinghamshire (NWT) 1987

GROUND INFORMATION

ENTRANCES Gatting Way off Park Road (players, officials, press/media, members, public and vehicles). There are additional entrances off Park Road to the rear of the scoreboard and from car park no. 4 at the Pavilion End.

MEMBERS' ENCLOSURE Pavilion and defined members' area in front of the pavilion and clubhouse.

PUBLIC ENCLOSURE Rest of the ground.

COVERED STANDS Pavilion and clubhouse.

OPEN STANDS Temporary seating both raised and at ground level surrounding the playing area.

NAME OF ENDS Pavilion End, Town End.

GROUND DIMENSIONS 124m × 122m.

REPLAY SCREEN If televised matches are staged at the ground the replay screen is sited at the Town End of the ground.

FIRST AID In the pavilion.

CODES OF DRESS Spectators are required to dress in an appropriate manner consistent with attending a cricket match. Bare torsos are not acceptable in, or in front of the pavilion. Executive Club/Suite users must wear a necktie and jacket.

BEHAVIOUR The club is keen that standards of behaviour should be maintained and members and spectators are urged to report immediately to the CEO any incident, or potential incident, where they feel action should be taken. Bad language is not acceptable at any match and the club will take prompt and strong action should this or any other ground regulation be ignored.

RECIPROCAL ARRANGEMENTS Members of Uxbridge CC can use the pavilion when Middlesex is playing on the ground.

SUPPORTERS' CLUB Seaxe Club £10 per annum, contact Middlesex CCC for details.

JUNIORS Junior Crusader Kids £10 per annum. Contact Membership Department for details.

CORPORATE ENTERTAINING Contact Middlesex CCC for details of corporate hospitality in marquees on ground.

FACILITIES FOR VISUALLY IMPAIRED SPECTATORS No reduction. Guide dogs are allowed. Contact club in advance.

FACILITIES AND ACCESS FOR PEOPLE WITH DISABILITIES INCLUDING WHEELCHAIR ACCESS TO GROUND Yes, from Gatting Way entrance.

DESIGNATED CAR PARK AVAILABLE INSIDE THE GROUND FOR PEOPLE WITH DISABILITIES Yes, there is a car parking area set aside on the rugby ground.

GOOD VIEWING AREAS INSIDE THE GROUND FOR PEOPLE USING WHEELCHAIRS Yes, generally around the whole boundary although because of the steps it is difficult to get into the pavilion.

DESIGNATED VIEWING AREAS FOR PEOPLE USING WHEELCHAIRS Yes.

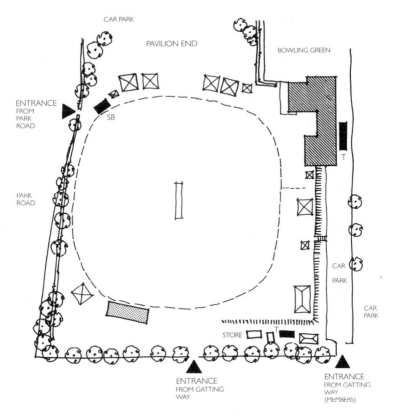

CAR PARK

PAVILION END

BOWLING GREEN

ENTRANCE
FROM
PARK
ROAD

SB

PARK
ROAD

T

CAR
PARK

CAR
PARK

STORE

T

ENTRANCE
FROM GATTING
WAY

ENTRANCE
FROM GATTING
WAY
(MEMBERS)

TOWN END

N

0   50   100

Approximate Metres

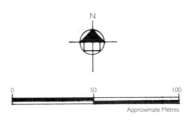

RAMPS TO PROVIDE EASY ACCESS TO BARS & REFRESHMENT OUTLETS FOR PEOPLE USING WHEELCHAIRS No.
FOOD & DRINK FULL RESTAURANT/DINING FACILITIES Members, yes. Public, yes. Food can be purchased from the outlet in the pavilion lounge area.
TEMPORARY FOOD/DRINK FACILITIES Members, yes. Public, yes.
FOOD SUITABLE FOR VEGETARIANS Members, yes. Public, yes.
BARS Members 1, Public 1.
VARIETIES OF BEER SOLD Various brands available.
CHILDREN'S FACILITIES Crèche, no. Play area, no.
CLUB SHOP Middlesex CCC have a mobile shop on the ground in the pavilion bar area.
CLUB MUSEUM No.
CRICKET COACHING FACILITIES Yes, contact Uxbridge CC.
CRICKET NETS Yes, contact Uxbridge CC.

OTHER SPORTING OR RECREATIONAL FACILITIES ON THE GROUND Rugby union, bowls, tennis, athletics, dry ski-slope and squash.

FACILITIES FOR HIRE OR WIDER COMMUNITY USE AT THE GROUND Rooms are available for functions, weddings, exhibitions, Christmas lunches, conferences and business and private entertainment. Contact Uxbridge CC for details.

WINTER CRICKET EVENTS No.

CAR PARKING FACILITIES Car parking available adjoining the ground off Gatting Way for members only and off Park Road for the general public and sponsors. Otherwise street parking is available in the streets close to Uxbridge Common opposite ground.

OTHER INFORMATION Secondhand book dealer Donald Scott of Brackley has a stall at most matches sited at the Town End.

GROUND CAPACITY 6,500.

ANTICIPATED GROUND DEVELOPMENTS None currently planned.

HOW TO GET THERE

 Uxbridge Underground Station (Metropolitan/Piccadilly lines) 0.75 mile.

 Buses 128, 129 and 223 pass near the ground ☎ 020 7222 1234

 There are cycle routes from Uxbridge and surrounding areas.

 From north: from M25 junction 16 continue east on M40, then on A40 (Western Avenue) to Swakeleys Roundabout, take B467 (Park Road), take B483 (Park Road), Gatting Way is the first turning on the left. **From south:** from M25 junction 16, then as for north. **From east:** from London take A40 (Western Avenue) to Swakeleys Roundabout then as for north. **From west:** from M40 junction 1 continue east on A40 (Western Avenue), then as for north.

 London Heathrow Airport ☎ 08700 000123

WHERE TO STAY

The Guest House (☎ 020 8574 3977), Master Brewer Hotel (☎ 01895 51199). For a further selection of places to stay in the Uxbridge area visit www.smoothhound.co.uk

WHERE TO EAT

There are a variety of restaurants in Uxbridge town centre 10 minutes' walk from the ground.

TOURIST INFORMATION Uxbridge Tourist Information Centre www.uxbridge.gov.uk

LOCAL RADIO STATIONS Greater London Radio (94.9 MHz FM/1458 KHz MW), Capital Radio (95.8 MHz FM/1548 KHz MW), LBC (97.3 MHz FM/1152 KHz MW).

LOCAL NEWSPAPERS *Evening Standard*

Northamptonshire

Northampton

NORTHAMPTONSHIRE COUNTY CRICKET CLUB, COUNTY CRICKET GROUND, WANTAGE ROAD, NORTHAMPTON NN1 4NJ

Telephone	01604 514455 **fax** 01604 514488
Shop	01604 514499
Indoor Cricket School	01604 514444
Catering	01604 514492
Website	www.nccc.co.uk
Email	post@nccc.co.uk

Founded 31 July 1878
Colours maroon
Crest Tudor Rose
National Cricket League Nickname Steelbacks
National Cricket League Colours maroon and yellow
Patrons The Earl of Dalkeith and The Earl Spencer
President L.A. Wilson
Chairman S.G. Schanschieff OBE
Chairman Cricket Committee J.A Scopes
Chief Executive S.P. Coverdale MA LLB
PA to Chief Executive L. Harris
Hon Treasurer F.D.G. Cattley
Medical Officer Dr D. Buckler
Commercial Manager Ms C. Horwood
Sales & Membership Manager G. Alsop
Conference & Events Co-ordinator F. Allbury
Club Shop Manager J. Alsop

Membership Secretary C. Hughes
First Team Manager K.C. Wessels
Technical Support Manager N.G.B. Cook
Academy Director D. J. Capel
Indoor Centre Manager A. Hodgson
Captain M.E.K. Hussey
Vice Captain A.L. Penberthy
Groundsman D. Bates
Scorer 1st XI A.C. Kingston
Scorer 2nd XI M. Woolley
Historian A. Radd
Sponsors Dr Martens
Newsletter *Northamptonshire News, The County, The County Brief*
Scorecard 60p
Yearbook £10.00
Frizzell County Championship Status Division 2
National Cricket League Status Division 2

ACHIEVEMENTS

County Championship 2nd 1912, 1957, 1965, 1976, Champions Division 2 2000
Minor Counties Championship Winners 1899 (shared), 1900 (shared), 1903, 1904
Gillette Cup Winners 1976, Finalists 1979
NatWest Trophy Winners 1992, Finalists 1981, 1987, 1989, 1995
Benson and Hedges Cup Winners 1980, Finalists 1987, 1996

John Player Sunday League 4th 1974
Refuge Assurance Sunday League 3rd 1991
Refuge Assurance Cup Semi-finalists 1991
Norwich Union National League Best 3rd Division 2 2000
Fenner Trophy Winners 1978
Tilcon Trophy Winners 1982, 1983, Finalists 1981

COUNTY CRICKET BOARD

Chairman S.G. Schanschieff OBE
Secretary I. Lucas
Treasurer F.D.G. Cattley
Cricket Development Officer D. Ripley
Women & Girls Secretary C. Tuck

Address   Northamptonshire County Cricket Board, County Cricket Ground, Wantage Road,
              Northampton NN1 4NJ
☎   01604 514456
Fax   01604 514488

GROUND

Northampton (County Cricket Ground, Wantage Road)
   Other grounds that have been used since 1969: Peterborough (Baker Perkins Sports Ground), Peterborough Town CC (Bretton Gate, Westwood), Kettering (Kettering CC, Northampton Road), Brackley (Brackley CC, off Buckingham Road), Bedford (Bedford School, Burnaby Road), Milton Keynes (Bletchley CC, Manor Fields, Bletchley), Milton Keynes (Campbell Park, The Boundary Organisation Limited), Wellingborough (Wellingborough School, Irthlingborough Road), Luton (Wardown Park, Old Bedford Road), Tring (Pound Meadow, Station Road), Finedon (Dolben Cricket Ground, Avenue Road) and Horton (Horton House CC, Horton)

SECOND XI GROUNDS

In addition to the above mentioned grounds the following are used for Second XI matches:
The Boundary Organisation Limited, The Pavilion, Campbell Park, Milton Keynes, Buckinghamshire
  ☎ 01908 694820
Isham CC, Orlingbury Road, Isham, Northamptonshire ☎ 01536 420068
Old Northamptonians CC, Cricket Ground, Rushmore Road, off Bedford Road, Northampton ☎ 01604 353435
Stowe School, School Grounds, Stowe, Buckingham MK18 5EH ☎ 01280 813164

Indoor Cricket Centre including club shop, executive boxes and suites at the Abington Avenue End.

NORTHAMPTON

Address County Cricket Ground, Wantage Road, Northampton NN1 4NJ
Prospects of Play ☎ 01604 514455

HISTORY OF GROUND AND FACILITIES

THE COUNTY CRICKET GROUND is sited between Abington Avenue and Wantage Road and is the second ground to be used for first-class cricket in the town. The first was the Northampton Racecourse Ground on the Promenade where a three-day match was staged between a United North of England XI and a United South of England XI between 2 and 4 September 1872. The match resulted in an 8 wickets win for the United South of England XI.

The County Cricket Ground was formed from land in the Abington district on the east side of Northampton and laid out by the Northampton County Cricket and Recreation Grounds Company Limited in 1885 at a cost of £2,000. The work was carried out under the guidance of Mr H.H. Stephenson, a former Surrey CCC cricketer. The county club moved to this venue in 1886. Alfred Cockerill guaranteed the cricket club possession of the ground in perpetuity and in 1923 handed it over for a small rent for 1,000 years. The whole area of 8.5 acres is now owned by the county cricket club.

The initial first-class match was staged between 5 and 7 June 1905 against neighbours Leicestershire. The County Cricket Ground was shared with Northampton Town Football Club from the 1897/8 season to the end of October 1994 during which time association football was staged at the northern end of the playing area. This restricted cricket games at the beginning and end of the season when it clashed with football matches. In 1994 the football club vacated the County Ground and moved approximately 2 miles to the west of the town centre to the purpose-built Sixfields Stadium not far from Northampton Saints Rugby Football Club at Franklins Gardens and near to the M1 motorway at Junction 15a.

The Ken Turner Stand (formerly the Main Stand) was built from funds provided by the Northamptonshire Cricket Supporters' Association and was opened by Mr G.A.T. Vials, President of NCCC, on 3 November 1958. The architect was Sir John Brown of A.E. Henson & Partners and the Contractor was Kottler & Heron. This building houses the press box, members' covered seating, members' areas, catering, toilets, a bar and the umpires' room. At the rear on the ground floor is the County Cricket Board headquarters. This is the oldest stand on the ground and it has remained unaltered, unlike the Old Pavilion.

The Old Pavilion was originally shared with the football and bowling clubs but is now in sole use of the cricket club. It was refurbished in the winter of 1990/1 and renamed the Spencer Pavilion in recognition of Earl Spencer, a great supporter of the county. The Spencer Pavilion now forms the members' main enclosure. On the ground floor of this building is the Long Room members' bar, and members' room. In 1979 a new players' pavilion was erected in place of the old Ladies' Pavilion. This is known as the Players' Pavilion and houses facilities for players, and the Cockerill and Lilford Hospitality Rooms and Executive Boxes at first floor level. The Players' Pavilion also houses the County Club Office, the

Spencer Pavilion, Ken Turner Stand and Players' Pavilion seen from the West Stand.

Marketing Department and the players' dining area where some memorabilia and honours boards are on view. The ground floor of the Players' Pavilion includes the Colin Milburn Room which was opened in 1990 and houses a fine display of blazers and caps belonging to the former Northamptonshire and England player. The Players' Pavilion was extended in 1987 and 1988.

During the 1992/3 close season the Wantage Road entrance was given a facelift with new splendid entrance gates and in 1996/7 at a cost of £100,000 the Spencer Pavilion was extended to provide additional seating. At the same time, at the Abington Avenue End of the ground a new wall and fence with entrance gates were built at a cost of £60,000. They are named after Dennis Brookes to commemorate his immense contribution to the club over many years. In 1997 the main entrance to the ground for all members and visitors was moved from Wantage Road to Abington Avenue through the Dennis Brookes Gate. The original Wantage Road entrance is now used by players, officials, press and guests only.

After the football club vacated the ground at the end of 1994 a huge amount of work took place. The floodlight pylons were taken down and sold by the football club to Sri Lanka, then the football stands and terracing were demolished (although the main timber football stand had been demolished earlier, following the fire at Valley Parade, Bradford). The old score box – where both scorers once sat on the first floor with the club cricket shop below – has retained its character but is now a quaint and indeed popular private room with a patio area used by the Supporters' Club. From this point northwards, that is the former Football Ground End, the entire ground has been totally rebuilt.

The West Stand was rebuilt in 1986 and in 1997 Northamptonshire's most ambitious and expensive infrastructure project began – construction of the new Indoor Cricket Centre at the Abington Avenue End. The building was designed by local architects Gotch Saunders and Surridge and was built by Swallow Construction. Building was completed in early August 1998. In the main hall there are six lanes allowing bowlers a full 20-yard run up with specially sprung floors which provide a cushioning effect. There is also a reception area, centre manager's office, video analysis and seminar rooms, changing and toilet facilities and on the ground floor a well-appointed and well-stocked NCCC club shop. In the bar area are cabinets displaying Northamptonshire CCC cricket memorabilia relating to great players who have represented the club in first-class and Test cricket. The building was opened on 30 August 1998 by Charles, 9th Earl Spencer. This building was partly funded by the National Lottery Sports Fund.

In January 2000 work began on a new Grandstand between the existing West Stand and the new Indoor Cricket Centre. This was partly funded by the Sports Ground Initiative Scheme. The North-West Stand features new seating with some specially designated disabled areas. The old garages on the eastern side of the ground were demolished to provide further car parking on the shingle areas close to the bowling green. Further essential work on the main scoreboard and the food preparation areas was carried out during the early part of 2000.

In 2001 a new membership scheme was introduced for Northamptonshire CCC members similar to that operated by some other counties who now favour computerised turnstiles using plastic swipe cards. During the winter of 2001/2 new turnstiles were installed between the new Indoor Cricket School and the bowling green.

The TV camera position is usually sited on the first floor of the Turner Stand adjoining the press box. There are two scoreboards on the ground: the main one houses the groundsman's equipment store on the ground floor and also a message board with computerised scores of other matches and significant performances attained during the match. The playing area is approximately 142 metres by 138 metres.

In 1920 at Northampton P.G.H. Fender of Surrey scored what was then the fastest century in first-class cricket. This remarkably free-scoring hitter not only scored his first century in first-class cricket, but it took him just 35 minutes.

Plaque commemorating the opening of the Main Stand, now called the Ken Turner Stand.

Another batting feat at the ground came in May 1973 when Glenn Turner of New Zealand scored his 1,000th run. It came off the bowling of Bishen Bedi, the Indian Test spinner.

In 1999 the ground hosted the Sri Lanka touring team for the World Cup. In two warm-up matches Northamptonshire took on Sri Lanka and Bangladesh. Later that summer Northampton hosted South Africa v Sri Lanka and Bangladesh v Pakistan. Floodlit matches were staged in 2000 with Worcestershire, in 2001 with Leicestershire and in 2002 with Sri Lanka and Derbyshire.

GROUND RECORDS AND SCORES

FIRST-CLASS MATCHES

Highest innings total for county 781 for 7 dec v Nottinghamshire 1995
Highest innings total against county 631 for 4 dec by Sussex 1938
Lowest innings total for county 15 v Yorkshire 1908
Lowest innings total against county 33 by Lancashire 1977
Highest individual innings for county 329* M.E. Hussey v Essex 2001
Highest individual innings against county 286 J.R. Freeman for Essex 1921
Highest wicket partnerships for county

1st	375 R.A. White & M.J. Powell	v	Gloucestershire	2002
2nd	344 G. Cook & R.J. Boyd-Moss	v	Lancashire	1986
3rd	320 L. Livingston & F. Jakeman	v	South Africans	1951
4th	370 R.T. Virgin & P. Willey	v	Somerset	1976
5th	401 M.B. Loye & D. Ripley	v	Glamorgan	1998
6th	255 D.J.G. Sales & D. Ripley	v	Leicestershire	1999
7th	293 D.J.G. Sales & D. Ripley	v	Essex	1999
8th	222 W.W. Timms & F.I. Walden	v	Warwickshire	1926
9th	156 R. Subba Row & S. Starkie	v	Lancashire	1955
10th	148 B.W. Bellamy & J.V. Murdin	v	Glamorgan	1925

Highest wicket partnerships against county

1st	279 P. Holmes & H. Sutcliffe	for	Yorkshire	1919
2nd	306 M.J. Powell & D.P. Ostler	for	Warwickshire	2000
3rd	303 H.A. Gomes & C.L. King	for	West Indians	1976
4th	282* M.W. Gatting & J.D. Carr	for	Middlesex	1994
5th	288 H.A. Peach & A. Ducat	for	Surrey	1920
6th	265 W.E. Alley & K.E. Palmer	for	Somerset	1961
7th	205 J.M. Dakin & D.J. Millns	for	Leicestershire	1997
8th	171 Shadab Kabir & Saqlain Mushtaq	for	Pakistanis	1996
9th	136 R.M. Ellison & A.P.E. Knott	for	Kent	1985
10th	138 R.I. Jefferson & D.A.D. Sydenham	for	Surrey	1963

Best bowling performance in an innings for county 9 for 43 G.E. Tribe v Worcestershire 1958
Best bowling performance in an innings against county 10 for 30 C. Blythe for Kent 1907
Best bowling performance in a match for county 15 for 31 G.E. Tribe v Yorkshire 1958
Best bowling performance in a match against county 17 for 48 C. Blythe for Kent 1907
Largest crowd 21,770 v Australians 1953

LIMITED-OVERS MATCHES

Highest innings total for county 360 for 2 v Staffordshire (NWT) 1990
Highest innings total against county 303 for 3 by Yorkshire (C&G) 2002
Lowest innings total for county 41 v Middlesex (SL) 1972
Lowest innings total against county 69 by Herefordshire (GC) 1976
Highest individual innings for county 134 R.J.Bailey v Gloucestershire (B&H) 1987
Highest individual innings against county 136* P.Johnson for Nottinghamshire (SL) 1995

Highest wicket partnerships for county

1st	166 A. Fordham & N.A. Felton	v	Staffordshire	(NWT)	1990
2nd	245 G. Cook & R.J. Bailey	v	Gloucestershire	(B&H)	1987
3rd	207* A.J. Lamb & R.J. Bailey	v	Hampshire	(SL)	1985
4th	164* D.J. Capel & K.M. Curran	v	Lancashire	(SL)	1992
5th	160 A.J. Lamb & D.J. Capel	v	Leicestershire	(B&H)	1986
6th	116* R.J. Warren & J.W. Cook	v	Gloucestershire	(B&H)	2002
7th	108 T.C. Walton & A.L. Penberthy	v	Warwickshire	(B&H)	1996
8th	66 R.J. Boyd-Moss & N.A. Mallender	v	Warwickshire	(SL)	1981
9th	50* A.L. Penberthy & M.N. Bowen	v	Glamorgan	(SL)	1994
10th	35 R.J. Bailey & J.P. Taylor	v	Warwickshire	(SL)	1994

Highest wicket partnerships against county

1st	159 D.E. Paynter & T.E. Coleman	for	Northamptonshire CB	(C&G)	2001
2nd	209 M.J. Smith & G.D. Barlow	for	Middlesex	(B&H)	1977
3rd	158 P. Johnson & C.L. Cairns	for	Nottinghamshire	(SL)	1995
4th	160 E.R. Dexter & J.M. Parks	for	Sussex	(GC)	1963
5th	111 A. McGrath & R.J. Blakey	for	Yorkshire	(SL)	1996
6th	90* P.A. Cottey & A.D. Shaw	for	Glamorgan	(SL)	1998
7th	86* N.J. Adams & A.M. Cade	for	Cambridgeshire	(NWT)	1992
8th	71* M. Watkinson & I.D. Austin	for	Lancashire	(NWT)	1993
9th	52* R.M. Ellison & C. Penn	for	Kent	(B&H)	1989
10th	50* E.E. Hemmings & M.K. Bore	for	Nottinghamshire	(SL)	1979

Best bowling performance in a match for county 7 for 37 N.A. Mallender v Worcestershire (NWT) 1984
Best bowling performance in a match against county 6 for 22 C.E.B. Rice for Nottinghamshire (B&H) 1991
Largest crowd 7,000 v Lancashire (NWT) 1981

ONE-DAY INTERNATIONALS

Highest innings total 223 for 9 by Bangladesh v Pakistan (WC) 1999
Lowest innings total for 110 by Sri Lanka v South Africa (WC) 1999
Highest individual innings 52* L. Klusener for South Africa v Sri Lanka (WC) 1999
Highest wicket partnerships

1st	69 Mehrab Hossain & Shahriar Hossain	for	Bangladesh v Pakistan	(WC)	1999
2nd	2 M.V. Boucher & H.H. Gibbs	for	South Africa v Sri Lanka	(WC)	1999
	2 Ijaz Ahmed & Saeed Anwar	for	Pakistan v Bangladesh	(WC)	1999
3rd	50 Akram Khan & Aminul Islam	for	Bangladesh v Pakistan	(WC)	1999
4th	29 D.J. Cullinan & J.H. Kallis	for	South Africa v Sri Lanka	(WC)	1999
5th	17 R.S. Mahanama & A. Ranatunga	for	Sri Lanka v South Africa	(WC)	1999
6th	55 Azhar Mahmood & Wasim Akram	for	Pakistan v Bangladesh	(WC)	1999
7th	20 U.D.U. Chandana & R.S. Mahanama	for	Sri Lanka v South Africa	(WC)	1999
8th	22 Moin Khan & Saqlain Mushtaq	for	Pakistan v Bangladesh	(WC)	1999
9th	44 S. Elworthy & L. Klusener	for	South Africa v Sri Lanka	(WC)	1999
10th	33* A.A. Donald & L. Klusener	for	South Africa v Sri Lanka	(WC)	1999

Best bowling performance 5 for 35 Saqlain Mushtaq for Pakistan v Bangladesh (WC) 1999
Largest crowd 7,326 South Africa v Sri Lanka (WC) 1999.

GROUND INFORMATION

ENTRANCES Dennis Brookes Gate in Abington Avenue (members and public), Wantage Road Gate (members on foot only, players, officials, press only).
MEMBERS' ENCLOSURE Spencer Pavilion and enclosure.
MEMBERS' ZONE In front of the Spencer Pavilion.
PUBLIC ENCLOSURE Rest of the ground.
COVERED STANDS Spencer Pavilion, Ken Turner Stand (upper) and West Stand.

OPEN STANDS Permanent tiered plastic tip up seating in North-West Stand and ground-level bench and plastic tip-up seating surrounding the playing area.

NAME OF ENDS Wantage Road End, Abington Avenue End.

GROUND DIMENSIONS 138m × 142m.

REPLAY SCREEN If televised matches are staged at the ground the replay screen is sited between the bowling green at the Abington Avenue End and the main scoreboard.

FIRST AID Situated at rear of Ken Turner Stand and in new Indoor Cricket School.

CODES OF DRESS Spectators are required to dress in an appropriate manner consistent with attending a cricket match. Bare torsos are not acceptable in, or in front of the Spencer Pavilion. Executive Club/Suite users must wear a necktie and jacket.

BEHAVIOUR The club is keen that standards of behaviour should be maintained and members and spectators are urged to report immediately to the CEO any incident, or potential incident, where they feel action should be taken. Bad language is not acceptable at any match and the club will take prompt and strong action should this or any other ground regulation be ignored.

RECIPROCAL ARRANGEMENTS Part of East Midlands Membership group with Derbyshire, Leicestershire, Nottinghamshire and Warwickshire, also offer certain days racing at Huntingdon and membership of Hong Kong CC, Queens Park CC in Trinidad and Western Australian CA at WACA in Perth.

SUPPORTERS' CLUB NCCSC membership £5 per annum. Special rates for concessions and husband and wife membership are available.

JUNIORS Junior Steelbacks membership for those under 16 as at 1 April £10.

CORPORATE ENTERTAINING Cockerill and Lilford Hospitality Rooms plus Thompson Suite in Main Pavilion and boxes in the new Indoor Cricket School. Corporate Brochure is available from Commercial Department at the club.

FACILITIES FOR VISUALLY IMPAIRED SPECTATORS No reduced admission. Guide dogs allowed by arrangement with club in advance.

FACILITIES AND ACCESS FOR PEOPLE WITH DISABILITIES INCLUDING WHEELCHAIR ACCESS TO GROUND Yes, from Abington Avenue.

DESIGNATED CAR PARK AVAILABLE INSIDE THE GROUND FOR PEOPLE WITH DISABILITIES Specially reserved areas for wheelchair disabled which must be reserved no more than 5 days in advance and 10 disabled car parking spaces between the main scoreboard and the Spencer Pavilion at a cost of £3 per day which must be reserved no more than 5 days in advance of the match.

GOOD VIEWING AREAS INSIDE THE GROUND FOR PEOPLE USING WHEELCHAIRS Specially reserved areas for wheelchair users which must be reserved no more than 5 days in advance and 10 disabled car parking spaces between the main scoreboard and the Spencer Pavilion at a cost of £3 per day which must be reserved no more than 5 days in advance of the match.

DESIGNATED VIEWING AREAS FOR PEOPLE USING WHEELCHAIRS Yes, in front of the Ken Turner Stand around the perimeter hard standing.

RAMPS TO PROVIDE EASY ACCESS TO BARS & REFRESHMENT OUTLETS FOR PEOPLE USING WHEELCHAIRS Yes.

FOOD & DRINK FULL RESTAURANT/DINING FACILITIES Members, yes. Public, yes. Restaurant service is available in the George Thompson Suite in the Main Pavilion. A cafeteria-style facility is available within the Ken Turner Stand where tea and coffee is also available with similar outlets in the Colin Milburn Room and the George Thompson Suite. Bookings must be made in person at the start of each match day for the restaurant only although it is recommended that bookings are made in advance for popular matches by telephoning the Catering Department. The Long Room of the Spencer Pavilion offers bar meals at lunchtime for members and a full bar. Further catering is available at 'Carlsberg-Tetley Corner' adjacent to the entrance to the new Indoor Cricket School at the Abington Avenue end of the ground.

TEMPORARY FOOD/DRINK FACILITIES Members, yes. Public, yes.

FOOD SUITABLE FOR VEGETARIANS Members, yes. Public, yes.

BARS Members 3, Public 3. Bars are available in the George Thompson Suite, Colin Milburn Room, new Indoor Cricket School and the Long Room of the Spencer Pavilion.

VARIETIES OF BEER SOLD Carlsberg-Tetley, Charles Wells and local beers.

CHILDREN'S FACILITIES Crèche, no. Bouncy castle, when available, for floodlit matches.

CLUB SHOP Northamptonshire CCC Shop located in Indoor Cricket School at Abington Avenue End of the ground.

CLUB MUSEUM No, but there are some cabinets displaying cricket memorabilia relating to Northamptonshire CCC in the upstairs bar in the New Indoor Cricket School at the Abington Avenue End of the ground.

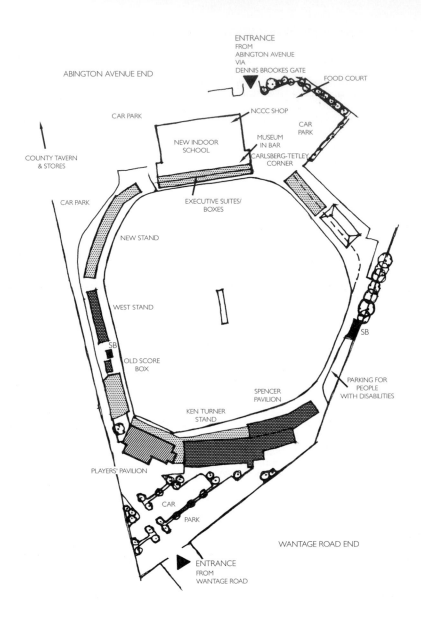

ENTRANCE
FROM
ABINGTON AVENUE
VIA
DENNIS BROOKES GATE

ABINGTON AVENUE END

FOOD COURT

CAR PARK

NCCC SHOP

CAR
PARK

NEW INDOOR
SCHOOL

MUSEUM
IN BAR

COUNTY TAVERN
& STORES

CARLSBERG-TETLEY
CORNER

CAR PARK

EXECUTIVE SUITES/
BOXES

NEW STAND

WEST STAND

SB

SB

OLD SCORE
BOX

PARKING FOR
PEOPLE
WITH DISABILITIES

SPENCER
PAVILION

KEN TURNER
STAND

PLAYERS' PAVILION

CAR
PARK

WANTAGE ROAD END

ENTRANCE
FROM
WANTAGE ROAD

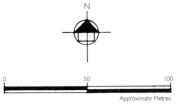

N

0   50   100
Approximate Metres

CRICKET COACHING FACILITIES Yes, new Indoor Cricket School at Abington Avenue End of ground.
CRICKET NETS Yes, winter only.
OTHER SPORTING OR RECREATIONAL FACILITIES ON THE GROUND Yes, Indoor Cricket School is available for hire.
FACILITIES FOR HIRE OR WIDER COMMUNITY USE AT THE GROUND The club can provide 18 conference rooms from 10 to 1,000 delegates with first-class catering and approximately 400 cars for meetings, seminars, exhibitions and private functions throughout the year. Contact Commercial Department for details.
WINTER CRICKET EVENTS Members' club dinners and lunches are staged in the Pavilion which is also used during the close season.
CAR PARKING FACILITIES Car parking within the ground is not guaranteed for members. Access is only via the Abington Avenue Gate. Sponsors' car parking is available in Roseholme Road, just off Wellingborough Road, which also serves as an overflow car parking area. For Sunday League matches members and spectators can park in the car park utilised by customers of Harris Wholesalers in Adnitt Road or in a similar car park in Ardington Road. Both are only two minutes' walk from the ground. For tourist and floodlit matches no car parking is available within the ground. For important matches street parking south of the ground is recommended.
OTHER INFORMATION A second-hand cricket book stall run by Donald Scott of Brackley is sited in front of the Ken Turner Stand at some matches. A 20-minute drive away is Althorp House, home of the Patron, which is open to visitors from 1 July to 30 September.
GROUND CAPACITY 6,500.
ANTICIPATED GROUND DEVELOPMENTS Club presently considering construction of new stands to eastern side of ground adjacent to main scoreboard.

HOW TO GET THERE

 Northampton station 2 miles ☎ 08457 484950, www.silverlink-trains.com

 Northampton Transport 1 or 51 from Northampton station to within 200m of ground also Northampton Transport 6, 8 and 15 from town centre to within 200m of ground, www.arriva.co.uk

 From north: from M1 junction 15 take A508 (north) to junction with A45 (Nene Valley Way), take A45 (north) to junction with A5095, take second exit at roundabout on to A5095 (Rushmere Road), continue on A5095 (Park Avenue), at junction with A4500 (Wellingborough Road) turn on to A4500 and follow signs to cricket ground. **From south:** from M1 junction 15 take A508 (north) then proceed as for north. **From east:** from A45, Weston Favell, continue on A45 to junction with A5095, take A5095 (north) then as for north. **From west:** from M1 junction 16 join A45 (east), continue on this road to junction with A5095, then as for north.

 London Luton ☎ 01582 405100, Birmingham ☎ 0121 767 5511, Cambridge ☎ 01223 373737

WHERE TO STAY

Broomhill Country House & Restaurant (☎ 01604 845959 www.broomhillhotel.co.uk), Coach House Hotel (☎ 01604 250981), Courtyard By Marriott (☎ 01327 349022), Grand Hotel (☎ 01604 34416), Green Park Hotel (☎ 01604 716777 www.greenpark-hotel.co.uk), Hilton Hotel (☎ 01604 700666 www.hilton.com), Lime Trees Hotel (☎ 01604 632188), Northampton Moat House Hotel (☎ 01604 739988 www.moathouse.com), Poplars Hotel (☎ 01604 643983), Stakis Country Court Hotel (☎ 01604 700666), The Aviator Hotel (☎ 01604 642111 www.aviatorhotel.com)
    Visit www.smoothhound.co.uk for details of other places to stay in and around Northampton.

WHERE TO EAT

Mem-Saab (☎ 01604 630214), The Althorp Coaching House Fox & Hounds (☎ 01604 770651 www.althorp-coaching-inn.co.uk), The Boat Inn (☎ 01604 862428 www.boatinn.co.uk), The Dusty Fox (☎ 01604 821122),The Imperial Oriental (☎/Fax 01604 627111), The Mirama Cantonese Restaurant (☎ 01604 233011)

The County Cricket Ground, Northampton.

TOURIST INFORMATION Northampton Tourist Information Centre, Mr Grant's House, St Giles Square, Northampton, Northamptonshire NN1 1DA ☎ 01604 233500 www.northamton.gov.uk, www.touristnetuk.com, www.northants-chamber.co.uk

OTHER USEFUL INFORMATION

Northampton Saints RFC ☎ 01604 751543, www.northamptonsaints.co.uk
www.northampton.gov.uk/museums
www.northantsfarmholidays.co.uk
www.althorp.com
www.nvr.org.uk

LOCAL RADIO STATIONS BBC Radio Northampton (104.2 MHz FM/1107 KHz MW), Hereward Radio (96.6 MHz FM/1557 KHz MW), Chiltern Radio (96.9 MHz FM/792 KHz MW)

LOCAL NEWSPAPERS *Chronicle and Echo*, *Evening Telegraph*, *Northampton Post*, *Mercury & Herald*, *Northamptonshire Image*

Nottinghamshire

NOTTS
OUTLAWS

Trent Bridge
Cleethorpes

NOTTINGHAMSHIRE COUNTY CRICKET CLUB, TRENT BRIDGE, NOTTINGHAM, NG2 6AG

Telephone main switchboard 0115 982 3000 **fax** 0115 945 5730
Ticket Office 0870 168 8888
Marketing Department 0115 982 3002
Email administration.notts@ecb.co.uk
Website www.nottsccc.co.uk, www.trentbridge.co.uk

Founded March/April 1841 substantial reorganisation 11 December 1866
Colours green and gold
Crest leaping stag
National Cricket League Nickname Outlaws
National Cricket League Colours green and gold
President Rt Hon K. Clarke QC MP
Chairman A. Bocking
Chief Executive Officer D.G. Collier
PA to CEO Ms L. Miles
Director of Cricket M. Newell
Captain J.E.R. Gallian
Vice Captain P.J. Franks
2nd XI Captain W. Noon
Cricket Secretary Ms B. Wynne-Thomas
Chairman Cricket Committee S. Foster
Sales & Marketing Manager Miss L.J. Pursehouse
Financial Controller Mrs H. Trinick
County Academy Director C.M. Tolley
Cricket Development Manager – Community D. Tighe

Cricket Development Manager – Performance & Excellence S. Burrows
Physiotherapist T. Leary
Head Groundsman S. Birks
Ground Manager K. Healy
Health & Safety Officer M. Whitt
Scorer 1st XI G. Stringfellow
Scorer 2nd XI B. Hewes
Hon Curator/Librarian, Statistician and Historian P. Wynne-Thomas
Sponsors PKF Accountants and Business Advisors
Shirt Sponsors PKF
Yearbook £7.50
Scorecard 30p (County) or 50p (Test/ODI)
National Cricket League Programme & Scorecard £2
Magazine *Covered* issued free to members
Frizzell County Championship Status Division 1
National Cricket League Status Division 2

ACHIEVEMENTS

County Championship Champions 1865, 1868, 1871, 1872, 1875, 1880, 1883, 1884, 1885, 1886, 1907, 1929, 1981, 1987, Joint Champions 1869, 1873, 1879, 1882, 1889
Gillette Cup Semi-finalists 1969
NatWest Trophy Winners 1987, Finalists 1985
Benson and Hedges Cup Winners 1989, Finalists 1982

John Player Sunday League 2nd 1984
Refuge Assurance Sunday League Champions 1991
Norwich Union National League Best 5th Division 1 2001
Refuge Assurance Cup Finalists 1989, Semi-finalists 1991
Tilcon Trophy Winners 1977, Finalists 1984, 1985

NOTTINGHAMSHIRE CRICKET BOARD

Chairman B. Pailing
Secretary R. Lafbery
Treasurer I. Hepburn
Cricket Development Officer D. Tighe
Development Manager Performance & Excellence S. Burrows

Address   Nottinghamshire Cricket Board, Trent Bridge, Nottingham, NG2 6AG
☎   0115 982 3000
Fax   0115 945 5730
Email   administration.notts@ecb.co.uk
Website   www.nottsccc.co.uk or www.trentbridge.co.uk

GROUNDS

Nottingham (Trent Bridge, West Bridgford) and Cleethorpes (Cleethorpes CC, Chichester Road)
   Other grounds used since 1969: Nottingham (John Player & Sons Sports Ground, Aspley Lane), Worksop (Town Ground, Central Avenue) and Newark-on-Trent (RHP Limited Sports Ground, Elm Avenue)

SECOND XI GROUNDS

Boots Ground, Nottingham ☎ 0115 949 2388
Farnsfield CC, Station Road, Farnsfield, Mansfield ☎ 01623 882986
Notts Unity Casuals CC, Brian Wakefield Memorial Ground, Lenton Lane, Nottingham ☎ 0115 986 8255
Welbeck Colliery CC, Oakfield Lane, Sherwood Street, Warsop, no ☎ on ground
Worksop College, Worksop ☎ 01909 472286

The Trent Bridge Inn behind the William Clarke Stand.

TRENT BRIDGE

Address Trent Bridge, Nottingham, NG2 6AG
Prospects of Play ☎ 0115 982 3000

HISTORY OF GROUND AND FACILITIES

TRENT BRIDGE became a cricket ground thanks to the enterprise of William Clarke. A bricklayer by trade, Clarke was also the organiser of the Nottingham First XI in the 1830s. In late 1837 he married a Mrs Chapman, the landlady and lessee of the Trent Bridge Inn and the open ground behind the building. He laid out a cricket ground at the back of his new home, known today to locals as the TBI. The first match at the ground was played on 10 July 1838 between T. Barker's XI and W. Clarke's XI, and in July 1840 the first county match was staged with Sussex the visitors.

William Clarke left Nottingham for London in 1846 and was succeeded by his stepson John Chapman but it was not until 1881 that the land's owners signed a 99-year lease for the area with Nottinghamshire CCC. In 1919 the club purchased both the inn, which they later sold, and the ground, which has been in their sole ownership since.

The present members' pavilion was built in 1886 and was designed by H.M. Townsend of Peterborough. It has been altered and extended but much of its original character remains. Developments over the years have made Trent Bridge one of the country's premier Test match venues; in the last 20 years a huge amount of money has been invested in the ground infrastructure.

In 1988 Nottinghamshire CCC celebrated 150 years of Trent Bridge. The proceeds of the celebrations, some £151,000, went towards the reconstruction of the Bridgford Road Stand and the creation of a new press lounge. A further £600,000 was provided by Rushcliffe Borough Council and £60,000 by a local businessman, Nat Puri.

The first Test match at Trent Bridge was played in 1899 when England met Australia. It is the third oldest Test venue after Lord's and Eden Gardens in Calcutta. In recent years the ground has seen many limited-overs international games including Prudential Cup, Prudential Trophy and Texaco Trophy matches. Over 1,300 Nottinghamshire CCC matches have been staged on the ground and all Test match nations, except Bangladesh, have played here.

Much has been written and spoken of Parr's Tree, which stood close to the Bridgford Road side of the ground behind the Parr Stand and was blown down during a gale in January 1976. It was an elm tree which gained its name in the last century from the frequency with which George Parr (1826–91, Nottinghamshire 1845–70) managed to hit balls into its branches. Mini cricket bats have been made from the tree. Indeed, the home of bat making, the Gunn & Moore factory, is only five minutes away by car.

Nottinghamshire CCC have played on four other grounds in the city; the most recent journey from headquarters was to the John Player & Sons Sports and Social Club Ground at Aspley Lane in 1973 for a John Player Sunday League match with Gloucestershire.

In 1990 the William Clarke Stand was built and it includes the club shop.

The Fox Road Stand, which offers a splendid view of the ground, is near the main scoreboard.

During the 1992/3 close season in some 26 weeks the Hound Road Stand was erected at a cost of £1.47m. This stand replaced the former Lowater Suite, Ladies' Pavilion and restaurant. The grandstand provides 1,715 seats with banqueting and catering facilities beneath for 300 people. The most recent additions to the ground include the £7.2m Radcliffe Road Stand, completed in 1998, which houses the press box, executive hospitality suites and public seating on the upper, middle and lower levels. The boxes in the Radcliffe Road Stand are named after famous Nottinghamshire cricketers: Attewell, Carr, Keeton, Butler, Shaw, Shrewsbury, Bolus, Robinson, Voce, Larwood, Simpson, Hardstaff, Barnes, Flowers, Whysall, Dooland, Broad, French, Hemmings and Rice. The Trent Bridge Cricket Centre is also within the Radcliffe Road Stand complex. It has indoor cricket nets and accommodation for those attending coaching and courses throughout the year. The £1.9m Fox Road Stand was opened by Ian Botham on 27 June 2002 ahead of the England versus Sri Lanka NatWest Series match. The stand features an architectural state-of-the-art 'aircraft wing' roof and has approximately 2,300 permanent seats.

The new library with a splendid collection of cricket memorabilia, which can be inspected on request, was opened in 2002 in the Squash Club Complex. The TV camera/commentary and radio commentary boxes are situated in the Radcliffe Road Stand.

Trent Bridge has been used for association football by both Nottingham Forest FC and Notts County FC, both of whose current grounds are within walking distance on either side of the nearby River Trent.

Ground records have included scores of over 200 from Charlie Macartney, A.O. Jones, Denis Compton and Frank Worrell. Tom Graveney took 258 off the West Indies during the 1950s. More recently, Vivian Richards scored 232 against

England in 1976. During the 1989 Cornhill Test match between England and Australia, the Australian openers Geoff Marsh (138) and Mark Taylor (219) added 329 for the 1st wicket. At the close of play on the first day the total was 301 for 0. In the same season Nottinghamshire scored 296 for 6 against Kent in the Benson and Hedges Cup beating the previous highest innings total recorded in 1968. The Nottingham public has seen some great players in action including William Clarke, George Parr, Alfred Shaw, Bill Voce, Harold Larwood, Reg Simpson, Gary Sobers, Clive Rice, Derek Randall, Richard Hadlee and Franklyn Stephenson.

GROUND RECORDS AND SCORES

FIRST-CLASS MATCHES

Highest innings total for county 739 for 7 dec v Leicestershire 1903
Highest innings total against county 706 for 4 dec by Surrey 1947
Lowest innings total for county 13 v Yorkshire 1901
Lowest innings total against county 16 by Derbyshire 1879
Highest individual innings for county 296 A.O. Jones v Gloucestershire 1903
Highest individual innings against county 345 C.G. Macartney for Australians 1921
Highest wicket partnerships for county

1st	303 A.O. Jones & J. Iremonger	v	Gloucestershire	1904
2nd	398 W. Gunn & A. Shrewsbury	v	Sussex	1890
3rd	367 W. Gunn & J.R. Gunn	v	Leicestershire	1903
4th	345 M. Newell & D.W. Randall	v	Derbyshire	1988
5th	247 J. Hardstaff jun & A. Staples	v	Middlesex	1937
6th	303* F.H. Winrow & P.F. Harvey	v	Derbyshire	1947
7th	201 R.H. Howitt & R. Bagguley	v	Sussex	1895
8th	220 G.F.H. Heane & R. Winrow	v	Somerset	1935
9th	165 W. McIntyre & G. Wootton	v	Kent	1869
10th	152 U. Afzaal & A.J. Harris	v	Worcestershire	2000

Highest wicket partnerships against county

1st	372* M.W. Goodwin & R.R. Montgomerie	for	Sussex	2001
2nd	349 C.S. Elliott & J.D. Eggar	for	Derbyshire	1947
3rd	321* A. Hearne & J.R. Mason	for	Kent	1899
4th	402 R.B. Kanhai & K. Ibadulla	for	Warwickshire	1968
5th	253* D.J. Bicknell & A.D. Brown	for	Surrey	1994
6th	315 P.A. de Silva & M.A. Ealham	for	Kent	1995
7th	271* E.H. Hendren & F.T. Mann	for	Middlesex	1925
8th	157 A. Hamer & E. Smith	for	Derbyshire	1955
9th	171 M.A. Ealham & P.A. Strang	for	Kent	1997
10th	141 J.T. Tyldesley & W. Worsley	for	Lancashire	1905

Best bowling performance in an innings for county 9 for 19 J. Grundy v Kent 1864
Best bowling performance in an innings against county 9 for 32 J.T. Hearne for Middlesex 1891, M.S. Nichols for Essex 1936
Best bowling performance in a match for county 17 for 89 F.C.L. Matthews v Northamptonshire 1923
Best bowling performance in a match against county 16 for 122 C.L. Townsend for Gloucestershire 1895
Largest crowd 35,000 v Surrey 1948

LIMITED-OVERS MATCHES

Highest innings total for county 329 for 6 v Derbyshire (SL) 1993
Highest innings total against county 352 for 8 by Northamptonshire (NWT) 1995
Lowest innings total for county 81 v Derbyshire (SL) 1972
Lowest innings total against county 84 by Surrey (SL) 1974
Highest individual innings for county 167* P. Johnson v Kent (SL) 1993

Highest individual innings against county 171 G.A. Gooch for Essex (SL) 1985
Highest wicket partnerships for county

1st	196 D.J. Bicknell & J.E.R. Gallian	v	Surrey	(SL)	2000
2nd	213* P. Johnson & R.T. Robinson	v	Kent	(SL)	1993
3rd	200 P. Johnson & G.F. Archer	v	Derbyshire	(SL)	1997
4th	190 J.E.R. Gallian & N. Boje	v	Leicestershire	(SL)	2002
5th	125 S.B. Hassan & R.J. Hadlee	v	Warwickshire	(B&H)	1982
6th	91 D.W. Randall & E.E. Hemmings	v	Essex	(SL)	1983
7th	119 P. Johnson & B.N. French	v	Staffordshire	(NWT)	1985
8th	65 C.M. Tolley & P.J. Franks	v	Yorkshire	(B&H)	2000
9th	84* J.R. Wileman & R.A. Pick	v	Essex	(SL)	1995
10th	49 E.E. Hemmings & K.E. Cooper	v	Gloucestershire	(SL)	1984

Highest wicket partnerships against county

1st	239 G.A. Gooch & B.R. Hardie	for	Essex	(SL)	1985
2nd	273 G.A. Gooch & K.S. McEwan	for	Essex	(SL)	1983
3rd	152 R.A. Smith & J.R. Wood	for	Hampshire	(SL)	1989
4th	159 J.B. Bolus & A.J. Borrington	for	Derbyshire	(B&H)	1974
5th	134 M. Maslin & D.N.F. Slade	for	Minor Counties East	(B&H)	1976
6th	123* Wasim Akram & W.K. Hegg	for	Lancashire	(B&H)	1998
7th	164 J.N. Snape & M.A. Hardinges	for	Gloucestershire	(SL)	2001
8th	95* D. Breakwell & K.F. Jennings	for	Somerset	(SL)	1976
9th	83 P.G. Newman & M.A. Holding	for	Derbyshire	(B&H)	1985
10th	52 N.M. McVicker & K. Higgs	for	Leicestershire	(SL)	1975

Best bowling performance in a match for county 6 for 12 R.J. Hadlee v Lancashire (SL) 1980
Best bowling performance in a match against county 7 for 41 A.N. Jones for Sussex (SL) 1986
Largest crowd 8,500 v Somerset (SL) 1979

TEST MATCHES

Highest innings total for England 658 for 8 v Australia 1938
Highest innings total against England 602 for 6 dec by Australia 1989
Lowest innings total for England 112 v Australia 1921
Lowest innings total against England 88 by South Africa 1960
Highest individual innings for England 278 D.C.S. Compton v Pakistan 1954
Highest individual innings against England 261 F.M.M. Worrell for West Indies 1950
Highest wicket partnerships for England

1st	219 C.J. Barnett & L. Hutton	v	Australia	1938
2nd	266 P.E. Richardson & T.W. Graveney	v	West Indies	1957
3rd	207 T.W. Graveney & P.B.H. May	v	West Indies	1957
4th	184 T.W. Graveney & P.H. Parfitt	v	Pakistan	1962
5th	237 D.C.S. Compton & N.W.D. Yardley	v	South Africa	1947
6th	215 G. Boycott & A.P.E. Knott	v	Australia	1977
7th	113* G.P. Thorpe & N. Hussain	v	Australia	1993
8th	93 P.H. Parfitt & J.M. Parks	v	South Africa	1965
9th	103 C. White & M.J. Hoggard	v	India	2002
10th	79* M. Watkinson & R. Illingworth	v	West Indies	1995

Highest wicket partnerships against England

1st	329 G.F. Marsh & M.A. Taylor	for	Australia	1989
2nd	170 W.A. Brown & D.G. Bradman	for	Australia	1938
3rd	319 A. Melville & A.D. Nourse	for	South Africa	1947
4th	283 F.M.M. Worrell & E. de. C. Weekes	for	West Indies	1950
5th	177 B.E. Congdon & V. Pollard	for	New Zealand	1973
6th	161 G.M. Wood & G.M. Ritchie	for	Australia	1985
7th	154 O.G. Smith & J.D.C. Goddard	for	West Indies	1957
8th	107 A.L. Hassett & R.R. Lindwall	for	Australia	1948
9th	66 A.C. Gilchrist & J.N. Gillespie	for	Australia	2001
10th	77 S.J. McCabe & L. Fleetwood-Smith	for	Australia	1938

Best bowling performance in an innings for England 8 for 107 B.J.T. Bosanquet v Australia 1905
Best bowling performance in an innings against England 7 for 54 W.J. O'Reilly for Australia 1934
Best bowling performance in a match for England 14 for 99 A.V. Bedser v Australia 1953
Best bowling performance in a match against England 11 for 129 W.J. O'Reilly for Australia 1934
Largest crowd 35,000 v Australia 1938

ONE-DAY INTERNATIONALS

Highest innings total for England in ODI 363 for 7 v Pakistan (TT) 1992
Highest innings total against England in ODI 282 for 5 by India (TT) 1990
Highest innings total in non-England ODI 330 for 6 by Pakistan v Sri Lanka (WC) 1975
Lowest innings total for England in ODI 157 v Pakistan (TT) 1987
Lowest innings total against England in ODI 165 by Pakistan (TT) 1992
Lowest innings total in non-England ODI 138 by Sri Lanka v Pakistan (WC) 1975
Highest individual innings for England in ODI 131 K.W.R. Fletcher v New Zealand (WC) 1975
Highest individual innings against England in ODI 109 Majid Khan for Pakistan (PT) 1974
Highest individual innings in non-England ODI 110 T.M. Chappell for Australia v India (WC) 1983
Highest wicket partnerships for England in ODI

1st	84 G.A. Gooch & A.J. Stewart	v	Pakistan	(TT)	1992
2nd	107 A.J. Lamb & C.J. Tavare	v	Pakistan	(PT)	1982
3rd	129 N.H. Fairbrother & R.A. Smith	v	Pakistan	(TT)	1992
4th	111 M.A. Atherton & R.A. Smith	v	India	(TT)	1990
5th	95 A.J. Stewart & R.C. Irani	v	Sri Lanka	(NWS)	2002
6th	88* A.J. Lamb & D.R. Pringle	v	Australia	(TT)	1989
7th	32 A.J. Stewart & M.A. Ealham	v	West Indies	(NWS)	2000
8th	23 P.A.J. de Freitas & J.E. Emburey	v	Pakistan	(TT)	1987
9th	13 J.E. Emburey & N.A. Foster	v	Pakistan	(TT)	1987
10th	8* A.R.C. Fraser & S.D. Udal	v	West Indies	(TT)	1995

Highest wicket partnerships against England in ODI

1st	113 Majid Khan & Sadiq Mohammad	for	Pakistan	(PT)	1974
2nd	114 S.L. Campbell & B.C. Lara	for	West Indies	(TT)	1995
3rd	97 S.V. Manjrekar & D.B. Vengsarkar	for	India	(TT)	1990
4th	47* Asif Iqbal & Mushtaq Mohammad	for	Pakistan	(PT)	1974
5th	77* Imran Khan & Javed Miandad	for	Pakistan	(TT)	1987
6th	53 P.J.L Dujon & C.H. Lloyd	for	West Indies	(TT)	1984
7th	20 C.H. Lloyd & M.D. Marshall	for	West Indies	(TT)	1984
	20 Ijaz Ahmed & Rashid Latif	for	Pakistan	(TT)	1996
8th	48 D.R. Hadlee & B.J. McKechnie	for	New Zealand	(WC)	1975
9th	24 Mushtaq Ahmed & Rashid Latif	for	Pakistan	(TT)	1992
10th	18 E.A.E. Baptiste & J. Garner	for	West Indies	(TT)	1984

Highest wicket partnerships in non-England ODI

1st	159 Majid Khan & Sadiq Mohammad	for	Pakistan v Sri Lanka	(WC)	1975
2nd	144 I.M. Chappell & K.J. Hughes	for	Australia v India	(WC)	1983
3rd	93 Salim Elahi & Yousuf Youhana	for	Pakistan v Australia	(NWS)	2001
4th	147* Imran Khan & Zaheer Abbas	for	Pakistan v New Zealand	(WC)	1983
5th	87 Asif Iqbal & Javed Miandad	for	Pakistan v Australia	(WC)	1979
6th	100 J.N. Rhodes & P.L. Symcox	for	South Africa v Sri Lanka	(Emir)	1998
7th	75* I.P. Butchart & D.A.G. Fletcher	for	Zimbabwe v Australia	(WC)	1983
8th	50* R.M. Hogg & R.W. Marsh	for	Australia v Zimbabwe	(WC)	1983
9th	59 J.P. Bracewell & J.V. Coney	for	New Zealand v Pakistan	(WC)	1983
10th	31 D.W. Fleming & J.N. Gillespie	for	Australia v Pakistan	(NWS)	2001

Best bowling performance for England in ODI 4 for 45 A.W. Greig v New Zealand (WC) 1975, A.J. Hollioake v Pakistan (TT) 1996
Best bowling performance against England in ODI 4 for 73 Waqar Younis for Pakistan (TT) 1992
Best bowling performance in non-England ODI 6 for 39 K.H. Macleay for Australia v India (WC) 1983
Largest crowd 15,365 v Sri Lanka (NWS) 2002

GROUND INFORMATION

ENTRANCES Members and public can use all entrances, except at international matches when restrictions apply, please contact venue for details. Dixon Gates & Dalling Gate (Hound Road) are for players' and officials' vehicles. Other entrances include Radcliffe Road and Fox Road.

MEMBERS' ENCLOSURE Pavilion, Larwood & Voce Tavern, Hound Road Stand (county matches only).

PUBLIC ENCLOSURE West Wing Lower/ Upper, Parr Stand Lower/Upper, Radcliffe Road Stand. Upper/Middle/Lower, Fox Round Stand and Hound Road Stand Upper/Lower.

COVERED STANDS West Wing Lower, Parr Stand Lower, Radcliffe Road Stand Lower (part), William Clarke Stand (part), Fox Road Stand (part) and Hound Road Stand Lower (part).

OPEN STANDS Pavilion, West Wing Upper, Parr Stand Upper, William Clarke Stand (part), Radcliffe Road Stand Upper/ Middle/ Lower (part), Fox Road Stand (part), Larwood and Voce Stand, and Hound Road Stand Upper and Lower (part).

NAME OF ENDS Radcliffe Road End, Hound Road End.

GROUND DIMENSIONS 141m × 144m.

REPLAY SCREEN If televised matches are staged at the ground the replay screen is sited directly behind the William Clarke Stand.

FIRST AID In Radcliffe Road Stand and in the Dixon Gate car park, near the Ticket Office.

CODES OF DRESS Spectators are required to dress in an appropriate manner consistent with attending a cricket match. Bare torsos are not acceptable in, or in front of the pavilion. In the Executive Suite and Hospitality facilities jeans, shorts and trainers are not allowed.

BEHAVIOUR The club is keen that standards of behaviour should be maintained and members and spectators are urged to report immediately to the CEO any incident, or potential incident, where they feel action should be taken. Abusive behaviour, entry on to the field of play, the throwing of any article or foul or abusive language will not be tolerated under any circumstances.

RECIPROCAL ARRANGEMENTS Members of Derbyshire, Leicestershire and Northamptonshire can gain free entry to County Championship matches on production of membership card when Nottinghamshire is not playing their own county.

JUNIORS Trent Bridge Junior Membership £10 per annum for under-16s. Contact Membership Department for details.

CORPORATE ENTERTAINING Trent Bridge Cricket Centre has 24 hospitality boxes, The Cricketers Suite and Bar. At the pavilion end there is the Long Room (members only), Derek Randall Banqueting Suite and Restaurant. Facilities vary for County, Test Match and one-day international fixtures. Contact Marketing Department for details and a brochure.

FACILITIES FOR VISUALLY IMPAIRED SPECTATORS Guide dogs allowed.

FACILITIES AND ACCESS FOR PEOPLE WITH DISABILITIES INCLUDING WHEELCHAIR ACCESS TO GROUND Yes, all gates.

DESIGNATED CAR PARK AVAILABLE INSIDE THE GROUND FOR PEOPLE WITH DISABILITIES Not at international matches. Very limited availability for Nottinghamshire CCC members who buy a parking permit for the season.

GOOD VIEWING AREAS INSIDE THE GROUND FOR PEOPLE USING WHEELCHAIRS Yes, special areas marked out in front of Fox Road Stand with disabled toilet facilities close by at rear of stand. Also Radcliffe Road Lower and Middle, West Wing Lower and Hound Road Lower and Upper.

RAMPS TO PROVIDE EASY ACCESS TO BARS & REFRESHMENT OUTLETS FOR PEOPLE USING WHEELCHAIRS Yes, the pavilion is accessed by a ramp at the front. Facilities in Radcliffe Road and Hound Road accessible by lift.

FOOD & DRINK FULL RESTAURANT/DINING FACILITIES Members, yes. Public, yes. Permanent restaurants at county matches for Public include Squash Club Bar and Cricketers Suite and Bar. Members' facilities include the pavilion and Derek Randall Banqueting Suite. Parr Bar Snack bar at the back of the William Clarke Stand.

TEMPORARY FOOD/DRINK FACILITIES Members, yes. Public, yes (international matches only).

FOOD SUITABLE FOR VEGETARIANS Members, yes. Public, yes.

BARS Members 4, Public 4 (depends on the match).

VARIETIES OF BEER SOLD Carling, Draught Worthington, London Pride.

CHILDREN'S FACILITIES Crèche, no. Play area, no.

CLUB SHOP Trent Bridge Shop is located to the rear of the William Clarke and is open on major match days and Monday to Friday at other times in the year.

CLUB MUSEUM In the pavilion. The Library with 7,000 books on cricket is now located in the Squash Club/Reception Building and is open throughout the year.

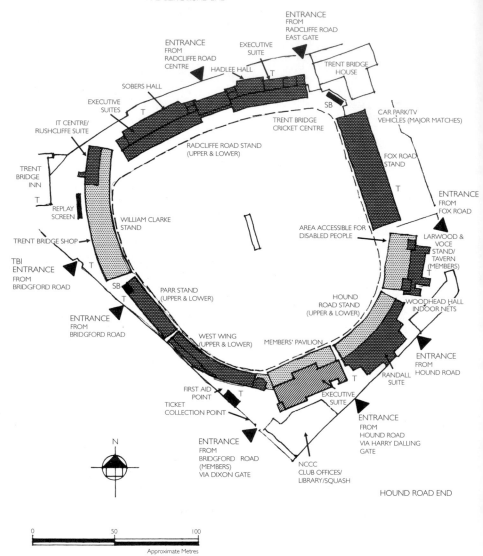

RADCLIFFE ROAD END

ENTRANCE FROM RADCLIFFE ROAD EAST GATE

ENTRANCE FROM RADCLIFFE ROAD CENTRE

EXECUTIVE SUITE

HADLEE HALL

TRENT BRIDGE HOUSE

SOBERS HALL

EXECUTIVE SUITES

CAR PARK/TV VEHICLES (MAJOR MATCHES)

IT CENTRE/ RUSHCLIFFE SUITE

SB

TRENT BRIDGE CRICKET CENTRE

FOX ROAD STAND

RADCLIFFE ROAD STAND (UPPER & LOWER)

TRENT BRIDGE INN

ENTRANCE FROM FOX ROAD

REPLAY SCREEN

WILLIAM CLARKE STAND

AREA ACCESSIBLE FOR DISABLED PEOPLE

LARWOOD & VOCE STAND/ TAVERN (MEMBERS)

TRENT BRIDGE SHOP

TBI ENTRANCE FROM BRIDGFORD ROAD

SB

PARR STAND (UPPER & LOWER)

HOUND ROAD STAND (UPPER & LOWER)

WOODHEAD HALL INDOOR NETS

ENTRANCE FROM BRIDGFORD ROAD

WEST WING (UPPER & LOWER)

MEMBERS' PAVILION

ENTRANCE FROM HOUND ROAD

FIRST AID POINT

RANDALL SUITE

TICKET COLLECTION POINT

EXECUTIVE SUITE

ENTRANCE FROM BRIDGFORD ROAD (MEMBERS) VIA DIXON GATE

ENTRANCE FROM HOUND ROAD VIA HARRY DALLING GATE

N

NCCC CLUB OFFICES/ LIBRARY/SQUASH

HOUND ROAD END

0   50   100
Approximate Metres

CRICKET COACHING FACILITIES Yes, in Trent Bridge Cricket Centre and Woodhead Hall throughout the year. Contact Cricket development Office for further information.

CRICKET NETS Yes, in Trent Bridge Cricket Centre and Woodhead Hall throughout the year.

OTHER SPORTING OR RECREATIONAL FACILITIES ON THE GROUND Gymnasium, Physiotherapy and Sports Injury Clinic. Squash in Trent Bridge Cricket Centre throughout the year including accommodation. ☎ 0115 982 3000 or email cricketcentre.notts@ecb.co.uk for a brochure and full details.

FACILITIES FOR HIRE OR WIDER COMMUNITY USE AT THE GROUND Yes, include Trent Bridge Cricket Centre with two state-of-the-art cricket schools, 24 hospitality boxes, syndicate rooms, bedroom accommodation, lecture theatre, Cricketer's Suite and Bar, Bodyline gymnasium, sauna, sports injury and physiotherapy clinic, the Long Room and Derek Randall Banqueting Suite. All facilities are available for parties, weddings, receptions, dinners, lunches, shows, exhibitions and trade fairs. Contact Marketing Department for details and a brochure. **CAR PARKING FACILITIES** No public car parking is available within the ground. Members can apply for a county match parking permit (limited availability). For international matches there is no parking on the ground. Members can purchase a pass in advance for the Bridge Fields Car Park. Executive Suite members can park at the Boots Ground. Public parking is available on the Embankment on north side of River Trent. TBI Car Park is for Executive Suite members only.

OTHER INFORMATION The Sport-in-Print Bookshop is located near the ground at 3 Radcliffe Road.

GROUND CAPACITY 15,365.

ANTICIPATED GROUND DEVELOPMENTS None planned.

HOW TO GET THERE

 Nottingham Midland station 1 mile ☎ 08457 125 678, www.midlandmainline.com

 Nottingham City Transport buses 1, 1X, 2, 4, 6, 7, 7X, 8, 9, 10, 11 pass ground and Trent Buses link Nottingham station with ground and city centre. Keyworth Connection, Cotgrave and Rushcliffe Buses also pass ground. ☎ 0115 950 6070, 0115 915 5215, 0870 608 2608

 There are cycle routes from surrounding areas of Nottingham to this part of West Bridgford.

 From north: from M1 junction 26 take A610 towards Nottingham, continue to junction with A6514, turn right on to Nottingham Ring Road (signposted Derby A52), continue on this road to junction with A52, continue on A52 (signposted Grantham) to junction with A453, keep left (signposted Grantham), at junction with B679 follow signs to West Bridgford, at junction with A60, turn left on to A60 (Nottingham), continue on this road (London Road) and follow signs to Trent Bridge. **From south:** from M1 junction 24 take A453 (north) towards West Bridgford, continue on this road to junction with A52, then as for north. **From east:** from A52 (Grantham Road) (west), at roundabout take the second exit on to A6011 (Radcliffe Road), continue on this road to junction with A60 (London Road), turn left and then left again on to Bridgford Road. **From west:** from A52, Breaston, Derby stay on A52 (east) and continue to junction with A453, then as for north.

 East Midlands Airport ☎ 01332 852852

WHERE TO STAY

Comfort Hotel (☎ 0115 947 5641), Radcliffe Road Bedrooms (☎ 0115 982 3000), Hilton East Midlands (☎ 01509 674000), Hilton Nottingham (☎ 0115 934 9700), Lace Market Hotel (☎ 0115 852 3232), Nottingham Royal Moat House Hotel (☎ 0115 936 9988), Posthouse Nottingham City (☎ 0115 988 4021), Rutland Square Hotel (☎ 0115 941 1114), Swans Hotel (☎ 0115 981 4042), Talbot House Hotel (☎ 0115 981 1123), The Gallery (☎ 0115 981 3651)

For other places to stay in Nottingham and the West Bridgford area visit www.smoothhound.co.uk, www.nottinghamcity.gov.uk.

WHERE TO EAT

Antonio's Italian on Trent Bridge (☎ 0115 982 0814), Bombay Brasserie Indian (☎ 0115 914 1818), Hart's (☎ 0115 911 0666), Mem Saab (☎ 0115 957 0009), Oriental Pearl (☎ 0115 945 5048), Shimla Pinks (☎ 0115 958 9899), Stratford Haven (☎ 0115 982 5981), Trent Bridge Inn (☎ 0115 982 2786)

TOURIST INFORMATION Nottingham Tourist Information Centre, 1–4 Smithy Row, Nottingham NG1 2BY ☎ 0115 915 5330, www.nottinghamcity.gov.uk

LOCAL RADIO STATIONS BBC Radio Nottingham (95.5 MHz FM/1584 KHz MW), Radio Trent (96.2 MHz FM/999 KHz MW)

LOCAL NEWSPAPERS *Nottingham Evening Post, Football Post* (Sunday only)

CLEETHORPES

Address Cleethorpes Cricket Club, The Pavilion and Squash Club, Chichester Road, Cleethorpes, North-East Lincolnshire DN35 0HZ
Prospects of Play ☎ 01472 691271

HISTORY OF GROUND AND FACILITIES

THE CHICHESTER ROAD GROUND is the home of Cleethorpes Cricket Club and is about 150 yards from the boating lake which forms part of the seafront. Cricket has been played at this ground since 1930. The first club match here was staged on 13 June 1931 against Scunthorpe CC in a Grimsby and District League match. The Cleethorpes Cricket Club First XI play in the Oxbridge Yorkshire ECB Premier League; the Second XI and Third XI play in the Lincolnshire League. Fixtures are staged at weekends throughout the season and some midweek matches take place in August. In 1981 the club celebrated the ground's golden jubilee. During the winter the playing area is used by Winteringham Ladies Hockey Club who have two pitches.

The first match of importance played at Chichester Road was in 1968 when Lincolnshire CCC staged a home match with the touring USA team. Since then Lincolnshire CCC have staged home Minor Counties Championship matches here with, among others, Staffordshire, Yorkshire II, Norfolk, Cambridgeshire, Cumberland and Northumberland. On 9 August 1970 a Lincolnshire County League team played the International Cavaliers XI which included Bob Barber, Eddie Barlow, Graeme Pollock, Ted Dexter, Brian Davison, Derek Murray, John Mitchell, Fred Trueman, Neil Hawke and Godfrey Evans. The International Cavaliers won by 116 runs. In 1974 a benefit match was staged for Jack Birkenshaw of Leicestershire CCC who brought a full county side plus one outsider, Bob Taylor, the Derbyshire and England wicketkeeper.

The former Test match umpire Don Oslear hails from the Cleethorpes club and his brother Roy is the Club Secretary and Coach of the Junior Section. Don Oslear played for the club First XI during the 1964 season. Martin Maslim, who represented Lincolnshire CCC and Minor Counties CA against the tourists for some years, still plays for the club. Martin won the man of the match award for scoring 62 n.o. for Lincolnshire CCC when they beat Glamorgan by 4 wickets at Swansea in the Gillette Cup 1st round in 1974.

The original pavilion, now demolished, was situated near the sightscreen at the Chichester Road End with the wicket at 90 degrees and the ground was originally leased from Sydney Sussex College, Cambridge. A new pavilion was constructed in 1963 and an extension with a couple of squash courts was added in 1978.

Nottinghamshire CCC staged first-class matches at Cleethorpes in 1980 against Worcestershire, in 1982 against Northamptonshire and twice against the Sri Lankan touring team in 1984 and 1990. A limited-overs John Player Sunday League match was staged against Middlesex in 1983. Other Nottinghamshire games have included: 30 July 1995 AXA Equity Law League against Yorkshire (Nottinghamshire won by 5 wickets), and 25 July 1999 CGU National League against Sussex (Nottinghamshire won by 46 runs). Matches have also been staged here by the Minor Counties Cricket Association for a Benson and Hedges Cup zonal tie between Minor Counties (North) and Nottinghamshire in 1972. An MCC 'A' fixture was staged with the Zimbabwe touring team in 1985. Nottinghamshire return to play matches at Cleethorpes in 2003.

Chichester Road Ground is to the south of the town centre. The only permanent buildings on the ground are the pavilion and squash club, scoreboard, groundsman's store, several areas of raised timber seating and some benches. The ground is enclosed by houses to the north, east and south of the playing area and by a school and trees to the west. At the Chichester Road End there are usually several marquees for sponsors as well as a press tent and radio commentary position. If required the TV camera/commentary box would be positioned on a gantry directly above and behind the sightscreen at the southern end of the ground. The playing area is circular in shape with dimensions of 128 metres by 118 metres and slopes from the Daggett Road End towards the Chichester Road End. The playing area is defined by a rope and some advertising boards. The ground capacity is 3,500. Seats are available for 80% of that number so spectators are advised to bring their own to popular matches.

GROUND RECORDS AND SCORES

FIRST-CLASS MATCHES

Highest innings total for county 319 v Northamptonshire 1981
Highest innings total against county 308 for 8 by Worcestershire 1980
Lowest innings total for county 251 v Sri Lankans 1990
Lowest innings total against county 85 by Northamptonshire 1981
Highest individual innings for county 115* R.T. Robinson v Sri Lankans 1984
Highest individual innings against county 114 R.S. Mahanama for Sri Lankans 1990
Highest wicket partnerships for county

1st	48 P.A. Todd & R.T. Robinson	v	Worcestershire	1980
2nd	90 R.T. Robinson & D.W. Randall	v	Sri Lankans	1984
3rd	104 R.T. Robinson & S.B. Hassan	v	Northamptonshire	1981
4th	104 P. Johnson & J.D. Birch	v	Sri Lankans	1984
5th	120 M. Newell & K.P. Evans	v	Sri Lankans	1990
6th	113* R.E. Dexter & B.N. French	v	Worcestershire	1980
7th	87 F.D. Stephenson & C.W. Scott	v	Sri Lankans	1990
8th	39 J.D. Birch & E.E. Hemmings	v	Northamptonshire	1981
9th	19 J.D. Birch & K.E. Cooper	v	Northamptonshire	1981
10th	22 J.D. Birch & M.K. Bore	v	Northamptonshire	1981

Highest wicket partnerships against county

1st	210 R.S. Mahanama & U.C. Hathurusingha	for	Sri Lankans	1990
2nd	65 D.M. von Hagt & S.A.R. Silva	for	Sri Lankans	1984
3rd	76 G.M. Turner & P.A. Neale	for	Worcestershire	1980
4th	110 Younis Ahmed & E.J.O. Hemsley	for	Worcestershire	1980
5th	102 Younis Ahmed & D.N. Patel	for	Worcestershire	1980
6th	31* A.P. Gurusinha & M.S. Atapattu	for	Sri Lankans	1990
7th	28 R.L. Dias & R.G. de Alwis	for	Sri Lankans	1984
8th	27 N. Gifford & H.L. Alleyne	for	Worcestershire	1980
9th	24 Sarfraz Nawaz & T.M. Lamb	for	Northamptonshire	1981
10th	19 R.G. de Alwis & M.M. Yusuf	for	Sri Lankans	1984

Best bowling performance in an innings for county 7 for 47 E.E. Hemmings v Sri Lankans 1984
Best bowling performance in an innings against county 4 for 39 N. Gifford for Worcestershire 1980
Best bowling performance in a match for county 8 for 69 R.J. Hadlee v Northamptonshire 1981

Best bowling performance in a match against county 5 for 124 N. Gifford for Worcestershire 1980
Largest crowd 5,000 v Worcestershire 1980

LIMITED-OVERS MATCHES

Highest innings total for county 246 for 4 v Sussex (SL) 1999
Highest innings total against county 200 for 8 by Sussex (SL) 1999
Lowest innings total for county 206 v Minor Counties North (B&H) 1972
Lowest innings total against county 151 by Minor Counties North (B&H) 1972
Highest individual innings for county 108* J.E.R. Gallian v Sussex (SL) 1999
Highest individual innings against county 64* J.R. Carpenter for Sussex (SL) 1999
Highest wicket partnerships for county

1st	103 G.E. Welton & J.E.R. Gallian	v	Sussex	(SL)	1999
2nd	32 J.E.R. Gallian & P. Johnson	v	Sussex	(SL)	1999
3rd	113 P.R. Pollard & C.L. Cairns	v	Yorkshire	(SL)	1995
4th	61 C.E.B. Rice & D.W. Randall	v	Middlesex	(SL)	1983
5th	11 G.St.A. Sobers & J.B. Bolus	v	Minor Counties North	(B&H)	1972
6th	34 G.St.A. Sobers & R.A. White	v	Minor Counties North	(B&H)	1972
7th	69* E.E. Hemmings & K. Saxelby	v	Middlesex	(SL)	1983
8th	9 G.St.A. Sobers & B. Stead	v	Minor Counties North	(B&H)	1972
9th	5 G.St.A. Sobers & D.A. Pullen	v	Minor Counties North	(B&H)	1972
10th	0 G.St.A. Sobers & W. Taylor	v	Minor Counties North	(B&H)	1972

Highest wicket partnerships for county

1st	20 R.G.P. Ellis & C.T. Radley	for	Middlesex	(SL)	1983
2nd	85 M.P. Vaughan & M.G. Bevan	for	Yorkshire	(SL)	1995
3rd	32 C.T. Radley & C.R. Cook	for	Middlesex	(SL)	1983
4th	34 P.A. Cottey & J.R. Carpenter	for	Sussex	(SL	1999
5th	18 M.G. Bevan & R.J. Blakey	for	Yorkshire	(SL)	1995
6th	28 R.J. Blakey & A.P. Grayson	for	Yorkshire	(SL)	1995
7th	49 G.D. Rose & N.F. Williams	for	Middlesex	(SL)	1983
8th	10 N.F. Williams & P.R. Downton	for	Middlesex	(SL)	1983
9th	48* J.R. Carpenter & B.V. Taylor	for	Sussex	(SL)	1999
10th	6 A.P. Grayson & M.A. Robinson	for	Yorkshire	(SL)	1995

Best bowling performance in a match for county 4 for 38 C.M. Tolley v Sussex (SL) 1999
Best bowling performance in a match against county 3 for 31 C.E.W. Silverwood for Yorkshire (SL) 1995
Largest crowd 2,500 v Middlesex (SL) 1983

GROUND INFORMATION

ENTRANCES Chichester Road (players, officials, members, public and vehicles), Daggett Road (members).
MEMBERS' ENCLOSURE Pavilion and Squash Club together with defined members' enclosure which extends from the sightscreen at the Chichester Road End, in front of the pavilion and at least a third of the way towards the scoreboard.
PUBLIC ENCLOSURE Rest of the ground.
COVERED STANDS Pavilion and Squash Club.
OPEN STANDS Temporary ground level seating surrounding the playing area together with several areas of raised timber seating and some benches.
NAME OF ENDS Daggett Road End, Chichester Road End.
GROUND DIMENSIONS 128m × 118m.
REPLAY SCREEN If televised matches are staged at the ground the replay screen is sited at the Chichester Road End of the ground.
FIRST AID In the pavilion.
CODES OF DRESS Spectators are required to dress in an appropriate manner consistent with attending a cricket match. Bare torsos are not acceptable in, or in front of the pavilion. Executive Club/Suite users must wear a necktie and jacket.
BEHAVIOUR The club is keen that standards of behaviour should be maintained and members and spectators are urged to report immediately to the CEO any incident, or potential incident, where they feel action should be taken. Abusive behaviour, entry on to the field of play, the throwing of any article or foul or abusive language will not be tolerated under any circumstances.

RECIPROCAL ARRANGEMENTS Members of Derbyshire, Leicestershire and Northamptonshire can gain free entry to County Championship matches on production of membership card when Nottinghamshire is not playing their own county.

SUPPORTERS' CLUB Details can be obtained from Notts CCSA, 85 Ingram Road, Bulwell, Nottingham NG6 9GP.

JUNIORS Junior Outlaws membership is £10 per annum for under-16s. Contact Membership Department for details.

CORPORATE ENTERTAINING Marquees and tents available, contact Marketing Department for details and a brochure.

FACILITIES FOR VISUALLY IMPAIRED SPECTATORS Reduced admission, although not for helpers. Guide dogs allowed.

FACILITIES AND ACCESS FOR PEOPLE WITH DISABILITIES INCLUDING WHEELCHAIR ACCESS TO GROUND Yes, via Chichester Road or Daggett Road entrance.

DESIGNATED CAR PARK AVAILABLE INSIDE THE GROUND FOR PEOPLE WITH DISABILITIES Yes, by arrangement in advance with Cleethorpes CC to rear of the pavilion. Entry from Chichester Road.

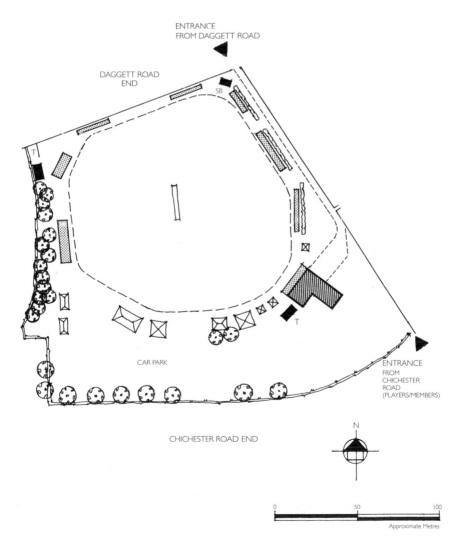

ENTRANCE
FROM DAGGETT ROAD

DAGGETT ROAD
END

SB

T

CAR PARK

T

ENTRANCE
FROM
CHICHESTER
ROAD
(PLAYERS/MEMBERS)

CHICHESTER ROAD END

N

0   50   100

Approximate Metres

GOOD VIEWING AREAS INSIDE THE GROUND FOR PEOPLE USING WHEELCHAIRS Yes, special areas marked out near sightscreen at Daggett Road End of the ground.

RAMPS TO PROVIDE EASY ACCESS TO BARS & REFRESHMENT OUTLETS FOR PEOPLE USING WHEELCHAIRS No.

FOOD & DRINK FULL RESTAURANT/DINING FACILITIES No.

TEMPORARY FOOD/DRINK FACILITIES Members, yes. Public, yes.

FOOD SUITABLE FOR VEGETARIANS Members, yes. Public, yes.

BARS Members 1, Public 1.

VARIETIES OF BEER SOLD Draught Worthington.

CHILDREN'S FACILITIES Crèche, no. Play area, no.

CLUB SHOP Trent Bridge Shop in a tent near the pavilion.

CLUB MUSEUM No, but there is a variety of pictures in the pavilion relating to Cleethorpes CC.

CRICKET COACHING FACILITIES Yes, contact Cleethorpes CC.

CRICKET NETS Yes, contact Cleethorpes CC.

OTHER SPORTING OR RECREATIONAL FACILITIES ON THE GROUND Hockey and squash.

FACILITIES FOR HIRE OR WIDER COMMUNITY USE AT THE GROUND WINTER CRICKET EVENTS None other than hockey or squash or events organised by Cleethorpes CC.

CAR PARKING FACILITIES Car parking is available to the rear of the pavilion and to the south of the playing area for approximately 300 cars. Additional car parking is available at the nearby Sports Centre and in adjoining streets.

OTHER INFORMATION Ground is 5 minutes walk from the seafront at Cleethorpes.

GROUND CAPACITY 3,500.

ANTICIPATED GROUND DEVELOPMENTS None planned.

HOW TO GET THERE

 Cleethorpes station 1.5 miles ☎ 08457 484950.

 From Cleethorpes station Grimsby-Cleethorpes Transport Company hopper bus 8, 8X or 9X for Chichester Road or Daggett Road. The buses pass Chichester Road ground entrance. ☎ 01472 358646

 There are cycle routes from central Cleethorpes to this area of the town.

 From north, south and west: from M180 junction 5 take A180 (east) towards Grimsby and Cleethorpes, continue on this road into Cleethorpes to roundabout junction with A1098, turn right on to A1098 (Isaacs Hill), turn right on to B1374 (St Peter's Avenue), turn right on to Highgate, turn left on to Thrunscoe Road, then cross on to Hardys Road, turn left on to Chichester Road for cricket ground.

 Humberside Airport ☎ 01652 688456

WHERE TO STAY

Hotel 77, 77 Kingsway (☎ 01472 692035), Wellow Hotel, Kings Road (01472 695589), The Grimsby Crest Hotel (☎ 01472 359771)

For other places to stay in the Cleethorpes and Grimsby area visit www.smoothhound.co.uk.

WHERE TO EAT

Rafters (☎ 01652 660669) or restaurants and fish and chip bars on Cleethorpes seafront

TOURIST INFORMATION Cleethorpes Tourist Information Centre ☎ 01472 342422, www.cleethorpes.gov.uk

LOCAL RADIO STATIONS BBC Radio Humberside (95.9 MHz FM/1485 KHz MW), Viking Radio (96.9 MHz FM/1161 KHz MW).

LOCAL NEWSPAPERS *Grimsby Evening Telegraph, Grimsby Gazette, Grimsby Target*

Somerset
COUNTY CRICKET CLUB

Somerset

**Taunton
Bath**

SOMERSET COUNTY CRICKET CLUB, THE COUNTY GROUND, ST JAMES'S STREET, TAUNTON, SOMERSET TA1 1JT

Telephone Main Office	01823 272946 **fax** 01823 332395
Marketing Department	01823 337598
Catering Department	01823 425305
Cricket Shop	01823 337597
Centre of Cricketing Excellence	01823 352266
Museum	01823 275893
Academy Gym	01823 350536
Email	somerset@ecb.co.uk
Website	www.somerset.cricinfo.com

Founded 18 August 1875
Colours black, silver and maroon
National Cricket League Nickname Sabres
National Cricket League Colours maroon, black and silver
Patron P.C. Ondaatje CBE, OC
Chairman G. Clarke
Vice Chairman R.D. Appleyard
Cricket Chairman V.J. Marks
Chief Executive Officer P.W. Anderson
Hon Treasurer R.A. O'Donnell
Head Coach K.J. Shine
2nd XI Coach M. Garaway
Captain M. Burns
Vice Captain M.E. Trescothick
Physiotherapist D. Veness
Head Groundsman P. Frost
Scorer 1st XI G.A. Stickley
Scorer 2nd XI H.V. Thorne
Cricket & Fixturing Secretary P.J. Robinson
Regional Academy Director M. Garaway
Youth Development & Academy Officer P. Sanderson
Executive Assistant S. Donoghue
Accounts Manager J. Fitzgerald
Accounts Assistant L. Southby

Marketing Manager G. Tesser
Marketing Assistant K. Rogers
Membership Secretary J. Arnold
Receptionist L. Faulkner
Catering Manager C. Bristow
Bars Manager M. Smith
Cricket Development Officer A.P. Moulding
Indoor Cricket School Manager G. Wolfenden
Hon Medical Officer Dr. P.L.B. Squire MB, BS
Fitness Trainer A. Hurry
Somerset Shop Manager (franchise to Boundary Sports) S. Abbhas
Somerset Cricket Museum Curator T. Steddal
Historian M.F. Hill
Statistician N. Johns
Shirt Sponsors Rowan Dartington & Company and Photo-scan Plc
Kit Sponsors Boundary Sports
Yearbook £7.50
Scorecard 50p
National Cricket League Match Official Programme & Scorecard £2
Newsletter *From the Pavilion* (issued free to members)
Frizzell County Championship Status Division 2
National Cricket League Status Division 2

ACHIEVEMENTS

County Championship 2nd Division 1 2001
Gillette Cup Winners 1979, Finalists 1967, 1978
NatWest Trophy Winners 1983, Finalists 2000
Cheltenham & Gloucester Trophy Winners 2001, Finalists 2002

Benson and Hedges Cup Winners 1981, 1982
John Player Sunday League Champions 1979
Tilcon Trophy Finalists 1976
Seeboard Trophy Semi-finalists 1991

COUNTY CRICKET BOARD

Chairman C.G. Clarke
Vice Chairman T. Davies
Secretary P.W. Anderson
Treasurer J. Davey
Youth Administrator P. Colbourne
Womens & Girls Secretary J. Goodman

Address Somerset Cricket Board, The County Ground, St James's Street, Taunton, Somerset
TA1 1JT
☎ 01823 272946
Fax 01823 332395

GROUNDS

Taunton (The County Ground, St James's Street) and Bath (Recreation Ground, William Street)
 Other grounds used since 1969: Bristol (Imperial Ground, West Town Lanes), Yeovil (Westland Sports Ground, Westbourne Close), Yeovil (Johnson Park, Boundary Close), Glastonbury (Morlands Athletic Sports Ground, Street Road), Torquay (Recreation Ground), Brislington (Ironmold Lane), Frome (Agricultural Showgrounds), Weston-super-Mare (Clarence Park, Walliscote Road), Weston-super-Mare (Devonshire Road Park Ground) and Street (Millfield School)

SECOND XI GROUNDS

In addition to the above, the following are used for Second XI matches:
Bristol Optimists CC, Imperial Ground, West Town Lanes, Bristol ☎ 01272 776659
Clevedon CC, Esmond Grove, Clevedon ☎ 01272 877585
Glastonbury CC, Tor Leisure Centre, 7 Street Road, Glastonbury ☎ 01458 273116
Millfield School, The Pavilion, Butleigh Road, Street, Somerset BA16 0ZY ☎ 01458 442291
North Perrott CC, Cricket Ground, North Perrott, nr Crewkerne ☎ 01460 77953
Winscombe CC, Recreation Ground, Winscombe ☎ 01934 842720

Colin Atkinson Pavilion, members' enclosure and main scoreboard at the County Ground, Taunton, seen from the top of the Ian Botham Stand.

TAUNTON

Address The County Ground, St James's Street, Taunton, Somerset TA1 1JT

Prospects of Play ☎ 01823 272946

HISTORY OF GROUND AND FACILITIES

THE COUNTY GROUND has been the headquarters of Somerset cricket since 1882, although admission to the County Championship was not granted until 1891.

Somerset County Cricket Club acquired the ground from the Taunton Athletic Company and secured a lease in 1885. The first first-class match was staged on the ground in 1882 when Somerset hosted Hampshire. The first championship match was against Lancashire in 1891. The club has worked to improve facilities at the ground by the River Tone ever since 1891 when a running track was built around the perimeter of the cricket pitch. The track was later used for greyhound racing.

The Old Pavilion was erected in 1891, together with the Ridley Stand which is situated under the shadow of St James's Church. The River Stand was built with funds generated from the Somerset Supporters' Club in 1955.

The past two decades have produced major advances for the club as a result of their achievements in limited-overs competitions. Developments include a new pavilion, executive boxes above the Vice Presidents' Stand with a gymnasium beneath and a new scoreboard, which was presented by Saab UK in 1981. In 1990 the new pavilion was named the Colin Atkinson Pavilion.

Since 1989 the club has refurbished a number of small barns on the Priory Bridge Road side of the ground for use as stores, offices and refreshment

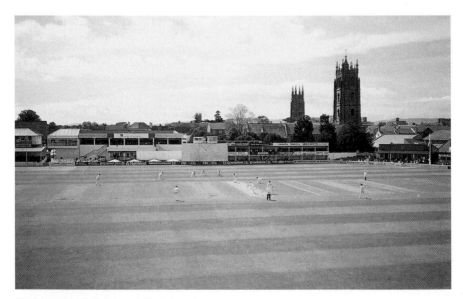

The County Ground with St James's Church beyond.

Ondaatje Pavilion and executive boxes viewed from the Ridley Stand.

facilities. The Somerset Cricket Museum is in Priory Barn and there is a splendid library and collection of cricket memorabilia.

The Ondaatje Cricket Pavilion with executive boxes, toilets and a new shop beneath was constructed on the site of the former cricket shop in 1995. In 1996 the Somerset Cricket School of Excellence was completed and this is located at the rear of the Ondaatje Pavilion. The facility has now been recognised by the England and Wales Cricket Board and awarded Regional Academy status, one of only seven in the country. The Ian Botham Stand and Suite at the River End of the ground were built in 1998 and house media and commentary boxes, executive boxes, additional seating for members and refreshment facilities.

The fencing at the entrance to the St James's Street End of the ground, new turnstiles and the J.C. White Memorial Gates were constructed during the 2001/2 close season. The Priory Bridge Road entrance also has new gates and turnstiles named the Sir Vivian Richards Gates. A new Riverside entrance was constructed in time for the 2002 season.

The County Cricket Ground will certainly be remembered as the stage where in 1925 Sir Jack Hobbs scored his 126th and 127th centuries to surpass W.G. Grace's record. Grace completed his century of centuries on this ground too, in 1895, and went on to score 288 for the visitors, Gloucestershire. Two more recent innings will be remembered by cricket followers at Taunton. Vivian Richards scored 322 against Warwickshire in 1985 in double quick time and Graeme Hick, the Worcestershire and England batsman, made a mammoth 405* in 1988 and so nearly reached the record 424 scored by A.C. MacLaren of Lancashire way back in 1895.

Somerset play the majority of their matches at Taunton, though there is a cricket week at Bath and an early season match was played at Millfield School in 2002 against Cardiff/Wales UCCE. The ground was used for one-day

Curator Tony Steddal with part of the collection at the Somerset Cricket Museum.

international limited-overs cricket in 1983 for the Prudential Cup match between England and Sri Lanka. Taunton hosted two matches during the 1999 World Cup: Kenya v Zimbabwe and India v Sri Lanka. Somerset also hosted two World Cup warm-up matches; Kenya and Australia were the visitors. There have also been several single-wicket competitions at Taunton. In 2002 the club had the honour of staging an England v India Women's Test match and two England Under-19 one-day internationals v India.

The ground has hosted several televised day/night matches when temporary lighting pylons are erected for one night only around the perimeter of the ground.

The playing area is approximately 127 metres by 140 metres and is an uneven oval shape. The shorter dimension is in the direction of the wicket so that a straight hit over the bowler's head will frequently fall in the River Tone barely 90 metres from the batsman.

It is often said by local followers of the great game that if you can see the Quantock Hills, it is going to rain and if you can't see them, it is already raining. However, the Colin Atkinson Pavilion has its back to the hills and members can no longer see them at all!

GROUND RECORDS AND SCORES

FIRST-CLASS MATCHES

Highest innings total for county 650 v Northamptonshire 2001
Highest innings total against county 801 by Lancashire 1895
Lowest innings total for county 48 v Yorkshire 1954
Lowest innings total against county 37 by Gloucestershire 1907
Highest individual innings for county 322 I.V.A. Richards v Warwickshire 1985

Highest individual innings against county 424 A.C. MacLaren for Lancashire 1895
Highest wicket partnerships for county

1st	346 L.C.H. Palairet & H.T. Hewett	v	Yorkshire	1892
2nd	262 R.T. Virgin & M.J. Kitchen	v	Pakistanis	1967
3rd	319 P.M. Roebuck & M.D. Crowe	v	Leicestershire	1984
4th	310 P.W. Denning & I.T. Botham	v	Gloucestershire	1980
5th	240 J.C. White & CCC Case	v	Gloucestershire	1927
6th	213 N.D. Burns & G.D. Rose	v	Gloucestershire	1990
7th	279 R.J. Harden & G.D. Rose	v	Sussex	1997
8th	172 A.R.K. Pierson & P.S. Jones	v	New Zealanders	1999
9th	179* N.F.M. Popplewell & D. Breakwell	v	Kent	1980
10th	112 J.W. Lee & W.T. Lukes	v	Kent	1934

Highest wicket partnerships against county

1st	265 B. Wood & D. Lloyd	for	Lancashire	1974
2nd	363 A.C. MacLaren & A.G. Paul	for	Lancashire	1895
3rd	316* W. Watson & A. Wharton	for	Leicestershire	1961
4th	237 L.E.G. Ames & A.P.F. Chapman	for	Kent	1928
5th	230 J. Seymour & J.R. Mason	for	Kent	1907
6th	411 R.M. Poore & E.G. Wynyard	for	Hampshire	1899
7th	248 A.P. Day & E. Humphreys	for	Kent	1908
8th	291 R.S.C. Martin-Jenkins & M.J.G. Davis	for	Sussex	2002
9th	170 J.C. Adams & K.P. Evans	for	Nottinghamshire	1994
10th	157 C.A.G. Russell & A.B. Hipkin	for	Essex	1926

Best bowling performance in an innings for county 10 for 49 E.J. Tyler v Surrey 1895
Best bowling performance in an innings against county 10 for 42 A.E. Trott for Middlesex 1900
Best bowling performance in a match for county 15 for 95 E.J. Tyler v Surrey 1895
Best bowling performance in a match against county 15 for 131 A.W. Mold for Lancashire 1891
Largest crowd 10,000 v Australians 1948

LIMITED-OVERS MATCHES

Highest innings total for county 367 for 5 v Herefordshire (NWT) 1997
Highest innings total against county 339 by Kent (C&G) 2002
Lowest innings total for county 63 v Yorkshire (GC) 1965
Lowest innings total against county 60 by Kent (SL) 1979
Highest individual innings for county 139* I.V.A. Richards v Warwickshire (GC) 1978
Highest individual innings against county 154* M.J. Proctor for Gloucestershire (B&H) 1972
Highest wicket partnerships for county

1st	176 S.J. Cook & P.M. Roebuck	v	Glamorgan	(SL)	1989
2nd	183 P.D. Bowler & S.C. Ecclestone	v	Surrey	(SL)	1996
3rd	195 P.M. Roebuck & C.J. Tavare	v	Essex	(NWT)	1989
4th	156 M.N. Lathwell & S. Lee	v	Warwickshire	(SL)	1996
5th	179 I.V.A. Richards & I.T. Botham	v	Hampshire	(SL)	1981
6th	106 G.D. Rose & S.C. Ecclestone	v	Kent	(SL)	1995
7th	122* G.D. Rose & A. Payne	v	Kent	(SL)	1993
8th	63* R.J. Turner & K.A. Parsons	v	British Universities	(B&H)	1996
9th	66* S.R. Waugh & A.N. Jones	v	Northamptonshire	(SL)	1988
10th	38 V.J. Marks & M.R. Davis	v	Sussex	(B&H)	1984

Highest wicket partnerships against county

1st	232 K.J. Barnett & J.E. Morris	for	Derbyshire	(SL)	1990
2nd	210 P.D. Bowler & J.E. Morris	for	Derbyshire	(B&H)	1990
3rd	179* N.H. Fairbrother & G.D. Lloyd	for	Lancashire	(SL)	1995
4th	170 M.J. Wood & D.S. Lehmann	for	Yorkshire	(SL)	2002
5th	138 M.E. Cassar & I.D. Blackwell	for	Derbyshire	(SL)	1999
6th	105 P. Bainbridge & J.N. Shepherd	for	Gloucestershire	(B&H)	1982
7th	80* D.R. Thomas & A.R. Fothergill	for	Minor Counties	(B&H)	1990
	80* R.B. Richardson & P.J. Hartley	for	Yorkshire	(SL)	1993

8th	75 T.C. Middleton & A.N. Aymes	for	Hampshire	(SL)	1994
9th	66 M.V. Fleming & D.D. Masters	for	Kent	(SL)	2000
10th	44* J.N. Graham-Brown & D.L. Underwood	for	Kent	(SL)	1975

Best bowling performance in a match for county 7 for 24 Mushtaq Ahmed v Ireland (B&H) 1997
Best bowling performance in a match against county 6 for 15 F.S. Trueman for Yorkshire (GC) 1965
Largest crowd 8,500 v Kent (GC) 1979, v Lancashire (NWBT) 1989

ONE-DAY INTERNATIONALS

Highest innings total for England in ODI 333 for 9 v Sri Lanka (WC) 1983
Highest innings total against England in ODI 286 by Sri Lanka (WC) 1983
Highest innings total in non-England ODI 373 for 6 for India v Sri Lanka (WC) 1999
Lowest innings total for England in ODI 333 for 9 v Sri Lanka (WC) 1983
Lowest innings total against England in ODI 286 by Sri Lanka (WC) 1983
Lowest innings total in non-England ODI 216 by Sri Lanka v India (WC) 1999
Highest individual innings for England in ODI 130 D.I. Gower v Sri Lanka (WC) 1983
Highest individual innings against England in ODI 58* R.G. de Alwis for Sri Lanka (WC) 1983
Highest individual innings in non-England ODI 183 S.C. Ganguly for India v Sri Lanka (WC) 1999
Highest wicket partnerships for England in ODI

1st	49 G. Fowler & C.J. Tavare	v	Sri Lanka	(WC)	1983
2nd	29 D.I. Gower & C.J. Tavare	v	Sri Lanka	(WC)	1983
3rd	96 D.I. Gower & A.J. Lamb	v	Sri Lanka	(WC)	1983
4th	19 M.W. Gatting & D.I. Gower	v	Sri Lanka	(WC)	1983
5th	1 I.T. Botham & D.I. Gower	v	Sri Lanka	(WC)	1983
6th	98 I.J. Gould & D.I. Gower	v	Sri Lanka	(WC)	1983
7th	6 G.R. Dilley & D.I. Gower	v	Sri Lanka	(WC)	1983
8th	35 G.R. Dilley & V.J. Marks	v	Sri Lanka	(WC)	1983
9th	0 P.J.W. Allott & V.J. Marks	v	Sri Lanka	(WC)	1983
10th	yet to be established.				

Highest wicket partnerships against England in ODI

1st	11 D.S.B.P. Kuruppu & S. Wettimuny	for	Sri Lanka	(WC)	1983
2nd	6 R.L. Dias & S. Wettimuny	for	Sri Lanka	(WC)	1983
3rd	75 L.R.D. Mendis & S. Wettimuny	for	Sri Lanka	(WC)	1983
4th	16 R.S. Madugalle & L.R.D. Mendis	for	Sri Lanka	(WC)	1983
5th	9 L.R.D. Mendis & A. Ranatunga	for	Sri Lanka	(WC)	1983
6th	51 D.S. de Silva & A. Ranatunga	for	Sri Lanka	(WC)	1983
7th	24 R.G. de Alwis & D.S. de Silva	for	Sri Lanka	(WC)	1983
8th	54 R.G. de Alwis & A.L.F. de Mel	for	Sri Lanka	(WC)	1983
9th	35 R.G. de Alwis & R.J. Ratnayake	for	Sri Lanka	(WC)	1983
10th	5 R.G. de Alwis & V.B. John	for	Sri Lanka	(WC)	1983

Highest wicket partnerships in non-England ODI

1st	81 G.W. Flower & N.C. Johnson	for	Zimbabwe v Kenya	(WC)	1999
2nd	318 R.S. Dravid & S.C. Ganguly	for	India v Sri Lanka	(WC)	1999
3rd	51 M.S. Atapattu & P.A. de Silva	for	Sri Lanka v India	(WC)	1999
4th	24 A. Flower & M.W. Goodwin	for	Zimbabwe v Kenya	(WC)	1999
5th	84 M.O. Odumbe & A.V. Vadher	for	Kenya v Zimbabwe	(WC)	1999
6th	34 P.A. de Silva & A. Ranatunga	for	Sri Lanka v India	(WC)	1999
7th	38 Asif Karim & T.M. Odoyo	for	Kenya v Zimbabwe	(WC)	1999
8th	16 R.S. Mahanama & K.E.A. Upashantha	for	Sri Lanka v India	(B&H)	1999
9th	1 R.S. Mahanama & G.P. Wickremasinghe	for	Sri Lanka v India	(WC)	1999
10th	12 M. Muralitharan & G.P. Wickremasinghe	for	Sri Lanka v Zimbabwe	(WC)	1999

Best bowling performance for England in ODI 5 for 39 V.J. Marks v Sri Lanka (WC) 1983
Best bowling performance against England in ODI 2 for 62 A.L.F. de Mel for Sri Lanka (WC) 1983
Best bowling performance in non-England ODI 5 for 31 R.R. Singh for India v Sri Lanka (WC) 1999
Largest crowd 6,778 India v Sri Lanka (WC) 1999

GROUND INFORMATION

ENTRANCES Priory Bridge Road (players and officials, members and public – pedestrians only), Riverside Entrance (members and public), St James's Street (members, public and vehicles).

MEMBERS' ENCLOSURE Colin Atkinson Pavilion, Ian Botham Stand, Old Pavilion, Ridley Stand and defined area between the New Pavilion and the Old Pavilion. Over half the ground is for members only.

PUBLIC ENCLOSURE River Stand and West Side enclosure of the ground.

COVERED STANDS Ian Botham Stand (part), Old Pavilion (Upper), Ridley Stand, Stragglers Pavilion (part), Executive Business Club (part) and River Stand.

OPEN STANDS Colin Atkinson Pavilion (part), East Side Enclosure, Old Pavilion (lower), Stragglers Pavilion (part), Executive Business Club (part) and West Side Enclosure.

NAME OF ENDS River End, Old Pavilion End.

GROUND DIMENSIONS 127m × 140m.

REPLAY SCREEN If televised matches are staged at the ground the replay screen is sited between the Vice Presidents' Stand and the Cricket Shop at the Old Pavilion End of the ground.

FIRST AID Situated to the rear of the Ondaatje Pavilion and Boxes near the Priory Barn Cricket Museum.

CODES OF DRESS Spectators are required to dress in an appropriate manner consistent with attending a cricket match. Bare torsos are not acceptable in, or in front of the pavilion. Executive Club/Suite users must wear a necktie and jacket. Swimwear is not permitted to be worn and footwear should be worn.

BEHAVIOUR The club is keen that standards of behaviour should be maintained and members and spectators are urged to report immediately to any steward any incident, or potential incident, where they feel action should be taken. Bad language is not acceptable at any match and the club will take prompt and strong action should this or any other ground regulation be ignored. Obstructing passageways, singing indecent songs, using indecent language, making unnecessary noise by means including persistent chanting, use of radios without an ear-piece, use of mobile telephones, possession of and/or waving of banners are not permitted.

RECIPROCAL ARRANGEMENTS Members of Glamorgan and Gloucestershire can gain entry free for County Championship matches on production of membership card when Somerset is not playing their own county.

SUPPORTERS' CLUB Somerset Wyverns membership £10 per annum. Special rates for concessions and husband and wife membership are available.

JUNIORS Junior Sabres Club for those under 21 is £25. Contact Membership Office ☎ 01823 272946 for further information.

CORPORATE ENTERTAINING Executive and Corporate membership is available for a season or can be arranged on a match basis. Facilities are available for between 25 and 100 guests in various sized hospitality boxes in the Ian Botham Stand, Ondaatje Pavilion and Deane Suite on the top of the Vice Presidents' Stand at the St James's Street End of the ground. Contact the Marketing Department for further information and a brochure, ☎ 01823 337598.

FACILITIES FOR VISUALLY IMPAIRED SPECTATORS No reduced admission. Guide dogs are allowed.

FACILITIES AND ACCESS FOR PEOPLE WITH DISABILITIES INCLUDING WHEELCHAIR ACCESS TO GROUND Yes, through entrance in St James's Street via J.C. White Gates.

DESIGNATED CAR PARK AVAILABLE INSIDE THE GROUND FOR PEOPLE WITH DISABILITIES Yes, in Car Park B at Old Pavilion End of the ground.

GOOD VIEWING AREAS INSIDE THE GROUND FOR PEOPLE USING WHEELCHAIRS Yes, particularly on areas of hard standing around the perimeter of the playing area. Please request position in advance.

DESIGNATED VIEWING AREAS FOR PEOPLE USING WHEELCHAIRS Yes, special enclosure in front of the Old Pavilion. Other locations are available around the ground, which are suitable for wheelchair viewing by prior arrangement with the club stewards. There are disabled toilets situated to the rear of the Old Pavilion and there are also additional facilities available in the Cricket School of Excellence, Colin Atkinson Pavilion and Ian Botham Stand.

RAMPS TO PROVIDE EASY ACCESS TO BARS & REFRESHMENT OUTLETS FOR PEOPLE USING WHEELCHAIRS Yes.

FOOD & DRINK FULL RESTAURANT/DINING FACILITIES Members, yes. Public, yes. Full restaurant service is available in the Colin Atkinson Pavilion for members only. Booking is recommended in advance for lunch, contact Catering Department in advance ☎ 01823 425305.

TEMPORARY FOOD/DRINK FACILITIES Members, yes. Public, yes. There are ample facilities for food within the ground for those attending including the Colin Atkinson Pavilion, a food outlet 'Hungry End Refreshments' beneath main scoreboard, Old Pavilion and fish and chip bar beneath Riverside Stand.

FOOD SUITABLE FOR VEGETARIANS Members, yes. Public, yes.

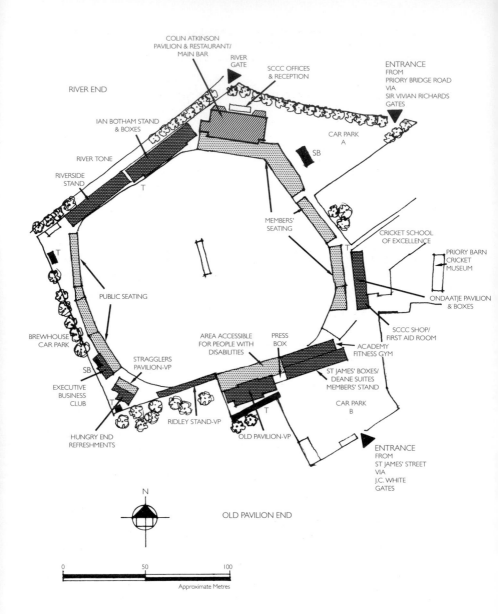

COLIN ATKINSON
PAVILION & RESTAURANT/
MAIN BAR

RIVER
GATE

SCCC OFFICES
& RECEPTION

ENTRANCE
FROM
PRIORY BRIDGE ROAD
VIA
SIR VIVIAN RICHARDS
GATES

RIVER END

IAN BOTHAM STAND
& BOXES

CAR PARK
A

SB

RIVER TONE

RIVERSIDE
STAND

T

MEMBERS'
SEATING

CRICKET SCHOOL
OF EXCELLENCE

PRIORY BARN
CRICKET
MUSEUM

T

ONDAATJE PAVILION
& BOXES

PUBLIC SEATING

BREWHOUSE
CAR PARK

SCCC SHOP/
FIRST AID ROOM

AREA ACCESSIBLE
FOR PEOPLE WITH
DISABILITIES

PRESS
BOX

ACADEMY
FITNESS GYM

SB

STRAGGLERS
PAVILION-VP

ST JAMES' BOXES/
DEANE SUITES
MEMBERS' STAND

EXECUTIVE
BUSINESS
CLUB

T

CAR PARK
B

RIDLEY STAND-VP

HUNGRY END
REFRESHMENTS

OLD PAVILION-VP

ENTRANCE
FROM
ST JAMES' STREET
VIA
J.C. WHITE
GATES

N

OLD PAVILION END

0   50   100

Approximate Metres

BARS Members 2, Public 1.
VARIETIES OF BEER SOLD Exmoor Ales (including Exmoor Ale, Fox, Gold, Hart, Stag, Beast and Seasonal),
Fosters, John Smiths' Extra Smooth, Kronenbourg 1664, Courage.
CHILDREN'S FACILITIES Crèche, no. Play area, no.
CLUB SHOP Boundary Sports/Somerset Cricket Shop is situated beneath the Ondaatje Pavilion and Boxes and
is a franchise facility which stocks Somerset CCC items together with cricket equipment, clothing, books,
sweets and newspapers. Open Monday to Friday 10.00 a.m. to 4.30 p.m. and Saturday 10.00 a.m. to 1.00
p.m. throughout the year.
CLUB MUSEUM In Priory Barn which dates back to the late fifteenth century. It is open Monday to Friday 10.00
a.m. to 4.00 p.m. April to November and is only open to cricket spectators who have paid the ground

admission charge on match days. There is a small admission charge. Inside there is a good library as well as cricket memorabilia including Harold Gimblett's blazer, a collection of china plates, an old scorecard printing press, pictures and ties. Membership is £5 per annum and entitles members to borrow books and videos from the library.

CRICKET COACHING FACILITIES Yes, in Cricket School of Excellence during winter months.

CRICKET NETS Yes, indoor nets in Cricket School of Excellence during winter months.

FACILITIES FOR HIRE OR WIDER COMMUNITY USE AT THE GROUND Rooms are available for seminars, trade shows, exhibitions, company lunches, dinner dances, private parties, training sessions and weddings throughout the year. Contact Catering Department ☎ 01823 425305.

WINTER CRICKET EVENTS Members' club dinners and lunches are staged in the pavilion which is also used by the Somerset Wyverns for an annual dinner.

CAR PARKING FACILITIES The St James's Street Car Park B may be used on match days, subject to space being available, by Vice Presidents, box holders and sponsors. Car parking will be on a first come first served basis. Vice Presidents must show their membership swipe cards and must be attending the match on the day in question. Parking is likely to be very limited on limited-overs match days. A charge is made for day parking. The Priory Bridge Road Car Park A is only available for officials, players and car park permit holders. All cars parked within the ground are at the owners' risk. Other car parking nearby is available in 'pay & displays' at Market, Brewhouse, Canon Street, Priory Bridge Road, Duke Street and Greenbrook Terrace.

OTHER INFORMATION Millichamp & Hall's cricket bat manufacturing base is on the ground behind Priory Barn. Here in Willow Yard cricket bats are crafted for Test, County and Club cricketers. For further information or a brochure ☎/Fax 01823 327755.

GROUND CAPACITY 8,000.

ANTICIPATED DEVELOPMENTS None presently planned.

HOW TO GET THERE

 Taunton station 0.5 mile ☎ 08457 484950, 08457 000125, 08457 222333, www.greatwesterntrains.co.uk, www.virgin.com/trains, www.railtrack.co.uk. West Somerset Steam Railway from Bishops Lydeard to Taunton ☎ 01643 704996

 The ground is 500m from the bus station. Also, a shuttle from town centre takes 5 minutes. Southern National Buses Information Line ☎ 01823 272033, Atmos Limited Buses ☎ 01823 358299, Berry's Coaches ☎ 01823 331356 www.berryscoaches.co.uk, National Express Coaches ☎ 08705 808080, www.nationalexpresscoaches.co.uk, www.gobycoach.com

 There are cycle routes from all parts of Taunton to this area of the town.

 From north: from M5 junction 25 exit roundabout on to A358, continue (west) to junction with A38 (Toneway) and follow signs round Taunton to cricket ground. **From south (A358):** from A358, Ruishton, stay on A358 (west) to junction with A38, continue (west) on A38, then as for north. **From south (M5):** leave M5 at junction 25 and proceed as for north. **From east:** from M5 junction 25 proceed as for north. **From west:** from Minehead (A358) continue on this road to Taunton and follow signs to cricket ground.

 Bristol International Airport ☎ 0870 1212 747, www.bristolairport.co.uk, Bournemouth International Airport ☎ 01202 364000 www.bournemouthairport.co.uk, Exeter Airport ☎ 01392 367433 www.exeterairport.co.uk

WHERE TO STAY

Best Western Shrubbery Hotel (☎ 01460 52108 www.shrubberyhotel.com), Blorenge House (☎ 01823 283005 www.blorengehouse.co.uk), Brookfield House (☎ 01823 272786 www.brookfieldguesthouse.uk.com), Corner House Hotel (☎ 01823 284683 www.corner-house.co.uk), Express by Holiday Inn (☎ 01823 624000 www.hiexpress.com/taunton), Heathfield Lodge (☎ 01823 432286), Holiday Inn (☎ 0870 400 9080), North Down Farm (☎ 01984 623730), Orchard House (☎ 01823 351783), Pyrland Farm (☎ 01823 334148) Rose & Crown (☎ 01823 698235 www.derek.mason.btinternet.co.uk), Rumwell Manor Hotel (☎ 01823 461902 www.runwellmanor.co.uk), Salisbury House Hotel (☎ 01823 272083 www.salisburyhousehotel.com),

The Castle Hotel (☎ 01823 272671 www.the-castle-hotel.com), The Falcon Hotel (☎ 01823 442502) For further places to stay in and around Taunton visit www.smoothhound.co.uk.

WHERE TO EAT

Brazz (☎ 01823 252000), Bindon Restaurant (☎ 01823 400070), Dynasty Indian Cuisine (☎ 01823 334361), The Castle Hotel (☎ 01823 272671 www.the-castle-hotel.com)

TOURIST INFORMATION Taunton Tourist Information Centre, Paul Street, Taunton, Somerset TA1 3XZ ☎ 01823 336344, www.heartofsomerset.com, www.somerset.gov.uk/tourism

OTHER USEFUL INFORMATION

Taunton Town FC ☎ 01823 278191
Taunton Rugby Football Club ☎ 01823 336363
Taunton Racecourse ☎ 01823 325035

LOCAL RADIO STATIONS BBC Radio Somerset Sound (1323 KHz MW), Orchard FM (102.6 MHz FM)

LOCAL NEWSPAPERS *Evening Post, Western Daily Press, Somerset County Gazette, West Somerset Free Press, Western Daily Press*

BATH

Address The Pavilion, The Recreation Ground, William Street,
off Great Pulteney Street, Bath
Prospects of Play 01823 272946

HISTORY OF GROUND AND FACILITIES

THE RECREATION GROUND is situated almost in the middle of the city close to the River Avon and Bath Abbey. For one week a year, usually in June, Somerset travel up from Taunton to play one County Championship and one limited-overs National Cricket League match at the ground, which is better known as the home of Bath Rugby Club. The Bath Sports & Leisure Centre, at the North Parade Road End of the ground, once caused the players to be called from the field on a sunny day because the batsmen were dazzled by the sun reflecting off the glass roof.

The first match staged at the Recreation Ground by Somerset was with Sussex in 1880; the initial first-class match was against Hampshire in 1884. In 1897 a match was staged with the touring Philadelphians and in 1898 there was a county match with Yorkshire.

The only permanent buildings are the small players' pavilion close to the main entrance in William Street and a block of toilets in the north-west corner of the ground. The rugby stands are some 70 metres from the cricket playing area and provide little benefit other than as a shelter in bad weather.

The playing area is approximately 133 metres by 131 metres and has a near circular boundary defined by advertising boards. The ground is now somewhat overshadowed by the Bath Sports & Leisure Centre to the south.

The Pavilion at the Recreation Ground, Bath.

In 1977 when Somerset hosted the Australian touring team at Bath, two silver birch trees were planted to the west of the pavilion by the two captains Brian Close and Greg Chappell. The latter played for Somerset in the early 1970s.

This is a local authority ground and the small cricket square is wedged between the hockey and rugby pitches, a part of each serving as the cricket outfield in summer. The ground is administered by Bath Council Leisure Services Department and has its own Facilities Manager responsible for its upkeep throughout the year.

The ground should not be confused with Bath Cricket Club on the other side of North Parade Road, or Lansdown Cricket Club, who have used the ground in the past.

The Bath Cricket Festival always attracts good crowds, usually around 5,000 each day, and attendances are boosted for limited-overs matches.

GROUND RECORDS AND SCORES

FIRST-CLASS MATCHES

Highest innings total for county 675 for 9 dec v Hampshire 1924
Highest innings total against county 609 for 4 dec by Australians 1905
Lowest innings total for county 35 Yorkshire 1898
Lowest innings total against county 37 by Derbyshire 1919

Highest individual innings for county 221 M. Burns v Yorkshire 2001
Highest individual innings against county 303* W.W. Armstrong for Australians 1905
Highest wicket partnerships for county

1st	225 L.C.H. Palairet & L.C. Braund	v	Lancashire	1901
2nd	245 A. Young & M.D. Lyon	v	Hampshire	1924
3rd	300 G. Atkinson & P.B. Wight	v	Glamorgan	1960
4th	216 M.N. Lathwell & A.N. Hayhurst	v	Surrey	1994
5th	194 P.M. Roebuck & B.C. Rose	v	Sussex	1978
6th	201* R.J. Harden & V.J. Marks	v	Kent	1989
7th	278* S. Lee & R.J. Turner	v	Worcestershire	1996
8th	163 M.D. Crowe & J.W. Lloyds	v	Lancashire	1984
9th	110 H.W. Stephenson & K.E. Palmer	v	Nottinghamshire	1962
10th	84 J.G. Lomax & B. Lobb	v	Yorkshire	1958

Highest wicket partnerships against county

1st	208 R. Relf & J. Vine	for	Sussex	1910
2nd	242* W. Rhodes & G.H. Hirst	for	Yorkshire	1906
3rd	320 W.W. Armstrong & M.A. Noble	for	Australians	1905
4th	216 S.J. O'Shaughnessy & D.P. Hughes	for	Lancashire	1984
5th	173 G.L. Jessop & C.S. Barnett	for	Gloucestershire	1908
6th	185 J.W.H. Makepeace & K.G. Macleod	for	Lancashire	1909
7th	143 H.S. Harrison & J.W. Hitch	for	Surrey	1922
8th	108 J.E. Walsh & J. Firth	for	Leicestershire	1952
9th	167 H. Verity & T.F. Smailes	for	Yorkshire	1936
10th	76 S.G. Smith & W.A. Buswell	for	Northamptonshire	1912

Best bowling performance in an innings for county 9 for 51 J.C. White v Glamorgan 1932
Best bowling performance in an innings against county 9 for 77 H. Dean for Lancashire 1910
Best bowling performance in a match for county 16 for 83 J.C. White v Worcestershire 1919
Best bowling performance in a match against county 16 for 80 D.V.P. Wright for Kent 1939
Largest crowd 6,500 v Australians 1905

LIMITED-OVERS MATCHES

Highest innings total for county 262 for 5 v Lancashire (SL) 1978
Highest innings total against county 244 for 6 by Yorkshire (SL) 2001
Lowest innings total for county 61 v Hampshire (SL) 1973
Lowest innings total against county 72 by Nottinghamshire (SL) 1982
Highest individual innings for county 131 D.B. Close v Yorkshire (SL) 1974
Highest individual innings against county 130* J.A. Hopkins for Glamorgan (SL) 1983
Highest wicket partnerships for county

1st	109 B.C. Rose & P.W. Denning	v	Essex	(SL)	1979
2nd	127 P.D. Bowler & P.C.L. Holloway	v	Nottinghamshire	(SL)	1999
3rd	127 P.M. Roebuck & I.T. Botham	v	Gloucestershire	(SL)	1983
4th	117 C.J. Tavare & R.J. Harden	v	Kent	(SL)	1989
5th	112 P.D. Bowler & I.D. Blackwell	v	Yorkshire	(SL)	2001
6th	83 P.M. Roebuck & V.J. Marks	v	Gloucestershire	(SL)	1981
7th	85* B.C. Rose & J. Garner	v	Surrey	(SL)	1982
8th	48 I.T. Botham & K.F. Jennings	v	Nottinghamshire	(SL)	1975
9th	33 D.J.S. Taylor & H.R. Moseley	v	Kent	(SL)	1981
10th	29 A.R. Caddick & H.R.J. Trump	v	Worcestershire	(SL)	1996

Highest wicket partnerships against county

1st	135 J.A. Hopkins & H. Morris	for	Glamorgan	(SL)	1983
2nd	126 B.C. Broad & C.E.B. Rice	for	Nottinghamshire	(SL)	1986
3rd	140* M.R. Ramprakash & J.D. Carr	for	Middlesex	(SL)	1993
4th	74 G.D. Barlow & M.W. Gatting	for	Middlesex	(SL)	1976
5th	88 P. Bainbridge & J.N. Shepherd	for	Gloucestershire	(SL)	1983
6th	78 D.R. Law & R.J. Rollins	for	Essex	(SL)	1998
7th	43* H.T. Tunnicliffe & R.A. White	for	Nottinghamshire	(SL)	1975

8th	50 T.G. Roshire & T.J. Barry	for	Buckinghamshire	(NWT)	1991
9th	36 S.A. Marsh & R.P. Davis	for	Kent	(SL)	1989
10th	28* M.P. Bicknell & M.A. Feltham	for	Surrey	(SL)	1988

Best bowling performance in a match for county 5 for 27 J. Garner v Yorkshire (SL) 1985
Best bowling performance in a match against county 5 for 44 E.E. Hemmings for Nottinghamshire (SL) 1982
Largest crowd 5,000 v Lancashire (SL) 1978

GROUND INFORMATION

ENTRANCES William Street, off Great Pulteney Street (players, officials, Vice Presidents, members, public and all vehicles), Spring Gardens Road via River Path (pedestrians only).
MEMBERS' ENCLOSURE Pavilion and defined area between Bath Rugby Club clubhouse and temporary members' seating enclosure to the east of the pavilion at the Great Pulteney Street End.
PUBLIC ENCLOSURE Rest of the ground.
COVERED STANDS None.
OPEN STANDS Temporary raised and ground level seating is erected surrounding the playing area.
NAME OF ENDS Pavilion End, North Parade End.
GROUND DIMENSIONS 133m × 131m.
REPLAY SCREEN If televised matches are staged at the ground the replay screen is sited to the rear of the temporary seats on the rugby ground.
FIRST AID In Bath rugby club pavilion and in temporary facility in caravan or tent.
CODES OF DRESS Spectators are required to dress in an appropriate manner consistent with attending a cricket match. Bare torsos are not acceptable in, or in front of the pavilion. Executive Club/Suite users must wear a necktie and jacket. Swimwear is not permitted and footwear should be worn.
BEHAVIOUR The club is keen that standards of behaviour should be maintained and members and spectators are urged to report immediately to any steward any incident, or potential incident, where they feel action should be taken. Bad language is not acceptable at any match and the club will take prompt and strong action should this or any other ground regulation be ignored. Obstructing passageways, singing indecent songs, using indecent language, making unnecessary noise by means including persistent chanting, use of radios without an ear-piece, use of mobile telephones, possession of and/or waving of banners is nor permitted.
RECIPROCAL ARRANGEMENTS Members of Glamorgan, Gloucestershire can gain entry free for County Championship matches on production of membership card when Somerset is not playing their own county.
SUPPORTERS' CLUB Somerset Wyverns membership £10 per annum. Special rates for concessions and husband and wife membership are available. Also there is a Friends of the Bath Festival Club ☎ 01225 859886 Membership £7.50 per annum.
JUNIORS Junior Sabres Club for those under 21 is £25. Contact Membership Office on ☎ 01823 272946 for further information.
CORPORATE ENTERTAINING Marquees are available at the Bath Cricket Festival and are fully furnished and have their own private viewing areas with outside seating provided. Contact the Marketing Department for further information and a brochure ☎ 01823 337598.
FACILITIES FOR VISUALLY IMPAIRED SPECTATORS No reduced admission. Guide dogs are allowed.
FACILITIES AND ACCESS FOR PEOPLE WITH DISABILITIES INCLUDING WHEELCHAIR ACCESS TO GROUND Yes, through main entrance in William Street off Great Pulteney Street.
DESIGNATED CAR PARK AVAILABLE INSIDE THE GROUND FOR PEOPLE WITH DISABILITIES In car park on rugby ground.
GOOD VIEWING AREAS INSIDE THE GROUND FOR PEOPLE USING WHEELCHAIRS Special area in front of members' enclosure.
DESIGNATED VIEWING AREAS FOR PEOPLE USING WHEELCHAIRS Yes, close to sightscreen at North Parade Road End of the ground. Other locations are available around the ground, which are suitable for wheelchair viewing by prior arrangement with the club stewards. There is a disabled toilet situated in the Bath RFC Pavilion.
RAMPS TO PROVIDE EASY ACCESS TO BARS & REFRESHMENT OUTLETS FOR PEOPLE USING WHEELCHAIRS

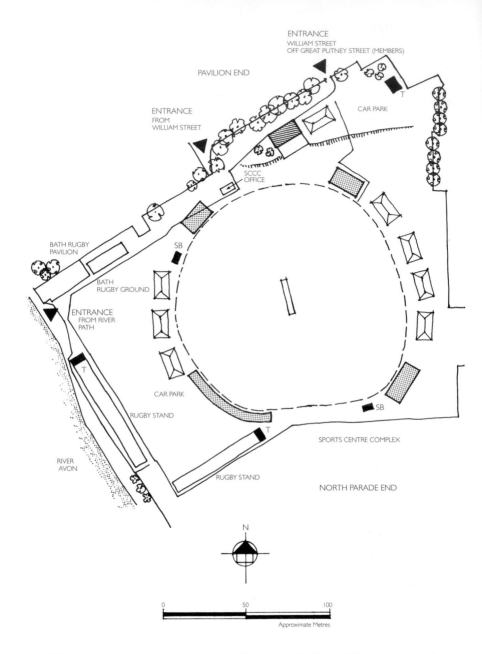

FOOD & DRINK FULL RESTAURANT/DINING FACILITIES Members, yes. Public, no. Full restaurant service in a marquee for Somerset CCC Vice Presidents and members only.
TEMPORARY FOOD/DRINK FACILITIES Members, yes. Public, yes.
FOOD SUITABLE FOR VEGETARIANS Members, yes. Public, yes.
BARS Members 2, Public 1.
VARIETIES OF BEER SOLD Exmoor Ales including Exmoor Ale, Fox, Gold, Hart, Stag, Beast and Seasonal, Fosters, John Smiths' Extra Smooth, Kronenbourg 1664, Courage.

CHILDREN'S FACILITIES Crèche, no. Play area, no.

CLUB SHOP Boundary Sports/Somerset Cricket Shop which stocks Somerset CCC items together with some cricket equipment, clothing, books, sweets and newspapers is usually in a tent on the ground.

CLUB MUSEUM No.

CRICKET COACHING FACILITIES No.

CRICKET NETS No.

OTHER SPORTING OR RECREATIONAL FACILITIES ON THE GROUND The ground is owned by Bath Council and is used during the winter months by Bath Rugby Football Club. There are ample facilities for lawn tennis, croquet and bowls on the Pulteney Street side.

FACILITIES FOR HIRE OR WIDER COMMUNITY USE AT THE GROUND Contact Bath Council and the adjacent Sports & Leisure Centre for further information.

WINTER CRICKET EVENTS The West of England branch of the Cricket Society hold meetings once a month between September and March at the Bath Cricket Club in North Parade Road.

CAR PARKING FACILITIES Available on the rugby ground (subject to weather conditions) for players, press/media, officials, Vice Presidents, members and public for which there is a small charge.

GROUND CAPACITY 8,000.

ANTICIPATED DEVELOPMENTS None presently planned.

HOW TO GET THERE

 Bath Spa station 0.5 mile ☎ 08457 484950, 08457 000125, 08457 222333, www.greatwesterntrains.co.uk, www.virgin.com/trains, www.railtrack.co.uk

 Badgerline 4 and 18 link Bath Spa station with ground ☎ 01225 464446. Other buses from surrounding areas to bus station, thence 0.5 mile walk to ground. National Express Coaches ☎ 08705 808080, www.nationalexpresscoaches.co.uk, www.gobycoach.com

 There are cycle paths and routes in this area of Bath.

 From north: from M5 junction 15 turn left on to M4 (east), continue on M4 to junction 18, take third exit at roundabout on to A46 (south) towards Bath, at junction with A4 turn right and continue into Bath on this road, follow A36 (Cleveland Place), bear right on to Henrietta Road, then left on to Henrietta Street, turn left at roundabout into Great Pulteney Street, turn right into William Street. **From south:** from A367 (Shepton Mallet) stay on A367 into Bath (Wellsway), turn right on to A3604 (Lower Bristol Road), follow signs to A36 (Lower Bristol Road), continue on A36 (Darlington Street), bear left on to Great Pulteney Street, turn left into William Street. **From east:** from M4 junction 18 take third exit at roundabout (A46) then as for from north. **From west:** from A39 stay on A39 (east) to junction with A4 (Bristol Road), bear left on to A36 (Lower Bristol Road), continue on this road to A36 (Darlington Street), then as for from south.

 Bristol International Airport ☎ 0870 1212 747 www.bristolairport.co.uk, Bournemouth International Airport ☎ 01202 364000 www.bournemouthairport.co.uk, Exeter Airport ☎ 01392 367433 www.exeterairport.co.uk

WHERE TO STAY

Bath Spa Hotel (☎ 01225 444424), Duke's Hotel (☎ 01225 463512 www.dukesbath.co.uk), Fernley Hotel (☎ 01225 61603), Kinlet Guest House (☎ 01225 420268), Queensberry Hotel (☎ 01225 447928 www.batholivetree.com), Royal Crescent Hotel (☎ 01225 319090), The Francis Hotel (☎ 01225 424257), The Saracens Head Hotel (☎ 01225 426518)

For further places to stay in Bath visit www.smoothhound.co.uk.

WHERE TO EAT

Browns (☎ 01225 461199 www.browns-restaurant.com), Demuth's (☎ 01225 446059 www.demuths.co.uk), Firehouse Rotisserie (☎ 01225 482070 www.firehouserotisserie.co.uk), Fishworks (☎ 01225 448707 www.fishworks.co.uk), Hole in the Wall (☎ 01225 425242), Mai Thai (☎ 01225 445557), Martin Blunos at Fitzroy's (☎ 01225 463512 www.dukesbath.co.uk), Moody Goose (☎ 01225 466688 www.moody-goose.com),

Olive Tree (☎ 01225 447928 www.batholivetree.com), Rajpoot (☎ 01225 466833 www.rajpoot.com), Richmond Arms (☎ 01225 316725), Sukhothai (☎ 01225 462463), The Eastern Eye (☎ 01225 422323 www.easterneye.co.uk), Tilley's Bistro (☎ 01225 484200 www.tilleysbistro.co.uk), Woods (☎ 01225 314812)

OTHER USEFUL INFORMATION

Friends of Bath Cricket Festival ☎ 01225 859886, Membership £7.50 per annum.
Bath Rugby Football Club ☎ 01225 325200, www.bathrugby.com
Somerset Talk www.Howzat.20m.com

TOURIST INFORMATION Bath Tourist Information Centre, Abbey Chambers, Abbey Church Yard, Bath BA1 1LY
☎ 01225 477101, www.tourismbath.gov.uk, www.heartofsomerset.com, www.somerset.gov.uk/tourism

LOCAL RADIO STATIONS BBC Radio Bristol (95.5 MHz FM/1548 KHz MW), BBC Radio Somerset Sound (1323 KHz MW), Orchard FM (102.6 MHz FM)

LOCAL NEWSPAPERS *Bath Chronicle, Evening Post, Western Daily Press*

Main entrance to the Recreation Ground through the William Street turnstiles.

SURREY
COUNTY CRICKET CLUB

Surrey

The AMP Oval
East Molesey – Metropolitan Police Sports Ground
Guildford
Whitgift School

SURREY COUNTY CRICKET CLUB, THE AMP OVAL, KENNINGTON, LONDON SE11 5SS

Telephone	020 7582 6660 **fax** 020 7735 7769
The AMP Oval Health & Fitness Centre	020 7820 5755
Ken Barrington Cricket Centre	020 7820 5739
The AMP Oval Equipment Shop	020 7820 5756
The AMP Oval Leisurewear Shop	020 7820 5714
Ticket Office	020 7582 7764
Membership Department	020 7820 5715
Surrey County Cricket Centre, Guildford	01483 598880
Email	enquiries@surreycricket.com
Website	www.surreycricket.com, www.ovalcricket.com

Founded Inauguration 18 October 1845
Colours Chocolate and silver
Crest Prince of Wales' Feathers
National Cricket League Nickname Surrey Lions
National Cricket League Colours Blue, red & yellow
Patron HRH The Prince of Wales
President B.G.K. Downing OBE
Chairman M.J. Soper
Chief Executive Officer P.C.J. Sheldon
PA to CEO Mrs C. Turner
Deputy Secretary Miss D.J. Thomas
Finance Director N. Rossiter
Corporate Development Director N.S. Cooke
Commercial Operations Director M. Lebus
Marketing Manager Miss A. Groves
Sponsorship Manager T. Codrington
Communications Manager J. Grave
Hospitality Manager Miss C. Holland
Retail Manager B. Green
Ken Barrington Cricket Centre Manager D. Gorrod
Surrey County Cricket Centre Manager M. Lane
Ticket Office Manager J. Callaghan

Membership Secretary Miss J. Blakesley
Hon Librarian J. Hancock
Chairman of Cricket R. Thompson
Cricket Manager K.T. Medlycott
2nd XI Coach A.R. Butcher
Academy Director G. Townsend
Cricket Secretary Miss A. Gibson
Captain A.J. Hollioake
Vice Captain M.A. Butcher
Physiotherapist D. Naylor
Scorer 1st XI K.R. Booth
Scorer 2nd XI C. J Hamm
Ground Manager P.D. Brind
Ground Sponsors AMP
Yearbook £7.50 (free to Surrey members)
Scorecard 30p (County) 50p (Test/ODI)
National Cricket League Programme & Scorecard £2
Magazine/Newsletter *Direct Hit* £3 (free to members)
Frizzell County Championship Status Division 1
National Cricket League Status Division 1

ACHIEVEMENTS

County Championship Champions 1864, 1887, 1888, 1890, 1891, 1892, 1894, 1895, 1899, 1914, 1952, 1953, 1954, 1955, 1956, 1957, 1958, 1971, 1999, 2000, 2002, Joint Champions 1889 and 1950
Gillette Cup Finalists 1969, 1980
NatWest Trophy Winners 1982, Finalists 1991
Benson and Hedges Cup Winners 1974, 1997, 2001, Finalists 1979, 1981

John Player Sunday League Best 5th 1969, 1980
Refuge Assurance Sunday League Best 5th 1988, 1989
AXA Sunday League Winners 1996
Norwich Union National League Best 8th Division 1 2001, Winners Division 2 2000
Tilcon Trophy Winners 1991, Finalists 1978, 1989
Seeboard Trophy Finalists 1990, Semi-finalists 1989

SURREY CRICKET BOARD

Chairman M.J. Soper
Vice Chairman A.R. Pannell
Treasurer D. Stewart
Cricket Development Manager C.K. Bullen (based at The AMP Oval)
Cricket Development Manager Miss S. Eyers (based at SCCC, Guildford)
Cricket Board Executive Mrs K. Meaney

Address	Surrey Cricket Board, AMP Oval, Kennington, London SE11 5SS
☎	020 7582 6660
Fax	020 7735 7769
Website	www.surreycricket.com

GROUNDS

The AMP Oval (Kennington, London), Croydon (Whitgift School, Nottingham Road), East Molesey (Metropolitan Police Sports Ground), Guildford CC (Woodbridge Road)

The other grounds that have been used since 1969 are: Byfleet (BAC Ground, Byfleet), Sunbury-on-Thames (Kenton Court Meadow, Lower Hampton Road), Leatherhead (St John's School), Sutton (Sutton CC, Cheam Road), Godalming (Charterhouse School), Tolworth (Decca Sports Ground) and Banstead (Banstead CC, Avenue Road)

SECOND XI GROUNDS

Bank of England Sports Ground, Priory Lane, Roehampton, London SW15 ☎ 020 8876 8417
Banstead CC, Avenue Road, Banstead, Surrey ☎ 01737 358838
Cheam CC, Peaches Close, off Station Way, Cheam, Surrey ☎ 020 8642 1817
East Molesey, Metropolitan Police CC, Imber Court, East Molesey ☎ 020 8398 1267
NatWest Bank Sports Ground, Turle Road, Norbury, London SW16 ☎ 020 8764 1170 (Pavilion), 020 8679 5638 (Office)
Normandy CC, Hunts Hill, Guildford Road, Normandy, nr Guildford, Surrey ☎ 01483 811519
Oxted CC, Master Park, Oxted, Surrey ☎ 01883 712792
Purley CC, The Ridge, off Foxley Lane, Purley, Surrey ☎ 020 8660 0608
Sutton CC, Cheam Road, Sutton, Surrey ☎ 020 8642 6888
Wimbledon CC, Church Road, Wimbledon, London SW19 ☎ 020 8946 7403

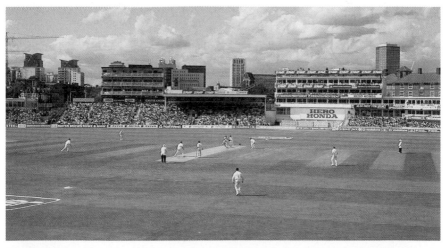

The Vauxhall End viewed from the members' balcony during the England v India Test match in 2002 with MI6 and St George's Wharf beyond.

THE AMP OVAL

Address AMP Oval, Kennington, London SE11 5SS
Prospects of Play ☎ 020 7820 5718

HISTORY OF GROUND AND FACILITIES

IN 1844 THE MONTPELIER CLUB, one of the most successful clubs in South London, was forced to moved from its ground at Walworth because the land had been sold for housing development. A member, Mr William Baker, suggested that Kennington Oval, a market garden and the property of the Duchy of Cornwall, might be used for cricket. The Duchy was willing to let it for use as a cricket ground and a thirty-one year lease was granted at £120 per year, with taxes which amounted to a further £20. At the time of its conversion to a cricket ground, Kennington Oval was mainly an open space with a small hedge surrounding it. It takes its name from the surrounding streets rather than the shape of the playing area itself. The original turf came from Tooting Common and was laid in March 1845 by Mr M. Turtle of Clapham Road at a cost of £300. The first match on the ground is recorded as having been played on 13 May 1845 between Mr Fould's XI and Mr Houghton's XI.

Following a meeting of the Montpelier Club on 22 August 1845 at the Horns Tavern, Kennington, more than a hundred members of different clubs in the county proposed the formation of a club for the County of Surrey. The resolution was carried amidst cheering and the formal inauguration took place at the Horns Tavern on 18 October 1845.

Members' pavilion with Laker and Lock Stands (left) and Bedser Stand (right).

The first Surrey match was on 21 and 22 August 1845 between the Gentlemen of Surrey and the Players of Surrey. The first Surrey County Cricket Club home match was staged with neighbours Kent in 1846, and the first County Championship fixture was staged in 1873 against Sussex. During the first Test match at The Oval in 1880 between England and Australia Dr W.G. Grace scored 152 for England and W.L. Murdoch replied for the Australians with 153*.

Association football was played at the ground in the nineteenth century and it was the venue for the FA Cup Final in 1872 and again between 1874 and 1892. At the Vauxhall End there was an ice skating rink in the 1880s but this was closed because members complained that the music was too loud! In 1971 The Oval was one of the first cricket grounds to host a pop concert with The Who and Rod Stewart and The Faces per-forming to sell-out crowds.

Main entrance to the pavilion for members beneath the famous Oval clock presented to the club by Lord Sandberg in 1995.

During the 'Great Stink' of 1858, when Parliament was suspended because of the stench of the River Thames, it was decided that the nearby River Effra, should be excavated and covered over. The soil was given to the Surrey County Cricket Club and was used to create the original mounds on which the Eastern Terrace, now the Peter May Stand, was constructed.

Rebuilding of the Mound Stand, including a number of fine executive boxes, was completed in 1984. The nets and the West Stand were demolished after the 1988 season to make way for the Bedser Stand development which includes the Ken Barrington Cricket Centre. The work was carried out by Eve Construction plc at a cost of £3m. The complex was completed in 1991 and was opened by Her Majesty The Queen on 31 July 1991 during the Surrey v Essex NatWest Trophy quarter-final match. On the very top floor there is a press room and media centre. The majority of this work was paid for by funds raised by the 'Save the Oval Fund' with assistance from Foster's Australian brewery.

The ground is known today as The AMP Oval. A highlight of the autumn sporting calendar for the last 15 years has been the annual Australian Rules Football match, which is staged between two of the top Australian sides for the Foster's Challenge Cup, later known as The AMP Challenge Cup. In 2002 the match was staged between Essendon Bombers and Richmond Tigers. Other tournaments held at The AMP Oval have included an International Batsman of the Year competition in 1979.

In 1990 Surrey County Cricket Club renamed the stands at The AMP Oval after famous players who have represented the county. They are: the Laker

Stand (formerly the Taverners Stand), the Lock Stand (formerly the Mound Stand), the Jardine Stand (formerly the Vauxhall East Stand), the Fender Stand (formerly the Vauxhall Centre Stand), the Gover Stand (formerly the Vauxhall West Stand), the Surridge Enclosure (formerly the West Terrace) and the Bedser Stand (formerly the West Stand and Nets Stand). The Peter May Enclosure has not been renamed.

The pavilion was built in 1898 and was designed by the architect Mr A.T. Muirhead who was also responsible for the pavilion at Old Trafford, Manchester. Although much altered in subsequent years it still retains much of its original character. Between 1993 and 1996 the pavilion was completely renovated and enlarged by adding two storeys to provide additional seating for members, executive suites, restaurants and an improved library. It has still to be cleared by a batsman. The shot that came nearest to achieving this distinction was by none other than Ali Brown who struck the red and green run-out lights. It is estimated that to clear the roof a batsman would need to hit over 115 yards.

There are many famous paintings and items of cricket memorabilia in the various parts of the pavilion as well as in the Surrey County Cricket Club Centenary Library on the top floor of the building, from where there is a splendid view of the ground. The world-famous Hobbs Gates form the main entrance to the ground at the rear of the pavilion. There is a splendid new clock above the members' main pavilion entrance, which was given to the club by Lord Sandberg in 1995. Near the main Hobbs Gate is a brick sculpture of Sir Leonard Hutton.

Like most Test match grounds, the facilities for members are good and except for the Peter May and Surridge Enclosures, all parts of the ground are covered.

The gas holders pictured during the England v India Test match in 2002.

In 1988 a new executive box area was constructed at the Vauxhall End. A large TV screen was installed high above the Vauxhall Stand to broadcast action replays of the cricket during the England v New Zealand Test match in 1983. This facility did not return until 1991 for the fifth Cornhill Insurance Test match between England and the West Indies. During this match the screen was situated on the Harleyford Road side of the ground.

The Oval wicket has 27 pitches, more than any other cricket venue in the world. At over 5.5 acres it provides the largest playing area for Test matches in the northern hemisphere. Only Melbourne Cricket Ground in Australia is bigger. The playing area is very large, extending to 168 metres by 148 metres, within which the actual playing area is defined by a rope stretched to the appropriate dimensions depending on the position of the playing strip being used, but usually about 136 metres by 142 metres.

This is very much an urban situation, overshadowed as it has been for so many years by the gasholders and blocks of flats. From the upper part of the pavilion there is a fine view of the tower of the Palace of Westminster, the NatWest Tower, Canary Wharf and the London Eye.

One of the most famous cricket records at The Oval is Sir Leonard Hutton's 364 against Australia in 1938. Also well remembered is the occasion in 1948 when Sir Donald Bradman was bowled for a duck on his last appearance in Test cricket by Eric Hollies of Warwickshire, thereby finishing his career with a Test match average of 99.94.

The Oval has staged matches in all major competitions for Surrey County Cricket Club and England as well as international matches not including England in the Prudential Cup competitions of 1975, 1979 and 1983, the Cricket World Cup in 1999 and NatWest ODI Series in 2000, 2001 and 2002. In 1999 Cricket World Cup warm-up matches were staged by Surrey v West Indies and Surrey v New Zealand. World Cup matches between England v South Africa, Pakistan v Zimbabwe and Australia v India were also played here.

Middlesex County Cricket Club have staged two matches at the Kennington Oval. The first was in 1870 when the home match with Surrey which was due to be played at Lille Bridge in West Brompton (north of Chelsea Football Ground) was transferred because the playing area was unfit. Then in 1939 the home County Championship match with Nottinghamshire was staged at Kennington Oval because Lord's was being used for the annual Eton versus Harrow school match.

GROUND RECORDS AND SCORES

FIRST-CLASS MATCHES

Highest innings total for county 811 v Somerset 1899
Highest innings total against county 863 by Lancashire 1990
Lowest innings total for county 16 v Nottinghamshire 1880
Lowest innings total against county 20 by Kent 1870 (1 man absent)
Highest individual innings for county 357* R. Abel v Somerset 1899
Highest individual innings against county 366 N.H. Fairbrother for Lancashire 1990
Highest wicket partnerships for county

1st	428 J.B. Hobbs & A. Sandham	v	Oxford University	1926
2nd	371 J.B. Hobbs & E.G. Hayes	v	Hampshire	1909
3rd	306 R. Abel & F.C. Holland	v	Cambridge University	1895

4th	448 R. Abel & T.W. Hayward	v	Yorkshire		1899
5th	308 J.N. Crawford & F.C. Holland	v	Somerset		1908
6th	298 A. Sandham & H.S. Harrison	v	Sussex		1913
7th	262 C.J. Richards & K.T. Medlycott	v	Kent		1987
8th	205 I.A. Greig & M.P. Bicknell	v	Lancashire		1990
9th	168 E.R.T. Holmes & E.W.J. Brooks	v	Hampshire		1936
10th	133* A. Sandham & W.J. Abel	v	Middlesex		1919

Highest wicket partnerships against county

1st	377* N.F. Horner & K. Ibadulla	for	Warwickshire		1960
2nd	325 G. Brann & K.S. Ranjitsinhji	for	Sussex		1899
3rd	364 M.A. Atherton & N.H. Fairbrother	for	Lancashire		1990
4th	314 Salim Malik & N. Hussain	for	Essex		1991
5th	340 E. Wainwright & G.H. Hirst	for	Yorkshire		1899
6th	376 R. Subba Row & A. Lightfoot	for	Northamptonshire		1958
7th	257 J.T. Morgan & F.R. Brown	for	Cambridge University		1930
8th	165 S. Haigh & Lord Hawke	for	Yorkshire		1902
9th	149 R.S. Lucas & J. Phillips	for	Middlesex		1894
	149 G.H. Hirst & D. Hunter	for	Yorkshire		1905
10th	249 C.T. Sarwate & S.N. Banerjee	for	Indians		1946

Best bowling performance in an innings for county 10 for 45 T. Richardson v Essex 1894
Best bowling performance in an innings against county 10 for 28 W.P. Howell for Australians 1899
Best bowling performance in a match for county 15 for 83 T. Richardson v Warwickshire 1898
Best bowling performance in a match against county 15 for 57 W.P. Howell for Australians 1899
Largest crowd 80,000 for Yorkshire 1906

LIMITED-OVERS MATCHES

Highest innings total for county 438 for 5 v Glamorgan (C&G) 2002
Highest innings total against county 429 by Glamorgan (C&G) 2002
Lowest innings total for county 74 v Kent (GC) 1967
Lowest innings total against county 44 by Glamorgan (SL) 1999
Highest individual innings for county 268 A.D. Brown v Glamorgan (C&G) 2002
Highest individual innings against county 180* T.M. Moody for Worcestershire (NWT) 1994
Highest wicket partnerships for county

1st	218 A.R. Butcher & G.P. Howarth	v	Gloucestershire	(SL)	1976
2nd	212 A.J. Stewart & G.P. Thorpe	v	Lancashire	(BHC)	1993
3rd	200 A.J. Stewart & G.P. Thorpe	v	Glamorgan	(SL)	1989
4th	181 I.J. Ward & A.J. Hollioake	v	Glamorgan	(SL)	2000
5th	166 M.A. Lynch & G.R.J. Roope	v	Durham	(NWT)	1982
6th	132 A.J. Stewart & M.A. Butcher	v	Hampshire	(BHC)	1996
7th	88* G.S. Clinton & R.D. Jackman	v	Nottinghamshire	(SL)	1980
8th	78* M.P. Bicknell & I.D.K. Salisbury	v	Derbyshire	(NWT)	1998
9th	58* M.A. Butcher & C.K. Bullen	v	Glamorgan	(SL)	1991
10th	30 P.I. Pocock & P.H. L. Wilson	v	Worcestershire	(SL)	1979

Highest wicket partnerships against county

1st	219 T.M. Moody & T.S. Curtis	for	Worcestershire	(SL)	1994
2nd	196 S.B.Hassan & C.E.B.Rice	for	Nottinghamshire	(SL)	1977
3rd	309* T.S. Curtis & T.M. Moody	for	Worcestershire	(NWT)	1994
4th	176 R.A. Smith & M.C.J. Nicholas	for	Hampshire	(NWT)	1989
5th	130* A.A. Metcalfe & D.L. Bairstow	for	Yorkshire	(SL)	1986
6th	124* J.J. Whitaker & P.A. Nixon	for	Leicestershire	(SL)	1992
7th	119 R.A. Smith & A.N. Aymes	for	Hampshire	(BHC)	1996
8th	110* C.L. Cairns & B.N. French	for	Nottinghamshire	(SL)	1993
9th	75 P.A. Nixon & T.J. Mason	for	Leicestershire	(BHC)	1997
10th	60 K.J. Dean & D.E. Malcolm	for	Derbyshire	(SL)	1996

Best bowling performance for county 7 for 30 M.P. Bicknell v Glamorgan (SL) 1999

Best bowling performance against county 7 for 15 A.L. Dixon for Kent (GC) 1967
Largest crowd 12,000 v Lancashire (NWT) 1988

TEST MATCHES

Highest innings total for England 903 for 7 dec v Australia 1938
Highest innings total against England 708 by Pakistan 1987
Lowest innings total for England 52 v Australia 1948
Lowest innings total against England 44 by Australia 1896
Highest individual innings for England 364 L. Hutton v Australia 1938
Highest individual innings against England 291 I.V.A. Richards for West Indies 1976
Highest wicket partnerships for England

1st	290 G. Pullar & M.C. Cowdrey	v	South Africa	1960
2nd	382 L. Hutton & M. Leyland	v	Australia	1938
3rd	264 L. Hutton & W.R. Hammond	v	West Indies	1939
4th	266 W.R. Hammond & T.S. Worthington	v	India	1936
5th	179 M. Leyland & L.E.G. Ames	v	South Africa	1935
6th	215 L. Hutton & J. Hardstaff jun.	v	Australia	1938
7th	142 J. Sharp & K.L. Hutchings	v	Australia	1909
8th	217 T.W. Graveney & J.T. Murray	v	West Indies	1966
9th	151 W.H. Scotton & W.W. Read	v	Australia	1884
10th	128 K. Higgs & J.A. Snow	v	West Indies	1966

Highest wicket partnerships against England

1st	213 S.M. Gavaskar & C.P.S. Chauhan	for	India	1979
2nd	451 W.H. Ponsford & D.G. Bradman	for	Australia	1934
3rd	243 P.A. de Silva & S.T. Jayasuriya	for	Sri Lanka	1998
4th	243 D.G. Bradman & A. Jackson	for	Australia	1930
5th	191 Javed Miandad & Imran Khan	for	Pakistan	1987
6th	196 C.L. Hooper & S. Chanderpaul	for	West Indies	1995
7th	110 R.J. Shastri & N. Kapil Dev	for	India	1990
8th	109* A. Mitchell & H. Tuckett	for	South Africa	1947
9th	190 Asif Iqbal & Intikhab Alam	for	Pakistan	1967
10th	88 W.L. Murdoch & W.H. Moule	for	Australia	1880

Best bowling performance in an innings for England 9 for 57 D.E. Malcolm v South Africa 1994
Best bowling performance in an innings against England 9 for 65 M. Muralitharan for Sri Lanka 1998
Best bowling performance in a match for England 13 for 57 S.F. Barnes v South Africa 1912
Best bowling performance in a match against England 16 for 220 M. Muralitharan for Sri Lanka 1998

ONE-DAY INTERNATIONALS

Highest innings total for England in ODI 322 for 6 v New Zealand (TT) 1983
Highest innings total against England in ODI 281 by West Indies (TT) 1995
Highest innings total in non-England ODI 328 for 5 by Australia v Sri Lanka (WC) 1975
Lowest innings total for England in ODI 103 v South Africa (Emir) 1999
Lowest innings total against England in ODI 165 by India (NWS) 2002
Lowest innings total in non-England ODI 123 by Zimbabwe v Pakistan (WC) 1999
Highest individual innings for England in ODI 114* D.I. Gower v Pakistan (PT) 1978
Highest individual innings against England in ODI 125* G.S. Chappell for Australia (PT) 1977
Highest individual innings in non-England ODI 119 I.V.A. Richards for West Indies v India (WC) 1983
Highest wicket partnerships for England in ODI

1st	161 D.L. Amiss & J.M. Brearley	v	Australia	(PT)	1977
2nd	144 M.A. Atherton & G.A. Hick	v	West Indies	(TT)	1995
3rd	159 A.J. Lamb & D.I. Gower	v	India	(PT)	1982
4th	115 A.J. Lamb & M.W. Gatting	v	New Zealand	(WC)	1983
5th	109* G.A. Gooch & R.C. Russell	v	New Zealand	(TT)	1990
6th	35 K.W.R. Fletcher & C.M. Old	v	West Indies	(PT)	1973

7th	76 G.A. Hick & M.A. Ealham	v	India	(TT)	1996
8th	35 K.W.R. Fletcher & G.G. Arnold	v	West Indies	(PT)	1973
9th	36 A.R. Caddick & R.D.B. Croft	v	Australia	(NWS)	2001
10th	21 A.R. Caddick & A.D. Mullally	v	Australia	(NWS	2001

Highest wicket partnerships against England in ODI

1st	111 G. Kirsten & H.H. Gibbs	for	South Africa	(Emir)	1999
2nd	163* S.M. Gavaskar & M. Azharuddin	for	India	(TT)	1986
3rd	110 Mudassar Nazar & Javed Miandad	for	Pakistan	(TT)	1987
4th	123 A.D.R. Campbell & A. Flower	for	Zimbabwe	(Emir)	2000
5th	113 M.G. Bevan & A.C. Gilchrist	for	Australia	(TT)	1997
6th	86 K.J. Hughes & R.W. Marsh	for	Australia	(PT)	1980
7th	47 J.R. Murray & W.K.M. Benjamin	for	West Indies	(TT)	1995
8th	65 N. Kapil Dev & S. Madan Lal	for	India	(PT)	1982
9th	52 M.D. Crowe & M.C. Snedden	for	New Zealand	(WC)	1983
10th	38 A. Kumble & A. Nehra	for	India	(NWS)	2002

Highest wicket partnerships in non-England ODI

1st	182 R.B. McCosker & A. Turner	for	Australia v Sri Lanka	(WC)	1975
2nd	166 Majid Khan & Zaheer Abbas	for	Pakistan v West Indies	(WC)	1979
3rd	132* I.V.A. Richards & H.A. Gomes	for	West Indies v Pakistan	(WC)	1983
4th	117 G.S. Chappell & K.D. Walters	for	Australia v Sri Lanka	(WC)	1975
5th	141 A.D. Jadeja & R.R. Singh	for	India v Australia	(WC)	1999
6th	99 R. Edwards & R.W. Marsh	for	Australia v West Indies	(WC)	1975
7th	42 D.P.M D. Jayawardene & W.P.U.J.C. Vaas	for	Sri Lanka v India	(NWS)	2002
8th	16 B.L. Cairns & B.F. Hastings	for	New Zealand v West Indies	(WC)	1975
9th	29 Shahid Afridi & Saqlain Mushtaq	for	Pakistan v Zimbabwe	(WC)	1999
10th	11* Saqlain Mushtaq & Shoaib Akhtar	for	Pakistan v Zimbabwe	(WC)	1999

Best bowling performance for England in ODI 5 for 26 R.C. Irani v India (NWS) 2002
Best bowling performance against England in ODI 4 for 17 A.A. Donald for South Africa (WC) 1999
Best bowling performance in non-England ODI 4 for 27 B.D. Julien for West Indies v New Zealand (WC) 1975
Largest crowd 18,665 England v South Africa (WC) 1999

GROUND INFORMATION

ENTRANCES Hobbs Gates (players, officials and vehicles), Kennington Oval including turnstiles 1–18, 19–22, 23–26 and 27–30 in Harleyford Road (members, public and sponsors), Vauxhall End – via West Gate (public and vehicles).
MEMBERS' ENCLOSURE Pavilion including areas A, B and C.
PUBLIC ENCLOSURE Rest of the ground including areas CC, D, E, F, G, H, J, K, L, M, N, P, Q, R, S, T, V, W, X, Y and Z.
COVERED STANDS Pavilion (part), Fender Stand (part), Lock Stand (part) and Laker Stand (part).
OPEN STANDS Pavilion (part), Fender Stand (part), Peter May Enclosure, Lock Stand (part), Laker Stand (part), Surridge Enclosure, Gover Stand, Stuart Surridge Enclosure and Bedser Stand.
NAME OF ENDS Pavilion End, Vauxhall End.
GROUND DIMENSIONS 168m × 148m (but usually set at 136m × 142m).
REPLAY SCREEN For all televised matches at the ground the replay screen is sited in the Surridge Stand at the Vauxhall End of the ground.
FIRST AID First Aid Room is located beneath the Bedser Stand Block E and there are two further points at the Vauxhall End and under the Peter May Stand during major matches.
CODES OF DRESS Spectators are required to dress in an appropriate manner consistent with attending a cricket match. Bare torsos are not acceptable in, or in front of, the pavilion. Executive Club/Suite users must wear a necktie and jacket.

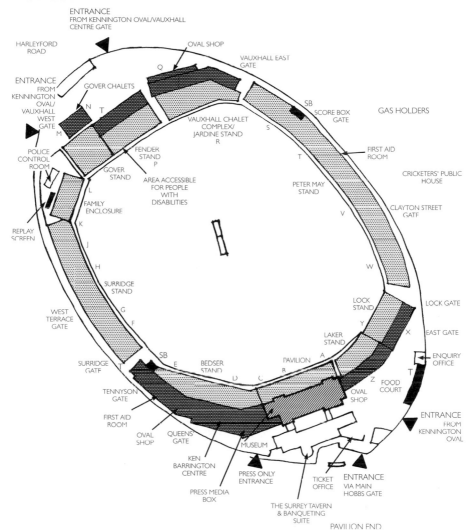

VAUXHALL END

ENTRANCE
FROM KENNINGTON OVAL/VAUXHALL
CENTRE GATE

HARLEYFORD
ROAD

OVAL SHOP

VAUXHALL EAST
GATE

ENTRANCE
FROM
KENNINGTON
OVAL/
VAUXHALL
WEST
GATE

GOVER CHALETS

Q

SB

SCORE BOX
GATE

GAS HOLDERS

N   T

M

VAUXHALL CHALET
COMPLEX/
JARDINE STAND
R

S

FIRST AID
ROOM

POLICE
CONTROL
ROOM

FENDER
STAND
P

T

CRICKETERS' PUBLIC
HOUSE

GOVER
STAND

L

AREA ACCESSIBLE
FOR PEOPLE
WITH
DISABILITIES

PETER MAY
STAND

FAMILY
ENCLOSURE

K

V

CLAYTON STREET
GATE

REPLAY
SCREEN

J

H

W

SURRIDGE
STAND

G

WEST
TERRACE
GATE

F

LOCK
STAND

LOCK GATE

Y

EAST GATE

SURRIDGE
GATE

SB

T

E

BEDSER
STAND

LAKER
STAND

A

PAVILION

X

ENQUIRY
OFFICE

B

Z

T

TENNYSON
GATE

D   C

OVAL SHOP

FOOD
COURT

FIRST AID
ROOM

OVAL
SHOP

QUEENS'
GATE

KEN
BARRINGTON
CENTRE

MUSEUM

ENTRANCE
FROM
KENNINGTON
OVAL

PRESS ONLY
ENTRANCE

TICKET
OFFICE

ENTRANCE
VIA MAIN
HOBBS GATE

PRESS MEDIA
BOX

THE SURREY TAVERN
& BANQUETING
SUITE

PAVILION END

N

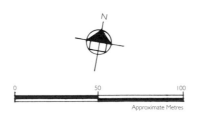

0   50   100
Approximate Metres

BEHAVIOUR The club is keen that standards of behaviour should be maintained and members and spectators are urged to report immediately to the CEO any incident, or potential incident, where they feel action should be taken. Bad language is not acceptable at any match and the club will take prompt and strong action should this or any other ground regulation be ignored.

RECIPROCAL ARRANGEMENTS Members of Surrey can enter Sydney Cricket Ground (Australia) and Western Province Cricket Club at Newlands Cricket Ground in Cape Town (South Africa) with supporters from these two venues attending The AMP Oval on a reciprocal basis.

SUPPORTERS' CLUB Surrey CCC Supporters' Club, membership £10 (SCCC members), £12 for (non-SCCC members). Quarterly newsletter *Oval World*. Special rates for concessions and husband and wife membership are available. Contact Marcus Hook at Flat 1, 67 Birdhurst Rise, South Croydon, Surrey CR2 7EJ, email mdevious@netcomuk.co.uk.

JUNIORS Junior Lions membership is available to under 18s at £10 per year. Contact the Membership Department on ☎ 020 7820 5715, email membership@surreycricket.com for further information.

CORPORATE ENTERTAINING The Executive Club, executive boxes, Pavilion Rooms, The Bedser Lounge, Banqueting Suite, Vauxhall Chalet Complex and Gover Chalets, Ken Barrington Cricket Centre, Montgomery Hall and Oval Way facilities are available for Test matches, one-day internationals and county and floodlit matches. Contact the Hospitality Department on ☎ 020 7820 5740/5717 for further details and a copy of the brochure.

FACILITIES FOR VISUALLY IMPAIRED SPECTATORS Guide dogs allowed.

FACILITIES AND ACCESS FOR PEOPLE WITH DISABILITIES INCLUDING WHEELCHAIR ACCESS TO GROUND Yes through Hobbs Gate and via Vauxhall Gate.

DESIGNATED CAR PARK AVAILABLE INSIDE THE GROUND FOR PEOPLE WITH DISABILITIES Limited car parking for members only at Vauxhall End and on Oval forecourt by arrangement in advance with club.

GOOD VIEWING AREAS INSIDE THE GROUND FOR PEOPLE USING WHEELCHAIRS There is a wheelchair area at the Vauxhall End of the ground in front of the Gover and Fender stands.

DESIGNATED VIEWING AREAS FOR PEOPLE USING WHEELCHAIRS There is a wheelchair area at the Vauxhall End of the ground in front of the Gover and Fender stands.

RAMPS TO PROVIDE EASY ACCESS TO BARS & REFRESHMENT OUTLETS FOR PEOPLE USING WHEELCHAIRS Yes, with a lift in the pavilion, Bedser Stand and Executive Suites at the Pavilion End of the ground.

FOOD & DRINK FULL RESTAURANT/DINING FACILITIES Members, yes. Public, Yes.

TEMPORARY FOOD/DRINK FACILITIES Members, yes. Public, yes.

FOOD SUITABLE FOR VEGETARIANS Members, yes. Public, yes.

BARS Members 2, Public 3.

VARIETIES OF BEER SOLD Fosters, Courage, Young's Real Ale.

CHILDREN'S FACILITIES Crèche, no. Play area, no.

CLUB SHOP The AMP Oval Shop is located on the forecourt near the members' entrance to the pavilion and sells replica merchandise, leisurewear, book and gifts relating to relating to Surrey CCC and The AMP Oval. The cricket equipment shop is located by entrance D of the Bedser Stand selling a large selection of cricket equipment supplied by all major cricket specialists. For major matches there are further temporary outlets at the rear of the Bedser Stand, at the Vauxhall End of the ground and on the main forecourt.

CLUB MUSEUM The Sandham Display room in the pavilion explains the history of Surrey CCC and The AMP Oval and contains Surrey and England memorabilia including the oldest known cricket bat in the world, all the trophies that Surrey have won over the years and the prototype stump camera, 1992. There is also a variety of pictures in the pavilion and a well equipped Library on the top floor.

CRICKET COACHING FACILITIES Contact Ken Barrington Cricket Centre for details.

CRICKET NETS Contact Ken Barrington Cricket Centre for details.

OTHER SPORTING OR RECREATIONAL FACILITIES ON THE GROUND Annual Australian Rules Football AMP Challenge Match is staged in October. The Ken Barrington Centre has facilities for a number of sports other than cricket nets including: martial arts, fitness, gymnasium, circuit training, five-a-side football, six-a-side hockey, badminton, volleyball, aerobics, netball, short tennis, table tennis, golf practice and yoga.

FACILITIES FOR HIRE OR WIDER COMMUNITY USE AT THE GROUND Contact the Club Office for further information.

WINTER CRICKET EVENTS Members' club dinners and lunches are staged in the pavilion, which is also used by the Surrey Dining Club. Membership is £10 per annum. Banqueting and conference facilities available to hire for further information contact Letheby & Christopher on ☎ 020 7820 5716.

CAR PARKING FACILITIES limited to players and officials only. Street car parking in area surrounding ground or (NCP) car parks in central London a short distance away.
GROUND CAPACITY 18,500.
ANTICIPATED GROUND DEVELOPMENTS Vauxhall End major development planned. Planning permission granted, currently awaiting approval of scheme and also finance.

HOW TO GET THERE

 Oval Underground (Northern Line) 50m Vauxhall (South-West Trains) and Vauxhall Underground (Victoria Line) 600m. London Transport enquiries ☎ 020 7222 1234

 3, 36, 36A, 36B, 59, 95, 109, 133, 155, 156, 157, 158, 159, 185, 196. London Transport information ☎ 020 7222 1234

 There are cycle routes from surrounding areas of London to this part of Kennington.

 The ground is currently outside the Central London Congestion Zone. **From north:** from M1 take A5 towards central London, continue on A5 (Edgware Road) to Marble Arch, turn right into Park Lane to Hyde Park Corner, follow signs to Victoria (A302) (Grosvenor Place), follow signs to Vauxhall Bridge Road (A202), cross Vauxhall Bridge, follows signs to AMP Oval.
From south: from M25 junction 8/7 continue on M23 (north) which becomes A23, continue on A23 towards central London, at junction with A202 (Camberwell New Road) turn left towards ground.
From east: from A2, continue on this road through Blackheath to junction with A202 at New Cross Road, bear left on to A202 (Queen's Road) and continue on A202 following signs to AMP Oval.
From west: from end of M4 continue on A4 (Great West Road) to junction with A3220 (Earls Court Road), turn right and continue to A3212 (Chelsea Embankment), at junction with Vauxhall Bridge Road (A202) turn right, then as for north.

 London Heathrow Airport ☎ 08700 000123 www.londonheathrowairport.co.uk, London City ☎ 020 7646 0000 www.londoncityairport.co.uk, London Gatwick Airport ☎ 08700 002468 www.londongatwickairport.co.uk

WHERE TO STAY

Dolphin Hotel (☎ 020 7834 3800 www.dolphinsquarehotel.co.uk), London Park Hotel, London SE1 (☎ 020 7735 9191)
For a further selection of numerous small hotels and guest houses in south/central London visit www.smoothhound.co.uk, www.london.gov.uk.

WHERE TO EAT

Fentiman Arms (☎ 020 7793 0126), Hanover Arms (☎ 020 7735 1576), Kennington Lane Restaurant and Bar (☎ 020 7793 8313), Kennington Tandoori (☎ 020 7735 9247), Pizza Express (☎ 020 7820 3877), Rhodes in the Square (☎ 020 7798 6767), The Beehive (☎ 020 7582 7608), The Greyhound (☎ 020 7735 2594)

TOURIST INFORMATION ☎ 020 8760 5630, 0839 123456, www.london.gov.uk

LOCAL RADIO STATIONS BBC London Live (94.9 MHz FM/1458 KHz MW), Capital Gold (95.8 MHz/1548 KHz MW), LBC (97.3 MHz FM/1152 KHz MW), LBC 1152AM

LOCAL NEWSPAPERS *Evening Standard, London Metro, South London Press, Croydon Advertiser, Surrey Comet*

EAST MOLESEY
Metropolitan Police Sports Ground

Address Metropolitan Police Cricket Club, Metropolitan Police Sports Club, Imber Court, Ember Lane, East Molesey, Esher, Surrey KT8 0BT
Prospects of Play ☎ 020 8398 1267 or 020 7230 7208

HISTORY OF GROUND AND FACILITIES

THE METROPOLITAN POLICE Cricket Club (MPCC) was established in 1919 and set up its headquarters at Imber Court Sports Club near Hampton Court. In fact cricket had been played at divisional level in the Force as far back as the nineteenth century. In 1893 Wandsworth Division were particularly strong and the annual report of that year records that twenty-seven matches were played and three trophies won, including the Commissioner's Silver Challenge Cup. The report expressed gratitude to the then Commissioner for permitting the game to be played; in his words, it 'prompted interest and healthy rivalry among the various teams in our Service'.

In the early days of the MPCC Walter 'Blossom' Fullwood joined the Force from Derbyshire CCC and was a fine wicket-keeper. Fixtures were staged at Imber Court, then in the countryside, against Cambridge University and Oxford University. A game against T.F. Blackwell's XI was always the last of the season. In 1938 *The Cricketer* magazine reported that the fixture with T.F. Blackwell's XI played at Berkhamsted in Hertfordshire was a timed match with two and half hours' batting each side. The Police made 310 for 3 and Blackwell's XI replied with 313 for 8, winning by 2 wickets with 3 minutes to spare.

From 1931 until 1953 police cricket achieved a significant profile thanks to the efforts of James Wills who joined the force from Cornwall CCC. He was a constable at Paddington Green station and he dominated police cricket during that period.

During the Second World War Imber Court hosted many representative matches attracting crowds of up to 5,000. Players who appeared here during this period included Lindsay Hassett, Learie Constantine, Denis and Leslie Compton, Cyril Washbrook, Bill Edrich and Les Ames. These matches raised many thousands of pounds for war charities and even had printed scorecards like games at Lord's and The Oval. After the war other police sports grounds were established at Bushey in Hertfordshire, Chigwell in Essex (near Chigwell School) and Hayes in Kent.

After many years of non-league cricket the MPCC joined the Surrey Cricketers' League in 1971 and enjoyed considerable success between 1975 and 1985. In 1987 the Cricketers' League amalgamated with the prestigious Surrey Championship League and the Metropolitan Police soon gained promotion to Division One which is acknowledged to be one of the strongest cricket competitions in the country.

The Police won the Surrey Championship 1st XI League in 1981, 1983, 1984 and 1986; the 2nd XI League in 1977, 1978, 1979, 1980 and 1985; and the Police Athletic Association Cup in 1980, 1981, 1982, 1983, 1985, 1986 and 1993. The

MPCC currently runs two representative XIs and boasts a fixture list including tour matches against visiting sides from overseas. Successful tours to South Africa and Australia have been made in recent years.

In 1983 a new and impressive pavilion was opened and this coincided with the only Surrey CCC 1st XI match to be staged at Imber Court when a John Player Sunday League match was played against Northamptonshire. The county side will return in 2003 for Twenty20 matches against Sussex and Essex.

Entry to the ground is from Imber Lane just off the A309 Hampton Court Way at the Embercourt Road roundabout and it is bounded by the River Ember, Imber Court and the Imber Court Trading Estate.

The Metropolitan Police Football Club, who play in the Ryman League Division 2, also use the ground.

GROUND RECORDS AND SCORES

LIMITED-OVERS MATCHES

Highest innings total for county 232 for 6 v Northamptonshire (SL) 1983
Highest innings total against county 234 for 5 by Northamptonshire (SL) 1983
Lowest innings total for county 232 for 6 v Northamptonshire (SL) 1983
Lowest innings total against county 234 for 5 by Northamptonshire (SL) 1983
Highest individual innings for county 70 M.A. Lynch v Northamptonshire (SL) 1983
Highest individual innings against county 72 A.J. Lamb for Northamptonshire (SL) 1983
Highest wicket partnerships for county

1st	55 A.R. Butcher & C.J. Richards	v	Northamptonshire	(SL)	1983
2nd	86 A.R. Butcher & M.A. Lynch	v	Northamptonshire	(SL)	1983
3rd	75 M.A. Lynch & D.J. Thomas	v	Northamptonshire	(SL)	1983
4th	5 M.A. Lynch & S.T. Clarke	v	Northamptonshire	(SL)	1983
5th	0 M.A. Lynch & A.J. Stewart	v	Northamptonshire	(SL)	1983
6th	4 M.A. Lynch & A. Needham	v	Northamptonshire	(SL)	1983
7th	7* A. Needham & I.R. Payne	v	Northamptonshire	(SL)	1983

8th to 10th yet to be established
Highest wicket partnerships against county

1st	40 R.J. Bailey & M.J. Bamber	for	Northamptonshire	(SL)	1983
2nd	41 M.J. Bamber & P. Willey	for	Northamptonshire	(SL)	1983
3rd	109 M.J. Bamber & A.J. Lamb	for	Northamptonshire	(SL)	1983
4th	27 A.J. Lamb & G. Cook	for	Northamptonshire	(SL)	1983
5th	7 G. Cook & R.G. Williams	for	Northamptonshire	(SL)	1983
6th	10* G. Cook & D.J. Wild	for	Northamptonshire	(SL)	1983

7th to 10th yet to be established
Best bowling performance in a match for county 3 for 46 I.R. Payne v Northamptonshire (SL) 1983
Best bowling analysis in a match against county 4 for 46 N.A. Mallender for Northamptonshire (SL) 1983
Largest crowd 4,000 v Northamptonshire (SL) 1983

GROUND INFORMATION

ENTRANCE From Ember Lane.
MEMBERS' ENCLOSURE Pavilion and defined members' enclosure.
PUBLIC ENCLOSURE Rest of the ground.
COVERED STANDS Pavilion (part).
OPEN STANDS Rest of the ground.
NAMES OF ENDS Football Ground End, Tennis Courts End.
GROUND DIMENSIONS 150m × 145m.
GROUND CAPACITY 6,000.
CAR PARKING FACILITIES In adjacent field.

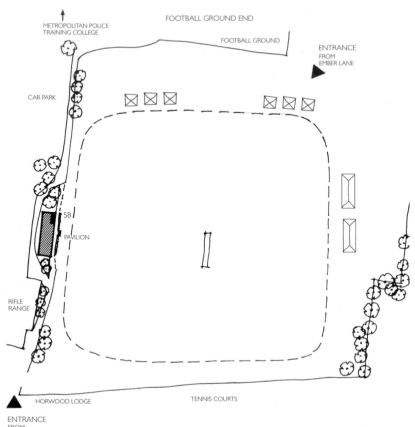

METROPOLITAN POLICE
TRAINING COLLEGE

FOOTBALL GROUND END

FOOTBALL GROUND

ENTRANCE
FROM
EMBER LANE

CAR PARK

SB

PAVILION

RIFLE
RANGE

HORWOOD LODGE

TENNIS COURTS

ENTRANCE
FROM
EMBER LANE

TENNIS COURTS END

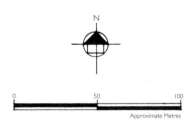

N

0   50   100

Approximate Metres

HOW TO GET THERE

 Hampton Court, ☎ 08457 484950. Trains connecting London Waterloo with Hampton Court are operated by South West Trains.

 London United Buses 411. Get off at East Molesey Police Station then 10 to 15 minute walk to ground.

 There are ample cycle routes to this area of East Molesey.

 From north: M25 take junction 13 and travel east along the A30. Continue on to the A308 across the Sunbury Cross roundabout and on to the Hampton Court roundabout. Turn right over Hampton Court Bridge and then travel south along Hampton Court Way (A309). Turn left at next roundabout into Embercourt Road. The ground is in front of you. **Or:** travel west along the A3 under the Hook underpass (A243). Take the next left on to the Kingston bypass (A309). **From south:** M25 take junction 10. Travel east along the A3 and turn left into Copsem Lane (A244). At the traffic lights in Esher turn right into Portsmouth Road (A307). At the Scilly Isles roundabout take the first left into Hampton Court Way (A309). Turn left at the first roundabout into Embercourt Road. The ground is in front of you. **From east:** travel west along the A3 under the Hook underpass (A243). Take the next left on to the Kingston bypass (A309). At the Scilly Isles roundabout turn right into Hampton Court Way (A309). Turn left at the first roundabout into Embercourt Road. The ground is in front of you. **From west:** Exit the M3 at the Sunbury Cross roundabout. Turn right into Staines Road East (A308). Turn right at the Hampton Court roundabout and go over Hampton Court Bridge. Travel south along Hampton Court Way (A309). Turn right at the next roundabout into Embercourt Road. The ground is in front of you.

 London Gatwick Airport ☎ 08700 002468, www.londongatwickairport.co.uk

WHERE TO STAY

Liongate Hotel (☎ 020 8977 8121). For other places to stay in the East Molesey/Esher area visit www.smoothhound.co.uk or email info@kingstonuponthames.gov.uk

WHERE TO EAT

Golden Curry (☎ 020 8941 1229), Blue Orchid (☎ 020 8979 1871), Palace Indian Restaurant (☎ 020 8941 3540), Shahee Mahal (☎ 020 8941 6952), New Anarkali (☎ 020 8979 5072)

LOCAL RADIO STATIONS BBC London Live (94.9 MHz FM/1458 KHz MW), Capital Gold (95.8 MHz/1548 KHz MW), LBC (97.3 MHz FM/1152 KHz MW)

LOCAL NEWSPAPERS *Surrey Advertiser, London Evening Standard, London Metro, South London Press, Croydon Advertiser, Surrey Comet and Guardian Series, Surrey Mirror*

GUILDFORD

Address Guildford Cricket Club, The Pavilion, Woodbridge Road,
Guildford, Surrey GU1 1AJ
Prospects of Play ☎ 01483 572181

HISTORY OF GROUND AND FACILITIES

THE EARLIEST KNOWN REFERENCE to the playing of cricket within the borders of Surrey is in a document of 1598 relating to a dispute over a plot of land at Guildford. The document speaks of a John Derrick, a scholar in the Free School of Guildford, and states that 'he and several of his fellows did run and play there at cricket'.

Guildford Cricket Club was founded in 1862 by two brothers, W. and J. Stevens, and the first mention of cricket played at the club appears in the *James Lillywhite Cricket Annual* of 1873. Mr J. Stevens scored 191 for the club during the 1874 season. At that time the ground was located near the cattle market, the present site of the law courts and car parks at the rear of the Guildford Sports Centre. Two famous players scored heavily in club matches at Guildford: C.T. Studd made 222* for Horsham Cricket Club against Guildford Cricket Club in 1881 and in the same season W.W. Read scored 263 for Reigate Priory Cricket Club.

The present Woodbridge Road Ground was given to the town by Sir Harry Waechter-Bart in 1911 for cricket, cycling, military parades and charitable purposes. Guildford Cricket Club disbanded between 1914 and 1922, though after 1918 the club's players played under the name of Guildford Wanderers Cricket Club. In May 1922 the players again wore the club colours of claret, pink and black when Guildford played against Woking, the first home match since 1914. The famous amateur football club, the Guildford Pinks, had the same colours and shared the Woodbridge Road Sports Ground until their demise in the early 1950s.

Guildford Cricket Club now play in the Surrey Championship. David Frith (the former editor of *Wisden Cricket Monthly*) is a former president. The present club chairman, who is responsible for the Guildford Cricket Festival, is Charles Woodhouse LLB. In 1988 Guildford Cricket Club celebrated a jubilee of county cricket in the county town. This was marked by a special tribute booklet compiled by David Frith.

The first visit to Guildford by Surrey County Cricket Club was in 1938 when Hampshire were the visitors. The first two days attracted a total of 10,000 spectators. Except for occasional breaks, the ground has been regularly used for County Championship matches. In recent years limited-overs Sunday League matches have also been played here. Most of the Surrey matches on the ground have been staged with neighbouring counties Sussex and Hampshire. In recent seasons the Guildford Cricket Festival has been restricted to a single County Championship fixture and a single limited-overs National Cricket League fixture.

Other matches staged have included a one-day game between the Club Cricket Conference and the touring South Africans in 1947 when the two sides scored a total of 715 runs. In 1957 The Queen and Duke of Edinburgh attended a match with Hampshire and met both teams. In recent years the Woodbridge Road Ground has hosted England women's international fixtures.

Covering some 8 acres the ground is lush and green with trees around most of the perimeter. The busy Woodbridge Road runs along the east side of the tree-lined area. The London–Guildford railway train line borders the northern end of the ground. The only permanent buildings are the pavilion, the groundsman's stores and the scoreboard. Woodbridge Road is reputed to be one of the few level playing areas in the City of Guildford. The playing area is approximately 113 metres by 119 metres. The main scoreboard is in the north-west corner of the cricket field with a smaller secondary scoreboard close to the Surrey County Cricket Club Executive Club marquees in the south-east corner of the ground. The press room/radio commentary box is located in the pavilion and there is also a press tent. If required the TV camera/commentary box positions are on the balcony of the pavilion at the southern end of the ground and on a gantry high above the sightscreen at the Railway End.

GROUND RECORDS AND SCORES

FIRST-CLASS MATCHES

Highest innings total for county 528 for 9 dec v Nottinghamshire 1995
Highest innings total against county 475 for 8 dec by Nottinghamshire 1989
Lowest innings total for county 76 v Kent 1992
Lowest innings total against county 48 by Hampshire 1946
Highest individual innings for county 228* D.J. Bicknell v Nottinghamshire 1995
Highest individual innings against county 203* A.J. Moles for Warwickshire 1994
Highest wicket partnerships for county

1st	255 R.E.C. Pratt & M.J. Stewart	v	Cambridge University	1956
	(256 runs were added for this wicket, D.G.W. Fletcher (0*) retiring ill when the score was 1)			
2nd	185 A.R. Butcher & A.J. Stewart	v	Worcestershire	1983
3rd	205 J.H. Edrich & R.D.V. Knight	v	Gloucestershire	1978
4th	162 B. Constable & R.A.E. Tindall	v	Sussex	1961
5th	155 J.F. Parker & E.W. Whitfield	v	Hampshire	1938
6th	145* G.P. Howarth & D.J. Thomas	v	Glamorgan	1982
7th	113 A.J. McIntyre & J.C. Laker	v	Northamptonshire	1955
8th	173 B. Constable & J.C. Laker	v	Cambridge University	1949
9th	97 D.J. Bicknell & C.G. Rackemann	v	Nottinghamshire	1995
10th	91 G.J. Kersey & R.M. Pearson	v	Sussex	1996

Highest wicket partnerships against county

1st	161 D.S. Sheppard & K.P.A. Matthews	for	Cambridge University	1951
2nd	160 V.P. Terry & M.C.J. Nicholas	for	Hampshire	1988
3rd	190 D.A. Reeve & J.R.T. Barclay	for	Sussex	1984
4th	201 R.C. Ontong & J.A. Hopkins	for	Glamorgan	1982
5th	214 D.P. Ostler & T.L. Penny	for	Warwickshire	1992
6th	164 C.W.J. Athey & P. Moores	for	Sussex	1996
7th	148 J. Birkenshaw & B. Dudleston	for	Leicestershire	1969
8th	123 A.N. Aymes & S.J. Renshaw	for	Hampshire	1997
9th	110 G. Welch & D.R. Brown	for	Warwickshire	1994
10th	51 R.E. East & J.K. Lever	for	Essex	1968

Best bowling performance in an innings for county 9 for 47 M.P. Bicknell v Leicestershire 2000
Best bowling performance in an innings against county 7 for 34 D. Shackleton for Hampshire 1958
Best bowling performance in a match for county 16 for 119 M.P. Bicknell v Leicestershire 2000
Best bowling performance in a match against county 9 for 109 V.H.D. Cannings for Hampshire 1952
Largest crowd 7,000 v Hampshire 1938

LIMITED-OVERS MATCHES

Highest innings total for county 344 for 5 v Hampshire (SL) 1997
Highest innings total against county 306 for 2 by Northamptonshire (SL) 1985
Lowest innings total for county 89 v Gloucestershire (SL) 1978
Lowest innings total against county 133 by Gloucestershire (SL) 1980
Highest individual innings for county 203 A.D. Brown v Hampshire (SL) 1997
Highest individual innings against county 132* A.J. Lamb for Northamptonshire (SL) 1985
Highest wicket partnerships for county

1st	90 A. R. Butcher & G.S. Clinton	v	Nottinghamshire	(SL)	1985
	90 A.D. Brown & A.J. Stewart	v	Hampshire	(SL)	1997
2nd	145 D.B. Pauline & R.D.V. Knight	v	Worcestershire	(SL)	1983
3rd	110 A.D. Brown & D.M. Ward	v	Warwickshire	(SL)	1994
4th	139* D.M. Smith & T.E. Jesty	v	Northamptonshire	(SL)	1987
5th	46 G.R.J. Roope & T.M.G. Hansall	v	Northamptonshire	(SL)	1988
6th	80 B.C. Hollioake & I.J. Ward	v	Somerset	(SL)	1999
7th	37 A.J. Hollioake & B.P. Julian	v	Sussex	(SL)	1996
8th	46 Intikhab Alam & A. Long	v	Gloucestershire	(SL)	1970

9th	30* N.M. Kendrick & J. Boiling	v	Warwickshire	(SL)	1994
10th	39 G.G. Arnold & P.I. Pocock	v	Somerset	(SL)	1975

Highest wicket partnerships against county

1st	119 D.M. Green & R.B. Nicholls	for	Gloucestershire	(SL)	1970
2nd	176 W. Larkins & A.J. Lamb	for	Northamptonshire	(SL)	1985
3rd	170* M. B. Loye & M. E. Hussey	for	Northamptonshire	(SL)	2001
4th	98 Zaheer Abbas & J.C. Foat	for	Gloucestershire	(SL)	1978
5th	99 J.S. Laney & S.D. Udal	for	Hampshire	(SL)	1997
6th	137 M.P. Speight & I.D.K. Salisbury	for	Sussex	(SL)	1996
7th	51 T.G. Twose & G. Welch	for	Warwickshire	(SL)	1994
8th	61* R.G. Twose & K.J. Piper	for	Warwickshire	(SL)	1994
9th	26* P.C.L. Holloway & A.R. Caddick	for	Somerset	(SL)	1999
10th	21 P.W. Jarvis & J.D. Lewry	for	Sussex	(SL)	1996

Best bowling performance for county 5 for 44 A.J. Hollioake v Sussex (SL) 1996
Best bowling performance against county 5 for 28 A.C.S. Pigott for Sussex (SL) 1982
Largest crowd 6,000 v Warwickshire (SL) 1994

GROUND INFORMATION

ENTRANCES Wharf Road (players, officials, members and vehicles), Woodbridge Road (members, public and vehicles).
MEMBERS' ENCLOSURE Pavilion and pavilion terrace together with defined area between the pavilion and Woodbridge Road.
PUBLIC ENCLOSURE Rest of the ground.
COVERED STANDS Pavilion (part).
OPEN STANDS Temporary raised plastic/timber seating together with ground level seating surrounding the playing area.
NAME OF ENDS Pavilion End, Railway End.
GROUND DIMENSIONS 113m × 119m.
REPLAY SCREEN If the match is televised then a replay screen is sited at the Railway End of the ground.
FIRST AID Position available in the pavilion and a tent or caravan at Railway End of the ground.
CODES OF DRESS Spectators are required to dress in an appropriate manner consistent with attending a cricket match. Bare torsos are not acceptable in, or in front of the pavilion. Executive Club/Suite users must wear a necktie and jacket.
BEHAVIOUR The club is keen that standards of behaviour should be maintained and members and spectators are urged to report immediately to the CEO any incident, or potential incident, where they feel action should be taken. Bad language is not acceptable at any match and the club will take prompt and strong action should this or any other ground regulation be ignored.
RECIPROCAL ARRANGEMENTS Members of Surrey can gain entry into Sydney Cricket Ground (Australia) and Western Province Cricket Club at Newlands Cricket Ground in Cape Town (South Africa) with supporters from these two venues attending The AMP Oval on a reciprocal basis.
SUPPORTERS' CLUB Surrey CCC Supporters' Club membership £10 (SCCC members), £12 (non-SCCC members). Quarterly newsletter *Oval World*. Special rates for concessions and husband and wife membership are available. Contact Marcus Hook at Flat 1, 67 Birdhurst Rise, South Croydon, Surrey CR2 7EJ, email mdevious@netcomuk.co.uk.
JUNIORS Junior Lions membership is available to under 18s at £10 per year. Contact the Membership Department on ☎ 020 7820 5715, email membership@surreycricket.com for further information.
CORPORATE ENTERTAINING Temporary chalets at Railway End, contact John Armstrong at Guildford City Council on ☎ 01483 505050 for further details.
FACILITIES FOR VISUALLY IMPAIRED SPECTATORS Guide dogs allowed.
FACILITIES AND ACCESS FOR PEOPLE WITH DISABILITIES INCLUDING WHEELCHAIR ACCESS TO GROUND Yes, via Wharf Road and through main entrance to car park at Railway End of Woodbridge Road.
DESIGNATED CAR PARK AVAILABLE INSIDE THE GROUND FOR PEOPLE WITH DISABILITIES Yes, car park at Railway End of ground entered from Woodbridge Road.
GOOD VIEWING AREAS INSIDE THE GROUND FOR PEOPLE USING WHEELCHAIRS Yes, near the pavilion and on Woodbridge Road side of the ground.

DESIGNATED VIEWING AREAS FOR PEOPLE USING WHEELCHAIRS Yes, near the pavilion and on Woodbridge Road side of the ground.

RAMPS TO PROVIDE EASY ACCESS TO BARS & REFRESHMENT OUTLETS FOR PEOPLE USING WHEELCHAIRS Yes, although ramps are only available within the pavilion.

FOOD & DRINK FULL RESTAURANT/DINING FACILITIES Members, yes. Public, yes.

TEMPORARY FOOD/DRINK FACILITIES Members, yes. Public, yes.

FOOD SUITABLE FOR VEGETARIANS Members, yes. Public, yes.

BARS Members 1, Public 1.

VARIETIES OF BEER SOLD Hogs Back TEA Bitter, Fosters, Carling.

CHILDREN'S FACILITIES Crèche, no. Play area, no.

CLUB SHOP An Oval Shop marquee is located at the Railway End of the ground.

CLUB MUSEUM No.

CRICKET COACHING FACILITIES The Surrey County Cricket Centre is located 5 mins drive away at the George Abbott School.

CRICKET NETS Yes, contact Guildford CC.

OTHER SPORTING OR RECREATIONAL FACILITIES ON THE GROUND Hockey.

FACILITIES FOR HIRE OR WIDER COMMUNITY USE AT THE GROUND No.

WINTER CRICKET EVENTS No.

CAR PARKING FACILITIES Limited car parking available at Railway End of the ground entered from Woodbridge Road for members only. Otherwise use multi-storey car parks in the city centre a short distance away.

OTHER INFORMATION The Woodbridge Road ground is a short walk away from Guildford city centre. Dapdune Wharf, a National Trust property on the River Wey, is reached via the towpath to the rear of the main scoreboard. There is a tea room which also offers lunches.

GROUND CAPACITY 7,500.

ANTICIPATED GROUND DEVELOPMENTS None planned.

HOW TO GET THERE

 Both Guildford and Guildford London Road stations are 0.75 miles from the ground ☎ 0845 6000 0650, 08457 484950, www.swtrains.co.uk, www.thetrainline.com, www.railtrack.co.uk

 Green Line buses from surrounding areas to bus station thence 0.5 mile ☎ 01483 575226, Travel Line ☎ 0870 6082608

 There are cycle routes to this area of the city.

 From north: from M25 junction 10 take A3 (Portsmouth Road), take A320 (south) towards Guildford city centre (Stoke Road), at junction with A246 (York Road) turn right, at roundabout turn right into Woodbridge Road (A322), Wharf Road is the second turning on the left. **From south:** from A3100 (Portsmouth Road) or A281 (Horsham Road) continue into Guildford, follow signs to A322 round central Guildford (Bridge Street, Onslow Street) to roundabout at junction with A246 (York Road), then as for north. **From east:** as for north from M25 junction 10. **From west:** from A3 or A31, follow A3 to junction signposted to Guildford city centre, Cathedral and University, at roundabout take left lane into Guildford (Midleton Road), turn right at traffic lights into Woodbridge Road (A322), ground is on the right-hand side immediately after railway bridge.

 London Heathrow Airport ☎ 08700 000123 www.londonheathrowairport.co.uk, London Gatwick Airport ☎ 08700 002468 www.londongatwickairport/co.uk

WHERE TO STAY

Crawford House Hotel (☎ 01483 579299 www.crawfordhousehotel.com), Hampton (☎ 01483 572012 www.hamptonbedandbreakfastco.uk), Hillside Hotel (☎ 01483 232051 www.thehillsidehotel.com), Holiday Inn Guildford (☎ 0870 400 9036), Jarvis Guildford Hotel (☎ 01483 564511 www.jarvis.co.uk), Manor House Hotel (☎ 01483 222624 www.manorhouse-hotel.com), Plaegan House (☎ 01483 822181), Stoke House (☎ 01483 453025), The Angel Posting House & Livery (☎ 01483 564555 www.shl.com www.johansens.com), The Carlton Hotel (☎ 01483 303030 www.hotelengland.com)

For a further selection of numerous small hotels and guest houses in the Guildford area visit www.smoothhound.co.uk.

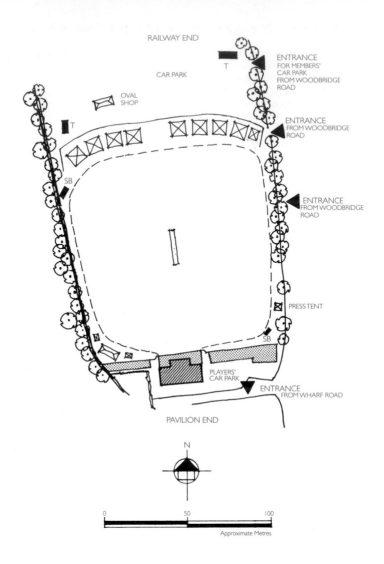

RAILWAY END

CAR PARK

T

OVAL
SHOP

ENTRANCE
FOR MEMBERS'
CAR PARK
FROM WOODBRIDGE
ROAD

ENTRANCE
FROM WOODBRIDGE
ROAD

T

SB

ENTRANCE
FROM WOODBRIDGE
ROAD

PRESS TENT

SB

PLAYERS'
CAR PARK

ENTRANCE
FROM WHARF ROAD

PAVILION END

N

0   50   100
Approximate Metres

WHERE TO EAT

Café de Paris (☎ 01483 534896), Cambio (☎ 01483 577702 www.cambiorestaurant.co.uk), Kinghams (☎ 01483 202168 www.kinghams-restaurant.co.uk), Rum Wong (☎ 01483 536092 www.rumwong.co.uk)

TOURIST INFORMATION Guildford Tourist Information Centre, 14 Tunsgate, Guildford, Surrey GU1 3QT. ☎ 01483 444333 www.guildfordborough.co.uk

LOCAL RADIO STATIONS BBC Southern Counties Radio (96.4 MHz FM/1476 KHz MW), Radio 2-Ten FM/Classic Gold (102.9 MHz FM/1431 KHz MW)

LOCAL NEWSPAPERS *Surrey Advertiser, Surrey Comet and Guardian Series*

WHITGIFT SCHOOL

Address Whitgift School, The Pavilion, North Field, Nottingham Road, Croydon, Surrey CR9 1AA
Prospects of Play ☎ 020 7582 6660

HISTORY OF GROUND AND FACILITIES

WHITGIFT SCHOOL WAS FOUNDED IN 1597 by John Whitgift, formerly of Trinity College, Cambridge, who became Archbishop of Canterbury in 1600. Cricket was first staged in Croydon in July 1707 when Croydon played London in an important match. Other games played in the town include Surrey v London in 1735, Caterham v Hambledon in 1767, Coulsdon & Caterham v XI of England in 1769 and Coulsdon v Sussex in 1775. No other matches are recorded as having been played until Surrey CCC travelled to Croydon to join the school's 400th anniversary celebrations on 9 August 2000 at the request of former Surrey cricketer David M. Ward, the cricket coach at the school.

At the end of the nineteenth century a number of fine cricketers were pupils at the school including V.F.S. Crawford who represented the Gentlemen in 1897 while still at the school, H.H.B. Hawkins (Cambridge University 1898–1900) and R.A. Sheppard (Surrey and Gentlemen). The most famous and without doubt the best cricketer to have represented the school is Raman Subba Row who was captain of the school 1st XI in 1950 before going up to Cambridge University. He went on to represent Cambridge University, Surrey, Northamptonshire and England as a fine top-order batsman. Now a much respected ICC match referee Raman Subba Row still lives locally and he is a frequent visitor to the school ground when Surrey matches are being staged here.

To date, four National Cricket League matches have been staged on the ground: against Warwickshire Bears in 2000 and 2001, and against Northamptonshire Steelbacks and Middlesex Crusaders in 2002.

The attractive pavilion, built in 1930, and main scoreboard are the only permanent cricket buildings on the ground. The rest of the facilities available during county matches are temporary.

The cricket ground is sited in a natural bowl beneath mature trees and within easy access of the main school building. The school has a splendid collection of rugby and cricket memorabilia on view in the main entrance hall. The school also has a rose named after it.

The players' pavilion.

GROUND RECORDS AND SCORES

LIMITED-OVERS MATCHES

Highest innings total for county 231 v Warwickshire (SL) 2001
Highest innings total against county 277 for 5 by Northamptonshire (SL) 2002
Lowest innings total for county 211 for 9 v Warwickshire (SL) 2001
Lowest innings total against county 108 by Warwickshire (SL) 2000, 108 by Warwickshire (SL) 2001
Highest individual innings for county 116 A.D. Brown v Warwickshire (SL) 2001
Highest individual innings against county 110 O. A. Shah for Middlesex (SL) 2002
Highest wicket partnerships for county

1st	89 D.M. Ward & S.A. Newman	v	Northamptonshire	(SL)	2002
2nd	43 A.J. Stewart & N. Shahid	v	Warwickshire	(SL)	2000
3rd	37 A.D. Brown & R. Clarke	v	Middlesex	(SL)	2002
4th	77 A.J. Stewart & A.D. Brown	v	Warwickshire	(SL)	2001
5th	64 A.D. Brown & B.C. Hollioake	v	Warwickshire	(SL)	2001
6th	56 A.D. Brown & G.J. Batty	v	Warwickshire	(SL)	2001
7th	24 J.N. Batty & Saqlain Mushtaq	v	Middlesex	(SL)	2002
8th	11 A.J. Tudor & M.P. Bicknell	v	Warwickshire	(SL)	2000
9th	13 M.P. Bicknell & I.D.K. Salisbury	v	Warwickshire	(SL)	2000
10th	22 P.J. Sampson & E.S.H. Giddins	v	Middlesex	(SL)	2002

Highest wicket partnerships against county

1st	55 M.E.K. Hussey & M.B. Loye	for	Northamptonshire	(SL)	2002
2nd	124 M.B. Loye & D.J.G Sales	for	Northamptonshire	(SL)	2002
3rd	90 A.J. Strauss & O.A. Shah	for	Middlesex	(SL)	2002
4th	44 O.A. Shah & E.C. Joyce	for	Middlesex	(SL)	2002
5th	54 O.A. Shah & P.N. Weekes	for	Middlesex	(SL)	2002
6th	12 T.L. Penney & A.F. Giles	for	Warwickshire	(SL)	2000
7th	5 A.F. Giles & N.M.K. Smith	for	Warwickshire	(SL)	2000
8th	35 A.F. Giles & K.J. Piper	for	Warwickshire	(SL)	2000
9th	13 T.L. Penney & M.A. Sheikh	for	Warwickshire	(SL)	2001
10th	0 C.E. Dagnall & A. Richardson	for	Warwickshire	(SL)	2001

Best bowling performance in a match for county 4 for 31 T.J. Murtagh v Warwickshire (SL) 2001
Best bowling performance in a match against county 4 for 56 D.R. Brown for Warwickshire (SL) 2001
Largest crowd 6,000 v Middlesex (SL) 2002

GROUND INFORMATION

ENTRANCES Nottingham Road (players, officials, press/media and members), Brighton Road (members and public, pedestrians only).
MEMBERS' ENCLOSURE Banked area between the pavilion and the southern end sightscreen.
PUBLIC ENCLOSURE Part of the banked area and the southern end of the ground.
COVERED STANDS None.
OPEN STANDS Entire ground with temporary plastic seats.
NAME OF ENDS North End, South End.
GROUND DIMENSIONS 132m × 105m.
REPLAY SCREEN If the match is televised the replay screen is sited at the North End of the ground.
FIRST AID Situated in tent near main school entrance.
CODES OF DRESS Spectators are required to dress in an appropriate manner consistent with attending a cricket match. Bare torsos are not acceptable in, or in front of the pavilion. Executive Club/Suite users must wear a necktie and jacket.
BEHAVIOUR The club is keen that standards of behaviour should be maintained and members and spectators are urged to report immediately to the CEO any incident, or potential incident, where they feel action should be taken. Bad language is not acceptable at any match and the club will take prompt and strong action should this or any other ground regulation be ignored.

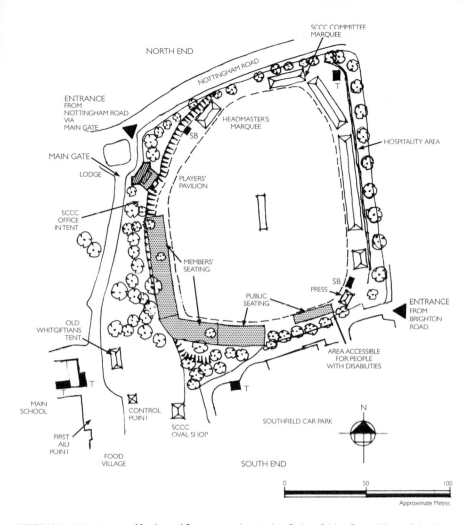

SCCC COMMITTEE MARQUEE

NORTH END

NOTTINGHAM ROAD

ENTRANCE FROM NOTTINGHAM ROAD VIA MAIN GATE

HEADMASTER'S MARQUEE

HOSPITALITY AREA

MAIN GATE

LODGE

SB

PLAYERS' PAVILION

SCCC OFFICE IN TENT

MEMBERS' SEATING

SB

PRESS

PUBLIC SEATING

ENTRANCE FROM BRIGHTON ROAD

OLD WHITGIFTIANS TENT

AREA ACCESSIBLE FOR PEOPLE WITH DISABILITIES

MAIN SCHOOL

CONTROL POINT

SCCC OVAL SHOP

SOUTHFIELD CAR PARK

N

FIRST AID POINT

FOOD VILLAGE

SOUTH END

0   50   100

Approximate Metres

RECIPROCAL ARRANGEMENTS Members of Surrey can gain entry into Sydney Cricket Ground (Australia) and Western Province Cricket Club at Newlands Cricket Ground in Cape Town (South Africa) with supporters from these two venues attending The AMP Oval on a reciprocal basis.

SUPPORTERS' CLUB Surrey CCC Supporters' Club membership £10 (SCCC members), £12 (non-SCCC members). Quarterly newsletter *Oval World*. Special rates for concessions and husband and wife membership are available. Contact Marcus Hook at Flat 1, 67 Birdhurst Rise, South Croydon, Surrey CR2 7EJ, email mdevious@netcomuk.co.uk.

JUNIORS Junior Lions membership is available to under 18s at £10 per year. Contact the Membership Department on ☎ 020 7820 5715, email membership@surreycricket.com for further information.

CORPORATE ENTERTAINING Temporary chalets at Brighton Road side of the ground, contact David Ward at Whitgift school on ☎ 020 8688 9222 for further details.

FACILITIES FOR VISUALLY IMPAIRED SPECTATORS Guide dogs allowed.

FACILITIES AND ACCESS FOR PEOPLE WITH DISABILITIES INCLUDING WHEELCHAIR ACCESS TO GROUND Yes, via Nottingham Road and Brighton Road.

DESIGNATED CAR PARK AVAILABLE INSIDE THE GROUND FOR PEOPLE WITH DISABILITIES Yes, car park near main school building entered from Nottingham Road.

GOOD VIEWING AREAS INSIDE THE GROUND FOR PEOPLE USING WHEELCHAIRS Yes, near sightscreen on raised timber plinths at South End of the ground.

DESIGNATED VIEWING AREAS FOR PEOPLE USING WHEELCHAIRS Yes, near sightscreen on raised timber plinths at South End of the ground.

RAMPS TO PROVIDE EASY ACCESS TO BARS & REFRESHMENT OUTLETS FOR PEOPLE USING WHEELCHAIRS Yes, into main school building otherwise only relative to defined area above.

FOOD & DRINK FULL RESTAURANT/DINING FACILITIES Members, yes. Public, yes.

TEMPORARY FOOD/DRINK FACILITIES Members, yes. Public, yes.

FOOD SUITABLE FOR VEGETARIANS Members, yes. Public, yes.

BARS Members 1, Public 1.

VARIETIES OF BEER SOLD Fosters, Carling.

CHILDREN'S FACILITIES Crèche, no. Play area, no.

CLUB SHOP The AMP Oval Shop is located at the Southern End in a marquee.

CLUB MUSEUM No, but collection of Raman Subba Row's cricket items is on display in the main school building.

CRICKET COACHING FACILITIES Yes, for school only.

CRICKET NETS Yes, for school only.

OTHER SPORTING OR RECREATIONAL FACILITIES ON THE GROUND Football.

FACILITIES FOR HIRE OR WIDER COMMUNITY USE AT THE GROUND No.

WINTER CRICKET EVENTS No.

CAR PARKING FACILITIES Limited car parking available near pavilion entered from Nottingham Road for players and officials only. Otherwise use car park in Southern Field a short distance walk away entered from Brighton Road or Nottingham Road.

GROUND CAPACITY 7,500.

ANTICIPATED GROUND DEVELOPMENTS None planned.

HOW TO GET THERE

 South Croydon station 0.5 mile ☎ 08457 484950, 0870 603 0405, www.connex.co.uk

 Buses from South Croydon station link with Nottingham Road ☎ 020 7222 1234

 There are cycle routes from surrounding areas of Croydon.

 From north: from The AMP Oval follow the A23 through Streatham and Thornton Heath to Purley (Purley Way), at Fiveways Corner take second exit into Denning Avenue (B275), follow this road into Warham Road, Nottingham Road is second turning on the right. **From south:** from M23 junction 8 stay on M23, after junction 7 continue on A23 (north), at Purley Cross follow signs to A235 (Brighton Road), Nottingham Road is approximately 2 miles further on the left hand side. **From east:** from M25 junction 7, follow M23 (north) then continue on A23 towards London, then as for south. **From west:** from M25 junction 7 as for east.

 London Gatwick ☎ 08700 002468 www.londongatwickairport.co.uk

WHERE TO STAY

Hayesthorpe Hotel (☎ 020 8688 8120), Alpine Hotel (☎ 020 8688 6116)
   Visit www.smoothhound.co.uk for details of other hotels, guesthouses and bed and breakfasts in and around Croydon.

WHERE TO EAT

Restaurants of various types in central Croydon within 15 minutes walk of ground.

TOURIST INFORMATION Croydon Tourist Information Centre www.croydon.gov.uk

LOCAL RADIO STATIONS BBC Southern Counties Radio (96.4 MHz FM/1476 KHz MW), Radio 2-Ten FM/Classic Gold (102.9 MHz FM/1431 KHz MW), BBC London Live (94.9 MHz FM/1458 KHz MW), Capital Gold (95.8 MHz/1548 KHz MW), LBC (97.3 MHz FM/1152 KHz MW), LBC 1152AM

LOCAL NEWSPAPERS *Evening Standard, London Metro, South London Press, Croydon Advertiser, Surrey Comet and Guardian* series, *Surrey Mirror*

play-cricket com

THE source of all information on Club Cricket.

Whether you are a player, supporter, coach, or official involved in club cricket, you should visit and register with www.play-cricket.com, the official ECB Club Cricket Network.

Play-Cricket provides all clubs with a free cricket administration system to enable clubs to:

- Manage fixtures, results and scorecards
- Assist with team selection and logistics
- Communicate with club members and promote and create their own club website.

For players and statisticians you can view all results and scorecards and even analyse your own personal performance against other players.

The online network already hosts over 1500 clubs and 150 leagues; the basic systems are free and require no technical knowledge to run. Save time and money for your club and ensure you always have access to the latest information on all aspects of the club game.

It's time to get online! Visit **www.play-cricket.com** and register today.

The **official** Club Cricket Network.

A successful opening partnership

For more details of C&G's mortgage and investment service call free on 0800 731 8500 or visit our website www.cheltglos.co.uk

C&G Cheltenham & Gloucester

TROPHY

CRICKET'S PREMIER ONE-DAY KNOCKOUT COMPETITION

Cheltenham & Gloucester Trophy 2003

(50 overs each side)

ECB

C&G Cheltenham & Gloucester
TROPHY

Wed	7	May	C&G Trophy Round 3		
			Bedfordshire	v Warwickshire	Luton
			Durham CB	v Glamorgan	Darlington
			Buckinghamshire	v Gloucestershire	Ascott Park, Wing
			Cambridgeshire	v Yorkshire	March
			Essex CB	v Essex	Chelmsford
			Kent CB	v Derbyshire	Canterbury
			Worcestershire CB	v Worcestershire	New Road
			Berkshire	v Durham	Reading
			Lincolnshire	v Nottinghamshire	Lincoln Lindum
			Cornwall	v Kent	Truro
			Staffordshire	v Surrey	Stone
			Scotland	v Somerset	The Grange
			Devon	v Lancashire	Exmouth
			Northumberland	v Leicestershire	Jesmond
			Northamptonshire	v Middlesex	Northampton **SKY**
			Hampshire	v Sussex	Rose Bowl
Wed	28	May	Round 4		**SKY**
Tue	10	June	Quarter-finals		**SKY**
Wed	11	June	Quarter-finals		**SKY**
Thur	7	Aug	Semi-final		**4**
Sat	9	Aug	Semi-final		**4**
Sat	30	Aug	Final	Lord's	**4**

Thur	28	Aug*	2004 Qualification (Round 1)		
			Scotland	v Cumberland	TBC
			Dorset	v Buckinghamshire	TBC
			Bedfordshire	v Cheshire	TBC
			Devon	v Suffolk	TBC
			Shropshire	v Northumberland	TBC
			Holland	v Cornwall	TBC
			Norfolk	v Lincolnshire	TBC
			Wales	v Denmark	TBC
			Oxfordshire	v Herefordshire	TBC
			Hertfordshire	v Ireland	TBC

(Fri 29 Aug reserve day)

*2004 Qualification round 1 matches can be played on Sun 31 Aug
(reserve day mon 1 Sept) if teams agree

4 Televised by Channel 4.   **SKY** Televised by Sky Sports

ENGLAND AND WALES CRICKET BOARD
Developing cricket from playground to Test arena
www.ecb.co.uk

Twenty20 Cup 2003

(20 overs each side, coloured clothing)

The Twenty20 Cup is ECB's newest domestic cricket competition. It has been introduced this year to replace the long standing 50-overs per side Benson & Hedges Cup.

The format of the Twenty20 Cup, as its name suggests, is 20-overs per side with just 15 minutes for the interval. This shortened format and the fact that matches will be played predominantly on midweek evenings after school and work, are the main reasons for its introduction.

There are many demands on people's leisure time and cricket does not currently attract sufficient women, children or young adults to County matches in particular. Extensive research has shown that these groups of people will find this form of the game attractive.

Although cricket will remain the centre-piece of the Twenty20 Cup we will be looking to create an all-round entertainment filled social event which will include music, Roadshows, children's activities etc.

Below is a brief summary of the format and playing conditions and opposite are the fixtures for 2003.

Format

Each team will play five zonal matches with either two or three of these being home matches. Matches are to be played between 13th and 24th June. The zonal groups are as follows:

NORTH	MID/WALES/WEST	SOUTH
Durham	Northamptonshire	Essex
Lancashire	Warwickshire	Middlesex
Yorkshire	Worcestershire	Surrey
Derbyshire	Glamorgan	Kent
Nottinghamshire	Gloucestershire	Hampshire
Leicestershire	Somerset	Sussex

The top teams from each group and the best second-placed team will progress to finals day on Saturday 19 July. Both semi-finals and the final will be played on that day. Zonal matches have no reserve days, finals day has one reserve day.

ECB

Fri	13	June	Durham	v Nottinghamshire	Riverside	
Sat	14	June	Yorkshire	v Derbyshire	Headingley	4
Mon	16	June	Leicestershire	v Yorkshire	Grace Road	
Mon	16	June	Nottinghamshire	v Lancashire	Trent Bridge	
Wed	18	June	Durham	v Leicestershire	Riverside	
Thur	19	June	Derbyshire	v Nottinghamshire	Derby	
Thur	19	June	Lancashire	v Yorkshire	Old Trafford	SKY
Fri	20	June	Leicestershire	v Lancashire	Grace Road	
Fri	20	June	Yorkshire	v Durham	Headingley	
Sat	21	June	Lancashire	v Derbyshire	Old Trafford	
Sat	21	June	Nottinghamshire	v Leicestershire	Trent Bridge	
Mon	23	June	Derbyshire	v Durham	Derby	
Tue	24	June	Lancashire	v Durham	Old Trafford	
Tue	24	June	Leicestershire	v Derbyshire	Grace Road	
Tue	24	June	Yorkshire	v Nottinghamshire	Headingley	SKY

NORTH

Fri	13	June	Hampshire	v Sussex	Rose Bowl	SKY
Fri	13	June	Surrey	v Middlesex	AMP Oval	
Sat	14	June	Surrey	v Essex	TBC	
Mon	16	June	Kent	v Hampshire	Beckenham	
Mon	16	June	Surrey	v Sussex	TBC	
Wed	18	June	Hampshire	v Essex	Rose Bowl	
Wed	18	June	Sussex	v Middlesex	Hove	
Thur	19	June	Middlesex	v Kent	Richmond	
Fri	20	June	Essex	v Kent	Chelmsford	
Sat	21	June	Sussex	v Essex	Hove	
Mon	23	June	Middlesex	v Hampshire	TBC	
Mon	23	June	Kent	v Surrey	Canterbury	SKY
Tue	24	June	Essex	v Middlesex	Chelmsford	
Tue	24	June	Hampshire	v Surrey	Rose Bowl	
Tue	24	June	Sussex	v Kent	Hove	

SOUTH

Fri	13	June	Somerset	v Warwickshire	Taunton	
Fri	13	June	Worcestershire	v Northamptonshire	New Road	
Mon	16	June	Glamorgan	v Northamptonshire	Sophia Gardens	SKY
Mon	16	June	Gloucestershire	v Worcestershire	Bristol	
Wed	18	June	Glamorgan	v Somerset	Sophia Gardens	
Wed	18	June	Worcestershire	v Warwickshire	New Road	SKY
Thur	19	June	Gloucestershire	v Northamptonshire	Bristol	
Fri	20	June	Northamptonshire	v Somerset	Northampton	
Fri	20	June	Warwickshire	v Glamorgan	Edgbaston	
Sat	21	June	Somerset	v Gloucestershire	Taunton	SKY
Mon	23	June	Glamorgan	v Worcestershire	Sophia Gardens	
Mon	23	June	Warwickshire	v Gloucestershire	Edgbaston	
Tue	24	June	Gloucestershire	v Glamorgan	Bristol	
Tue	24	June	Northamptonshire	v Warwickshire	Northampton	
Tue	24	June	Worcestershire	v Somerset	New Road	

MID / WALES / WEST

Sat	19	July	Semi-Finals		Venue tbc	
Sat	19	July	Final		Venue tbc	SKY

© Floodlit match   4 Televised by Channel 4   **SKY** Televised by Sky Sports   Broadcast by BBC Radio Five Live

ENGLAND AND WALES CRICKET BOARD
Developing cricket from playground to Test arena

www.ecb.co.uk

As part of our commitment to developing kids cricket, npower supports the ECB initiative to get every boy and girl learning, watching, playing and enjoying cricket.

Transfer your gas or electricity to npower and we'll make a donation to your favourite county cricket club for the development of youth cricket in England and Wales.

Call us today on
0808 180 0808

Take the
npower Test

npower®

Developing cricket from playground to Test arena

ECB

DISTRICT CRICKET

CLUB CRICKET

SECONDARY SCHOOLS CRICKET

PRIMARY SCHOOLS CRICKET

ENGLAND AND WALES CRICKET BOARD
Developing cricket from playground to Test arena
www.ecb.co.uk

Sussex

Hove
Arundel
Eastbourne
Hastings
Horsham

SUSSEX COUNTY CRICKET CLUB, COUNTY CRICKET GROUND, EATON ROAD, HOVE, EAST SUSSEX BN3 3AN

Switchboard	01273 827100 **fax** 01273 771549
Membership	01273 827133
Scores & Prospects of Play	01273 827145
Development	01273 827115
Commercial	01273 827102
Press Office	01273 827103
Catering	01273 827143
Indoor Cricket Nets	01273 827135
Pro Cricket Department	01273 827105
Email	info@sussexcricket.co.uk
Website	www.sussexcricket.co.uk

Founded 1 March 1839

Colours dark blue, light blue and gold

Crest shield with six martlets

National Cricket League Nickname Sharks

National Cricket League Colours black with red trim

Patron The Duke of Richmond and Gordon FCA

President The Right Reverend Lord D.S. Sheppard

Chairman D.E. Green

Chairman Cricket Committee J.R.T. Barclay

Chief Executive H.H. Griffiths

Director of Cricket P. Moores

Corporate Development Manager I.C. Waring

Marketing Manager N.J. Lenham

Development Director S.H. Peyman

Acting Finance Manager A. Alcott

Head Groundsman D.J. Traill

Club Coach M.A. Robinson

ECB Academy Director K. Greenfield

County Youth Manager C.E. Waller

Media Relations Officer Miss F. Watson

Membership Secretary Miss P.A. Carr

Cricket Development Officers A.C. Winstone, N.J. Wilton

Indoor School Manager C.G. Pickett

Retail Manager R.J. Petrides

Pro Cricket Administrator S.J. Dyke

Marketing Administrator Miss J. Bayford

Maintenance Technician J. Mitchell

Deputy Head Groundsman L.J. Gosling

Groundstaff J.P. Marchant

Physiotherapist S. Osborne Grad.Dip.Phys, MCSP, SRP

1st XI Scorer J. Hartridge

2nd XI Scorer M.J. Charman

Hon Librarian R. Boddie

Hon Treasurer D.J. Stoner FCA

Hon Medical Officer Dr P. Forsdick

Hon Dental Surgeon M.J. Sharpe, LDS, RCS

Statisticians R. Packham (First Class), N. Beck (One Day)

Sponsors Pav i.t. services

Yearbook £10

Scorecard 50p

National Cricket League Programme & Scorecard £2

Magazine/Newsletter *Hove and Away* issued twice yearly free to Members

Frizzell County Championship Status Division 1

National Cricket League Status Division 2

ACHIEVEMENTS

County Championship Champions Division 2 2001, 2nd 1902, 1903, 1932, 1933, 1934, 1953, 1981

Gillette Cup Winners 1963, 1964, 1978, Finalists 1968, 1970, 1973

NatWest Trophy Winners 1986, Finalists 1993

Benson and Hedges Cup Semi-finalists 1982, 1999

John Player Sunday League Champions 1982

Refuge Assurance Sunday League 13th 1989, 1990, 1991

Norwich Union National League Division 1 9th 2000

National Cricket League Champions Division 2 1999

Tilcon Trophy Winners 1979

Seeboard Trophy Winners 1989, 1991, Semi-finalists 1990

SUSSEX CRICKET BOARD

Chairman J.R.T. Barclay
Secretary M. Beckwith
Treasurer The Revd K. Jeffrey
Cricket Development Officer N.J. Wilton
Women & Girls Secretary J. Russell

Address Sussex Cricket Board, County Cricket Ground, Eaton Road, Hove, East Sussex BN3 3AN
☎ 01273 827105
Fax 01273 771549

GROUNDS

Hove (County Ground, Eaton Road), Horsham (Horsham CC, Cricketfield Road), Eastbourne (Eastbourne Saffrons Sports Club, The Saffrons), Hastings (Horntye Park, St Leonards-on-Sea) and Arundel Castle (The Friends of Arundel Castle CC, Arundel Castle, Castle Park)

   Other grounds used since 1969: Pagham (Pagham CC, Nyetimber Lane, Pagham) and Hastings (Central Cricket Ground, Priory Meadow)

SECOND XI GROUNDS

Stirlands CC, Church Lane, Main Road, Birdham, Chichester ☎ 01243 514124
Worthing CC, Manor Ground, Broadwater Road, Worthing ☎ 01903 238329

The Tate Gates at the main entrance to the ground in Eaton Road, Hove.

HOVE

Address County Cricket Ground, Eaton Road, Hove, East Sussex BN3 3AN
Prospects of Play ☎ 01273 827145

HISTORY OF GROUND AND FACILITIES

EATON ROAD has been the headquarters of Sussex cricket since 1872. Previously the club played on the Royal Brunswick cricket ground, which opened in 1848. This area is now Fourth Avenue. The Royal Brunswick land was leased in 1858 to Tom Box, the wicket-keeper, who also managed the local hotel, but in 1863 the lease was transferred to Sussex County Cricket Club, providing it with its own ground for the first time. The last important match was played there in August 1871. When the club moved to Eaton Road, the Brunswick turf was removed, transported and relaid at the new headquarters.

The first first-class match staged here by Sussex was against Gloucestershire in June 1872 and county matches have been played at Eaton Road ever since. Today Sussex play most of their matches at Hove, but games are also staged at Eastbourne, Horsham, Hastings (at two different venues) and, since 1990, at Arundel.

Plaque commemorating the centenary of Sussex CCC in 1972. It is next to the Tate Gates.

The pavilion was built in the 1880s, with additions in 1921, and major refurbishment and extension in 1933; the upper pavilion was reconstructed in 1961. The Gilligan Stand was opened in 1971 and currently hosts a council-run Child Study Support Centre. The main scoreboard, which dates from the 1930s, was paid for by the Harmsworth family. The clock tower was dedicated to the memory of Umer Rashid in April 2003. He tragically died with his brother Burhan on the squad's pre-season tour of Grenada in April 2002. The squash rackets club to the north-west of the playing area and the Cox Memorial Garden were demolished in 2001/2 and have been replaced by a totally new facility including the players' dressing rooms, indoor cricket nets and improved facilities for the Sussex/ECB Academy. The new building was opened by Jim Parks on 17 January 2003.

Pavilion and Members' enclosure viewed from the Cromwell Road End.

The club was bequeathed £4 million by past President, Spen Cama. This money is being spent wisely on upgrading existing facilities and improving the ground generally.

The ball can be lost against the stands or flats which surround the ground on three sides and the sea mist or 'fret' at Hove can provide quickly changing conditions for the seafront is only a short walk away.

Sussex was the home of William Lillywhite, James Dean and John Wisden, founder of the *Wisden Cricketers' Almanack*.

The chalet behind the Sussex Cricketer pub houses the Sussex CCC shop and John Newbery Limited's cricket bat workshop and sales office. The TV camera and commentary position and radio commentary boxes are located in the Arthur Gilligan Stand.

The playing area is 130 metres by 150 metres and is defined by a rope and advertising boards. The pitch slopes towards the Sea End and there is also a plastic wicket within the square for practice use. In 1998 Hove became the first English county ground to install permanent floodlights.

Sussex is the oldest county cricket club and there is much cricket memorabilia in the pavilion and in the club library, which is currently housed in temporary buildings at the Sea End of the ground under the stewardship of Rob Boddie.

Many great players have played at Hove including Prince Ranjitsinhji, C.B. Fry, K.S. Duleepsinhji, M.W. Tate, the Gilligans and the Langridges. Ted Alletson, playing for Nottinghamshire in 1911, threatened the ground with demolition with 189 in 90 minutes, the last 142 coming in 40 minutes after lunch. Alletson hit Killick for 34 in one over and this record was not beaten until Gary Sobers scored 36 off Malcolm Nash at Swansea in 1968.

In 1999 Sussex hosted one Cricket World Cup match between South Africa and India which was attended by a crowd of 6,216.

GROUND RECORDS AND SCORES

FIRST-CLASS MATCHES

Highest innings total for county 670 for 9 dec v Northamptonshire 1921
Highest innings total against county 703 for 9 dec by Cambridge University 1890
Lowest innings total for county 19 v Nottinghamshire 1873
Lowest innings total against county 23 by Kent 1859
Highest individual innings for county 333 K.S. Duleepsinghji v Northamptonshire 1930
Highest individual innings against county 322 E. Paynter for Lancashire 1937
Highest wicket partnerships for county

1st	490 E.H. Bowley & J.G. Langridge	v	Middlesex	1933
2nd	385 E.H. Bowley & M.W. Tate	v	Northamptonshire	1921
3rd	298 K.S. Ranjitsinghji & E.H. Killick	v	Lancashire	1901
4th	303* A.P. Wells & C.M. Wells	v	Kent	1987
5th	246 K.S. Ranjitsinghji & A. Collins	v	Kent	1900
6th	255 K.S. Duleepsinghji & M.W. Tate	v	Northamptonshire	1930
7th	184 I.J. Gould & A.C.S. Pigott	v	Hampshire	1989
8th	229* C.L.A. Smith & G. Brann	v	Kent	1902
9th	138 J. Vine & F.W. Tate	v	Nottinghamshire	1901
10th	130 G.R. Cox & G.A. Stannard	v	Essex	1919

Highest wicket partnerships against county

1st 3	55 A.F. Rae & J.B. Stollmeyer	for	West Indians	1950
2nd	306 F.B. Watson & G.E. Tyldesley	for	Lancashire	1928
3rd	301 E.T. Killick & E.H. Hendren	for	Middlesex	1928
4th	261 M.L. Hayden & J.L. Langer	for	Young Australians	1995
5th	275 M.A. Noble & J. Darling	for	Australians	1905
6th	428 M.A. Noble & W.W. Armstrong	for	Australians	1902
7th	289 D.R. Brown & A.F. Giles	for	Warwickshire	2000
8th	136 P.J.P. Burge & F.M. Misson	for	Australians	1961
9th	183 C.J. Tavare & N.A. Mallender	for	Somerset	1990
10th	177 J.H. Naumann & A.E.R. Gilligan	for	Cambridge University	1919

Best bowling performance in an innings for county 9 for 35 J.E.B.B.P.Q.C. Dwyer v Derbyshire 1906
Best bowling performance in an innings against county 9 for 11 A.P. Freeman for Kent 1922
Best bowling performance in a match for county 16 for 100 J.E.B.B.P.Q.C. Dwyer v Derbyshire 1906
Best bowling performance in a match against county 17 for 67 A.P. Freeman for Kent 1922
Largest crowd 14,500 v Australians 1948

LIMITED-OVERS MATCHES

Highest innings total for county 323 for 8 v Surrey (C&G) 2002
Highest innings total against county 337 for 3 by Surrey (C&G) 2002
Lowest innings total for county 59 v Glamorgan (SL) 1996
Lowest innings total against county 39 by Ireland (NWT) 1985
Highest individual innings for county 141* G.D. Mendis v Warwickshire (GC) 1980
Highest individual innings against county 198* G.A. Gooch for Essex (B&H) 1982
Highest wicket partnerships for county

1st	248 D.M. Smith & C.W.J. Athey	v	Hampshire	(NWT)	1993
2nd	189 P.W.G. Parker & C.M. Wells	v	Warwickshire	(SL)	1983
3rd	208 N.R. Taylor & M. Newell	v	Gloucestershire	(B&H)	1997
4th	154 P.W.G. Parker & C.M. Wells	v	Ireland	(NWT)	1985
5th	141 B. Zuiderent & W.J. House	v	Lancashire	(SL)	2000
6th	108* P.J. Graves & Imran Khan	v	Warwickshire	(SL)	1977
7th	107 A.P. Wells & N.J. Lenham	v	Glamorgan	(NWT)	1993
8th	84* K.J. Innes & M.J.G. Davis	v	Surrey	(SL)	2002
9th	56 V.C. Drakes & P.W. Jarvis	v	Yorkshire	(NWT)	1996
10th	46 P.W. Jarvis & J.D. Lewry	v	Surrey	(B&H)	1996

Highest wicket partnerships against county

1st	221 C.G. Greenidge & V.P. Terry	for	Hampshire	(SL)	1985
2nd	188 P.M. Roebuck & M.D. Crowe	for	Somerset	(NWT)	1984
3rd	268* G.A. Gooch & K.W.R. Fletcher	for	Essex	(B&H)	1982
4th	157 A.J. Lamb & P. Willey	for	Northamptonshire	(GC)	1979
5th	145 R.J. Harden & K.A. Parsons	for	Somerset	(SL)	1996
6th	178 J.P. Crawley & I.D. Austin	for	Lancashire	(NWT)	1997
7th	81* S.E. Leary & G.W. Johnson	for	Kent	(SL)	1970
8th	81 S.D. Thomas & Waqar Younis	for	Glamorgan	(B&H)	1998
9th	53 M.V. Fleming & A.P. Igglesden	for	Kent	(SL)	1981
10th	37 D.L. Bowett & A.M. Shimmons	for	Shropshire	(NWT)	1997

Best bowling performance in a match for county 6 for 14 M.A. Buss v Lancashire (SL) 1983
Best bowling performance in a match against county 8 for 21 M.A. Holding for Derbyshire (NWT) 1988
Largest crowd 6,000 v Middlesex (GC) 1980

ONE-DAY INTERNATIONALS

Highest innings total in ODI 254 for 6 by South Africa v India (WC) 1999
Lowest innings total in ODI 253 for 5 by India v South Africa (WC) 1999
Highest individual innings in ODI 97 S.C. Ganguly for India v South Africa (WC) 1999
Highest wicket partnerships in ODI

1st	67 S.C. Ganguly & S.R. Tendulkar	for	India v South Africa	(WC)	1999
2nd	130 R.S. Dravid & S.C. Ganguly	for	India v South Africa	(WC)	1999
3rd	46 M.V. Boucher & J.H. Kallis	for	South Africa v India	(WC)	1999
4th	48 D.J. Cullinan & J.H. Kallis	for	South Africa v India	(WC)	1999
5th	64 W.J. Cronje & J.H. Kallis	for	South Africa v India	(WC)	1999
6th	47 J.H. Kallis & J.N. Rhodes	for	South Africa v India	(WC)	1999
7th	27* J.N. Rhodes & L. Klusener	for	South Africa v India	(WC)	1999

8th to 10th yet to be established.
Best bowling performance in ODI 3 for 66 L. Klusener for South Africa v India (WC) 1999
Largest crowd 6,216 India v South Africa (WC) 1999

GROUND INFORMATION

ENTRANCES Eaton Road via Tate Gates (players, officials, Members, public and vehicles), Palmeira Avenue via North-East Gate (Members, public and vehicles).
MEMBERS' ENCLOSURE Pavilion, pavilion terrace, Wilbury Stand and defined area under trees Cromwell Road End sightscreen.
PUBLIC ENCLOSURE Rest of the ground.
COVERED STANDS Pavilion (part), Wilbury Stand and East Stand (part).
OPEN STANDS Pavilion (part), Arthur Gilligan Stand and East Stand (part) together with permanent and temporary raised and ground-level seating, including deckchairs, surrounding the playing area.
NAME OF ENDS Sea End, Cromwell Road End.
GROUND DIMENSIONS 130m × 150m.
REPLAY SCREEN If televised matches are staged at the ground the replay screen is sited at the Cromwell Road End of the ground.
FIRST AID St John Ambulance First Aid caravan located within the disabled car parking area at the Cromwell Road End of the ground near the North-East Gate.
CODES OF DRESS Spectators are required to dress in an appropriate manner consistent with attending a cricket match. Bare torsos are not acceptable in, or in front of the pavilion. This area includes the Jim Parks Bar, the Dexter Room, pavilion seating and benches and deck chairs from the pavilion to the Cromwell Road End sightscreen. Executive Club/Suite users must wear a necktie and jacket.
BEHAVIOUR The club is keen that standards of behaviour should be maintained and Members and spectators are urged to report immediately to the CEO any incident, or potential incident, where they feel action should be taken. Bad language is not acceptable at any match and the club will take prompt and strong action should this

or any other ground regulation be ignored. Mobile telephones are not permitted, please ensure that mobile telephones are switched off before entering the spectator areas of the ground.

RECIPROCAL ARRANGEMENTS Members of Essex, Hampshire and Kent free except when Sussex are playing their own county. Sussex CCC Members can also gain free or reduced admission to race events on reciprocal dates at Plumpton, Fontwell Park, Goodwood and Brighton racecourses and Hickstead showgrounds.

SUPPORTERS' CLUB Sussex County Cricket Supporters' Club: subscription £4 (adults), £2 (senior citizens and under-16s) per annum. Regular newsletters are issued throughout the year. Membership details and information about events can be obtained from SCCSC, Freepost, County Ground, Eaton Road, Hove BN3 3AN.

JUNIORS Membership for those aged up to 16 on 1 January is £10 per annum. Contact Membership Department ☎ 01273 827133 for full details.

CORPORATE ENTERTAINING Executive Membership is available and includes use of hospitality boxes and marquees. Facilities available for conferences, lunches, dinners, wedding receptions throughout the year. Contact Commercial Department for details and a brochure ☎ 01273 827101.

FACILITIES FOR VISUALLY IMPAIRED SPECTATORS Reduced admission, group bookings only accepted and guide dogs allowed. Dogs or any other animals are not allowed to be taken into the Jim Parks Bar, the Dexter Room, the Wilbury Bar or any places on the ground where food or drinks are served. The club reserves the right to ask dog owners to remove animals from the spectating areas.

FACILITIES AND ACCESS FOR PEOPLE WITH DISABILITIES INCLUDING WHEELCHAIR ACCESS TO GROUND Yes, via Tate Gate and North-East Gate.

DESIGNATED CAR PARK AVAILABLE INSIDE THE GROUND FOR PEOPLE WITH DISABILITIES Car parking is available within the ground for 15 vehicles with disabled stickers whose occupants have serious mobility problems or use wheelchairs. Otherwise vehicles are parked on the grass area at the Cromwell Road End of the ground.

GOOD VIEWING AREAS INSIDE THE GROUND FOR PEOPLE USING WHEELCHAIRS Special area plus car parking spaces opposite main pavilion, north of main scoreboard with entrance from Palmeira Avenue via North-East Gate.

RAMPS TO PROVIDE EASY ACCESS TO BARS & REFRESHMENT OUTLETS FOR PEOPLE USING WHEELCHAIRS Yes, special area opposite pavilion, to the north of the main scoreboard.

FOOD & DRINK FULL RESTAURANT/DINING FACILITIES Members, yes. Public, yes. Members' Pavilion offers full meals, bar snacks, coffee and tea. Jim Parks Bar offers drinks including tea, coffee and bar snacks. Dexter Room in pavilion offers a full English breakfast at £4.50 from 9.30 a.m. and also full meals. Bookings can be made in advance with the Catering Office ☎ 01273 827143. Catering at the County Cricket Ground is offered by Kings Cuisine ☎ 01273 744038 or 01273 827143.

TEMPORARY FOOD/DRINK FACILITIES Members, yes. Public, yes.

FOOD SUITABLE FOR VEGETARIANS Members, yes. Public, yes.

BARS Members 1 (Jim Parks Bar), Public 2.

VARIETIES OF BEER SOLD Shepherd Neame.

CHILDREN'S FACILITIES Crèche, no. Play area, yes, for certain matches.

CLUB SHOP Sussex CCC shop is situated in the chalet building behind the Sussex Cricketer pub and sells cricket books, items of Sussex memorabilia and clothing. The shop is open throughout the year and mail order brochures are available ☎ 01273 827127 www.sussexcricket.co.uk, opening times 10 a.m. to 6 p.m. Tuesday to Friday, 10 a.m. to 1 p.m. Saturday non-match days. Open throughout play on match days.

CLUB MUSEUM No, but there are many pictures in the pavilion. For further information regarding exhibitions and the Sussex Collection contact Rob Boddie, the Hon Librarian, at the club ☎ 01273 827112/7. Back copies of scorecards and programmes can be obtained direct from Librarian at cost. Please send a stamped addressed envelope.

CRICKET COACHING FACILITIES Yes, available throughout the year in the Indoor Cricket School. Contact Sussex CCC Development Office for details ☎ 01273 827135 or speak direct to Coach Co-ordinator David Lewry ☎ 01903 767319.

CRICKET NETS Yes, available throughout the year in the Indoor Cricket School. Contact Sussex CCC for details.

FACILITIES FOR HIRE OR WIDER COMMUNITY USE AT THE GROUND Dining and conference facilities throughout the year. Contact Neil Lenham on 01273 827101 for full details and a copy of the Corporate Brochure.

WINTER CRICKET EVENTS The Sussex Cricket Society meet for lunches between November and February and have meetings in October, December, January and March. Membership is £5 (single) and £7.50 (family),

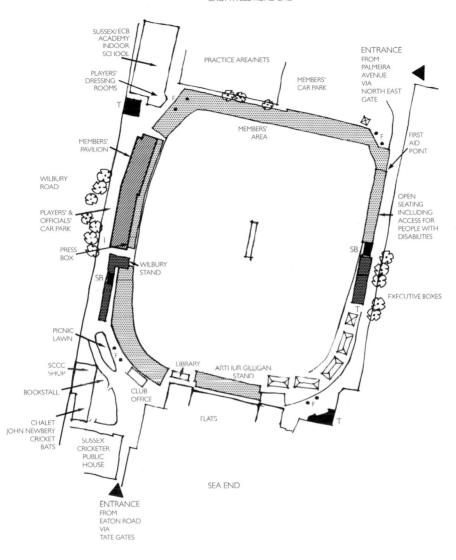

CROMWELL ROAD END

SUSSEX/ECB
ACADEMY
INDOOR
SCHOOL

PRACTICE AREA/NETS

ENTRANCE
FROM
PALMEIRA
AVENUE
VIA
NORTH EAST
GATE

PLAYERS'
DRESSING
ROOMS

MEMBERS'
CAR PARK

MEMBERS'
AREA

FIRST
AID
POINT

MEMBERS'
PAVILION

WILBURY
ROAD

PLAYERS' &
OFFICIALS'
CAR PARK

OPEN
SEATING
INCLUDING
ACCESS FOR
PEOPLE WITH
DISABILITIES

PRESS
BOX

WILBURY
STAND

EXECUTIVE BOXES

PICNIC
LAWN

LIBRARY

ARTHUR GILLIGAN
STAND

SCCC
SHOP

BOOKSTALL

CLUB
OFFICE

FLATS

CHALET
JOHN NEWBERY
CRICKET
BATS

SUSSEX
CRICKETER
PUBLIC
HOUSE

SEA END

ENTRANCE
FROM
EATON ROAD
VIA
TATE GATES

N

0   50   100
Approximate Metres

contact Pauline Brabyn, 4 Wolstonbury Walk, Shoreham-by-Sea, East Sussex BN43 5GU or www.sussexcs.cricket.org for full details. In November the club hosts a Cricket Book Fair which is now in its fifth year. Contact Neil Beck at Ivymead, Castle Road, Pevensey, East Sussex BN24 5LG for details.

CAR PARKING FACILITIES Car parking is available within the ground for players, officials and some Members at £5 per car subject to space being available. Cars are brought into the ground at the owner's risk. There is car parking in neighbouring streets at £2 from 10 a.m. to 8 p.m. daily although space is limited. Other car parking is available a short distance walk away from the ground at Hove station car park £2.50 per day, Hove Town Hall multi-storey car park £1.40 per day. Wilbury Road (north of Eaton Road), Cromwell Road (east of The Drive) and Palmeira Avenue have no parking restrictions.

OTHER INFORMATION The club has its own pub adjoining the ground at the Sea End – Sussex Cricketer. **GROUND CAPACITY** 6,500.

ANTICIPATED GROUND DEVELOPMENTS Development at the Sea End including a public pavilion and hospitality boxes to replace the Gilligan Indoor School and Stand.

HOW TO GET THERE

Hove station 0.5 mile, Brighton (Thameslink) station 1 mile ☎ 08457 484950, www.connex.co.uk, www.railtrack.co.uk, www.thetrainline.co.uk, www.thameslink.co.uk

Brighton & Hove Metro Line Bus 6, 6A, 7, 7A from Brighton station link with Hove station to Cromwell Road for ground every 6 minutes Monday to Saturday and every 10 minutes on Sunday ☎ 01273 206666, 01273 886200, 01273 700406, 0870 608 2608, www.buses.co.uk. Brighton & Hove Metro Line Buses 1, 2, 3, 5, 5B, 6, 19, 26, 33, 37, 43, 43A, 46, 49, 59 and 81B (81B from Churchill Square) pass close to the ground in Cromwell Road, Palmeira Avenue, Palmeira Square or Selborne Road. Railbus tickets are available and discount is available to Sussex CCC members on production of a valid membership card on days when cricket is being played at Hove. National Express buses and coaches pass close to ground and link with Brighton ☎ 08705 808080, 08706 082608, www.gobycoach.com.

There are cycle routes from all parts of Brighton and Hove.

From north: from A23 take A27 (west), follow signs to Hove, at roundabout take second exit (Brighton), turn right on to Woodland Drive, take third turning on left into Shirley Drive, continue on this road, at third set of traffic lights turn left on to Eaton Road. **From east:** from Brighton continue on A27 (west), then as for north. **From west:** from Worthing take A27 to Hove exit, turn right at roundabout, at next roundabout take Brighton exit, turn right on to Woodland Drive, then as for north.

London Gatwick Airport ☎ 08700 002468 www.londongatwickairport.co.uk, London Heathrow Airport ☎ 08700 000123 www.londonheathrowairport.co.uk, Shoreham Airport ☎ 01273 296900.

WHERE TO STAY

Adelaide Hotel (☎ 01273 205286), Alexandra Hotel (☎ 01273 202722), Belgrave Hotel (☎ 01273 323221 www.thebelgravehotel.brighton.cwc.net), Courtlands Hotel (☎ 01273 731055), Imperial Hotel (☎ 01273 731121), Malvern Hotel (☎ 01273 324302), Princes Marine Hotel (☎ 01273 207660 www.brighton.co.uk/hotels/princes), Ramada Jarvis Brighton (☎ 01273 225519 www.ramadajarvis.co.uk), The Brighton Hotel (☎ 01273 820555 www.brighton.co.uk), The De Vere Grand (☎ 01273 224300 www.grandbrighton.co.uk), The Dudley Hotel (☎ 01273 736266), The Kings Hotel (☎ 01273 820854), The Marina House Hotel (☎ 01273 605349), The Old Tollgate Restaurant and Hotel (☎ 01273 879494 www.oldtollgatehotel.com), The Queens Hotel (☎ 01273 321222), Thistle Brighton Hotel (☎ 01273 206700 www.thistlehotels.com)

For other places to stay in and around Brighton visit www.smoothhound.co.uk or www.visitbrighton.com.

WHERE TO EAT

Ashoka (☎ 01273 736463), Aumthong Thai (☎ 01273 773922 www.aumthong.com), Browns (☎ 01273 323501 www.browns-restaurants.com), Cactus Canteen Mexican & American Food (☎ 01273 725700), English's of Brighton Seafood Restaurant (☎ 01273 327980 www.englishs.co.uk), Gingerman (☎ 01273 326688), Hove Place (☎ 01273 738266), Indian Summer (☎ 01273 733090), La Fourchette (☎ 01273 722556), La Piazza (☎ 01273 771739 www.brightonpages.co.uk/lapiazza), Redz Bar & Brasserie (☎ 01273 329001 www.paramount-hotels.co.uk), Saucy (☎ 01273 324080 www.saucyrestaurant.com), Thai Bycee (☎ 01273 324878), The Greenhouse Effect (☎ 01273 204783), The Old Tollgate Restaurant (☎ 01273 879494 www.oldtollgatehotel.com), Tin Drum (☎ 01273 777575), Topolino Duo (☎ 01273 725726), Wheeler's Fish Restaurant (☎ 01273 325135)

TOURIST INFORMATION Hove Tourist Information Centre, King Alfred Leisure Centre, Kingsway, Hove, East Sussex BN3 2WW ☎ 01273 746100, www.brighton-hove.gov.uk. Brighton Tourist Information Centre, Bartholomew Square, The Lanes, Brighton BN1 1NS ☎ 0906 7112255 (calls cost 50p per minute), 08457 573512 (Accommodation Guide Line), www.visitbrighton.com

OTHER USEFUL INFORMATION

Brighton & Hove Travel Advice Line ☎ 01273 292480
Brighton & Hove Bus Company ☎ 01273 886200
Access in Brighton ☎ 01273 680796
Cycle Route Information Brighton & Hove ☎ 01273 292475
NCP Car Parking ☎ 01273 329145, 0870 606 7050, www.ncp.co.uk
Council Car Parking ☎ 01273 293225
Brighton & Hove Voucher Car Parking ☎ 01273 292242
Hoverspeed (Newhaven–Dieppe) ☎ 08705 240241, www.hoverspeed.com
South Central Railways Customer Services ☎ 0870 830 6000 (calls cost 50p per minute)
Guide Friday Tours ☎ 01273 540893, www.guidefriday.com
Brighton Racecourse ☎ 01273 603580, www.brighton-racecourse.co.uk
Brighton Streamline Taxi-Cab Limited ☎ 01273 747474, www.brighton-streamline.co.uk

LOCAL RADIO STATIONS BBC Radio Southern Counties (104.5 MHz FM/1161 KHz MW), Southern FM (103.4 MHz FM/1332 KHz MW)

LOCAL NEWSPAPERS *The Argus, Brighton & Hove Leader*

ARUNDEL – Arundel Park

For a history of the ground and other information including where to stay and how to get there please refer to the Friends of Arundel Castle CC section of this guide.

GROUND RECORDS AND SCORES

FIRST-CLASS MATCHES

Highest innings total for county 392 v Yorkshire 2002
Highest innings total against county 566 for 8 dec by Leicestershire 1999
Lowest innings total for county 71 v Worcestershire 1997
Lowest innings total against county 87 by Middlesex 1994
Highest individual innings for county 192 C.J. Adams v Derbyshire 2001
Highest individual innings against county 216 D.S. Lehmann for Yorkshire 2002

Highest wicket partnerships for county

1st	93 N.J. Lenham & C.W.J. Athey	v	Middlesex	1994
2nd	96 W.G. Khan & M. Newell	v	South Africans	1998
3rd	141 C.J. Adams & B. Zuiderent	v	Derbyshire	2001
4th	77 A.P. Wells & M.P. Speight	v	Hampshire	1990
5th	150 P.A. Cottey & R.S.C. Martin-Jenkins	v	Essex	2000
6th	156 C.J. Adams & M.J. Prior	v	Derbyshire	2001
7th	139 C.M. Wells & P. Moores	v	Hampshire	1990
8th	88 M.J. Prior & M.J.G. Davis	v	Yorkshire	2002
9th	45 N.J. Wilton & J.D. Lewry	v	Leicestershire	1999
10th	59* A.C.S. Pigott & B.T.P. Donelan	v	Hampshire	1990

Highest wicket partnerships against county

1st	147 D.J. Bicknell & R.I. Alikhan	for	Surrey	1991
2nd	126 P.J. Prichard & D.D.J. Robinson	for	Essex	2000
3rd	79 D.D.J. Robinson & S.G. Law	for	Essex	2000
4th	238 D.S. Lehmann & M.J. Lumb	for	Yorkshire	2002
5th	136 V.P. Terry & M. Keech	for	Hampshire	1996
6th	62* C.L. Smith & J.R. Ayling	for	Hampshire	1990
7th	50 A. Habib & C.D. Crowe	for	Leicestershire	1999
8th	99 A. Habib & M.S. Kasprowicz	for	Leicestershire	1999
9th	87 S.J. Rhodes & P.J. Newport	for	Worcestershire	1997
10th	38 U. Afzaal & R.J. Chapman	for	Nottinghamshire	1995

Best bowling performance in an innings for county 6 for 45 R.J. Kirtley v Derbyshire 2001
Best bowling performance in an innings against county 8 for 47 C.L. Cairns for Nottinghamshire 1995
Best bowling performance in a match for county 8 for 116 R.J. Kirtley v Derbyshire 2001
Best bowling performance in a match against county 15 for 83 C.L. Cairns for Nottinghamshire 1995
Largest crowd 8,000 v Surrey 1993

LIMITED-OVERS MATCHES

Highest innings total for county 297 for 5 v Middlesex (SL) 1999
Highest innings total against county 288 for 6 by Middlesex (SL) 1999
Lowest innings total for county 107 v Hampshire (SL) 1998
Lowest innings total against county 202 by Yorkshire (SL) 2000
Highest individual innings for county 163 C.J. Adams v Middlesex (SL) 1999
Highest individual innings against county 134 O.A. Shah for Middlesex (SL) 1999
Highest wicket partnerships for county

1st	76 C.J. Adams & R.R. Montgomerie	v	Yorkshire	(SL)	2000
2nd	91 M.J. DiVenuto & C.J. Adams	v	Middlesex	(SL)	1999
3rd	120 M.W. Goodwin & B. Zuiderent	v	Derbyshire	(SL)	2001
4th	125 C.J. Adams & J.R. Carpenter	v	Middlesex	(SL)	1999
5th	116 A.P. Wells & K. Greenfield	v	Middlesex	(SL)	1994
6th	50 J.M. Parks & P.J. Graves	v	Gloucestershire	(SL)	1972
7th	28 J.M. Parks & J. Denman	v	Gloucestershire	(SL)	1972
8th	55 V.C. Drakes & I.D.K. Salisbury	v	Hampshire	(SL)	1996
9th	22 M. Newell & M.A. Robinson	v	Worcestershire	(SL)	1997
10th	34 P.W. Jarvis & J.D. Lewry	v	Hampshire	(SL)	1996

Highest wicket partnerships against county

1st	160 O.A. Shah & J.L. Langer	for	Middlesex	(SL)	1999
2nd	78 D.L. Haynes & M.R. Ramprakash	for	Middlesex	(SL)	1994
3rd	84* S.G. Koenig & O.A. Shah	for	Middlesex	(SL)	2002
4th	111* K.R. Spiring & D.A. Leatherdale	for	Worcestershire	(SL)	1997
5th	61 R.D.V. Knight & D.R. Shepherd	for	Gloucestershire	(SL)	1972
	61 G.F. Archer & J.R. Wileman	for	Nottinghamshire	(SL)	1995
6th	67 C.W.G. Bassano & K.M. Krikken	for	Derbyshire	(SL)	2001
7th	29 K.R. Brown & P.N. Weekes	for	Middlesex	(SL)	1994
8th	68 D.S. Lehmann & R.J. Sidebottom	for	Yorkshire	(SL)	2000

| 9th | 33 A.N. Aymes & P.J. Hartley | for | Hampshire | (SL) | 1998 |
| 10th | 7 R.L. Johnson & P.C.R. Tufnell | for | Middlesex | (SL) | 1994 |

Best bowling performance in a match for county 5 for 24 F.D. Stephenson v Middlesex (SL) 1994
Best bowling performance in a match against county 5 for 10 M.J. Procter for Gloucestershire (SL) 1972
Largest crowd 6,500 v Middlesex (SL) 1994

EASTBOURNE

Address Eastbourne Cricket Club, Eastbourne Saffrons Sports Club, The
Saffrons, Compton Place Road, Eastbourne, East Sussex BN21 1EA
Prospects of Play ☎ 01323 724328

HISTORY OF GROUND AND FACILITIES

THE SAFFRONS GROUND is the home of Eastbourne Cricket Club, founded in
1855. They play in the Sussex County Cricket League. The outfield is shared with
Eastbourne Town Football Club and the sports complex is now known as the
Eastbourne Saffrons Sports Club.

Cricket has been played in Eastbourne for about 255 years, a fact which may
surprise many followers of the game, but the Saffrons has not always been the
venue. The earliest ground was at Paradise, now the Royal Eastbourne Golf
Club. The Dental Estimates Board offices now stand on the second ground and
the third ground at Ashford Road was on the site now occupied by the multi-
storey car park near Eastbourne railway station. The Aboriginals played on this
ground in 1868. In 1870 Dr W.G. Grace visited with a United South of England XI
and played an Eastbourne team of XVII. In 1874 the club moved to Devonshire
Park which was given to the town by the Duke of Devonshire. The move to the
Saffrons was made in 1884 but Sussex CCC did not play there until 1897 when
Middlesex were the visitors.

The Saffrons Cricket Ground viewed from the Sea End looking towards the Larkins Field End.

The original pavilion was destroyed by fire in 1947 and was replaced by the current building, which was itself damaged by fire in 1977. Plans are in hand for the refurbishment of the pavilion and car parking area to the rear. A number of squash courts have already been constructed. On the old white pavilion, known as the War Memorial Pavilion, and squash courts is a plaque bearing the name of the illustrious D.R. Jardine. The other pavilion on the ground is the Harry Bartlett Pavilion, which is also at the Meads Road End.

The name 'Saffrons' originates from the original use of the land over a century ago when saffron was grown for dyeing and medicinal purposes. The part of the ground known as Larkin's Field dates from the 1700s when a saddler named Larkin rented land there to graze the cattle he raised for their hides.

Many of the game's most famous players have appeared at the Saffrons: the Hide brothers, both Eastbourne men; M.W. Tate when a Sussex Colt; and Dr W.G. Grace. Jack Hobbs played here only once, in a Festival match. Archie MacLaren's Young Amateurs defeated the formidable Australians in 1921 at the Saffrons; this is probably the most famous match to have taken place on this ground.

As well as playing championship matches here, Sussex CCC have staged limited-overs matches on the ground, the first in 1969. The ground has also been used by Sussex for matches against the touring sides, Derek Robins' XI, H.D.G. Leveson-Gower's XI and Col H.C. Stevens' XI. The former Sussex captain J.R.T. Barclay and R.J. Parks, the Hampshire wicket-keeper, both played for the Saffrons club before graduating to first-class cricket.

The Eastbourne club has been served well by groundsmen, notably Wilf Wooller for 54 years from 1922 to 1976 and his father for 50 years from 1884 to 1934. Between them they prepared over 5,000 wickets.

The scoreboard is situated on the north, football ground side with a groundsman's store which has the press box below. The football terraces are some distance away from the cricket field and only provide shelter during poor weather. On the east side, directly behind the sightscreen, are the TV camera and commentary position, radio commentary box and first aid tent. The playing area is 120 metres by 130 metres and defined by a rope on one side and on the other by some advertising boards.

GROUND RECORDS AND SCORES

FIRST-CLASS MATCHES

Highest innings total for county 540 for 6 dec v Glamorgan 1938
Highest innings total against county 586 by Gloucestershire 1936
Lowest innings total for county 38 v Hampshire 1950
Lowest innings total against county 57 by Nottinghamshire 1962
Highest individual innings for county 272* R.R. Relf v Worcestershire 1909
Highest individual innings against county 310 H. Gimblett for Somerset 1948
Highest wicket partnerships for county

1st	163 J. Vine & J.G.C. Scott	v	Oxford University	1907
2nd	275 J.G. Langridge & H.W. Parks	v	Glamorgan	1938
3rd	259 D.S. Sheppard & G. Cox	v	Glamorgan	1949
4th	198 R.J. Langridge & F.R. Pountain	v	Oxford University	1965
5th	185 J. Langridge & H.W. Parks	v	Derbyshire	1936
6th	241 M.P. Speight & P. Moores	v	Nottinghamshire	1993

7th	218 T.E.R. Cook & A.F. Wensley	v	Worcestershire	1933
8th	188 R.L. Holdsworth & A.E.R. Gilligan	v	Lancashire	1927
9th	119* K.G. Suttle & P.A. Kelland	v	Worcestershire	1952
10th	112 A.E. Relf & H.E. Roberts	v	Lancashire	1914

Highest wicket partnerships against county

1st	233* W. Place & C. Washbrook	for	Lancashire	1947
2nd	219 G. Atkinson & P.B. Wight	for	Somerset	1961
3rd	215 A.E. Alderman & L.F. Townsend	for	Derbyshire	1938
4th	214 B.R. Hardie & K.W.R. Fletcher	for	Essex	1987
5th	209 H. Gimblett & M. Coope	for	Somerset	1948
6th	148 R.B. Nicholls & A.R. Windows	for	Gloucestershire	1965
7th	171 V.F.S. Crawford & W.W. Odell	for	Leicestershire	1908
8th	202 D. Davies & J.J. Hills	for	Glamorgan	1928
9th	142 L.O.S. Poidevin & A. Kermode	for	Lancashire	1907
10th	55 H.I. Young & W. Mead	for	Essex	1903

Best bowling performance in an innings for county 8 for 25 A.A. Jones v Lancashire 1968
Best bowling performance in an innings against county 9 for 62 A.G. Nicholson for Yorkshire 1967
Best bowling performance in a match for county 12 for 86 J. Langridge v Hampshire 1950
Best bowling performance in a match against county 14 for 106 R.C. Robertson-Glasgow 1923
Largest crowd 5,000 v Somerset 1948

LIMITED-OVERS MATCHES

Highest innings total for county 262 v Nottinghamshire (SL) 1993
Highest innings total against county 207 for 2 by Yorkshire (SL) 1996
Lowest innings total for county 117 v Worcestershire (SL) 1995
Lowest innings total against county 63 by Minor Counties East (B&H) 1978
Highest individual innings for county 109 R.D.V. Knight v Leicestershire (SL) 1976
Highest individual innings against county 93* C.E.B. Rice for Nottinghamshire (SL) 1980
Highest wicket partnerships for county

1st	108 R.K. Rao & K. Greenfield	v	Yorkshire	(SL)	1996
2nd	120 M.A. Buss & R.M. Prideaux	v	Derbyshire	(SL)	1973
3rd	67 G.A. Greenidge & J.M. Parks	v	Surrey	(SL)	1971
4th	97 P.J. Graves & Imran Khan	v	Minor Counties East	(B&H)	1978
5th	60 J.J. Groome & M.A. Buss	v	Gloucestershire	(SL)	1975
6th	46* C.M. Wells & C.P. Phillipson	v	Essex	(SL)	1986
7th	66 C.P. Phillipson & G.S. LeRoux	v	Kent	(SL)	1981
8th	46 J.R.T. Barclay & T.J. Head	v	Nottinghamshire	(SL)	1980
9th	21 P. Moores & I.D.K. Salisbury	v	Nottinghamshire	(SL)	1993
10th	25* J.R.T. Barclay & A. Buss	v	Nottinghamshire	(SL)	1974

Highest wicket partnerships against county

1st	76 G.A. Gooch & P.J. Prichard	for	Essex	(SL)	1986
2nd	114 D. Byas & M.P. Vaughan	for	Yorkshire	(SL)	1996
3rd	102 M.B. Loye & D.J.G. Sales	for	Northamptonshire	(SL)	2000
4th	78 J.E. Morris & T.J.G. O'Gorman	for	Derbyshire	(SL)	1992
5th	89 A.W. Stovold & J.C. Foat	for	Gloucestershire	(SL)	1975
6th	64 G.W. Johnson & J.N. Shepherd	for	Kent	(SL)	1979
7th	47 M.A. Crawley & B.N. French	for	Nottinghamshire	(SL)	1993
8th	58 W.P.C. Weston & S.J. Rhodes	for	Worcestershire	(SL)	1995
9th	24 T.M. Tremlett & R.J. Parks	for	Hampshire	(SL)	1982
	24 B.N. French & R.A. Pick	for	Nottinghamshire	(SL)	1993
10th	24 N. Gifford & J. Cumbes	for	Worcestershire	(SL)	1978

Best bowling performance in a match for county 5 for 19 M.A. Buss v Minor Counties East (B&H) 1978
Best bowling performance in a match against county 5 for 29 M.G. Bevan for Yorkshire (SL) 1996
Largest crowd 8,000 v Kent (SL) 1978

GROUND INFORMATION

ENTRANCES Compton Place Road (players, officials, members and vehicles), Meads Road (members and public), Old Orchard Road/Saffrons Road (members, public and vehicles).

MEMBERS' ENCLOSURE Pavilion and temporary members' stand enclosure of raised and ground-level seating

PUBLIC ENCLOSURE Rest of the ground.

COVERED STANDS Pavilion, Football Stand (part), War Memorial Pavilion and Harry Bartlett Pavilion.

OPEN STANDS Temporary raised and ground level seating including deck chairs surrounding the playing area.

NAME OF ENDS Larkins Field End, Sea End.

GROUND DIMENSIONS 120m × 130m.

REPLAY SCREEN If televised matches are staged at the ground the replay screen is sited on the football ground side of the ground opposite the pavilion.

FIRST AID In caravan at Meads Road End of the ground.

CODES OF DRESS Spectators are required to dress in an appropriate manner consistent with attending a cricket match. Bare torsos are not acceptable in, or in front of the pavilion. Executive Club/Suite users must wear a necktie and jacket.

BEHAVIOUR Sussex are keen that standards of behaviour should be maintained and members and spectators are urged to report immediately to the CEO any incident, or potential incident, where they feel action should be taken. Bad language is not acceptable at any match and the club will take prompt and strong action should this or any other ground regulation be ignored. Mobile telephones are not permitted, please ensure that mobile telephones are switched off before entering the spectator areas of the ground.

RECIPROCAL ARRANGEMENTS Members of Essex, Hampshire and Kent free except when Sussex are playing their own county. Sussex CCC members can also gain free or reduced admission to race events on reciprocal dates at Plumpton, Fontwell Park, Goodwood and Brighton racecourses and Hickstead showgrounds.

SUPPORTERS' CLUB Sussex County Cricket Supporters' Club: subscription £4 (adults), £2 (senior citizens and under-16s) per annum. Regular newsletters are issued throughout the year. Membership details and information about events can be obtained from SCCSC, Freepost, County Ground, Eaton Road, Hove BN3 3AN.

JUNIORS Membership for those aged up to 16 on 1 January is £10 per annum. Contact Sussex CCC Membership Department ☎ 01273 827133 for full details.

CORPORATE ENTERTAINING Executive Membership is available and includes use of temporary marquees. Facilities available for conferences, lunches, dinners, wedding receptions throughout the year. Contact Commercial Department for details and a brochure ☎ 01273 827101.

FACILITIES FOR VISUALLY IMPAIRED SPECTATORS Yes, via Compton Place Road and Meads Road entrances.

FACILITIES AND ACCESS FOR PEOPLE WITH DISABILITIES INCLUDING WHEELCHAIR ACCESS TO GROUND Yes, special area available on football ground side of ground.

DESIGNATED CAR PARK AVAILABLE INSIDE THE GROUND FOR PEOPLE WITH DISABILITIES Yes, special area available on football ground side of ground.

DESIGNATED VIEWING AREAS FOR PEOPLE USING WHEELCHAIRS Yes, special area available on football ground side of ground.

RAMPS TO PROVIDE EASY ACCESS TO BARS & REFRESHMENT OUTLETS FOR PEOPLE USING WHEELCHAIRS No.

FOOD & DRINK FULL RESTAURANT/DINING FACILITIES Members, yes. Public, no.

TEMPORARY FOOD/DRINK FACILITIES Members, yes. Public, yes.

FOOD SUITABLE FOR VEGETARIANS Members, yes. Public, no.

BARS Members 1, Public 1.

VARIETIES OF BEER SOLD Shepherd Neame.

CHILDREN'S FACILITIES Crèche, no. Play area, no.

CLUB SHOP Sussex CCC temporary shop is situated at the Meads Road End of the ground in a mobile unit. Local secondhand book dealer Neil Beck sells cricket books and items of Sussex memorabilia.

CLUB MUSEUM No, but there are some pictures on view in the main pavilion.

CRICKET COACHING FACILITIES No.

CRICKET NETS No.

OTHER SPORTING OR RECREATIONAL FACILITIES ON THE GROUND Hockey, croquet, squash and football.

FACILITIES FOR HIRE OR WIDER COMMUNITY USE AT THE GROUND WINTER CRICKET EVENTS No

CAR PARKING FACILITIES There is a large car park available at the rear of the football stand at the Saffrons End of the ground which is entered off Old Orchard Road/Saffrons Road. Alternative car parking can be found in neighbouring streets and town centre car parks.

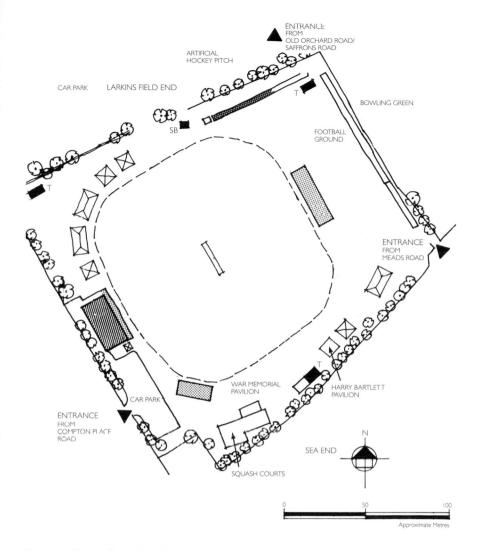

ENTRANCE FROM OLD ORCHARD ROAD/ SAFFRONS ROAD

ARTIFICIAL HOCKEY PITCH

CAR PARK   LARKINS FIELD END

BOWLING GREEN

FOOTBALL GROUND

SB

ENTRANCE FROM MEADS ROAD

WAR MEMORIAL PAVILION

HARRY BARTLETT PAVILION

CAR PARK

ENTRANCE FROM COMPTON PLACE ROAD

SEA END

N

SQUASH COURTS

0   50   100

Approximate Metres

OTHER INFORMATION The Saffrons Ground is a short walk away from Devonshire Park where the International Women's Tennis Tournament is staged in June. ☎ 01323 412000 for information and full details, www.eastbourne-tennis.co.uk.
GROUND CAPACITY 4,500.
ANTICIPATED GROUND DEVELOPMENTS Nothing planned.

HOW TO GET THERE

 Eastbourne station 0.5 mile ☎ 08457 484950, www.connex.co.uk, www.railtrack.co.uk, www.thetrainline.co.uk

 From surrounding areas to within 0.5 mile of ground also Eastbourne Bus 8B from town centre passes ground. Eastbourne Coach Station ☎ 01323 416416, National Express Coaches 08705 808080, 0870 6082608, www.gobycoach.com, www.bus.co.uk

 There are cycle routes from surrounding areas of Eastbourne to this part of the town.

From north: from A22, Polegate, continue on A22 (Willingdon Road) following signs to town centre (Upperton Road) (A259), at roundabout take second exit on to Grove Road, at junction turn right and then right again into Saffrons Road. **From east:** from Hastings take A259 (west), at Pevensey continue on A259 towards Eastbourne (Pevensey Bay Road) on to Seaside, then Seaside Road, at Trinity Trees take A25 (South Street), turn right on to Gildredge Road, turn left into Terminus Road, at roundabout turn left on to Grove Road, turn right and then right again on to Saffrons Road. **From west:** from Seaford stay on A259 (east) to junction with Upperton Road, continue on this road as for north.

London Gatwick Airport ☎ 08700 002468 www.londongatwickairport.co.uk, London Heathrow Airport ☎ 08700 000123 www.londonheathrowairport.co.uk, Lydd Airport ☎ 01797 322411, Shoreham Airport ☎ 01273 296900

WHERE TO STAY

Afton Hotel (☎ 01323 733162), Chatsworth Hotel (☎ 01323 411016 www.chatsworth-hotel.com), Cherry Tree Hotel (☎ 01323 722406 www.eastbourne.org/cherrytree-hotel), Claremont Hotel (☎ 01983 861111), Devonshire Park Hotel (☎ 01323 728144 www.devonshire-park-hotel.co.uk), Haddon Hall Hotel (☎ 01323 640953), Hadleigh Hotel (☎ 01323 417365), Heatherleigh Hotel (☎ 01323 721167), Imperial Hotel (☎ 01983 861111), York House Hotel (☎ 01323 412918 www.yorkhousehotel.co.uk)
    For places to stay in Eastbourne ☎ 01323 410000, visit www.smoothhound.co.uk, www.eastbourne.org.

WHERE TO EAT

The Mirabelle at the Grand Hotel (☎ 01323 412345 www.grandeastbourne.co.uk). There are numerous other places to eat in Eastbourne.

TOURIST INFORMATION Eastbourne Tourist Information Centre, Cornfield Road, Eastbourne, East Sussex BN21 4QL ☎ 01323 411400

OTHER USEFUL INFORMATION

Cycle Hire ☎ 01323 870310
Royal Eastbourne Golf Club ☎ 01323 736986
Devonshire Park Theatre ☎ 01323 412000

LOCAL RADIO STATIONS BBC Radio Southern Counties (104.5 MHz FM/1161 KHz MW), Southern FM (103.4 MHz FM/1332 KHz MW)

LOCAL NEWSPAPERS *The Argus, Eastbourne News, Eastbourne Gazette and Herald*

HASTINGS

Address Hastings & Leonard's Priory Cricket Club, Horntye Park Sports Complex, The Pavilion, Bohemia Road, St Leonards-on-Sea, Hastings, East Sussex TN34 1EX
Prospects of Play ☎ 01424 424546

HISTORY OF GROUND AND FACILITIES

HASTINGS PRIORY MEADOW Central Cricket Ground was one of England's most famous and historic cricket grounds. Established in 1864 it hosted some 230 first-class cricket matches over the years with no fewer than 625 different first-class cricketers playing here, including W.G. Grace, Gilbert Jessop, Fred Spofforth,

Horntye Park has a splendid pavilion with a distinctive lime green roof.

Tom Richardson, Prince Ranjitsinhji, Maurice Tate, Harold Larwood, Prince Duleepsinhji, Donald Bradman, Les Ames, Denis Compton, Colin Cowdrey, Ted Dexter, Tony Greig, Alan Knott, Derek Underwood and John Snow. The Hastings Cricket Festival was a regular event and Hastings played host to visiting touring teams – the Australians played here on 18 occasions. In 1986 the site was purchased by Boots Properties plc for the development of a multi-million pound shopping complex. The last first-class match staged at the Central Cricket and Recreation Ground was in 1989 when Middlesex were the visitors.

One of the conditions of the compulsory purchase order was that a suitable alternative site for a replacement sports facility be found and that appropriate compensation be paid. Horntye Park was settled upon and a sports complex developed. The Priory Meadow Shopping Mall was opened by HM The Queen on 6 June 1997 by which time Horntye Park was already being used for cricket in the summer and football in the winter. The Horntye Park complex covers more than 11 acres whereas the old Priory Meadow ground covered only 4.

Horntye Park was constructed at a cost of £4.5m with the Sports Council contributing a further £3.2m towards the scheme. There are facilities for cricket, football, hockey, basketball, volleyball, table tennis, indoor cricket, cricket nets, badminton, netball, five-a-side football and all types of training. The complex was formally opened on 25 April 2000 by Sport England. There is also a floodlit all-weather hockey pitch to the rear of the pavilion. The complex is without doubt one of the finest in the south of England with excellent ancillary facilities and parking for up to 200 cars.

The ground is the home of Hastings & St Leonards Priory Cricket Club, South Saxons Hockey Club, Hastings Town 2000 Football Club, Monarchs Table Tennis Club, Hastings & District Cricket Association, The Civil Service Badminton Club and Springfield Badminton Club.

A substantial amount of time has gone into the development of a first-class cricket square and this was nurtured to such a standard that first-class cricket returned to Hastings in 2000 when Sussex hosted the touring Zimbabwe team. Further matches followed with Kent in the Benson and Hedges zonal round in 2001 and with Bradford UCCE in 2002. Other matches have included Sussex 2nd XI games and an Old England XI versus France.

The Horntye Park cricket ground, with its magnificent pavilion and electronic scoreboard, is set in a man-made bowl. It is a sheltered area ideal for both players and spectators. The ground was constructed to the County Cricket Specifications set out by the ECB and is only the third cricket facility of this standard to be built from scratch in this country. The others are Riverside and The Rose Bowl.

The only permanent buildings on the ground are the pavilion, groundsman's house, utility building including toilets and an electronic scoreboard. The pavilion offers facilities for players, officials, members and the press. It includes excellent changing, catering and function rooms. Facilities during matches include a restaurant.

GROUND RECORDS AND SCORES

Sussex played Bradford UCCE in 2002; this match was not first-class.
Scores: Sussex 400 (M.J. Prior 151, K.J. Innes 53, S. Noach 5 for 83) and 163 for 5 dec (B. Zuiderent 84) beat Bradford UCCE 164 (J.W.N. Lucas 49, J.D. Lewry 4 for 48, W.J. House 4 for 10) and 199 (S. Noach 52, J.D. Lewry 5 for 35) by 200 runs. Largest crowd: 1,500 v Bradford UCCE 2002.

LIMITED-OVERS MATCHES

Highest innings total for county 264 for 4 v Zimbabweans (F) 2000
Highest innings total against county 267 for 2 by Zimbabweans (F) 2000
Lowest innings total for county 180 for 5 v Kent (SL) 2001
Lowest innings total against county 175 by Kent (SL) 2001
Highest individual innings for county 129 R.R. Montgomerie v Zimbabweans (F) 2000
Highest individual innings against county 107 N.C. Johnson for Zimbabweans (F) 2000
Highest wicket partnerships for county

1st	40 R.R. Montgomerie & M.W. Goodwin	v	Kent	(SL)	2001
2nd	176 R.R. Montgomerie & P.A. Cottey	v	Zimbabweans	(F)	2000
3rd	38 R.R. Montgomerie & U.B.A. Rashid	v	Zimbabweans	(F)	2000
4th	61 B. Zuiderent & W.J. House	v	Kent	(SL)	2001
5th	12 W.J. House & U.B.A. Rashid	v	Kent	(SL)	2001
6th	34 U.B.A. Rashid & R.R.C. Martin-Jenkins	v	Kent	(SL)	2001

7th to 10th yet to be established.
Highest wicket partnerships against county

1st	104 N.C. Johnson & G.W. Flower	for	Zimbabweans	(F)	2000
2nd	115 N.C. Johnson & M.W. Goodwin	for	Zimbabweans	(F)	2000
3rd	48* N.C. Johnson & A.D.R. Campbell	for	Zimbabweans	(F)	2000
4th	16 M.J. Walker & M.A. Ealham	for	Kent	(SL)	2001
5th	49 M.J. Walker & P.A. Nixon	for	Kent	(SL)	2001
6th	26 M.J. Walker & J.B. Hockley	for	Kent	(SL)	2001
7th	0 M.J. Walker & M.J. McCague	for	Kent	(SL)	2001
8th	7 M.J. Walker & J.M. Golding	for	Kent	(SL)	2001
9th	11 J.M. Golding & M.M. Patel	for	Kent	(SL)	2001
10th	9 J.M. Golding & D.D. Masters	for	Kent	(SL)	2001

Best bowling performance in a match for county 4 for 29 M.A. Robinson v Kent (SL) 2001
Best bowling performance in a match against county 2 for 34 M.M. Patel for Kent (SL) 2001
Largest crowd 4,000 v Zimbabweans (F) 2000

GROUND INFORMATION

ENTRANCES Bohemia Road (players, officials, press, members and public; players' and officials' cars only), Brescoe's Walk (pedestrians only).
MEMBERS' ENCLOSURE Pavilion and defined members' area.
PUBLIC ENCLOSURE Rest of the ground.
COVERED STANDS Pavilion.
OPEN STANDS Rest of ground on temporary seating including deck chairs and plastic tip up seats.
NAME OF ENDS Pavilion End, Sea End.

GROUND DIMENSIONS 168m × 152m.

REPLAY SCREEN If televised matches are staged at the ground the replay screen is sited at the Sea End.

FIRST AID Caravan near groundsman's utility building and toilets.

CODES OF DRESS Spectators are required to dress in an appropriate manner consistent with attending a cricket match. Bare torsos are not acceptable in, or in front of the pavilion. Executive Club/Suite users must wear a necktie and jacket.

BEHAVIOUR Sussex are keen that standards of behaviour should be maintained and members and spectators are urged to report immediately to the CEO any incident, or potential incident, where they feel action should be taken. Bad language is not acceptable at any match and the club will take prompt and strong action should this or any other ground regulation be ignored. Mobile telephones are not permitted, please ensure that mobile telephones are switched off before entering the spectator areas of the ground.

RECIPROCAL ARRANGEMENTS Members of Essex, Hampshire and Kent free except when Sussex are playing

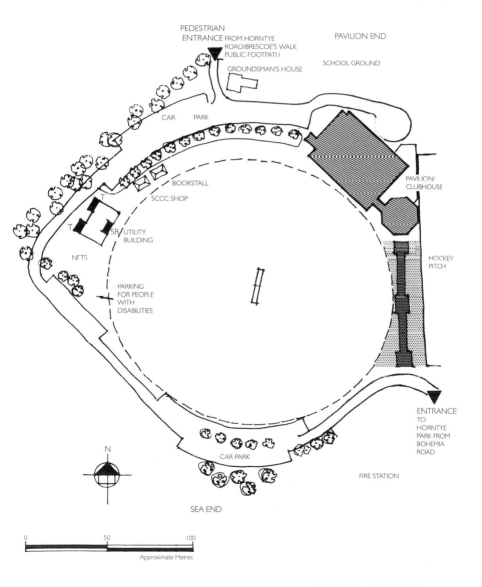

their own county. Sussex CCC members can also gain free or reduced admission to race events on reciprocal dates at Plumpton, Fontwell Park, Goodwood and Brighton racecourses and Hickstead showgrounds.

SUPPORTERS' CLUB Sussex County Cricket Supporters' Club: subscription £4 (adults), £2 (senior citizens and under-16s) per annum. Regular newsletters are issued throughout the year. Membership details and information about events can be obtained from SCCSC, Freepost, County Ground, Eaton Road, Hove BN3 3AN.

JUNIORS Membership for those aged up to 16 on 1 January is £10 per annum. Contact Sussex CCC Membership Department ☎ 01273 827133 for full details.

CORPORATE ENTERTAINING Executive Membership is available and includes use of temporary marquees also Cornwallis Suite. Facilities available for conferences, lunches, dinners, wedding receptions throughout the year. Contact Commercial Department for details and a brochure ☎ 01273 827101 or 01424 424546.

FACILITIES FOR VISUALLY IMPAIRED SPECTATORS Yes, via Bohemia Road entrance to the ground.

FACILITIES AND ACCESS FOR PEOPLE WITH DISABILITIES INCLUDING WHEELCHAIR ACCESS TO GROUND Yes, special area available at Sea End of the ground.

DESIGNATED CAR PARK AVAILABLE INSIDE THE GROUND FOR PEOPLE WITH DISABILITIES No.

DESIGNATED VIEWING AREAS FOR PEOPLE USING WHEELCHAIRS Yes, special area available at Sea End of the ground.

RAMPS TO PROVIDE EASY ACCESS TO BARS & REFRESHMENT OUTLETS FOR PEOPLE USING WHEELCHAIRS Yes, access to the pavilion is possible.

FOOD & DRINK FULL RESTAURANT/DINING FACILITIES Members, yes. Public, yes. Lunch is available in the pavilion. Daily catering available throughout the year from 12.30 p.m. open to non-members.

TEMPORARY FOOD/DRINK FACILITIES Members, yes. Public, yes.

FOOD SUITABLE FOR VEGETARIANS Members, yes. Public, no.

BARS Members 1, Public 1.

VARIETIES OF BEER SOLD Shepherd Neame.

CHILDRENS FACILITIES Crèche, no. Play area, no.

CLUB SHOP Sussex CCC shop is situated near the groundsman's utility building in a mobile unit (☎ 01273 827127 www.sussexcricket.co.uk) and secondhand book dealer Neil Beck sells cricket books.

CLUB MUSEUM No, but there are some pictures on display in the pavilion.

CRICKET COACHING FACILITIES No.

CRICKET NETS Outdoor nets, contact Horntye Park Sports Complex for details ☎ 01424 424546.

OTHER SPORTING OR RECREATIONAL FACILITIES ON THE GROUND Hockey, five-a-side football, volleyball, netball, basketball and all types of training, contact Horntye Park Sports Complex for details ☎ 01424 424546.

FACILITIES FOR HIRE OR WIDER COMMUNITY USE AT THE GROUND Catering and Meeting Rooms plus Cornwallis Suite available throughout the year, contact Horntye Park Sports Complex for details ☎ 01424 424546.

WINTER CRICKET EVENTS No.

CAR PARKING FACILITIES 200 car parking spaces within the ground for players, officials, committee, press/media and sponsors only. Some parking is available for disabled drivers and Sussex CCC members at £5 per vehicle. Otherwise car parking is available in surrounding streets or in town centre car parks approximately 10 to 15 minutes' walk from the ground.

GROUND CAPACITY 4,500.

ANTICIPATED GROUND DEVELOPMENTS Nothing planned.

HOW TO GET THERE

 Hastings station is approximately 10 minutes walk from ground: go past multi-storey car park and walk up Bohemia Road. ☎ 08457 484950, www.connex.co.uk, www.railtrack.co.uk, www.thetrainline.co.uk

 Local bus services from Hastings connect with St Leonards-on-Sea and pass the ground in Bohemia Road. Get off near the fire station; the ground is situated directly behind the fire service building. National Express coaches 08705 808080, 08706 082608, www.gobycoach.com

 There are cycle routes from Hastings and St Leonards-on-Sea to this area of the town.

 From north: from A21 stay on follow signs to town centre, Horntye Park is on the left immediately after the fire station. **From east:** from Rye take A259 to Hastings, turn right at junction with A21,

Horntye Park is on the right hand side immediately before the fire station. **From west:** from Bexhill-on-Sea (De la Warr Road) take A259 (east) (Hastings Road) and continue into Hastings to junction with A21, turn left on to A21, then as for east.

 London Gatwick Airport ☎ 08700 002468 www.londongatwickairport.co.uk, London Heathrow Airport ☎ 08700 000123 www.londonheathrowairport.co.uk, Lydd Airport ☎ 01797 322411

WHERE TO STAY

Chatsworth Hotel (☎ 01424 720188 www.chatsworthhotel.com), Croft Place (☎ 01424 433004 www.croftplace.co.uk), Crowhurst Park (☎ 01424 773344 www.crowhurstpark.co.uk), Grand Hotel (☎ 01424 428510), Parkside Hotel (☎ 01424 433096), The Eagle House Hotel (☎ 01424 430535 www.eaglehousehotel.com), The Lansdowne Hotel (☎ 01424 429605 www.lansdowne-hotel.com), Tower House Hotel (☎ 01424 427217 www.towerhousehotel.com)
    For other places to stay in and around Hastings visit www.smoothhound.co.uk or www.hastings.gov.uk.

WHERE TO EAT

The Mermaid Café (☎ 01424 438100)

TOURIST INFORMATION Hastings & St Leonards Tourist Information Centre, Queens Square, Priory Meadow, Hastings, East Sussex TN34 1TL ☎ Freephone 0500 21 1066, www.hastings.gov.uk

LOCAL RADIO STATIONS BBC Radio Southern Counties (104.5 MHz FM/1161 KHz MW), Southern FM (103.4 MHz FM/1332 KHz MW)

LOCAL NEWSPAPERS *The Argus, Hastings Observer, Hastings Citizen*

HORSHAM

Address Horsham Cricket & Sports Club, The Pavilion, Cricketfield Road, Worthing Road, Horsham, West Sussex RH13 6BG
Prospects of Play ☎ 01403 254628

HISTORY OF GROUND AND FACILITIES

HORSHAM CRICKET CLUB were founded in 1771 and have played home fixtures at Cricketfield Road since 1851. The club play in the Sussex County Cricket League and share facilities with Horsham Caledonians Cricket Club, founded in 1949. The Horsham club celebrated their 200th anniversary in 1971 with a match between Sussex and Cambridge University.
    Four other grounds in the town have been used for cricket: the Artillery Ground, the Common in North Parade at the south side of the junction with Hurst Road, Denne Park and Stanford's or the 'New Ground'. Sussex first appeared at Horsham as a representative side in 1853.
    The county have played on the present Cricketfield Road ground since 1908 when the first first-class match was staged with Essex. Matches were played during the following periods: 1908 to 1910, 1912 to 1914, 1920 to 1939 and 1946 to 1956. Sussex visited in 1971 and 1974 to play against Oxford and Cambridge Universities but championship cricket did not return to Horsham until

1983. The county have made many visits to this delightful rural setting since 1974 for limited-overs Sunday League fixtures. Horsham Cricket Club have hosted a cricket festival week over the years but recently this has comprised only one championship and one limited-overs match, usually in June.

The first pavilion was situated close to the footbridge crossing the railway line but was demolished. The present pavilion was built in 1921. To the north the ground is bounded by the River Arun which runs close to the area where willow trees were planted by Ben Warsop, the former cricket bat manufacturer. The ball has been hit into the river once, by 'Jacko' Watson, the mightiest of Sussex's hitters. At the southern end of the ground is the railway line. Horsham CC own the ground and there has been talk in recent years of improving the facilities to attract more county matches to Cricketfield Road.

Spectators who visited the ground during the 1980s will recall Garth le Roux's swashbuckling knock against Hampshire to set up a Sussex victory in a Sunday League match. Vivian Richards kept wicket here for Somerset one Sunday in 1985 after Trevor Gard was injured warming up on the slippery outfield.

The only permanent building is the large pavilion/club house on the west side of the ground, which has been extended in recent years by adding two storeys. The main scoreboard is opposite the pavilion. The playing area is approximately 126 metres by 122 metres and is bounded by advertising boards. The radio commentary position is usually in the press marquee at the Town End of the ground. The TV camera/commentary box is located on a gantry high above the sightscreen at the Railway End. Seats are provided for about 35% of the ground's 4,500 capacity.

Pavilion at Cricketfield Road.

GROUND RECORDS AND SCORES

FIRST-CLASS MATCHES

Highest innings total for county 519 v Leicestershire 1921
Highest innings total against county 593 by Derbyshire 1998
Lowest innings total for county 35 v Glamorgan 1946
Lowest innings total against county 51 by Leicestershire 1924
Highest individual innings for county 176 E.H. Bowley v Warwickshire 1927
Highest individual innings against county 224 C.P. Mead for Hampshire 1921
Highest wicket partnerships for county

1st	258 J.G. Langridge & J.H. Parks	v	Surrey	1934
2nd	187 A.M. Green & P.W.G. Parker	v	Surrey	1985
3rd	200 E.H. Bowley & T.E.R. Cook	v	Warwickshire	1927
4th	200 G.D. Mendis & C.M. Wells	v	Northamptonshire	1984
5th	152 H.W. Parks & J.Y. Oakes	v	Worcestershire	1947
6th	141 G. Cox & J.Y. Oakes	v	Nottinghamshire	1950
7th	180 M.W. Tate & A.E. Relf	v	Hampshire	1921
8th	90 M.W. Tate & A.E.R. Gillingham	v	Glamorgan	1923
9th	178 H.W. Parks & A.F. Wensley	v	Derbyshire	1930
10th	67 T.E.R. Cook & W.L. Cornford	v	Glamorgan	1929

Highest wicket partnerships against county

1st	187 W.W. Keeton & C.B. Harris	for	Nottinghamshire	1934
2nd	178* L.B. Fishlock & H.T. Barling	for	Surrey	1939
3rd	243 A.J. Stewart & G.P. Thorpe	for	Surrey	1995
4th	254 K.J. Barnett & M.E. Cassar	for	Derbyshire	1998
5th	159 F.R. Santall & H.E. Dollery	for	Warwickshire	1936
6th	123 M.A. Roseberry & D.C. Nash	for	Middlesex	2000
7th	174* D.R. Pringle & M.A. Garnham	for	Essex	1989
8th	130* N.A. Foster & A.G.J. Fraser	for	Essex	1991
9th	100 G. Fowler & P.J.W. Allott	for	Lancashire	1990
10th	183 S.A. Marsh & B.J. Phillips	for	Kent	1997

Best bowling performance in an innings for county 9 for 50 G.R. Cox v Warwickshire 1926
Best bowling performance in an innings against county 9 for 35 V. Broderick for Northamptonshire 1948
Best bowling performance in a match for county 17 for 106 G.R. Cox v Warwickshire 1926
Best bowling performance in a match against county 12 for 133 G.E. Tribe for Northamptonshire 1952
Largest crowd 6,000 v Northamptonshire 1948

LIMITED-OVERS MATCHES

Highest innings total for county 293 for 4 v Worcestershire (SL) 1980
Highest innings total against county 275 for 4 by Durham (SL) 1992
Lowest innings total for county 140 v Worcestershire (SL) 2001
Lowest innings total against county 165 by Northamptonshire (SL) 1984
Highest individual innings for county 109* C.W.J. Athey v Kent (SL) 1997
Highest individual innings against county 147 G.M. Turner for Worcestershire (SL) 1980
Highest wicket partnerships for county

1st	96 K.C. Wessels & J.A. Snow	v	Lancashire	(SL)	1977
2nd	100 C.W.J. Athey & K. Greenfield	v	Kent	(SL)	1997
3rd	156 P.W.G. Parker & Imran Khan	v	Worcestershire	(SL)	1980
4th	89 P.W.G. Parker & A.P. Wells	v	Northamptonshire	(SL)	1984
5th	55 Imran Khan & C.M. Wells	v	Nottinghamshire	(SL)	1985
6th	79 D.R. Law & P. Moores	v	Surrey	(SL)	1995
7th	51 P.W.G. Parker & C.P. Phillipson	v	Worcestershire	(SL)	1982
8th	57 P.W.G. Parker & A.C.S. Pigott	v	Derbyshire	(SL)	1988
9th	39 J.R.T. Barclay & G.G. Arnold	v	Warwickshire	(SL)	1981
10th	16 R.J. Kirtley & M.A. Robinson	v	Derbyshire	(SL)	1998

Highest wicket partnerships against county

1st	107 W. Larkins & J.D. Glendenen	for	Durham	(SL)	1992
2nd	86 M.J. Walker & A.P. Wells	for	Kent	(SL)	1997
3rd	101 G.P. Napier & A. Flower	for	Essex	(SL)	2002
4th	121* M.A. Atherton & J.E.R. Gallian	for	Lancashire	(SL)	1994
5th	89 G.P. Thorpe & A.J. Hollioake	for	Surrey	(SL)	1995
6th	59 L. Potter & P.A. Nixon	for	Leicestershire	(SL)	1993
7th	24 J.E. Morris & B.J.M. Maher	for	Derbyshire	(SL)	1988
	24 C.C. Lewis & J.M. Dakin	for	Leicestershire	(SL)	2000
8th	61* V.J. Wells & J.M. Dakin	for	Leicestershire	(SL)	1993
9th	30 J. Abrahams & N.H. Fairbrother	for	Lancashire	(SL)	1983
10th	26 J.E. Benjamin & C.G. Rackemann	for	Surrey	(SL)	1995

Best bowling performance in a match for county 5 for 19 M.A. Buss v Minor Counties East (B&H) 1978
Best bowling performance in a match against county 5 for 29 M.G. Bevan for Yorkshire (SL) 1996
Largest crowd 6,500 v Worcestershire (SL) 1978

GROUND INFORMATION

ENTRANCES Cricketfield Road, via Worthing Road (B2237) (players, officials, members, public and vehicles), Barrackfield Walk via St Mary's Churchyard (pedestrians only).

MEMBERS' ENCLOSURE Pavilion and defined members enclosure in front of the pavilion.

PUBLIC ENCLOSURE Rest of the ground.

COVERED STANDS Pavilion/clubhouse.

OPEN STANDS Temporary raised and ground-level seating surrounding the playing area.

NAME OF ENDS Railway End, Town End.

GROUND DIMENSIONS 126m × 122m.

REPLAY SCREEN If televised matches are staged at the ground the replay screen is sited at the Railway End of the ground.

FIRST AID In tent at Railway End.

CODES OF DRESS Spectators are required to dress in an appropriate manner consistent with attending a cricket match. Bare torsos are not acceptable in, or in front of the pavilion. Executive Club/Suite users must wear a necktie and jacket.

BEHAVIOUR Sussex are keen that standards of behaviour should be maintained and members and spectators are urged to report immediately to the CEO any incident, or potential incident, where they feel action should be taken. Bad language is not acceptable at any match and the club will take prompt and strong action should this or any other ground regulation be ignored. Mobile telephones are not permitted, please ensure that mobile telephones are switched off before entering the spectator areas of the ground.

RECIPROCAL ARRANGEMENTS Members of Essex, Hampshire and Kent except when Sussex are playing their own county. Sussex CCC members can also gain free or reduced admission to race events on reciprocal dates at Plumpton, Fontwell Park, Goodwood and Brighton racecourses and Hickstead showgrounds.

SUPPORTERS' CLUB Sussex County Cricket Supporters' Club: subscription £4 (adults), £2 (senior citizens and under-16s) per annum. Regular newsletters are issued throughout the year. Membership details and information about events can be obtained from SCCSC, Freepost, County Ground, Eaton Road, Hove BN3 3AN.

JUNIORS Membership for those aged up to 16 on 1 January is £10 per annum. Contact Sussex CCC Membership Department ☎ 01273 827133 for full details.

CORPORATE ENTERTAINING Executive Membership is available and includes use of temporary marquees. Facilities available for conferences, lunches, dinners, wedding receptions throughout the year. Contact Commercial Department for details and a brochure ☎ 01273 827101.

FACILITIES FOR VISUALLY IMPAIRED SPECTATORS Yes, via Cricketfield Road entrance to rear of the pavilion.

FACILITIES AND ACCESS FOR PEOPLE WITH DISABILITIES INCLUDING WHEELCHAIR ACCESS TO GROUND Yes, special area available at Railway End of the ground.

DESIGNATED CAR PARK AVAILABLE INSIDE THE GROUND FOR PEOPLE WITH DISABILITIES Yes.

GOOD VIEWING AREAS INSIDE THE GROUND FOR PEOPLE USING WHEELCHAIRS No.

DESIGNATED VIEWING AREAS FOR PEOPLE USING WHEELCHAIRS No.

RAMPS TO PROVIDE EASY ACCESS TO BARS & REFRESHMENT OUTLETS FOR PEOPLE USING WHEELCHAIRS No.

FOOD & DRINK FULL RESTAURANT/DINING FACILITIES Members, yes. Public, no.

TEMPORARY FOOD/DRINK FACILITIES Members, yes. Public, yes.

FOOD SUITABLE FOR VEGETARIANS Members, yes. Public, no.

BARS Members 1, Public 1.

VARIETIES OF BEER SOLD Shepherd Neame, King & Barnes.

CHILDREN'S FACILITIES Crèche, no. Play area, no.

CLUB SHOP Sussex CCC shop in a mobile unit at the Railway End sells cricket books, items of Sussex memorabilia and clothing ☎ 01273 827127 www.sussexcricket.co.uk.

CLUB MUSEUM No, but there are pictures in the pavilion.

CRICKET COACHING FACILITIES Contact Horsham Cricket & Sports Club for details.

CRICKET NETS Contact Horsham Cricket & Sports Club for details.

OTHER SPORTING OR RECREATIONAL FACILITIES ON THE GROUND Hockey, squash and tennis.

FACILITIES FOR HIRE OR WIDER COMMUNITY USE AT THE GROUND WINTER CRICKET EVENTS No.

CAR PARKING FACILITIES There is a large area for car parking to the south and east of the ground at £4 per car, together with nearby street parking and central car parks in the town centre a short distance walk away from the ground.

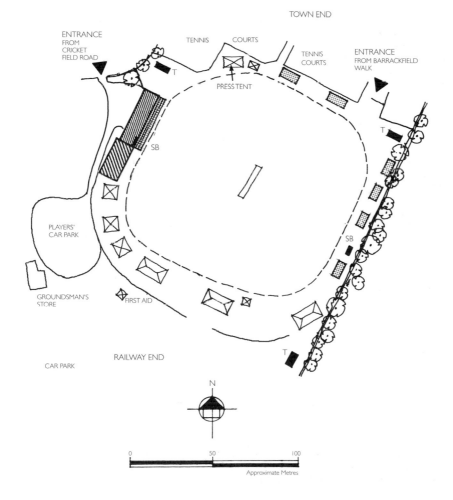

OTHER INFORMATION Neil Beck, a local cricket book dealer, usually has a caravan at the Railway End where he sells second-hand cricket books and memorabilia.
GROUND CAPACITY 4,500.
ANTICIPATED GROUND DEVELOPMENTS Nothing planned.

HOW TO GET THERE

 Horsham station 1 mile, approximately 25 minutes' walk from ground. ☎ 08457 484950, www.connex.co.uk, www.railtrack.co.uk, www.thetrainline.co.uk

 London Country (SW) H1, H2 and H5 link Horsham station with ground, ☎ 020 8668 7261 or 0345 959099. National Express Coaches ☎ 08705 808080, 08706 082608, www.gobycoach.com

 There are cycle routes from Horsham to this area of the town.

 From north: from M23 junction 11 take A264 (west), continue on this road and follow signs to Horsham town centre, follow one-way system and signs to Worthing, at traffic lights continue straight ahead, turn right at roundabout into Worthing Road, Cricketfield Road is on the left. From Guildford take A281 and follow this road to Horsham town centre, then as for M23. **From south:** from Brighton take A23, then bear left on to A281, follow this road into Horsham town centre, follow signs to Worthing, then as for north. **From east:** from Haywards Heath take A272 (west) to Cowfold, turn right on to A281 and follow signs to Horsham town centre, follow one-way system and signs to Worthing, then as for north. **From west:** Billingshurst, take A272 (east), at traffic lights junction with A24, turn left on A24 and continue on this road to second roundabout, take third exit signposted Christ's Hospital and amenity tip (Worthing Road), Cricketfield Road is on the right hand side.

 London Gatwick Airport ☎ 08700 002468 www.londongatwickairport.co.uk, London Heathrow Airport ☎ 08700 000123 www.londonheathrowairport.co.uk

WHERE TO STAY

Travel Lodge adjacent to Horsham station (☎ 08700 850950), Ye Olde King's Head (☎ 01403 253126). For other places to stay in and around Horsham visit www.smoothhound.co.uk or www.horsham.gov.uk.

WHERE TO EAT

Dining Room 2 (☎ 01444 417755), Fleur de Sel (☎ 01903 742331), Jeremys at Bordehill (☎ 01444 441102), Ockenden Manor (☎ 01444 416111)

TOURIST INFORMATION Horsham Tourist Information Centre, 9 Causeway, Horsham, West Sussex RH12 1HE ☎ 01403 211661, www.horsham.gov.uk

LOCAL RADIO STATIONS BBC Radio Southern Counties (104.5 MHz FM/1161 KHz MW), Southern FM (103.4 MHz FM/1332 KHz MW)

LOCAL NEWSPAPERS *The Argus, West Sussex County Times, Crawley Observer, West Sussex Gazette*

WARWICKSHIRE
COUNTY CRICKET CLUB

Warwickshire

Edgbaston

WARWICKSHIRE COUNTY CRICKET CLUB, THE COUNTY GROUND, EDGBASTON, BIRMINGHAM, WEST MIDLANDS B5 7QU

Club Office	0121 446 4422 **fax** 0121 440 7516
Membership and General Enquiries	0121 446 4422
Ticket Office	0121 446 5506
Marketing Department	0121 446 4777
Edgbaston Cricket Centre	0121 446 3633
The Shop at Edgbaston	0121 446 3636
Catering/Conference & Banqueting Department	0121 440 0747
Harpers Fitness Club	0121 256 1500
Website	www.thebears.co.uk
Email	info@thebears.co.uk

Founded 8 April 1882, substantial reorganisation 19 January 1884

Colours dark blue, gold and silver

Crest bear and ragged staff

National Cricket League Nickname The Bears

National Cricket League Colours silver, black and white

President The Rt Hon The Lord Guernsey

Chairman W.N. Houghton FCA

Vice Chairman I.R. Metcalfe

Chairman Cricket Committee T.A. Lloyd

Chief Executive Officer D.L. Amiss MBE

PA to CEO Mrs J. Jones

Operations Manager K.V. Cook

Head of Marketing P. Thompson

Director of Coaching R.J. Inverarity

1st XI Coach R.N. Abberley

2nd XI Coach S.P. Perryman

Captain M.J. Powell

Vice Captain D.R. Brown

Scorer 1st XI D.E. Wainwright

Scorer 2nd XI R. Burrows

Hon Treasurer S.G. Mills FCA

Accountant A. Wilkes

Assistant Accountant P. Kimberley

Edgbaston Cricket Centre Manager C. Howell

Ticket Office Manager Mrs S. Davies

Assistant Ticket Office Manager Mrs. M. Nelson

Development Manager P.J. Macdonald

Academy Director R.J. Newman

Head Groundsman S.J. Rouse

Catering General Manager (Letheby & Christopher) Ms A. Tooley

Ground Manager M.F. White

Shop Manager K. Butler

Historian/Librarian R.W. Brooke

Sponsors Banks's

Shirt Sponsors Banks's

Yearbook £5

Scorecard 40p (County) 50p (Test/ODI)

National Cricket League Programme & Scorecard £2

Newsletter/Magazine *Beyond The Boundary*

Frizzell County Championship Status Division 1

National Cricket League Status Division 1

ACHIEVEMENTS

County Championship Champions 1911, 1951, 1972, 1994, 1995

Gillette Cup Winners 1966, 1968, Finalists 1964, 1972

NatWest Trophy Winners 1989, 1993, 1995, Finalists 1982

Benson and Hedges Cup Winners 1994, 2002, Finalists 1984

John Player Sunday League Champions 1980

AXA Equity & Law League/AXA League Champions 1994, 1997

Fenner Trophy Finalists 1974

Tilcon Trophy Winners 1985, 1990, Finalists 1986, 1988

Seeboard Trophy Semi-finalists 1990

COUNTY CRICKET BOARD

Chairman R. Ball
Secretary D.L. Amiss MBE
Treasurer M. Timms
Director of Cricket R.M. Cox
Cricket Development Officer Foundation K. Evenson
Cricket Development Officer Participation E. McCabe
Cricket Development Officer (Senior) Performance G. Steer
Cricket Development Administrator A. Sweeney
Cricket Development Secretary A. Smart
Womens & Girls Director of Cricket R.M. Cox
Newsletter *Time to Declare*

Address Warwickshire Cricket Board, The County Ground, Edgbaston, Birmingham, West
Midlands B5 7QU
☎ 0121 446 3615
Fax 0121 440 8297
Website www.wcb.org.uk

GROUND

Birmingham (County Ground, Edgbaston)
   Other grounds used since 1969: Coventry (Courtaulds Sports Ground, Lockhurst Lane), Coventry (Coventry & North Warwickshire CC, Bull's Head Ground) and Nuneaton (Griff & Coton Sports Ground, Heath End Road).

SECOND XI GROUNDS

In addition to the above mentioned grounds the following are used for Second XI matches:
Coventry & North Warwickshire CC, Bull's Head Ground, Binley Road, Stoke, Coventry ☎ 01203 451426
Harborne CC, Old Church Avenue, Harborne, Birmingham ☎ 0121 427 4110
Kenilworth Wardens CC Glasshouse Park, Glasshouse Lane, Kenilworth, Warwickshire ☎ 01926 852476
Knowle & Dorridge CC, Station Road, Dorridge, Solihull, West Midlands ☎ 01564 774338
Leamington CC, Arlington Avenue, Leamington Spa, Warwickshire ☎ 01926 423854
Moseley CC, Streetsbrook Road, Solihull, West Midlands ☎ 0121 744 5694
Stratford-on-Avon CC, Swans Nest Lane, Stratford-on-Avon, Warwickshire ☎ 01789 297968
Studley CC, Washford Fields, Birmingham Road, Studley, Warwickshire ☎ 01527 853668
Walmley CC, Eldon Drive, off Penns Lane, Walmley, Sutton Coldfield, West Midlands ☎ 0121 351 1349
West Bromwich Dartmouth CC Sandwell Park, West Bromwich ☎ 0121 533 0168

EDGBASTON

Address The County Ground, Edgbaston Road, Edgbaston, Birmingham,
West Midlands B5 7QU
Prospects of Play ☎ 0121 446 4422

HISTORY OF GROUND AND FACILITIES

EDGBASTON IS THE THIRD GROUND in Birmingham to be used by Warwickshire County Cricket Club. The main part of the ground was acquired by Warwickshire in 1886 and the freehold land has been added to piecemeal at intervals since then. It has now been developed into one of the best-equipped cricket grounds in the country, second only, perhaps, to Lord's.

The ground was used for a Test match for the first time in 1902 when England played Australia in the first Test of that series. Test matches continued to be played there until 1929 but there was then a gap until the England v West Indies game in 1957 since when it has remained one of six regular Test venues in England.

The ground was originally a 'meadow of rough grazing land' and belonged to Lord Calthorpe until he allowed the club to lease it for cricket purposes. The original pavilion is still here but so much alteration has taken place that, except for the distinctive, red-tiled roof, it is difficult to recognise it among all the new additions at the Pavilion End. The William Ansell Stand was built during the 1950s from funds raised by the Warwickshire CCSA and was named after the first key figure in Warwickshire and Edgbaston's history. In 1975 an executive suite was added to the William Ansell Stand and in recent seasons more sponsors' suites and seating have been installed.

Most of the building at the ground took place in 1946, and during the 1950s and 1960s various additions were made. The most recent addition is the R.E.S. Wyatt Stand which was built during the winter of 1994/5 and includes the press and media box. The Thwaite Memorial Scoreboard was constructed in 1950 but was moved and reconstructed during the winter of 1988/9 because of the improvements made to the Stanley Barnes Stand and seating at the City End.

Edgbaston is one of the few grounds where the press box is still

Sydney Barnes Wicket Gate at the Pavilion End.

William Ansell and Leslie Deakins Stands seen from the Priory Stand.

immediately behind the sightscreen at the opposite end of the ground to the pavilion. The Edgbaston Cricket Museum is in the pavilion and many items of Warwickshire cricket memorabilia can be viewed. At the rear of the William Ansell Stand is the Calthorpe Library which is open for members on match days and houses the club's cricket book collection. On the Edgbaston Road frontage of the ground the observant visitor will note the Sydney Barnes Wicket Gate.

In February 1999, construction started on the new Edgbaston Cricket Centre to replace the existing indoor facility. It was completed thirteen months later in February 2000. The centre was designed by David Morley Architects and Bryant Priest Newman Architects. Extensive use has been made of glass panels in the construction. On the Pershore Road side of the building the elevation is clad with terracotta and written on the face are the words 'All over the world, Wherever they play, Stars of tomorrow are starting today'. The new building cost £2,233,300 and 65% of this was provided by Sport England. It covers 2,740 square metres.

The most recent development at Edgbaston has been the reconstruction of the former Rea Bank Stand, now the Eric Hollies Stand, which took place during the winter of 2001/2 at a cost of £2m. The roof of the stand is rather unusual as it was designed by Bryant Priest Newman Architects to keep out the sun rather than the rain.

In 1975, 1979 and 1983 Edgbaston hosted World Cup matches and in 1999 Warwickshire played two World Cup warm-up matches against the West Indies and Zimbabwe. Later when the tournament was in full flow, Edgbaston hosted three matches: in Group A England v India and in the Super 6 round South Africa v New Zealand. Finally, and probably the best match of the competition,

Edgbaston saw the semi-final between Australia and South Africa which resulted in a tied match. Australia, however, progressed into the final against Pakistan at Lord's.

During the 1990s Edgbaston hosted the Refuge Assurance Cup Finals between Lancashire and Worcestershire and Derbyshire and Middlesex. Warwickshire CCC were one of the first clubs to pioneer floodlit cricket in the UK and staged the first ever competitive day/night match on 23 July 1997 against Somerset in the Norwich Union National League. Around 15,000 spectators watched this historic game.

In 2002 Edgbaston celebrated 100 years as a venue for Test cricket and on 21 June the ground hosted the second Hill House Hammond Zone 6 City Cricket Challenge, the first having been staged at Bristol in 2001.

The TV camera/commentary box position is at the Pavilion End above the members' enclosure and scorers'/public address boxes. The radio commentary box is situated on the first floor of the pavilion overlooking the playing area which measures 148 metres by 145 metres. The actual playing area for a particular match will depend on the position of the playing strip selected and boundaries defined by ropes may vary, though for Test matches boundaries will only vary between 68 metres and 70 metres.

A premier cricket ground, Edgbaston is perhaps more of a stadium these days, surrounded on all sides by tiers of seats and expansive stands. However, a backcloth of trees is still visible in many areas and Cannon Hill Park is only five minutes' walk away to the south of the ground.

R.E.S. Wyatt stand with executive boxes, press box and open seating for the public seen from the Raglan Stand in 2002.

The Eric Hollies Stand in 2002.

GROUND RECORDS AND SCORES

FIRST-CLASS MATCHES

Highest innings total for county 810 for 4 dec v Durham 1994
Highest innings total against county 887 by Yorkshire 1896
Lowest innings total for county 35 v Yorkshire 1963
Lowest innings total against county 15 by Hampshire 1922
Highest individual innings for county 501* B.C. Lara v Durham 1994
Highest individual innings against county 250 by P. Holmes for Yorkshire 1931
Highest wicket partnerships for county

1st	333 J.F. Byrne & S.P. Kinneir	v	Lancashire	1905
2nd	465* J.A. Jameson & R.B. Kanhai	v	Gloucestershire	1974
3rd	327 S.P. Kinneir & W.G. Quaife	v	Lancashire	1901
4th	319 R.E.S. Wyatt & H.E. Dollery	v	Lancashire	1937
5th	322* B.C. Lara & K.J. Piper	v	Durham	1994
6th	204 H.E. Dollery & R.E. Hitchcock	v	Leicestershire	1952
7th	199 H.E. Dollery & T. Collin	v	Gloucestershire	1935
8th	203 G.W. Humpage & W.A. Bourne	v	Sussex	1976
9th	154 G.W. Stephens & A.J.W. Croom	v	Derbyshire	1925
10th	214 N.V. Knight & A. Richardson	v	Hampshire	2002

Highest wicket partnerships against county

1st	406* D.J. Bicknell & G.E. Welton	for	Nottinghamshire	2000
2nd	333 P. Holmes & E. Oldroyd	for	Yorkshire	1922
3rd	349 D.M. Jones & T.M. Moody	for	Australians	1989
4th	230 N.H. Fairbrother & G.D. Lloyd	for	Lancashire	1996
5th	393 E.G. Arnold & W.B. Burns	for	Worcestershire	1909
6th	268 J.N. Shepherd & D.A. Graveney	for	Gloucestershire	1983
7th	162 J. Iddon & P.T. Eckersley	for	Lancashire	1933
8th	292 R. Peel & Lord Hawke	for	Yorkshire	1896
9th	197 C.P. Mead & W.R.D. Shirley	for	Hampshire	1923
10th	149 G. Boycott & G.B. Stevenson	for	Yorkshire	1982

Best bowling performance in an innings for county 10 for 49 W.E. Hollies v Nottinghamshire 1946
Best bowling performance in an innings against county 10 for 67 E.A. Watts for Surrey 1939

Best bowling performance in a match for county 14 for 93 v T.L. Pritchard v Glamorgan 1951
Best bowling performance in a match against county 15 for 154 H.I. Young for Essex 1899
Largest crowd 28,000 v Lancashire 1951

LIMITED-OVERS MATCHES

Highest innings total for county 392 for 5 v Oxfordshire (NWT) 1984
Highest innings total against county 339 for 9 by Somerset (NWT) 1995
Lowest innings total for county 86 v Surrey (SL) 1969
Lowest innings total against county 56 by Yorkshire (SL) 1995
Highest individual innings for county 206 A.I. Kallicharran v Oxfordshire (NWT) 1984
Highest individual innings against county 163* C.G.Greenidge for Hampshire (SL) 1979
Highest wicket partnerships for county

1st	185 N.V. Knight & A. Singh	v	Hampshire	(NWT)	2000
2nd	197 K.D. Smith & A.I. Kallicharran	v	Oxfordshire	(NWT)	1984
3rd	169 B.C. Lara & D.L. Hemp	v	Kent	(NWT)	1998
4th	175* M.J.K. Smith & D.L. Amiss	v	Yorkshire	(SL)	1970
5th	143 D.A. Reeve & P.A. Smith	v	Lancashire	(SL)	1991
6th	94 A.I. Kallicharran & N.M. McVicker	v	Glamorgan	(GC)	1972
7th	137 A.J. Moles & A.F. Giles	v	Norfolk	(NWT)	1997
8th	83 W. Blenkiron & N.M. McVicker	v	Nottinghamshire	(SL)	1971
9th	47 Asif Din & A.A. Donald	v	Surrey	(SL)	1989
10th	39* R.G.D. Willis & D.J. Brown	v	Derbyshire	(SL)	1975

Highest wicket partnerships against county

1st	211* M.D. Moxon & A.A. Metcalfe	for	Yorkshire	(B&H)	1987
2nd	167 S.B. Hassan & G.StA. Sobers	for	Nottinghamshire	(SL)	1971
3rd	190 K.S. McEwan & D.R. Pringle	for	Essex	(SL)	1985
4th	149 M.P. Vaughan & A. McGrath	for	Yorkshire	(SL)	1999
5th	107 J.M. Brearley & G.D. Barlow	for	Middlesex	(GC)	1975
6th	121 N.A. Gie & W.M. Noon	for	Nottinghamshire	(B&H)	1998
7th	81 B.F. Smith & G.J. Parsons	for	Leicestershire	(B&H)	1996
8th	67* A.N. Hayhurst & R.P. Lefebvre	for	Somerset	(NWT)	1991
9th	59 D.J. Millns & T.J. Mason	for	Leicestershire	(B&H)	1996
10th	51 B.E.A. Edmeades & J.K. Lever	for	Essex	(B&H)	1975

Best bowling performance in a match for county 7 for 32 R.G.D. Willis v Yorkshire (B&H) 1981
Best bowling performance in a match against county 6 for 32 P.A. Strang for Nottinghamshire (SL) 1998
Largest crowd 14,750 v Yorkshire (NWT) 1982

TEST MATCHES

Highest innings total for England 633 for 5 dec v India 1979
Highest innings total against England 608 for 7 dec by Pakistan 1971
Lowest innings total for England 101 v Australia 1975, (lowest 89 for 9 v West Indies 1995 1 absent hurt)
Lowest innings total against England 30 by South Africa 1924
Highest individual innings for England 285* P.B.H. May v West Indies 1957
Highest individual innings against England 274 Zaheer Abbas for Pakistan 1971
Highest wicket partnerships for England

1st	179 M.A. Atherton & M.A. Butcher	v	South Africa	1998
2nd	331 R.T. Robinson & D.I. Gower	v	Australia	1985
3rd	227 A.J. Stewart & R.A. Smith	v	Pakistan	1992
4th	411 P.B.H. May & M.C. Cowdrey	v	West Indies	1957
5th	101 E.R. Dexter & P.J. Sharpe	v	West Indies	1963
6th	165* D.I. Gower & G. Miller	v	India	1979
7th	159 A.P.E. Knott & P. Lever	v	Pakistan	1971
8th	70 A.R. Caddick & A.J. Tudor	v	New Zealand	1999
9th	92 D.R. Pringle & C.C. Lewis	v	West Indies	1991
10th	103 A.J. Stewart & A.R. Caddick	v	Australia	2001

Highest wicket partnerships against England

1st	171 R.H. Catterall & B. Mitchell	for	South Africa	1929
2nd	291 Zaheer Abbas & Mushtaq Mohammad	for	Pakistan	1971
3rd	206 H.A. Gomes & I.V.A. Richards	for	West Indies	1984
4th	322 Javed Miandad & Salim Malik	for	Pakistan	1992
5th	153 M.E. Waugh & S.R. Waugh	for	Australia	1993
6th	190 O.G. Smith & F.M.M. Worrell	for	West Indies	1957
7th	107 I.A. Healy & M.G. Hughes	for	Australia	1993
8th	104 L. Klusener & J.N. Rhodes	for	South Africa	1998
9th	150 E.A.E. Baptiste & M.A. Holding	for	West Indies	1984
10th	63 A.C. Gilchrist & G.D. McGrath	for	Australia	2001

Best bowling performance in an innings for England 7 for 17 W. Rhodes v Australia 1902
Best bowling performance in an innings against England 7 for 49 S. Ramadhin for WIndies 1957
Best bowling performance in a match for England 12 for 119 F.S. Trueman v West Indies 1963
Best bowling performance in a match against England 10 for 188 C. Sharma for India 1986
Largest crowd 32,000 West Indies 1957

ONE-DAY INTERNATIONALS

Highest innings total for England in ODI 320 for 8 v Australia (PT) 1980
Highest innings total against England in ODI 280 for 4 by Australia (TT) 1993
Highest innings total in non-England ODI 309 for 5 for New Zealand v East Africa (WC) 1975
Lowest innings total for England in ODI 161 v Pakistan (NWS) 2001
Lowest innings total against England in ODI 70 by Australia (PT) 1977
Lowest innings total in non-England ODI 105 by Canada v Australia (WC) 1979
Highest individual innings for England in ODI 167* R.A. Smith v Australia (TT) 1993
Highest individual innings against England in ODI 113 M.E. Waugh for Australia v England (TT) 1993
Highest individual innings in non-England ODI 171* G.M. Turner for New Zealand v East Africa (WC) 1975

Highest wicket partnerships for England in ODI

1st	158 D.L. Amiss & B. Wood	v	East Africa	(WC)	1975
2nd	69 M.A. Atherton & G.A. Hick	v	South Africa	(TT)	1994
3rd	113 G.A.Hick & N.V.Knight	v	South Africa	(Emir)	1998
4th	81 A.J.Stewart & G.P.Thorpe	v	Zimbabwe	(NWS)	2000
5th	142 R.A. Smith & G.P. Thorpe	v	Australia	(TT)	1993
6th	47 I.T. Botham & M.W. Gatting	v	Australia	(PT)	1981
7th	41 D.I. Gower & V.J. Marks	v	New Zealand	(WC)	1983
8th	55 J.K. Lever & C.M. Old	v	Australia	(PT)	1977
9th	42 P.A.J. de Freitas & N.A. Foster	v	Pakistan	(PT)	1987
10th	23* M.A. Atherton & R.K. Illingworth	v	West Indies	(TT)	1991

Highest wicket partnerships against England in ODI

1st	53 J. Dyson & B.M. Laird	for	Australia	(PT)	1980
2nd	86 G.M. Wood & G.N. Yallop	for	Australia	(PT)	1981
3rd	150 Inzamam-ul-Haq & Saeed Anwar	for	Pakistan	(NWS)	2001
4th	168 A.R. Border & M.E. Waugh	for	Australia	(TT)	1993
5th	97 C.L. Hooper & A.L. Logie	for	West Indies	(TT)	1988
6th	65 A.R. Border & S.P. O'Donnell	for	Australia	(TT)	1985
7th	70 J.V. Coney & R.J. Hadlee	for	New Zealand	(WC)	1983
8th	35 G.F. Lawson & D.K. Lillee	for	Australia	(PT)	1981
9th	52* C.A. Walsh & C.E.L. Ambrose	for	West Indies	(TT)	1991
10th	35* Imran Khan & Mohsin Kamal	for	Pakistan	(TT)	1987

Highest wicket partnerships in non-England ODI

1st	176 H.H. Gibbs & G. Kirsten	for	South Africa v New Zealand	(WC)	1999
2nd	62 Majid Khan & Zaheer Abbas	for	Pakistan v West Indies	(WC)	1975
3rd	149 J.M. Parker & G.M. Turner	for	New Zealand v East Africa	(WC)	1975
4th	62 Mushtaq Mohammad & Wasim Raja	for	Pakistan v West Indies	(WC)	1975
5th	91 R.S. Dravid & Yuvraj Singh	for	India v Sri Lanka	(NWS)	2002
6th	46 J.V. Coney & M.D. Crowe	for	New Zealand v Pakistan	(WC)	1983

7th	49 M.G. Bevan & S.K. Warne	for	Australia v South Africa	(WC)	1999
8th	36 K.D. Ghavri & G.R. Vishwanath	for	India v West Indies	(WC)	1979
9th	55 K.M. Curran & P.W.E. Rawson	for	Zimbabwe v West Indies	(WC)	1983
10th	64* D.L. Murray & A.M.E. Roberts	for	West Indies v Pakistan	(WC)	1975

Best bowling performance for England in ODI 4 for 11 J.A. Snow for England v East Africa (WC) 1975
Best bowling performance against England in ODI 5 for 18 G.J. Cosier for Australia v England (PT) 1977
Best bowling performance in non-England ODI 5 for 21 A.G. Hurst for Australia v Canada (WC) 1979
Largest crowd 19,639 Australia v South Africa (WC) 1999

GROUND INFORMATION

ENTRANCES Edgbaston Road (players, officials, members, public and vehicles), Constance Road (members, press/media, public and vehicles), Pershore Road (members, public and vehicles).

MEMBERS' ENCLOSURE William Ansell Stand, R.V. Ryder Stand, Leslie Deakins Stand and Centre Pavilion only. Also, part of the Priory Stand for Test and one-day international matches if required.

PUBLIC ENCLOSURE Rest of the ground, including Priory Stand, Raglan Stand, R.E.S. Wyatt Stand, Press Box Stand, Stanley Barnes Stand and Eric Hollies Stand. For important matches all seats are reserved and numbered except in some parts of the members' enclosure.

COVERED STANDS Centre Pavilion (part), William Ansell Stand (part) including Tom Dollery Lounge and Cyril Goodway Suite, Priory Stand (part), Aylesford Executive Suites, Raglan Stand (part), R.E.S. Wyatt Executive Suites, R.E.S. Wyatt Stand (part), Press Box (lower) Stand (part), Calthorpe Suite, Eric Hollies Stand and R.V. Ryder Stand (part).

OPEN STANDS Pavilion (part), William Ansell Stand (part), Priory Stand (part), Raglan Stand (part), R.E.S. Wyatt Stand (part), Press Box (upper), Press Box Stand (lower), Stanley Barnes Stand, Leslie Deakins Stand, Eric Hollies Stand (part) and R.V. Ryder Stand (part).

NAME OF ENDS Pavilion End, City End.

GROUND DIMENSIONS 148m × 145m.

REPLAY SCREEN If televised matches are staged at the ground the replay screen is sited between the Eric Hollies Stand and the Stanley Barnes Stand at the City End of the ground.

FIRST AID First Aid room at rear of Priory Stand.

CODES OF DRESS Consistent with the prestige of attending a cricket match at Edgbaston members are expected to dress and behave in an appropriate manner. In the members' refreshment areas, smart casual dress is required. Bare torsos, bare feet and swimwear are unacceptable as is all ripped and torn clothing.

BEHAVIOUR Members are also expected to observe a standard of conduct which will enhance the reputation of the club, and in the interest of all members any foul language or abusive behaviour will not be tolerated. To avoid embarrassment, members are reminded that they have a responsibility to ensure that their guests observe these requirements.

GROUND REGULATIONS The club has a policy to prevent the importation of alcohol into the ground by non-members, members are restricted to four cans of beer or one bottle of wine. These drinks must be consumed in the membership areas only. Non-members will be able to obtain alcoholic beverages once inside the ground. The club reserves the right to refuse admission or to eject from the ground any person under the influence of alcohol.

RECIPROCAL ARRANGEMENTS None.

SUPPORTERS' CLUB Warwickshire CCC organise coaches to away matches. ☎ 0121 446 4422 for further information and specific details.

JUNIORS Membership of the Junior Bears costs £20 and is available to youngsters under 18. For further information contact club ☎ 0121 446 4422, www.thebears.co.uk

CORPORATE ENTERTAINING Executive and Corporate membership is available for a season or can be arranged on a match basis. Facilities are available for between 12 and 30 guests in various sized sponsors' executive boxes. Corporate hospitality offers from catering for 3 to 3,000 guests. The Edgbaston Club is ideal for smaller parties from 2 to 10 guests. Contact the Marketing Department for further information and a brochure ☎ 0121 446 4422.

FACILITIES FOR VISUALLY IMPAIRED SPECTATORS Yes, £20 charge for wheelchair users for an entire season with free pass for helpers if required.

FACILITIES AND ACCESS FOR PEOPLE WITH DISABILITIES INCLUDING WHEELCHAIR ACCESS TO GROUND Yes, through main gates in Edgbaston Road or via entrances in Pershore or Constance Road for vehicles.

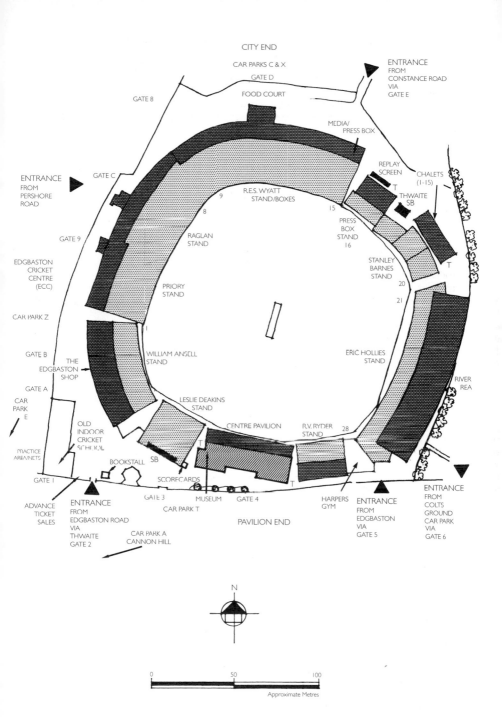

CITY END

CAR PARKS C & X

GATE D

GATE 8

FOOD COURT

MEDIA/
PRESS BOX

REPLAY
SCREEN

CHALETS
(1-15)

GATE C

THWAITE
SB

ENTRANCE
FROM
PERSHORE
ROAD

R.E.S. WYATT
STAND/BOXES

9

8

15

RAGLAN
STAND

PRESS
BOX
STAND

16

GATE 9

STANLEY
BARNES
STAND

EDGBASTON
CRICKET
CENTRE
(ECC)

PRIORY
STAND

20

CAR PARK Z

21

GATE B

THE
EDGBASTON
SHOP

WILLIAM ANSELL
STAND

ERIC HOLLIES
STAND

RIVER
REA

GATE A

CAR
PARK
E

LESLIE DEAKINS
STAND

OLD
INDOOR
CRICKET
SCHOOL

CENTRE PAVILION

R.V. RYDER
STAND

28

PRACTICE
AREA/NETS

T

BOOKSTALL

SB

T

GATE 1

SCORECARDS

T

ADVANCE
TICKET
SALES

ENTRANCE
FROM
EDGBASTON ROAD
VIA
THWAITE
GATE 2

GATE 3

MUSEUM

GATE 4

HARPERS
GYM

ENTRANCE
FROM
EDGBASTON
VIA
GATE 5

ENTRANCE
FROM
COLTS
GROUND
CAR PARK
VIA
GATE 6

CAR PARK T

CAR PARK A
CANNON HILL

PAVILION END

N

0   50   100

Approximate Metres

WARWICKSHIRE • EDGBASTON   359

DESIGNATED CAR PARK AVAILABLE INSIDE THE GROUND FOR PEOPLE WITH DISABILITIES Yes, situated in Car Park B at St James's Street End of the ground and in Car Park A accessed from Priory Bridge Road near main scoreboard.

GOOD VIEWING AREAS INSIDE THE GROUND FOR PEOPLE USING WHEELCHAIRS Yes, in front of Thwaite Scoreboard and the Eric Hollies Stand and in other area by special arrangement in advance with club.

DESIGNATED VIEWING AREAS FOR PEOPLE USING WHEELCHAIRS Yes, special enclosure in front of the Old Pavilion. Other locations are available around the ground by prior arrangement with the club stewards. There are disabled toilets situated to the rear R.E.S. Wyatt Stand, to the rear of Stanley Barnes Stand and in the Pavilion Annexe area.

RAMPS TO PROVIDE EASY ACCESS TO BARS & REFRESHMENT OUTLETS FOR PEOPLE USING WHEELCHAIRS Yes, but not many, however, lifts are available within the William Ansell Stand, Eric Hollies Stand and the R.E.S. Wyatt Stand.

FOOD & DRINK FULL RESTAURANT/DINING FACILITIES Members, yes. Public, some matches only. Full restaurant service is available in the William Ansell Stand in the Tom Dollery Bar & Restaurant. Contact Catering Department in advance ☎ 0121 440 0747 to book.

TEMPORARY FOOD/DRINK FACILITIES Members, yes. Public, yes. There is also a food village at the City End during major matches.

FOOD SUITABLE FOR VEGETARIANS Members, yes. Public, yes.

BARS Members 2, Public 5+ for major matches.

VARIETIES OF BEER SOLD Banks's.

CHILDREN'S FACILITIES Crèche, no. Play area, yes on National Cricket League match days only.

CLUB SHOP The shop at Edgbaston is one of the largest and best stocked in the country. It offers an extensive range of Warwickshire CCC items together with England items and over 500 current titles of cricket books, plus videos, CDs and audio tapes. It also has basics such as suntan lotion, sweets and batteries. Open Monday to Saturday 9 a.m. to 5 p.m. throughout the year and Sunday 9 a.m. to close of play on any match day ☎ 0121 446 3633, www.thebears.co.uk.

CLUB MUSEUM In the main pavilion area is the Edgbaston Museum which has a splendid collection of Warwickshire, England and Edgbaston cricket memorabilia. There are many display cabinets and numerous pictures, bats, balls, trophies and caps on view. New features in 2002 included a computerised visual display and audio presentations. There is a cabinet devoted to Midlands cricket and items on Warwickshire's Championship years starting in 1911. The museum is open on match days only or by request in advance. Contact club for information about winter opening hours. The club library is located to the rear of the William Ansell stand.

CRICKET COACHING FACILITIES Yes, in Edgbaston Cricket Centre open throughout the year.

CRICKET NETS Yes, indoor nets in Edgbaston Cricket Centre open throughout the year.

OTHER SPORTING OR RECREATIONAL FACILITIES ON THE GROUND Harpers Fitness Club and Gymnasium. For further information ☎ 0121 256 1500.

FACILITIES FOR HIRE OR WIDER COMMUNITY USE AT THE GROUND The Edgbaston Conference and Banqueting Centre can accommodate from 10 to 400 delegates with car parking for 700 vehicles. Rooms are available for seminars, trade shows, exhibitions, company lunches, dinner dances, private parties, training sessions and weddings throughout the year by arrangement with Marketing Department ☎ 0121 446 4777.

WINTER CRICKET EVENTS Members' club dinners, lunches, fun day, end of season reception, members' night, forums and Christmas lunches. The Midlands branch of The Cricket Society holds regular monthly meetings at Edgbaston in the William Ansell Stand between September and March.

CAR PARKING FACILITIES Members holding a valid car park season ticket will be able to use the car park subject to space being available and the club hopes to have additional spaces available off site to supplement the main members' car park. Please contact the club in advance of the match you wish to attend. Arrangements for car parking vary from match to match. Additional car parking will be made available for Test and one-day international matches. Official car parks will be clearly signposted from approach roads. West Midlands Police do not permit parking on many of the local streets. For further information contact the Ticket Office in advance of the match.

OTHER INFORMATION Near the Main Gate in Edgbaston Road is the stall owned by Tim Beddow. He offers a wide selection of second-hand and out-of-print cricket and football books and other items of cricket memorabilia as well as daily newspapers. At major matches he has other outlets around the ground. For further information ☎ 0121 421 7117.

GROUND CAPACITY 21,000.

ANTICIPATED DEVELOPMENTS None presently planned.

HOW TO GET THERE

 Birmingham New Street station 1.75 miles, Birmingham Snow Hill station 2 miles from ground. Taxi services are available. ☎ 08457 484950, 08457 000125, 08457 222333, 08700 006060, 01296 332113, 08709 00 0766, 0121 214 7072, 08705 165165, www.virgin.com/trains, www.silverlink-trains.com, www.centraltrains.com, www.chilternrailways.co.uk, www.walesandwest.co.uk, www.thetrainline.co.uk, www.railtrack.co.uk

 West Midlands Travel Bus 45 and 47 link New Street station and city centre with ground via Pershore Road (A441). Buses 61, 62 and 63 from Navigation Street via Bristol Road (A38) to ground and Bus 1 from Five Ways (A456) to Acocks Green via Edgbaston Road (B4217) to ground. ☎ 0121 200 2601, Centro Hotline 0121 200 2700, Travel Line 0870 608 2608, www.centro.co.uk, National Express Coaches ☎ 08705 808080, www.travelwm.co.uk, www.nationalexpresscoaches.co.uk, www.gobycoach.com

 There are cycle routes from surrounding areas to this part of the city. The ground is adjacent to the Rea Valley Cycle Way.

 From north: from M6 junction 6 continue towards Birmingham on A38(M) (Aston Expressway), continue through city centre following signs to A441, continue on A441 following signs to Edgbaston and County Cricket Ground. **From south:** from M42 junction 3 take third exit from roundabout on to A435 (Alcester Road), continue on this road to junction with B4217 (Salisbury Road), take Salisbury Road, then bear left on to Edgbaston Road and follow signs to County Cricket Ground. **From east:** from A45 (Coventry) continue towards Birmingham to junction with A435 (Alcester Road), take A435 and continue to junction with A4217, following signs to County Cricket Ground. **From west:** from M5 junction 3 exit roundabout on to A456 (Quinton Expressway), continue on A456 (Hagley Road), at roundabout take fourth exit on to B4217 (Calthorpe Road) and continue on B4217 (Church Road, Priory Road, Edgbaston Road) following signs to County Cricket Ground.

 Birmingham International Airport ☎ 0121 767 5511, Flight Enquiries 0121 767 7798/9 www.bhx.co.uk

WHERE TO STAY

Beech House Hotel (☎ 0121 373 0620), Birmingham Marriott (☎ 0121 452 1144), Celtic Court Hotel (☎ 0121 604 8111), Cobden Hotel (☎ 0121 454 6621), Copthorne Hotel (☎ 0121 200 2727 www.millennium-hotels.com), Crowne Plaza (☎ 0121 224 5053 www.crownplaza.com), Days Inn (☎ 0121 643 9344 www.daysinn.com), Edgbaston Hotel (☎ 0121 455 9606), Holiday Inn Hotel (☎ 0121 357 7444), Hotel Campanile (☎ 0121 359 3330), Hyatt Regency (☎ 0121 643 1234 www.hyatt.com), Ibis Centre Hotel (☎ 0121 622 6010 www.ibis.co.uk), J.D. Wetherspoon Briar Rose (☎ 0121 634 8100), Plough & Harrow (☎ 0121 454 4111 www.corushotels.com/ploughandharrow), Strathallan Hotel (☎ 0121 455 9777), The Burlington Hotel (☎ 0121 643 9191 www.burlingtonhotel.com), The De Vere Belfry (☎ 01675 470033 www.devereonline.co.uk), The Grand Hotel (☎ 0121 236 7951), The Holiday Inn Albany (☎ 0121 631 2528), The Norfolk Hotel (☎ 0121 454 8071), Thistle Edgbaston (☎ 0121 606 4500 www.thistlehotels.com), Wentsbury Hotel, Selly Oak (☎ 0121 472 1258)

For other places to stay in Birmingham contact Birmingham Convention & Visitor Bureau ☎ 0121 780 4321, 0121 643 2514, 01206 255800, 0870 606 7204, 08000 726 999, www.birmingham.org.uk or www.smoothhound.co.uk.

WHERE TO EAT

52 Degrees North (☎ 0121 622 5250 www.fiftytwodegreesnorth.co.uk), Bank (☎ 0121 633 4466 www.bankrestaurants.com), Café Ikon (☎ 0121 248 3226), Chez Jules (☎ 0121 633 4664), Chung Ying Garden (☎ 0121 666 6622 www.chungying.co.uk), Fish (☎ 020 7234 3333 www.fishdiner.co.uk), Henry's Cantonese (☎ 0121 200 1136 www.henrysrestaurant.co.uk), Imran's (☎ 0121 449 6440 www.imrans.co.uk), Kababish (☎ 0121 449 5556), Le Petit Blanco (☎ 0121 633 7333 www.petitblanc.com), Maharaja (☎ 0121 622 2641), Nando's (☎ 0800 975 8181 www.nandos.co.uk), Shimla Pinks (☎ 0121 633 0366

R.V. Ryder Stand, pavilion and Leslie Deakins Stand pictured from the Eric Hollies Stand, 2002.

www.shimlapinks.bite2enjoy.com), Siam Thai (☎ 0121 444 0906 www.siamrestaurant.co.uk), Thai Edge (☎ 0121 643 3993), The Jam House (☎ 0121 200 3030 www.thejamhouse.com)

TOURIST INFORMATION Birmingham Convention & Visitor Bureau, Visitor Information Centre, 2 City Arcade, Birmingham B2 4TX ☎ 0121 643 2514, 130 Colmore Row, Victoria Square, Birmingham B3 3AP ☎ 0121 693 6300, 26 Waterloo Street, Victoria Square, Birmingham B2 5TJ ☎ 0121 603 2000 www.tourismbirmingham.gov.uk

OTHER USEFUL INFORMATION

Aston Villa Football Club ☎ 0121 372 5353 www.avfc.co.uk
Birmingham & Solihull Rugby Football Club ☎ 0121 705 0409
Birmingham Canals ☎ 0121 507 0477
Birmingham City Football Club ☎ 0121 772 0101 www.bcfc.co.uk
Birmingham Museum & Art Gallery ☎ 0121 303 2834 www.bmag.org.uk
Birmingham Tour Bus Company ☎ 0121 693 6300
Birmingham Visitor Information ☎ 0121 693 6300
Cadbury World ☎ 0121 451 4180 www.cadburyworld.co.uk
Coventry City Football Club ☎ 024 7623 4000 www.ccfc.co.uk
Hall Green Stadium ☎ 0121 777 8439
Moseley Rugby Football Club ☎ 0121 415 2207
Museum of Jewellery Quarter ☎ 0121 554 3598 www.bmag.co.uk
The De Vere Belfry ☎ 01675 47033 www.thebelfry.com
Walsall Football Club ☎ 01922 622791 www.walsallfc.co.uk
West Bromwich Albion Football Club ☎ 0121 525 8888 www.baggies.co.uk
Wolverhampton Wanderers Football Club ☎ 01902 655000 www.wwfc.co.uk

LOCAL RADIO STATIONS BBC Radio WM (95.6 MHz FM/1468 KHz MW), BRMB-FM/Capital Gold (96.4 MHz FM/1152 KHz MW), Mercia FM/Classic Gold Digital (97.0 MHz FM/1359 KHz MW), Beacon FM/Classic Gold WABC (97.2 MHz FM/990 KHz MW)

LOCAL NEWSPAPERS *Birmingham Post*, *Birmingham Evening Mail*, *Sports Argus* (weekends only), *Express & Star*, *Sunday Mercury*

Worcestershire

Worcester
Kidderminster

WORCESTERSHIRE COUNTY CRICKET CLUB, COUNTY CRICKET GROUND, NEW ROAD, WORCESTER, WORCESTERSHIRE WR2 4QQ

Main Switchboard	01905 748474 **fax** 01905 748005
New Road One	01905 337922
Catering Department	01905 337940
Ticket Office	01905 337921
Website	www.wccc.co.uk
Email	webmaster@wccc.co.uk

Founded 5 March 1865
Colours dark green and black
Crest shield argent bearing a fess between three pears stable
National Cricket League Nickname Royals
National Cricket League Colours black, dark green and white
President N.H. Whiting
Chairman Cricket Committee J. Elliott
Hon Treasurer P. Seward FCA
Captain B.F. Smith
Vice Captain S.J. Rhodes
Chief Executive Officer M. Newton
Director of Cricket T.M. Moody
Assistant Coach D.B. D'Oliveira
PA to Chief Executive/Director of Cricket Mrs J. Grundy
Director of Finance and Operations M. Tagg
Head Groundsman T. Packwood
Stadium Manager P. Phillips

Accounts Supervisor Ms L. Serjeant
Accounts Administrator Mrs H. Wainwright
Commercial Director T. Sears
Corporate Hospitality Manager Ms E. Underwood
Membership Secretary Ms R. Hooper
Shop Manager Ms S. Gray
Director of Catering S. Gibbs
Catering Administrator Mrs C. Bradley
Heritage Group Chairman B. Bridgewater
Scorer 1st XI W. Clarke
Scorer 2nd XI N. Smith
Sponsors Apollo 2000, Coors Brewers
Yearbook £10
Scorecards 50p each
National Cricket League Match Programme £2
Newsletter *New Road News* issued twice yearly free to members
Club Shop New Road One, www.newroad1.co.uk
Frizzell County Championship Status Division 2
National Cricket League Status Division 1

ACHIEVEMENTS

County Championship Champions 1964, 1965, 1974, 1988, 1989, Runners-up 1907, 1962, 1966, 1979, 1993
Gillette Cup Finalists 1963, 1966
NatWest Trophy Winners 1994, Finalists 1988
Benson and Hedges Cup Winners 1991, Finalists 1973, 1976, 1990
John Player Sunday League Champions 1971

Refuge Assurance League Champions 1987, 1988
CGU National Cricket League Runners-up 1999
Norwich Union National League Runners-up Division 1 2002, Runners-up Division 2 2001
Refuge Assurance Cup Winners 1991, Finalists 1988
Tilcon Trophy Winners 1981, 1989
Minor Counties Champions 1895, 1896, 1897, 1898

COUNTY CRICKET BOARD

Chairman M. Gilhooly
Secretary A. Scrafton
Treasurer R. Viner
Cricket Development Officer S.R. Lampitt
Women & Girls Secretary C. Penwarden

Address   Worcestershire Cricket Board, County Cricket Ground, New Road, Worcester,
Worcestershire WR2 4QQ
☎   01905 429137
Fax   01905 429137
Email worcscricketboard@talk21.com

GROUNDS

Worcester (County Cricket Ground, New Road) and Kidderminster (Kidderminster CC, Chester Road)
   Other grounds used since 1969: Hereford (Racecourse Ground, Grandstand Road), Dudley (County Ground, Tipton Road), Stourbridge (Stourbridge War Memorial Ground, Amblecote), Stourport-on-Severn (Parsons Controls Holdings Limited, The Chainwire Club Sports Ground, Minister Road) and Halesowen (Halesowen CC, Sports Ground, Grange Road)

SECOND XI GROUNDS

In addition to the above mentioned grounds the following are used for Second XI matches:
Barnt Green CC, Cherry Hill Road, Barnt Green ☎ 0121 445 1684
Kidderminster CC, Chester Road, Kidderminster ☎ 01562 824175
Old Hill CC, Haden Hill Park, Cradley Heath ☎ 01384 566827
Ombersley CC, Cricket Ground, Ombersley, no ☎ on ground

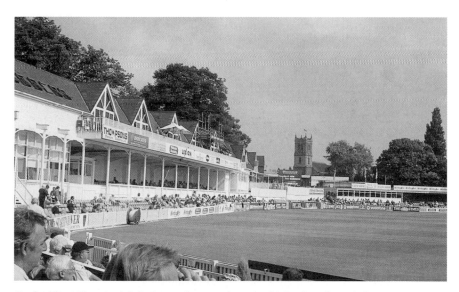

New Road Stand, Worcester, including the press box, scorers' room, members' seating and executive boxes.

WORCESTER

Address County Cricket Ground, New Road, Worcester,
Worcestershire WR2 4QQ
Prospects of Play ☎ 01905 748474

HISTORY OF GROUND AND FACILITIES

THE COUNTY CRICKET GROUND at Worcester is situated in New Road, west of the bridge over the River Severn and within walking distance of the city centre. It is probably the most attractive county ground in the country and was the property of Worcester Cathedral until purchased by Worcestershire County Cricket Club in 1976 for £30,000. The view of the playing area from the pavilion enclosure has the fourteenth-century cathedral as its backcloth.

The county club moved to New Road in 1899 from Boughton Park and the first first-class match staged on the ground was with Yorkshire between 4 and 6 May that year. So urgent were the preparations that the sightscreen was still being painted by ground staff on the morning of the match.

The members' pavilion was built in 1898/9 and appears unchanged externally, although internal alterations have taken place. Since the Worcestershire County Cricket Supporters' Association was founded in 1951 by the Lord Lieutenant of the County, Admiral Sir William Tennant, much money has been raised to improve the county ground. Changes have included the addition of new seating in 1952 (which was replaced during the 1990s), a scoreboard in 1954 and two years later a Ladies Pavilion. In 1965, the championship year, the Severn Bar on the east side was rebuilt and in the winter of 1973/4 major additions were made

The main scoreboard with the cathedral behind.

Floodlit cricket at New Road in 2001. The Worcestershire Royals beat the Durham Dynamos in the Norwich Union National League.

to the New Road Stand notably a roof, press box/scorers' room and the secretary's office. In 1984/5 further development was undertaken when an executive suite was built on the site of the old supporters' association offices, scorers' room and press box. The scorers' room and press boxes have since been moved to the other end of the New Road Stand, near to the pavilion. The supporters' association is now housed in the offices of the club's marketing department. New executive boxes on top of the New Road Stand were constructed in 1989/90.

Regular floods from the nearby Rivers Teme and Severn have introduced fishing, boating, swimming, wind surfing and even ice skating to the County Ground on occasions! In the members' pavilion there is a brass plate showing the highest water level in 1947 – at least a metre above the floor and several metres above the playing area outside. Flooding usually occurs around Christmas but in 1987 the waters came in March, only a few weeks before the start of the season, and in 2001 there were more in February.

The ground has staged Test trial and international matches including the 1983 Prudential Cup match between West Indies and Zimbabwe, a Young England against Young Australia Test match in 1983, the 1979 ICC Trophy final between Sri Lanka and Canada and a Ladies' Test match in 1984 between England and New Zealand. This was the third Women's Test match staged at Worcester. World Cup matches were staged at New Road in 1999 when Australia played Scotland and Sri Lanka played Zimbabwe.

For several years following the restructuring of the Minor Counties Cricket Association in 1983 the winners of the two divisions, East and West, met at New Road to decide the championship. In 1990 the final was transferred to Wardown Park, Luton but New Road again hosted the championship decider between

1993 and 1995. In 2002 the final of the ECB County Board Cup between Devon and Warwickshire was staged at the ground.

For many years Worcester was traditionally the first county match for the touring side, but this has altered in recent years and many touring sides now begin their tours at Arundel Castle.

During Queen Elizabeth's Golden Jubilee weekend, 2 and 3 June 2002, two concerts were staged at the County Ground: XS 2002 featuring Blue, H & Claire and 3SL was followed the next day by the English Symphony Orchestra.

The main radio commentary point is in the New Road Stand and the TV camera position is at the Diglis End on a gantry directly above and behind the sightscreen. The press box and scorers' room are in the New Road Stand. The playing area falls slightly towards the west and is defined by a rope and white fence with advertising boards. It measures 145 metres by 158 metres and is roughly circular in shape.

GROUND RECORDS AND SCORES

FIRST-CLASS MATCHES

Highest innings total for county 670 for 7 dec v Somerset 1995
Highest innings total against county 701 for 4 dec by Leicestershire 1906
Lowest innings total for county 40 v Leicestershire 1971
Lowest innings total against county 30 by Hampshire 1903
Highest individual innings for county 315* G.A. Hick v Durham 2002
Highest individual innings against county 331* J.D.B. Robertson for Middlesex 1949
Highest wicket partnerships for county

1st	306 F.L. Bowley & F.A. Pearson	v	Gloucestershire	1913
2nd	300 W.P.C. Weston & G.A. Hick	v	Indians	1996
3rd	314 M.J. Horton & T.W. Graveney	v	Somerset	1962
4th	277 H.H.I. Gibbons & B.W. Quaife	v	Middlesex	1931
5th	227 T.S. Curtis & M.J. Weston	v	Surrey	1985
6th	220 P.A. Neale & R.K. Illingworth	v	Nottinghamshire	1990
7th	205 G.A. Hick & P.J. Newport	v	Yorkshire	1988
8th	145* F. Chester & W.H. Taylor	v	Essex	1914
9th	181 J.A. Cuffe & R.D. Burrows	v	Gloucestershire	1907
10th	119 W.B. Burns & G.A. Wilson	v	Somerset	1906

Highest wicket partnerships against county

1st	380 C.J.B. Wood & H. Whitehead	for	Leicestershire	1906
2nd	336 F.B. Watson & G.E. Tyldesley	for	Lancashire	1929
3rd	285 M.R. Benson & C.J. Tavare	for	Kent	1987
4th	277 D.G. Bradman & C.L. Badcock	for	Australians	1938
5th	301* C.E. Pellew & C.B. Willis	for	AIF	1919
6th	260 A.C. MacLaren & R. Whitehead	for	Lancashire	1910
7th	173 Younis Ahmed & Intikhab Alam	for	Surrey	1975
8th	183 D.J. Insole & R. Smith	for	Essex	1937
9th	146 G.H. Hirst & W. Rhodes	for	Yorkshire	1901
10th	141 A.F. Giles & T.A. Munton	for	Warwickshire	1996

Best bowling performance in an innings for county 9 for 23 C.F. Root v Lancashire 1931
Best bowling performance in an innings against county 10 for 51 J. Mercer for Glamorgan 1936
Best bowling performance in a match for county 15 for 106 R.T.D. Perks v Essex 1937
Best bowling performance in a match against county 15 for 175 J.C. White for Somerset 1921
Largest crowd 14,000 v Australians 1948

LIMITED-OVERS MATCHES

Highest innings total for county 404 for 3 v Devon (NWT) 1987
Highest innings total against county 328 for 6 for Hampshire (NWT) 1996
Lowest innings total for county 70 v Gloucestershire (B&H) 2002
Lowest innings total against county 45 by Hampshire (SL) 1988
Highest individual innings for county 172* G.A.Hick v Devon (NWT) 1987
Highest individual innings against county 158 R.A.Smith for Hampshire (NWT) 1996
Highest wicket partnerships for county

1st	198 T.S. Curtis & T.M. Moody	v	Kent	(SL)	1991
2nd	174 T.S. Curtis & D.M. Smith	v	Warwickshire	(B&H)	1985
3rd	190* D.M. Smith & G.A. Hick	v	Nottinghamshire	(B&H)	1986
4th	152 G.A. Hick & P.A. Neale	v	Cumberland	(NWT)	1988
5th	131 J.M. Parker & T.J. Yardley	v	Leicestershire	(B&H)	1975
6th	121 P.A. Neale & S.J. Rhodes	v	Yorkshire	(B&H)	1988
7th	66 S.J. Rhodes & S.R. Lampitt	v	Oxfordshire	(SL)	1994
8th	79 T.S. Curtis & R.K. Illingworth	v	Yorkshire	(SL)	1994
9th	51 S.R. Lampitt & R.K. Illingworth	v	Leicestershire	(SL)	1993
10th	50 S.R. Lampitt & P.J. Newport	v	Surrey	(SL)	1993

Highest wicket partnerships against county

1st	157 A.W. Stovold & Zaheer Abbas	for	Gloucestershire	(B&H)	1976
	(224 was shared by Sadiq Mohammed & A.W. Stovold and Zaheer Abbas in the above match, A.W. Stovold retiring hurt at 57 for 0.)				
2nd	200* R.T. Robinson & C.E.B. Rice	for	Nottinghamshire	(SL)	1984
3rd	188 A.J. Lamb & R.G. Williams	for	Northamptonshire	(SL)	1981
4th	156 A.I. Kalllcharran & G.W. Humpage	for	Warwickshire	(B&H)	1985
5th	123 R.W. Tolchard & P.B. Clift	for	Leicestershire	(B&H)	1976
6th	108* R.B. Kanhai & P.R. Oliver	for	Warwickshire	(B&H)	1977
7th	134 S.M. Pollock & T.L. Penney	for	Warwickshire	(SL)	2002
8th	95* A.S. Rollins & P.A.J. de Freitas	for	Derbyshire	(B&H)	1998
9th	83 M.P. Bicknell & Saqlain Mushtaq	for	Surrey	(SL)	1997
10th	51 I.D. Austin & J. Stanworth	for	Lancashire	(B&H)	1987

Best bowling performance in a match for county 6 for 14 J.A. Flavell v Lancashire (GC) 1963
Best bowling performance in a match against county 6 for 14 H.P. Cooper for Yorkshire (SL) 1975
Largest crowd 8,500 v Lancashire (NWT) 1989

ONE-DAY INTERNATIONALS

Highest innings total in ODI 218 for 2 by West Indies v Zimbabwe (WC) 1983
Lowest innings total in ODI 181 by Scotland v Australia (WC) 1999
Highest individual innings in ODI 105* C.G. Greenidge for West Indies v Zimbabwe (WC) 1983
Highest wicket partnerships in ODI

1st	21 A. Flower & N.C. Johnson	for	Zimbabwe v Sri Lanka	(WC)	1999
2nd	84 R.T. Ponting & M.E. Waugh	for	Australia v Scotland	(WC)	1999
3rd	195* H.A. Gomes & C.G. Greenidge	for	West Indies v Zimbabwe	(WC)	1983
4th	40 M.E. Waugh & S.R. Waugh	for	Australia v Scotland	(WC)	1999
5th	92 D.A.G. Fletcher & D.L. Houghton	for	Zimbabwe v West Indies	(WC)	1983
6th	62 J.E. Brinkley & G.M. Hamilton	for	Scotland v Australia	(WC)	1999
7th	68 S.V. Carlisle & A. Flower	for	Zimbabwe v Sri Lanka	(WC)	1999
8th	34* D.A.G. Fletcher & G.E. Peckover	for	Zimbabwe v West Indies	(WC)	1983
9th	14 E.A. Brandes & H.H. Streak	for	Zimbabwe v Sri Lanka	(WC)	1999
10th	21* E.A. Brandes & H.E. Olonga	for	Zimbabwe v Sri Lanka	(WC)	1999

Best bowling performance in ODI 3 for 30 G.P. Wickramasinghe for Sri Lanka v Zimbabwe (WC) 1999
Largest crowd 5,107 Sri Lanka v Zimbabwe (WC) 1999

GROUND INFORMATION

ENTRANCES New Road through main gate (players, officials, press/media, members, public and vehicles), New Road Turnstiles near club office (pedestrians only).

MEMBERS' ENCLOSURE Pavilion, Pavilion Terrace, Ladies' Pavilion, Ladies' Terrace, Diglis End and New Road Stand (upper covered area).

PUBLIC ENCLOSURE Rest of the ground including open pitch side seats in front of New Road Stand.

COVERED STANDS Pavilion (part) and New Road Stand (part).

OPEN STANDS Pavilion (part), New Road Stand (part), Pavilion (Terrace), Ladies' Pavilion (part), Diglis End seats and seats in front of New Road One shop, WCCSA shop and the secondary scoreboard.

NAME OF ENDS New Road End, Diglis End.

GROUND DIMENSIONS 145m × 158m.

REPLAY SCREEN If televised matches are staged at the ground the replay screen is sited at the Diglis End of the ground.

FIRST AID At the Diglis End of the ground.

CODES OF DRESS Spectators are required to dress in an appropriate manner consistent with attending a cricket match. Bare torsos are not acceptable in, or in front of, the pavilion. Executive Club/Suite users must wear smart casual clothing.

BEHAVIOUR The club is keen that standards of behaviour should be maintained and members and spectators are urged to report immediately any incident, or potential incident, where they feel action should be taken. Bad language and racist behaviour is not acceptable at any match and the club will take prompt and strong action should this or any other ground regulation be ignored.

RECIPROCAL ARRANGEMENTS Members of Glamorgan, Gloucestershire and Somerset can gain entry free for championship matches on production of membership card when Worcestershire is not playing their own county.

SUPPORTERS' CLUB Worcestershire CC Supporters' Association £5 for (WCCC members) and £10 for (non WCCC members). Special rates for concessions and husband and wife membership are available.

JUNIORS Under-16s can go free under the 'Kids Go Free Scheme'. Contact the Membership Office on ☎ 01905 748474 for further information.

CORPORATE ENTERTAINING Various packages are available including full corporate hospitality in the Cricket Suite or in either the Perks or Foster Rooms. There are 10 boxes on the upper level of the New Road Stand behind the bowler's arm and a marquee seating up to 200 at the Diglis End of the ground. Contact the Commercial Department for further information and a brochure on ☎ 01905 748474.

FACILITIES FOR VISUALLY IMPAIRED SPECTATORS Reduced admission on request including helper. Guide dogs are allowed but please give one day's warning of attendance.

FACILITIES AND ACCESS FOR PEOPLE WITH DISABILITIES INCLUDING WHEELCHAIR ACCESS TO GROUND Yes, through main gate to rear of pavilion in New Road. Most buildings are raised 6-8 feet above ground and are accessible only by steps.

DESIGNATED CAR PARK AVAILABLE INSIDE THE GROUND FOR PEOPLE WITH DISABILITIES Yes, at the Diglis End of the ground. Subject to space being available vehicles can be parked adjacent to the Diglis End from where cricket can be watched.

GOOD VIEWING AREAS INSIDE THE GROUND FOR PEOPLE USING WHEELCHAIRS Yes, particularly on areas of hard standing around the perimeter of the playing area. Please request position in advance.

DESIGNATED VIEWING AREAS FOR PEOPLE USING WHEELCHAIRS Yes, at both the Diglis End and New Road Ends of the ground on hard standing. There is a designated viewing area in front of the main scoreboard at the Diglis End of the ground where there is also a limited area for disabled car parking. Other locations are available around the ground which are suitable for wheelchair viewing by prior arrangement with the club stewards. There are disabled toilets situated to the rear of the Ladies' Pavilion adjacent to the large marquee and there is also an additional facility available for gentlemen only by the main club office reception.

RAMPS TO PROVIDE EASY ACCESS TO BARS & REFRESHMENT OUTLETS FOR PEOPLE USING WHEELCHAIRS Yes.

FOOD & DRINK FULL RESTAURANT/DINING FACILITIES Members, yes, Public, yes.

TEMPORARY FOOD/DRINK FACILITIES Members, yes. Public, yes.

FOOD SUITABLE FOR VEGETARIANS Members, yes. Public, yes.

BARS Members 1, Public 1.

VARIETIES OF BEER SOLD Bass, Worthington, Guinness, Carling.

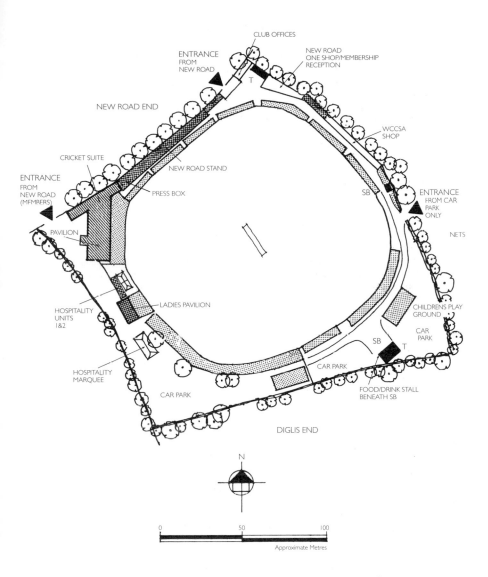

CLUB OFFICES

ENTRANCE FROM NEW ROAD

NEW ROAD ONE SHOP/MEMBERSHIP RECEPTION

NEW ROAD END

T

WCCSA SHOP

CRICKET SUITE

NEW ROAD STAND

ENTRANCE FROM NEW ROAD (MEMBERS)

PRESS BOX

SB

ENTRANCE FROM CAR PARK ONLY

NETS

PAVILION

HOSPITALITY UNITS 1&2

LADIES PAVILION

CHILDRENS PLAY GROUND

CAR PARK

SB

T

HOSPITALITY MARQUEE

CAR PARK

CAR PARK

FOOD/DRINK STALL BENEATH SB

DIGLIS END

N

0   50   100
Approximate Metres

CHILDREN'S FACILITIES Crèche, no. Children's play area with swings near main scoreboard at Diglis End of the ground.

CLUB SHOP New Road One Shop and the Worcestershire CCSA both have well-appointed shops with a good stock of cricket items including clothing, ties, books, pictures, china and Worcestershire souvenirs.

CLUB MUSEUM No, although in the pavilion there are several display cabinets and a fine selection of photographs. There is a library in the Ladies' Pavilion. A voluntary Heritage Group archives and protects all club memorabilia.

CRICKET COACHING FACILITIES Indoor, no. Outdoor, yes.

CRICKET NETS Yes, outdoor only to rear of secondary scoreboard adjoining grass car park between River Severn and ground.

OTHER SPORTING OR RECREATIONAL FACILITIES ON THE GROUND Outdoor concert venue for up to 25,000.

FACILITIES FOR HIRE OR WIDER COMMUNITY USE AT THE GROUND Rooms are available for functions, weddings, formal dinners, dinner dances, birthday parties, christenings, seminars, Christmas parties, exhibitions and conferences throughout the year by arrangement with Marketing Department ☎ 01905 748474 and Catering Department ☎ 01905 337940.

WINTER CRICKET EVENTS Members' club dinners and lunches are staged in the pavilion which is also used by the Worcestershire Cricket Society. Membership is £10 per annum and meetings are held once a month between September and March.

CAR PARKING FACILITIES Car parking is available to the rear of the pavilion for players, officials and press/media. There is also car parking for members, sponsors and hospitality guests around the perimeter of the ground at the Diglis End. Additional car parking is available for members only on production of valid WCCC car park pass in the adjoining field between the ground and the River Severn. Street parking and nearby car parks are within a short walk over the bridge into the city centre or within the park opposite the entrance in New Road.

OTHER INFORMATION Groups of school children, disabled people and the disadvantaged can usually gain entry to ground only for championship matches if requested to the management in advance. Contact club for details. Tea and a variety of home-made cakes are always available in the Ladies' Pavilion at teatime.

GROUND CAPACITY 8,500.

ANTICIPATED GROUND DEVELOPMENTS New stand with 700 seats, toilet facilities, refreshment facilities and a new scoreboard due to be ready for 2004 season.

HOW TO GET THERE

 Worcester Foregate Street station 0.5 mile, Worcester Shrub Hill station 1 mile. ☎ 08457 484950, 08457 000125, 0121 643 4444, www.greatwesterntrains.co.uk, www.centraltrains.co.uk

 Midland Red West 23, 24, 25, 26, 33, 44 and 46 link Angel Place (200 metres from Worcester Foregate station) with ground ☎ 01905 763888, 0345 125436. National Express Coachway stops located at Three Pears and Warndon on outskirts of the City Centre thence Midland Red West to New Road ☎ 08705 808080, www.midlandredwest.co.uk, www.nationalexpresscoaches.com.

 From north: from M5 junction 7, exit on to A44 (north) and continue on this road to Worcester city centre (Whittington Road, London Road, Sidbury, College Street, Deansway), cricket ground is on the left hand side after crossing the bridge over the River Severn. **From south:** from M5 junction 7, then as for north. **From east:** from A422, Alcester, continue on this road to roundabout junction with A4440 (Swinesherd Way), take second exit at roundabout on to A44, then as for north. **From west:** from A44, Evesham, stay on A44 (east) to New Road and cricket ground is on right hand side just before the bridge over the River Severn.

 Birmingham International Airport ☎ 0121 767 5511, www.bhx.co.uk

WHERE TO STAY

Bank House Hotel Golf & Country Club (☎ 01886 833551), Burbage House (☎ 01905 25396), Farm Stays (☎ 01905 381807 www.farmstayworcs.co.uk), Gifford Heritage Hotel (☎ 01905 27155), Hilton Puckrup Hall (☎ 01684 296200 www.tewkesbury.hilton.com), Home Farm (☎ 01299 896825), The Chandlery (☎ 01886 888318), The Diglis House Hotel (☎ 01905 353518), The Elms (☎ 01299 896666 www.theelmshotel.co.uk), The Five Ways Hotel including The Stump & Divot Bar (☎ 01905 616980), The Fownes Hotel (☎ 01905 613151), The Star Hotel (☎ 01905 24308), Three Pears Beefeater & Travel Inn (☎ 01905 451240), Ye Olde Talbot Hotel (☎ 01905 23573).

For other places to stay in and around Worcester visit www.smoothhound.co.uk.

WHERE TO EAT

Browns Restaurant (☎ 01905 26263), Glass House (☎ 01905 611120), Il Pescatore (☎ 01905 21444), Little Venice (☎ 0800 0260721 www.littlevenice.uk.com), Monsoon Indian Restaurant (☎ 01905 726333), Ostlers at No 1 (☎ 01905 612300), Strollers Bistro (☎ 01905 616167), The Elms (☎ 01905 896666 www.theelmshotel.co.uk), The Fruiterer's Arms (☎ 01905 820462), The Lemon Tree (☎ 01905 27770 www.thelemontree.co.uk)

OTHER USEFUL INFORMATION

Worcester Racecourse ☎ 0870 220 2772, www.worcester-racecourse.co.uk

Royal Worcester Visitor Centre ☎ 01905 746000
Worcester Cathedral ☎ 01905 28854
River Boat Trips on the River Severn ☎ 01905 422499
Worcester Rugby Football Club ☎ 01905 454183 www.wrfc.co.uk

TOURIST INFORMATION Worcester Tourist Information Centre, The Guildhall, High Street, Worcester, Worcestershire WR1 2EY ☎ 01905 726311

LOCAL RADIO STATIONS Classic Gold WABC (95.4/1530AM), Radio Wyvern FM (102/1530AM), BBC Radio WM (95.6/1468AM), BBC Radio Hereford & Worcester (95.6/1468AM)

LOCAL NEWSPAPERS *Worcester Evening News, Worcester Standard*

KIDDERMINSTER

Address Kidderminster Cricket Club, Chester Road Sports Club, Offmore Lane, Chester Road, Kidderminster, Worcestershire DY10 1TH
Prospects of Play ☎ 01562 824175

HISTORY OF GROUND AND FACILITIES

THE CHESTER ROAD GROUND was established in 1870 but cricket has been played in the town since 1850.

The present Kidderminster Cricket Club was formed in 1890 and its ground is located close to the main Chester Road. The club played previously at Worcester Road until the land was purchased to make a steeplechasing racecourse. For the next two years the club played at Comberton Road on a field provided by the Kidderminster Grammar School but then had to move again. This time Kidderminster were more fortunate and rented some land close to Offmore Farm which was part of the Earl of Dudley's estate.

The ground opened on 20 August 1870. By 1896 the club had secured the lease direct from the Earl of Dudley and this was renewed annually until 1918 when the Dudley property was sold by auction. A local carpet manufacturer, Michael Tomkinson, then President of the club, purchased the freehold for £1,287 10s on 31 December 1918. The Old Pavilion, which dates from 1896, was brought from the Worcester Road ground and rebuilt on its present site. The new pavilion was built in 1925 at a cost of £886 subscribed by members to commemorate winning the Birmingham League in 1924. Close to this is a recreation and tea room for members, known as the Long Room.

Kidderminster Cricket Club joined the Birmingham Cricket League in 1895. The club won the league for the first time in 1899 and has done so on eleven occasions since, the last being in 1991. In 1984 the association between Kidderminster Cricket Club, the Kidderminster Hockey Club (who use the ground during the winter months) and the Old Carolians was formalised with the creation of the Chester Road Sporting Club, in which the land and buildings are now vested.

The first Worcestershire County Cricket Club match staged at Kidderminster was in 1921 when Glamorgan were the visitors. After visiting Kidderminster for 46

The players' pavilion and part of the adjoining Long Room.

consecutive seasons Worcestershire's long run at the ground ended in 1973 – possibly because they were bowled out for 63 by the visitors, Northamptonshire. In 1987, however, first-class cricket returned with Nottinghamshire the visitors. The ground has also been used by the county for Second XI championship fixtures. ICC Trophy matches have been staged at Chester Road since 1979, with Denmark, Malaysia (twice) and Bangladesh taking part.

Surprisingly, only three Worcestershire limited-overs matches have been staged at Kidderminster. The first was in 1969 when the visitors, Middlesex, were bowled out for only 56. The other two matches took place within a day of each other when the county club decided to switch venues to Kidderminster because of flooding at New Road. On 29 April 2001 Sussex were the visitors in the Norwich Union National League, and on 30 April 2001 Worcestershire hosted Northamptonshire in the Benson and Hedges Cup zonal round, Worcestershire winning by 96 runs.

The association between the Kidderminster Cricket Club and Worcestershire County Cricket Club has meant that players of the calibre of Laddie Outschoorn, Fred Rumsey, Basil D'Oliveira and latterly Graeme Hick have represented the club.

The scoreboard is at the Lyndholm Road end of the ground, known as the Railway End because of the railway cutting just behind the metal fencing. The playing area is 131 metres by 121 metres and is defined by a rope and advertising boards. The ground is very flat with a slight fall towards the Chester Road in the direction of the main entrance gates. There is no fixed seating except near the pavilion. The ground capacity is 5,500 but seats are provided for only about one-third of that number.

GROUND RECORDS AND SCORES

FIRST-CLASS MATCHES

Highest innings total for county 560 v Derbyshire 1993
Highest innings total against county 551 for 7 dec by Leicestershire 1929
Lowest innings total for county 63 v Northamptonshire 1973
Lowest innings total against county 71 by Leicestershire 1933
Highest individual innings for county 259 D. Kenyon v Yorkshire 1956
Highest individual innings against county 210* D.J.G. Sales for Northamptonshire 1996
Highest wicket partnerships for county

1st	210 C.F.Walters & H.H.I.Gibbons	v	Warwickshire	1934
2nd	218 E. Cooper & R. Howorth	v	Northamptonshire	1946
3rd	269 T.S. Curtis & T.M. Moody	v	Northamptonshire	1996
4th	159 T.M.Moody & D.A.Leatherdale	v	Derbyshire	1995
5th	181 P.A. Neale & M.J. Weston	v	Sussex	1988
6th	114 C.D.Fearnley & D.W.Richardson	v	Derbyshire	1966
7th	138 W.V. Fox & M.K. Foster	v	Derbyshire	1926
8th	184 S.J. Rhodes & S.R. Lampitt	v	Derbyshire	1991
9th	79 S.J. Rhodes & R.K. Illingworth	v	Leicestershire	1989
10th	94 C.F. Root & R.T.D. Perks	v	Derbyshire	1930

Highest wicket partnerships against county

1st	243 D. Brookes & P.C. Davis	for	Northamptonshire	1946
2nd	317* J.H.Kallis & M.R.Ramprakash	for	Middlesex	1997
3rd	243 D.J. Capel & D.J.G. Sales	for	Northamptonshire	1996
4th	123* D.J.G.Sales & K.M.Curran	for	Northamptonshire	1996
5th	185 S.G.Law & S.D.Peters	for	Essex	2000
6th	140 W.W.Timms & J.E.Timms	for	Northamptonshire	1925
7th	123 N.F.Armstrong & G.Geary	for	Leicestershire	1929
8th	123 I.D. Austin & N.H. Fairbrother	for	Lancashire	1990
9th	88 A.R. Roberts & D. Ripley	for	Northamptonshire	1996
10th	95 D. Ripley & J.P. Taylor	for	Northamptonshire	1996

Best bowling performance in an innings for county 9 for 56 J.A. Flavell v Middlesex 1964
Best bowling performance in an innings against county 7 for 35 A.R. Gover for Surrey 1938
Best bowling performance in a match for county 13 for 96 J.A. Flavell v Somerset 1965
Best bowling performance in a match against county 14 for 85 A.R. Gover for Surrey 1938
Largest crowd 7,000 v Yorkshire 1956

LIMITED-OVERS MATCHES

Highest innings total for county 227 for 7 v Northamptonshire (B&H) 2001
Highest innings total against county 154 for 9 by Sussex (SL) 2001
Lowest innings total for county 116 for 9 v Middlesex (SL) 1969
Lowest innings total against county 56 by Middlesex (SL) 1969
Highest individual innings for county 69 P.R. Pollard v Northamptonshire (B&H) 2001
Highest individual innings against county 53 B. Zuiderent for Sussex (SL) 2001
Highest wicket partnerships for county

1st	15 P.R. Pollard & A. Singh	v Northamptonshire	(B&H)	2001
2nd	60 G.M. Turner & B.L. D'Oliveira	v Middlesex	(SL)	1969
3rd	57 P.R. Pollard & V.S. Solanki	v Northamptonshire	(B&H)	2001
4th	45 V.S. Solanki & D.A. Leatherdale	v Northamptonshire	(B&H)	2001
5th	60 D.A. Leatherdale & A.J. Bichel	v Northamptonshire	(B&H)	2001
6th	82* G.A. Hick & S.J. Rhodes	v Sussex	(SL)	2001
7th	2 D.N.F. Slade & J.A. Standen	v Middlesex	(SL)	1969
8th	13* W.P.C. Weston & S.R. Lampitt	v Northamptonshire	(B&H)	2001
9th	4 D.N.F. Slade & L.J. Coldwell	v Middlesex	(SL)	1969
10th	yet to be established			

Highest wicket partnerships against county

1st	22 R.R. Montgomerie & M.W. Goodwin	for	Sussex	(SL)	2001
2nd	11 M.E.K. Hussey & J.W. Cook	for	Northamptonshire	(B&H)	2001
3rd	22 P.H. Parfitt & C.T. Radley	for	Middlesex	(SL)	1969
4th	26 J.W. Cook & A.L. Penberthy	for	Northamptonshire	(B&H)	2001
5th	55 B. Zuiderent & R.S.C. Martin-Jenkins	for	Sussex	(SL)	2001
6th	6 B. Zuiderent & M.J. Prior	for	Sussex	(SL)	2001
7th	44 B. Zuiderent & M.H. Yardy	for	Sussex	(SL)	2001
8th	7 M.H. Yardy & M.J.G. Davis	for	Sussex	(SL)	2001
9th	7 R.S. Herman & J.S.E. Price	for	Middlesex	(SL)	1969
	7 G.P. Swann & D.M. Cousins	for	Northamptonshire	(B&H)	2001
10th	13 G.P. Swann & J.F. Brown	for	Northamptonshire	(B&H)	2001

Best bowling performance in a match for county 4 for 37 S.R. Lampitt v Sussex (SL) 2001
Best bowling performance in a match against county 4 for 23 D.M. Cousins for Northamptonshire (B&H) 2001
Largest crowd 3,500 v Middlesex (SL) 1969

GROUND INFORMATION

ENTRANCES Offmore Lane (players, officials, members and vehicles), Chester Road (members and public).
MEMBERS ENCLOSURE Defined area between Pavilion, Long Room and Old Pavilion.
PUBLIC ENCLOSURE Rest of the ground.
COVERED STANDS Pavilion, Long Room and Old Pavilion.
OPEN STANDS Temporary raised plastic/timber seating together with ground level seating surrounding the playing area.
NAME OF ENDS Pavilion End, Railway End.
GROUND DIMENSIONS 131m × 121m.
REPLAY SCREEN If televised matches are staged at the ground the replay screen is sited near the main scoreboard at the Railway End of the ground.
FIRST AID In main pavilion.
CODES OF DRESS Spectators are required to dress in an appropriate manner consistent with attending a cricket match. Bare torsos are not acceptable in, or in front of the pavilion. Executive Club/Suite users must wear a necktie and jacket.
BEHAVIOUR The club is keen that standards of behaviour should be maintained and members and spectators are urged to report immediately to the CEO any incident, or potential incident, where they feel action should be taken. Bad language is not acceptable at any match and the club will take prompt and strong action should this or any other ground regulation be ignored.
RECIPROCAL ARRANGEMENTS Members of Glamorgan, Gloucestershire and Somerset can gain entry free on production of membership card when Worcestershire is not playing their own county.
SUPPORTERS' CLUB Worcestershire CC Supporters' Association £5 for (WCCC members) and £10 for (non WCCC members). Special rates for concessions and husband and wife membership are available.
JUNIORS Under-16s can go free under the 'Kids Go Free Scheme'. Contact the Membership Office on ☎ 01905 748474 for further information.
CORPORATE ENTERTAINING Various packages are available full corporate hospitality in the marquees on the pavilion side of the ground. Contact the Commercial Department for further information and a brochure on ☎ 01905 748474.
FACILITIES FOR VISUALLY IMPAIRED SPECTATORS Reduced admission on request including helper. Guide dogs are allowed but please give one day's warning of attendance.
FACILITIES AND ACCESS FOR PEOPLE WITH DISABILITIES INCLUDING WHEELCHAIR ACCESS TO GROUND Yes, through main gate from Chester Road.
DESIGNATED CAR PARK AVAILABLE INSIDE THE GROUND FOR PEOPLE WITH DISABILITIES Yes, on the boundary on the Chester Road side of the ground.
GOOD VIEWING AREAS INSIDE THE GROUND FOR PEOPLE USING WHEELCHAIRS Yes, particularly on areas of hard standing in front of the Long Room at the Offmore Lane end of the ground. Please request position in advance.
DESIGNATED VIEWING AREAS FOR PEOPLE USING WHEELCHAIRS Yes, at both the Offmore Lane and the Railway

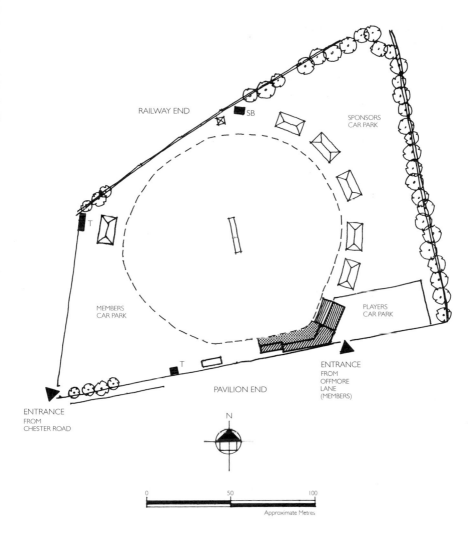

Ends of the ground by the sightscreens. Other locations are available around the ground by prior arrangement with the club stewards. There are no disabled toilets on the ground.

RAMPS TO PROVIDE EASY ACCESS TO BARS & REFRESHMENT OUTLETS FOR PEOPLE USING WHEELCHAIRS Yes.

FOOD & DRINK FULL RESTAURANT/DINING FACILITIES Members, yes. Public, yes by prior arrangement only.

TEMPORARY FOOD/DRINK FACILITIES Members, yes. Public, yes.

FOOD SUITABLE FOR VEGETARIANS Members, yes. Public, yes.

BARS Members 1, Public 1.

CHILDREN'S FACILITIES None.

CLUB SHOP New Road One Shop and the Worcestershire CCSA both have temporary outlets in marquees on the ground.

CLUB MUSEUM No, although in the pavilion there is a collection of signed cricket bats from County Championship matches staged on the ground since 1983. Several old photographs and prints in the pavilion and Long Room bar relate to Kidderminster cricket and the history of the Chester Road ground.

CRICKET COACHING FACILITIES Yes.

CRICKET NETS Yes, members only.

OTHER SPORTING OR RECREATIONAL FACILITIES ON THE GROUND Hockey and snooker.

FACILITIES FOR HIRE OR WIDER COMMUNITY USE AT THE GROUND Function Room is available for hire. Contact club on ☎ 01562 824175.

WINTER CRICKET EVENTS Staged by County Associations and International Police Cricket Sections.

CAR PARKING FACILITIES Car parking is available within the ground via Chester Road for members with car park pass otherwise £3.50 per car, members 330 spaces, 110 spaces non members. Otherwise street parking in surrounding area or car parking within the town centre 7 to 10 minutes' walk away.

OTHER INFORMATION Groups of school children, the disabled and disadvantaged can usually gain entry to ground only for championship matches if requested to the management in advance. Contact club for details. A second-hand cricket book stall is available at some matches.

GROUND CAPACITY 5,500.

ANTICIPATED GROUND DEVELOPMENTS None presently planned.

HOW TO GET THERE

 Kidderminster station 0.5 mile ☎ 08457 484950, 08457 000125, 0121 643 4444, www.greatwesterntrains.co.uk, www.centraltrains.co.uk

 Midland Red from surrounding areas to bus station, thence 0.75 mile; Midland Red 7 passes ground. ☎ 01905 763888, 0345 125436, www.midlandredwest.co.uk

 From north: from M5 junction 3 take A456 (west) towards Hagley and Kidderminster, continue on this road into Kidderminster (Birmingham Road), at junction with A449 (Chester Road North) turn left on to A449, Offmore Lane is on the left. **From south:** from M5 junction 5 take A38 towards Droitwich, at roundabout take A442 (Kidderminster) exit and continue on this road to junction with A449, bear right on to A449 and continue to roundabout, take third exit (A449) (Chester Road), continue to Chester Road North, Offmore Lane is a turning on the right shortly after junction with A448 (Comberton Road). **From east:** from M5 junction 4 take A491 towards Hagley, at roundabout junction with A456 take first exit (Kidderminster Road), then as for north. **From west:** from A456, stay on A456 (east) towards Kidderminster, follow A456 Ringway to junction with A448 Comberton Hill, turn left in to A449 Chester Road North, Offmore Lane is on the left.

 Birmingham International Airport ☎ 0121 767 5511, www.bhx.co.uk

WHERE TO STAY

Bank House Hotel Golf & Country Club (☎ 01886 833551), Bewdley Hill House (☎ 01562 60473), Cedars Hotel (☎ 01562 745869), Dowlescroft (☎ 01299 253810), Farm Stays (☎ 01905 381807 www.farmstayworcs.co.uk), Gainsborough House Hotel (☎ 01562 754041), Home Farm (☎ 01299 896825), Talbot House Hotel (☎ 01299 270036), The Elms (☎ 01299 896666 www.theelmshotel.co.uk), The Granary Hotel (☎ 01562 777535), The Old Bake House (☎ 01299 270193), Victoria Hotel (☎ 01562 67240)

For other places to stay in and around Kidderminster visit www.smoothhound.co.uk.

WHERE TO EAT

Brockencote Hall (☎ 01562 777876), Kings Arms (☎ 01905 620142), Talbot Restaurant (☎ 01886 821235), The Granary Restaurant (☎ 01562 777535)

OTHER USEFUL INFORMATION

Kidderminster Harriers Football Club, Aggborough Stadium ☎ 01562 823931. www.harriers.co.uk.

TOURIST INFORMATION Kidderminster Tourist Information Centre, Severn Valley Railway Station, Comberton Hill, Kidderminster, Worcestershire DY10 1QX ☎ 01562 829400

LOCAL RADIO STATIONS BBC Radio Hereford & Worcester (95.6/1468AM), BBC Radio WM (95.6/1468AM), Classic Gold WABC (95.4/1530AM), Radio Wyvern FM (102/1530AM), BRMB (96.4 MHz FM/1152 KHz MW)

LOCAL NEWSPAPERS *Worcester Evening News, Worcester Standard, Kidderminster Shuttle, Kidderminster Chronicle*

THE YORKSHIRE COUNTY
CRICKET CLUB

Yorkshire

**Headingley
Scarborough**

YORKSHIRE COUNTY CRICKET CLUB, HEADINGLEY CRICKET GROUND, HEADINGLEY, LEEDS, LS6 3BU

Main Switchboard	0113 278 7394 **fax** 0113 278 4099
Ticket Freephone	0800 032 6644
Cricket Office	0113 203 3651
Yorkshire White Rose Merchandise Shop	0113 2740460
Marketing Department	0113 203 3621
Email	cricket@yorkshireccc.org.uk
Website	www.yorkshireccc.org.uk

Founded 8 January 1863

Colours Oxford dark blue, Cambridge light blue and gold

Crest white rose of Yorkshire

National Cricket League Nickname Phoenix

National Cricket League Colours black and orange with white trim

Patroness HRH The Duchess of Kent

Patrons The Earl of Mexborough, The Earl of Harewood and Lord Savile

President R.A. Smith TD, LLB, DL

Chairman of the Board R.A. Smith TD, LLB, DL

Board R.A. Smith TD, LLB, DL, C.J. Graves, G.A. Cope, B. Bouttell

Chief Executive Officer C.J. Graves

PA to CEO S. Beckett

Company Secretary/Finance Director B. Bouttell

Director of Cricket G.A. Cope

Chief Accountant D.M. Ryder

Ground Manager M. Dooley

Marketing Assistant S. Bore

Marketing & Sponsorship Manager L. Sutcliffe

Sales Marketing Manager V. Stanworth

Marketing Executive M. Senior

Marketing Director I. Bishop

Membership Manager Miss L. Battye

Stadium Ticket Office Manager B. Howard

Cricket Secretary Miss R. O'Halloran

Academy Director S. Oldham

Cricket Centre Manager A. Rowsell

Coach (Batting) K. Sharp

Coach (Bowling) A. Sidebottom

Captain A. McGrath

Vice Captain R.T. Blakey

1st XI Physiotherapist S. McAllister

Medical Consultant W. Morton MCSP, SRP, MACP, OM

Medical Officer Dr J.W.D. Moxon MRCGP

Head Groundsman A.W. Fogarty

Scorer 1st XI J.T. Potter

Scorer 2nd XI M. Snook

Statistician R.D. Wilkinson (First-Class), P.E. Dyson (Limited-Overs)

Sponsors Yorkshire Tea (Taylors of Harrogate), Western Union, Exito, Leeds & Holbeck Building Society

Kit Sponsors Exito

Yearbook £15 (hardback), £26 (hardback, leather)

Scorecard 50p (County) and 50p (Test/ODI)

National Cricket League Programme & Scorecard £2

Magazine/Newsletter *The White Rose* £2.95 (issued free to members)

Frizzell County Championship Status Division 2

National Cricket League Status Division 1

ACHIEVEMENTS

County Championship Champions 1867, 1870, 1893, 1896, 1898, 1900, 1901, 1902, 1905, 1908, 1912, 1919, 1922, 1923, 1924, 1925, 1931, 1932, 1933, 1935, 1937, 1938, 1939, 1946, 1959, 1960, 1962, 1963, 1966, 1967, 1968, 2001; Joint Champions 1869, 1949

Gillette Cup Winners 1965, 1969

NatWest Trophy Semi-finalists 1982

Cheltenham & Gloucester Trophy Winners 2002

Benson and Hedges Cup Winners 1987, Finalists 1972

John Player Sunday League Champions 1983

Refuge Assurance Sunday League 6th 1990

Norwich Union National League 2nd Division 1 2000

Fenner Trophy Winners 1972, 1974, 1981, Finalists 1973, 1975, 1976, 1978, 1979

Asda Trophy Winners 1987, Finalists 1984

Ward Four Counties Knockout Competition Winners 1989, Finalists 1988, Semi-finalists 1990

Tilcon Trophy Winners 1978, 1988, Finalists 1983, 1990

Joshua Tetley Festival Trophy Winners 1991

YORKSHIRE CRICKET BOARD

Chairman R.K. Platt
Secretary I. Chappell
Cricket Development Officers I. Powell, T. Bowry, I. Dews, A. Watson
Women & Girls Secretary B. Nicholson

Address   Yorkshire Cricket Board, Headingley Cricket Ground, St Michael's Lane, Headingley, Leeds, LS6 3BU
☎   0113 278 7394
Fax   0113 278 4099
Email   ichappell@ycb-yca.fsnet.co.uk
Website www.ycb-yca.org.uk

GROUNDS

Leeds (Headingley Cricket Ground, St Michael's Lane) and Scarborough (Scarborough CC, North Marine Road)

Other grounds used since 1969: Bradford (Park Avenue), Sheffield (Abbeydale Park, Abbeydale Park Road South, Dore), Huddersfield (Fartown), Sheffield (Bramall Lane), Barnsley (Clarence Ground, Shaw Lane), Middlesbrough (Acklam Park, Green Lane), Castleford (Savile Park), Harrogate (St George's Road) and Hull (The Circle, Anlaby Road).

SECOND XI GROUNDS

Bradford & Bingley CC, Wagon Lane, Cottingley Bridge, Bingley ☎ 01274 775441
Castleford CC, Savile Park, Castleford ☎ 01924 249500 or match days ☎ 01836 335135
Elland Cricket Athletic and Bowling Club, Hullen Edge, Elland, Leeds ☎ 01422 372682
Harrogate CC, St George's Road, Harrogate ☎ 01423 561301
New Rover CC, Richmond Oval, Smithy Mill Lane, Adel, Leeds LS16 8HF ☎ 0113 261 3923
Pudsey Congs CC, Britannia Ground, Pudsey, no ☎ on ground
Stamford Bridge CC, Stamford Bridge, York ☎ 01759 371545
Todmorden CC, Centre Vale, Burnley Road, Todmorden ☎ 01706 813140
York CC, Clifton Park, Shipton Road, York ☎ 01904 623602

Sir Leonard Hutton Memorial Gates, the entrance to Headingley from the Kirkstall Lane End.

HEADINGLEY

Address Headingley Cricket Ground, St Michael's Lane, Headingley, Leeds,
West Yorkshire LS6 3BU
Prospects of Play ☎ 0113 278 7394

HISTORY OF GROUND AND FACILITIES

THE ORIGINAL HEADQUARTERS of Yorkshire cricket was at Bramall Lane, Sheffield, from 1863. However, in 1888 a group of wealthy developers who were also sportsmen joined together to buy Lot 17a, a plot of land in the north-west of the City of Leeds, at an auction by the Cardigan Estate. They formed the Leeds Cricket, Football and Athletic Company Limited. Their chairman was Lord Hawke who captained Yorkshire County Cricket Club from 1883 to 1910. The purchase was the first step towards the establishment of the county's headquarters at Headingley.

Cricket and rugby football have been played at Headingley since 1890. That year the first important cricket match on the ground was staged between the North of England XI and the touring Australians. Yorkshire County Cricket Club's first county match, which was with Derbyshire, and the first first-class match – against Kent – were staged on the ground in 1891. Headingley hosted its first Test match between England and Australia in 1899. Yorkshire CCC moved its headquarters to the City of Leeds in 1903. The county once leased offices in Park Row but is now based at Headingley.

Much of the development at Headingley was carried out by Sir Edwin Airey, a local building contractor, who in 1932 undertook improvements designed to

Walkways beneath the West Stand.

The Members' Pavilion Stand and Leeds Pavilion from the top of the Wintershed Stand.

establish this as a major cricketing venue. The Main Stand was built in 1933 at a cost of £20,000 following a fire which destroyed the original Rugby Stand during a Leeds v Bradford rugby league match in 1932. The double-sided Main Stand stretches along the southern boundary of the field so that cricket can be watched from the north side and rugby from the south. The Leeds Pavilion, constructed in 1888/9, is the oldest building on the ground. Additions have included the Kirkstall Lane End and the Wintershed Stand, which contains executive boxes and ample seating. In 1985 Headingley became one of the first grounds to have a computerised scoreboard.

During the early 1990s there was considerable debate and speculation about the ground's future, and Yorkshire CCC members approved the possibility of moving to a new greenfield site at Durkar, near Wakefield. A team of experts was brought together to design and construct a new state-of-the-art home for Yorkshire CCC. Despite the location, the quality of the chosen site and the possibility of funding, Yorkshire decided to stay at Headingley thanks to the enthusiastic vision of Paul Caddick.

In October 1996 Castleford-born Paul Caddick, a chartered civil and municipal engineer, stepped in to take over the struggling Leeds Cricket, Football and Athletic Company. He now owns the ground and is Leeds CAFC's chairman. In 1999 strategic plans for the comprehensive redevelopment of Headingley were prepared and these included a £32m project to rebuild the Western Terrace and provide new facilities. The West Stand Development, with seating for 7,500, was officially opened by the Yorkshire President, Robin A. Smith, at the Ashes Test match against Australia on Wednesday 15 August 2001.

In 2001 the Sir Leonard Hutton Gates were commissioned and are now installed at the Kirkstall Lane entrance to the ground. The design of the gates has proved controversial. Also in 2001 the Dickie Bird Clock was erected on the Western Stand; this was provided by Philip Stoner Jewellery of Yorkshire and was unveiled by Dickie Bird himself.

During the winter of 2001/2 further work took place. The construction of the East Stand began on 12 November 2001 on the St Michael's Lane side of the ground where the temporary hospitality chalets used to be sited during major matches. The East Stand, which was constructed in 40 weeks and completed on 16 August 2002 ready for the 2002 Test match between England and India, has seating for over 1,700 members on the open terrace and has three levels. On the ground floor there are classrooms, coaches' and reception rooms, indoor cricket nets, changing rooms, umpires' room and other facilities. On Level 1 there is a huge members' bar and large reception areas. On Level 2 there are 32 executive boxes which double up as rooms for the Headingley Lodge Hotel. The executive boxes are named after former Yorkshire players and the choice of titles was decided by a vote among YCCC members. The East Stand was opened by Freddie Trueman, Brian Close, Geoffrey Boycott and Ray Illingworth.

Further developments in 2002 included a new car parking area to the rear of the East Stand, and a new Yorkshire shop and rugby sales outlet close to the rear of the Leeds members' pavilion. Further work is likely to include the reconstruction of the Rugby Stand to accommodate 23 executive boxes, new media/TV and commentary points, an enlarged press gallery, new Yorkshire offices and further refurbished seating areas.

Today, Headingley is the home to three world-class teams: Yorkshire Cricket, Leeds Tykes (who have joined the elite band of teams in the Zurich Premiership) and the Leeds Rhinos rugby league team (who play in the Tetley's Super League). The Headingley Stadium has hosted international fixtures for all three sports.

Achievements on the field at Headingley include Geoffrey Boycott's 100th hundred, scored in a Test match against Australia in 1977 in front of his home crowd. Big scores have included innings from Don Bradman, Herbert Sutcliffe, Allan Lamb and John Edrich. Other feats at Headingley include England's first Test win over South Africa in June 1907. Hat-tricks have been achieved here by Jack Hearne (1899), Peter Loader (1957) and Andy Caddick (2000). Cricket-lovers will recall a day of pure genius from Ian Botham who, having put Kim Hughes' Australian team under the hammer, put England on the way to regaining the Ashes in 1981 under the captaincy of Mike Brearley. Significant bowling

performances over the years have been achieved by Colin Blythe, Hedley Verity, Richard Peel, Richard Hutton and Bob Willis. Darren Gough took 6 for 42 for England v South Africa in August 1998 and in an incredible 48 hours of Test cricket in 2000 England beat West Indies by an innings and 39 runs. Then in 2001 Mark Butcher single-handedly led England to victory against Australia when the home side achieved their second highest

Dickie Bird clock in the Western Stand.

Headingley viewed from the North Stand looking towards the Kirkstall Lane End during the England v India Test match in 2002.

ever successful run chase against the Australians. (The highest came in 1928/9 with 332 scored to win the Test.)

Headingley spectators have also seen some strange sights including the George Davis protests in 1975 and the burst pipe episode with Curtley Ambrose and Dickie Bird in 1988.

The playing area is oval in shape, measures 145 metres by 142 metres and is defined by advertising boards. The actual playing area for a match is defined by a rope within the boards and this provides an area of approximately 130 metres by 134 metres, depending on the location of the wicket. Headingley has 11 first-class wickets; in 1986 number 7 was famously relaid by Keith Boyce, then Head Groundsman.

GROUND RECORDS AND SCORES

FIRST-CLASS MATCHES

Highest innings total for county 560 for 6 dec v Leicestershire 1921
Highest innings total against county 630 by Somerset 1901
Lowest innings total for county 33 v Lancashire 1924
Lowest innings total against county 23 by Australians 1902
Highest individual innings for county 270 H. Sutcliffe v Sussex 1932
Highest individual innings against county 235 A.J. Lamb for Northamptonshire 1990
Highest wicket partnerships for county

1st	290 P. Holmes & H. Sutcliffe	v	Middlesex	1928
2nd	237 H. Sutcliffe & D. Denton	v	Gloucestershire	1919
	237 M.D. Moxon & K. Sharp	v	Sri Lankans	1988
3rd	317 A. McGrath & D.S. Lehmann	v	Lancashire	2002
4th	205 W. Watson & E.I. Lester	v	Somerset	1953

5th	196* R. Kilner & G.H. Hirst	v	Gloucestershire	1919
6th	252 C. White & R.J. Blakey	v	Lancashire	1996
7th	138 D. Denton & G.H. Hirst	v	Sussex	1905
8th	180 W. Barber & T.F. Smailes	v	Sussex	1935
9th	118 S. Haigh & W. Rhodes	v	Somerset	1901
10th	118 Lord Hawke & D. Hunter	v	Kent	1896

Highest wicket partnerships against county

1st	222 L.C.H. Palairet & L.C. Braund	for	Somerset	1901
2nd	156 E.H. Bowley & K.S. Duleepsinhji	for	Sussex	1932
3rd	393 A. Fordham & A.J. Lamb	for	Northamptonshire	1990
4th	326* James Langridge & G. Cox	for	Sussex	1949
5th	170 M.R. Ramprakash & K.R. Brown	for	Middlesex	1995
6th	191 T.R. Ambrose & M.J. Prior	for	Sussex	2002
7th	248 G.D. Lloyd & I.D. Austin	for	Lancashire	1997
8th	148 F.R. Brown & E.W. Watts	for	Surrey	1939
9th	120 J. Wood & G. Keedy	for	Lancashire	2002
10th	70 H.R. Murrell & W.F. Lord	for	Middlesex	1919

Best bowling performance in an innings for county 10 for 10 H. Verity v Nottinghamshire 1932
Best bowling performance in an innings against county 9 for 57 F.A. Tarrant for Middlesex 1906
Best bowling performance in a match for county 15 for 50 R. Peel v Somerset 1895
Best bowling performance in a match against county 15 for 154 T. Richardson for Surrey 1897
Largest crowd 44,507 v Lancashire 1948

LIMITED-OVERS MATCHES

Highest innings total for county 345 for 5 v Nottinghamshire (NWT) 1996
Highest innings total against county 297 for 3 by Australians (Tour) 1989
Lowest innings total for county 75 v Kent (SL) 1995
Lowest innings total against county 23 by Middlesex (SL) 1974
Highest individual innings for county 137 M.D. Moxon v Nottinghamshire (NWT) 1996
Highest individual innings against county 172 D.C. Boon for Australians (Tour) 1989
Highest wicket partnerships for county

1st	242* M.D. Moxon & A.A. Metcalfe	v	Warwickshire	(NWT)	1990
2nd	202 G. Boycott & C.W.J. Athey	v	Kent	(GC)	1980
3rd	184 M.P. Vaughan & D.S. Lehmann	v	Durham	(NWT)	1998
4th	207 S.A. Kellett & C. White	v	Ireland	(B&H)	1995
5th	160* G.M. Fellows & C. White	v	Surrey	(C&G)	2001
6th	115 M.P. Vaughan & B. Parker	v	Northamptonshire	(NWT)	1997
7th	102 D.L. Bairstow & C.M. Old	v	Worcestershire	(B&H)	1982
8th	79 P.J. Hartley & D. Gough	v	Ireland	(NWT)	1997
9th	74* R.A. Hutton & H.P. Cooper	v	Lancashire	(SL)	1973
10th	64 R.J. Blakey & R.J. Sidebottom	v	Glamorgan	(SL)	2002

Highest wicket partnerships against county

1st	135 B.C. Rose & P.W. Denning	for	Somerset	(B&H)	1981
2nd	184 D.C. Boon & D.M. Jones	for	Australians	(Tour)	1989
3rd	131 R.J. Bailey & A.J. Lamb	for	Northamptonshire	(NWT)	1995
4th	154* N.J. Speak & N.H. Fairbrother	for	Lancashire	(SL)	1992
5th	104 I.V.A. Richards & I.T. Botham	for	Somerset	(NWT)	1985
6th	122* A. Habib & W.F. Stelling	for	Leicestershire	(B&H)	2000
7th	115 I.J. Gould & G.S. le Roux	for	Sussex	(NWT)	1986
8th	61 M.A. Ealham & P.A. Strang	for	Kent	(SL)	1997
9th	62 D. Ripley & N.G.B. Cook	for	Northamptonshire	(SL)	1993
10th	81 S. Turner & R.E. East	for	Essex	(NWT)	1982

Best bowling performance in a match for county 7 for 15 R.A. Hutton v Worcestershire (SL) 1969
Best bowling performance in a match against county 6 for 25 G. Chapple for Lancashire (SL) 1998
Largest crowd 16,500 v Northamptonshire (NWT) 1995

TEST MATCHES

Highest innings total for England 550 for 4 v India 1967
Highest innings total against England 653 for 4 dec by Australia 1993
Lowest innings total for England 76 v South Africa 1907
Lowest innings total against England 61 by West Indies 2000
Highest individual innings for England 310* J.H. Edrich v New Zealand 1965
Highest individual innings against England 334 D.G. Bradman for Australia 1930
Highest wicket partnerships for England

1st	168 L. Hutton & C. Washbrook	v	Australia	1948
	168 M.A. Atherton & G.A. Gooch	v	Pakistan	1992
2nd	369 J.H. Edrich & K.F. Barrington	v	New Zealand	1965
3rd	194* C.A. Milton & P.B.H. May	v	New Zealand	1958
4th	252 G. Boycott & B.L. D'Oliveira	v	India	1967
5th	133 J.P. Crawley & N. Hussain	v	Australia	1997
6th	152 A.W. Greig & A.P.E. Knott	v	West Indies	1976
7th	98 G.A. Gooch & D.R. Pringle	v	West Indies	1991
	98 G.A. Hick & M.P. Vaughan	v	West Indies	2000
8th	117 I.T. Botham & G.R. Dilley	v	Australia	1981
9th	108 C. Geary & G.G. Macaulay	v	Australia	1926
10th	61 D.J. Brown & D.L. Underwood	v	Australia	1968

Highest wicket partnerships against England

1st	192 R.C. Fredericks & C.G. Greenidge	for	West Indies	1976
2nd	301 A.R. Morris & D.G. Bradman	for	Australia	1948
3rd	229 D.G. Bradman & A.F. Kippax	for	Australia	1930
4th	388 W.H. Ponsford & D.G. Bradman	for	Australia	1934
5th	332* S.R. Waugh & A.R. Border	for	Australia	1993
6th	117 B.M. McMillan & J.N. Rhodes	for	South Africa	1998
7th	147 S.R. Waugh & M.G. Hughes	for	Australia	1989
8th	105 P.J.P. Burge & N.J.N. Hawke	for	Australia	1964
9th	89 P.J.P. Burge & A.T.W. Grout	for	Australia	1964
10th	103 H.G. Owen-Smith & A.J. Bell	for	South Africa	1929

Best bowling performance in an innings for England 8 for 43 R.D.G. Willis v Australia 1981
Best bowling performance in an innings against England 7 for 37 J.N. Gillespie for Australia 1997
Best bowling performance in a match for England 15 for 99 C. Blythe v South Africa 1907
Best bowling performance in a match against England 11 for 85 C.G. Macartney for Australia 1909
Largest crowd 39,000 England v Australia 1948

ONE-DAY INTERNATIONALS

Highest innings total for England in ODI 295 for 6 v New Zealand (TT) 1990
Highest innings against England in ODI 298 for 6 by New Zealand (TT) 1990
Highest innings total in non-England ODI 278 for 7 for Australia v Pakistan (WC) 1975
Lowest innings total for England in ODI 93 v Australia (WC) 1975
Lowest innings against England in ODI 136 by Sri Lanka (WC) 1983
Lowest innings total in non-England ODI 120 by East Africa v India (WC) 1975
Highest individual innings for England in ODI 128 R.A. Smith v New Zealand (TT) 1990
Highest individual innings against England in ODI 112 S.T. Jayasuriya for Sri Lanka (NWS) 2002
Highest individual innings in non-England ODI 120* S.R. Waugh for Australia v South Africa (WC) 1999
Highest wicket partnerships for England in ODI

1st	133 C.J. Tavare & B. Wood	v	India	(PT)	1982
2nd	113 G.A. Gooch & R.A. Smith	v	New Zealand	(TT)	1990
3rd	50 A.J. Lamb & R.A. Smith	v	New Zealand	(TT)	1990
4th	83 J.H. Edrich & K.W.R. Fletcher	v	India	(PT)	1974
5th	135* A.J. Hollioake & G.P. Thorpe	v	Australia	(TT)	1997
6th	66 P.R. Downton & D.R. Pringle	v	West Indies	(TT)	1988
	66 P.D. Collingwood & A.J. Stewart	v	Sri Lanka	(NWS)	2002

7th	44 C.J. Tavare & D.L. Bairstow	v	West Indies	(PT)	1980
8th	67 B.C. Hollioake & D. Gough	v	Pakistan	(NWS)	2001
9th	43 R.W. Taylor & R.G.D. Willis	v	Pakistan	(WC)	1979
10th	24 C.J. Tavare & J.K. Lever	v	West Indies	(PT)	1980

Highest wicket partnerships against England in ODI

1st	97 A.H. Jones & J.G. Wright	for	New Zealand	(TT)	1990
2nd	130 G.M. Wood & G.N. Yallop	for	Australia	(PT)	1981
3rd	118 M.D. Crowe & M.J. Greatbatch	for	New Zealand	(TT)	1990
4th	70 F.M. Engineer & A.L. Wadekar	for	India	(PT)	1974
5th	58 J.V. Coney & J.J. Crowe	for	New Zealand	(TT)	1986
6th	45 R.J. Shastri & Yashpal Sharma	for	India	(PT)	1982
7th	55* G.J. Gilmour & K.D. Walters	for	Australia	(WC)	1975
8th	52 M.V. Boucher & S.M. Pollock	for	South Africa	(TT)	1998
9th	38 N. Kapil Dev & S.V. Nayak	for	India	(PT)	1982
10th	33 V.B. John & R.J. Ratnayake	for	Sri Lanka	(WC)	1983

Highest wicket partnerships in non-England ODI

1st	123* F.M. Engineer & S.M. Gavaskar	for	India v East Africa	(WC)	1975
2nd	95 D.J. Cullinan & H.H. Gibbs	for	South Africa v Australia	(WC)	1999
3rd	80* B.A. Edgar & G.M. Turner	for	New Zealand v India	(WC)	1979
4th	126 R.T. Ponting & S.R. Waugh	for	Australia v South Africa	(WC)	1999
5th	113 M.G. Bevan & S.R. Waugh	for	Australia v Pakistan	(WC)	1999
6th	144 Imran Khan & Shahid Mahboob	for	Pakistan v Sri Lanka	(WC)	1983
7th	48 R. Edwards & M.H.N. Walker	for	Australia v Pakistan	(WC)	1975
8th	35* R. Edwards & J.R. Thomson	for	Australia v Pakistan	(WC)	1975
9th	41 W.W. Daniel & M.A. Holding	for	West Indies v Australia	(WC)	1983
10th	25 A.L.F. de Mel & V.B. John	for	Sri Lanka v Pakistan	(WC)	1983

Best bowling performance for England in ODI 4 for 15 M. Hendrick v Pakistan (WC) 1979
Best bowling performance against England in ODI 7 for 36 Waqar Younis for Pakistan (NWS) 2001
Best bowling performance in non-England ODI 7 for 51 W.W. Davis for West Indies v Australia (WC) 1983
Largest crowd 15,479 Australia v South Africa (WC) 1999

GROUND INFORMATION

ENTRANCES St Michael's Lane, via Main Gates (players, officials, members, public and vehicles), Kirkstall Lane via Sir Leonard Hutton Memorial Gates (members and public).
MEMBERS' ENCLOSURE Leeds Pavilion and East Stand and seating area.
PUBLIC ENCLOSURE North Enclosure seating A, B, C and D, Wintershed Stand Upper, West Terrace Enclosure seating A, B, C, D, E, F, G, H and I, Main Stand Upper (including Grandstand Bar) and Main Stand Lower.
COVERED STANDS Leeds Pavilion (part), Main Stand Balcony and Lower (part).
OPEN STANDS Leeds Pavilion (part), East Stand, North Enclosure seating N, O, and P, Wintershed Stand Upper and Lower, West Terrace Enclosure seating A, B, C, D, E, F, and Main Stand Lower (part).
NAME OF ENDS Rugby Stand End, Kirkstall Lane End.
GROUND DIMENSIONS 145m × 142m (although for matches the playing area is limited to 130m × 134m).
REPLAY SCREEN This is sited at the rear of the West Stand for all major matches.
FIRST AID At various First Aid Points around the ground.
CODES OF DRESS Spectators are required to dress in an appropriate manner consistent with attending a cricket match. Bare torsos are not acceptable in, or in front of the pavilion. Executive Club/Suite users must wear a necktie and jacket.
BEHAVIOUR The club is keen that standards of behaviour should be maintained and members and spectators are urged to report immediately to the CEO any incident, or potential incident, where they feel action should be taken. Bad language is not acceptable at any match and the club will take prompt and strong action should this or any other ground regulation be ignored.
RECIPROCAL ARRANGEMENTS Yorkshire CCC members can gain free entry to designated Yorkshire Racecourses.

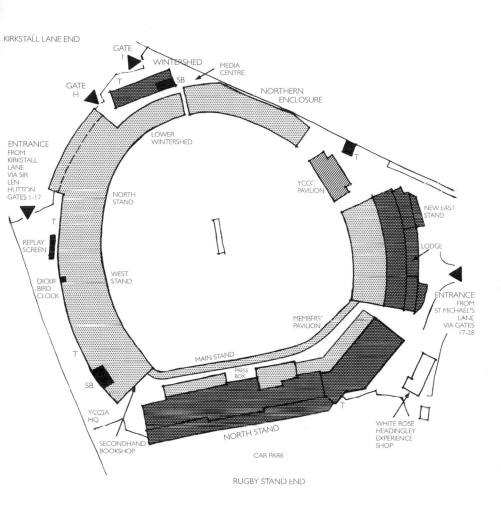

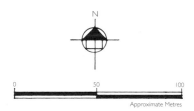

SUPPORTERS' CLUB Yorkshire County Cricket Supporters' Association can be contacted at 19 Staybrite Avenue, Cottingley, Bingley, West Yorks BD16 1PR, membership is £4 per annum. Details of membership of Yorkshire Exiles, the Southern Group, £9 per annum, can be obtained from PO Box 6024, Leighton Buzzard, Beds LU7 2ZS.

JUNIORS Junior Vikings membership available for under-18s. Contact Membership Secretary for full details ☎ 0113 278 7394, www.juniorvikings.com

CORPORATE ENTERTAINING Corporate entertaining facilities are available at all matches, including Executive Club membership, county hospitality, day/night hospitality, match sponsorship, match ball, mascot, Man of the Match, scorecard sponsorship and full corporate entertainment. Facilities are also available for conferences, training events, sporting dinners and parties. Contact Marketing Department ☎ 0113 278 7394 for full details together with brochure.

FACILITIES FOR VISUALLY IMPAIRED SPECTATORS Concessionary admission rates available which include helper. Guide dogs allowed but please give club a few days notice of your visit.

FACILITIES AND ACCESS FOR PEOPLE WITH DISABILITIES INCLUDING WHEELCHAIR ACCESS TO GROUND Yes, access to the ground through main entrance in St Michael's Lane.

DESIGNATED CAR PARK AVAILABLE INSIDE THE GROUND FOR PEOPLE WITH DISABILITIES Yes, limited space available, via Kirkstall Lane entrance.

GOOD VIEWING AREAS INSIDE THE GROUND FOR PEOPLE USING WHEELCHAIRS Yes, good facilities available including disabled toilets around ground including positions at the Kirkstall Lane and Rugby Stand Ends at pitch level on hard standing perimeter and in East Stand members' area.

DESIGNATED VIEWING AREAS FOR PEOPLE USING WHEELCHAIRS Yes, several positions are clearly marked and offer excellent views of the playing area.

RAMPS TO PROVIDE EASY ACCESS TO BARS & REFRESHMENT OUTLETS FOR PEOPLE USING WHEELCHAIRS Yes, including a lift in the new East Stand.

FOOD & DRINK FULL RESTAURANT/DINING FACILITIES Members, yes. Public, no.

TEMPORARY FOOD/DRINK FACILITIES Members, yes. Public, yes.

FOOD SUITABLE FOR VEGETARIANS Members, yes. Public, yes.

BARS Members 3, Public 4.

VARIETIES OF BEER SOLD Websters, Tetley's Bitter, Yorkshire Pride, Black Sheep Draught Bitter

CHILDREN'S FACILITIES Crèche, no. Play area, no.

CLUB SHOP The Headingley Retail Shop (joint venture between Yorkshire CCC and Leeds Rugby) facility is located in new premises near the main gate in St Michael's Lane and is open throughout the year. There is a secondary equipment-based shop available within the Yorkshire CCC Cricket Centre in St Michael's Lane opposite the main gates to the ground.

CLUB MUSEUM No, but there are many pictures in the pavilion and future plans include a museum.

CRICKET COACHING FACILITIES Available in Yorkshire Cricket Centre located in St Michael's Lane opposite the main gates. Contact Yorkshire CCC for full details.

CRICKET NETS Available throughout the year in the Yorkshire Cricket Centre. Contact Yorkshire CCC for full details.

OTHER SPORTING OR RECREATIONAL FACILITIES ON THE GROUND Leeds Rhinos rugby league and Leeds Tykes rugby union clubs both play matches on the adjacent Leeds rugby football ground.

FACILITIES FOR HIRE OR WIDER COMMUNITY USE AT THE GROUND WINTER CRICKET EVENTS Facilities are available within the Leeds Pavilion and the new East Stand for wedding receptions, parties, conferences, banquets and sporting dinners. Contact Marketing Department for full details and a brochure. In 2002 a hotel was opened at Headingley Lodge on the upper levels of the new East Stand. This offers en-suite rooms with views of the ground. Secure free overnight car parking for hotel guests is available within the ground, enter via St Michael's Lane entrance.

CAR PARKING FACILITIES Some car parking is available on the rugby ground car park, but this is severely limited. Car parking is available in neighbouring streets or local parking areas at Beckett Park and Woodhouse Moor. There is limited members' car parking off St Michael's Lane on the practice area of the rugby ground and main ground. For international matches tickets must be obtained in advance. A special Park and Ride facility is also available on major match days from various Leeds car parks to the north of the ground.

GROUND CAPACITY 16,500.

ANTICIPATED GROUND DEVELOPMENTS Demolition of Yorkshire CCC offices and relocation to the East Stand by beginning of the 2004 season.

HOW TO GET THERE

 Headingley (MetroLine) 0.5 mile, Burley Park (MetroLine) 0.45 mile on Leeds/Harrogate and York Metro Line from Leeds Central station 2.5 miles. ☎ 08457 484950, 08457 225225, 0870 602 3322, www.gner.co.uk, www.northern-spirit.co.uk, MetroLine ☎ 0113 245 7676, www.metro-wyorks.co.uk, www.wymetro.com

 Yorkshire Rider 74, 75, 76 and 77 link Leeds Central station with ground as well as many other routes. Buses from Bradford, Horsforth, Ilkley, Otley, Shipley and Skipton also pass near the ground. ☎ 0113 245 7676 for timetables or MetroLine ☎ 0113 245 7676, www.metro-wyorks.co.uk. National Bus Enquiries ☎ 0870 608 2608

 There are cycle routes from surrounding areas of Leeds to Headingley.

 From north: from A1(M) junction 45 take fourth exit from roundabout on to A64 towards Leeds, at junction with Ring Road (A6120) (Seacroft Roundabout) take A6120 signposted Harrogate, continue on A6120 (Ring Road) to roundabout junction with A660 (West Park Roundabout), take first exit A660 to city centre, bear left on to B6157 (Headingley), take right hand land and turn right into North Lane (B6157) signposted Kirkstall, Bradford, cricket ground is on the left hand side. **From south:** from M1 junction 43 take M621 towards Leeds city centre, continue on M621 to junction 2, at roundabout take A643 signposted Wetherby, at A58/A62 junction take A58 and continue towards Leeds to junction with A64/B6154, at roundabout take A65, turn right at traffic lights on to B6157 (Kirkstall), follow signs to Headingley station and cricket ground. **From east:** from Selby stay on A63 to junction with A64, bear left on to A64 (York Road), continue on this road to junction with A58(M), bear right on to A58(M) (York Road), continue on A64(M) (New York Road), bear left on to A660 and follow signs to cricket ground. **From west:** from A647 turn left (north) on to Swinnow Lane (B6157), continue on this road, following signs to Kirkstall and cricket ground.

✈ Leeds/Bradford Airport ☎ 0113 250 9696 www.leedsbradfordairport.co.uk

WHERE TO STAY

Headingley Lodge Hotel (☎ 0113 278 5323), 44 The Calls (☎ 0113 244 0099), Crowne Plaza (☎ 0113 244 2200 www.leeds.crowneplaza.com), Golden Lion Hotel (☎ 0113 243 6454), Le Meridien Queen's Hotel (☎ 0870 400 8696 www.lemeridien.com), Malmaison Hotel (☎ 0113 398 1000 www.malmaison.com), Merevale Hotel (☎ 0113 265 8933), Pinewood Hotel (☎ 0113 262 2581 or 0800 0967463), The Boundary Hotel (☎ 0113 275 7700), The Metropole Hotel (☎ 0113 243 5081), The Village Hotel, (☎ 0113 2781000), Weetwood Hall (☎ 0113 230 6000 www.weetwood.co.uk)

For further places to stay in Leeds visit www.smoothhound.co.uk, www.leeds.gov.uk, www.yorkshirevisitor.com.

WHERE TO EAT

Art's Bar Café (☎ 0113 243 8243 www.artscafe.co.uk), Brasserie Forty Four (☎ 0113 234 3232 www.dine-services.com), Bryan's (☎ 0113 278 5679), Clockhouse Café (☎ 0113 294 5464), Gueller (☎ 0113 245 9922 www.guellers.com), Headingley Taps (☎ 0113 220 0931), Malmaison (☎ 0113 398 1000 www.malmaison.com), Pool Court at 42 (☎ 0113 244 4242), Rascasse (☎ 0113 244 6611 www.rascasse-leeds.co.uk), Salvo's (☎ 0113 275 5017 www.salvos.co.uk), Shogun Teppanyaki (☎ 0113 245 1856 www.shogunteppanyaki.btconnect.co.uk), Tariq's (☎ 0113 275 1881), Thai Siam (☎ 0113 245 1608 www.thai-siam.co.uk), The Three Horseshoes (☎ 0113 275 7222), Trio (☎ 0113 203 6090)

TOURIST INFORMATION Gateway Yorkshire/Leeds Tourist Information Centre, Station Arcade, PO Box 244, Leeds, West Yorkshire LS1 1PL ☎ 0113 242 5242, www.leeds.gov.uk, www.yorkshirevisitor.com

Leeds Rhinos Rugby League Club ☎ 0113 278 6181
Leeds Tykes Rugby Football Club ☎ 0113 230 4242
Leeds United Football Club ☎ 0113 226 6000, www.leedsunited.com
GNER Hotel Booking Service ☎ 01904 671111
Yorkshire Tourist Board ☎ 01904 773371, www.yorkshirevisitor.com
English Tourism Council www.visitbritain.com, www.travelengland.org.uk

LOCAL RADIO STATIONS BBC Radio Leeds (95.3 MHz FM/774 KHz MW), Radio Aire/Magic 828 (96.3 MHz FM/828 KHz MW)

LOCAL NEWSPAPERS *Yorkshire Evening Post, Yorkshire Post, York Evening Press, Bradford Telegraph & Argus*

SCARBOROUGH

Address Scarborough Cricket Club, The Pavilion, North Marine Road,
Scarborough, North Yorkshire YO12 7TJ
Prospects of Play ☎ 01723 365625

HISTORY OF GROUND AND FACILITIES

SCARBOROUGH CRICKET CLUB leased the North Marine Road cricket ground for £15 a year from 1863 until 1878 when it purchased the land.

Cricket has been played in Scarborough since 1849 when Scarborough Cricket Club was established. Their first matches were staged at Castle Hill, also known as the Queen's Cricket Ground, which has long since been built over. Yorkshire County Cricket Club staged matches at Castle Hill between 1874 and 1877 and have visited the seaside resort on the North Yorkshire coast ever since. The first match staged by Yorkshire CCC at the North Marine Road Ground was against I'Zingari in 1878. The first cricket festival was staged in 1876 when New Forest Rangers Cricket Club, Yorkshire County Cricket Club, MCC and Scarborough Cricket Club took part.

The original pavilion erected in 1874 was replaced at a cost of £2,150 in 1895 by a new pavilion in the north-west corner of the ground. The pavilion clock was presented by Mr and Mrs J. Compton-Rickett and Mr J.H. Morton in 1896 before the first County Championship match between Yorkshire and Leicestershire. In 1902 a new seating enclosure was erected using funds generated from a very successful festival; this enclosure was added to in 1903 and 1907. In 1903 a press box/score' room was constructed at a cost of £250. A concrete stand was built in the north-east corner in 1926. The most recent addition to the ground is the West Stand, built in 1956. Yorkshire CCC play two championship fixtures and one limited-overs match at Scarborough each season, usually one in June and others in August or September.

The Scarborough Cricket Festival takes place annually. Yorkshire CCC used to compete with three other invited counties for the Festival Trophy. The limited-overs competition was established in 1971 and consisted of two 50-over matches involving four first-class counties; the winners of the two matches meet in the final.

Games have also been staged at Scarborough between the Gentlemen and the Players and against various touring teams. In 1988 MCC staged a match with a Michael Parkinson's XI and this is now an annual feature of the festival as is Yorkshire CCC versus The Yorkshiremen XI. Other visiting teams have included C.I. Thornton's, H.D.G. Leveson Gower's, Lord Londesborough's, T.N. Pearce's and D.B. Close's XIs. In 1986 Ken Rutherford scored 317 against D.B. Close's XI which included eight Test players.

Scarborough Cricket Club play in the Yorkshire League and Websters Cricket League and field three XIs throughout the season. They also enter the National Knockout Cup and have reached the final at Lord's. In 1976 and 1978 the ground hosted one-day internationals between England and the West Indies and England and New Zealand.

Many great cricketers have played at Scarborough: G.J. Bonnor the 'Colonial Hercules', Sir Jack Hobbs, Sir Donald Bradman, Denis Compton and Richie Benaud have all notched up notable achievements on this ground. Sir Donald Bradman is said to have considered his innings of 132 against H.D.G. Leveson Gower's XI in 1934 one of his best, if not his best, innings ever played in England! Sir Jack Hobbs scored 266* for the Players in 1925 which remains the record highest individual innings for a Gentlemen versus Players match.

The playing area is 132 metres by 128 metres and is defined by a rope and some advertising boards. The TV camera/commentary box position is at the Trafalgar Square End with the radio commentary box adjoining the pressroom.

GROUND RECORDS AND SCORES

FIRST-CLASS MATCHES

Highest innings total for county 600 for 4 dec v Worcestershire 1995
Highest innings total against county 517 for 7 dec by Northamptonshire 1999
Lowest innings total for county 37 v I'Zingari 1877
Lowest innings total against county 31 by MCC 1877
Highest individual innings for county 223* J.V. Wilson v Scotland 1951
Highest individual innings against county 208* M.P. Donnelly for MCC 1948
Highest wicket partnerships for county

1st	228 H. Halliday & J.V. Wilson	v	Scotland	1951
2nd	302 W. Watson & J.V. Wilson	v	Derbyshire	1948
3rd	293* A.A. Metcalfe & P.E. Robinson	v	Derbyshire	1990
4th	258 P.E. Robinson & D. Byas	v	Kent	1989
5th	191 M.G. Bevan & A.A. Metcalfe	v	West Indians	1995
6th	140 F.S. Jackson & F.W. Milligan	v	Somerset	1898
7th	170 G.S. Blewett & G.M. Hamilton	v	Northamptonshire	1999
8th	159 E. Smith (Morley) & W. Rhodes	v	MCC	1901
9th	149* R.J. Blakey & A.K.D. Gray	v	Leicestershire	2002
10th	75 J.A. Richardson & T.F. Smailes	v	MCC	1936

Highest wicket partnerships against county

1st	180 G.D. Mendis & N.J. Speak	for	Lancashire	1991
2nd	148 A. Jones & G.A. Gooch	for	International XI	1975
3rd	321 M.W. Gatting & M.R. Ramprakash	for	Middlesex	1993
4th	190 K.L.T. Arthurton & J.R. Murray	for	West Indians	1995
	190 R.J. Warren & D.J.G. Sales	for	Northamptonshire	1999

5th	142 D.N. Patel & C.N. Boynes	for	Worcestershire	1976
6th	166 N.G. Featherstone & H.A. Gomes	for	Middlesex	1975
7th	214 A.L. Penberthy & D. Ripley	for	Northamptonshire	1999
8th	172 W.E. Astill & A.E.R. Gilligan	for	MCC	1923
9th	98 R.E. Hitchcock & A.C. Smith	for	Warwickshire	1963
10th	82 I.D. Austin & P.J. Martin	for	Lancashire	1991

Best bowling performance in an innings for county 9 for 28 J.M. Preston v MCC 1888
Best bowling performance in an innings against county 8 for 33 J.A. Young for MCC 1946
Best bowling performance in a match for county 13 for 63 J.M. Preston v MCC 1888
Best bowling performance in a match against county 13 for 45 R. Henderson for l'Zingari 1877
Largest crowd 22,946 v Derbyshire 1947

LIMITED-OVERS MATCHES

Highest innings total for county 352 for 6 v Nottinghamshire (SL) 2001
Highest innings total against county 375 for 4 by Surrey (SL) 1994
Lowest innings total for county 91 v Surrey (SL) 1970
Lowest innings total against county 87 by Derbyshire (SL) 1973
Highest individual innings for county 191 D.S. Lehmann v Nottinghamshire (SL) 2001
Highest individual innings against county 133 A.D. Brown for Surrey (SL) 1994
Highest wicket partnerships for county

1st	190 G. Boycott & R.G. Lumb	v	Nottinghamshire	(SL)	1976
2nd	141 A.A. Metcalfe & K. Sharp	v	Gloucestershire	(SL)	1984
3rd	172 A. McGrath & D.S. Lehmann	v	Nottinghamshire	(SL)	2001
4th	146 R.B. Richardson & R.J. Blakey	v	Sussex	(SL)	1993
5th	94 A. McGrath & R.J. Harden	v	Kent	(SL)	1999
6th	105 S.N. Hartley & D.L. Bairstow	v	Warwickshire	(SL)	1984
7th	69 D.L. Bairstow & M.D. Moxon	v	Surrey	(SL)	1981
8th	89 R.J. Blakey & R.K.J. Dawson	v	Leicestershire	(SL)	2002
9th	40 D.L. Bairstow & C.M. Old	v	Middlesex	(SL)	1979
10th	50* P. Carrick & S. Oldham	v	Warwickshire	(SL)	1984

Highest wicket partnerships against county

1st	142 G.W. Humpage & K.D. Smith	for	Warwickshire	(SL)	1984
2nd	160 A.D. Brown & G.P. Thorpe	for	Surrey	(SL)	1994
3rd	116 G.S. Clinton & M.A. Lynch	for	Surrey	(SL)	1981
4th	125 M.A. Buss & A.W. Greig	for	Sussex	(SL)	1976
5th	105 A.W. Greig & Javed Miandad	for	Sussex	(SL)	1976
6th	74 R.J. Boyd-Moss & Sarfraz Nawaz	for	Northamptonshire	(SL)	1980
7th	60* J.W. Lloyds & D.V. Lawrence	for	Gloucestershire	(SL)	1991
8th	47 R.P. Lefebvre & I.G. Swallow	for	Somerset	(SL)	1990
9th	45 M.S. Kasprowicz & D. Williamson	for	Leicestershire	(SL)	1999
10th	36 G. Welch & T.A. Munton	for	Warwickshire	(SL)	1994

Best bowling performance in a match for county 5 for 19 C. White v Somerset (SL) 2002
Best bowling performance in a match against county 5 for 41 C.L. Cairns for Nottinghamshire (SL) 1996
Largest crowd 12,000 v Worcestershire (SL) 1989

ONE-DAY INTERNATIONALS

Highest innings total for England in ODI 206 for 8 v New Zealand (PT) 1978
Highest innings total against England in ODI 207 for 4 by West Indies (PT) 1976
Lowest innings total for England in ODI 202 for 8 v West Indies (PT) 1976
Lowest innings total against England in ODI 187 for 8 by New Zealand (PT) 1978
Highest individual innings for England in ODI 94 G.A. Gooch v New Zealand (PT) 1978
Highest individual innings against England in ODI 119* I.V.A. Richards for West Indies (PT) 1976
Highest wicket partnerships for England in ODI

1st	67 J.M. Brearley & G.A. Gooch	v	New Zealand	(PT)	1978
2nd	111 G.A. Gooch & C.T. Radley	v	New Zealand	(PT)	1978

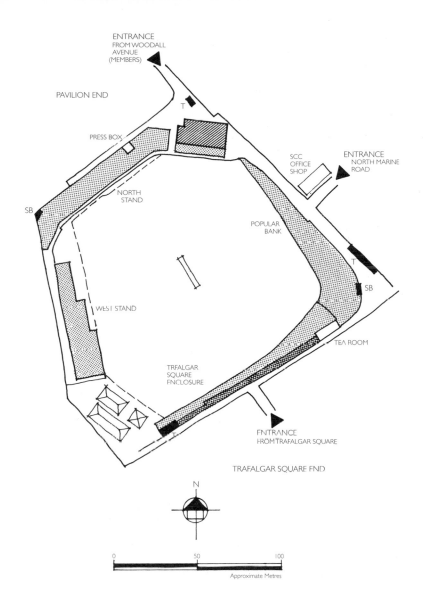

ENTRANCE
FROM WOODALL
AVENUE
(MEMBERS)

PAVILION END

T

PRESS BOX

SCC
OFFICE
SHOP

ENTRANCE
NORTH MARINE
ROAD

NORTH
STAND

SB

POPULAR
BANK

N

T

SB

WEST STAND

TEA ROOM

TRAFALGAR
SQUARE
ENCLOSURE

T

ENTRANCE
FROM TRAFALGAR SQUARE

TRAFALGAR SQUARE END

N

0   50   100
Approximate Metres

3rd	5 D.L. Amiss & R.A. Woolmer	v	West Indies	(PT)	1976
4th	49 D.L. Amiss & G.D. Barlow	v	West Indies	(PT)	1976
5th	64 G.D. Barlow & G.A. Gooch	v	West Indies	(PT)	1976
6th	13 G. Miller & G.R.J. Roope	v	New Zealand	(PT)	1978
7th	36 G.D. Barlow & A.P.E. Knott	v	West Indies	(PT)	1976
8th	21 G.D. Barlow & D.L. Underwood	v	West Indies	(PT)	1976
9th	8* M. Hendrick & J.K. Lever	v	New Zealand	(PT)	1978
10th	yet to be established.				

Highest wicket partnerships against England in ODI

1st	28 R.W. Anderson & J.G. Wright	for	New Zealand	(PT)	1978
2nd	74 C.G. Greenidge & I.V.A. Richards	for	West Indies	(PT)	1976

3rd	39 C.H. Lloyd & I.V.A. Richards	for	West Indies	(PT)	1976
4th	60 I.V.A. Richards & L.G. Rowe	for	West Indies	(PT)	1976
5th	31* C.L. King & I.V.A. Richards	for	West Indies	(PT)	1976
6th	6 R.J. Hadlee & G.P. Howarth	for	New Zealand	(PT)	1978
7th	8 B.E. Congdon & G.P. Howarth	for	New Zealand	(PT)	1978
8th	68 B.L. Cairns & B.E. Congdon	for	New Zealand	(PT)	1978
9th	14* R.O. Collinge & B.E. Congdon	for	New Zealand	(PT)	1978
10th	yet to be established.				

Best bowling performance for England in ODI 2 for 29 G.A. Gooch for England v New Zealand (PT) 1978
Best bowling performance against England in ODI 5 for 28 B.L. Cairns for New Zealand v England (PT) 1978
Largest crowd 12,000 v West Indies (PT) 1976

GROUND INFORMATION

ENTRANCES North Marine Road (players, officials, members, public and vehicles), Trafalgar Square (members and public), Woodall Avenue (vehicles).
MEMBERS' ENCLOSURE Pavilion, Pavilion terrace, North Stand enclosure and Trafalgar Square Stand and Enclosure (part).
PUBLIC ENCLOSURE Popular Bank, West Stand Upper (including 'Dropped Catch' Bar beneath) and Trafalgar Square Stand and Enclosure (part).
COVERED STANDS Pavilion (part) and Trafalgar Square Stand including Tearoom Bar.
OPEN STANDS Pavilion terrace (part), North Stand Enclosure, West Stand Upper, Trafalgar Square Enclosure and Popular Bank.
NAME OF ENDS Pavilion End, Trafalgar Square End.
GROUND DIMENSIONS 132m × 128m.
REPLAY SCREEN If televised matches are staged at the ground the replay screen is sited to the west of the playing area.
FIRST AID In the pavilion and in Scarborough Cricket Club offices near main entrance from North Marine Road.
CODES OF DRESS Spectators are required to dress in an appropriate manner consistent with attending a cricket match. Bare torsos are not acceptable in, or in front of the pavilion. Executive Club/Suite users must wear a necktie and jacket.
BEHAVIOUR The club is keen that standards of behaviour should be maintained and members and spectators are urged to report immediately to the CEO/Scarborough Cricket Club official, any incident, or potential incident, where they feel action should be taken. Bad language is not acceptable at any match and the club will take prompt and strong action should this or any other ground regulation be ignored.
RECIPROCAL ARRANGEMENTS Yorkshire CCC members can gain free access to designated Yorkshire Racecourses.
SUPPORTERS' CLUB Yorkshire County Cricket Supporters' Association can be contacted at 19 Staybrite Avenue, Cottingley, Bingley, West Yorks BD16 1PR, membership is £4 per annum. Details of membership of Yorkshire Exiles, the Southern Group, £9 per annum, can be obtained from PO Box 6024, Leighton Buzzard, Beds LU7 2ZS.
JUNIORS Junior Vikings membership available for under-18s. Contact Membership Secretary for full details ☎ 0113 278 7394 www.juniorvikings.com.
CORPORATE ENTERTAINING Corporate entertaining facilities are available at all matches. Contact Scarborough CC for full details.
FACILITIES FOR VISUALLY IMPAIRED SPECTATORS Concessionary rates apply which include helper. Guide dog is allowed but please give club a few days' notice of your visit.
FACILITIES AND ACCESS FOR PEOPLE WITH DISABILITIES INCLUDING WHEELCHAIR ACCESS TO GROUND Yes, access to the ground through main entrance in North Marine Road.
DESIGNATED CAR PARK AVAILABLE INSIDE THE GROUND FOR PEOPLE WITH DISABILITIES No.
GOOD VIEWING AREAS INSIDE THE GROUND FOR PEOPLE USING WHEELCHAIRS Yes, good facilities at various points around the playing area perimeter, plus special area situated within the Trafalgar Square enclosure and at the Pavilion End.

DESIGNATED VIEWING AREAS FOR PEOPLE USING WHEELCHAIRS Yes, several positions are clearly marked and offer excellent views of the playing area and there is a special area situated within the Trafalgar Square enclosure.

RAMPS TO PROVIDE EASY ACCESS TO BARS & REFRESHMENT OUTLETS FOR PEOPLE USING WHEELCHAIRS Yes, ramps are available to gain access into the pavilion and other bars and the tea room at the Trafalgar Square End of the ground.

FOOD & DRINK FULL RESTAURANT/DINING FACILITIES Members, no. Public, no.

TEMPORARY FOOD/DRINK FACILITIES Members, yes. Public, yes.

FOOD SUITABLE FOR VEGETARIANS Members, no. Public, no.

BARS Members 1, Public 2.

VARIETIES OF BEER SOLD Websters, Yorkshire Pride, Burton Ales.

CHILDREN'S FACILITIES Crèche, no. Play area, no.

CLUB SHOP The Headingley shop and Scarborough CC have souvenir outlets on the North Marine Road side of the ground and in the Scarborough CC Office in North Marine Road.

CLUB MUSEUM No, but there are pictures in the pavilion.

CRICKET COACHING FACILITIES Yes, contact Scarborough CC for full details.

CRICKET NETS Yes, contact Scarborough CC for full details.

OTHER SPORTING OR RECREATIONAL FACILITIES ON THE GROUND No.

FACILITIES FOR HIRE OR WIDER COMMUNITY USE AT THE GROUND No.

WINTER CRICKET EVENTS No.

CAR PARKING FACILITIES No car parking is available within the ground. Members and public are advised to use one of the town centre car parks or neighbouring streets, some of which are metered, or the park ride facilities.

GROUND CAPACITY 11,500.

ANTICIPATED GROUND DEVELOPMENTS Nothing planned.

HOW TO GET THERE

 Scarborough central station 0.75 mile ☎ 08457 484950, 0870 602 3322, www.gner.co.uk, www.northern-spirit.co.uk

 United Automobile Services from Whitby and Middlesbrough, East Yorkshire Motor Services from Bridlington and Hull, West Yorkshire Road Car Company from Malton, York and Leeds to town centre Bus Station. Contact Scarborough Bus Station for details of timetable and cost ☎ 01723 375463.

 There are cycle routes to this area of the town.

 From north: from A171, continue to junction with A165, bear left on to A165 (Coastal Road), continue on Burniston Road and Columbus Ravine to junction with B1364 (Peasholm Road), turn left in to Peasholm Road, continue on North Marine Road and follow signs to cricket ground. **From south:** from A64 turn right on to A170 (High Street), continue on A170 along Stepney Road to Falsgrave Road, bear left on to Victoria Road and follow it to North Marine Road. **From west:** from A170 (Thirsk, Pickering), continue on A170 into Scarborough, then as for south.

 Leeds/Bradford Airport ☎ 0113 250 9696 www.leedsbradfordairport.co.uk, Teesside Airport ☎ 01325 332811 www.teessideairport.co.uk

WHERE TO STAY

Burghcliffe Hotel (☎ 01723 361524), Esplanade Hotel (☎ 01723 360382), Glywin Guesthouse (☎ 01723 371311), Hackness Grange Hotel (☎ 01723 882345), Holbeck Hall (☎ 01723 374374, La Baia Hotel (☎ 01723 370780), Ox Pasture Hall Country Hotel (☎ 01723 365295 www.s-h-systems.co.uk/hotels/oxpasture.html), Philamon Guesthouse (☎ 01723 373107), Red Lea Hotel (☎ 01723 362431 www.redleahotel.co.uk), Ryndle Court Hotel (☎ 01723 375188 www.ryndlccourt.co.uk), Smugglers Rock Country House (☎ 01723 870044 www.smugglersrock.co.uk), The Falcon Inn (☎ 01723 870717), The New Southlands Hotel (☎ 01723 361461 www.southlandshotel.co.uk), The Wickets Guesthouse (☎ 01723 373472), White Rails Guesthouse (☎ 01723 362800)

The pavilion and Scarborough's North Marine Road ground pictured from the Trafalgar Square End, 1996.

For further places to stay in the Scarborough/Whitby area visit www.smoothhound.co.uk, www.scarborough.gov.uk. Stay on a Farm ☎ 0870 241 3746, 01271 336141, www.farmsstaynorth.co.uk.

WHERE TO EAT

Lanterna Ristorante (☎ 01723 363616), The Falcon Inn (☎ 01723 870717), Wacker's (☎ 01723 353758)

TOURIST INFORMATION Scarborough Tourist Information Centre, Pavilion House, Valley Bridge Road, Scarborough, North Yorkshire YO11 1UY ☎ 01723 373333, www.scarborough.gov.uk

OTHER USEFUL INFORMATION

English Tourism Council www.visitbritain.com, www.travelengland.org.uk
GNER Hotel Booking Service ☎ 01904 671111
Middlesborough Football Club ☎ 01642 877700 www.mfc.co.uk
York City Football Club ☎ 01904 624447 www.ycfc.net
Yorkshire Tourist Board ☎ 01904 773371 www.yorkshirevisitor.com

LOCAL RADIO STATION BBC Radio York (95.5 MHz FM/1260 KHz MW)

LOCAL NEWSPAPERS *Scarborough Evening News, Northern Echo, Yorkshire Evening Post, Yorkshire Post, Evening Press, The Mercury, Whitby Gazette*

University Centres of Cricketing Excellence

Bradford/Leeds UCCE – Bradford Park Avenue
Cambridge UCCE – Fenner's
Cardiff/Glamorgan UCCE – Abergavenny
Durham UCCE – Durham University
Loughborough UCCE – Loughborough University
Oxford UCCE – University Parks

BRADFORD/LEEDS UCCE

Physical Recreation Department, Sports Centre, University of Bradford, Richmond Road, Bradford, West Yorkshire BD7 1DP

Telephone 01274 234867 **fax** 01274 235510
Email j.s.teasdale@bradford.ac.uk

UCCE Founded 2000
UCCE Administrator S. Teasdale
UCCE Senior Coach R. Horner

GROUND
Bradford (Bradford Park Avenue). No other grounds are used for matches.

BRADFORD

Address Bradford/Leeds UCCE, Bradford Park Avenue Cricket Ground, Canterbury Avenue, Bradford, West Yorkshire
Prospects of Play ☎ 07711 981163

HISTORY OF GROUND AND FACILITIES

YORKSHIRE COUNTY CRICKET CLUB played at two venues in Bradford: the first ground was at Great Horton Road (also known as Easby Road) and it was used between 1863 and 1874. Then in 1881 Yorkshire CCC played their first game at Horton Park Avenue, known today as Bradford Park Avenue. After 104 years the link with this venue was severed because of the stringent regulations imposed following the Taylor Report after the fire at Bradford City's Valley Parade. Yorkshire's last game for seven years at Bradford Park Avenue was a limited-overs match with Surrey on 14 July 1985 in the John Player Sunday League. The ground is now the home venue for Bradford/Leeds UCCE matches.

As soon as cricket ceased being played at Bradford in 1985, a society, The Friends of Park Avenue, was formed to win back first-class status to this historic Yorkshire venue. The society has staged many fund raising events and its president is Brian Close. Thanks to support from the society and Yorkshire CCC the Yorkshire Academy of Cricket (YAC) was founded on 15 May 1989.

The ground is owned by Bradford Metropolitan Council and they offered considerable support to this venture with a 999-year lease at nominal rent, £15,000 per annum for five years towards upkeep of the grounds and £40,000 towards ground improvements. A further £60,000 has been obtained from sponsorship, donations and other fund-raising activities. Yorkshire returned to the ground in August 1992 when Surrey were the visitors for a Britannic Assurance County Championship match.

The YAC play a number of matches against local universities, cricket clubs, league XIs, club touring teams, colleges and county second XIs throughout the season from April to September at Bradford Park Avenue. Players who have represented the YAC include Jeremy Batty, Matthew Doidge, Darren Gough, Paul Grayson and Stuart Milburn.

Bradford Park Avenue FC used to adjoin the ground but has now gone and at one end is the privately owned Fitness First facility. The only permanent structures on the ground are the concrete terraces, scoreboard and groundsman's stores.

The playing area is rather small – measuring 130 metres by 124 metres – and over the years some spinners have found it difficult to contain a batsman in full flow on this ground. The old pavilion end of the ground has been cleared and levelled to create ample car parking space. The playing area at the southern end is approximately six feet higher than that at the northern end.

Since the inception of the Bradford/Leeds UCCE in 2000, very considerable effort has gone into reinstating the playing surface to its former quality and over £90,000 has been spent on this process. The pitch is now as good, if not better, than it has ever been.

GROUND RECORDS AND SCORES

FIRST-CLASS MATCHES

(No UCCE matches – Yorkshire records on ground)
Highest innings total for Yorkshire 540 for 7 dec v Warwickshire 1928
Highest innings total against Yorkshire 681 for 7 dec for Leicestershire 1996
Lowest innings total for Yorkshire 40 v Kent 1967
Lowest innings total against Yorkshire 28 by Worcestershire 1907
Highest individual innings for Yorkshire 275 P. Holmes v Warwickshire 1928
Highest individual innings against Yorkshire 234 C.B. Fry for Sussex 1903
Highest wicket partnerships for Yorkshire

1st	248 G. Boycott & A.A. Metcalfe	v	Nottinghamshire	1983
2nd	243 G. Boycott & J.D. Love	v	Nottinghamshire	1976
3rd	258* J.T. Brown & F. Mitchell	v	Warwickshire	1901
4th	271 B.B. Wilson & W. Rhodes	v	Sussex	1914
5th	187 J.T. Brown & G.H. Hirst	v	Somerset	1903
6th	200 D. Denton & G.H. Hirst	v	Essex	1902
7th	161 R.G. Lumb & C.M. Old	v	Worcestershire	1980
8th	128 H. Verity & T.F. Smailes	v	Indians	1936
9th	179 R.A. Hutton & G.A. Cope	v	Pakistanis	1971
10th	108 G. Boycott & M.K. Bore	v	Nottinghamshire	1973

Highest wicket partnerships against Yorkshire

1st	186 G. Gunn & W.W. Whysall	for	Nottinghamshire	1927
2nd	224 W.H. Ashdown & F.E. Woolley	for	Kent	1931
3rd	174 C.B. Fry & K.S. Ranjitsinghji	for	Sussex	1903
4th	218 V.J. Wells & J.J. Whitaker	for	Leicestershire	1996
5th	184 J.D. Eggar & A.C. Revill	for	Derbyshire	1949
6th	294 D.R. Jardine & P.G.H. Fender	for	Surrey	1928
7th	126 J.J. Whitaker & P.A. Nixon	for	Leicestershire	1996
8th	124 R.J. Hadlee & E.E. Hemmings	for	Nottinghamshire	1981
9th	86 M.L. Jaisimha & R.B. Desai	for	Indians	1959
10th	89 G.D. Rose & M. Dimond	for	Somerset	1994

Best bowling performance in an innings for Yorkshire 9 for 36 E. Robinson v Lancashire 1920
Best bowling performance in an innings against Yorkshire 9 for 30 A.E. Thomas for Northamptonshire 1920
Best bowling performance in a match for Yorkshire 14 for 68 H. Verity v Glamorgan 1939
Best bowling performance in a match against Yorkshire 15 for 75 G.E. Tribe for Northamptonshire 1955
Largest crowd 30,790 v Gloucestershire 1947

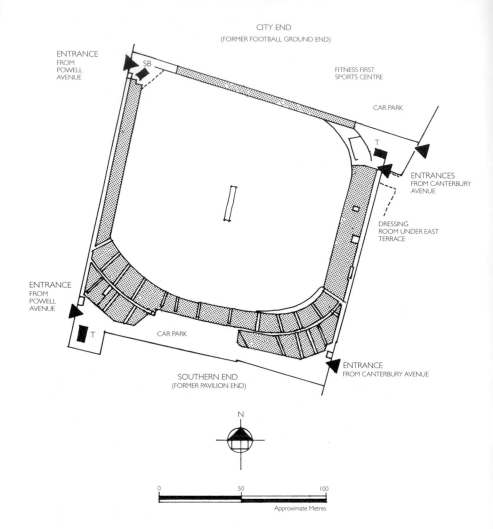

CITY END
(FORMER FOOTBALL GROUND END)

ENTRANCE FROM POWELL AVENUE

SB

FITNESS FIRST SPORTS CENTRE

CAR PARK

T

ENTRANCES FROM CANTERBURY AVENUE

DRESSING ROOM UNDER EAST TERRACE

ENTRANCE FROM POWELL AVENUE

T

CAR PARK

ENTRANCE FROM CANTERBURY AVENUE

SOUTHERN END
(FORMER PAVILION END)

N

0   50   100
Approximate Metres

LIMITED-OVERS MATCHES

Highest innings total for Yorkshire 263 for 8 v Surrey (SL) 1985
Highest innings total against Yorkshire 262 for 6 by Surrey (SL) 1985
Lowest innings total for Yorkshire 91 v Essex (SL) 1971
Lowest innings total against Yorkshire 66 by Nottinghamshire (SL) 1969
Highest individual innings for Yorkshire 118* J.D. Love v Scotland (B&H) 1981
Highest individual innings against Yorkshire 136 M.A. Lynch for Surrey (SL) 1985
Highest wicket partnerships for Yorkshire

1st	135* G. Boycott & J.H. Hampshire	v	Middlesex	(SL)	1976
2nd	107* G. Boycott & R.G. Lumb	v	Essex	(SL)	1975
3rd	146 G. Boycott & K. Sharp	v	Northamptonshire	(B&H)	1984
4th	54 G. Boycott & R.A.J. Townsley	v	Somerset	(SL)	1975
5th	64 C. Johnson & D.L. Bairstow	v	Worcestershire	(SL)	1974
6th	85 P.J. Sharpe & J.G. Binks	v	Northamptonshire	(SL)	1969
7th	149* J.D. Love & C.M. Old	v	Scotland	(B&H)	1981

8th	41* J.D. Love & P. Carrick	v	Leicestershire	(SL)	1984
9th	27* D.L. Bairstow & A.G. Nicholson	v	Derbyshire	(B&H)	1975
10th	32* P. Carrick & S. Stuchbury	v	Warwickshire	(SL)	1982

Highest wicket partnerships against Yorkshire

1st	106 G. Cook & P. Willey	for	Northamptonshire	(SL)	1976
2nd	116 N.E. Briers & P. Willey	for	Leicestershire	(SL)	1984
3rd	99 R.G. Williams & A.J. Lamb	for	Northamptonshire	(B&H)	1980
4th	110 M.A. Lynch & A. Needham	for	Surrey	(SL)	1985
5th	61 G.I. Burgess & P.W. Denning	for	Somerset	(SL)	1973
6th	57 C.E.B. Rice & H.T. Tunnicliffe	for	Nottinghamshire	(GC)	1978
7th	44 M.S.A. McEvoy & J.D. Inchmore	for	Worcestershire	(SL)	1984
8th	42* R.J. Finney & B.J.M. Maher	for	Derbyshire	(SL)	1983
9th	29 K.F. Jennings & H.R. Moseley	for	Somerset	(SL)	1975
10th	16* J.D. Inchmore & R.K. Illingworth	for	Worcestershire	(B&H)	1985

Best bowling performance in a match for Yorkshire 5 for 24 A.G. Nicholson v Derbyshire (B&H) 1975
Best bowling performance in a match against Yorkshire 5 for 16 B.S. Crump for Northamptonshire (SL) 1969
Largest crowd 8,000 v Nottinghamshire (GC) 1969

HOW TO GET THERE

 Bradford interchange 1.25 miles ☎ 08457 484950, www.gner.com

 West Yorkshire Metro ☎ 0113 384 8484, First Bus ☎ 01274 734833, from surrounding areas to Bradford interchange thence approximately 0.75 miles to ground.

 There are cycle routes from surrounding areas of Bradford to this part of the city.

 From north: take A650, A6038 or A658 signposted Bradford and city centre then follow signs for Halifax, the ground is situated to the south-west of the city centre and is off Great Horton Road (A647) to Halifax. **From south:** from M1 junction 42, follow M62 junction 26, then M606, then follow signs Bradford and city centre, then as north or A650, A641, A638 or A6036 signposted Bradford and city centre, then as north. **From east:** from A647, A650, A6120 or M62 junction 26 take M606, then follow signs Bradford and city centre, then as north. **From west:** from A647, B6145, A6025 or M62 junction 26 take M606, then follow signs Bradford and city centre, then A647 for the ground.

 Leeds/Bradford Airport ☎ 0113 250 9696

WHERE TO STAY

Bradford College (☎ 01274 733291), Cedar Court Hotel (☎ 01274 406 606), Dubrovnik Hotel & Restaurant (☎ 01274 543 511), Ivy Guest House (☎ 01274 727 060), Marriott Hollins Hall (☎ 01274 530 053), Norland House (☎ 01274 571698), Stakis Bradford (☎ 01274 734734), The Bradford Hilton (☎ 01274 734734), The Guide Post Hotel (☎ 01274 607 866), The Victoria Hotel (☎ 01274 728706), University of Bradford (☎ 01274 234 881), Westleigh Hotel (☎ 01274 727 089)

For further small hotels and guest houses in the Bradford area visit www.smoothhound.co.uk, www.visitbradford.org or www.bradford.gov.uk.

WHERE TO EAT

Aagrah (☎ 01274 668818 www.aagrah.com), Akbars Balti (☎ 01274 773311 www.akbars.com), Clarks (☎ 01274 499890 www.clarksrestaurant.co.uk), Karachi (☎ 01274 732015), Kashmir (☎ 01274 726513), Mumtaz Paan House (☎ 01274 571861 www.mumtaz.co.uk), Nawaab (☎ 01274 720371 www.nawaab.com)

TOURIST INFORMATION Bradford Tourist Information Centre ☎ 01274 753678, www.visitbradford.org

LOCAL RADIO STATIONS BBC Radio Leeds (95.3 MHz FM/774 KHz MW), Radio Aire (96.3 MHz FM/828 KHz MW)

LOCAL NEWSPAPERS *Yorkshire Post, Yorkshire Evening Post, Bradford Telegraph and Argus*

CAMBRIDGE UNIVERSITY CC
AND CAMBRIDGE UCCE

Cambridge UCCE/Cambridge University Cricket Club, Fenner's University
Cricket Ground, Mortimer Road, Cambridge, Cambridgeshire CB1 2EL

Telephone 01223 353552 (Club office)

CUCC founded 1820
UCCE founded 2000
Colours light blue
CUCC Crest University crest
President Professor A.D. Buckingham, CBE, ScD,
FRS
Fixtures Secretary R.J.A. Abraham
Senior Treasurer Professor K. Siddle, PhD
UCCE Administrator T. Lemons
CUCC Administrator G.P. Jones, BA

Coach (CUCC and Cambridge UCCE) C.W. Scott
CUCC Captain A. Shankar
UCCE Captain S.J. Marshall
Secretary D.E.T. McGrath
Head Groundsman J.R. Moden
Scorer/Statistician R. Markham
Newsletter *Cambridge University Cricket Club Notes
for Members*
Scorecard 50p

ACHIEVEMENTS
Varsity Match won 56, drawn 51, lost 49, abandoned 1

GROUND
Cambridge (Fenner's University Cricket Ground). No other grounds have been used for matches.

CAMBRIDGE – FENNER'S

Address Cambridge UCCE/Cambridge University CC, Fenner's University
Cricket Ground, Mortimer Road, Cambridge, Cambridgeshire CB1 2EL
Prospects of Play 01223 353552

HISTORY OF GROUND AND FACILITIES

CAMBRIDGE UNIVERSITY may first have played cricket against Cambridge Town in
1710, presumably on Parkers' Piece. However, the first formally recorded match
against Cambridge Town was in 1821. Cambridge University Cricket Club was
founded in 1820 and the first match against Oxford University was played at
Lord's in 1827.

Since 1848 all home matches have been played at Fenner's University Cricket
Ground in the centre of the city. In 1846 Mr F.P. Fenner leased a field to the east
of Parkers' Piece from Gonville and Caius College and opened a cricket ground.
Two years later he sub-let it to Cambridge University Cricket Club, and while the
ground has continued to retain the name Fenner's, it has been the home of
University cricket since then. The freehold of the ground was acquired from
Gonville and Caius in 1894 and assigned to a company which held it in trust.
Then in 1976 the University assumed full financial responsibility for the ground.

By the latter part of the nineteenth century Cambridge could give any side in
England a good game. Regular fixtures were arranged with the first-class

The memorial in
the pavilion to the
members of
Cambridge
University Cricket
Club who fell in
the First World
War.

counties and these have continued to the present day. In 2000 Cambridge became a University Centre of Cricketing Excellence and the current UCCE Cambridge squad includes players from Cambridge University and Anglia Polytechnic University cricket clubs. The Cambridge UCCE coach is Christopher Scott, the former Nottinghamshire CCC wicket-keeper/batsman, who took over the position from Derek Randall of Nottinghamshire and England.

The UCCE play three county matches, five one-day matches in the Halifax BUSA Championship and five two-day matches in the Inter-UCCE Competition. In addition to the one-day Varsity match against Oxford at Lord's and a four-day Oxford game, CUCC still play their traditional fixtures against Quidnuncs, Free Foresters, Combined Services, MCC Young Cricketers, Earl of Arundel's XI, Sir Paul Getty's XI, MCC and Lashings CC.

Like Oxford University CC, Cambridge University CC is afforded first-class status although this has been questioned in recent years. The universities team no longer play the touring team individually but play as a British Universities which is made up of players from the six UCCEs (Cambridge, Loughborough, Durham, Bradford/Leeds, Cardiff and Oxford) with the fixtures usually rotating between the university grounds.

Over seventy Cambridge men have played for England, and many of them have also captained their country from the Hon Ivo Bligh in 1882 through Doug Insole, Ted Dexter, Peter May, Tony Lewis and Mike Brearley to Michael Atherton (1993–8). Other international players and Cambridge men include Trevor Bailey, Raman Subba Row, Richard Hutton, Hubert Doggart, John Dewes, Peter Roebuck, Derek Pringle, John Crawley, Andy Whittall (Zimbabwe) and Greg Loveridge (New Zealand).

Until the 1950s the ground was shared with the University athletes and there was a running track surrounding the playing area but this has since been removed. The ground is still used for tennis in summer and hockey and soccer in the winter.

Fenner's, which is renowned for its true pitches and even outfield, is partly enclosed by walls and adjoining buildings. Earlier pavilions were on the south-west side backing on to Gresham Road, but in 1972 a new pavilion designed by architect Colin Stansfield-Smith RIBA (Cricket Blue 1954–7) was built on the Wollaston Road side to the north-east.

The administrator's office is in the J.D.W. 'Jack' Davies Room, named in memory of the former secretary, player and official of the club who played for Cambridge University, Kent and MCC. He was President of MCC and in 1934 bowled Sir Donald Bradman for 0 when the touring Australians played at Fenner's against the Light Blues.

The pitch is disposed in a north–south direction and the playing area is 147 metres by 148 metres. The groundsman, John Moden, was specially commended by the ECB Pitches Advisory Group in their national survey in 2000 and 2001. In 2001 he was the UCCE Groundsman of the Year.

The ground is also used by Cambridgeshire CCC for home Minor Counties Championship matches and during the 1980s the Minor Counties English Estates Knockout Trophy Finals were played here.

GROUND RECORDS AND SCORES

FIRST-CLASS MATCHES

Highest innings total for University 594 for 4 dec v West Indians 1950
Highest innings total against University 730 for 3 for West Indians 1950
Lowest innings total for University 30 v Yorkshire 1928
Lowest innings total against University 43 by Warwickshire 1936
Highest individual innings for University 254* K.S.Duleepsinghi v Middlesex 1927
Highest individual innings against University 304* E.de C.Weekes for West Indians 1950
Highest wicket partnerships for University

1st	262 F.G. Mann & J.R. Thompson	v	Leicestershire	1939
2nd	429* J.G. Dewes & G.H.G. Doggart	v	Essex	1949
3rd	284 E.T. Killick & G.C. Grant	v	Essex	1929
4th	275 R. de W.K. Winlaw & J.G. Human	v	Essex	1934
	275 J.R. Thompson & P.M. Studd	v	Free Foresters	1938
5th	219 C.H.M. Ebden & K.R.B. Fry	v	H.D.G.Leveson-Gower XI	1902
6th	193 R.Q. Cake & W.J. House	v	Derbyshire	1996
7th	159 R.de W.K. Winlaw & J.H. Human	v	Free Foresters	1933
8th	175 E.L. Kidd & F.S.G. Calthorpe	v	Sussex	1912
9th	149* B.K.K. Fryer & R.D. Pearsall	v	Middlesex	1948
10th	95 G.A. Rotherham & J.H. Naumann	v	AIF	1919

Highest wicket partnerships against University

1st	278 J. Cox & P.D. Bowler	for	Somerset	1999
2nd	302 V.P. Terry & T.E. Jesty	for	Hampshire	1984
3rd	291 P.A. Perrin & F.H. Gillingham	for	Essex	1910
4th	324 J.R. Reid & W.M. Wallace	for	New Zealanders	1949
5th	300 G.S. Grimston & C.W.C. Page	for	The Army	1939
6th	194* G.R.J. Roope & D.M. Smith	for	Surrey	1976
7th	144 M.J. Smedley & E.E. Hemmings	for	Nottinghamshire	1979
8th	174 H.W. Parks & A.F. Wensley	for	Sussex	1936
9th	128 G. Woodcock & E.C. Baker	for	Somerset	1921
10th	156 G.R. Cox & H.R. Butt	for	Sussex	1908

Best bowling performance in an innings for University 9 for 55 M.J.C. Allom v The Army 1927
Best bowling performance in an innings against University 9 for 17 H.L. Jackson for Derbyshire 1959
Best bowling performance in a match for University 15 for 138 H.C. McDonnell v Surrey 1904
Best bowling performance in a match against University 14 for 76 N. Gifford for Worcestershire 1972
Largest crowd 9,000 v West Indians 1950

LIMITED-OVERS MATCHES

Highest innings total for Combined Universities 312 for 8 v Glamorgan (B&H) 1996
Highest innings total against Combined Universities 314 for 2 by Glamorgan (B&H) 1996
Lowest innings total for Combined Universities 59 v Glamorgan (B&H) 1983
Lowest innings total against Combined Universities 92 by Worcestershire (B&H) 1975
Highest individual innings for Combined Universities 147 G.A. Khan v Glamorgan (B&H) 1996
Highest individual innings against Combined Universities 121* S.P. James for Glamorgan (B&H) 1996
Highest wicket partnerships for Combined Universities

1st	127 G.A. Khan & A.C. Ridley	v	Glamorgan	(B&H)	1996
2nd	82 G.A. Khan & A. Singh	v	Glamorgan	(B&H)	1996
3rd	92 M.A. Crawley & C.M. Tolley	v	Lancashire	(B&H)	1990
4th	54 M.J. Chilton & W.J. House	v	Sussex	(B&H)	1997
5th	59 J.I. Longley & P.C.L. Holloway	v	Worcestershire	(B&H)	1991
6th	71 D.R. Pringle & I.G. Peck	v	Worcestershire	(B&H)	1980
7th	43 S.P. Henderson & S.J.G. Doggart	v	Kent	(B&H)	1983
8th	55 S.P. Henderson & J.G. Varey	v	Kent	(B&H)	1983
9th	58* J.M. Knight & D. Surridge	v	Northamptonshire	(B&H)	1979
10th	15 M.N. Field & M.E.W. Brooker	v	Essex	(B&H)	1974

Highest wicket partnerships against Combined Universities

1st	134 G. Cook & W. Larkins	for	Northamptonshire	(B&H)	1979
2nd	95 T.M. Moody & G.A. Hick	for	Worcestershire	(B&H)	1991
3rd	189* G.A. Gooch & N. Hussain	for	Essex	(B&H)	1995
4th	107 K.S. McEwan & D.R. Pringle	for	Essex	(B&H)	1984
5th	41 V.C. Drakes & K. Newell	for	Sussex	(B&H)	1997
6th	113* M.A. Atherton & I.D. Austin	for	Lancashire	(B&H)	1990
7th	117 Javed Miandad & E.W. Jones	for	Glamorgan	(B&H)	1983
8th	17* B.R. Hardie & N.A. Foster	for	Essex	(B&H)	1987
9th	9 E.W. Jones & M.A. Nash	for	Glamorgan	(B&H)	1983
10th	32* C.K. Bullen & A.J. Murphy	for	Surrey	(B&H)	1989

Best bowling performance in an innings for Combined Universities 5 for 26 M.J. Chilton v Sussex (B&H) 1997
Best bowling performance in an innings against Combined Universities 5 for 28 M.A. Feltham by Surrey (B&H) 1989
Largest crowd 4,500 v Australians (Tour) 1985

HOW TO GET THERE

 Cambridge station 0.75 mile ☎ 08457 484950, 0990 468468, www.wagn.co.uk

 Stagecoach Cambus Services No 142 or 143 from bus station to ground. Stagecoach in Cambridge ☎ 01223 423578, 01223 317740, www.ukpti.org.uk

 There are cycle paths and routes in all areas of Cambridge.

 From north: from A10 (south) continue to A14 junction 33, take third exit on to A1309 (Milton Road), turn left on to Victoria Road, then Chesterton Road, turn right on to Elizabeth Way and continue to crossroads (A1303/A14) (Newmarket Road), cross into East Road (A603) and continue to Mill Road, turn left into Mill Road and right into Mortimer Road. **From south:** from M11 junction 11/A10 take A1309 (Hauxton Road), continue on this road towards Cambridge, continue on A1134 (Trumpington Road), turn right on to A603 (Lensfield Road), continue on this road into Gonville

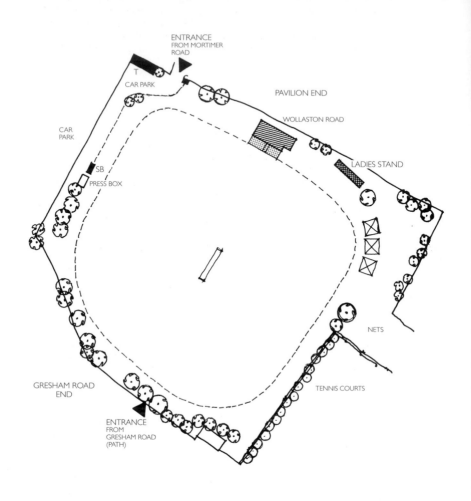

ENTRANCE
FROM MORTIMER
ROAD

T

CAR PARK

CAR
PARK

SB

PRESS BOX

PAVILION END

WOLLASTON ROAD

LADIES STAND

NETS

GRESHAM ROAD
END

ENTRANCE
FROM
GRESHAM ROAD
(PATH)

TENNIS COURTS

N

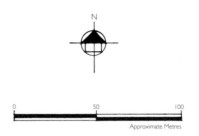

0   50   100
Approximate Metres

Place, turn right on to Mill Road and right again into Mortimer Road. **From east:** from A14 take A1303, turn left at junction with A603 (East Road) then as for north. **From west:** from A428 (St Neots) continue towards Cambridge, at junction take A1303 (St Neots Road) and continue on Madingley Road to junction with A1134 (Queens Road), turn right and follow this road into Newnham Road, turn left on to Fen Causeway, turn left on to Trumpington Road, turn left then as for south.

 London Stansted ☎ 08700 000303, London Luton ☎ 01582 405100

WHERE TO STAY

Best Western Gonville Hotel (☎ 01223 366611 www.gonvillehotel.co.uk), Cambridge Garden House Moat House (☎ 01223 259988 www.gardenhousehotel.co.uk), Cambridgeshire Moat House (☎ 01954 249988 www.moathousehotels.co.uk), Conduit Hotel (☎ 01223 464673), Crowne Plaza Cambridge (☎ 01223 464466 www.crowneplaza.com), Dykelands Guest House (☎ 01223 244300), Hamilton Hotel (☎ 01223 365664 www.hamiltonhotelcambridge.co.uk), Holiday Inn Cambridge (☎ 0870 4009015), Holiday Inn Express (☎ 0870 4009015 www.holidayinn.co.uk), Lensfield Hotel (☎ 01223 355017 www.lensfieldhotel.co.uk), Leys Cottage Guest House (☎ 01223 262482), Lovell Lodge Guest House (☎ 01223 425478), Meadowcroft Hotel (☎ 01223 346120 www.meadowcrofthotel.co.uk), Royal Cambridge Hotel (☎ 01223 351631 www.zoffanyhotels.co.uk), Sleeperz Hotel (☎ 01223 304050 www.sleeperz.com), Sorrento Hotel and Restaurant (☎ 01223 243533 www.sorrentohotel.com), University Arms Hotel (☎ 01223 351241 www.devereonline.co.uk)
    For other places to stay in and around Cambridge visit www.smoothhound.co.uk.

WHERE TO EAT

Browns Restaurant & Bar (☎ 01223 461655), Café Eleven (☎ 01223 369157), Curry Queen (☎ 01223 351027), Dojo (☎ 01223 363471), Hobbs Pavilion Restaurant (☎ 01223 367480), Hole in the Wall (☎ 01223 812282), Lawyers (☎ 01223 566887), Loch Fyne Oyster Bar (☎ 01223 362433), Michel's Brasserie & Wine Bar (☎ 01223 353110), Midsummer House (☎ 01223 369299), No 1 Kings Parade (☎ 01223 359506), Old Orleans ☎ (01223 322777), Parisa Café Bar (☎ 01223 306051), Peking Restaurant (☎ 01223 354755), The Galleria (☎ 01223 362054), The Panos (☎ 01223 212958), The Queen Adelaide (☎ 01223 208278), Venue (☎ 01223 367333)

TOURIST INFORMATION Cambridge Tourist Information, The Old Library, Wheeler Street, Cambridge, Cambridgeshire CB2 3QB ☎ 01223 322640, www.cambridge.gov.uk, www.cam.ac.uk, www.touristnetuk.com, www.tourismcambridge.com. Guided Tours ☎ 01223 547574, Accommodation Bookings ☎ 01223 457581, Destination Cambridge ☎ 01223 457577.

LOCAL RADIO STATIONS BBC Radio Cambridgeshire (96.0 MHz FM/1026 KHz MW), Hereward Radio (96.6 MHz FM/1557 KHz MW), Q103 Cambridge 103.0 MHz FM

LOCAL NEWSPAPER *Cambridge Evening News*

CARDIFF/GLAMORGAN UCCE

Faculty of Education and Sport, University of Wales Institute, Cardiff,
Cyncoed Campus, Cyncoed Road, Cardiff CF2 6XD

Telephone 029 2041 6590 **fax** 029 2041 6589
Email dcobner@uwic.ac.uk

UCCE Founded 2000
Administrator D. Cobner
Head Coach K.J. Lyons

GROUNDS

Abergavenny (Pen-y-Pound, Avenue Road). In addition the following venues are also used occasionally for matches: Pontypridd (Ynysangharad Park) (see Wales Minor Counties), Usk (see Glamorgan CCC section) and Cardiff (Sophia Gardens) (see Glamorgan CCC section).

ABERGAVENNY

Address Abergavenny Cricket Club, The Pavilion, Pen-y-Pound Cricket
Ground, Avenue Road, Abergavenny, Gwent
Prospects of Play 01873 852350

HISTORY OF GROUND AND FACILITIES

AVENUE ROAD is the home of Abergavenny Cricket Club, which was established in 1834. The ground is known as Pen-y-Pound. It is situated on the northern outskirts of Abergavenny, off Avenue Road and adjoining Avenue Crescent and is used by Cardiff/Glamorgan UCCE for matches against first-class counties and other UCCEs. The 4.5 acre ground was opened in 1896 when a match was staged between a South Wales XI and an Abergavenny XI.

During its early years the club moved from one ground to another until in 1895 an approach was made to the Marquess of Abergavenny, a keen follower of cricket and a one-time President of Kent CCC, who leased the ground to the club. The ground took its name from the nearby lane, Pen-y-Pound. The Marquess provided the original pavilion in 1915 after generously giving further land in 1910 and again in 1912.

Like Ebbw Vale CC, the ground was also used by Monmouthshire CCC for minor county matches. Glamorgan CCC first played Second XI matches on the ground in 1948. The club has often staged benefit matches for players from some of the first-class counties. Abergavenny Cricket Club play in the South Wales Premier League; the best known player to have represented club and county is Malcolm Nash.

Glamorgan CCC were so impressed with the Pen-y-Pound wicket and facilities that following several Second XI, club and ground and benefit matches, they decided to play more cricket in Gwent. The first Glamorgan county match was with Worcestershire in the John Player Sunday League in 1981. Thanks to the work of the local ground staff, the match went ahead despite torrential rain during the morning. As a result of this successful visit another Sunday League match was staged in 1982. In 1983 the initial first-class County Championship match was staged on the ground when Worcestershire were again the visitors.

The ground has two scoreboards, a manual one near the pavilion and another electronic one which has been used since 1985. The electronic scoreboard is dedicated to the memory of Bill McPherson who was groundsman for many years. The pavilion was rebuilt in 1977 after a fire. The clock over the entrance door survived the fire; its plaque notes that it was presented to the club by Mr and Mrs Lyons in 1921.

The pavilion is situated to the north of the playing area, close to the bowling green and at right angles to the wicket. The playing area is 117 metres by 112 metres and is circular. It is defined by a rope and some advertising boards. The radio commentary box and TV camera/commentary box position is at the Avenue Road End of the ground situated directly behind and above the sightscreen on a gantry.

There are also ample facilities for hockey, bowls and tennis at the ground.

GROUND RECORDS AND SCORES

(No UCCE matches – Glamorgan records on ground)

FIRST-CLASS MATCHES

Highest innings total for Glamorgan 514 for 9 dec v Gloucestershire 1981
Highest innings total against Glamorgan 514 for 4 dec by Worcestershire 1990
Lowest innings total for Glamorgan 168 v Derbyshire 1986
Lowest innings total against Glamorgan 158 by Gloucestershire 1993
Highest individual innings for Glamorgan 164 M.P. Maynard v Gloucestershire 1995
Highest individual innings against Glamorgan 254* A. Symonds for Gloucestershire 1995
Highest wicket partnerships for Glamorgan

1st	256 A.R. Butcher & H. Morris	v	Worcestershire	1990
2nd	145 H. Morris & D.L. Hemp	v	Gloucestershire	1995
3rd	306 D.L. Hemp & M.P. Maynard	v	Gloucestershire	1995
4th	216 A.R. Butcher & R.J. Shastri	v	Middlesex	1989
5th	186 D.L. Hemp & P.A. Cottey	v	Kent	1994
6th	124 A.R. Butcher & N.G. Cowley	v	Worcestershire	1990
7th	88* R.J. Shastri & C.P. Metson	v	Middlesex	1989
8th	85 O.D. Gibson & C.P. Metson	v	Kent	1994
9th	73 S.D. Thomas & N.M. Kendrick	v	Gloucestershire	1995
10th	58 S.D. Thomas & S.L. Watkin	v	Gloucestershire	1995

Highest wicket partnerships against Glamorgan

1st	200* T.S. Curtis & W.P.C. Weston	for	Worcestershire	1996
2nd	192 T.S. Curtis & G.A. Hick	for	Worcestershire	1988
3rd	264 G.A. Hick & D.B. D'Oliveira	for	Worcestershire	1990
4th	121 M.W. Alleyne & A. Symonds	for	Gloucestershire	1995
5th	84 N.D. Burns & G.D. Rose	for	Somerset	1992
6th	213 A. Symonds & R.C.J. Williams	for	Gloucestershire	1995
7th	79 K.M. Curran & J.P. Taylor	for	Northamptonshire	1997
8th	84 A. Symonds & J. Srinath	for	Gloucestershire	1995
9th	83 G.D. Hodgson & C.A. Walsh	for	Gloucestershire	1993
10th	67 A. Symonds & V.J. Pike	for	Gloucestershire	1995

Best bowling performance in an innings for Glamorgan 6 for 56 Waqar Younis v Northamptonshire 1997
Best bowling performance in an innings against Glamorgan 9 for 76 J. Srinath for Gloucestershire 1995
Best bowling performance in a match for Glamorgan 10 for 134 Waqar Younis v Northamptonshire 1997

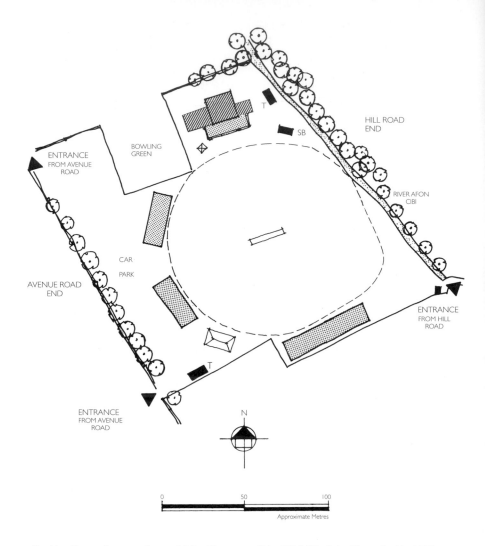

Best bowling performance in a match for Glamorgan 13 for 150 J. Srinath for Gloucestershire 1995
Largest crowd 5,000 v Worcestershire 1988

LIMITED-OVERS MATCHES

Highest innings total for Glamorgan 229 for 7 v Northamptonshire (SL) 1982
Highest innings total against Glamorgan 170 for 7 by Worcestershire (SL) 1981
Lowest innings total for Glamorgan 152 v Worcestershire (SL) 1981
Lowest innings total against Glamorgan 153 for 7 by Northamptonshire (SL) 1982
Highest individual innings for Glamorgan 100 R.C. Ontong v Northamptonshire (SL) 1982
Highest individual innings against Glamorgan 43 E.J.O. Hemsley for Worcestershire (SL) 1981
Highest wicket partnerships for Glamorgan

1st	27 A. Jones & J.A. Hopkins	v	Worcestershire	(SL)	1981
2nd	21 A.L. Jones & D.A. Francis	v	Northamptonshire	(SL)	1982
3rd	68 D.A. Francis & R.C. Ontong	v	Northamptonshire	(SL)	1982
4th	47 R.C. Ontong & J.A. Hopkins	v	Northamptonshire	(SL)	1982

5th	16 R.C. Ontong & J.G. Thomas	v	Northamptonshire	(SL)	1982
6th	38 R.C. Ontong & H.A. Moseley	v	Worcestershire	(SL)	1981
7th	38 R.C. Ontong & B.J. Lloyd	v	Northamptonshire	(SL)	1982
8th	9* B.J. Lloyd & E.W. Jones	v	Northamptonshire	(SL)	1982
9th	31 H.A. Moseley & B.J. Lloyd	v	Worcestershire	(SL)	1981
10th	7 B.J. Lloyd & S.R. Barwick	v	Worcestershire	(SL)	1981

Highest wicket partnerships against Glamorgan

1st	20 G.M. Turner & J.A. Ormrod	for	Worcestershire	(SL)	1981
2nd	16 G.M. Turner & Younis Ahmed	for	Worcestershire	(SL)	1981
3rd	40 A.J. Lamb & G. Cook	for	Northamptonshire	(SL)	1982
4th	43 G. Cook & R.G. Williams	for	Northamptonshire	(SL)	1982
5th	30 E.J.O. Hemsley & D.J. Humphries	for	Worcestershire	(SL)	1981
6th	25 R.G. Williams & G. Sharp	for	Northamptonshire	(SL)	1982
7th	36 E.J.O. Hemsley & J.D. Inchmore	for	Worcestershire	(SL)	1981
8th, 9th and 10th – yet to be established					

Best bowling performance in a match for Glamorgan 2 for 21 M.A. Nash v Northamptonshire (SL) 1982
Best bowling performance in a match against Glamorgan 3 for 17 J. Birkenshaw for Worcestershire (SL) 1981
Largest crowd 3,000 v Northamptonshire (SL) 1982

HOW TO GET THERE

 Abergavenny station 2 miles ☎ 08457 484950, www.greatwestern.co.uk

 National Welsh 20 Newport to Hereford and 21 Newport to Brecon go to bus station, thence 1.5 mile walk to ground ☎ 01222 371331

 There are cycle routes from all areas of Abergavenny to this part of the town.

 From north: from A465 or A40 follow signs Abergavenny, ground is in Avenue Road off A40 Brecon Road. **From south:** from M4 junction 26, take A4042 follow signs Abergavenny, then as north. **From east:** from A40 to Abergavenny, then as north. **From west:** A465 or A40 then as north.

 Cardiff International Airport ☎ 01446 7111111

WHERE TO STAY

Angel Hotel (☎ 01873 857121). For other places to stay in the Abergavenny area visit www.smoothhound.co.uk

WHERE TO EAT

Walnut Tree (☎ 01873 852797 www.thewalnuttreeinn.com)

TOURIST INFORMATION Abergavenny Tourist Information Centre, Swan Meadow, Monmouth Road, Abergavenny NP7 5HH ☎ 01873 857588

LOCAL RADIO STATIONS BBC Radio Wales (882 KHz MW), BBC Radio Cymru (93.1 MHz FM/882 KHz MW)

LOCAL NEWSPAPERS *South Wales Evening Post, Western Mail, Abergavenny Chronicle, Abergavenny Gazette, South Wales Argus*

DURHAM UCCE

Durham University Sports Centre, Maiden Castle, Durham City DH6 5LS

Telephone 0191 374 4519 **fax** 0191 384 0230
Email p.a.warburton@durham.ac.uk

UCCE founded 2000
Durham University CC founded 1842
UCCE President G. Holland
UCCE Administrator P. Warburton
UCCE Senior Coach G. Fowler

DURHAM UNIVERSITY

Address Durham UCCE/Durham University Cricket Club, The Pavilion, The Racecourse Ground, Green Lane, Durham City
Prospects of Play ☎ 0191 374 3404

HISTORY OF GROUND AND FACILITIES

THE RACECOURSE GROUND is the home of Durham UCCE and was used by Durham County Cricket Club from 1992 to 1995.

In April 1992 Durham County Cricket Club played their inaugural home matches in the Sunday League against Lancashire, the Benson and Hedges Cup match against Glamorgan and the Britannic Assurance County Championship match with Leicestershire on this ground.

The Racecourse Ground is situated between Green Lane and the River Wear. To the east is the Durham City Cricket Club ground which was last used for a Durham Second XI match with Leicestershire in June 1992. Durham Rugby Union Football Ground, the University Rowing Club boat house, swimming baths, squash and tennis courts, and a bowling green are within a stone's throw of the Racecourse Ground.

The ground takes its name from the old Durham Racecourse which was on this land. It is now only used by Durham UCCE for university matches and games in the Halifax BUSA Championship Senior and Junior sections.

In 1990 Durham University beat Exeter University at Aigburth Cricket Ground, Liverpool, to win the UAU Championship. The Durham University team included several players with first-class experience: Brian Evans (Hertfordshire CCC), Jon Longley (Kent CCC), Wasim Raja (Pakistan), James Boiling (Surrey and Durham), Sean Morris (Hampshire), Jeremy Snape (Northamptonshire, Gloucestershire and Leicestershire) and James Foster (Essex). Durham University CC were finalists in the UAU Championships for seven consecutive years between 1985 and 1992.

While the standard of cricket at both Cambridge and Oxford universities has declined since the early 1970s, Durham University's Racecourse Ground has emerged as the setting for one of the new nurseries of county cricket. Five former old boys have already represented their country: Paul Allott, Graeme

Fowler (now UCCE coach), Tim Curtis, John Stephenson and Nasser Hussain. More than a dozen other former students of Durham University CC have established themselves on the county circuit.

In 1989 for the first time Durham University students were selected for inclusion in the Combined Universities team for the Benson and Hedges Cup – in previous years the team had been selected only from Cambridge and Oxford students. The Combined Universities team recorded zonal group victories over Surrey and Worcestershire and were beaten in the quarter-finals by Somerset at Taunton. The team which played in that quarter-final match included five Durham University students – James Boiling, Tim O'Gorman, Martin Speight, Jon Longley and Nasser Hussain.

The pavilion is situated to the south-east of the playing area with a small adjoining scoreboard, press tent and scorers' tent. The dimensions of the playing area are 148 metres by 118 metres and it is defined by a rope and advertising boards. The TV camera/commentary box is positioned directly above and behind the sightscreen on a gantry at the Pavilion End of the ground.

GROUND RECORDS AND SCORES

FIRST-CLASS MATCHES

Highest innings total for UCCE 251 v Lancashire 2001
Highest innings total against UCCE 372 by Lancashire 2002
Lowest innings total for UCCE 244 for 7dec v Lancashire 2002
Lowest innings total against UCCE 279 for 5dec by Lancashire 2002
Highest individual innings for UCCE 78 J.S. Foster v Lancashire 2001
Highest individual innings against UCCE 120 A. Flintoff for Lancashire 2001
Highest wicket partnerships for UCCE

1st	81 M.J. Brown & J.G.C. Rowe	v	Lancashire	2001
2nd	47 M.J. Brown & M.J. Banes	v	Lancashire	2002
3rd	73 M.J. Banes & T.J. Phillips	v	Lancashire	2002
4th	52 A.G.R. Loudon & J.S. Foster	v	Lancashire	2001
5th	17 J.S. Foster & H.J.H. Loudon	v	Lancashire	2001
6th	16 A.G.R. Loudon & R.S. Ferley	v	Lancashire	2002
7th	33 R.S. Ferley & M.L. Creese	v	Lancashire	2002
8th	89 J.S. Foster & C.G. van der Gucht	v	Lancashire	2001
9th	9 J.S. Foster & M. Thorburn	v	Lancashire	2001
10th	8 M. Thorburn & J.T.A. Bruce	v	Lancashire	2001

Highest wicket partnerships against UCCE

1st	28 R.C. Driver & M.J. Chilton	for	Lancashire	2001
2nd	166 M.J. Chilton & J.J. Haynes	for	Lancashire	2002
3rd	65 J.J. Haynes & A. Flintoff	for	Lancashire	2001
4th	55 A. Flintoff & T.W. Roberts	for	Lancashire	2001
5th	76 A. Flintoff & C.P. Schofield	for	Lancashire	2001
6th	55 C.P. Schofield & G. Yates	for	Lancashire	2001
7th	51 G. Yates & K.W. Hogg	for	Lancashire	2001
8th	17 K.W. Hogg & J. Wood	for	Lancashire	2001
9th	8 J. Wood & G. Keedy	for	Lancashire	2001
10th	0 J. Wood & M.P. Smethurst	for	Lancashire	2001

Best bowling performance in an innings for UCCE 3 for 52 R.S. Ferley v Lancashire 2001
Best bowling performance in an innings against UCCE 3 for 17 K.W. Hogg for Lancashire 2001
Best bowling performance in a match for UCCE 3 for 52 R.S. Ferley v Lancashire 2001
Best bowling performance in a match against UCCE 3 for 30 K.W. Hogg for Lancashire 2001
Largest crowd 500 v Lancashire 2001 (5,000 Durham v Australians 1993)

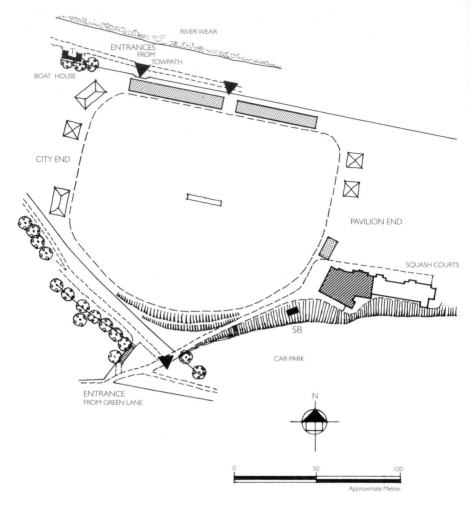

LIMITED-OVERS MATCHES

(No UCCE limited-overs matches – Durham records on ground)
Highest innings total for Durham 281 for 2 v Derbyshire (SL) 1993
Highest innings total against Durham 330 for 6 by Surrey (SL) 1992
Lowest innings total for Durham 194 for 9 v Sussex (SL) 1993
Lowest innings total against Durham 169 by Derbyshire (SL) 1993
Highest individual innings for Durham 124 G. Fowler v Derbyshire (SL) 1993
Highest individual innings against Durham 125 D.J. Bicknell for Surrey (SL) 1993
Highest wicket partnerships for Durham

1st	184 G. Fowler & P.W.G. Parker	v	Derbyshire	(SL)	1993
2nd	87 W. Larkins & D.M. Jones	v	Lancashire	(SL)	1992
3rd	72 D.M. Jones & P. Bainbridge	v	Lancashire	(SL)	1992
4th	62 P.W.G. Parker & I.T. Botham	v	Glamorgan	(BH)	1992
5th	57 I.T. Botham & M.P. Briers	v	Surrey	(SL)	1992
6th	71 M.P. Briers & A.R. Fothergill	v	Surrey	(SL)	1992
7th	13 A.R. Fothergill & J. Wood	v	Surrey	(SL)	1992
	13 S. Hutton & I. Smith	v	Sussex	(SL)	1993

8th	7 I.T. Botham & S.P. Hughes	v	Glamorgan	(BH)	1992
9th	36 C.W. Scott & D.A. Graveney	v	Sussex	(SL)	1993
10th	38* D.A. Graveney & S.P. Hughes	v	Sussex	(SL)	1993

Highest wicket partnerships against Durham

1st	117 D.J. Bicknell & A.D. Brown	for	Surrey	(SL)	1992
2nd	172 P.V. Simmons & V.J. Wells	for	Leicestershire	(SL)	1994
3rd	64 D. Byas & C. White	for	Yorkshire	(SL)	1994
4th	73 A.P. Wells & N.J. Lenham	for	Sussex	(SL)	1993
5th	85 C.S. Cowdrey & P.A. Cottey	for	Glamorgan	(BH)	1992
6th	46 C.S. Cowdrey & R.D.B. Croft	for	Glamorgan	(BH)	1992
7th	32 N.J. Speak & P.A.J. de Freitas	for	Lancashire	(SL)	1992
8th	15 B. Parker & D. Gough	for	Yorkshire	(SL)	1994
9th	24 N.J. Speak & P.J.W. Allott	for	Lancashire	(SL)	1992
10th	21 R.W. Sladdin & D.E. Malcolm	for	Derbyshire	(SL)	1993

Best bowling performance in a match for Durham 3 for 21 P. Bainbridge v Sussex (SL) 1993
Best bowling performance in a match against Durham 5 for 28 N.J. Lenham for Sussex (SL) 1993
Largest crowd 6,000 v Lancashire (SL) 1992

HOW TO GET THERE

 Durham station 1.25 mile ☎ 08457 225225, 0870 602 3322, 0191 387 1387, www.gner.co.uk, www.northern-spirit.co.uk, www.railtrack.com, www.thetrainline.co.uk, www.chester-le-track.co.uk

 20, 41 and 57 United/Gardiners/OK Travel buses pass 0.25 mile from ground; 20 links Durham Station with Old Elvet leading to Green Lane and ground ☎ 0191 386 4411, Bus Information Line ☎ 0845 6060 260. National Express Coaches ☎ 08705 808080, www.nationalexpress.co.uk

 There are cycle routes from all parts of Durham to this area.

 From north: from A1(M) junction 62 signposted to Durham City follow A690 for Durham and city centre, then take New Elvet Bridge and take left into Old Elvet for Green Lane and ground. **From south:** from A1(M) junction 61 to Durham City follow A177 for Durham and city centre, then as north, or take A167, turn right on to A177 to Durham City, then as for north. **From east:** follow A690 for Durham and city centre then as north or A181 for Durham and city centre, then as north. **From west:** from A698 follow signs Durham and city centre take Leazes Bridge and New Elvet Bridge, then as north.

 Newcastle Airport ☎ 0191 286 0966, Teesside Airport ☎ 01950 460 654

WHERE TO STAY

Beamish Park (☎ 01207 281260), Bees Cottage (☎ 0191 384 5775), Dun Cow Inn (☎ 01740 20894), Kings Lodge Hotel (☎ 0191 370 9977), Lambton Arms Hotel (☎ 0191 388 3265), Peterlee Lodge (☎ 0191 586 2161), Rainton Lodge (☎ 0191 512 0540), The Cookson Public House (☎ 0191 389 2044), The Old Manse (☎ 0191 410 2486), Waldridge Hall Farm (☎ 0191 388 4210).

For other places to stay in Chester-le-Street, Durham or Washington ☎ 0191 384 3720, 0191 375 3046, 0191 384 3720 or visit www.smoothhound.co.uk, www.visitnorthumbria.com, www.durham.gov.uk.

WHERE TO EAT

Barn Again Bistro (☎ 0191 230 3338), Bistro 21 (☎ 0191 384 4354), Dragon House (☎ 0191 232 0868), Fisherman's Lodge (☎ 0191 281 3281), Francesca's (☎ 0191 281 6586), Leela's (☎ 0191 230 1261), Lisann's Restaurant (☎ 0191 383 0352), Pani's (☎ 0191 232 4366 www.pani.net), Paradiso (☎ 0191 221 1240 www.paradiso.co.uk), Shaheens Indian Bistro (☎ 0191 386 0960), The Rose Tree (☎ 0191 386 8512), Valley Junction 397 (☎ 0191 281 6397), Vujon (☎ 0191 221 0601).

TOURIST INFORMATION Durham Tourist Information Centre, Market Place, Durham, County Durham ☎ 0191 384 3720, www.durham.gov.uk.

OTHER USEFUL INFORMATION

Newcastle United Football Club ☎ 0191 201 8400 www.nufc.co.uk
Sunderland Football Club ☎ 0191 551 5000 www.safc.com
Northumbria Tourist Board ☎ 0191 375 3046 www.visitnorthumbria.com
Hotel Booking Line with GNER Trains ☎ 01904 671111

LOCAL RADIO STATIONS BBC Radio Newcastle (96.0 MHz FM/1458 KHz MW), BBC Radio Cleveland (95.0 MHz FM/1548 KHz MW), TFM Radio (96.6 MHz FM/1170 KHz MW)

LOCAL NEWSPAPERS *The Northern Echo, The Journal, Evening Gazette, Hartlepool Mail*

LOUGHBOROUGH UCCE

Director of Cricket, Sports Development Centre, Loughborough University,
Loughborough, Leicestershire LE11 3TU

Telephone 01509 226102 **fax** 01509 226126
Email g.a.m.jackson@lboro.ac.uk

Loughborough University CC founded 1966
UCCE founded 2000
UCCE Administrator Dr G. Jackson
UCCE Senior Coach G.R. Dilley

ACHIEVEMENTS
UCCE Championship winners 2001, 2002
UCCE Challenge Final winners 2001, 2002
British Universities Champions 1996, 1998, 2000, 2001, 2002

LOUGHBOROUGH UNIVERSITY

Address Loughborough UCCE, c/o Director of Cricket, Sports Development
Centre, Loughborough University, Loughborough,
Leicestershire LE11 3TU
Prospects of Play ☎ 01509 226102

HISTORY OF GROUND AND FACILITIES

LOUGHBOROUGH UNIVERSITY has established itself as the training ground for many of the nation's most successful sports men and women. The sports facilities on campus are among the most extensive in the country and include facilities for athletics, basketball, volleyball, netball, badminton, swimming, squash, tennis indoor and outdoor, hockey, soccer, rugby and, of course, cricket.

The University campus is south-west of the town centre and at the junction of Ashby Road (A512) which leads from M1 junction 23 and Epinal Way (A6004). The main entrance to the campus is from Epinal Way. The Haslegrave Cricket

Ground together with the pavilion and the new ECB Cricket Academy and Centre of Excellence (presently under construction) are located nearby off University Road. The Senior Coach is Graham Dilley, the former Kent, Worcestershire and England quick bowler, and the administrator is Dr Guy Jackson.

Loughborough have dominated University cricket in recent years, winning the British Universities Championship for the last three years and all ECB UCCE Championships and play-offs since their inception in 2000.

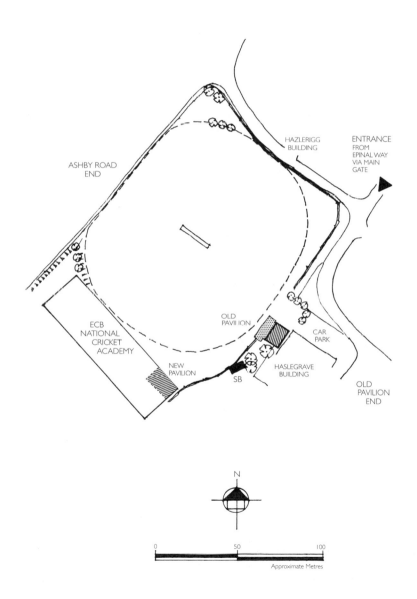

GROUND RECORDS AND SCORES

No first-class or limited-overs matches.

HOW TO GET THERE

 Loughborough station 10 minutes by taxi to ground, ☎ 08457 484950, www.midlandmainline.co.uk

 University Shuttle Bus 3 runs every 20 minutes from Radmoor Road between town, university and railway station ☎ 01509 816161. National Express Coaches ☎ 08705 808080, www.nationalexpress.co.uk

 There are cycle paths and routes from all parts of the town to the university.

 From M1 junction 23 or the A6, follow the signs to the Loughborough University for campus and ground.

 East Midlands Airport ☎ 01332 852852, www.eastmidlandsairport.co.uk, Birmingham International Airport ☎ 0121 767 5511, www.birminghaminternationalairport.co.uk

WHERE TO STAY

Quality Hotel (☎ 01509 211800), Great Central Hotel (☎ 01509 263405)
    For other places to stay in the Loughborough area visit www.smoothhound.co.uk or www.loughborough.gov.uk.

WHERE TO EAT

Canteen and shop on campus including Towers Bar and Sofi de France or other restaurants in Loughborough town centre.

TOURIST INFORMATION Loughborough Tourist Information Centre www.loughborough.gov.uk, Leicester Tourist Information Centre, 7–9 Every Street, Town Hall Square, Leicester, Leicestershire LE1 6AG. ☎ 0116 299 8888, 0116 265 7039, 0116 265 7302, 0116 265 7038, 0116 265 7333, www.leicester.gov.uk, www.discoverleicester.com, www.leicestershire.gov.uk

LOCAL RADIO STATIONS BBC Radio Leicester (95.1 MHz FM/837 KHz MW), Leicester Sound (105.4 MHz FM/1260 KHz MW)

LOCAL NEWSPAPER *Leicester Mercury*

OXFORD UNIVERSITY CC AND OXFORD UCCE

Oxford UCCE/Oxford University CC, The Pavilion, The University Parks, Oxford

Telephone	01865 557106 (season only)
All enquiries	01865 241335

OUCC founded 1800
UCCE founded 2000
Colours dark blue
OUCC Crest two crowns above OUCC
President A.C. Smith, CBE
Senior Treasurer E. Peel
Chairman Dr S.R. Porter, MA, DPhil

OUCC and UCCE Administrator M. Huddleston
OUCC and UCCE Coach G. Charlesworth
OUCC Captain 2002/3 J. Dalrymple
UCCE Captain 2002/3 J. Sayers
Senior Groundsman R. Sula
Scorer/Statistician N. Harris

ACHIEVEMENTS

Varsity Match won 49, drawn 51, lost 56, abandoned 1
UCCE championship Oxford UCCE runners-up 2002, lost final in play-off 2002

GROUND

Oxford (The University Parks). In addition Marston Ground, Edgeway Road, Oxford and Christ Church Cricket Ground, Iffley Road, Oxford are used occasionally.

OXFORD – UNIVERSITY PARKS

Address Oxford UCCE/Oxford University CC, The Pavilion, University Parks, Parks Road, Oxford
Prospects of Play ☎ 01865 557106

DESCRIPTION OF GROUND AND FACILITIES

THE FIRST MENTION OF CRICKET IN OXFORD seems to have been in 1727 but the first reliably recorded match was in 1795 when Bullingdon Club played the MCC. The direct forerunner of Oxford University Cricket Club was Magdalen Club, which was established in about 1800, although a reference to Oxford University Cricket Club playing in a match did not appear until 1827.

The early matches were played on Cowley Marsh until in 1881 Dr Evans, Master of Pembroke College, succeeded in obtaining a lease on 10 acres of land in the University Parks. This venue has remained the club's ground for all home matches and many consider it to be one of the most attractive in the country. The University Parks cover about 65 acres and are open to the public. The cricket ground lies within the Parks but is not in any way separated from them. Thus, apart from the small pavilion complex, no part of the ground is enclosed, except by trees on the north, east and south sides. Entrance fees cannot therefore be charged and no crowd numbers have been established. Because of this, other grounds have been used for matches against touring sides where admission charges are necessary.

The pavilion at the University Parks, Oxford.

The first match was played in 1881, by which time the pavilion had been constructed to the designs of Sir Thomas G. Jackson, architect of many nineteenth- and early twentieth-century Oxford buildings. The pavilion is the main focus of the ground; it is a most impressive building with three striking gables in its steeply pitched roof which is surmounted by a cupola. A part of the veranda has been enclosed to provide a press box. The Long Room is reminiscent of a university hall with its great roof trusses. The walls are in panelled oak on which the names of all Blues are recorded in gold lettering. A small scoreboard is situated to the side of the pavilion, while on the other side a single-storey modern building houses the Assistant Secretary's office and refreshment facilities.

The playing area is 132 metres by 140 metres and the pitch is positioned approximately north–south with the pavilion to the south. The boundary is marked by a rope.

As early as 1884 Oxford University defeated the Australian touring team by seven wickets, no mean feat as the Australian team differed little from the one which had won the Ashes in 1882.

Many fine cricketers played at Oxford in the years before 1914 including P.F. 'Plum' Warner, R.E. Foster and C.B. Fry. Later players who experienced their early first-class cricket at the Parks include D.R. Jardine, England captain in the bodyline series of 1932–3, Colin Cowdrey and M.J.K. Smith, who has the unique achievement of a century in each of his three Varsity Matches at Lord's. Alan C. Smith CBE, who is now President, led the club to six victories against first-class counties in 1959 and later became the Chief Executive of the Test & County Cricket Board after having served Warwickshire County Cricket Club as Secretary.

The ground has seen many outstanding performances, beginning in 1886 when W.G. Grace took all 10 Oxford wickets for 49 runs when playing for MCC. This followed his 104 runs in the same match.

The Parks is the home of both OUCC and Oxford UCCE. The latter team is made up of students from Oxford University and Oxford Brookes University and they now play county matches. OUCC's team still play fixtures throughout the season, culminating in the Varsity Matches at the end of the year.

GROUND RECORDS AND SCORES

FIRST-CLASS MATCHES

Highest innings total for University 589 v Gentlemen of England 1908
Highest innings total against University 627 for 2 dec for Gloucestershire 1930
Lowest innings total for University 24 v Leicestershire 1985
Lowest innings total against University 45 by New Zealanders 1958
Highest individual innings for University 236 S.R.T. Holmes v Free Foresters 1927
Highest individual innings against University 266* by W. Place for Lancashire 1947
Highest wicket partnerships for University

1st	338 T. Bowring & H. Teesdale	v	Gentlemen of England	1908
2nd	225 M.R. Barton & N.S. Mitchell-Innes	v	Leicestershire	1937
3rd	273 F.C. de Saram & N.S. Mitchell-Innes	v	Gloucestershire	1934
4th	218 M.P. Donnelly & R.H. Maudsley	v	Lancashire	1946
5th	256* A.A. Baig & C.A. Fry	v	Free Foresters	1959
6th	270 D.R. Walsh & S.A. Westley	v	Warwickshire	1969
7th	197 B.J.T. Bosanquet & J.W.F.A. Crawford	v	London county	1900
8th	138 R.C.M. Kimpton & A.P. Singleton	v	Gloucestershire	1935
9th	157 H.M. Garland-Wells & C.K.H. Hill-Wood	v	Kent	1928
10th	134 A.F. Gofton & S.H. Khan	v	Northamptonshire	2000

Highest wicket partnerships against University

1st	395 D.M. Young & R.B. Nicholls	for	Gloucestershire	1962
2nd	343 F.A. Lowson & J.V. Wilson	for	Yorkshire	1956
3rd	269 D. Byas & R.J. Blakey	for	Yorkshire	1991
4th	366* P.R. Umrigar & V.S. Hazare	for	Indians	1952
5th	243 D.B. D'Oliveira & D.A. Leatherdale	for	Worcestershire	1991
6th	227 E.J.O. Hemsley & D.N. Patel	for	Worcestershire	1976
7th	218 J.H. Camerson & E.A.V. Williams	for	West Indians	1939
8th	137 K.J. Key & H. Martyn	for	A.J. Webb's XI	1901
9th	113 R.H.B. Bettington & A.F. Dunglass	for	Free Foresters	1924
10th	101 H.D.G. Leveson-Gower & R.H. Fox	for	Gentlemen of England	1904

Best bowling performance in an innings for University 9 for 38 R.B. Raikes v The Army 1924
Best bowling performance in an innings against University 9 for 75 by G.A. Wilson v Worcestershire 1904
Best bowling performance in a match for University 14 for 112 V.R. Price v Gentlemen of England 1919
Best bowling performance in a match against University 16 for 225 J.E. Walsh for Leicestershire 1953
Largest crowd No crowd figures established. Police estimates give a figure of 6,000 for the Saturday play of the British Universities v West Indians 1995.

LIMITED-OVERS MATCHES

Highest innings total for Combined Universities 284 for 8 v Hampshire (B&H) 1997
Highest innings total against Combined Universities 366 for 4 by Derbyshire (B&H) 1991
Lowest innings total for Combined Universities 112 v Somerset (B&H) 1988
Lowest innings total against Combined Universities 250 by Kent (B&H) 1996
Highest individual innings for Combined Universities 113 T.P. Hodgson v Hampshire (B&H) 1997

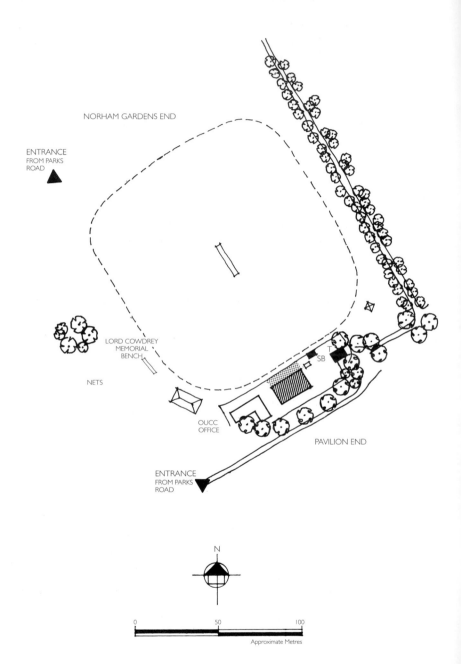

NORHAM GARDENS END

ENTRANCE
FROM PARKS
ROAD

LORD COWDREY
MEMORIAL
BENCH

NETS

OUCC
OFFICE

T
SB

PAVILION END

ENTRANCE
FROM PARKS
ROAD

N

0   50   100
Approximate Metres

HIghest individual innings against Combined Universities 133 by C.G. Greenidge for Hampshire (B&H) 1987

Highest wicket partnerships for Combined Universities

1st	62 G.I. Macmillan & I.J. Sutcliffe	v	Hampshire	(B&H)	1995
2nd	168 T.P. Hodgson & U.B.A. Rashid	v	Hampshire	(B&H)	1997
3rd	93 A.J.T. Miller & J.D. Carr	v	Surrey	(B&H)	1984
4th	103 A. Odendaal & J.O.D. Orders	v	Yorkshire	(B&H)	1980
5th	94 M.J. Chilton & L.D. Sutton	v	Kent	(B&H)	1998
6th	47* N. Hussain & M.J. Cann	v	Hampshire	(B&H)	1987
7th	33 M.A. Atherton & A. Dale	v	Middlesex	(B&H)	1989
8th	64 D.R. Pringle & J.G. Varey	v	Gloucestershire	(B&H)	1982
9th	49* R.J. Turner & A.M. Smith	v	Surrey	(B&H)	1990
10th	12* D.R. Gurr & R. IeQ. Savage	v	Sussex	(B&H)	1977

Highest wicket partnerships against Combined Universities

1st	194 C.G. Greenidge & V.P. Terry	for	Hampshire	(B&H)	1987
2nd	148* G. Boycott & C.W.J. Athey	for	Yorkshire	(B&H)	1980
3rd	91 K.C. Wessels & R.D.V. Knight	for	Sussex	(B&H)	1977
4th	107 J.A. Hopkins & P.D. Swart	for	Glamorgan	(B&H)	1978
5th	103* M.V. Fleming & M.A. Ealham	for	Kent	(B&H)	1998
6th	61 G. Sharpe & Sarfraz Nawaz	for	Northamptonshire	(B&H)	1975
7th	48 A.P.E. Knott & R.A. Woolmer	for	Kent	(B&H)	1976
8th	40* Imran Khan & I.J. Gould	for	Sussex	(B&H)	1985
9th	51 M.A. Ealham & M.M. Patel	for	Kent	(B&H)	1996
10th	13* S.T.Clarke & P.I. Pocock	for	Surrey	(B&H)	1984

Best bowling performance in an innings for Combined Universities 5 for 36 A.D.H. Grimes v Sussex (B&H) 1985

Best bowling performance in an innings against Combined Universities 5 for 28 R.W. Hills by Kent (B&H) 1976

Largest crowd No crowd figures established

HOW TO GET THERE

 Oxford station 1 mile ☎ 08457 484950, www.thamestrains.co.uk

 Oxford 2/A, 10/A from Cornmarket Street, 52 links Oxford Station with Cornmarket Street, City Circuit Electric Bus 5, 7, 7A, 10, 25, 25A and 27 all stop at Wycliffe Hall, ☎ 01865 711312. National Express Coaches ☎ 0870 608 2608, www.gobycoach.com

 There are cycle paths and routes throughout the city.

 From north: from M40 junction 9 take A34 towards Oxford, continue on A34 to junction with A44, take second exit on to A44 signposted Oxford and Cheltenham, at roundabout junction with A4144 (Wolvercote Roundabout) take third exit A4144 Woodstock Road, turn left on to B4495 (Moreton Road), turn right on to A4165 Banbury Road, turn left into Norham Gardens, then bear right into Parks Road **From south:** from A34, at roundabout take fourth exit on to A423, at roundabout take first exit on to A4144, bear left on to A4144 (Abingdon Road), bear left on to St Aldates, bear left on to A420 (Thames Street, then Oxpens Road), bear right on to Hollybush Row, bear right on to A4144 (Hythe Bridge Street), bear left on to Worcester Street, bear right on to Beaumont Street, turn left on to A4144 (St Giles), turn right on to Norham Gardens, bear right on to Parks Road. **From east:** from M40 junction 8, continue on A40 round the Ring Road to junction with A4165 (Banbury Road), then as for north. **From west:** from A40 continue to Wolvercote Roundabout (A4144) then as for north.

 London Heathrow Airport ☎ 08700 000123

The Colin Cowdrey Memorial bench in the University Parks.

WHERE TO STAY

Cotswold Lodge Hotel (☎ 01865 512121 www.cotswoldlodgehotel.co.uk), Eastgate (☎ 0870 400 8201 www.heritage-hotels.com), Holiday Inn Oxford (☎ 0870 400 9086 www.holiday-inn.com), Old Bank Hotel (☎ 01865 799599 www.oxford-hotels-restaurants.co.uk), Oxford Spires Four Pillars Hotel (☎ 0800 374 692 www.four-pillars.co.uk), Royal Oxford Hotel (☎ 01865 248432), The Old Parsonage Hotel (☎ 01865 310210 www.oxford-hotels-restaurants.co.uk), The Randolph (☎ 0870 400 8200 www.heritage-hotels.com)

For other places to stay in Oxford ☎ 01865 726871 or visit www.smoothhound.co.uk, www.visitoxford.org or www.oxford.gov.uk.

WHERE TO EAT

Al Shami (☎ 01865 310066), Bangkok House (☎ 01865 200705), Chaing Mai (☎ 01865 202233), Chutney's (☎ 01865 724241), Edamame (☎ 01865 246916), Elizabeth's (☎ 01865 242230), Quod at Old Bank Hotel (☎ 01865 202505)

TOURIST INFORMATION Oxford Tourist Information Centre, The Old School, Gloucester Green, Oxford, Oxfordshire OX1 2DA ☎ 01865 726871, www.visitoxford.org

LOCAL RADIO STATIONS BBC Radio Oxford (95.2 MHz FM/1485 KHz MW), Radio 210 (102.9 MHz FM/1431 KHz MW)

LOCAL NEWSPAPERS *Oxford Mail, Oxford Times*

Minor
Counties

BEDFORDSHIRE

BEDFORDSHIRE COUNTY CRICKET CLUB, 35 AMBERLEY GARDENS, BEDFORD MK40 3BT

Telephone 01234 327935 (Secretary: home) 01234 261391 (Secretary: work)
Fax 01234 327588 (Secretary: work)
Email philip.august@ecb.co.uk, john@paugust.fsnet.co.uk
Minor Counties Web www.mcca.cricket.org

Founded 1899
Colours purple and black
Crest rampant lion with three shells (taken from
Duke of Bedford's insignia)
President D.E. Wood CBE
Chairman M.E. Green

Secretary P.G.M. August
Treasurer I.D. Smith
Team Manager J.W.G. Howells
Captain A.R. Roberts
Scorers C. Mountain, R. Heley
Cricket Development Officer D.J.M. Mercer

ACHIEVEMENTS

Minor Counties Championship Champions 1970, 1972
Minor Counties Knockout Cup/Holt Cup/ECB 38 Counties Winners 1999

BEDFORDSHIRE CRICKET BOARD

Chairman M. Noble
Secretary P.G.M. August
Treasurer A. Gilbert
Cricket Development Officer D.J.M. Mercer
Womens & Girls Secretary D.J.M. Mercer

GROUNDS

Bedford Town CC, Goldington Bury, Church Lane, Goldington, Bedford (☎ 01234 352458). Goldington Bury is in Church Lane off Goldington Road on the A428 to Cambridge.
Dunstable Town CC, Lancot Park, Tottenhoe, Dunstable (☎ 01582 663735). Follow signs for Tring and take right turn off B489 to Tottenhoe. Lancot Park is on the outskirts of the village.
Flitwick CC, Ampthill Road, Flitwick (☎ 01525 715100). From M1 junction 12, take A5120 towards Ampthill. Ground is on the right by garden centre on Westoning side of Flitwick.
Luton Town CC, Wardown Park, Old Bedford Road, Luton (01582 727855). (see details opposite)
Southill Park CC, Southill Park, near Biggleswade (no ☎ at ground). To the north of Shefford, follow signs to Southill Park, and enter Southill Park Estate through white gates past lodge house.

LUTON

Address Luton Town Cricket Club, Wardown Park, Old Bedford Road, Luton
Prospects of Play ☎ 01582 727855

HISTORY OF GROUND AND FACILITIES

FOUNDED IN 1906 Luton Town Cricket Club is probably one of the strongest club sides in the county and fields three XIs throughout the season. The club plays in the Saracens Hertfordshire Cricket League.

Wardown Park has been used by Bedfordshire County Cricket Club for home Minor Counties Championship matches together with Gillette Cup, NatWest Trophy and Cheltenham & Gloucester Trophy first round ties. Northamptonshire County Cricket Club staged a John Player Sunday League match with Nottinghamshire here in 1973 for the first time. Each season thereafter the ground was used for Sunday League matches and in 1986 Northamptonshire staged its first first-class match at Wardown Park against Yorkshire.

The ground was formed from an area in the north of Wardown Park and the town gardens. The Luton Nomads Cricket Club and the Bedfordshire Eagles Hockey Club also use the ground and its facilities.

There have been crowds of up to 5,000 for Northamptonshire matches. The record attendance was for a benefit match in 1961 for Tom Clark of Surrey CCC when 6,000 were present. Photographs taken during this match can be viewed on the stairs of the pavilion. Northamptonshire's championship match with Middlesex in 1988 attracted 4,000 and the Sunday League match with Warwickshire in 1983 approximately 4,500.

One of Tom Graveney's benefit matches was held at Wardown Park on the rest day of the first England v West Indies Test at Old Trafford in 1969. Graveney attended the benefit and as a result lost his Test match place.

The 1990 and 1991 Minor Counties Championship finals were staged at Wardown Park with Hertfordshire beating Berkshire in 1990 and Staffordshire beating Oxfordshire in 1991. In May 1992 the England Amateur XI played the touring Pakistan team at Luton in a one-day match. Bedfordshire played Hertfordshire and Holland at Luton in August 2002 in the first round of the C&G Trophy. The ground hosts Bedfordshire against Warwickshire in the C&G third round tie in 2003.

This is a very pleasant tree-enclosed ground which has been levelled so that a raised area exists to the eastern, Old Bedford Road side, backed by trees and a timber fence. This provides a most advantageous position from which to view the cricket. The pavilion is a new extension to an existing building which still houses the players' changing rooms. The main scoreboard, which is now electronic, is on the western side of the ground as is the area for sponsors' tents. The members' enclosure is in front of the pavilion and to either side of the players' entrance. There are a good number of seats so it is not always necessary to take your own, except to popular limited-overs matches. A rope and advertising boards define the playing area which is approximately circular in shape with dimensions of 131 metres by 132 metres. The main TV camera position is situated on a gantry high above the sightscreen at the Pavilion End when required. The press box and radio commentary positions are located on the first floor of the pavilion and balcony area.

Entry to the ground is from Wardown Park and pedestrians can approach from either Old Bedford Road or New Bedford Road through the park. In the event of bad weather, an hour or so can be spent visiting Wardown House Museum which is situated a short walk away in Wardown Park adjoining the players' and officials' car park. Here one can learn the methods and history of hat making in Luton and other historical information about the Bedfordshire town.

GROUND RECORDS AND SCORES

LIMITED-OVERS MATCHES

Highest innings total for county 223 for 3 v Huntingdonshire (NWT) 1999
Highest innings total against county 275 for 3 by Lancashire (GC) 1973
Lowest innings total for county 111 v Northumberland (GC) 1977
Lowest innings total against county 96 by Holland (C&G) 2002
Highest individual innings for county 93 D.R. Clarke v Northamptonshire CB (NWT) 2000
Highest individual innings against county 88 B. Wood for Lancashire (GC) 1973
Highest wicket partnerships for county

1st	97* D.J. Roberts & N.A. Stanley	v	Holland	(C&G)	2002
2nd	74 W. Larkins & D.R. Clarke	v	Huntingdonshire	(NWT)	1999
3rd	134* D.R. Clarke & S. Young	v	Hertfordshire	(C&G)	2002
4th	61* A.R. Roberts & D.J.M. Mercer	v	Huntingdonshire	(NWT)	1999
5th	121 D.R. Clarke & O.J. Clayson	v	Nottinghamshire CB	(C&G)	2001
6th	23 A.W. Durley & R.O. Demming	v	Lancashire	(GC)	1973
	23 D.J.M. Mercer & J.A. Knott	v	Yorkshire	(C&G)	2001
7th	48 J.A. Knott & A.J. Trott	v	Yorkshire	(C&G)	2001
8th	38 P.D.B. Hoare & J.R. Wake	v	Gloucestershire	(NWT)	1985
9th	36 I.J. Davison & G.M. Jarrett	v	Northamptonshire	(GC)	1967
10th	31 P.G.M. August & C.G. Proudman	v	Gloucestershire	(NWT)	1985

Highest wicket partnerships against county

1st	129 D. Lloyd & B. Wood	for	Lancashire	(GC)	1973
2nd	111 A.S. Rollins & M.E. Cassar	for	Derbyshire	(NWT)	1999
3rd	80 B. Wood & F.C. Hayes	for	Lancashire	(GC)	1973
4th	43 R.M. Prideaux & Mushtaq Mohammad	for	Northamptonshire	(GC)	1967
5th	72 B.M. Shafayat & A.F.D. Jackman	for	Nottinghamshire CB	(C&G)	2001
6th	79 D.S. Lehmann & G.M. Hamilton	for	Yorkshire	(C&G)	2001
7th	10 A.F.D. Jackman & R.M. Wyld	for	Nottinghamshire CB	(C&G)	2001
8th	38 A.F.D. Jackman & T.E. Savill	for	Nottinghamshire CB	(C&G)	2001
9th	13* T.E. Savill & A.C. Thomas	for	Nottinghamshire CB	(C&G)	2001
10th	12 S.N. Abbas & S. Weurman	for	Holland	(C&G)	2002

Best bowling performance in a match for county 5 for 28 A.R.Roberts v Huntingdonshire (NWT) 1999
Best bowling performance in a match against county 4 for 39 R.J.Sidebottom for Yorkshire (C&G) 2001
Largest crowd 3,000 v Lancashire (GC) 1973 (5,000 Northamptonshire v Middlesex (SL) 1988)

HOW TO GET THERE

Luton station, Midland and Thameslink services, 1 mile ☎ 08457 484950, www.midlandmainline.com, www.thameslink.co.uk

Luton & District 24, 25 and 26 from Mill Street (200m from Luton station) to ground ☎ 01582 404074, Bus Line ☎ 0870 608 2608, 0345 788788. Green Line Bus 757 to Luton bus station thence Bus 6 from town centre to ground.

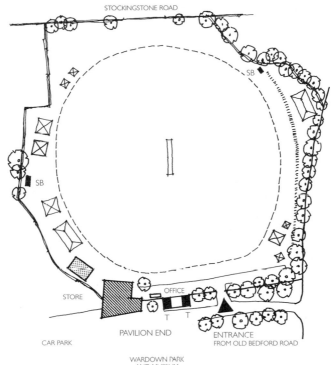

STOCKINGSTONE ROAD END

STOCKINGSTONE ROAD

SB

SB

STORE

OFFICE

T   T

PAVILION END

CAR PARK

ENTRANCE
FROM OLD BEDFORD ROAD

WARDOWN PARK
AND MUSEUM

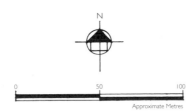

N

0   50   100

Approximate Metres

There are cycle routes from central and surrounding areas of Luton to this part of the town.

 From north: M1 junction 11, then follow signs for Luton A505 into Dunstable Road for town centre, follow signs A6 from town centre to New Bedford Road for Wardown Park and main car park. The ground is half a mile from the town centre. **From south:** Leave M1 at junction 10/10a, then follow signs for Luton and town centre, then signs for A6 from town centre to New Bedford Road for Wardown Park. **From east:** take A505 signposted Luton to town centre, then as north. **From west:** take A505 signposted Luton, then as north.

 London Luton Airport ☎ 01582 405100

WHERE TO STAY

Chiltern Hotel (☎ 01582 575911), Strathmore Thistle Hotel (☎ 01582 734199). For other places to stay in the Luton area visit www.smoothhound.co.uk or www.luton.gov.uk

TOURIST INFORMATION Luton Tourist Information Centre, The Bus Station, Bute Street, Luton, Bedfordshire LU1 2EY ☎ 01582 401579 Fax 01582 487886, www.luton.gov.uk

LOCAL RADIO STATIONS Chiltern Radio (96.9 MHz FM/792 KHz MW) BBC 3 Counties Radio (95.5 MHz FM/1161 KHz MW)

LOCAL NEWSPAPERS *Luton News, The Luton Herald*

BERKSHIRE

BERKSHIRE COUNTY CRICKET CLUB, 41 HOLYROOD CLOSE, CAVERSHAM, READING RG4 6PZ

Telephone	0118 947 7959 (Home) **fax** 0118 946 3422
Email	berkscricksec@hotmail.com
Web	www.berkshire.cricinfo.com
Minor Counties Web	www.mcca.cricket.org

Founded 1895
Colours narrow old gold stripe between broad stripes of purple and green
Crest a white hart passing under a polled oak with a dark green background
President G.A. Clift
Chairman L.A. Sears

Secretary R.M. New
Treasurer G.G. Fyffe
Team Manager G.E.J. Child
Captain J.R. Wood
Scorer R. Arnold
Statistician R.M. New

ACHIEVEMENTS

Minor Counties Championship Champions 1924, 1928, 1953
Minor Counties Championship Finalists 1990
Minor Counties Knockout Cup/Holt Cup/ECB 38 Counties Quarter-finalists 1987

BERKSHIRE CRICKET BOARD

Chairman L.A. Sears
Secretary R.M. New
Treasurer G.G. Fyffe
Youth Administrator A. Kingstone
Cricket Development Officer S. Ayres
Women & Girls Secretary C. Bosley

GROUNDS

Falkland CC, Wash Common, Essex Street, off Andover Road, nr Newbury RG14 6RQ (☎ 01635 47658).
Ground is in Essex Street, off Andover Road A343 to the south of Newbury.
Finchampstead CC, Memorial Ground, Finchampstead RG40 4JR (☎ 0118 973 2890). Ground is on B3348 in village, 4 miles south of Wokingham.
Reading CC, The Pavilion, Sonning Lane, off London Road, Sonning, Reading RG4 0ST (☎ 0118 969 9049).
(see details below)
Thatcham CC, Brownsfield Road, Thatcham, Newbury RG13 4AG (☎ 01635 865521). M4 junction 12 towards Newbury. Brownsfield Road is next to the War Memorial.

READING

Address Reading Cricket Club, The Pavilion, Sonning Lane, off London Road,
Sonning, Reading, Berkshire RG4 0ST
Prospects of Play ☎ 0118 969 9049

HISTORY OF GROUND AND FACILITIES

SONNING LANE off London Road is the home of Reading Cricket Club who play in the Home Counties Premier League. The ground has been used by Berkshire County Cricket Club for Minor Counties Championship matches together with NatWest Trophy and Cheltenham & Gloucester Trophy first to third round matches. The ground hosted a Minor Counties CA versus Australia 'A' tour match in 1995.

Reading Cricket Club is one section of Reading Cricket and Hockey Club. The cricket club is the older of the two sections, having been founded in 1859. The hockey club became affiliated to the cricket club in 1959. In 1985 the club moved to its present location in Sonning Lane and Reading Cricket and Hockey Club was properly formed. The move benefited both sections by providing a magnificent pavilion and the space in which to enjoy and advance both cricket and hockey.

For the cricket section, two squares were laid, each having full-size boundaries. Cricket was first played at Sonning Lane in 1986 and it is now regarded as one of the best places to play the game in Berkshire. With the growth in popularity of hockey at the time, the outfield provided enough space for six grass pitches. This facility has since been enhanced by the laying of a floodlit water-based artificial pitch. Reading has been at the forefront of national developments in hockey, including the foundation of the National League. Reading Hockey Club is presently one of the most successful clubs in the UK with National League and Cup honours.

Reading Cricket and Hockey Club Pavilion.

Sonning Lane is regularly used for important and prestigious cricket games. These have included Minor Counties Festival 1995, Minor Counties v Australia 'A', Minor Counties v West Indies, Berkshire v Hampshire (NatWest Trophy 1994), Women's World Cup, and a Malcolm Marshall benefit match. Berkshire County matches are played here every year, including Berkshire Representative games and the Berkshire v Essex Cheltenham & Gloucester Trophy fixture in 2001.

Reading Cricket Club were among the founding members of the Thames Valley League in 1972. The club have won the 1st XI Championship five times in 1974, 1975, 1977, 1981 and 1992. The 2nd XI Championship has been won on three occasions in 1983, 1989 and 1991. Up to and including the 1999 season, four sides were entered into this competition.

Reading have also enjoyed success in the National Club Knockout Competition with two trips to Lord's for the final in 1979 and 1985. Unfortunately, on both occasions Reading were runners-up. Success in this competition has meant numerous victories in the regional final and participation in the last eight. As a result, Reading is regarded by the Cricket Club Conference as one of the top twenty clubs nationally.

With the formation of the Home Counties Premier League, which started in 2000, Reading is once again at the forefront of cricket development. Reading CC is also used for Women's Super Fours fixtures.

The permanent buildings on the ground include a pavilion, scoreboard and groundsman's store. The ground is enclosed by bushes and hedges with some trees at the London Road End. The playing area is 135 metres by 140 metres making this a small ground by club standards; it is defined by rope and advertising boards.

GROUND RECORDS AND SCORES

LIMITED-OVERS MATCHES

Highest innings total for county 150 for 4 v Warwickshire CB (NWT) 1999
Highest innings total against county 218 for 9 by Essex (C&G) 2001
Lowest innings total for county 149 v Essex (C&G) 2001
Lowest innings total against county 119 by Norfolk (C&G) 2002
Highest individual innings for county 56 G.E. Loveday v Warwickshire CB (NWT) 1999
Highest individual innings against county 55 R.C. Irani for Essex (C&G) 2001
Highest wicket partnerships for county

1st	42 G.E. Loveday & S.A. Seymour	v	Warwickshire CB	(NWT)	1999
2nd	25 G.E. Loveday & T.D. Fray	v	Warwickshire CB	(NWT)	1999
3rd	74 J. Moss & J.R. Wood	v	Essex	(C&G)	2001
4th	70 G.E. Loveday & S.D. Myles	v	Warwickshire CB	(NWT)	1999
5th	27 M.L. Simmons & P.J. Oxley	v	Hampshire	(NWT)	1991
6th	8 S.A. Seymour & S.S. Patel	v	Essex	(C&G)	2001
7th	10 S.A. Seymour & C.J. Batt	v	Essex	(C&G)	2001
8th	6 S.A. Seymour & N.P. Harvey	v	Essex	(C&G)	2001
9th	9 N.P. Harvey & N.E.L. Gunter	v	Essex	(C&G)	2001
10th	2 N.E.L. Gunter & T.L. Lambert	v	Essex	(C&G)	2001

Highest wicket partnerships against county

1st	93* V.P. Terry & R.A. Smith	for	Hampshire	(NWT)	1991
2nd	47 C.J. Rogers & S.C. Goldsmith	for	Norfolk	(C&G)	2002
3rd	28 S.C. Goldsmith & M.E. Parlane	for	Norfolk	(C&G)	2002
4th	38 R.C. Irani & S.D. Peters	for	Essex	(C&G)	2001
5th	66 R.C. Irani & A.P. Grayson	for	Essex	(C&G)	2001
6th	23 J.O. Troughton & S. McDonald	for	Warwickshire CB	(NWT)	1999
7th	32 R.S. Clinton & B.J. Hyam	for	Essex	(C&G)	2001
8th	23 B.J. Hyam & A.P. Cowan	for	Essex	(C&G)	2001
9th	31 S.J.B. Livermore & J.P. Taylor	for	Norfolk	(C&G)	2002
10th	13*B.J.Hyam & T.J.Mason	for	Essex	(C&G)	2001

Best bowling performance in a match for county 4 for 8 S.D. Myles v Norfolk (C&G) 2002
Best bowling performance in a match against county 3 for 37 R.C. Irani for Essex (C&G) 2001
Largest crowd 3,500 v Hampshire (NWT) 1991

HOW TO GET THERE

 Reading station 2 miles, Thames Trains and Great Western Railways ☎ 08457 484950, www.greatwesterntrains.co.uk, www.thamestrains.co.uk

 Local buses connect London Road with Reading city centre and Reading railway station, ☎ 0870 608 2608

 There are cycle paths and routes from central and surrounding areas of Reading to this area of Sonning.

 From north: from A4074, A4155 follow signs to Reading and town centre, then follow A4 east (London Road) to Sonning. Sonning Lane is left turn just after railway bridge. **From south:** A327, A33 or M4 junction 11 follow signs to Reading town centre, then as north. **From east:** A4 through Twyford, Sonning Lane is right turn just before railway bridge, from M4 junction 10 take A329(M)

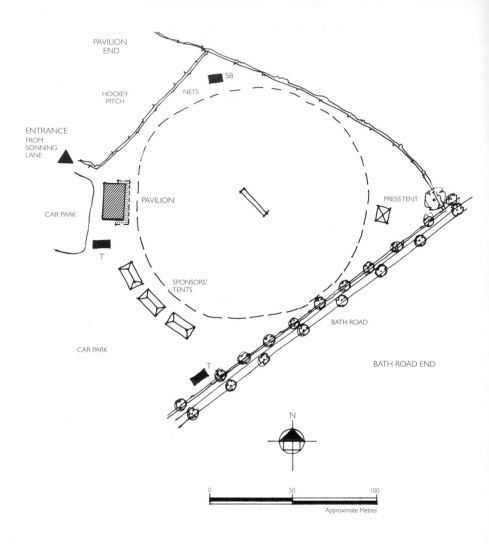

signposted to Reading, at roundabout take A4 (London Road) then as north. **From west:** A329, A4, or M4 junction 12 follow signs to Reading town centre, then as north.

✈ London Heathrow Airport ☎ 08700 000123

WHERE TO STAY

Holiday Inn Reading (☎ 0800 500 500), St Anne's Lodge (☎ 0118 946 2490), Country View Lodge (☎ 07710 855262).

For other places to stay in the Reading area visit www.smoothhound.co.uk or www.reading.gov.uk.

TOURIST INFORMATION Reading Tourist Information Centre ☎ 0118 956 6226, www.reading.gov.uk

LOCAL RADIO STATIONS 2-Ten FM (97.0 MHz FM/102.9 MHz FM), BBC Radio Berkshire (104.4MHz FM)

LOCAL NEWSPAPERS *Reading Evening Post, Reading Chronicle*

BUCKINGHAMSHIRE

BUCKINGHAMSHIRE COUNTY CRICKET CLUB, 49 AMERSHAM ROAD, LITTLE CHALFONT, AMERSHAM, BUCKINGHAMSHIRE HP6 6SW

Telephone	01494 763516 (home)
Email	kevin.beaumont@tesco.net
Web	not yet available
Minor Counties Web	www.mcca.cricket.org

Founded 1891
Colours green with silver and white stripes
Crest chained swan
President K. Drucquer
Chairman S. York
Secretary K.A. Beaumont
Assistant Secretary K.D.T. Hillier

Treasurer N.A. Relph
Team Secretary S. Lynch
Cricket Development Officer S.R. Goldthorpe
Captain P.D. Atkins
Scorers Mrs L. Hawkins/J. Goodman/T. Davidson
Statistician D.H. Miller

ACHIEVEMENTS

Minor Counties Championship Champions 1922, 1923, 1925, 1932, 1938, 1952, 1968, 1987, Joint Champions 1899

Minor Counties Championship Final Winners 1987
Minor Counties Knockout Cup/Holt Cup/ECB 38 Counties Winners 1990

BUCKINGHAMSHIRE CRICKET BOARD

Chairman C. Pocock
Secretary M. Watts
Treasurer R. Judge
Youth Administrator M. Watts
Cricket Development Officer S. Goldthorpe
Women & Girls Secretary E. Powell

GROUNDS

Aylesbury Town CC, Aylesbury Sports Club, Wendover Road, Aylesbury (☎ 01296 415187). Ground is on Wendover Road A413 on left going out of town.

Beaconsfield CC, Wilton Park, Oxford Road, Beaconsfield (☎ 01494 674134) On Oxford Road on the London side of Beaconsfield Old Town on A40, easily accessible from M40 junction 2.

Dinton CC, Oxford Road, Dinton, nr Aylesbury (☎ 01296 747254). On main Thame to Oxford road (A418) 5 miles from Aylesbury.

Gerrards Cross CC, Dukes Lane, Gerrards Cross (☎ 01753 886610), On A40, ½ mile east of junction with B416, turn into Dukes Wood Avenue for Dukes Wood Avenue for Dukes Lane.

High Wycombe CC, London Road, High Wycombe (☎ 01494 522611). On A40 London Road going out of town centre towards Beaconsfield.

Marlow CC, Pound Lane, off High Street, Marlow (☎ 01628 483638). At the river end of the High Street. Turn right before bridge.

Milton Keynes, Campbell Park, Milton Keynes (☎ 01908 694820). Campbell Park is near M1 junction 14 M1 between H6 (A509) and V10 (A4146) roads close to the Grand Union Canal.
Wing, Ascott Park CC, Aylesbury Road, Wing, nr Leighton Buzzard (☎ 01296 688242). (see details below)
Wormsley, Sir Paul Getty's Ground, Wormsley Estate, off Ibstone Road, Wormsley, nr Stokenchurch (no telephone on ground). Wormsley Estate is the private ground of Sir Paul Getty on Ibstone Road, near Stokenchurch. Anyone wishing to attend this ground must contact the Buckinghamshire CCC Secretary no later than 10 days in advance of the game.

ASCOTT PARK, WING

Address Ascott Park Cricket Club, The Estate Office, Wing, near Leighton
Buzzard, Bedfordshire LU7 OPS
Prospects of Play ☎ 01296 688942

HISTORY OF GROUND AND FACILITIES

THE ASCOTT PARK CRICKET GROUND is located within the grounds of Ascott House, which is the home of the Rothschild family. The house and estate were given over to the National Trust in 1949. The extensive Ascott Park gardens, which include the cricket ground, are a mixture of both formal and natural gardens which are self contained within areas of fine trees, shrubs, a herbaceous walk, lily pond, Dutch garden and a remarkable topiary sundial. The gardens are open from 1 April to 26 September. The house is open from 1 April to 14 September but is closed on Mondays.

The only permanent buildings on the cricket ground are the attractive timber pavilion built in 1890 and the scoreboard. Cricket has always formed an important part of life at Ascott. The first match took place on 28 August 1880 when an XI brought from London played an XI selected by Mr Tennant, partly from London and partly from the neighbouring Leighton Buzzard area. Leopold de Rothschild was present to watch the first match played on his new cricket ground.

Before the First World War many invitation teams played cricket weeks. An Ascott XI played regular fixtures. The records for 1911 show Anthony de Rothschild scored 513 runs in 14 innings for an average of 36.64. The Revd J. Cuthbertson topped the bowling with an average of 18.28.

Buckinghamshire County Cricket Club was formed in 1891 through the interest of the Rothschild family and regularly played at Ascott until 1979. The county first team returned to Ascott in 1998 to play a one-day fixture and since then matches have been played each year. Buckinghamshire are scheduled to play Gloucestershire at Ascott Park in 2003 in the third round of the Cheltenham & Gloucester Trophy.

The senior side Buckinghamshire County Cricket Colts and Schools teams are regular visitors to Ascott. The groundsman and Estate Manager is Victor Demain who is responsible for co-ordination of cricket matches on the estate throughout the season. The Estate does not have a team but the ground is used regularly by Ascott Park CC and Wing CC.

Other matches to have been staged at Ascott Park include Bunbury CC v NatWest Primary Club on 12 September 1999 and Ascott Park CC v Old England XI on 31 August 1998 and 13 July 2002.

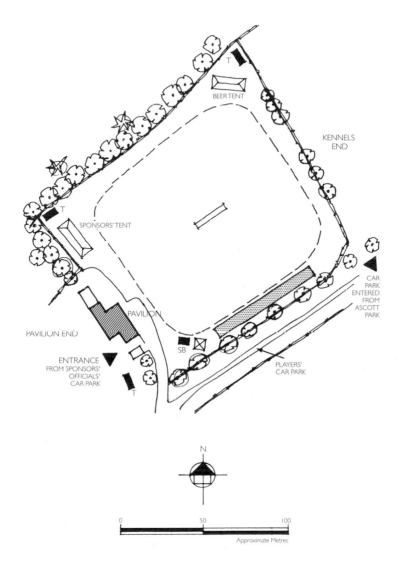

The pavilion is located at the southern end of the ground, which is nearest to the main estate buildings. It has facilities for players, officials and umpires only. TV and radio commentary positions and a press tent would be positioned at the Pavilion End if necessary.

The semi-finals and final of the Coronation Cup, a midweek competition for local village clubs, are staged at Ascott. The cup was one of the first limited-overs competitions played in the country. It has frequently been won by Stewkley CC and Long Marston CC. However, in 2002, in the 49th Coronation Cup, Edlesbrough CC beat Soulbury CC in the final.

Other wandering clubs play here including Harrow Wanderers, The Stragglers of Asia, Hottentot CC, Chase Farmers CC, and the Harlequins Rugby Football Club Supporters' Club CC.

The delightful pavilion at Ascott Park, Wing.

GROUND RECORDS AND SCORES

LIMITED-OVERS MATCHES

No C&G limited-overs matches played to date.

HOW TO GET THERE

 Leighton Buzzard station 2 miles ☎ 08457 484950, www.silverlink-trains.com. Aylesbury station 5 miles, www.chilternrailways.co.uk

 Arriva The Shires X15, 65 Aylesbury to Milton Keynes pass close by ☎ 0870 608 2608

 There are cycle routes from surrounding areas of Leighton Buzzard and Aylesbury.

 The Ascott Park estate, including cricket ground, is located half a mile east of Wing, which is 2 miles south-west of Leighton Buzzard on the south side of the A418 between Leighton Buzzard and Aylesbury. The entrance to the estate is on the left hand side of the road on the Leighton Buzzard side of Tring travelling towards Aylesbury.

 London Luton Airport ☎ 01582 405100

WHERE TO STAY

Holiday Inn (Aylesbury) (☎ 0800 500 500 www.holidayinn.com). For other places to stay in the Aylesbury, Leighton Buzzard, Tring or Wing area visit www.smoothhound.co.uk

TOURIST INFORMATION National Trust ☎ 01296 681904, 01525 402051/406464

LOCAL RADIO STATION Chiltern Radio (97.6 MHz FM/828 KHz MW), BBC 3 Counties Radio (95.6MHz FM/1161 KHz MW)

LOCAL NEWSPAPERS *Bucks Herald, Bucks Advertiser, Bucks Free Press*

CAMBRIDGESHIRE

CAMBRIDGESHIRE COUNTY CRICKET CLUB, THE REDLANDS, OAKINGTON ROAD, COTTENHAM, CAMBRIDGE, CAMBRIDGESHIRE CB4 4TW

Telephone 01954 250429 (home)
Minor Counties Web www.mcca.cricket.org

Founded 1844
Colours blue, maroon and straw
Crest a shield supported by two bustards
President D.H.R. Fairey
Chairman M. Stephenson

Secretary P.W. Gooden
Treasurer R. Stevens
Cricket Development Officer R.J. Doel
Team Manager K. Coburn
Captain Ajaz Akhtar

ACHIEVEMENTS

Minor Counties Championship Champions 1963
Minor Counties Championship Finalists 1988

Minor Counties Knockout Cup/Holt Cup/ECB 38 Counties Winners 1995

CAMBRIDGESHIRE CRICKET BOARD

Chairman P. Gooden
Secretary R. Wardle
Treasurer L. Cooke
Youth Manager S. Kay
Cricket Development Officer R. Doel
Women & Girls Secretary R. Doel

GROUNDS

Cambridge University CC, Fenner's University Cricket Ground, Cambridge (☎ 01223 353552). (see details in Cambridge UCCE section)
March Town CC, Avenue Ground, Burrowmoor Road, March (☎ 01354 652029). (see details over)
Wisbech Town CC, Harecroft Road, Wisbech (☎ 01945 585429). From town centre, over river bridge to T-junction. Turn left and go past rugby ground.

MARCH

Address March Town Cricket Club, The Pavilion, Sports Ground,
Burrowmoor Road, March, Cambridgeshire
Prospects of Play ☎ 01354 652029

HISTORY OF GROUND AND FACILITIES

THE AVENUE SPORTS GROUND is situated off Burrowmoor Road to the south-east
of the market town of March and is the home of March Town Cricket Club.

The ground is used by Cambridgeshire County Cricket Club for Minor
Counties Championship matches, the NatWest Trophy and Cheltenham &
Gloucester Trophy matches. The first Cambridgeshire match to be staged on the
ground was the 1st round NatWest Trophy tie in 1989 when Worcestershire were
the visitors. Worcestershire won by 9 wickets thanks to 91* from Tim Curtis. Ian
Lawrence top scored for Cambridgeshire with 74.

The ground is enclosed and permanent facilities include a pavilion, clubhouse,
groundsman's store, toilets, scoreboard and a bowling green pavilion. The south
of the ground is surrounded by trees and to the south-east of the playing area is
a car park. The playing area is 108 metres by 125 metres and is defined by a
rope with some advertising boards. The only entrance to the ground is from
Burrowmoor Road and observant visitors will notice that the nearby housing
estate is called Cricketer's Close.

GROUND RECORDS AND SCORES

LIMITED-OVERS MATCHES

Highest innings total for county 221 v Somerset (C&G) 2001
Highest innings total against county 289 for 3 by Derbyshire (NWT) 1995
Lowest innings total for county 107 v Hampshire (NWT) 1994
Lowest innings total against county 146 by Derbyshire (C&G) 2001
Highest individual innings for county 92 G.W. Ecclestone v Kent (NWT) 1996
Highest individual innings against county 119* D.J. Cullinan for Derbyshire (NWT) 1995
Highest wicket partnerships for county

1st	36 S.A. Kellett & N.T. Gadsby	v	Derbyshire CB	(C&G)	2001
2nd	19 S.A. Kellett & M. Mohammed	v	Derbyshire CB	(C&G)	2001
3rd	98 I.S. Lawrence & N.J. Adams	v	Worcestershire	(NWT)	1989
4th	11 N.J. Adams & D.P. Norman	v	Worcestershire	(NWT)	1989
	11 G.W. Ecclestone & N. Mohammed	v	Kent	(NWT)	1996
5th	32 N.T. Gadsby & D.G. Wilson	v	Cumberland	(NWT)	2000
6th	121 S.A. Kellett & Ajaz Akhtar	v	Somerset	(C&G)	2001
7th	40 N.T. Gadsby & Ajaz Akhtar	v	Cumberland	(NWT)	2000
8th	26 Ajaz Akhtar & T.S. Smith	v	Cumberland	(NWT)	2000
9th	29 R.D. Powell & T.S. Smith	v	Warwickshire CB	(C&G)	2001
10th	32 B.T.P. Donelan & D.F. Ralfs	v	Derbyshire	(NWT)	1995

Highest wicket partnerships against county

1st	49 S.T. Knox & D.J. Pearson	for	Cumberland	(NWT)	2000
2nd	170* T.S. Curtis & G.A. Hick	for	Worcestershire	(NWT)	1989
3rd	169 W.A. Dessaur & D.J. Cullinan	for	Derbyshire	(NWT)	1995
4th	104 N.J. Llong & M.A. Ealham	for	Kent	(NWT)	1996

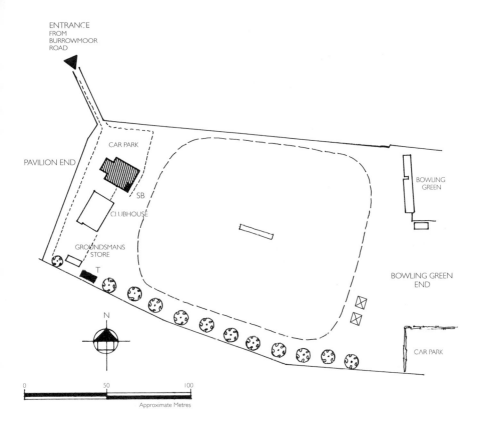

5th	80 M.N. Lathwell & M. Burns	for	Somerset	(C&G)	2001
6th	96* N.J. Llong & M.J. Walker	for	Kent	(NWT)	1996
7th	52 D.S. Steele & Sarfraz Nawaz	for	Northamptonshire	(GC)	1975
8th	6 R.J. Turner & J.I.D. Kerr	for	Somerset	(C&G)	2001
9th	25 R.J. Turner & P.S. Jones	for	Somerset	(C&G)	2001
10th	4 D.S. Steele & J.C.J. Dye	for	Northamptonshire	(GC)	1975

Best bowling performance in a match for county 4 for 29 Ajaz Akhtar v Warwickshire CB (C&G) 2001
Best bowling performance in a match against county 5 for 28 P.A.J. de Freitas for Derbyshire (NWT) 1995
Largest crowd 2,500 v Worcestershire (NWBT) 1989

HOW TO GET THERE

 March station 1 mile ☎ 08457 484950, www.wagn.co.uk

 From surrounding areas to March with links to Peterborough, Wisbech and Ely ☎ 0870 608 2608

 There are cycle routes from surrounding areas of March to this part of the town.

 From north: A141 or B1101 signposted March and town centre, then follow signs county cricket. **From east:** B1099 signposted March and town centre, then as north. **From west:** B1093 and A605 and A141 signposted March and town centre, then as north. **From south:** A141 and B1101 signposted March and town centre, then as north.

 Cambridge Airport ☎ 01223 373737

Holiday Inn, Peterborough (☎ 01733 240209) or stay in March or Ely. For other places to stay in the March area visit www.smoothhound.co.uk.

LOCAL RADIO STATIONS BBC Radio Cambridgeshire (95.7 MHz FM/1026 KHz MW), Hereward Radio (96.6 MHz FM/1557 KHz MW)

LOCAL NEWSPAPER *Cambridge Evening News*

CHESHIRE

THE HON SECRETARY, CHESHIRE COUNTY CRICKET CLUB, 36 LANDSWOOD PARK, HARTFORD, NORTHWICH, CHESHIRE CW8 1NF

Telephone 01606 74970 (home) **fax** 01606 79357
Web www.cheshire-county-cricket-club.org.uk
Minor Counties Web www.mcca.cricket.org

Founded 1908
Colours purple, silver black or blue with optional wheatsheaf in silver and gold
Crest a wheatsheaf
Patron The Duke of Westminster
Hon President J.B. Pickup
Hon Chairman G.C. Hardstaff
Hon Secretary J.B. Pickup
Hon Vice Chairman/Hon Membership Secretary A.B. Percival

Hon Assistant Secretary Mrs E. Scrimgeour
Hon Treasurer A.G. Hall
Hon Team Secretary/Assistant Treasurer D.W. Sharp
Cricket Development Officer R. Newton
Publicity/Press Officer T. Everatt
Captain A.J. Hall
Scorer J. Hempstock
Sponsor Lees Brewery

ACHIEVEMENTS

Minor Counties Championship Champions 1967, 1985, 1988, 2001 (joint)
Minor Counties Championship Finalists 1984, 1993

Minor Counties Knockout Cup/Holt Cup/ECB 38 Counties Winners 1983, 1987, 1996, Finalists 2000

CHESHIRE CRICKET BOARD

Chairman J.P.H. Campey
Secretary D.W. Sharp
Treasurer M.D. Roff
Cricket Development Officer R.C. Newton
Cricket Development Officer P.A. Hancock
Administrator M. Alder
Women & Girls Secretary A. Cutler

GROUNDS

Alderley Edge CC, Moss Lane, Alderley Edge (☎ 01625 584733, www.alderleyedgecricket.com)

Bowdon CC, South Downs Road, Bowdon, Altrincham (☎ 0161 928 1358). (see details below)

Cheadle Hulme CC, Grove Park, Grove Lane, off Meadway Road, Cheadle Hulme (☎ 0161 485 3733 then dial 24 for bar)

Chester Boughton Hall CC, Boughton Hall Avenue, off Filkins Lane, Chester (☎ 01244 326072)

Nantwich CC, Whitehouse Lane, Nantwich (☎ 01270 626155)

Neston CC, Parkgate, South Wirral (☎ 0151 336 4199 www.collyer.force9.co.uk/neston)

New Brighton CC, Rake Lane, Liscard, Wallasey (☎ 0151 639 4900)

Oxton CC, Townfield Lane, Birkenhead, Wirral (☎ 0151 652 1331)

Toft CC, Booth's Park, Chelford Road, Knutsford (☎ 01565 632734)

BOWDON

Address Bowdon Cricket Club, The Pavilion, South Downs Road,
Bowdon, Cheshire
Prospects of Play ☎ 0161 928 1358

HISTORY OF GROUND AND FACILITIES

SOUTH DOWNS ROAD is the home of Bowdon Cricket Club. The ground has been used by Cheshire CCC for Minor Counties Championship matches together with Gillette Cup, NatWest Trophy and Cheltenham & Gloucester Trophy fixtures. The ground was also used by Minor Counties and Minor Counties (North) for matches in the Benson and Hedges Cup zonal rounds.

The only permanent buildings on the ground are the pavilion, squash club, groundsman's store and scoreboard. Temporary facilities are installed when county matches are staged here.

In 1990 Bowdon CC played Lancashire CCC in aid of Paul Allott's Benefit Year.

GROUND RECORDS AND SCORES

LIMITED-OVERS MATCHES

Highest innings total for county 204 for 9 v Kent (NWT) 1999
Highest innings total against county 312 for 7 by Kent (NWT) 1999
Lowest innings total for county 107 for 9 v Durham (NWT) 1994
Lowest innings total against county 108 for 9 by Durham (NWT) 1994
Highest individual innings for county 57 N.D. Cross v Kent (NWT) 1999
Highest individual innings against county 123 N.J. Llong for Kent (NWT) 1999
Highest wicket partnership for county

1st	9 P.R.J. Bryson & J.D. Bean	v	Kent	(NWT)	1999
2nd	1 J.D. Bean & R.G. Hignett	v	Kent	(NWT)	1999
3th	29 R.G. Hignett & I. Cockbain	v	Kent	(NWT)	1999
4th	62 R.G. Hignett & N.D. Cross	v	Kent	(NWT)	1999
5th	50 N.D. Cross & D. Leather	v	Kent	(NWT)	1999

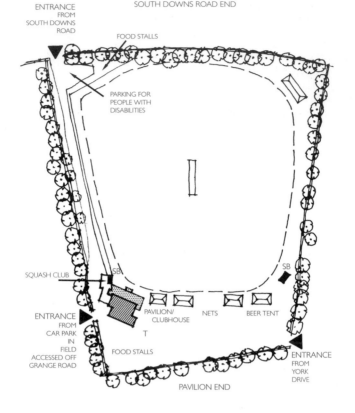

ENTRANCE
FROM
SOUTH DOWNS
ROAD

SOUTH DOWNS ROAD END

FOOD STALLS

PARKING FOR
PEOPLE WITH
DISABILITIES

SQUASH CLUB

SB

SB

ENTRANCE
FROM
CAR PARK
IN
FIELD
ACCESSED OFF
GRANGE ROAD

PAVILION/
CLUBHOUSE

NETS

BEER TENT

T

FOOD STALLS

ENTRANCE
FROM
YORK
DRIVE

PAVILION END

N

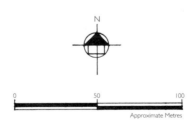

0   50   100

Approximate Metres

6th	17 J.D. Gray & R.G. Hignett	v	Durham	(NWT)	1994
7th	24 J.D. Gray & J.D. Bean	v	Durham	(NWT)	1994
8th	3 J.D. Gray & S. Bramhall	v	Durham	(NWT)	1994
9th	35 J.D. Gray & S.J. Renshaw	v	Durham	(NWT)	1994
10th	1* P.J. Cottrell & S. Bramhall	v	Kent	(NWT)	1999

Highest wicket partnership against county

1st	11 T.R. Ward & E.T. Smith	for	Kent	(NWT)	1999
2nd	38 W. Larkins & J.E. Morris	for	Durham	(NWT)	1994
3rd	28 M.J. Walker & A. Symonds	for	Kent	(NWT)	1999
4th	29 J.E. Morris & P. Bainbridge	for	Durham	(NWT)	1994
5th	22 P. Bainbridge & S. Hutton	for	Durham	(NWT)	1994

6th	226 N.J. Llong & M.V. Fleming	for	Kent	(NWT)	1999
7th	16 M.V. Fleming & S.A. Marsh	for	Kent	(NWT)	1999
8th	8* M.V. Fleming & M.J. McCague	for	Kent	(NWT)	1999

9th and 10th – yet to be established

Best bowling performance for county 3 for 34 CC Finegan v Kent (NWT) 1999
Best bowling performance against county 5 for 22 S.J.E. Brown for Durham (NWT) 1994
Largest crowd 2,500 v Kent (NWT) 1999

HOW TO GET THERE

 Altrincham station ☎ 08457 484950, www.virgintrains.com. Metrolink Tram GMTR from Manchester Piccadilly station to Altrincham ☎ 0161 228 7811, 0161 205 2000, www.GMPTE.com

 GMT Buses pass close to the ground in South Downs Road and link Altrincham station and Tram Link station with Bowdon village centre. ☎ 0870 608 2608, www.gobybus.co.uk

 There are cycle routes from Altrincham and surrounding areas to Bowdon.

 The ground is signposted from the A56 south of Altrincham town centre. The A56 is the main road from M6 junction 19 to the Old Trafford district of Manchester.

 Manchester International Airport ☎ 0161 489 3000

WHERE TO STAY

Cresta Court Hotel (☎ 0161 927 7272), Lowry Hotel (☎ 0161 827 4000), Malmaison Hotel (☎ 0161 278 1000), Old Trafford Lodge (☎ 0161 874 3333), Travel Inn Metro (☎ 0870 238 3315). For further small hotels and guest houses in Bowdon area visit www.smoothhound.co.uk or www.altrinchaml.gov.uk.

TOURIST INFORMATION Manchester Visitor Information Centre & Gift Shop, Town Hall Extension, Lloyd Street, St Peters Square, Manchester ☎ 0161 234 3157, www.destinationmanchester.com, www.manchesteronline.co.uk

LOCAL RADIO STATIONS BBC Radio Greater Manchester Radio (GMR) (95.1 MHz FM/ KHz MW), Key 103/Magic 1152 (103 MHz FM/1152 KHz MW), BBC Radio Lancashire (104.5 MHz FM/1557 KHz MW)

LOCAL NEWSPAPERS *Manchester Evening News, Sunday Sports Pink*

CORNWALL

CORNWALL COUNTY CRICKET CLUB, THE LOGAN ROCK INN, TREEN, ST LEVAN, PENZANCE, CORNWALL TR19 6LG

Telephone 01736 810495 (home) **fax** 01736 810177
Website www.cornwall-cricket.org
Minor Counties Web www.mcca.cricket.org

Founded 1895
Colours red, yellow and black
Crest black chough
President F. J. Williams
Chairman Col R. Potts
Secretary Mrs A. George JP
Assistant Secretary The Revd Canon K. Rogers

Treasurer D. Nance
Team Secretary/Manager G. Furse
Under-21s (2003) W.R. Collins
Captain T.G. Sharp
Scorer B. Holder
Statistician M. Weeks

ACHIEVEMENTS

Minor Counties Championship 2nd 1974, 1976
Minor Counties Knockout Cup/Holt Cup/ECB 38 Counties Quarter-finalists 1988, 2nd Round Proper 1990, 2nd Round 1994 (MCC Trophy)

CORNWALL CRICKET BOARD

Chairman Col. R. Potts
Secretary M. Harland
Treasurer/Youth Administrator M. Broad MBE
Cricket Development Officer T. Marrion
Women & Girls Secretary T. Marrion

GROUNDS

Camborne CC, Roskear, Camborne (☎ 01209 715478). From the centre of Camborne, take road for Roskear, turn left adjacent to All Saints Church and ground is on left.
Falmouth CC, Trescobeas Cricket Ground, Falmouth (☎ 01326 374000). Trescobeas Cricket Ground is on the road from Penryn, turn right at the Dracaena traffic lights and follow the road, turning right at Falmouth School.
St Austell CC, Wheal Eliza, Bethel, St Austell (☎ 01726 72588). From east end of by-pass, turn left at fourth set of traffic lights after roundabout taking A391, turn left at first roundabout and ground is on left.
St Just, Cape Cornwall School, Cape Cornwall Road, St Just, nr Penzance (☎ 01736 787495). From Penzance, turn left from St Just square into Cape Cornwall School. Ground is 400 yards on right.
Truro CC, Boscawen Park, Truro (☎ 01872 277468). (see details opposite)

TRURO

Address Truro Cricket Club, Boscawen Park, Malpas Road, Truro
Prospects of Play ☎ 01872 277468

HISTORY OF GROUND AND FACILITIES

TRURO CRICKET CLUB began playing at Boscawen Park in 1961, having previously shared a ground with Truro City Football Club. Truro City Council owns the ground and has granted the club a long lease, enabling them to continue further enhancement of the ground and facilities. The council maintains the cricket pitch on the adjoining ground, on which the club's 3rd and 4th XIs play their matches.

The present ground is on land reclaimed from the Truro River, having formerly been the Truro landfill site, as indeed is the entire Boscawen Park complex. The club began work to level the surface, lay drains and spread soil in the mid/late 1950s. Much of the work was carried out by a dedicated band of volunteers, backed by generous donations from Truro businessmen, notably Messrs Radmore, Frank and Smith. Grants from sporting organisations have ensured that this is now the finest ground and amenities in the Duchy. In recent years the pavilion has been extended, the scoreboard has been improved and the nets replaced with much more satisfactory facilities.

This is the most scenic ground in Cornwall, situated as it is right on the river. Truro is still a relatively active port and play can occasionally be delayed while a ship passes behind the bowler's arm.

Cornwall have played five matches at Truro in the Gillette Cup/NatWest Trophy and Cheltenham & Gloucester Trophy: v Glamorgan 1970, Lancashire 1977, Norfolk 2000, Sussex 2001 and Worcestershire 2002. The match against Worcestershire was staged with less than 24 hours' notice when the umpires decided that the St Austell ground would be unfit for play on the designated days. A Cheltenham & Gloucester Trophy match will be staged against Kent in 2003. Somerset County Club have also played one-day pre-season friendly matches here.

The TV camera position, when required, is on a gantry directly behind the City End sightscreen. Temporary tents for press, first aid facilities, etc. are erected when necessary. Spectators are advised to bring their own seats as only about 300 are provided.

GROUND RECORDS AND SCORES

LIMITED-OVERS MATCHES

Highest innings total for county 220 for 8 v Sussex (C&G) 2001
Highest innings total against county 253 for 6 by Sussex (C&G) 2001
Lowest innings total for county 62 v Lancashire (GC) 1977
Lowest innings total against county 125 for 7 by Worcestershire (C&G) 2002
Highest individual innings for county 56 S.C. Pope v Norfolk (NWT) 2000
Highest individual innings against county 89* C.J. Adams for Sussex (C&G) 2001

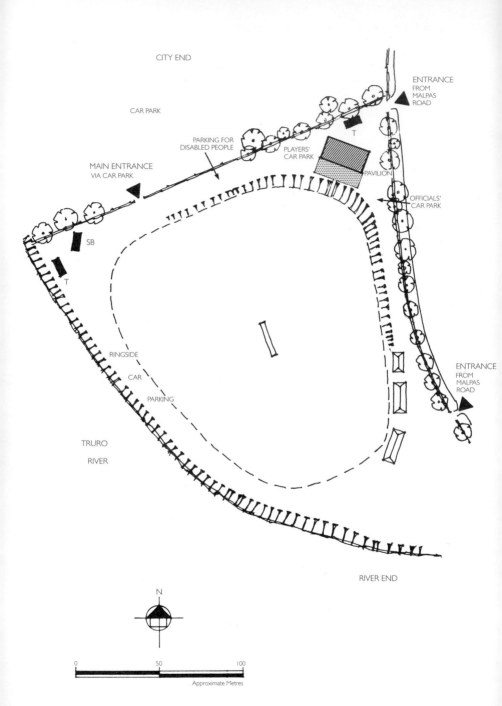

CITY END

CAR PARK

PARKING FOR
DISABLED PEOPLE

PLAYERS'
CAR PARK

ENTRANCE
FROM
MALPAS
ROAD

T

MAIN ENTRANCE
VIA CAR PARK

PAVILION

OFFICIALS'
CAR PARK

SB

T

RINGSIDE

CAR

PARKING

TRURO

RIVER

ENTRANCE
FROM
MALPAS
ROAD

RIVER END

N

0   50   100
Approximate Metres

Highest wicket partnerships for county

1st	32 G.M. Thomas & S.M. Williams	v	Norfolk	(NWT)	2000
2nd	76 S.M. Williams & S.C. Pope	v	Norfolk	(NWT)	2000
3rd	51 J.M. Hands & N.S. Curnow	v	Sussex	(C&G)	2001
4th	39 B. Laity & M.S.T. Dunstan	v	Glamorgan	(GC)	1970
5th	62 J.P. Kent & T.G. Sharp	v	Sussex	(C&G)	2001
6th	11 T.G. Sharp & G.D. Edwards	v	Sussex	(C&G)	2001
7th	33 J.P. Kent & G.D. Edwards	v	Worcestershire	(C&G)	2002
8th	32 G.D. Edwards & T. Edwards	v	Sussex	(C&G)	2001
9th	4 J. Hurrell & B. Read	v	Glamorgan	(GC)	1970
10th	6 J. Hurrell & W.J. Lawry	v	Glamorgan	(GC)	1970

Highest wicket partnerships against county

1st	88 D. Lloyd & B. Wood	for	Lancashire	(GC)	1977
2nd	94 M.W. Goodwin & C.J. Adams	for	Sussex	(C&G)	2001
3rd	41 C.J. Adams & B. Zuiderent	for	Sussex	(C&G)	2001
4th	61 G.A. Hick & D.A. Leatherdale	for	Worcestershire	(C&G)	2002
5th	36 A.R. Lewis & P.M. Walker	for	Glamorgan	(GC)	1970
6th	33 P.M. Walker & K.J. Lyons	for	Glamorgan	(GC)	1970
7th	46* C.J. Rogers & P.J. Free	for	Norfolk	(NWT)	2000
8th	44 J. Simmons & R.M. Ratcliffe	for	Lancashire	(GC)	1977
9th	16* J. Simmons & J. Lyon	for	Lancashire	(GC)	1977
10th	yet to be established				

Best bowling performance in a match for county 5 for 19 C.E. Shreck v Worcestershire (C&G) 2002
Best bowling performance in a match against county 5 for 21 P.M. Walker for Glamorgan (GC) 1970
Largest crowd 2,000 v Worcestershire (C&G) 2002

HOW TO GET THERE

 Truro railway station is situated less than 2 miles from the ground, a comfortable walk away, 08457 484950, www.greatwesternrailways.co.uk. Taxis are always available at the station, City Taxis 0800 318708.

 There are cycle routes to this area of Truro.

 From east: leave A30 at the Carland Cross roundabout at Mitchell (large wind farm) taking the exit to Trispen and Truro, follow signs to Truro city centre, take second exit at the first large roundabout, signposted Malpas. The cricket ground is about 1 mile further on. **From west:** take the Ring Road round the city centre following signs to St Austell, then follow signs to Malpas.

 Plymouth Airport 01752 204090, Newquay Airport 01637 860551

WHERE TO STAY

Alverton Manor (01872 276633), Bay Tree Guest House (01872 240274), Brookdale Hotel (01872 273513), Marcorrie Hotel (01872 277374). For other places to stay in Truro visit www.smoothhound.co.uk.

WHERE TO EAT

Heron Inn, Malpas (01872 272773), Shanaz Indian Restaurant (01872 262123), Stars Restaurant at Hall for Cornwall (01872 262389)

TOURIST INFORMATION Truro Information Bureau, Boscawen Street, Truro, Cornwall 01872 274555, www.truro.gov.uk

LOCAL RADIO STATIONS Radio Cornwall (103.9 MHz), Pirate Radio (102.8 MHz)

LOCAL NEWSPAPERS *West Briton, Western Morning News*

CUMBERLAND

CUMBERLAND COUNTY CRICKET CLUB, 47 BEECH GROVE, STANWIX, CARLISLE, CUMBERLAND CA3 9BG

Telephone	01228 528858
Email	kion47bg@aol.com
Minor Counties Web	www.mcca.cricket.org

Founded 1853
Colours bottle green, gold and red
Crest original Cumberland county crest
Patron R. Bowan
President J.H. Millican
Chairman A.G. Wilson

Secretary K. Ion
Treasurer E. Carter
Team Manager G.W. Johnstone
Cricket Development Officer R. Simpson
Captain J.M. Lewis
Scorer/Statistician G. Minshaw

ACHIEVEMENTS

Minor Counties Championship Champions 1986, 1999
Minor Counties Championship Final Winners 1986

Minor Counties Knockout Cup/Holt Cup/ECB 38 Counties Winners 1989

CUMBERLAND CRICKET BOARD

Chairman A. Wilson
Vice Chairman A. Pemberton
Secretary D. Fallows
Treasurer D. Morewood
Director of Coaching D. Bell
Director of Cricket I. Heath
Director of School & Youth Cricket J. Bryson
Director of Planning & Strategy N. Williamson
Cricket Development Officer R. Simpson
Women & Girls Secretary R. Simpson

GROUNDS

Barrow-in-Furness CC, Ernest Pass Ground, Abbey Road, Barrow-in-Furness (☎ 01229 825201).
Carlisle CC, Edenside, Stanwix Bank, Carlisle (☎ 01228 528593). Just over the bridge on A7 going north out of the City of Carlisle. Ground is left at end of the bridge.
Keswick CC, Fitz Park, Keswick (no ☎ on ground). Leave M6 at junction 40 then take A66 towards Keswick. Take A591 to Keswick. Turn right on to A5271 Penrith Road. Turn right on to Station Road near the Ravensworth Hotel. The cricket ground is on the left.
Millom CC, St. George's Road, Millom (☎ 01657 722839). Enter Millom on A5093. Turn right at T-junction in town centre, and ground is on the left.
Netherfield CC, K Shoes, Parkside Road, Kendal (☎ 01539 724051). (see details opposite)

KENDAL

Address Netherfield Cricket Club, The Pavilion, Netherfield Sports Ground,
Parkside Road, Kendal, Cumbria
Prospects of Play ☎ 01539 724051

HISTORY OF GROUND AND FACILITIES

NETHERFIELD IS A SUBURB of Kendal, situated peacefully in the valley of the River Kent. Parkside Road is the home of Netherfield CC which was established in the 1890s. The club plays in the Northern Cricket League. The original ground was situated opposite the current one, which was bought by K Shoes as a recreation ground for its employees. As K's workforce dwindled, non-employees were allowed to join the cricket club and now make up 90% of the membership.

The 5-acre ground has two cricket fields and also provides facilities for bowls, hockey, soccer and tennis. The playing area measures 138 metres by 140 metres. The pavilion was built in 1960 and has been much extended and improved since then. Netherfield CC field four XIs throughout the season and three junior teams. Some club members have also represented the county.

Cumberland CCC used the ground, one of many in the county, on alternate years until 1982. Since then the improved wicket and facilities have encouraged the county club to use it each season. Several NatWest Trophy 1st round matches have been staged here.

Many past and present Test players have played at Netherfield including Carlisle Best, Rohan Kanhai, Cammie Smith, Mushtaq Mohammad, Collis King, Trevor Franklin, Karsen Ghavri, Brendon Kuruppu, Ravi Shastri, Chetan Sharma, Franklyn Stephenson and Mark Greatbatch.

There is ample car parking available and the ground capacity is 4,500.

GROUND RECORDS AND SCORES

LIMITED-OVERS MATCHES

Highest innings total for county 314 for 9 v Cornwall (NWT) 1999
Highest innings total against county 216 for 4 by Sussex (NWT) 1999
Lowest innings total for county 84 v Lancashire (NWT) 1989
Lowest innings total against county 86 for 6 by Lancashire (NWT) 1989
Highest individual innings for county 138 A.A. Metcalfe v Cornwall (NWT) 1999
Highest individual innings against county 73* J.G. Wright for Derbyshire (NWT) 1984
Highest wicket partnership for county

1st	55 D.J. Pearson & S. Sharp	v	Leicestershire	(NWT)	1994
2nd	43 J.D. Glendenen & A.A. Metcalfe	v	Cornwall	(NWT)	1999
3th	53 M.D. Woods & D. Lloyd	v	Derbyshire	(NWT)	1984
4th	175 A.A. Metcalfe & S.J. O'Shaughnessy	v	Cornwall	(NWT)	1999
5th	99 T.A. Hunte & S.T. Knox	v	Sussex	(NWT)	1999
6th	33 C.J. Stockdale & S.M. Dutton	v	Lancashire	(NWT)	1989
7th	32 D.J. Makinson & D.T. Smith	v	Leicestershire	(NWT)	1994
8th	23 D.J. Parsons & A.G. Wilson	v	Derbyshire	(NWT)	1984
9th	38 M.D. Woods & D. Halliwell	v	Lancashire	(NWT)	1989
10th	5 A.G. Wilson & W.N. Boustead	v	Derbyshire	(NWT)	1984

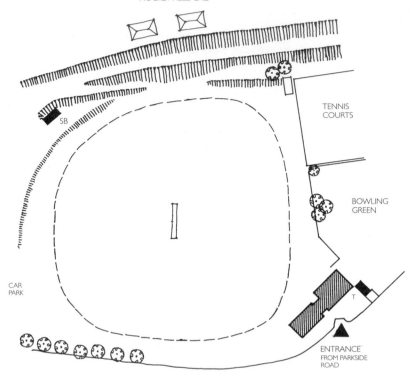

HOCKEY FIELD END

SB

TENNIS COURTS

BOWLING GREEN

CAR PARK

T

ENTRANCE FROM PARKSIDE ROAD

PARKSIDE ROAD END

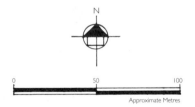

N

| 0 | 50 | 100 |

Approximate Metres

Highest wicket partnership against county

1st	120 R.R. Montgomerie & M.J. DiVenuto	for	Sussex	(NWT)	1999
2nd	60 R.R. Montgomerie & C.J. Adams	for	Sussex	(NWT)	1999
3rd	21 T.G. Sharp & B.F.S. Purchase	for	Cornwall	(NWT)	1999
4th	148* J.J. Whitaker & B.F. Smith	for	Leicestershire	(NWT)	1994
5th	28* R.R. Montgomerie & G.R. Haywood	for	Sussex	(NWT)	1999
6th	31 M. Watkinson & Wasim Akram	for	Lancashire	(NWT)	1989
7th	22 B.F.S. Purchase & C.M. Gazzard	for	Cornwall	(NWT)	1999
8th	9 C.M. Gazzard & C.J. Ellison	for	Cornwall	(NWT)	1999
9th	4 C.M. Gazzard & J.C.J. Stephens	for	Cornwall	(NWT)	1999
10th	16 J.C.J. Stephens & CC Shreck	for	Cornwall	(NWT)	1999

Best bowling performance for county 3 for 24 S. Wall v Lancashire (NWT) 1989
Best bowling performance against county 6 for 24 K.J. Barnett for Derbyshire (NWT) 1984
Largest crowd 2,000 v Derbyshire (NWT) 1984

Kendal station 1 mile, Oxenholme station 1 mile ☎ 08457 484950, www.virgintrains.com

 National Express coaches link Kendal with major cities and towns and local buses link Kendal with the Lake District, ☎ 0870 608 2608, www.gobybus.co.uk

 There are cycle routes to this area of Kendal.

 From north: from M6 junction 37, follow A684 signposted Kendal and town centre for Netherfield Sports Ground situated off Parkside Road or A6 signposted Kendal and town centre. **From south:** from M6 junction 36, follow A590, A591 and A6 signposted Kendal and town centre or A65 signposted Natland and Kendal and town centre, then as north. **From east:** A684 or B6254 signposted Kendal and town centre, then as for north. **From west:** B5284, A591 and A6 signposted Kendal and town centre, then as for north.

WHERE TO STAY

County Hotel (☎ 01539 722461), Grey Gables, Grayrigg (☎ 01539 84345), Riverside Hotel (☎ 01539 724707), Woolpack Hotel (☎ 01539 723852). For other places to stay in the Kendal area visit www.smoothhound.co.uk

TOURIST INFORMATION Kendal Tourist Information Centre

LOCAL RADIO STATION BBC Radio Cumbria (95.6 MHz FM/756 KHz MW)

LOCAL NEWSPAPERS *Barrow Evening Mail, Lancashire Evening Post, Westmorland Gazette*

DEVON

DEVON COUNTY CRICKET CLUB, BLUEBERRY HAVEN, 20 BOUCHER ROAD, BUDLEIGH SALTERTON, DEVON EX9 6JF

Telephone 01395 445216 **fax** 01395 445334
Email geoff.evans@ecb.co.uk
Minor Counties Web www.mcca.cricket.org

Founded 1862
Colours navy blue and sky blue or black, gold and sky-blue
Crest rampant lion or quartered shield in gold depicting crest of Courtenay family (Earls of Devon)
President D.H. Cole
Chairman R. C. Moylan-Jones
Secretary G.R. Evans

Treasurer J. Tozer
Cricket Development Officer S. M. Priscott
Team Manager M.S. Woodward
MCCA Organiser G.R. Evans
Captain R.I. Dawson
Scorer H. Shaw
Statistician H. Shaw

ACHIEVEMENTS

Minor Counties Championship Champions 1978, 1994, 1995, 1996, 1997
Minor Counties Knockout Cup/Holt Cup/ECB 38 Counties Winners 1992, 1994, 1998, 2001

GROUNDS

Bovey Tracey CC, The Recreation Ground, Newton Road, Bovey Tracey (☎ 01626 832061). From A38 follow signs to Bovey Tracey. At roundabout on outskirts of town, take town centre sign and ground is in Newtown Road half a mile on the left.

Exmouth CC, The Pavilion, The Maer Ground, Queens Drive, Exmouth EX8 2AY (☎ 01395 272771). (see details below)

Sidmouth CC, The Fortfield, Sidmouth (☎ 01395 513229). The ground is in Fortfield Terrace just off the seafront.

Torquay CC, Recreation Ground, The Seafront, Torquay (☎ 01803 292001). Head for the Grand Hotel on the seafront and Torquay Railway Station, the ground is opposite behind the trees.

EXMOUTH

Address Exmouth Cricket Club, The Pavilion, The Maer, Queens Drive,
Exmouth, Devon EX8 2AY
Prospects of Play ☎ 01395 272771

HISTORY OF GROUND AND FACILITIES

THE EARLIEST MENTION OF EXMOUTH fielding a club side dates from 1843 when an Exmouth team were reported in *Trueman's Flying Post*, the local newspaper. In all probability they played their matches at Webbers Field in the grounds of what is now the Imperial Hotel. The club moved a quarter of a mile to its present location on the Maer in 1867. The same journal, dated 10 July 1867, reads: 'Since last season the field has been considerably enlarged and the club have erected a very commodious clubhouse, which supplies all the requisites of cricketers.'

Although the pavilion and changing rooms were enlarged in the 1980s, the original character of the pavilion remains with the changing rooms on the ground floor and the clubhouse upstairs. The views over the ground to the south remain as described in 1867 with the western coastline of Lyme Bay and the Exe Estuary set against the backdrop of Haldon Hills. A local historian believes that cricket in the 1860s was something of a diversion for upper class gentlemen who regularly visited the Exmouth and Sidmouth area. This state of affairs persisted well into the 1900s when Exmouth boasted a fixture list that included the MCC, Free Foresters and I' Zingari.

The season of 1912 proved a very wet one, the club ran into financial difficulties and a letter appeared in the *Exmouth Journal* appealing for funds. Following the onset of the First World War in 1914 cricket continued fitfully and most matches involved teams from the services. The club was re-established in

The pavilion at Exmouth CC.

the 1920s and since then has continued to grow. The next watershed in the club's history was in 1950 when Sunday cricket was introduced. This rapidly improved both the playing and financial viability of the club and large crowds were often entertained by an Exmouth Sunday XI playing touring sides and others including the Sunday Crusaders. In 1972 the Devon League was instituted and the quality of Sunday cricket gradually deteriorated. Exmouth was one of the fourteen founding clubs and has gone on to become the league's most successful team, having been league champions on ten occasions with a record of six consecutive titles between 1990 and 1995.

Exmouth CC have always been a strong supporter of Devon County Cricket Club and the demise of Sunday club cricket has coincided with an increase in the number of county representative sides playing at the Maer Ground. The club first hosted Devon playing first-class opposition in 1986 in the NatWest Trophy when Nottinghamshire were the visitors led by Clive Rice and including Derek Randall. Since that time Devon have entertained Essex, Derbyshire, Yorkshire, Leicestershire and Surrey; all played at Exmouth in the early rounds of the NatWest Trophy and subsequently the Cheltenham & Gloucester Trophy. In 2003 Lancashire will play Devon at Exmouth in May with additional one-day and Minor Counties Championship matches taking place during the summer.

The club's entrance is on Queens Drive, the seafront road. The pavilion is on the far side of the ground immediately opposite the entrance below what was once the sea cliff and set alongside lime, chestnut and other deciduous trees. The playing area is large, allowing 60-metre boundaries and still having considerable capacity for spectators and members to drive on to the ground to watch. Visitors are often surprised to find a large fast-draining cricket ground with 18 wickets when the surrounding area is mostly sand dunes. The ground drains very quickly and matches often proceed on time even when the weather leading up to the match has been atrocious.

In the north-west corner of the ground is the equipment building with a spacious scorebox above on the first floor. To the rear of the scorebox is the club's tea hut and tea gardens. The club successfully obtained lottery funding in 1994 for an all-weather enclosed practice area with three full-size nets situated in the north-eastern side of the ground.

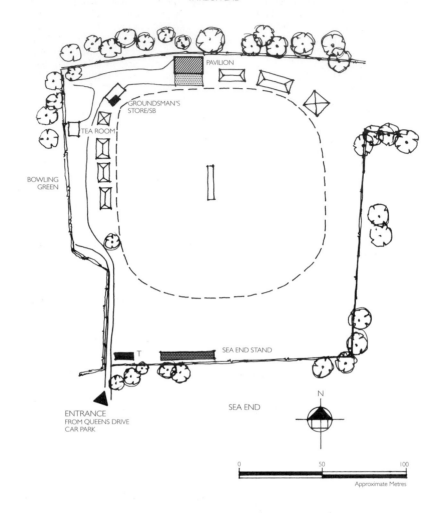

PAVILION END

PAVILION

GROUNDSMAN'S STORE/SB

TEA ROOM

BOWLING GREEN

SEA END STAND

T

SEA END

N

ENTRANCE
FROM QUEENS DRIVE
CAR PARK

0   50   100

Approximate Metres

GROUND RECORDS AND SCORES

LIMITED-OVERS MATCHES

Highest innings total for county 285 for 6 v Cumberland (C&G) 2002
Highest innings total against county 266 for 7 by Derbyshire (NWT) 1993
Lowest innings total for county 80 v Yorkshire (NWT) 1998
Lowest innings total against county 158 by Cumberland (C&G) 2002
Highest individual innings for county 138 R.I. Dawson v Cumberland (C&G) 2002
Highest individual innings against county 103* I.J. Sutcliffe for Leicestershire (NWT) 1997
Highest wicket partnerships for county

1st	38 G.T.J. Townsend & D.F. Lye	v	Bedfordshire	(C&G)	2001
2nd	172 M.P. Hunt & R.I. Dawson	v	Cumberland	(C&G)	2002
3rd	88 N.G. Folland & N.R. Gaywood	v	Nottinghamshire	(NWT)	1986

4th	100 M.J. Wood & D.F. Lye	v	Surrey	(NWT)	2000
5th	100 R.I. Dawson & J.J. Williams	v	Bedfordshire	(C&G)	2001
6th	42 P.M. Roebuck & K. Donohue	v	Derbyshire	(NWT)	1993
7th	39 K. Donohue & T.W. Ward	v	Derbyshire	(NWT)	1993
8th	32 P.A. Brown & R.C. Turpin	v	Nottinghamshire	(NWT)	1986
9th	9* P.M. Roebuck & M.C. Theedom	v	Worcestershire	(NWT)	1999
10th	38 A.C. Cottam & P.M. Warren	v	Leicestershire	(NWT)	1997

Highest wicket partnerships against county

1st	129 A.R. Roberts & N.A. Stanley	for	Bedfordshire	(C&G)	2001
2nd	90 A.D. Brown & A.J. Stewart	for	Surrey	(NWT)	2000
3rd	95* A.J. Stewart & G.P. Thorpe	for	Surrey	(NWT)	2000
4th	35 P.R. Pollard & G.R. Haynes	for	Worcestershire	(NWT)	1999
5th	63 C. White & D.S. Lehmann	for	Yorkshire	(C&G)	2002
6th	87 M.D. Moxon & C. White	for	Yorkshire	(NWT)	1994
7th	67 I.J. Sutcliffe & T.J. Mason	for	Leicestershire	(NWT)	1997
8th	15 I.J. Sutcliffe & G.J. Parsons	for	Leicestershire	(NWT)	1997
9th	44* I.J. Sutcliffe & D.J. Millns	for	Leicestershire	(NWT)	1997
10th	34 D.B. Pennett & M.A. Sharp	for	Cumberland	(C&G)	2002

Best bowling performance in a match for county 4 for 22 M.A.E. Richards v Cumberland (C&G) 2002
Best bowling performance in a match against county 4 for 18 D.G. Cork for Derbyshire (NWT) 1993
Largest crowd 2,000 v Yorkshire (C&G) 2002

HOW TO GET THERE

 A regular train service links Exeter Central and Exeter St David's stations with Exmouth ☎ 08457 484950, www.greatwesternrailways.co.uk

 There is a bus service from the bus station in the centre of the town to the seafront and buses connect Exmouth with Exeter, Budleigh Salterton and Sidmouth.

 There are cycle routes from Exmouth and surrounding areas to this part of the town.

 The Maer Cricket Ground is located on the seafront, to the east of the town centre. From M5 at Exeter take A376 and follow signs for Exmouth town centre passing through Topsham and Lympstone. The cricket ground is off Queens Drive.

 Exeter Airport ☎ 01392 367433

WHERE TO STAY

Aliston House Hotel (☎ 01395 274119), Aston Court Hotel (☎ 01395 263002), Devoncourt Hotel (☎ 01395 272277), Hansard House Hotel (☎ 01395 442773, www.hansardhousehotel.co.uk) Manor Hotel (☎ 01395 274477), Royal Beacon Hotel (☎ 01395 264886). For other places to stay in the Exmouth area visit www.smoothhound.co.uk

WHERE TO EAT

Galley Seafood, Topsham (☎ 01392 876078), Salterton Arms, Budleigh Salterton (☎ 01395 445048), The Clinton Arms (☎ 01395 264054), The Globe Inn, Lympstone (☎ 01395 263166)

TOURIST INFORMATION Exmouth Tourist Information Bureau, Alexandra Terrace, Exmouth EX8 1NZ ☎ 01395 222299, www.exmouthguide.co.uk

LOCAL RADIO STATION BBC Radio Devon

LOCAL NEWSPAPER *Western Morning News*

DORSET

DORSET COUNTY CRICKET CLUB, THE BARN, HIGHER FARM, BAGBER COMMON, STURMINSTER NEWTON, DORSET DT10 2HB

Telephone	01258 473394
Minor Counties Web	www.mcca.cricket.org

Founded 1896
Colours green
Crest three leopards
President D.J.W. Bridge TD
Chairman D.A. Graham
Secretary K.H. House
Assistant Secretary A.J.G. Jones

Treasurers D. Read/N. Woodruffe
Team Manager P. Moxam
Team Secretary K.H. House
Cricket Development Officer K. Brewer
Captain S.W.D. Rintoul
Scorer/Statistician C. Drew

ACHIEVEMENTS

Minor Counties Championship Champions 2000
Minor Counties Knockout Cup/Holt Cup/ECB 38 Counties Winners 1988

DORSET CRICKET BOARD

Chairman K.H. House
Secretary C. Moore
Treasurer J. Ridout
Cricket Development Officer K. Brewer
Women & Girls Secretary J. Bell

GROUNDS

Bournemouth University CC, Dean Park, Cavendish Road, off Wimborne Road, Bournemouth. (see details opposite)
Bournemouth, Bournemouth Sports Club, Chapel Gate Ground, Kinson Park Road, Near Hurn Airport, East Parley, Bournemouth (☎ 01202 581933). Chapel Gate Ground is off B3073 and adjacent to Hurn Airport in East Parley.

BOURNEMOUTH

Address Bournemouth University Cricket Club, The Pavilion, Dean Park, Cavendish Road, Bournemouth, Dorset
Prospects of Play ☎ 01202 25872

HISTORY OF GROUND AND FACILITIES

THE DEAN PARK GROUND was laid out in 1869 and the first match took place in 1871. It was once in Hampshire but boundary changes mean it is now in Dorset. The first county match to be staged here was between Hampshire and Somerset in 1882. In 1897 the initial first-class match took place with the touring Philadelphians. The first County Championship match was played here in 1898 between Hampshire and Somerset.

In 1927 the county club formed a company to take over the lease of the Bournemouth ground from the Cooper-Dean family and in 1948 the ground was taken under the direct control of the Hampshire CCC. Colonel R.A.W. Binny was appointed to manage the club facilities. Formerly part of the Cooper-Dean family estate, Dean Park was one of the few privately owned cricket grounds. It is now leased by Bournemouth University CC. The family continue to support the club and in 1974 Miss A. Ellen Cooper-Dean presented a new scoreboard. This is situated opposite the pavilion which was built in 1902. The ground, which is located in the northern suburb of the town, extends to 4.5 acres and is enclosed by fine trees and residential properties. The entrances are from Cavendish Road, which can be quite difficult to find.

The pavilion, adjoining covered stand, press/scorers' building and players' dining room are permanent structures, together with a new scoreboard and enclosure of tiered benches adjoining the pavilion and groundsman's stores. The playing area is 140 metres by 135 metres, roughly circular, and defined by a rope and advertising boards.

Bournemouth is one of the most pleasant Dorset grounds. W.G. Grace played in the first Bournemouth Festival Week on the ground in 1902.

Dean Park is the ground where Hampshire won the Championship for the first time in 1961 and also where in 1978 they defeated Middlesex to win the John Player Sunday League.

The ground is used by Dorset CCC for Minor Counties Championship matches and home matches in the Cheltenham & Gloucester Trophy.

GROUND RECORDS AND SCORES

LIMITED-OVERS MATCHES

Highest innings total for county 197 for 9 v Bedfordshire (C&G) 2001
Highest innings total against county 333 for 4 for Glamorgan (NWT) 2000
Lowest innings total for county 111 v Essex (NWT) 1983
Lowest innings total against county 71 by Norfolk (NWT) 2000
Highest individual innings for county 81 M.G. Miller v Glamorgan (NWT) 2000
Highest individual innings against county 156 M.T.G. Elliott for Glamorgan (NWT) 2000

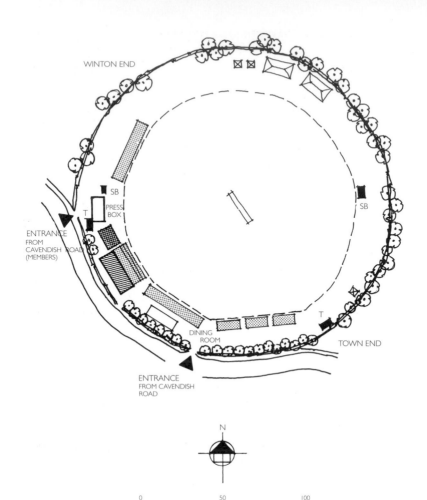

WINTON END

SB

PRESS
BOX
T

SB

ENTRANCE
FROM
CAVENDISH ROAD
(MEMBERS)

DINING
ROOM

T

TOWN END

ENTRANCE
FROM CAVENDISH
ROAD

N

0   50   100
Approximate Metres

Highest wicket partnership for county

1st	25 G.S. Calway & J.A. Claughton	v	Lancashire	(NWT)	1991
2nd	38 J.A. Claughton & J.M.H. Graham-Brown	v	Lancashire	(NWT)	1991
3th	33 R.V. Lewis & S.J. Halliday	v	Essex	(NWT)	1983
4th	64 M. Keech & P.J. Deakin	v	Bedfordshire	(C&G)	2001
5th	44 A.J. Sexton & G.D. Reynolds	v	Norfolk	(NWT)	2000
6th	58 M. Keech & S.W.D. Rintoul	v	Bedfordshire	(C&G)	2001
7th	12 G.D. Reynolds & S.W.D. Rintoul	v	Norfolk	(NWT)	2000
8th	82 M.G. Miller & V.J. Pike	v	Glamorgan	(NWT)	2000
9th	37 S.W.D. Rintoul & K.J. Wilson	v	Bedfordshire	(C&G)	2001
10th	35 V.J. Pike & S.M. Forshaw	v	Glamorgan	(NWT)	2000

Highest wicket partnership against county

1st	246 K. Newell & M.T.G. Elliott	for	Glamorgan	(NWT)	2000
2nd	24 M.T.G. Elliott & A.G. Wharf	for	Glamorgan	(NWT)	2000

3rd	83 M.A. Atherton & N.H. Fairbrother	for	Lancashire	(NWT)	1991
4th	179 R.A. Smith & A.N. Aymes	for	Hampshire	(NWT)	1998
5th	65 R.A. Smith & N.A.M. McLean	for	Hampshire	(NWT)	1998
6th	71* R.A. Smith & A.D. Mascarenhas	for	Hampshire	(NWT)	1998
7th	1 S.J.B. Livermore & P.J. Free	for	Norfolk	(NWT)	2000
8th	1 P.J. Free & J.P. Garner	for	Norfolk	(NWT)	2000
9th	7 J.P. Garner & P.G. Newman	for	Norfolk	(NWT)	2000
10th	0 J.P. Garner & A.R. Clarke	for	Norfolk	(NWT)	2000

Best bowling performance for county 5 for 10 V.J. Pike v Norfolk (NWT) 2000
Best bowling performance against county 4 for 20 S.D.Udal for Hampshire (NWT) 1998
Largest crowd 2,000 v Hampshire (NWT) 1988 (6,000 Hampshire v Middlesex (SL) 1978)

HOW TO GET THERE

 Bournemouth station about 0.5 mile from ground ☎ 08457 484950, www.southwesttrains.co.uk

 Numerous local services to within 0.25 mile of the ground ☎ 0870 608 2608

 There are cycle routes from Bournemouth and surrounding areas to this part of the town.

 From north: from M27 junction 1 take A31. Dean Park is signposted from the A347 junction with the A338 or A348 and A341 to town centre then Wimborne Road for County Cricket. **From east:** from A35 to town centre then as north. **From west:** from A31, A35, A350 or A341 to town centre then as north. Dean Park is situated 1 mile north of the seafront between the A347 Wimborne Road and B3064 Lansdowne Road.

 Bournemouth Airport ☎ 01202 364000

WHERE TO STAY

Belvedere Hotel (☎ 0500 657895), Carlton Hotel (☎ 01202 552011), Pavilion Hotel (☎ 01202 291266). For other places to stay in the Bournemouth area visit www.smoothhound.co.uk or www.bournemouth.gov.uk.

TOURIST INFORMATION Bournemouth Tourist Information Centre, www.bournemouth.gov.uk

LOCAL RADIO STATIONS BBC Radio Solent (96.1 MHz FM/1359 KHz MW), Two Counties Radio (97.2 MHz FM/828 KHz MW), Ocean Sound (103.2 MHz FM/1557 KHz MW)

LOCAL NEWSPAPERS *Bournemouth Evening Echo*, *Southern Evening Echo*, *The News*

HEREFORDSHIRE

HEREFORDSHIRE COUNTY CRICKET CLUB, 5 DALE DRIVE, HOMER GRANGE, HEREFORD HR4 9RF

Telephone	01432 264703
Web	www.mcca.cricket.org
Email	pete.sykes@freeuk.com
Minor Counties Web	www.mcca.cricket.org

Founded 1991
Colours maroon and azure
Crest lion and bull either side of the River Wye
Patron Sir Paul Getty KBE
President J.E. Chadd
Chairman G. Jones
Secretary P. Sykes
Treasurer D.R. Wood

Fixture Secretary J. Sandford
Membership Secretary D. James
Match Manager, Advertising and Sponsorship D. Hince
Team Secretary B. Smith
Promotions J. Beaman
Captain C.W. Boroughs
Scorer/Statistician J. Morris

ACHIEVEMENTS

Minor Counties Championship Champions 2002
Minor Counties Knockout Cup/Holt Cup/ECB 38 Counties Champions 2000, Runners-up 1995

HEREFORDSHIRE CRICKET BOARD

Chairman M. Cronin
Secretary P. Sykes
Treasurer J. Beaman
Cricket Development Officer C. Dirkin

GROUNDS

Brockhampton CC, The Parks, nr Brockhampton Court Hotel, Brockhampton (no ☎ on ground). Signposted off Hereford to Ross-on-Wye road (B4224) between Fownhope (1.6 miles) and How Caple.
Colwall CC, Cricket Ground, nr Railway Bridge, Stowe Lane, Colwall (☎ 01684 541050). Entering village from Ledbury (B4218), pass over railway bridge. Stowe Lane is on the immediate left as you leave the bridge.
Hereford City CC, Hereford City Sports Club, Racecourse Cricket Ground, Grandstand Road, Hereford (☎ 01432 354221). (see details below)
Kington CC, Recreation Ground, Kington (☎ 01544 230095). Ground is in the centre of town. Bear left past the Burton Hotel and the ground is 200 yards on the left.
Luctonians CC, Kingsland Village, Kingsland (☎ 01568 708345). From Hereford take (A4110) towards Knighton. The ground is on the left, at junction with the (B4360), as you leave Kingsland village.
Leominster, Dales CC, F.H. Dale & Company Sports Ground, Mill Street, Leominster (no ☎ on ground). At the roundabout at the northern end roundabout of the bypass, turn left into town over level crossing. Ground is on the left.

HEREFORD

Address Hereford Cricket Club, Hereford City Sports Club, Racecourse Cricket Ground, Grandstand Road, Hereford
Prospects of Play ☎ 01432 354221

HISTORY OF GROUND AND FACILITIES

THE GROUND IS PART of the Hereford racecourse complex and has been the home of the town's cricket club since 1909. The club was founded in 1836 and played at Widemarsh Common until the move to the present ground.

Widemarsh Common and the Westfield racecourse were both part of the same area until separated by a new road. The pavilion, which was built at the common in 1889, is still in use today. The first first-class match was in 1919 when Worcestershire played H.K. Foster's XI; the game was part of the county's programme after they decided not to re-enter the County Championship after the First World War. Hereford hosted later matches for H.K. Foster's XI, including a match with the Australian Imperial Forces touring side. In another friendly first-class match in 1947, Worcestershire played the Combined Services XI. With the formation of the County of Hereford and Worcestershire, first-class cricket returned to the Racecourse Ground after 34 years with the visit of Glamorgan in 1981. Subsequent games included visits from Kent and Leicestershire. In 1983 the first limited-overs match was staged with Nottinghamshire in the John Player Sunday League and later years have seen Sunday League matches with Gloucestershire and Surrey in the Refuge Assurance Sunday League. Middlesex were due to visit in 1984 but the fixture was transferred to Worcester.

The Old Grandstand Pavilion was demolished in 2001 and a special needs school was built on the site. This structure incorporates a new cricket pavilion. Because the ground is in the middle of the racecourse the playing area is some way from the pavilion. Players therefore view the match from a tent adjoining the press and scorers' tents in the south-west corner of the ground. The playing area is 140 metres by 120 metres and is defined by a rope and advertising boards. The radio commentary and TV camera/commentary box positions are at the Grandstand Road End.

Until 2002, Hereford CC played in the Three Counties League which was formed in 1968 and includes club sides from Hereford, Gloucestershire and South Wales. The club won the First XI League nine times after 1972 and the Second XI on three occasions. They are now members of the Worcestershire County League. Reg Perks and Peter Richardson both played for Hereford CC and represented Worcestershire CCC and England during their careers.

Since 1992 the Racecourse Ground has been used for home Minor Counties Championship matches by Herefordshire CCC.

GROUND RECORDS AND SCORES

LIMITED-OVERS MATCHES

(No Herefordshire matches – Worcestershire records on ground)
Highest innings total for Worcestershire 233 for 6 v Gloucestershire (SL) 1986
Highest innings total against Worcestershire 230 by Gloucestershire (SL) 1986
Lowest innings total for Worcestershire 195 for 9 v Nottinghamshire (SL) 1983
Lowest innings total against Worcestershire 154 by Surrey (SL) 1987
Highest individual innings for Worcestershire 86 P.A. Neale v Nottinghamshire (SL) 1983
Highest individual innings against Worcestershire 108 R.C. Russell for Gloucestershire (SL) 1986
Highest wicket partnerships for Worcestershire

1st	130 T.S. Curtis & I.T. Botham	v	Surrey	(SL)	1987
2nd	52 D.N. Patel & P.A. Neale	v	Nottinghamshire	(SL)	1983
3rd	81 T.S. Curtis & D.N. Patel	v	Gloucestershire	(SL)	1986
4th	22 D.N. Patel & P.A. Neale	v	Gloucestershire	(SL)	1986
5th	41 P.A. Neale & D.B. D'Oliveira	v	Nottinghamshire	(SL)	1983
6th	3 S.J. Rhodes & M.J. Weston	v	Gloucestershire	(SL)	1986
7th	29* M.J. Weston & P.J. Newport	v	Gloucestershire	(SL)	1986
8th	16 P.A. Neale & P. Moores	v	Nottinghamshire	(SL)	1983
9th	4 P. Moores & A.P. Pridgeon	v	Nottinghamshire	(SL)	1983
10th	yet to be established				

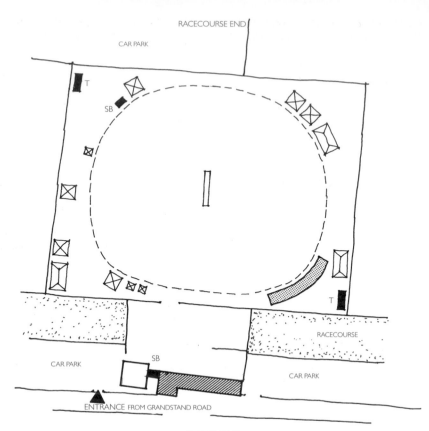

RACECOURSE END

CAR PARK

T

SB

RACECOURSE

CAR PARK

SB

CAR PARK

ENTRANCE FROM GRANDSTAND ROAD

PAVILION END

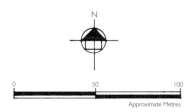

N

0	50	100

Approximate Metres

Highest wicket partnerships against Worcestershire

1st	55 P.W. Romaines & R.C. Russell	for	Gloucestershire	(SL)	1986
2nd	112 S.B. Hassan & C.E.B. Rice	for	Nottinghamshire	(SL)	1983
3rd	51 C.E.B. Rice & J.D. Birch	for	Nottinghamshire	(SL)	1983
4th	33 R.C. Russell & K.P. Tomlins	for	Gloucestershire	(SL)	1986
5th	77 R.C. Russell & M.W. Alleyne	for	Gloucestershire	(SL)	1986
6th	36 M.W. Alleyne & A.J. Wright	for	Gloucestershire	(SL)	1986
7th	10 C.J. Richards & I.A. Greig	for	Surrey	(SL)	1987
8th	3 M.W. Alleyne & P.H. Twizell	for	Gloucestershire	(SL)	1986
9th	45 C.K. Bullen & A.H. Gray	for	Surrey	(SL)	1987
10th	5 M.W. Alleyne & D.A. Burrows	for	Gloucestershire	(SL)	1986

Best bowling performance in a match for Worcestershire 3 for 23 A.P. Pridgeon v Gloucestershire (SL) 1986
Best bowling performance in a match against Worcestershire 2 for 39 M. Hendrick for Nottinghamshire (SL) 1983
Largest crowd 7,500 v Surrey (SL) 1987

HOW TO GET THERE

 Hereford station 1.5 miles ☎ 08457 484950, 08457 000125, 0121 643 4444,
www.greatwesterntrains.co.uk, www.centraltrains.co.uk

 Midland Red West 102, 112 from city centre (104, 105 and 115 link Hereford station with city centre)
☎ 0870 608 2608

 There are cycle routes to this area of the city.

 From north: A49 or A4110 signposted Hereford and city centre, follow signs Racecourse and Grandstand Road for Hereford Sports Club. **From south:** A49 or B4224 or B4399 signposted Hereford and city centre, then follow signs Leominster A49 into Grandstand Road. **From east:** A465 or A438 signposted Hereford and city centre, then as south. **From west:** A438 or A465 signposted Hereford and city centre, then as south.

WHERE TO STAY

Green Dragon Hotel (☎ 01432 272506), Three Counties Hotel (☎ 01432 299955)
    For other places to stay in and around Hereford visit www.smoothhound.co.uk or www.hereford.gov.uk.

TOURIST INFORMATION Hereford Tourist Information Centre, www.hereford.gov.uk

LOCAL RADIO STATIONS Radio Wyvern (102 MHz FM/1530 KHz MW), Severn Sound (95.0 MHz FM/774 KHz MW), BBC Radio Hereford & Worcestershire (94.7 MHz FM)

LOCAL NEWSPAPER *Hereford Times*

HERTFORDSHIRE

HERTFORDSHIRE COUNTY CRICKET CLUB, 16 LANDFORD CLOSE, RICKMANSWORTH, HERTFORDSHIRE WD3 1NG

Telephone 01923 772755 (home) **fax** 01923 711683
Email mulhollandbrian@aol.com
Minor Counties Web www.mcca.cricket.org

Founded 1876
Colours blue, green and yellow
Crest white hart on blue background
President R.G. Simons
Chairman A.G. Buchanan

Match Manager B. Mulholland
Treasurer R.J.A. Abraham
Captain D.M. Ward
Scorers/Statisticians B. Mulholland/A.C.S. Gibbs

ACHIEVEMENTS

Minor Counties Championship Champions 1936, 1975, 1983, 1990
Minor Counties Championship Final Winners 1990

Minor Counties Knockout Cup/Holt Cup/ECB 38 Counties Winners 1984

HERTFORDSHIRE CRICKET ASSOCIATION

President D.W.S. Beynon
Chairman A. Buchanan
Secretary D.S. Dredge
Treasurer R.J.A. Abraham
Youth Administrator C. Stringer
Membership Secretary M.J. Arnold
Women & Girls Secretary S. Humphrey

GROUNDS

Bishop's Stortford CC, The Pavilion, Cricket Field Lane, Bishop's Stortford (☎ 01279 654463). (see details below)

Harpenden CC, The Common. Harpenden (☎ 01582 763620). The Common is on A1081 opposite Rothamsted Experimental Station.

Hertford CC, Balls Park, Mangrove Road, Hertford (☎ 01992 581983). From A10 take A414 to Hertford and turn left at sign to Balls Park, take third left along Mangrove Road.

Long Marston CC, Marlins Ground, Cheddington Lane, Long Marston, nr Tring (☎ 01296 661706). Six miles east of Aylesbury. From Hemel Hempstead, leave A41(M) at end and take second exit, turn left in 1 mile at roundabout, and follow signs for Long Marston. Turn right at crossroads in Long Marston Village and ground is on left behind wooden open fence.

Radlett CC, Pavilion, Brunton Memorial Ground, Cobden Hill, Watling Street, Radlett (☎ 01923 856348). Ground is located off A5 (Watling Street), Radlett High Street, at London side of town. Left between houses into Cobden Hill for Tabard Rugby Club and Radlett Cricket Club beyond.

Welwyn Garden City CC, Digswell Park, Knightsfield, Welwyn Garden City (☎ 01727 327354). Leave A1(M) at junction 6. Follow signs for Welwyn Garden City, pass school and take first right at roundabout into Knightsfield. Digswell Park is half a mile on left. Look for the giant topiary chicken!

BISHOP'S STORTFORD

Address Bishop's Stortford Cricket Club, The Pavilion, Cricket Field Lane, Bishop's Stortford, Hertfordshire
Prospects of Play ☎ 01279 654463

HISTORY OF GROUND AND FACILITIES

CRICKET FIELD LANE is the home of Bishop's Stortford Cricket Club which was established in 1825. The earliest recorded match on the ground took place on 16 June 1834 when Matching played Stortford. In 1844 matches were staged with the Cambridge Town Club both at Bishop's Stortford and at Fenner's in Cambridge and by 1856 games were being played against Southgate CC for the first time. In 1862 and 1867 the club played All England XIs and in 1903 and 1904 the club side included A.E.J. Collins who had amassed 628 at Clifton College, Bristol, in 1899.

Bishop's Stortford play in the Saracens Hertfordshire County League and have reached Lord's twice in the John Haig/William Younger Cup – in 1978 v Cheltenham and in 1984 v Old Hill.

The club has always had a strong Lancashire connection and the Manchester-based county regularly visit Cricket Field Lane for benefit matches, other fixtures permitting. Recent years have seen matches staged for Neil Fairbrother and Ian Austin, as well as Lord's Taverners and Minor Counties Championship games. Bishop's Stortford has only once hosted a first-class county in a NatWest Trophy match: on 26 and 27 June 1991 when Hertfordshire defeated Derbyshire in a bowl-out – the first ever in the competition although a match at The Oval between Surrey and Oxfordshire was decided by the same method two hours later on the same day.

The only permanent buildings on the ground are the pavilion, clubhouse, scoreboard and groundsman's store.

GROUND RECORDS AND SCORES

LIMITED-OVERS MATCHES

Highest innings total for county 213 for 3 v Sussex CB (NWT) 1999
Highest innings total against county 209 for 9 by Sussex CB (NWT) 1999
Lowest innings total for county 213 for 3 v Sussex CB (NWT) 1999
Lowest innings total against county 209 for 9 by Sussex CB (NWT) 1999
Highest individual innings for county 83* D.M. Ward v Sussex CB (NWT) 1999
Highest individual innings against county 92 M. Newell for Sussex (NWT) 1999
Highest wicket partnership for county

1st	24 M.H. James & M.A. Everett	v	Sussex CB	(NWT)	1999
2nd	26 M.H. James & D.M. Ward	v	Sussex CB	(NWT)	1999
3th	45 D.M. Ward & K. Jahangir	v	Sussex CB	(NWT)	1999
4th	118* D.M. Ward & A.D. Griffin	v	Sussex CB	(NWT)	1999
5th–10th – yet to be established

Highest wicket partnership against county

1st	16 P.J. Stephens & M.H. Yardy	for	Sussex CB	(NWT)	1999
2nd	0 P.J. Stephens & I. Cox	for	Sussex CB	(NWT)	1999
3rd	54 I. Cox & M. Newell	for	Sussex CB	(NWT)	1999
4th	32 M. Newell & C.M. Mole	for	Sussex CB	(NWT)	1999
5th	62 M. Newell & B. Smith	for	Sussex CB	(NWT)	1999
6th	2 M. Newell & D.A. Alderman	for	Sussex CB	(NWT)	1999
7th	10 M. Newell & S. Simmonds	for	Sussex CB	(NWT)	1999
8th	6 S. Simmonds & S.J. Jurgensen	for	Sussex CB	(NWT)	1999
9th	1 S. Simmonds & B.A. Chambers	for	Sussex CB	(NWT)	1999
10th	26* S. Simmonds & J.J. Newell	for	Sussex CB	(NWT)	1999

Best bowling performance for county 3 for 34 S.J.W. Andrew v Sussex CB (NWT) 1999
Best bowling performance against county 2 for 50 S. Simmonds for Sussex CB (NWT) 1999
Largest crowd 1,000 v Sussex CB (NWT) 1999

HOW TO GET THERE

 Bishop's Stortford station 0.5 mile ☎ 08457 484950, www.wagntrains.co.uk

 There are buses from most areas of Hertfordshire and Essex to Bishop's Stortford ☎ 0870 608 2608

 There are cycle routes to this area of the town.

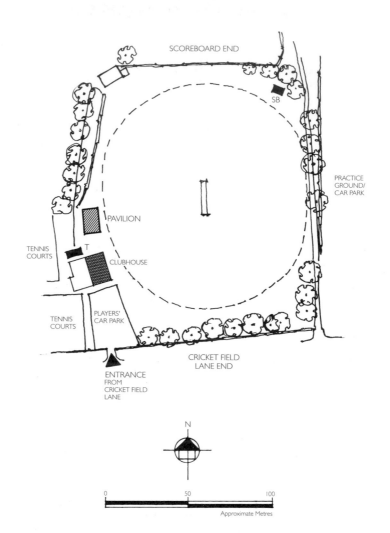

 The ground in Cricket Field Lane is 0.25 mile from the A120 and A1250 road junction to the west of Bishop's Stortford town centre.

 Cambridge Airport ☎ 01223 373737, London Stansted Airport ☎ 08700 000303

WHERE TO STAY

For a selection of places to stay in the Bishop's Stortford area visit www.smoothhound.co.uk

TOURIST INFORMATION Hertford Tourist Information Centre, www.hertford.gov.uk

LOCAL RADIO STATIONS Greater London Radio (94.9 MHz FM/1458 KHz MW), Capital Radio (95.8 MHz FM/1548 KHz MW), LBC (97.3 MHz FM/1152 KHz MW)

LOCAL NEWSPAPERS *Evening Standard, Hertfordshire Advertiser*

LINCOLNSHIRE

LINCOLNSHIRE COUNTY CRICKET CLUB, FIRST FLOOR, 27 THE FORUM, NORTH HYKEHAM, LINCOLN, LINCOLNSHIRE LN6 9HW

Telephone 01522 688008 (office) 01522 688093 (home)
Fax 01522 688073 (home)
Minor Counties Web www.mcca.cricket.org

Founded 1870
Colours gold and green
Crest a Lincoln imp
President W.A. Bradford
Chairman E.N. Hamilton
Secretary C.A. North

Treasurer C.J. Thomas
Cricket Development Officer M.A. Fell
Captain M.A. Fell
Scorers L. Freeman, S. Clayton
Statistician L. Freeman

ACHIEVEMENTS

Minor Counties Championship Champions 1966, 2001 (Joint)

Minor Counties Knockout Cup/Holt Cup/ECB 38 Counties Finalists 1990

LINCOLNSHIRE CRICKET BOARD

Secretary C.A. North
Treasurer D. Savage
Cricket Development Officer M. Fell
Women & Girls Secretary N. Young

GROUNDS

Sleaford CC, London Road, Sleaford (☎ 01529 303368). The ground is just off the town centre, off the A153 in London Road, south of the railway level crossing in Bourne Road.
Grantham CC, Gorse Lane, Grantham (☎ 01476 563953). Go south on the old A1 towards Colsterworth. The ground is about 1 mile from town centre on the right.
Lincoln, Lindum Sports Association CC, St Giles Avenue, Wragby Road, Lincoln (☎ 01522 526592). (see details over)
Cleethorpes CC, Chichester Road, Cleethorpes (☎ 01472 691271). (see details in Nottinghamshire section)

LINCOLN

Address Lindum Sports Club, Pavilion, St Giles Avenue, Lincoln
Prospects of Play ☎ 01522 526592

HISTORY OF GROUND AND FACILITIES

THE LINDUM SPORTS CLUB is one of the venues used by Lincolnshire County Cricket Club for home Minor Counties Championship fixtures.

In 1969 the Minor Counties played the New Zealand touring team at Lindum Sports Club. Four other one-day matches have been staged at the ground: 1974 Lincolnshire v Surrey in the Gillette Cup, 1979 Minor Counties North v Kent in the Benson and Hedges Cup zonal round, 1997 Lincolnshire v Derbyshire in the NatWest Trophy 1st round and in 2001 Lincolnshire v Berkshire in the Cheltenham & Gloucester Trophy 1st round. In May 2003 Lincolnshire are due to host neighbours Nottinghamshire at Lindum Sports Club in the Cheltenham & Gloucester Trophy 1st round.

In 1982 a Vivian Richards Benefit Match was staged at the ground between a Vic Lewis All Stars XI and Somerset CCC.

The pavilion is extensive and is sited to the north-west of the playing area. The scoreboard is to the south-east.

GROUND RECORDS AND SCORES

LIMITED-OVERS MATCHES

Highest innings total for county 243 for 8 v Berkshire (C&G) 2001
Highest innings total against county 266 for 5 by Surrey (GC) 1974
Lowest innings total for county 116 v Derbyshire (NWT) 1997
Lowest innings total against county 157 by Berkshire (C&G) 2001
Highest individual innings for county 76 J. Trower v Berkshire (C&G) 2001
Highest individual innings against county 76 Younis Ahmed by Surrey (GC) 1974
Highest wicket partnerships for county

1st	7 G. Robinson & T. Johnson	v	Surrey	(GC)	1974
2nd	45 J. Trower & R.W.J. Howitt	v	Berkshire	(C&G)	2001
3rd	69 J. Trower & J. Clarke	v	Berkshire	(C&G)	2001
4th	26 M.R. Gouldstone & M.A. Fell	v	Derbyshire	(NWT)	1997
5th	15 M.A. Fell & S.N. Warman	v	Berkshire	(C&G)	2001
6th	62 M. Maslin & C.A. Richardson	v	Surrey	(GC)	1974
7th	35 M.A. Fell & D.A. Christmas	v	Berkshire	(C&G)	2001
8th	50 M.A. Fell & S.A. Bradford	v	Derbyshire	(NWT)	1997
9th	18* M.A. Fell & D.J. Pipes	v	Berkshire	(C&G)	2001
10th	5 S.A. Bradford & S. Oakes	v	Derbyshire	(NWT)	1997

Highest wicket partnerships against county

1st	40 G.P. Howarth & J.H. Edrich	for	Surrey	(GC)	1974
2nd	63 A.S. Rollins & C.J. Adams	for	Derbyshire	(NWT)	1997
3rd	136 D.R. Owen-Thomas & Younis Ahmed	for	Surrey	(GC)	1974
4th	38 Younis Ahmed & S.J. Storey	for	Surrey	(GC)	1974
5th	2 Younis Ahmed & G.R.J. Roope	for	Surrey	(GC)	1974
6th	48* G.R.J. Roope & R.D. Jackman	for	Surrey	(GC)	1974
7th	31 R.P. Davis & T.L. Lambert	for	Berkshire	(C&G)	2001

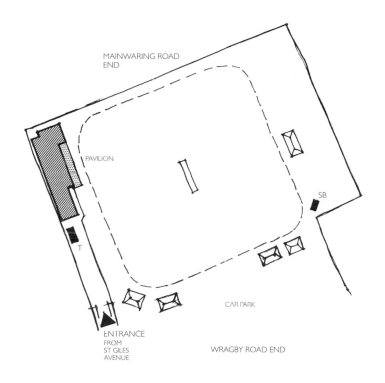

MAINWARING ROAD END

PAVILION

SB

T

CAR PARK

ENTRANCE FROM ST GILES AVENUE

WRAGBY ROAD END

N

0   50   100

Approximate Metres

8th	51 R.P. Davis & M.J. O'Sullivan	for	Berkshire	(C&G)	2001
9th	0 R.P. Davis & J.K. Barrow	for	Berkshire	(C&G)	2001
10th	5 R.P. Davis & N.A. Denning	for	Berkshire	(C&G)	2001

Best bowling performance in a match for county 4 for 18 R.J. Chapman v Berkshire (C&G) 2001
Best bowling performance in a match against county 5 for 15 G.G. Arnold by Surrey (GC) 1974
Largest crowd 2,000 v Derbyshire (NWT) 1997

HOW TO GET THERE

 Lincoln station 1.5 miles ☎ 08457 225225, www.gner.co.uk

 Local buses to Lincoln bus station thence 10 minute walk to ground ☎ 0870 608 2608

 There are cycle paths and routes from surrounding areas of Lincoln to this area of the city.

From all directions: Ground is located in St Giles Avenue off Wragby Road. Follow A158 north through Lincoln city centre, pass the Cathedral in the distance on the left, and the Lincoln Lindum Cricket Ground is behind the fencing on the left-hand side of the road.

WHERE TO STAY

D'isney Place Hotel (☎ 01522 538881), Washingborough Hall (☎ 01522 790340), The Castle Hotel (☎ 01522 538801)

For other places to stay in and around Lincoln visit www.smoothhound.co.uk or www.lincoln.gov.uk.

LOCAL RADIO STATION BBC Radio Lincolnshire (95.9 MHz FM/1485 KHz MW)

LOCAL NEWSPAPER *Lincolnshire Echo*

NORFOLK

S.J. SKINNER, HONORARY SECRETARY, NORFOLK COUNTY CRICKET CLUB, 27 COLKETT DRIVE, OLD CATTON, NORWICH, NORFOLK NR6 7ND

Telephone	01603 485940 (home) 01603 624236 (office)
Minor Counties Web	www.mcca.cricket.org

Founded 1827
Colours blue and white
Crest county arms of Norfolk
Patrons HM The Queen, HRH Prince Philip
  The Duke of Edinburgh
President D.J.M. Armstrong

Chairman K. Bray
Hon Secretary S.J. Skinner
Treasurer D.S. Honnor
Captain P.J. Bradshaw
Scorer/Statistician R.D. Grimes

ACHIEVEMENTS

Minor Counties Championship Champions 1905, 1910, 1913, Joint Champions 1895, 2002

Minor Counties Knockout Cup/Holt Cup/ECB 38 Counties Winners 1986, 1997, 2001

NORFOLK CRICKET BOARD

Chairman D.R. Goodrum
Secretary/Treasurer D.P. Cousins
Cricket Development Officer G. Batley
Women & Girls Secretary V. Boon

GROUNDS

Horsford CC, Manor Park Cricket Ground, Holt Road, Horsford, Hellesdon, Norwich (☎ 01603 424635). (see details opposite)

HORSFORD

Address Horsford Cricket Club, Manor Park Cricket Ground,
Holt Road, Horsford, Hellesdon, Norwich, Norfolk
Prospects of Play ☎ 01603 424635

MANOR PARK SPORTS CLUB is the home of Horsford Cricket Club. The ground staged two one-day matches in 1986, but has since been redeveloped to replace Lakenham Cricket Ground as the home of Norfolk cricket from the end of the 2000 season. The Manor Park Sports Club ground is used by Norfolk CCC for the annual Norfolk Cricket Festival of Minor Counties Championship matches. The ground is fully equipped with a pavilion, scoreboard, groundsman's buildings and ample marquees, tents and, when necessary, temporary facilities.

The ground was first used for a Cheltenham & Gloucester Trophy match with Wales MC in 2001.

GROUND RECORDS AND SCORES

LIMITED-OVERS MATCHES

Highest innings total for county 317 for 8 v Leicestershire CB (ECB38) 2001
Highest innings total against county 341 for 6 by Kent (C&G) 2002
Lowest innings total for county 151 v Wales MC (C&G) 2001
Lowest innings total against county 86 by Huntingdonshire (ECB38) 2002
Highest individual innings for county 139* C.J. Rogers v Holland (C&G) 2001
Highest individual innings against county 77 R.W.T. Key for Kent (C&G) 2002
Highest wicket partnership for county

1st	64 C. Amos & C.J. Rogers	v	Kent	(C&G)	2002
2nd	180 C.J. Rogers & J.R. Walker	v	Holland	(C&G)	2001
3rd	164 C. Amos & S.C. Goldsmith	v	Leicestershire CB	(ECB38)	2001
4th	118 S.C. Goldsmith & S.J.B. Livermore	v	Nottinghamshire CB	(ECB38)	2002
5th	48 S.J.B. Livermore & C.R. Borrett	v	Leicestershire CB	(ECB38)	2001
6th	75 R.D. Huggins & D.E. Mattocks	v	Suffolk	(MCCA KO)	1986
7th	43* D.E. Mattocks & R.A. Bunting	v	Suffolk	(MCCA KO)	1986
8th	52 C. Brown & P.J. Bradshaw	v	Kent	(C&G)	2002
9th	19* P.J. Bradshaw & J.P. Taylor	v	Kent	(C&G)	2002
10th	24* P.J. Bradshaw & P.G. Newman	v	Nottinghamshire CB	(ECB38)	2002

Highest wicket partnership against county

1st	79 M.V. Fleming & R.W.T. Key	for	Kent	(C&G)	2002
2nd	65 R.W.T. Key & J.B. Hockley	for	Kent	(C&G)	2002
3rd	84 H.J.C. Mol & D.J. Reekers	for	Holland	(C&G)	2001
4th	58 J.B. Hockley & D.P. Fulton	for	Kent	(C&G)	2002
5th	68 D.P. Fulton & M.A. Ealham	for	Kent	(C&G)	2002
6th	43 M.A. Ealham & P.A. Nixon	for	Kent	(C&G)	2002
7th	26 A. Akhtar & M.W. Thomas	for	Cambridgeshire	(ECB38)	2001
8th	37 L.O. Jones & A.D. Towse	for	Wales MC	(C&G)	2001
9th	36* S.R. Porter & K.A. Arnold	for	Oxfordshire	(MCCA KO)	1986
10th	16 A. Raja & S.N. Abbas	for	Holland	(C&G)	2001

Best bowling performance for county 4 for 22 C.R. Borrett v Leicestershire CB (ECB38) 2001
Best bowling performance against county 5 for 18 M.P.L. Bulbeck for Somerset CB (C&G) 2001
Largest crowd 713 v Kent (C&G) 2002

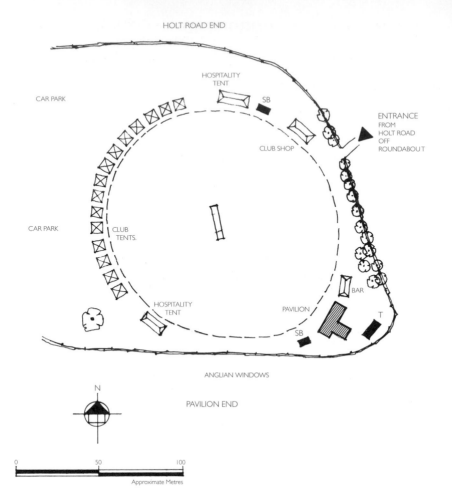

HOLT ROAD END

HOSPITALITY
TENT

CAR PARK

SB

ENTRANCE
FROM
HOLT ROAD
OFF
ROUNDABOUT

CLUB SHOP

CAR PARK

CLUB
TENTS.

HOSPITALITY
TENT

PAVILION

BAR

T

SB

ANGLIAN WINDOWS

N

PAVILION END

0   50   100

Approximate Metres

HOW TO GET THERE

 Norwich 5 miles ☎ 08459 505000, 020 7247 5488, www.yourtrain.co.uk

 ☎ 0870 608 2608, www.gobybus.co.uk

 There are cycle routes from Norwich to this area.

 Manor Park Sports Club is the home of Horsford Cricket Club and is located off the roundabout at the junction of the A140 and B1149 (the Cromer and Holt roads), about 1 mile beyond Norwich Airport.

 Norwich Airport ☎ 01603 411923

WHERE TO STAY

Barnham Broom Hotel (☎ 01603 759393), Quality Hotel (☎ 01603 741161), Petersfield House Hotel (☎ 01692 630741)

For further small hotels and guest houses in this area visit www.smoothhound.co.uk or www.norwich.gov.uk
TOURIST INFORMATION Norwich Tourist Information Centre www.norwich.gov.uk

LOCAL RADIO STATION BBC Radio Norfolk (95.1FM, 855MW (East); 104.4FM, 873 MW (West))

LOCAL NEWSPAPER *Eastern Daily Press, Eastern Evening News*

NORTHUMBERLAND

NORTHUMBERLAND COUNTY CRICKET CLUB, COUNTY CRICKET GROUND, OSBORNE AVENUE, JESMOND, NEWCASTLE UPON TYNE NE2 1JS

Telephone 0191 281 2738 (Club office) 0191 213 1152 (home)
Minor Counties Web www.mcca.cricket.org

Founded 1895
Colours red, green and gold
Crest county shield of Northumberland
President W.J. Peacock
Chairman A. McKenna
Secretary A.B. Stephenson
Treasurer N. Walton

Team Manager W.H. Graham
Captain P.J. Nicholson
Cricket Development Officer I. Wardle
Groundsman B. Marshall
Scorers R. Dodds, P.W.R. Lough
Historian/Statistician J.H. Jude

ACHIEVEMENTS

Minor Counties Championship Runners-up after play-offs 1924, 1925, 1955, 1956

NORTHUMBERLAND CRICKET BOARD

Chairman S. Lunn
Secretary R. Ayton
Treasurer T.D. Spraggon
Delegate R. Perry
Cricket Development Officer I. Wardle

GROUNDS

County Cricket Ground, Osborne Avenue, Jesmond, Newcastle-upon-Tyne (☎ 0191 281 0775). (see details over)
South Northumberland CC, Roseworth Terrace, Gosforth (☎ 0191 285 6716). Leave city centre on B1318 north to Gosforth, turn right at Lloyds Bank off Gosforth High Street. A car park is next to the ground.
Tynemouth CC, Preston Avenue, adjacent Percy Park Rugby Football Club Ground, Tynemouth, North Shields (☎ 0191 257 6865). Take the A1058 coast road from Newcastle city centre to Billy Mount roundabout, into Queen Alexandra Road, turn left into Preston Road and right into Preston Avenue. Ground is next to Percy Park RFC.

JESMOND

Address Northumberland County Cricket Club, The Pavilion, County Cricket
Ground, Osborne Avenue, Jesmond, Newcastle-upon-Tyne NE2 1JS
Prospects of Play ☎ 0191 281 2738

HISTORY OF GROUND AND FACILITIES

THE CRICKET GROUND AT OSBORNE AVENUE, Jesmond, was opened in 1887 and
was then known as the new Recreation Ground for the Newcastle Police
Constabulary.

Northumberland CCC was founded in December 1895 and acquired the
ground in March 1897. The county's first match here was against Durham CCC
on 7 and 8 June 1897. Northumberland's previous matches had been staged at
three grounds in Newcastle – South Northumberland CC, Burdon Terrace and
Heaton Lane – and at Tynemouth CC.

Mr F.G.H. Clayton, a committee member, took it upon himself to improve the
county ground between October 1897 to January 1898. The work included
building a seating area at the Osborne Road End next to the Swiss chalet pavilion,
which was built for the Queen Victoria Jubilee Exhibition on the Town Moor in
1887 and was transferred to the ground to serve as a members' pavilion after the
exhibition ended. Further benches were constructed during this period. After 1945
much of this seating was removed and a more substantial seating area was built
to the south of the pavilion. The Swiss chalet pavilion itself was demolished on 19
March 1962 and a new one was constructed at a cost of £25,000 ready for the
beginning of the next season. It was opened on 3 June 1963 by Mr R.H. Houston
during the Bank Holiday Minor Counties match with Durham CCC.

Northumberland play the majority of their home fixtures in the minor counties
and knockout competitions at Jesmond with three other grounds hosting one or
two games each year on a rotational basis. These are Benwell Hill, South
Northumberland and Tynemouth. In addition Club and Ground sides participate
in the local league competitions, for which Jesmond is their home ground.
Previously known as County Club, these sides now play under the name of
Newcastle. They are presently members of the North East Premier League and
also take part in cup competitions.

Since the 1920s the ground's seating capacity and the excellent playing
surface have enabled the club to host many games against international touring
sides, both as a county and on behalf of the Minor Counties XI.

For thirteen years from 1981 the ground at Osborne Avenue was used for a
cricket festival, initially sponsored by Callers-Pegasus. The festival included two
55-over matches in early August each season played under Benson and Hedges
Cup rules. From about half way through the festival's history the matches were
played by the Rest of the World XI and an England XI.

The ground is bounded to the north by Osborne Avenue and to the east and
south by All Saints' Cemetery. The pavilion includes seating for members and
bars/restaurant at ground level, and players' changing rooms, secretary's office,
radio commentary position and press room on the first floor/balcony level. To the
south-west of the playing area is the scoreboard/scorers' room and

groundsman's store. The playing area is rectangular with dimensions of 138 metres by 117 metres and is defined by a rope, white fence and flower beds in front of the pavilion and advertising boards. When required the TV camera/ commentary box can be positioned at the Cemetery End with additional cameras at the northern Osborne Avenue End and on the pavilion balcony.

GROUND RECORDS AND SCORES

LIMITED-OVERS MATCHES

Highest innings total for county 352 v Yorkshire CB (C&G) 2002
Highest innings total against county 344 for 6 by Nottinghamshire (NWT) 1994
Lowest innings total for county 71 v Essex (NWT) 1987
Lowest innings total against county 164 by Bedfordshire (NWT) 2000
Highest individual innings for county 108 B. Parker v Yorkshire CB (C&G) 2002
Highest individual innings against county 146 P. Johnson for Nottinghamshire (NWT) 1994
Highest wicket partnerships for county

1st	118 G.D. Halliday & K. Pearson	v	Essex	(NWT)	1986
2nd	59 M.P. Speight & C.J. Hewison	v	Yorkshire CB	(C&G)	2002
3rd	128 W. Falla & G. Hallam	v	Ireland	(NWT)	1999
4th	99 J.M. Crawhall & J. van Geloven	v	Lincolnshire	(GC)	1971
5th	94 B. Parker & J.B. Windows	v	Yorkshire CB	(C&G)	2002
6th	96 J.A. Graham & J.B. Windows	v	Staffordshire	(C&G)	2001
7th	79* P.N.S. Dutton & S. Tiffin	v	Surrey	(NWT)	1989
8th	26 M.E. Younger & K. Corby	v	Middlesex	(NWT)	1984
9th	31 M.E. Younger & P.H. Twizell	v	Middlesex	(NWT)	1984
10th	13 D.J. Rutherford & G. Angus	v	Yorkshire CB	(C&G)	2002

Highest wicket partnerships against county

1st	176 G. Robinson & C.D. Fearnley	for	Lincolnshire	(GC)	1971
2nd	68 G.S. Clinton & A.J. Stewart	for	Surrey	(NWT)	1989
3rd	112 R.T. Robinson & P. Johnson	for	Nottinghamshire	(NWT)	1994
4th	198* G.F. Archer & O.D. Gibson	for	Staffordshire	(C&G)	2001
5th	126 D.I. Stevens & CC Lewis	for	Leicestershire	(NWT)	2000
6th	57* A.R. Dunlop & E.C. Joyce	for	Ireland	(NWT)	1999
7th	57 C.T. Radley & J.E. Emburey	for	Middlesex	(NWT)	1984
8th	60 A.W. Lilley & D.E. East	for	Essex	(NWT)	1986
9th	24 C.T. Radley & N.F. Williams	for	Middlesex	(NWT)	1984
10th	20 C.T. Brice & S.A. Patterson	for	Yorkshire CB	(C&G)	2002

Best bowling performance in a match for county 6 for 52 S.J. Foster v Leicestershire (NWT) 2000
Best bowling performance in a match against county 6 for 10 K.P. Evans for Nottinghamshire (NWT) 1994
Largest crowd 3,500 v Middlesex (NWT) 1984

HOW TO GET THERE

 Newcastle upon Tyne Central station 2 miles ☎ 08457 225225, www.gner.co.uk. Jesmond Zone 26 (Tyne & Wear Metro) (Green/Red/Yellow Lines) 0.50 mile

 80 Newcastle–Jesmond from city centre and station. Newcastle Central buses OK Travel/Newcastle Busways pass Jesmond via Osborne Avenue ☎ 0191 222 0404, 0870 608 2608

 There are cycle routes from surrounding areas of Newcastle to this part of the city.

 From north: from A167, A69, A696 or A1 (Great North Road) signposted Newcastle and city centre, then follow signs to Jesmond and county cricket, turn left into Clayton Road before reaching the North West Radial road for Osborne Road and Osborne Avenue. **From south:** take A189, A1(M)

OSBORNE AVENUE END

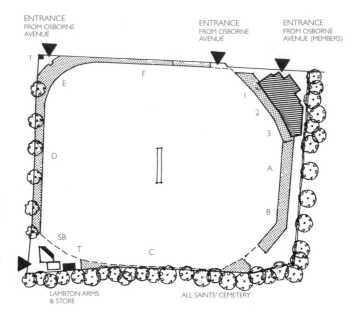

ENTRANCE
FROM OSBORNE
AVENUE

ENTRANCE
FROM OSBORNE
AVENUE

ENTRANCE
FROM OSBORNE
AVENUE (MEMBERS)

ENTRANCE
FROM LOVERS'
LANE VIA
CLAYTON
ROAD

LAMBTON ARMS
& STORE

ALL SAINTS' CEMETERY

CEMETERY END

N

0   50   100
Approximate Metres

then A1, B1307, A167, A184 or A19(M) signposted Newcastle and city centre, then as for north. **From east:** from A1058, B1307, A187 or A186 signposted Newcastle and city centre, then as for north. **From west:** from A187, A167, A186, B1311 or A695 signposted Newcastle and city centre, then as for north.

 Newcastle Airport ☎ 0191 286 0966

WHERE TO STAY

Cairn Hotel (☎ 0191 281 1358), Caledonian Hotel (☎ 0191 281 7881), Imperial Swallow Hotel (☎ 0191 281 5511), Northumbria Hotel (☎ 0191 281 4961), Quality Inn (☎ 0191 232 5025). For other places to stay in and around Newcastle visit www.smoothhound.co.uk.

TOURIST INFORMATION Newcastle upon Tyne Tourist Information Centre ☎ 0191 277 8000, www.newcastle.gov.uk

LOCAL RADIO STATION BBC Radio Newcastle (96.0 MHz FM/1458 KHz MW)

LOCAL NEWSPAPERS *Newcastle Journal, Newcastle Evening Chronicle, Northern Echo, Sunday Sun*

OXFORDSHIRE

OXFORDSHIRE COUNTY CRICKET CLUB, 4 BROOKSIDE, THAME, OXFORDSHIRE OX9 3DE

Telephone 01844 260439 (home)
Minor Counties Web www.mcca.cricket.org

Founded 1779, re-formed 1895 and 1921
Colours blue, gold and magenta
Crest an ox crossing a ford
Joint Presidents J.E.O. Smith MBE, W.W. Bennett
Chairman Dr S.R. Porter
Secretary P.R.N O'Neill

Treasurer R.S. Berryman
Captain K.A. Arnold
38 County Competition Organiser P.R.N O'Neill
Cricket Development Officer R.A. Evans
Scorer R. Clarke
Statistician J. Lawton Smith

ACHIEVEMENTS

Minor Counties Championship Champions 1929, 1974, 1982, 1989
Minor Counties Championship Final Winners 1989, Finalists 1986

Minor Counties Knockout Cup/Holt Cup/ECB 38 Counties Semi-finalists 1990

OXFORDSHIRE CRICKET BOARD

Chairman Dr S.R. Porter
Secretary P.R.N. O'Neill
Treasurer R.S. Berryman
Cricket Development Officer R.A. Evans
Women & Girls Secretary R.A. Evans

GROUNDS

Banbury CC, White Post Road, Bodicote, Banbury (☎ 01295 264368 or 277884).
Challow & Childrey CC, Vicarage Hill, East Childery, nr Wantage (☎ 01235 763335).
Thame Town CC, Church Road, off High Street, Thame (☎ 01844 217799). (see details below)

THAME

Address Thame Town Cricket Club, Pavilion, Church Meadow, Church Road, off High Street, Thame, Oxfordshire OX9 3AJ
Prospects of Play ☎ 01844 217799

HISTORY OF GROUND AND FACILITIES

CHURCH MEADOW CRICKET GROUND is the home of Thame Town Cricket Club, founded in the 1840s. Thame Town CC, or Thame Cricket Club as it was known until 1973, can trace a continuous existence from 1884, although the chairman of the club in 1900 spoke of having had an association with the club for over 40 years.

In 1884 the club played on the Southern Road Recreational Ground which had been opened in 1872. A South of England XI, which included Dr W.G. Grace, played at Southern Road in 1873 against a South Oxfordshire XX. In 1948 the club moved to a new ground in Thame Park and from there in 1966 they moved again to share facilities with Thame United Football Club in Windmill Road. It was in 1972 that the Town Council granted the club permission to use the town crest and in 1973 it became known as Thame Town CC. In 1976 the club acquired the lease of Church Meadow from Oxfordshire County Council after the Town Conservation Study Report mentioned that Church Meadow was 'suitable for cricket'. The first game was played here in 1977 but the ground came into full use in 1978.

Having declined the opportunity to join the Cherwell League when it was founded because it already had a strong fixture list, the club became a founder member of the Trinity League, though still regarding league cricket as 'inevitable rather than desirable'. In 1990 the club accepted an invitation to join the Cherwell League, now called the Cherwell Cricket League. Thame Town CC won promotion to the Home Counties Premier League for 2003. The club field three Saturday and two Sunday XIs throughout the season.

The tranquil Church Meadow ground is located close to Lower High Street and is accessed from Church Road. The entrance to the ground is via the car park adjoining the Thame Barns Centre, which is sited near to the pavilion and clubhouse. Pedestrians can also access the ground at its south-eastern corner from Aylesbury Road. The pavilion is unique in character, having been converted from the barns that were on the site, and has been developed over time in keeping with the conservation area in which it lies. It includes a scoreboard built within the roof structure and houses players' dressing rooms, press room, bar and refreshment facilities. Close to the pavilion are artificial and grass nets. The ground is bounded to the west by the parish church of St Mary the Virgin and a stone wall and to the east by the main A418 Thame to Aylesbury Road.

Parking is available to the rear of the Thame Barns Centre in the cricket club car park, and there is provision for cars around the boundary during representative matches. Street parking is also available within easy walking distance in the neighbouring area. The view of the cricket is excellent from all parts of the ground. The only permanent buildings are the pavilion/clubhouse, scorebox and groundsman's store. The majority of facilities for matches are temporary and include chairs, sponsors' marquees, refreshment/beer tents and a small OCCC club tent. The members' enclosure is in front of the pavilion and toilets are available in the clubhouse.

The ground is reasonably flat and is defined by boundary rope and flags. The dimensions of the playing area are 130 metres by 150 metres. When required the radio commentary point is sited near the pavilion.

The ground has been used by Oxfordshire CCC for Minor Counties Championship matches and fixtures in the 38 County Knock-out Trophy.

AYLESBURY ROAD END

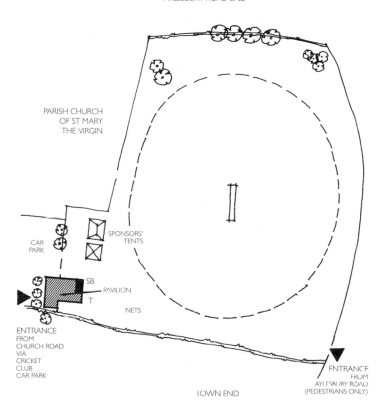

PARISH CHURCH
OF ST MARY
THE VIRGIN

CAR
PARK

SPONSORS'
TENTS

SB

PAVILION

T

NETS

ENTRANCE
FROM
CHURCH ROAD
VIA
CRICKET
CLUB
CAR PARK

ENTRANCE
FROM
AYLESBURY ROAD
(PEDESTRIANS ONLY)

TOWN END

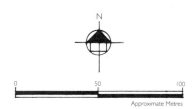

N

0   50   100
Approximate Metres

GROUND RECORDS AND SCORES

LIMITED-OVERS MATCHES

No C&G limited-overs matches played to date.

HOW TO GET THERE

 Haddenham and Thame Parkway 5 miles ☎ 08705 165165, www.chilternrailways.co.uk

 Arriva Bus 280 links Thame with Oxford, Wheatley and Aylesbury ☎ 0345 788788 and Wycombe Bus Company links Thame with High Wycombe via Princes Risborough and Chinnor ☎ 01494 520941. The ground is a short walk from Lower High Street and Cornmarket.

 There are cycle routes to this area of Thame.

 From north: M40 junction 8/8a follow A418 signposted Thame. Turn opposite Six Bells pub in Lower High Street – there is a sign to Thame Cricket Club on the road. Turn right after Booker Tate offices into the ground, which is at the rear of the Thame Barns Centre. **From south:** M40 junction 7/8 then as north. **From east:** from Aylesbury take A418 signposted Thame then as north. **From west:** from M40 junction 8/8a follow A418 signposted Thame then as north.

 London Luton Airport ☎ 01582 405100, London Heathrow Airport ☎ 08700 000123

WHERE TO STAY

The Oxford Belfry Hotel (☎ 01844 279381), The Swan Hotel & Restaurant (☎ 01844 261211), The Black Horse Hotel (☎ 01844 212886), Studley Priory Hotel (☎ 01844 351203), The Old Trout Hotel & Restaurant (☎ 01844 212146), Spread Eagle Hotel (☎ 01844 213661). For other places to stay in and around Thame ☎ 01865 726871 or visit www.smoothhound.co.uk or www.thame.net.

WHERE TO EAT

Farmhouse Kitchen (☎ 01844 217560), Thame Tandoori (☎ 01844 212175), Mia Capri (☎ 01844 213016), Pizza House (☎ 01844 216266)

TOURIST INFORMATION Oxford Tourist Information Centre, The Old School, Gloucester Green, Oxford OX1 2DA ☎ 01865 726871, fax 01865 240261, www.visitoxford.org or www.oxfordshire.gov.uk or www.thame.net

LOCAL RADIO STATIONS BBC Radio Oxford (95.2 MHz FM/1485 KHz MW), Radio 210 (102.9 MHz FM/1431 KHz MW)

LOCAL NEWSPAPERS *Oxford Mail*, *Oxford Times*

SHROPSHIRE

SHROPSHIRE COUNTY CRICKET CLUB, FOUR WINDS, 24 RIDGEBOURNE ROAD, SHREWSBURY SY3 9AB AND C/O SHREWSBURY CC, THE PAVILION, LONDON ROAD, SHREWSBURY SY2 6PT

Telephone	01743 233650 (home)
Minor Counties Web	www.mcca.cricket.org

Founded 1850
Colours blue and gold
Crest Loggerhead (county crest)
President Mrs V. Holt DL
Chairman J.B. Foulkes
Vice Chairman P. Bradley

Secretary N.H. Birch
Chairman of Finance M.P.T.W. Jones
Captain G.L. Home
Cricket Development Officer C. Patel
Scorer/Statistician C. Barthorpe

ACHIEVEMENT

Minor Counties Championship Champions 1973
Minor Counties Knockout Cup/Holt Cup/ECB 38 Counties Semi-finalists 1986

SHROPSHIRE CRICKET BOARD

Chairman J. Bennett
Secretary P. Wilkinson
Treasurer G. Murrall
Cricket Development Officer C. Patel
Women & Girls Secretary C. Patel
Administrator S.G. Aston

GROUNDS

Oswestry CC, Cricket Ground, Morda Road, Oswestry (☎ 01691 653006). Leave town on Welshpool road, go over traffic lights into Morda Road. Ground is on left.
Shifnal CC, Shrewsbury Road, Shifnal (☎ 01952 462003). From M54 junction 4 take A464 and follow signs for Shifnal. The ground is on the right.
Shrewsbury CC, London Road, Shrewsbury (☎ 01952 363655). London Road is south of the town centre, on Ring Road opposite crematorium.
Telford, St George's CC, St George's Cricket Ground, Cricketers Lane off Church Road, Telford (☎ 01952 612911). (see details over)
Wellington CC, Orleton Park, Haygate Road, Wellington (☎ 01952 251539). From M54 junction 7 turn right towards Wellington. Haygate Road is on the left and the entrance to ground is first left.
Whitchurch CC, Heath Road, Whitchurch (☎ 01948 663923). Heath Road is main road from Shrewsbury to Whitchurch. Ground is on left once you reach Whitchurch town signs.

TELFORD

Address St George's Cricket Club, The Pavilion, St George's Cricket Ground, Church Road, St George's, Telford, Shropshire
Prospects of Play ☎ 01952 612911

HISTORY OF GROUND AND FACILITIES

ST GEORGE'S CRICKET CLUB was founded on 9 March 1922. The St George's recreation committee purchased the field close to Vicarage Drive in 1924 but four years later in 1928 the club lost some of its best cricketers due to the Lilleshall Company closing down its new works yard. In the first season after the Second World War St George's CC were unbeaten throughout the season. In 1948 the club entered a National Cricket Competition organised by the *News Chronicle* and were runners-up. During the same season a new pavilion was constructed and was opened by the Earl Granville who was then the Governor of Northern Ireland. In 1949 Wolverhampton Wanderers Football Club, the FA Cup winners, staged a friendly match with the cricket club and the Cup was on display during the match. Using the proceeds from this match the club was able to install electricity in the pavilion and make other ground improvements including a new scoreboard and the re-laying of some of the square.

Funds were raised in 1964 to pay for the construction of a new clubhouse and during the same year the club moved to the new ground at Church Road.

Since 1984 the ground has been used by Shropshire CCC for NatWest Trophy 1st round matches, the highlight being the defeat of Yorkshire in 1984 thanks to a splendid performance from the former Pakistani Test captain Mushtaq Mohammad. Other matches have been staged with Hampshire, Leicestershire, Northamptonshire, Middlesex and Somerset.

St George's Cricket Club play in the Furrows Shropshire Cricket League and field three XIs throughout the season.

GROUND RECORDS AND SCORES

LIMITED-OVERS MATCHES

Highest innings total for county 235 for 9 v Somerset (NWT) 2000
Highest innings total against county 301 for 4 by Somerset (NWT) 1993
Lowest innings total by county 149 v Middlesex (NWT) 1992
Lowest innings total against county 192 by Yorkshire (NWT) 1984
Highest individual innings for county 102* J.T. Ralph v Somerset (NWT) 2000
Highest individual innings against county 130 G. Cook for Northamptonshire (NWT) 1985
Highest wicket partnership for county

1st	51 J. Foster & J.B.R. Jones	v	Hampshire	(NWT)	1988
2nd	68 J.B.R. Jones & J.V. Anders	v	Somerset	(NWT)	2000
3rd	114 J.B.R. Jones & T. Parton	v	Hampshire	(NWT)	1988
4th	153 J. Abrahams & M.R. Davies	v	Leicestershire	(NWT)	1989
5th	43 Mushtaq Mohammad & B. Perry	v	Yorkshire	(NWT)	1984
6th	51 J.B.R. Jones & P.M. Blakeley	v	Somerset	(NWT)	1993
7th	59 J.T. Ralph & A.B. Byram	v	Somerset	(NWT)	2000
8th	38 J.T. Ralph & K.P. Evans	v	Somerset	(NWT)	2000

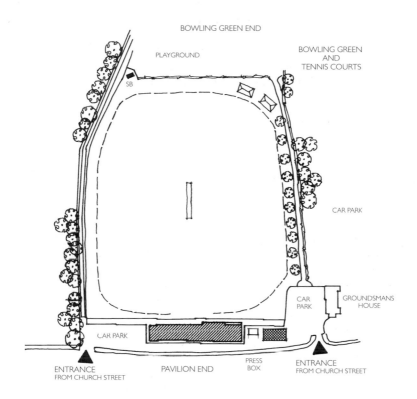

BOWLING GREEN END

PLAYGROUND

BOWLING GREEN
AND
TENNIS COURTS

SB

CAR PARK

CAR
PARK

GROUNDSMANS
HOUSE

CAR PARK

ENTRANCE
FROM CHURCH STREET

PAVILION END

PRESS
BOX

ENTRANCE
FROM CHURCH STREET

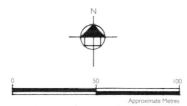

N

0   50   100

Approximate Metres

9th	13 P.M. Blakeley & A.B. Byram	v	Somerset	(NWT)	1993
10th	36 A.B. Byram & G. Edmunds	v	Somerset	(NWT)	1993

Highest wicket partnership against county

1st	199 D.L. Haynes & M.A. Roseberry	for	Middlesex	(NWT)	1992
2nd	150 G. Cook & R.J. Boyd-Moss	for	Northamptonshire	(NWT)	1985
3rd	104 D.I. Gower & P. Willey	for	Leicestershire	(NWT)	1989
4th	102 G.D. Rose & C.J. Tavare	for	Somerset	(NWT)	1993
5th	19* D.I. Gower & L. Potter	for	Leicestershire	(NWT)	1989
6th	44 M.E. Trescothick & I.D. Blackwell	for	Somerset	(NWT)	2000
7th	64 P. Carrick & G.B. Stevenson	for	Yorkshire	(NWT)	1984
8th	11* R.J. Sims & N.F. Williams	for	Middlesex	(NWT)	1992
9th	20 S. Oldham & S.J. Dennis	for	Yorkshire	(NWT)	1984
10th	21 S.J. Dennis & P.A. Booth	for	Yorkshire	(NWT)	1984

Best bowling performance for county 6 for 47 G.J. Toogood v Middlesex (NWT) 1992

Best bowling performance against county 5 for 20 D.W. Headley for Middlesex (NWT) 1992
Largest crowd 5,000 v Yorkshire 1984

HOW TO GET THERE

 Telford station 2 miles ☎ 08457 484950, 0121 643 4444, www.centraltrains.co.uk

 From surrounding areas including Shrewsbury, Newport, Bridgnorth and Wolverhampton to Telford
☎ 0870 608 2608

 There are cycle routes from Telford and surrounding areas to this part of the town.

 From north: take A442 or A518 signposted Telford, then follow signs for county cricket to Church
Road and cricket ground. **From south:** take A442, A464 or A4169 signposted Telford, then as for
north **From east:** from M54 junction 5 take A442 signposted Telford, then follow signs for county
cricket as north. **From west:** from A5 then M54 junction 5, take A442signposted Telford, then as
north.

WHERE TO STAY

Madeley Court Hotel (☎ 01952 680068), Prince Rupert Hotel, Shrewsbury (☎ 01743 236000),
The Shrewsbury Hotel (☎ 01743 231246). For further small hotels and guest houses in Shrewsbury and
Telford area visit www.smoothhound.co.uk, www.telford.gov.uk.

TOURIST INFORMATION Telford Tourist Information Centre, www.telford.gov.uk

LOCAL RADIO STATION BBC Radio Shropshire (756 KHz FM/397 MHz MW)

LOCAL NEWSPAPERS *Shropshire Star, Shrewsbury Chronicle*

STAFFORDSHIRE

STAFFORDSHIRE COUNTY CRICKET CLUB, 10 THE PAVEMENT, BREWOOD, STAFFORD, STAFFORDSHIRE ST19 9BZ

Telephone 01902 850325 (home)
Minor Counties Web www.mcca.cricket.org

Founded 1871
Colours green and gold
Crest Stafford knot
President Lord Stafford
Secretary W.S. Bourne
Assistant Secretary N.J. Archer

Treasurer A. Butters
Coach G. Warner
Captain R.P. Harvey
Cricket Development Officer R. Mitchell
Scorer/Statistician K. O'Connell

ACHIEVEMENTS

Minor Counties Championship Champions 1906, 1908, 1911, 1914 (title disputed), 1920, 1921, 1927, 1991, 1992, 1993, 1998

Minor Counties Knockout Cup/Holt Cup/ECB 38 Counties Winners 1991 and 1993

STAFFORDSHIRE CRICKET BOARD
Secretary W.S. Bourne
Treasurer J. Bosson
Youth Chairman R. Cherry
Cricket Development Officer R. Mitchell
Women & Girls Secretary M. Barraclough

GROUNDS

Leek CC, Highfield, Macclesfield Road, Leek (☎ 01538 383693). Ground is on A523 towards Rudyard, past Leek Town Football Club and at top of hill on right in Highfield.

Longton CC, Trentham Road, Blurton, Stoke-on-Trent (☎ 01782 312278). Follow Longton signs from the Trentham roundabout. The ground is on the left off the main road in Blurton.

Porthill Park CC, Porthill Park Ground, Basford Park Road, Wolstanton, Newcastle-under-Lyme (☎ 01782 626350). From A500 take A53 towards Newcastle-under-Lyme. Take third right into Basford Park Road and the ground is 1 mile on right.

Stone CC, Priory Road, off Lichfield Road, Stone (☎ 01785 813068). (see details below).

Tamworth CC, Hints Road, Tamworth (☎ 01827 63428). From M42 junction 10, take the old A5 through Wilnecote to Mile Oak. At Mile Oak pub, turn right and second left at island signposted Lichfield and Hopwas. Ground is in Hints Road on right-hand side.

Walsall CC, Gorway Cricket Ground, Gorway Road, Gorway, Walsall (☎ 01922 622094). From M6 junction 7, take A34. Go over Boundary Hotel island, turn left and then left again for Gorway Road for Walsall Cricket Club.

STONE

Address Stone Cricket Club, The Pavilion, Priory Road, Stone, Staffordshire
Prospects of Play ☎ 01785 813068

HISTORY OF GROUND AND FACILITIES

STONE CRICKET CLUB is bounded by Lichfield Road, Willow Walk and Priory Road within a residential area not far from the Trent and Mersey Canal. The wicket is oriented east–west and the ends are named the Pavilion End and Lichfield Road End. A rope and some advertising boards define the playing area. The dimensions are 105 metres by 122 metres.

This venue has been used for Gillette Cup/NatWest Trophy/Cheltenham & Gloucester Trophy matches since the first match in 1973 with Dorset. Other matches have been staged with Essex, Northamptonshire, Sussex, Warwickshire, Hampshire, Kent, Glamorgan, Gloucestershire, Derbyshire and in 2003 Surrey are due to be the visitors for the 3rd round Cheltenham & Gloucester Trophy match. Matches against touring sides have also been staged here. The last visit was by the Australian touring team in 1997.

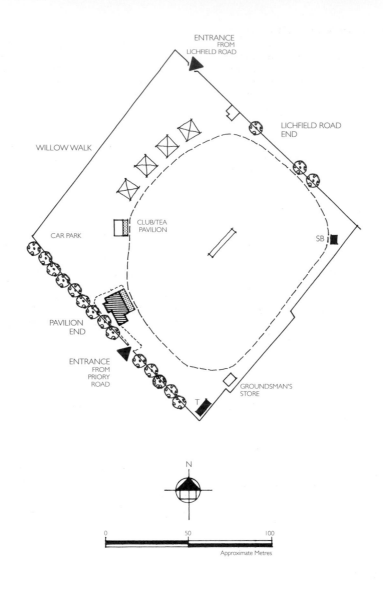

ENTRANCE
FROM
LICHFIELD ROAD

LICHFIELD ROAD
END

WILLOW WALK

CLUB/TEA
PAVILION

CAR PARK

SB

PAVILION
END

ENTRANCE
FROM
PRIORY
ROAD

GROUNDSMAN'S
STORE

T

N

0   50   100

Approximate Metres

GROUND RECORDS AND SCORES

LIMITED-OVERS MATCHES

Highest innings total for county 258 for 6 v Kent (NWT) 1995
Highest innings total against county 349 for 8 by Kent (NWT) 1995
Lowest innings total for county 108 v Northamptonshire (NWT) 1991
Lowest innings total against county 84 by Dorset (GC) 1973
Highest individual innings for county 105* L. Potter v Kent (NWT) 1995
Highest individual innings against county 145 R.J. Bailey for Northamptonshire (NWT) 1991

Highest wicket partnerships for county

1st	75 D.A. Hancock & G.S. Warner	v	Essex	(GC)	1976
2nd	37 P.F. Shaw & J.A. Waterhouse	v	Derbyshire	(NWT)	1996
3rd	140 D.A. Hancock & Nasim-ul-Ghani	v	Sussex	(GC)	1978
4th	55 G.F. Archer & P.F. Shaw	v	Warwickshire	(C&G)	2002
5th	42 A.J. Dutton & N.J. Archer	v	Hampshire	(NWT)	1993
6th	49 L. Potter & N.J. Archer	v	Kent	(NWT)	1995
7th	61* L. Potter & M.I. Humphries	v	Kent	(NWT)	1995
8th	37 C.G. Feltham & P.M. Ridgway	v	Derbyshire	(NWT)	1996
9th	52 P.M. Ridgway & D.J. Brock	v	Derbyshire	(NWT)	1996
10th	9* B.G. Gessner & K.H. Stride	v	Sussex	(GC)	1978

Highest wicket partnerships against county

1st	173 B.E.A. Edmeades & B.R. Hardie	for	Essex	(GC)	1976
2nd	117 T.C. Middleton & R.A. Smith	for	Hampshire	(NWT)	1993
3rd	131* T.J.G. O'Gorman & C.J. Adams	for	Derbyshire	(NWT)	1996
4th	100 N.R. Taylor & G.R. Cowdrey	for	Kent	(NWT)	1995
5th	39 N.V. Knight & S.M. Pollock	for	Warwickshire	(C&G)	2002
6th	36 G.R. Cowdrey & M.V. Fleming	for	Kent	(NWT)	1995
7th	19 S.M. Pollock & N.M.K. Smith	for	Warwickshire	(C&G)	2002
8th	71* R.C. Ontong & T. Davies	for	Glamorgan	(NWT)	1986
9th	43 S.C. Willis & M.J. McCague	for	Kent	(NWT)	1995
10th	18 T.J. Hall & D. Shackleton	for	Dorset	(GC)	1973

Best bowling performance in a match for county 4 for 62 P.M. Ridgway v Kent (NWT) 1995
Best bowling performance in a match against county 5 for 35 A. Richardson for Warwickshire (C&G) 2002
Largest crowd 3,500 v Essex (GC) 1976

HOW TO GET THERE

 Stone station 1 mile ☎ 08457 484950, www.virgin-trains.co.uk

 PMT buses pass close to ground and link Stone station with bus station in town centre ☎ 01782 747000, 0870 608 2608.

 There are cycle routes to this area of the town.

 From north: from A34, A520 or M6 junction 15 signposted Stone and town centre, follow A51 Lichfield Road, ground entrance is off Priory Road. **From south:** from A51, A34 or M6 junction 14, follow A34 signposted Stone and town centre, then as north. **From east:** from A51, B5027 or A520 signposted Stone and town centre, then as north. **From west:** from A51 or B5026 signposted Stone and town centre, then as north.

 Manchester International Airport ☎ 0161 489 3000

WHERE TO STAY

Holiday Inn Hotel (☎ 01782 717171). For other places to stay in the Stone and Stoke-on-Trent area visit www.smoothhound.co.uk, www.visitstoke.org, www.stokeontrent.gov.uk

LOCAL RADIO STATIONS BBC Radio Stoke-on-Trent (94.6 MHz FM/1503 KHz MW), Radio Signal (102.6 MHz FM/1170 KHz MW)

LOCAL NEWSPAPER *Evening Sentinel*

SUFFOLK

SUFFOLK COUNTY CRICKET CLUB, 94 HENLEY ROAD, IPSWICH, SUFFOLK IP1 4NJ

Telephone 01473 213288 (home) 01473 232121 (office)
Minor Counties Web www.mcca.cricket.org

Founded 1864
Colours maroon and old gold
Crest rampant lion
President G.C. Perkins
Chairman N.P. Atkins MBE
Secretary T.J. Pound

Treasurer N. Hammond
Director of Cricket K. Brooks
Captain P.J. Caley
Cricket Development Officer R. Blackmore
Scorer/Statistician A. Broome

ACHIEVEMENTS

Minor Counties Championship Champions 1946, 1977 and 1979
Minor Counties Championship Final Finalists 1985

Minor Counties Knockout Cup/Holt Cup/ECB 38 Counties Quarter-finalists 1986

SUFFOLK CRICKET BOARD

Chairman N.P. Atkins MBE
Secretary T.J. Pound
Treasurer N. Hammond
Cricket Development Officer R. Blackmore
Women & Girls Secretary R. Blackmore

GROUNDS

Bury St Edmunds CC, The Victory Ground, Nowton Road, Bury St Edmunds (☎ 01284 754592). (see details opposite)

Copdock & Old Ipswichians CC, Old London Road, Copdock (☎ 01473 730752). Leave the A12 for Copdock. The ground is on the right almost opposite the County Hotel.

Exning CC, Village Cricket Ground, Exning (no ☎ on ground). Leave A14 at junction with A142, at Exning village, turn right at T-junction and the ground is on the right.

Mildenhall CC, Wamil Way, off Queensway, Mildenhall (☎ 01638 712018). Wamil Way is approached via Queensway leading from the town centre.

Ipswich, Ransome's Sports Club, Sidegate Avenue, Ipswich (☎ 01473 726134).

Woodbridge, Woodbridge School, School Ground, Woodbridge (☎ 01394 385547). Six miles east of Ipswich on the A12. In Woodbridge, turn right at T-junction and school entrance is second on the left.

BURY ST EDMUNDS

Address Bury St Edmunds Cricket Club, The Pavilion,
The Victory Ground, Nowton Road, Bury St Edmunds, Suffolk
Prospects of Play ☎ 01284 754759

HISTORY OF GROUND AND FACILITIES

THE VICTORY GROUND in Nowton Road is the home of Bury St Edmunds CC. The ground is used on a regular basis by Suffolk CCC for Minor Counties Championship and one-day NatWest Trophy, now Cheltenham & Gloucester Trophy, matches.

The only permanent buildings on the ground are the pavilion, groundsman's store and the scoreboard. All other facilities are temporary.

County matches staged here date from 1981 when Derbyshire visited on 11 June in the NatWest Trophy 1st round. Further games followed: 1983 v Derbyshire, 1985 v Lancashire, 1989 v Northamptonshire, 1990 v Worcestershire, 1993 v Essex, 1999 v Hampshire CB, 2001 v Herefordshire and 2002 v Northamptonshire.

GROUND RECORDS AND SCORES

LIMITED-OVERS MATCHES

Highest innings total for county 284 for 8 v Hampshire CB (NWT) 1999
Highest innings total against county 290 for 3 by Hampshire CB (NWT) 1999
Lowest innings total for county 99 v Derbyshire (NWT) 1981
Lowest innings total against county 151 by Herefordshire (C&G) 2001
Highest individual innings for county 109* K.M. Wijesuriya v Hampshire CB (NWT) 1999
Highest individual innings against county 105* M.S. Compton for Hampshire CB (NWT) 1999
Highest wicket partnership for county

1st	34 R.J. Catley & I.D. Graham	v	Herefordshire	(C&G)	2001
2nd	107 M.S.A. McEvoy & J.W. Edrich	v	Worcestershire	(NWT)	1990
3th	123 K.M. Wijesuriya & D.J. Callaghan	v	Hampshire CB	(NWT)	1999
4th	85 K.M. Wijesuriya & P.J. Caley	v	Hampshire CB	(NWT)	1999
5th	28 D.J. Callaghan & A.J. Squire	v	Herefordshire	(C&G)	2001
6th	49 S.M. Clements & R.J. Bond	v	Derbyshire	(NWT)	1983
7th	92 C.P. Seal & C.J. Warn	v	Herefordshire	(C&G)	2001
8th	40 C.A. Swallow & K.G. Shaw	v	Northamptonshire	(C&G)	2002
9th	14* C. Rutterford & R.C. Green	v	Derbyshire	(NWT)	1983
10th	29 S.A. Westley & C. Rutterford	v	Derbyshire	(NWT)	1981

Highest wicket partnership against county

1st	64 P.J. Prichard & J.P. Stephenson	for	Essex	(NWT)	1993
2nd	179 M.S. Compton & C.J. Nevin	for	Hampshire CB	(NWT)	1999
3rd	84* G.A. Hick & D.B. D'Oliveira	for	Worcestershire	(NWT)	1990
4th	167 A.J. Lamb & D.J. Capel	for	Northamptonshire	(NWT)	1989
5th	69 D.J. Capel & N.A. Felton	for	Northamptonshire	(NWT)	1989
6th	51 N.H. Fairbrother & M. Watkinson	for	Lancashire	(NWT)	1985
7th	28 C.W. Boroughs & K. Pearson	for	Herefordshire	(C&G)	2001
8th	7 R.J. Warren & J.A.R. Blain	for	Northamptonshire	(C&G)	2002

| 9th | 23 R.J. Warren & D.M. Cousins | for | Northamptonshire | (C&G) | 2002 |
| 10th | 22 C.W. Boroughs & P.A. Thomas | for | Herefordshire | (C&G) | 2001 |

Best bowling performance for county 4 for 33 A.J. Hall v Northamptonshire (C&G) 2002
Best bowling performance against county 5 for 22 S.R. Lampitt for Worcestershire (NWT) 1990
Largest crowd 2,000 v Northamptonshire (C&G) 2002

HOW TO GET THERE

 Bury St Edmunds station. Trains connect Bury St Edmunds with Cambridge, Ipswich and the London/Norwich line ☎ 08457 484950

 National Express Coaches run to Bury St Edmunds from all over the country. Visit Suffolk County Council's TraveLine on the internet and try out the Suffolk Journey Planner.

 There are cycle routes from surrounding areas of Bury St Edmunds.

 From north From the Midlands or the North, follow the A14. Leave A14 at the Butterfly Hotel roundabout, head towards the town and turn left at third roundabout into Nowton Road. **From south:** (London), take the M25 and M11/A11. **From east:** take A14 from Ipswich **From west:** as for north.

 Norwich Airport ☎ 01603 411923, London Stansted Airport ☎ 08700 000303

WHERE TO STAY

Angel Hotel (☎ 01284 714000), Chantry Hotel (☎ 01284 767427), South Hill House (☎ 01284 755650). For other places to stay in the Bury St Edmunds area visit www.smoothhound.co.uk.

WHERE TO EAT

Maison Bleue (☎ 01284 760623), Stone's at 42 (☎ 01284 764179)

TOURIST INFORMATION Bury St Edmunds Tourist Information, 6 Angel Hill, Bury St Edmunds IP33 1UZ, ☎ 01284 764667 or 757083

LOCAL RADIO STATION BBC Radio Suffolk

LOCAL NEWSPAPER *East Anglian Daily Times*

WALES MINOR COUNTIES

WALES MINOR COUNTIES CRICKET ASSOCIATION, 59A KING EDWARD ROAD, SWANSEA, WALES SA1 4LN

Telephone 01792 462233 (home) **fax** 01792 643931
Minor Counties Web www.mcca.cricket.org

Founded 1969
Colours green, red and yellow
Crest Duke of Edinburgh's crown above three dragons
Patron HRH The Prince Philip, Earl of Merioneth
President The Rt Hon Lord Gibson-Watt MC, DL, PC, BA

Chairman H. Benyon
Secretary W. Edwards
Treasurer G. Crimp
Team Manager H. Williams
Captain C.P. Metson
Scorer J. Jones
Statistician H.S. Evans

ACHIEVEMENTS

Minor Counties Championship 8th 1990
Minor Counties Knockout/Holt Cup/ECB 38 Counties 1st Round 1989

CRICKET BOARD OF WALES

Chairman D. Morgan
Secretary M.J. Fatkin
Treasurer G. Crimp
Director of Cricket M. Frost
Cricket Development Officers G. Paulson, J. Huband, B. Higginson, S.L. Watkin, J. Cartwright
Women & Girls Secretary J. Collins

GROUNDS

Abergavenny CC, The Pavilion, Pen-y-Pound Cricket Ground, Avenue Road, Abergavenny (☎ 01873 852350). (see details in Cardiff UCCE section)
Pontarddulais CC, Pontarddulais Park, off Main Street, Pontarddulais (☎ 01792 882556). Leave M4 at junction 48. Ground is left off main street through Pontarddulais.
Pontypridd CC, The Pavilion, Ynysangharad Park, Pontypridd, Mid Glamorgan (☎ 01443 400785). (see details over)
Swansea CC, The Pavilion, St Helen's Cricket Ground, Bryn Road, Swansea (☎ 01792 466321). (see details in Glamorgan section)

PONTYPRIDD

Address Pontypridd Cricket Club, The Pavilion, Ynysangharad Park, Pontypridd,
Mid Glamorgan
Prospects of Play ☎ 01443 400785

HISTORY OF GROUND AND FACILITIES

THE YSANGHARAD PARK GROUND is the home of Pontypridd Cricket Club which
was formed in 1870 and plays in the Glamorgan Cricket League. The park is also
the town's war memorial and is located in a flat parkland area on the eastern
side of the River Taff between the river and the main A470 trunk road. The
parkland was originally given to the town by the Lenox family as a memorial to
servicemen from the town who died in the First World War. The Park was opened
in 1923 by Field-Marshal Lord Allenby and between 1924 and 1930 the facilities
were also used by Pontypridd Rugby Football Club until they moved to Sardis
Road during the late 1970s.

The first visit by Glamorgan CCC to the ground was in 1926 when Derbyshire
were the visitors and during the late 1920s matches were staged annually; these
included a tour match with the South African touring team in 1929.

Over the years the ground has had problems with rain and this has affected
many matches at Pontypridd.

The county continued to play County Championship matches at Pontypridd
until 1971 when these were discontinued due to falling attendances and unlucky
weather. The last limited-overs matches were a Benson and Hedges Cup zonal
group game against Somerset and a John Player Sunday League match against
Essex in 1972. Not until 1988, as part of the county club's centenary
celebrations, did Glamorgan return to Ynysangharad Park. They played
Lancashire in a Refuge Assurance Sunday League fixture, only for the match to
be ruined by rain. In September 1989 the county staged a four-day County
Championship match with Worcestershire and Glamorgan scored 230 for 9
before the weather had the last laugh yet again. In 1991 a single limited-overs
Refuge Assurance League match was staged with Essex, but again the heavens
opened and the match was washed out.

The ground is enclosed by a fence and mature grounds. The only permanent
buildings are the pavilion, terrace and scoreboard. A radio commentary position
and press tent are usually located close to the pavilion as is the TV
camera/commentary box position. The playing area is 120 metres by 114 metres
and is defined by a line and advertising boards. The playing area is flat and there
is ample space surrounding it for temporary facilities.

The ground is used regularly by Glamorgan CCC, Wales Minor Counties and
Cardiff/Wales UCCE.

GROUND RECORDS AND SCORES

FIRST-CLASS MATCHES

(No Wales Minor Counties matches – Glamorgan records on ground)
Highest innings total for Glamorgan 421 v Warwickshire 1937

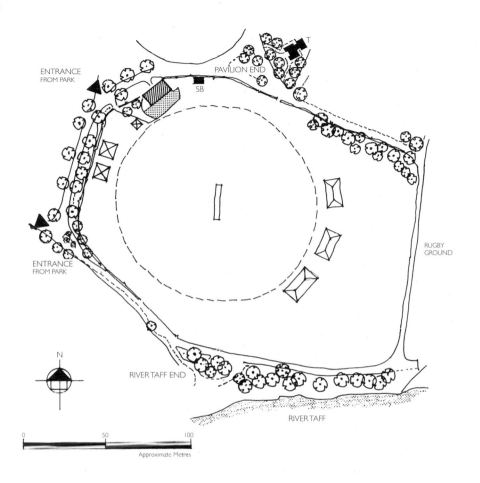

Highest innings total against Glamorgan 461 for 2 dec by Pakistanis 1996
Lowest innings total for Glamorgan 68 v Leicestershire 1929
Lowest innings total against Glamorgan 53 by Somerset 1946
Highest individual innings for Glamorgan 150* J.S. Presdee v Cambridge University 1965
Highest individual innings against Glamorgan 219* Saeed Anwar for Pakistanis 1996
Highest wicket partnerships for Glamorgan

1st	175 A.H. Dyson & D.E. Davies	v	Sussex	1939
2nd	107 W.G.A. Parkhouse & L.N. Devereux	v	Derbyshire	1957
3rd	89* M.J.L. Turnbull & R.G. Duckfield	v	Northamptonshire	1934
4th	141 D.L. Hemp & P.A. Cottey	v	South Africans	1994
5th	104 D.L. Hemp & A.J. Dalton	v	South Africans	1994
6th	130 N.V.H. Riches & J.C. Clay	v	Derbyshire	1926
7th	84 R.D.B. Croft & C.P. Metson	v	Worcestershire	1989
8th	69 D.E. Davies & J.C. Clay	v	Sussex	1939
9th	59 J.E. MC.Connon & H.G. Davies	v	Kent	1952
10th	58 J.B. Evans & D.J. Shepherd	v	Worcestershire	1960

Highest wicket partnerships against Glamorgan

1st	106 M.J. Horton & R.G.A. Headley	for	Worcestershire	1960
2nd	104 R.J. Langridge & E.R. Dexter	for	Sussex	1964
3rd	362* Saeed Anwar & Inzamam-ul-Haq	for	Pakistanis	1996
4th	99 J.G. Langridge & J. Langridge	for	Sussex	1939

5th	121 A.C. Revill & J.M. Kelly	for	Derbyshire	1953
6th	84* P.D. Johnson & P.H. Edmonds	for	Cambridge University	1971
7th	121 R.E.S. Wyatt & P. Cranmer	for	Warwickshire	1937
8th	70 M.D. Marshall & A.N. Aymes	for	Hampshire	1990
9th	80* W.T. Greensmith & L.H.R. Ralph	for	Essex	1955
10th	58 H.D. Burrough & W.T. Luckes	for	Somerset	1935

Best bowling performance in an innings for Glamorgan 8 for 60 J. Mercer v South Africans 1929
Best bowling performance in an innings against Glamorgan 10 for 18 G. Geary for Leicestershire 1929
Best bowling performance in a match for Glamorgan 14 for 119 J. Mercer v South Africans 1929
Best bowling performance in a match against Glamorgan 16 for 96 G. Geary for Leicestershire 1929
Largest crowd 6,000 v Gloucestershire 1933

LIMITED-OVERS MATCHES

Highest innings total for Glamorgan 294 for 4 v Surrey (SL) 1999
Highest innings total against Glamorgan 236 for 9 by Essex (SL) 1995
Lowest innings total for Glamorgan 129 v Essex (SL) 1970
Lowest innings total against Glamorgan 121 by Somerset (B&H) 1972
Highest individual innings for Glamorgan 155* J.H. Kallis v Surrey (SL) 1999
Highest individual innings against Glamorgan 74* N.J. Speak for Durham (SL) 1997
Highest wicket partnerships for Glamorgan

1st	133 S.P. James & H. Morris	v	Essex	(SL)	1995
2nd	66 R.D.B. Croft & J.H. Kallis	v	Surrey	(SL)	1999
3rd	204 J.H. Kallis & M.P. Maynard	v	Surrey	(SL)	1999
4th	33 R.J. Shastri & R.C. Ontong	v	Lancashire	(SL)	1988
5th	64* P.A. Cottey & S.P. James	v	Durham	(SL)	1997
6th	59 M.P. Maynard & A. Dale	v	Essex	(SL)	1995
7th	33 J. Derrick & C.P. Metson	v	Essex	(SL)	1991
8th	6 M.P. Maynard & S.L. Watkin	v	Leicestershire	(SL)	1998
9th	11 R.C. Davis & D.J. Shepherd	v	Essex	(SL)	1970
10th	5 M.P. Maynard & O.T. Parkin	v	Leicestershire	(SL)	1998

Highest wicket partnerships for Glamorgan

1st	59 M.E. Waugh & P.J. Prichard	for	Essex	(SL)	1995
2nd	32 I.J. Ward & J.D. Ratcliffe	for	Surrey	(SL)	1999
3rd	60 K.W.R. Fletcher & K.D. Boyce	for	Essex	(SL)	1970
4th	66 G.A. Gooch & R.C. Irani	for	Essex	(SL)	1995
5th	68 P.A. Nixon & CC Lewis	for	Leicestershire	(SL)	1998
6th	57 D.J. Bicknell & G.P. Butcher	for	Surrey	(SL)	1999
7th	35 CC Lewis & J.M. Dakin	for	Leicestershire	(SL)	1998
8th	15 T.W. Cartwright & D.J.S. Taylor	for	Somerset	(SL)	1972
9th	12 D.J. Bicknell & J.E. Benjamin	for	Surrey	(SL)	1999
10th	1 D.J. Bicknell & I.E. Bishop	for	Surrey	(SL)	1999

Best bowling performance in a match for Glamorgan 3 for 8 S.R.Barwick v Lancashire (SL) 1988
Best bowling performance in a match against Glamorgan 4 for 12 G.I.Burgess for Somerset (B&H) 1972
Largest crowd 3,000 v Essex (SL) 1970

HOW TO GET THERE

 Pontypridd station 0.25 mile ☎ 08457 484950, www.walesandwesttrains.co.uk

 Local bus to Ynysangharad Park via Ynysybwl Road. From surrounding areas to Pontypridd bus station, thence 0.5 mile ☎ 0870 608 2608

 From north: from A470 follow signs to Pontypridd, ground is situated off B4273 Ynysybwl Road adjoining Ynysangharad Park. **From south and east:** from M4 junction 32, follow A470 signs to Pontypridd and town centre, then as north. **From west:** from A4058 or A473 follow signs Pontypridd and town centre, then as north.

WHERE TO STAY

The Graig Hotel (☎ 01443 402844). For other places to stay in the Pontypridd visit www.smoothhound.co.uk

TOURIST INFORMATION Pontypridd Tourist Information Centre ☎ 01443 402077

LOCAL RADIO STATIONS BBC Radio Wales (882 KHz MW), Red Dragon Radio (97.4 MHz FM/1359 KHz MW)

LOCAL NEWSPAPERS *South Wales Evening Post, South Wales Echo, Western Mail, Pontypridd Observer*

WILTSHIRE

WILTSHIRE COUNTY CRICKET CLUB, PO BOX 10, FAIRFORD, GLOUCESTERSHIRE GL7 4YR

Telephone	01285 810809 (home) **fax** 01285 810809
Email	chris.sheppard@ecb.co.uk
Minor Counties Web	www.mcca.cricket.org

Founded 1881
Colours green and white
Crest white horse
President J. Hardstaff MBE
Chairman J.R. Collins
Secretary C.R. Sheppard

Treasurer/Team Manager B.H. White
Cricket Development Officer R. Gulliver
Captain R.J. Rowe
Scorer/Statistician S. Rice
Sponsor Wadworth & Co

ACHIEVEMENTS

Minor Counties Championship Champions 1902, 1909
Minor Counties Knockout Cup/Holt Cup/ECB 38 Counties Semi-finalists 1983

WILTSHIRE CRICKET BOARD

Chairman N. Peters
Secretary/Administrator C.R. Sheppard
Financial Controller B. White
Cricket Development Officers R. Gulliver, A. Crouch
Women & Girls Secretary A. Gray

GROUNDS

Chippenham CC, Hardenhuish Park, Chippenham (☎ 01249 652867). From M4 junction 17, take A350 into Chippenham and follow by-pass. At roundabout take A420 left towards town centre. Hardenhuish Park is on left after double roundabout.
Corsham CC, Station Road, Corsham (☎ 01249 713929). From A4 (Chippenham to Bath road) take left at traffic lights at Cross Keys. Turn left at T-junction and ground is on right in Station Road.
South Wiltshire CC, Bemerton Sports Ground, Wilton Road, Salisbury (☎ 01722 327108). Take A36 out of Salisbury towards Wilton and Bristol. Cross railway bridge and ground is on left.
Swindon Town CC, County Ground, County Road, off Gorse Hill, Swindon (☎ 01793 523088). (see details over)
Warminster CC, Sambourne Road, Warminster (☎ 01985 219039). From A350 or A36 follow signs to town

centre. At mini-roundabout (Farmers Hotel) turn into Sambourne Road and the ground is 200 yards on the right. Westbury & District CC, Leighton Sports Ground, Wellhead Lane, Westbury (☎ 01373 826438). On A350 Westbury to Warminster road, the ground is 1 mile out of town. Turn left into Wellhead Lane.

SWINDON

Address Swindon Cricket Club, The Pavilion, The County Ground,
County Road, Swindon, Wiltshire
Prospects of Play ☎ 01793 523088

HISTORY OF GROUND AND FACILITIES

SWINDON CRICKET CLUB was formed in 1844 when home and away fixtures were played with Malmesbury. In 1844 the club's home ground was in the area where Upham Road now is. It was in this era that one of the most famous cricketers ever to represent Swindon CC, E.H. Budd, played; in 1848 at the age of 63 he took 10 wickets in a match against Stroud CC. In the prime of his career E.H. Budd played for the Gentlemen against the Players.

In 1849 the club moved to a ground in the Greywethers Avenue area of the town; records indicate that during this period the club had no pavilion and instead used tents. In 1860 Swindon CC merged with the Swindon Rangers Football Club; they played at a ground called the Sands in the Goddard Avenue area. Then in the early 1890s a small group of businessmen formed a company with capital of £700 to acquire and develop the club's 5.5 acre present headquarters at the County Ground. It was at this time that the Great Western Railway CC and Swindon CC combined to form the Swindon CC as we know it today. The new club moved to the present ground, which is at the rear of Swindon Town FC's ground, in 1895.

In the ground's first year Bobby Reynolds scored 192 against Chippenham CC, to this day the highest individual innings here. Another feat was that of Billy Overton who played regularly for Wiltshire CCC and in 1903 was the first bowler to take 100 wickets in a Minor Counties season. Playing for the MCC against the club in 1903 he took 6 for 3 as Swindon were dismissed for just 10. Other Swindon players to have made a significant contribution to Minor Counties cricket were Ted Nash and Bert Lloyd. Ted Nash kept wicket for the county and made almost 200 appearances. Bert Lloyd is best remembered for his 196 against Surrey Second XI at The Oval when he is alleged to have tamed the Bedser twins. In 1940 the County Ground was requisitioned by the War Department and became a temporary prisoner-of-war camp.

In 1967 the Minor Counties CA staged a match here with the Pakistan touring team. This was the first important match at the County Ground. The ground was first used by Gloucestershire CCC in 1970 when a John Player Sunday League match was staged with Sussex. The ground is also used by Wiltshire CCC for Minor Counties Championship matches and NatWest Trophy 1st round games have been staged with Leicestershire and Northamptonshire.

The pavilion, which includes first-floor seating for members as well as two large groundsman's stores, is situated at the northern end of the ground, close to the bowling club. The ground is overshadowed by the back of the Swindon Town Football

Stand and tall floodlight pylons to the south of the playing area. There is a scoreboard in the south-east corner and the TV camera/commentary box is sited directly behind the bowler's arm at the Football Ground End. A press and scorers' tent is situated close to the pavilion and a secondary scoreboard is sited in the pavilion for county matches. The ground is close to the recreation ground and athletics track but is enclosed by trees and a hedge to the east and houses and hedges to the west and north. The playing area is 148 metres by 142 metres and is defined by a rope and some advertising boards.

GROUND RECORDS AND SCORES

LIMITED-OVERS MATCHES

Highest innings total for county 209 for 6 v Leicestershire (NWT) 1984
Highest innings total against county 354 for 7 by Leicestershire (NWT) 1984
Lowest innings total for county 120 v Northamptonshire (NWT) 1983
Lowest innings total against county 285 for 6 by Northamptonshire (NWT) 1983
Highest individual innings for county 75* J.M. Rice v Leicestershire (NWT) 1984
Highest individual innings against county 155 J.J. Whitaker for Leicestershire (NWT) 1984
Highest wicket partnership for county

1st	43 B.H. White & R.J. Lanchbury	v	Leicestershire	(NWT)	1984
2nd	1 B.H. White & J.M. Rice	v	Leicestershire	(NWT)	1984
3th	21 P.L. Thorn & R.C. Cooper	v	Northamptonshire	(NWT)	1983
4th	13 R.C. Cooper & J.J. Newman	v	Northamptonshire	(NWT)	1983
5th	34 J.M. Rice & M.J. Bailey	v	Leicestershire	(NWT)	1984
6th	89 J.M. Rice & D.P. Simpkins	v	Leicestershire	(NWT)	1984
7th	35* J.M. Rice & J.J. Newman	v	Leicestershire	(NWT)	1984
8th	2 R.G.J. Meale & R.J. Gulliver	v	Northamptonshire	(NWT)	1983
9th	2 R.G.J. Meale & R. Wilson	v	Northamptonshire	(NWT)	1983
10th	21 R. Wilson & T.H. Barnes	v	Northamptonshire	(NWT)	1983

Highest wicket partnership against county

1st	44 G. Cook & W. Larkins	for	Northamptonshire	(NWT)	1983
2nd	45 W. Larkins & P. Willey	for	Northamptonshire	(NWT)	1983
3rd	125 W. Larkins & A.J. Lamb	for	Northamptonshire	(NWT)	1983
4th	10 A.J. Lamb & N. Kapil Dev	for	Northamptonshire	(NWT)	1983
5th	34 J.J. Whitaker & G.J. Parsons	for	Leicestershire	(NWT)	1984
6th	89 J.J. Whitaker & M.A. Garnham	for	Leicestershire	(NWT)	1984
7th	168 J.J. Whitaker & T.J. Boon	for	Leicestershire	(NWT)	1984
8th	12* T.J. Boon & P.B. Clift	for	Leicestershire	(NWT)	1984

9th and 10th – yet to be established
Best bowling performance for county 4 for 82 A.J. Spencer v Leicestershire (NWT) 1984
Best bowling performance against county 3 for 16 R.G. Williams for Northamptonshire (NWT) 1983
Largest crowd 3,500 v Leicestershire (NWT) 1984

HOW TO GET THERE

 Swindon station 0.75 mile ☎ 08457 484950, www.greatwesterntrains.co.uk

 Thamesdown 7, 16, 17 or 18 from Swindon station also Swindon TPT from surrounding areas to bus station thence 0.5 mile walk ☎ 0870 608 2608

 From north: A419, A361 or A420 to town centre, ground situated off County Road adjoining Swindon Town FC. **From south:** from A346 follow signs to Swindon and town centre, then as north. **From east:** from M4 junction 15 follow A419 and signs to town centre, then as north. **From west:** from M4 junction 16, follow signs Swindon and town centre, then as north.

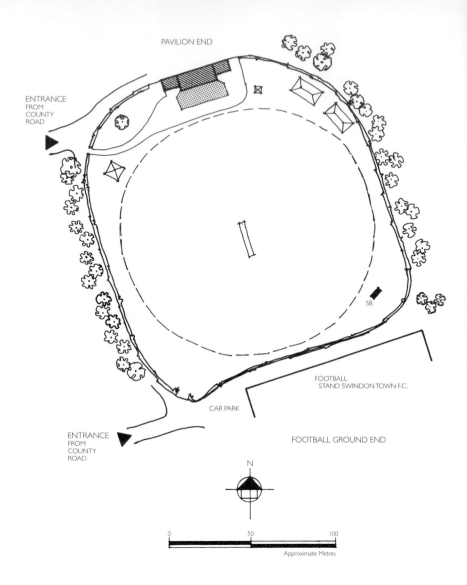

PAVILION END

ENTRANCE
FROM
COUNTY
ROAD

SB

FOOTBALL
STAND SWINDON TOWN F.C.

CAR PARK

ENTRANCE
FROM
COUNTY
ROAD

FOOTBALL GROUND END

N

0   50   100
Approximate Metres

WHERE TO STAY

Goddard Arms (☎ 01793 692313). For other places to stay in the Swindon area visit www.smoothhound.co.uk or www.swindon.gov.uk

TOURIST INFORMATION Swindon Tourist Information Centre www.swindon.gov.uk

LOCAL RADIO STATION GWR Radio (96.3 MHz FM/1260 KHz MW)

LOCAL NEWSPAPERS *Swindon Evening Advertiser, Swindon Messenger, Wiltshire Star, Wiltshire Gazette and Herald*

Friends of
Arundel Castle

Arundel

ARUNDEL

Address Friends of Arundel Castle Cricket Club, The Cricket Office, Arundel Park, Arundel, West Sussex BN18 9LH
Prospects of Play ☎ 01903 882462

HISTORY OF GROUND AND FACILITIES

A CRICKET CLUB existed at Arundel probably as long ago as 1774, but it was not until 1894/5 that the present ground and pavilion to the north of Arundel Castle were constructed under the aegis of the fifteenth Duke of Norfolk. This is a quite perfect setting for a cricket arena, and the work on ground development was continued by Bernard, the sixteenth Duke of Norfolk, at one time president of MCC and in 1962/3 Manager of the MCC Tour of Australia. The club played as the Duke of Norfolk's XI. The first recorded match on the ground was between the Castle Works XI and the *West Sussex Gazette*.

In 1975 Lavinia, Duchess of Norfolk, decided that, as a memorial to her late husband, cricket should continue at Arundel Park with the object of sustaining its unique character and to aid 'the promotion, encouragement and maintenance of the playing of cricket'. With the assistance of two former secretaries of the MCC, Ronnie Aird and Billy Griffith, and Eddie Harrison of Sussex Martlets and Lord Cowdrey of Tonbridge CBE, she set about establishing the Friends of Arundel Castle Cricket Club. Since then some forty-five matches have been played every year by teams assembled from various sources. The more important matches are played as Lavinia, Duchess of Norfolk's XI, and of these the major fixture is always the annual match against the touring side. The first match with a touring team was in 1977 against the Australian side when a crowd of some 6,000 attended. A members' dinner was held in July 2000 in the pavilion to celebrate the silver jubilee of the team.

Visiting teams also play at Arundel. In 2000 the West Indies played a three-day match with Zimbabwe, in 2002 West Indies 'A' played India and in 2003 India 'A' are due to play South Africa. In 2001 MCC played Australia – Australia 390 and 294 for 8 declared, MCC 124 and 280 – Australia won by 280 runs.

Other regular games are played by the Earl of Arundel's XI against the Australian Crusaders, Melbourne XXIX Club, Oxford and Cambridge Universities, Cambridge Quidnuncs, Oxford Harlequins, Ireland, Midland Club Cricket Conference, ECB Development XI, West Indies Under-19s, St Barnabas Hospice and an Old England XI. Other matches have included fixtures with MCC Young Cricketers, Arabs, Sussex Martlets, Lord's Taverners, South African Cavaliers, Arundel Cricket Club, Hampshire Hogs and I'Zingari.

In recent years the Arundel Castle Cricket Foundation has been established assisted by a generous donation from Sir Paul Getty with the aim of providing cricket and cricket coaching for youngsters. The former captain of Sussex, John Barclay, was appointed Director of Cricket and Coaching. In 1989 a new indoor cricket school was opened at the rear of the present pavilion. The pavilion is 22 yards long, the length of a cricket pitch.

A scoreboard has been erected on the north-west side and this also houses the scorers. The ground slopes naturally from north-west to south-east but the cricket area has been levelled and is approximately circular, 152 metres by 140 metres. The pitch is aligned in a north–south direction. The area is enclosed within a surround of mature landscaped trees which provide a green backcloth to all activities on the field. The hurricane in October 1987 felled many of the trees in the south and south-east areas but this has opened a better vista of the Castle from the Park End.

In 1990 championship cricket made a welcome first appearance at Castle Park when Sussex entertained neighbours Hampshire, since when a championship match and a limited-overs league match have been staged annually at the ground by Sussex, usually in July.

GROUND RECORDS AND SCORES

FIRST-CLASS MATCHES

(First-class matches excluding Sussex)
Highest innings total 407 for West Indies v Zimbabwe 2000
Lowest innings total 124 MCC v Australians 2001
Highest individual innings 176 B.C. Lara for West Indies v Zimbabwe 2000
Highest wicket partnerships

1st	63 T.R. Gripper & C.B. Wishart	for	Zimbabwe v West Indies	2000
2nd	76 Asif Mujtaba & D.M. Ward	for	MCC v Australians	2001
3rd	276 S.L. Campbell & B.C. Lara	for	West Indies v Zimbabwe	2000
4th	158 S.R. Waugh & D.R. Martyn	for	Australians v MCC	2001
5th	103 M.W. Goodwin & D.P. Viljoen	for	Zimbabwe v West Indies	2000
6th	49 S.M. Katich & W.A. Seccombe	for	Australians v MCC	2001
7th	190 S.M. Katich & S.K. Warne	for	Australians v MCC	2001
8th	20 S.M. Katich & J.N. Gillespie	for	Australians v MCC	2001
9th	24 M.V. Nagamootoo & F.A. Rose	for	West Indies v Zimbabwe	2000
10th	27 J.C. Adams & C.M. Willoughby	for	MCC v Australians	2001

Best bowling performance in an innings 5 for 68 B.C. Strang for Zimbabwe v West Indies 2000
Best bowling performance in a match 7 for 128 C.R. Miller for Australians v MCC 2001
Largest crowd 12,000 MCC v Australians 2001

LIMITED-OVERS MATCHES – Lavinia, Duchess of Norfolk's XI/Duke of Norfolk's XI

Highest innings total for Lavinia, Duchess of Norfolk's XI/Duke of Norfolk's XI 277 for 6 v New Zealanders 1990

Highest innings total against Lavinia, Duchess of Norfolk's XI/Duke of Norfolk's XI 314 for 7 by Australians 1989

Lowest innings total for Lavinia, Duchess of Norfolk's XI/Duke of Norfolk's XI 122 for 9 v West Indians 1980

Lowest innings total against Lavinia, Duchess of Norfolk's XI/Duke of Norfolk's XI 106 by Australians 1981

Highest individual innings for Lavinia, Duchess of Norfolk's XI/Duke of Norfolk's XI 131 A.I.C. Dodemaide v New Zealanders 1990

Highest individual innings against Lavinia, Duchess of Norfolk's XI/Duke of Norfolk's XI 114 D.C. Boon for Australians 1989

Best bowling performance in a match for Lavinia, Duchess of Norfolk's XI/Duke of Norfolk's XI 3 for 17 R.A. Woolmer v Australians 1977

Best bowling performance in a match against Lavinia, Duchess of Norfolk's XI/Duke of Norfolk's XI 4 for 18 G.J. Cosier for Australians 1977

GROUND INFORMATION

ENTRANCES London Road, via stables (players, officials, members and vehicles), London Road, via Arundel Park (members, public and vehicles).
MEMBERS' ENCLOSURE Pavilion and defined members' enclosure between main scoreboard and members refreshment tent.
PUBLIC ENCLOSURE Rest of the ground.
COVERED STANDS Pavilion.
OPEN STANDS Temporary seats surrounding the playing area.
NAME OF ENDS Castle End, Park End.
GROUND DIMENSIONS 152m × 140m.
REPLAY SCREEN If televised matches are staged at the ground the replay screen is sited at the Castle End of the ground.
FIRST AID In Friends of Arundel Castle CC Office and in the pavilion.
CODES OF DRESS Spectators are required to dress in an appropriate manner consistent with attending a cricket match. Bare torsos are not acceptable in, or in front of the pavilion. Executive Club/Suite users must wear a necktie and jacket.
BEHAVIOUR The club is keen that standards of behaviour should be maintained and members and spectators are urged to report immediately to the club secretary any incident, or potential incident, where they feel action should be taken. Bad language is not acceptable at any match and the club will take prompt and strong action should this or any other ground regulation be ignored. Mobile telephones are not permitted, please ensure that mobile telephones are switched off before entering the spectator areas of the ground.
RECIPROCAL ARRANGEMENTS Members of Essex, Hampshire and Kent gain free access to Sussex matches only, except when Sussex are playing their own county. Sussex members can also gain free or reduced admission to race events on reciprocal dates at Plumpton, Fontwell Park, Goodwood and Brighton Racecourses and Hickstead Showgrounds. Members of The Friends of Arundel Castle CC can gain admission to Sussex CCC matches free of charge.
SUPPORTERS' CLUB Sussex County Cricket Supporters' Club: subscription £4 (adults), £2 (senior citizens and under-16s) per annum. Regular newsletters are issued throughout the year. Membership details and information about events can be obtained from SCCSC, Freepost, County Ground, Eaton Road, Hove BN3 3AN.
JUNIORS Sussex membership for those aged up to 16 on 1 January is £10 per annum. Contact Membership Department ☎ 01273 827133 for full details.
CORPORATE ENTERTAINING Sussex executive membership is available and includes use of temporary tents and marquees. Facilities available for conferences, lunches, dinners, wedding receptions throughout the year. Contact Business Manager for details and a brochure ☎ 01273 827102.

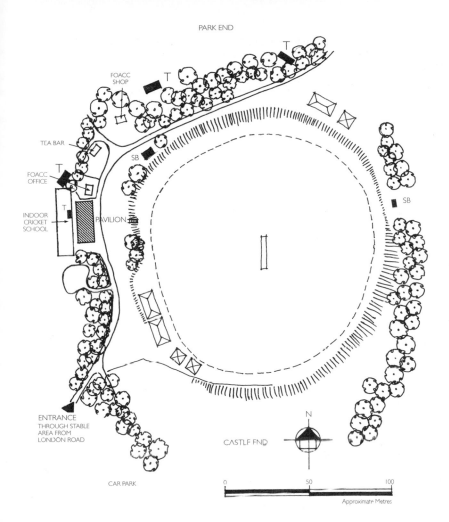

PARK END

FOACC SHOP

TEA BAR

FOACC OFFICE

INDOOR CRICKET SCHOOL

PAVILION

SB

SB

ENTRANCE
THROUGH STABLE
AREA FROM
LONDON ROAD

CASTLE END

N

CAR PARK

0   50   100

Approximate Metres

FACILITIES FOR VISUALLY IMPAIRED SPECTATORS Yes, via stable area from London Road or via Park Gate at Park End of the ground.

FACILITIES AND ACCESS FOR PEOPLE WITH DISABILITIES INCLUDING WHEELCHAIR ACCESS TO GROUND Yes, special area available Park End at top of bank.

DESIGNATED CAR PARK AVAILABLE INSIDE THE GROUND FOR PEOPLE WITH DISABILITIES Yes, special area available Park End at top of bank.

GOOD VIEWING AREAS INSIDE THE GROUND FOR PEOPLE USING WHEELCHAIRS Yes, at Park End at top of bank.

DESIGNATED VIEWING AREAS FOR PEOPLE USING WHEELCHAIRS Yes, adjacent to the pavilion on path or at Park End at top of bank.

RAMPS TO PROVIDE EASY ACCESS TO BARS & REFRESHMENT OUTLETS FOR PEOPLE USING WHEELCHAIRS No.

FOOD & DRINK FULL RESTAURANT/DINING FACILITIES Members, yes. Public, yes.

TEMPORARY FOOD/DRINK FACILITIES Members, yes. Public, yes.

FOOD SUITABLE FOR VEGETARIANS Members, yes. Public, yes.

BARS Members 2, Public 2.

VARIETIES OF BEER SOLD Gales Bitter.

CHILDREN'S FACILITIES Crèche, no. Play area, no.

CLUB SHOP Sussex CCC shop at Park End in a mobile unit sells cricket books, items of Sussex memorabilia and clothing during Sussex matches. A mail order brochure is available – ☎ 01273 827127 Fax 01273 771549 www.sussexcricket.co.uk. The Friends of Arundel Castle CC shop is in a mobile unit near the Pavilion Members' entrance – ☎ 01903 882462 for details of mail order items.

CLUB MUSEUM No, but there are pictures in the Pavilion, not accessible to members or public on Sussex county match days.

CRICKET COACHING FACILITIES Yes, contact Friends of Arundel Castle CC for details.

CRICKET NETS Yes, contact Friends of Arundel Castle CC for details.

OTHER SPORTING OR RECREATIONAL FACILITIES ON THE GROUND No.

FACILITIES FOR HIRE OR WIDER COMMUNITY USE AT THE GROUND No.

WINTER CRICKET EVENTS Friends of Arundel Castle CC stage members' luncheons during the winter. Contact Friends of Arundel Castle CC for details.

CAR PARKING FACILITIES Car parking in Arundel Park to the north of the playing area is accessed through the Park Gate approximately 2 miles north of the playing area and costs £4 per car. To the south of the ground cars can be positioned close to the playing area if space is available. Members of Arundel Castle CC and Sussex CCC members with car park passes are admitted free.

OTHER INFORMATION Neil Beck, a cricket book dealer from Pevensey Bay, usually has a caravan at the Park End where he sells second-hand cricket books and memorabilia.

GROUND CAPACITY 12,000.

ANTICIPATED GROUND DEVELOPMENTS Nothing planned.

HOW TO GET THERE

 Arundel, 1 mile, approximately 30 minutes' walk from the ground ☎ 08457 484950, www.connex.co.uk, www.railtrack.co.uk, www.thetrainline.co.uk

 Southdown Buses 212 and 230 from Worthing to and from Arundel Castle. Bus 11 from Arundel station to London Road. Walk from there to the ground via Stable Entrance. ☎ 01903 237661, 0345 959099. National Express Coaches 08705 808080, 08706 082608, www.gobycoach.com, www.bus.co.uk

 There are cycle routes in the Arundel area.

 From north: from A29, (Guildford, Dorking) continue to junction with A284 signposted Arundel (London Road), follow signs to castle and cricket ground. **From south:** from A284 (north) continue to junction with A27, take first exit from roundabout (Lyminster Road), continue towards Arundel, at roundabout junction with A284 (north) (London Road) turn right and follow signs to castle and cricket ground. **From east:** from A27 at Brighton on A27 (west) to junction with A284 (north) then as for south. **From west:** from A27, Chichester, stay on A27 to roundabout junction with A284 (north (London Road) then as for north.

 London Gatwick Airport ☎ 08700 002468 www.londongatwickairport.co.uk, London Heathrow Airport ☎ 08700 000123 www.londonheathrowairport.co.uk

WHERE TO STAY

Bailiffscourt Hotel (☎ 01903 723511 www.hshotels.co.uk), Bridge Hotel (☎ 01903 882242), Norfolk Arms (☎ 01903 882101).

For other places to stay in the Arundel area visit www.smoothhound.co.uk.

WHERE TO EAT

Amberley Castle (☎ 01798 831992), Bailiffscourt Hotel (☎ 01903 723511 www.hshotels.co.uk), Comme Ça (☎ 01243 788724), Fleur de Sel (☎ 01903 742331), George & Dragon (☎ 01903 883131), White Horse (☎ 01243 535219)

TOURIST INFORMATION Arundel Tourist Information Centre, 61 High Street, Arundel, West Sussex BN18 9AJ ☎ 01243 882268

LOCAL RADIO STATIONS BBC Radio Southern Counties (104.5 MHz FM/1161 KHz MW), Southern FM (103.4 MHz FM/1332 KHz MW) ☎ 01273 430111

LOCAL NEWSPAPERS *The Argus, West Sussex Gazette*

Scotland

Dundee
Edinburgh – Raeburn Place
Forfar
Glasgow – Hamilton Crescent
Glasgow – Titwood

Telephone 0131 313 7420 **fax** 0131 313 7430
Email admin.scu@btinternet.com

Founded 1909 (present Cricket Union – previous Scottish Cricket Union existed 1880/3)
Colours blue and white
Crest thistle
President C.H. Carruthers
Chairman C.K. Oliver
Hon Secretary R.W. Barclay

Chief Executive Officer G.A. Jones
Operations Director E.J.McIntyre
Captain C.M. Wright
Scorer/Statistician N.J. Leitch
National Cricket League Status Division 2 initial season 2003

ACHIEVEMENTS

Benson and Hedges Cup Zonal Rounds 1980 to 1996
NatWest Trophy 1st Round 1983 to 1999
Cheltenham & Gloucester Trophy 1st Round 2000 to 2002

GROUNDS

Forfarshire CC (Forthill, Broughty Ferry, Dundee), Grange CC (Raeburn Place, Edinburgh), Strathmore County CC (Lochside Park, Forfar), West of Scotland CRGP CC (Hamilton Crescent, Partick, Glasgow) and Teacher's Clydesdale CC (Titwood, Pollokshields, Glasgow)

DUNDEE

Address Forfarshire Cricket Club, The Pavilion, Forthill, Fintry Place, Broughty Ferry, Dundee
Prospects of Play ☎ 01382 475550

HISTORY OF GROUND AND FACILITIES

FORFARSHIRE CRICKET CLUB was established in the 1880s at a meeting at the Royal British Hotel. The first match was with Glenalmond College and later games were staged with near neighbours Perthshire CC. The club field four XIs throughout the season with a number of junior teams and play in the Scottish Championship, Shish Mahal Trophy, Beneagles Quaich Trophy and Haig National club knock-out competition. Their Broughty Ferry ground is regarded as one of the best in Scotland.

In 1882 the name of W.R. Sharp first appeared in the records. He was a prolific batsman and indeed a genuine all-rounder who kept wicket and bowled occasionally. In 1885 'W.R.' was elected club captain and held this office for 40 years. He made the highest score on the ground for the club and the main entrance gates were erected in his memory.

The club has long been regarded as one of the major teams in Scotland and a number of Forfarshire's cricketers have represented Scotland, including Alex Steele and Peter Rhind. The ground has a fine playing surface and many high-scoring matches have been staged here. Scotland have held a number of international matches on the ground against Australia, India, New Zealand and the West Indies. Many county teams have also played here.

In 1970 the Forthill Sports Club was established and in 1972 the new pavilion was built. A match was staged between Forfarshire CC and The Lord's Taverners in 1972 to celebrate the opening of the pavilion.

The only permanent buildings are the pavilion/clubhouse, small covered stand and scoreboard together with the groundsman's store. The pavilion/clubhouse is situated to the north-west of the playing area with the scoreboard and covered stand sited to the east. The wicket is sited in a north–south disposition. The playing area is 108 metres by 130 metres and is defined by a rope and some advertising boards. The TV camera/commentary box and radio commentary point are positioned in the elevated viewing area of the pavilion.

GROUND RECORDS AND SCORES

FIRST-CLASS MATCHES

Highest innings total for Scotland 390 for 6 dec v Ireland 1992
Highest innings total against Scotland 472 for 8 dec by New Zealanders 1978
Lowest innings total for Scotland 81 v Indians 1932
Lowest innings total against Scotland 134 by Ireland 1924
Highest Individual innings for Scotland 118 G. Salmond v Ireland 1992
Highest Individual innings against Scotland 200* L. Outshoorn for Worcestershire 1951
Highest wicket partnerships for Scotland

1st	111 B.M.W. Patterson & I.L. Philip	v	Ireland	1992
2nd	103 N.J. McRae & M.J.de G. Allingham	v	South Africa Academy	1999
3rd	38 I.L. Philip & G. Salmond	v	Ireland	1992
4th	114 G. Salmond & A.B. Russell	v	Ireland	1992
5th	66 G. Salmond & D.A. Orr	v	Ireland	1992
6th	30 F.O. Thomas & J.D. Henderson	v	Worcestershire	1951
7th	35 C.M. Wright & J.E. Brinkley	v	South Africa Academy	1999
8th	68 G.F. Goddard & J.E. Ker	v	New Zealanders	1978
9th	31 C.S. Paterson & W.W. Anderson	v	Ireland	1924
10th	47 W.W. Anderson & C.S. Scobie	v	Ireland	1924

Highest wicket partnerships against Scotland

1st	26 J.G. Heaslip & A.H. Robinson	for	Ireland	1924
2nd	258 B.W. Anderson & B.A. Edgar	for	New Zealanders	1978
3rd	43* A.M. Amla & A. Jacobs	for	South Africa Academy	1999
4th	159 A. Jacobs & A.M. van den Berg	for	South Africa Academy	1999
5th	62 A.M. van den Berg & W.R. Wingfield	for	South Africa Academy	1999
6th	80 T.J.T. Patterson & C. McCrum	for	Ireland	1992
7th	108 L. Outshoorn & H. Yarnold	for	Worcestershire	1951
8th	29 F.W. Jackson & G.N.B. Kelly	for	Ireland	1924
9th	62* R.O.Collinge & S.L. Boock	for	New Zealanders	1978
10th	104 Wasir Ali & J.G. Navle for	for	Indians	1932

Best bowling performance in an innings for Scotland 6 for 32 J.H. Melville v Indians 1932
Best bowling performance in an innings against Scotland 5 for 41 R.O. Jenkins for Worcestershire 1951
Best bowling performance in a match for Scotland 9 for 156 J.W. Govan v Ireland 1992
Best bowling performance in a match against Scotland 10 for 110 R.O. Jenkins for Worcestershire 1951
Largest crowd 3,000 v Indians 1932

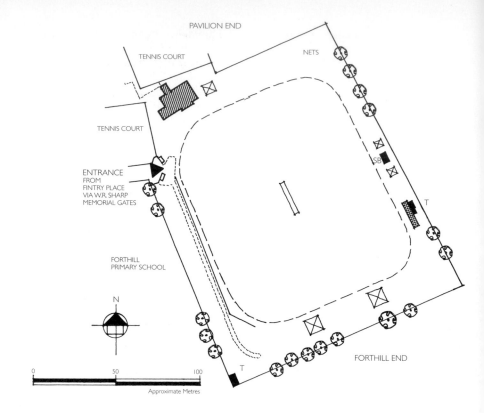

PAVILION END

TENNIS COURT

NETS

TENNIS COURT

ENTRANCE
FROM
FINTRY PLACE
VIA W.R. SHARP
MEMORIAL GATES

SB

T

FORTHILL
PRIMARY SCHOOL

N

FORTHILL END

T

0   50   100

Approximate Metres

HOW TO GET THERE

 Dundee station 2 miles, Broughty Ferry station 0.25 miles (peak times only) ☎ 08457 550033

 Tayside Buses 7/8 from Dundee, Seagate bus station and Dundee city centre to Forthill, 9/10/11 and 12 from Dundee city centre to Nursery Road thence 5 minute walk for ground, also some buses from surrounding areas. Strathtay Scottish Stagecoach from Dundee city centre to Broughty Ferry post office thence 10 minute walk.

 From north: take A929 or A92 signposted Dundee, then follow signs Broughty Ferry for Forthill Cricket Ground. **From south:** A92 taking Tay Road Bridge or M90 junction 10, then M85 junction 1, then A85 and A972 signposted Dundee, then follow signs Broughty Ferry for Forthill Cricket Ground. **From east:** A930 or A92 signposted Dundee then follow signs Broughty Ferry on eastern outskirts of Dundee. **From west:** A972 and A92 or A85 and A930 follow signs Dundee, then as for south.

 Dundee Airport ☎ 01382 643242

WHERE TO STAY

Craigtay Hotel (☎ 01382 451142), Fisherman's Tavern Hotel (☎ 01382 775941), The Sandford Country House Hotel (☎ 01382 541802), The Shaftesbury Hotel (☎ 01382 669216). For further places to stay in Dundee and surrounding towns visit www.smoothhound.co.uk.

LOCAL RADIO STATION Radio Tay (102.8 MHz FM/1161 KHz MW)

LOCAL NEWSPAPERS *Dundee Courier, Evening Telegraph, The Scotsman, Scotland on Sunday*

EDINBURGH
Raeburn Place

Address Grange Cricket Club, The Pavilion, Raeburn Place,
Edinburgh EH4 1HQ
Prospects of Play ☎ 0131 332 2148

HISTORY OF GROUND AND FACILITIES

GRANGE CRICKET CLUB in Raeburn Place, Edinburgh, was established in 1895.
The pavilion was erected during the winter of 1894 and was officially opened on
29 June 1895 by Lord Moncrieff on the occasion of a match between Scotland
and Gloucestershire. The Gloucestershire team included Dr W.G. Grace.

The pavilion served solely as a cricket pavilion until 1972 when it was
incorporated with the Grange Club. Over the last 30 years the Grange Club has
expanded rapidly and now has a membership of over 700 members spread across
the cricket, hockey, tennis, squash and lacrosse teams. In 1995 the club launched
a Pavilion Centenary Appeal and since then the ground has staged most of the
important cricket matches in Scotland. These include two Cricket World Cup
matches in 1999 between Scotland and Australia and Scotland and New Zealand
and many NatWest Trophy and Cheltenham & Gloucester Trophy matches, as well
as matches with touring teams. In 2003 the ground will host eight National Cricket
League Division 2 matches.

GROUND RECORDS AND SCORES

FIRST-CLASS MATCHES

Highest innings total for Scotland 411 for 6 dec v Ireland 1956
Highest innings total against Scotland 443 by South Africans 1907
Lowest innings total for Scotland 51 v Pakistanis 1954
Lowest innings total against Scotland 64 by Ireland 1936
Highest individual innings for Scotland 143* B.R. Tod v Ireland 1936
Highest individual innings against Scotland 149 W. Bardsley for Australians 1912

The delightful Grange Cricket
Club pavilion.

Highest wicket partnerships for Scotland

1st	95 H.F. Sheppard & R.H.E. Chisholm	v	Northamptonshire	1951
2nd	143 L.C. Dudman & R.W. Young	v	Warwickshire	1963
3rd	110 J. Aitchison & G.W.L. Courtenay	v	Derbyshire	1955
4th	72 M.R. Dickson & G. MacGregor	v	Australians	1905
5th	80 J. Aitchison & S.H. Cosh	v	Pakistanis	1954
6th	190 A.K. McTavish & B.R. Tod	v	Ireland	1936
7th	59 G.W.A. Alexander & C. Melville	v	Ireland	1928
	59 W.A. Edward & S.H. Cosh	v	Northamptonshire	1951
8th	47 B.R. Tod & W.W. Anderson	v	Ireland	1936
9th	67 J. Kerr & W.L. Fraser	v	Ireland	1913
10th	44* W.M.R. Drinnen & T. Watson	v	Ireland	1928

Highest wicket partnerships against Scotland

1st	148 H. Martin & S.F. Bergin	for	Ireland	1956
2nd	192 D.F. Hills & M.J. DiVenuto	for	Australia A	1998
3rd	116 A.W. Nourse & G.A. Faulkner	for	South Africans	1912
4th	172 W. Bardsley & C. Kelleway	for	Australians	1912
5th	176 B.A. Barnett & A.F. Kippax	for	Australians	1934
6th	58 R.W. Power & J.F. Kempster	for	Ireland	1920
7th	58 J. Darling & D.R.A. Gehrs	for	Australians	1905
8th	76 N.W.D. Yardley & R. Aspinall	for	Yorkshire	1950
9th	43 N.F. McNamara & G.W.F.B. Kelly	for	Ireland	1913
10th	61 V. Broderick & S. Starkie	for	Northamptonshire	1951

Best bowling performance in an innings for Scotland 7 for 71 R.W. Sievwright v Australians 1912
Best bowling performance in an innings against Scotland 9 for 46 E. Smith for Derbyshire 1955
Best bowling performance in a match for Scotland 11 for 146 W. Ringrose v Nottinghamshire 1908
Best bowling performance in a match against Scotland 14 for 112 E. Smith for Derbyshire 1955
Largest crowd 2,500 v Ireland 1991

LIMITED-OVERS MATCHES

Highest innings total for Scotland 147 v Surrey (NWT) 1999
Highest innings total against Scotland 246 for 2 by Surrey (C&G) 2002
Lowest innings total for Scotland 63 for 4 v Surrey (C&G) 2002
Lowest innings total against Scotland 148 for 3 by Surrey (NWT) 1999
Highest individual innings for Scotland 33 R.A. Parsons v Surrey (NWT) 1999
Highest individual innings against Scotland 101* M.R. Ramprakash for Surrey (C&G) 2002
Highest wicket partnerships for Scotland

1st	15 J.G. Williamson & N.J. McRae	v	Surrey	(C&G)	2002
2nd	56 B.G. Lockie & C.J. Richards	v	Surrey	(NWT)	1999
3rd	14 C.J. Richards & R.A. Parsons	v	Surrey	(NWT)	1999
4th	25 J.G. Williamson & R.R. Watson	v	Surrey	(C&G)	2002
5th	46 R.A. Parsons & C.J.O. Smith	v	Surrey	(NWT)	1999
6th	2 C.J.O. Smith & C.M. Wright	v	Surrey	(NWT)	1999
7th	2 C.M. Wright & J.E. Brinkley	v	Surrey	(NWT)	1999
8th	12 C.M. Wright & S. Gourlay	v	Surrey	(NWT)	1999
9th	2 C.M. Wright & K.L.P. Sheridan	v	Surrey	(NWT)	1999
10th	0 K.L.P Sheridan & Asim Butt	v	Surrey	(NWT)	1999

Highest wicket partnerships against Scotland

1st	0 A.D. Brown & A.J. Stewart	for	Surrey	(NWT)	1999
2nd	111 I.J. Ward & M.R. Ramprakash	for	Surrey	(C&G)	2002
3rd	135* M.R. Ramprakash & N. Shahid	for	Surrey	(C&G)	2002
4th to 10th – yet to be established					

Best bowling performance in a match for Scotland 1 for 21 C.M. Wright v Surrey (NWT) 1999
Best bowling performance in a match against Scotland 4 for 17 Saqlain Mushtaq for Surrey (NWT) 1999
Largest crowd 2,500 v Surrey (NWT) 1999

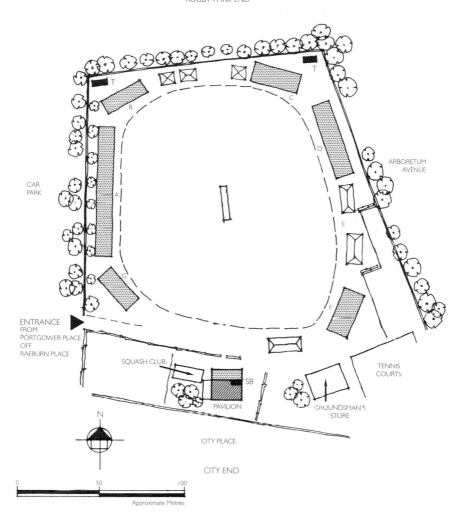

RUGBY PARK END

CAR
PARK

ARBORETUM
AVENUE

ENTRANCE
FROM
PORTGOWER PLACE
OFF
RAEBURN PLACE

SQUASH CLUB

SB

PAVILION

TENNIS
COURTS

GROUNDSMAN'S
STORE

N

CITY PLACE

CITY END

0   50   100

Approximate Metres

ONE-DAY INTERNATIONALS

Highest innings total for Scotland in ODI 163 v Bangladesh (WC) 1999
Highest innings total against Scotland in ODI 185 for 9 by Bangladesh (WC) 1999
Lowest innings total for Scotland in ODI 121 v New Zealand (WC) 1999
Lowest innings total against Scotland in ODI 123 for 4 by New Zealand (WC) 1999
Highest individual innings for Scotland in ODI 63 G.M. Hamilton v Bangladesh (WC) 1999
Highest individual innings against Scotland in ODI 68* Minhajul Abedin for Bangladesh (WC) 1999
Highest wicket partnerships for Scotland in ODI

1st	2 M.J.deG. Allingham & M.J. Smith	v	New Zealand	(WC)	1999
2nd	9 M.J.deG. Allingham & G. Salmond	v	New Zealand	(WC)	1999
3rd	1 M.J.deG. Allingham & G.M. Hamilton	v	New Zealand	(WC)	1999
4th	54 G.M. Hamilton & I.M. Stanger	v	New Zealand	(WC)	1999
5th	12 G.M. Hamilton & I.M. Stanger	v	Bangladesh	(WC)	1999

6th	34 G.M. Hamilton & J.E. Brinkley	v	Bangladesh	(WC)	1999
7th	55 G.M. Hamilton & A.G. Davies	v	Bangladesh	(WC)	1999
8th	20 A.G. Davies & J.A.R. Blain	v	Bangladesh	(WC)	1999
9th	10 Asim Butt & A.G. Davies	v	New Zealand	(WC)	1999
10th	11 A.G. Davies & N.R. Dyer	v	New Zealand	(WC)	1999

Highest wicket partnerships against Scotland in ODI

1st	6 Khaled Mashud & Mehrab Hossain	for	Bangladesh	(WC)	1999
2nd	19 N.J. Astle & C.D. McMillan	for	New Zealand	(WC)	1999
3rd	62 C.D. McMillan & R.G. Twose	for	New Zealand	(WC)	1999
4th	11 Akram Khan & Faruq Ahmed	for	Bangladesh	(WC)	1999
5th	31* R.G. Twose & C.L. Cairns	for	New Zealand	(WC)	1999
6th	69 Minhajul Abedin & Naimur Rahman	for	Bangladesh	(WC)	1999
7th	1 Minhajul Abedin & Khaled Mahmud	for	Bangladesh	(WC)	1999
8th	37 Minhajul Abedin & Emanul Haque	for	Bangladesh	(WC)	1999
9th	31 Minhajul Abedin & Hasibul Hossain	for	Bangladesh	(WC)	1999
10th	21* Minhajul Abedin & Manjural Islam	for	Bangladesh	(WC)	1999

Best bowling performance for Scotland in ODI 4 for 37 J.A.R. Blain v New Zealand (WC) 1999
Best bowling performance against Scotland in ODI 4 for 7 C.Z. Harris for New Zealand (WC) 1999
Largest crowd 5,217 v New Zealand (WC) 1999

GROUND INFORMATION

ENTRANCES Port Gower Place off Raeburn Place (players, officials, members, public and vehicles).
MEMBERS' ENCLOSURE Pavilion and defined members' enclosure.
PUBLIC ENCLOSURE Rest of the ground.
COVERED STANDS Pavilion.
OPEN STANDS Temporary raised and ground-level seating surrounding the playing area.
NAME OF ENDS City End, Rugby Park End.
GROUND DIMENSIONS 140m × 125m.
CAR PARKING FACILITIES Available inside ground for players, officials and members only. Parking in neighbouring streets.
GROUND CAPACITY 5,500.

HOW TO GET THERE

 Edinburgh Waverley station – 20 minute walk ☎ 08457 550033, 08457 225225, www.gner.co.uk

 Buses link ground with Edinburgh city centre and Waverley railway station.

 From north: M90 and A90 signposted Edinburgh to city centre then follow signs B900 for Grange CC ground in Raeburn Place. **From south:** A70, A71, A702, A703, A7, A68 signposted Edinburgh to city centre then as north. **From east:** A1, A68 signposted Edinburgh to city centre then as north. **From west:** M9 and A90 or M8 and A80 signposted Edinburgh to city centre then as north.

 Edinburgh Airport ☎ 0131 333 1000

WHERE TO STAY

Raeburn House Hotel (☎ 0131 622 6800), The Barnton Thistle Hotel (☎ 0131 339 1144), Menzies Belford Hotel (☎ 0131 332 2545). For further places to stay contact Edinburgh Tourist Board ☎ 0131 557 1700 or visit www.smoothhound.co.uk.

LOCAL RADIO STATIONS BBC Radio Scotland (92.5 MHz FM/810 KHz MW), Radio Forth (97.3 MHz FM/1548 KHz MW)

LOCAL NEWSPAPERS *Daily Record, The Scotsman*

FORFAR

Address Strathmore County Cricket Club, The Pavilion, Lochside Park, Forfar
Prospects of Play ☎ 01307 564289

HISTORY OF GROUND AND FACILITIES

STRATHMORE COUNTY CRICKET CLUB was established in 1868 and played at Zoar until the move to their present home in 1873. The first match was with Brechin. It was not until 1923 that the pavilion was built with a further extension in 1926. Mr J.A. Grant gifted the tea pavilion in 1935 and the scorebox was built in 1937. After a fire following a break-in during 1971 the pavilion was rebuilt and opened by the Earl of Strathmore. Recent years have seen the introduction of a new scoreboard, ground equipment, an artificial wicket and an improved square.

The ground is located near to Forfar Loch north-west of the town centre. The permanent buildings include the pavilion with bar, 50 seats and changing facilities, tea room verandah, store and scoreboard, together with nets. For Scotland matches most of the facilities are temporary, including seating, hospitality marquees and refreshment tents. The playing area is defined by a rope and some advertising boards; it measures 135 metres by 125 metres. A press box and radio commentary box are in a caravan. Six Benson and Hedges Cup Zonal group matches have been staged here.

GROUND RECORDS AND SCORES

LIMITED-OVERS MATCHES

Highest innings total for Scotland 190 for 9 v Northamptonshire (B&H) 1992
Highest innings total against Scotland 235 for 6 by Northamptonshire (B&H) 1992
Lowest innings total for Scotland 106 for 8 v Essex (B&H) 1993
Lowest innings total against Scotland 107 for 1 by Essex (B&H) 1993
Highest individual innings for Scotland 96 B.M.W. Patterson v Northamptonshire 1992
Highest individual innings against Scotland 103 A. Fordham for Northamptonshire 1992
Highest wicket partnerships for Scotland

1st	75 B.M.W. Patterson & I.L. Philip	v	Northamptonshire	(B&H)	1996
2nd	75 I.L. Philip & J.G. Williamson	v	Northamptonshire	(B&H)	1996
3rd	16 B.G. Lockie & R.A. Parsons	v	Derbyshire	(B&H)	1998
4th	73 N.J. Smith & J.G. Williamson	v	Durham	(B&H)	1997
5th	29 J.G. Williamson & M.J.deG. Allingham	v	Derbyshire	(B&H)	1998
6th	48 A.B. Russell & J.W. Govan	v	Lancashire	(B&H)	1991
7th	57 B.M.W. Patterson & J.W. Govan	v	Northamptonshire	(B&H)	1992
8th	31 D.J. Haggo & A.W. Bee	v	Lancashire	(B&H)	1991
9th	33 S. Gourley & C.M. Wright	v	Derbyshire	(B&H)	1998
10th	17* P.G. Duthie & K.L.P. Sheridan	v	Northamptonshire	(B&H)	1992

Highest wicket partnerships against Scotland

1st	97 G.D. Mendis & G. Fowler	for	Lancashire	(B&H)	1991
2nd	101 D.J. Capel & R.J. Bailey	for	Northamptonshire	(B&H)	1996
3rd	87 A. Fordham & A.J. Lamb	for	Northamptonshire	(B&H)	1992
4th	32* N.H. Fairbrother & M. Watkinson	for	Lancashire	(B&H)	1991
5th	23 A. Fordham & K.M. Curran	for	Northamptonshire	(B&H)	1992
6th	15 K.J. Barnett & V.P. Clarke	for	Derbyshire	(B&H)	1998
7th	23* R.G. Williams & A.L. Penberthy	for	Northamptonshire	(B&H)	1992

| 8th | 61* T.A. Tweats & K.M. Krikken | for | Derbyshire | (B&H) | 1998 |

9th–10th yet to be established

Best bowling performance in an innings for Scotland 4 for 55 J.W. Govan v Northamptonshire (B&H) 1992
Best bowling performance in an innings against Scotland 5 for 21 M.C. Ilott for Essex (B&H) 1993
Largest crowd 2,500 v Lancashire (BHC) 1991

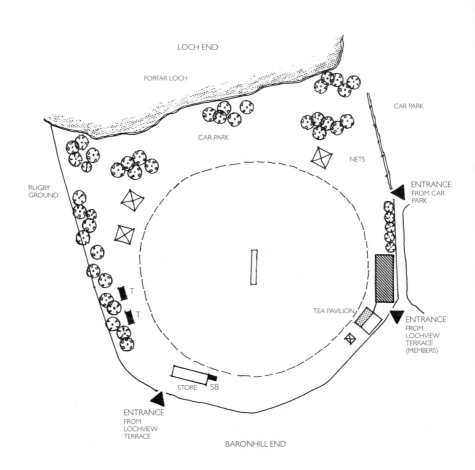

HOW TO GET THERE

 Dundee station 12 miles ☎ 08457 550033, 08457 225225, www.gner.co.uk

 City Link buses serve Dundee, then take local Scottish Buses from Dundee and surrounding areas to Forfar town centre.

 From north: A94 and B9128 signposted Forfar and town centre, then follow signs for Lochside Park for Strathmore County CC ground. **From south:** A929 and A932 or B9128 signposted Forfar and town centre, then as north. **From east:** B9134, B9133 or A932 signposted Forfar and town centre, then as north or as north. **From west:** A929 and A932 or A94 or A928 signposted Forfar and town centre, then as north.

 Dundee Airport ☎ 01382 643242

WHERE TO STAY

Castle House Hotel (☎ 01307 840340), Finavon Farmhouse (☎ 01307 850269), Royal Hotel (☎ 01307 462691) plus smaller guesthouses in Forfar or stay in Dundee. Visit www.smoothhound.co.uk.

LOCAL RADIO STATION Radio Tay (102.8 MHz FM/1161 KHz MW)

LOCAL NEWSPAPERS *Dundee Courier and Advertiser, Forfar Dispatch* (weekly)

GLASGOW
Hamilton Crescent

Address West of Scotland Cricket Club, The Pavilion, Hamilton Crescent,
Peel Street, Partick, Glasgow G11 5LU
Prospects of Play ☎ 0141 339 0688

HISTORY OF GROUND AND FACILITIES

THE WEST OF SCOTLAND CRICKET CLUB was founded in 1862 in the suburban village of Partick, north-west of central Glasgow, by a group of local businessmen under the presidency of Colonel Buchanan, later Sir David Carrick Buchanan. In the early days, because of the facilities and support, the ground was much in use for more than just cricket. Between 1870 and 1872 Scotland played England in association football international matches at Hamilton Crescent and the 1876 Scottish Cup Final between Queen's Park and Third Lanark was staged at the ground. Hockey internationals were staged by Scotland between 1914 and the late 1960s. Partick was home of the West of Scotland Rugby Football Club from 1870 to 1939 and four Scottish rugby internationals were staged here.

The first note of cricket at Hamilton Crescent dates from 1878 when the club became famous for organising matches against England XIs which included W.G. Grace, J.T. Tyldesley and C.B. Fry. The Australian touring team were frequent visitors and have played here several times.

West of Scotland CC play in the Western District Cricket Union which was formed in 1893 and includes nine other clubs within the wider district. The club have nearly always engaged a professional for his playing and coaching ability and these have included: Harry Preston, Bert Wensley, Charlie Harris, Frank Vigar and Tom Atkinson. In later years the club relied on overseas professionals including: Intikhab Alam, Salahuddin, Trevor Bayliss, Clive Rice and Mark Harper. West of Scotland CC field three XIs during the season named the Eleven, Partick XI and Hamilton Crescent XI. There are also under-18, -15 and -12 colts teams.

The ground is owned by the club and is self-contained with permanent facilities including a pavilion, tea room, scoreboard, indoor cricket school and some seating. The cricket square has approximately 36 wickets and the playing area is well drained. The pavilion is in the north-west corner of the ground. A scoreboard is sited in the north-east corner of the ground and houses the scorers. A press tent is adjacent. Close to the pavilion is the groundsman's store and to the rear of the pavilion is the West of Scotland Indoor Cricket School which is also used as an area for hospitality suites. The TV camera/commentary box is positioned on a gantry at the southern end of the ground when required. The playing area is rectangular and the dimensions are 110 metres by 123 metres. It is defined by a rope and a white fence which surrounds the perimeter of the playing area.

The Scottish Knockout Cup Final, Divisional Games and Scotland 'B' matches are staged on the ground each season. During the winter months the ground is used for hockey by two local clubs.

Scotland will host the touring Pakistanis here in 2003.

GROUND RECORDS AND SCORES

FIRST-CLASS MATCHES

Highest innings total for Scotland 381 for 9 v Yorkshire 1952
Highest innings total against Scotland 433 by Surrey 1923
Lowest innings total for Scotland 36 v South Africans 1924
Lowest innings total against Scotland 137 by Ireland 1948
Highest individual innings for Scotland 150 J. Aitchison v Yorkshire 1952
Highest individual innings against Scotland 183 B. Sutcliffe for New Zealanders 1949
Highest wicket partnerships for Scotland

1st	169 G.L. Willatt & T.R. Crosskey	v	New Zealanders	1949
2nd	188 A.C. Storie & B.M.W. Patterson	v	Ireland	1994
3rd	178 J. Aitchison & J.A.S. Taylor	v	Yorkshire	1952
4th	60 G.W.A. Alexander & J.M'W. Tennent	v	Ireland	1922
5th	130 J.M. Allan & D. Barr	v	MCC	1967
6th	144 T.N. Gallagher & J.M. Allan	v	New Zealanders	1965
7th	141* J.R. Laing & K.M. Hardie	v	Ireland	1976
8th	54 J.M. Allan & J. Brown	v	New Zealanders	1965
9th	51 J. Brown & K.M. Hardie	v	MCC	1967
10th	39 J.F. Gibson & C.F. Younger	v	South Africans	1912

Highest wicket partnerships against Scotland

1st	154 D. Kenyon & L. Outschoorn	for	Worcestershire	1955
2nd	119 A. Sandham & A. Ducat	for	Surrey	1923
3rd	130 H.G.H. Mulholland & R.A. Lloyd	for	Ireland	1911

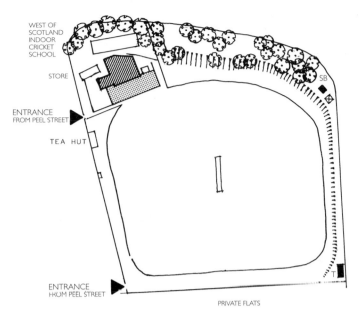

WEST OF
SCOTLAND
INDOOR
CRICKET
SCHOOL

STORE

SB

ENTRANCE
FROM PEEL STREET

TEA HUT

ENTRANCE
FROM PEEL STREET

T

PRIVATE FLATS

BURGH HALL STREET END

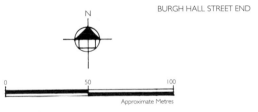

N

0   50   100

Approximate Metres

4th	225* D.A. Lewis & G.D. Harrison	for	Ireland	1994
5th	126 B. Sutcliffe & F.B. Smith	for	New Zealanders	1949
6th	141* G.A.L. Hearne & H.G. Deane	for	South Africans	1924
7th	138 P.J. Dineen & A.J. O'Riordan	for	Ireland	1968
8th	88 W.J. Abel & H.A. Peach	for	Surrey	1923
9th	73 H.B. Cave & J. Cowie	for	New Zealanders	1949
10th	32 G.H. Padgett & W.E.N. Holdsworth	for	Yorkshire	1952

Best bowling performance in an innings for Scotland 7 for 39 W. Nichol v Ireland 1948
Best bowling performance in an innings against Scotland 8 for 45 R. Wood for Yorkshire 1952
Best bowling performance in a match for Scotland 12 for 78 W. Nichol v Ireland 1948
Best bowling performance in a match against Scotland 11 for 68 J.C. Boucher for Ireland 1948
Largest crowd 3,500 v New Zealanders 1949

LIMITED-OVERS MATCHES

Highest innings total for Scotland 245 for 7 v Dorset (NWT) 1999
Highest innings total against Scotland 319 for 8 by Kent (B&H) 1991
Lowest innings total for Scotland 90 v Gloucestershire (B&H) 1983
Lowest innings total against Scotland 165 by Dorset (NWT) 1999

Highest individual innings for Scotland 70 C.J. Richards v Dorset (NWT) 1999
Highest individual innings against Scotland 110 N.R. Taylor for Kent (B&H) 1991
Highest wicket partnerships for Scotland

1st	93 I.L. Philip & C.G. Greenidge	v	Essex	(B&H)	1990
2nd	62 R.A. Keith & C.J. Richards	v	Dorset	(NWT)	1999
3rd	63 O. Henry & R.G. Swan	v	Leicestershire	(B&H)	1984
4th	48 B.M.W. Patterson & A.B. Russell	v	Essex	(B&H)	1990
5th	68 R.G. Swann & A.B. Russell	v	Yorkshire	(B&H)	1987
6th	67 O. Henry & D.L. Snodgrass	v	Northamptonshire	(B&H)	1989
7th	34 D.L. Snodgrass & J.W. Govan	v	Northamptonshire	(B&H)	1989
8th	38 D.J. Haggo & A.W. Bee	v	Kent	(B&H)	1991
9th	25 A.W. Bee & D. Cowan	v	Kent	(B&H)	1991
10th	16 D.N. DeNeef & W. Morton	v	Gloucestershire	(B&H)	1983

Highest wicket partnerships against Scotland

1st	130* M.D. Moxon & M.P. Vaughan	for	Yorkshire	(B&H)	1995
2nd	111 A.A. Metcalfe & R.J. Blakey	for	Yorkshire	(B&H)	1987
3rd	80 P.J. Prichard & M.E. Waugh	for	Essex	(B&H)	1990
4th	65 P.J. Prichard & D.R. Pringle	for	Essex	(B&H)	1990
5th	54 P.J. Prichard & M.A. Garnham	for	Essex	(B&H)	1990
6th	49 M.V. Fleming & R.M. Ellison	for	Kent	(B&H)	1991
7th	42 R.C. Russell & D.A. Graveney	for	Gloucestershire	(B&H)	1983
8th	10 R.A. Pyman & E.T. Elliot-Square	for	Dorset	(NWT)	1999
9th	28 E.T. Elliot-Square & V.J. Pike	for	Dorset	(NWT)	1999
10th	3 E.T. Elliot-Square & S.M. Forshaw for Dorset (NWT) 1999				

Best bowling performance in a match for Scotland 4 for 42 A.B. Russell v Kent (B&H) 1991
Best bowling performance in a match against Scotland 4 for 21 P.J. Hartley for Yorkshire (B&H) 1995
Largest crowd 3,500 v Australians (Tour) 1989

GROUND INFORMATION

ENTRANCE Peel Street (players, officials, members, public and vehicles).
MEMBERS' ENCLOSURE Pavilion and defined members' enclosure.
PUBLIC ENCLOSURE Rest of the ground.
COVERED STANDS Pavilion.
OPEN STANDS Pavilion terrace together with temporary ground level seating surrounding the playing area.
NAME OF ENDS Pavilion End, Burgh Hall Street End.
GROUND DIMENSIONS 110m × 123m.
CAR PARKING FACILITIES Car parking is not available within the ground. Street parking is available within the neighbouring streets; Peel Street, Fortrose Street and Burgh Hall Street for members and public.
GROUND CAPACITY 4,500.

HOW TO GET THERE

Partick station 100m from Glasgow Queen's Street station ☎ 08457 550033

Strathclyde Buses 6, 16, 62 and 64, Kelvin Bus 5 link ground with Glasgow city centre and Partick

From north: A81, A879, A803 or A80 follow signs Partick and Partickhill for Hamilton Crescent cricket ground which is entered from Peel Street close to Partick Railway Station. **From south:** M74, M73 then M8 junction 17, then follow A82 and Dumbarton for Partick and Peel Street or A749, A726, A77 or A736 to Glasgow city centre, then follow A82 for Partick. **From east:** M8 junction 17 then follow A82 and Dumbarton for Partick and Peel Street or A80, A8, A74 or A724 to Glasgow city centre, then follow A82 for Partick. **From west:** M8 junction 25 then follow A739 signposted Partick for Hamilton Crescent or A82, A8 or A737 to Glasgow city centre, then follow A82 for Partick.

Glasgow Airport ☎ 0141 887 1111

Barrisdale Guesthouse (☎ 0141 339 7589), Wickets Hotel (☎ 0141 334 9334), Park Hotel (☎ 0141 339 1559), Manor Park Hotel (☎ 0141 339 2143), Lochgilvie (☎ 0141 357 1593). For other places to stay contact Glasgow Tourist Board ☎ 0141 204 4400 or visit www.smoothhound.co.uk.

LOCAL RADIO STATIONS Radio Clyde (102.5 MHz FM/1152 KHz MW), BBC Radio Scotland (92.5 MHz FM/810 KHz MW)

LOCAL NEWSPAPERS *Herald, Daily Record*

GLASGOW – Titwood

Address Clydesdale Cricket Club, The Pavilion, Titwood Athletic Grounds,
Beaton Road, Pollokshields, Glasgow G41 4LA
Prospects of Play ☎ 0141 423 1463

HISTORY OF GROUND AND FACILITIES

THE CLYDESDALE CRICKET CLUB was established in 1848 and its founder and guiding light for the first twenty-five years was Archie Campbell from Hawick. A cricket ball presented to Mr Campbell while club president in 1873 is on display in the pavilion trophy cabinet. Around that time the Clydesdale CC players spent their winters playing association football and became founder members of the Scottish Football Association with Mr Campbell as the first president. Clydesdale were one of the big four football teams of their time. In 1874 they were finalists in the first ever Scottish Cup Final, but they lost to Queen's Park at Hampden Park.

Clydesdale CC moved from their first ground in Kinning Park to their present location, though the original Titwood ground was on adjacent land where Hutcheson's Grammar School is now situated. The Kinning Park ground was sold to a little-known up-and-coming young football club established in 1873 called Glasgow Rangers! Clydesdale have always had a tradition of Rangers support since then.

Clydesdale CC are one of the oldest clubs in Scotland and were founder members of Scotland's top cricket league, the Western District Cricket Union, established in 1903. The club have won the league several times and have also taken the Scottish Knock-out Cup. In 1977 the Titwood Athletic Grounds were chosen by the Scottish Sports Council as the National Sports Facility for cricket. The club, therefore, host many international matches.

In 1986 the ground was purchased by the Titwood Sports Ground Trust. In 1989 the club embarked on a five-year programme to develop the ground with improved wickets and three new hockey pitches.

The ground is enclosed and is overlooked by flats and houses to the north, south and west; Hutchesons' Grammar School is to the east. Facilities for cricket include an enormous cricket square over 100 metres long with an integral non-turf pitch at the western end. There are also two non-turf practice nets and some grass nets to the north-west of the playing area. During the cricket season the club expects to stage cricket seven days a week and frequently two matches are being played at the same time, one at each end of the square. The 7.5-acre ground is picturesque and very flat with the wicket sited in a north–south disposition. There is a slight slope away from the cricket table at the south-western corner. The original pavilion built early in the twentieth century has been much added to, but the cluster of permanent buildings in the north-east corner of the ground also includes a separate junior cricket pavilion. The press tent is situated adjacent to the scoreboard and the TV camera/commentary box is sited in the North Stand. The dimensions of the playing area are 138 metres by 130 metres. The field is almost circular and is defined by a rope and some advertising boards.

GROUND RECORDS AND SCORES

FIRST-CLASS MATCHES

Highest innings total for Scotland 396 for 7 dec v Ireland 1986
Highest innings total against Scotland 356 by Ireland 1984
Lowest innings total for Scotland 193 v MCC 1963
Lowest innings total against Scotland 186 by Ireland 1986
Highest individual innings for Scotland 145 I.L. Philip v Ireland 1986
Highest individual innings against Scotland 95 J.D. Monteith for Ireland 1984
Highest wicket partnerships for Scotland

1st	90 W.A. Donald & C.J. Warner	v	Ireland	1984
2nd	98 I.L. Philip & R.G. Swan	v	Ireland	1986
3rd	98 C.J. Warner & R.G. Swan	v	Ireland	1984
4th	50 I.L. Philip & A.B. Russell	v	Ireland	1986
5th	21 R.W. Young & J.M.C. Ford	v	MCC	1963
	21 T.B. Racionzer & D.J. Simpson	v	Ireland	1984
6th	12 I.L. Philip & D.G. Moir	v	Ireland	1986
7th	91 I.L. Philip & P.G. Duthie	v	Ireland	1986
8th	56 T.B. Racionzer & J.E. Ker	v	Ireland	1984
9th	15* J.E. Ker & W.A. McPate	v	Ireland	1984
10th	9 J. Brown & R.W. Wilson	v	MCC	1963

Highest wicket partnerships against Scotland

1st	61 A.H. Phebey & J.H. Hampshire	for	MCC	1963
2nd	77 S.J.S. Warke & M.F. Cohen	for	Ireland	1986
3rd	53 S.J.S. Warke & R.T. Wills	for	Ireland	1984
4th	58 J.V. Wilson & R.A.E. Tindall	for	MCC	1963
5th	118 J.A. Prior & G.D. Harrison	for	Ireland	1984
6th	118 G.D. Harrison & S.C. Corlett	for	Ireland	1986
7th	61 T.J.T. Patterson & J.D. Monteith	for	Ireland	1984
8th	35 J.D. Monteith & S.C. Corlett	for	Ireland	1984
9th	52 S.C. Corlett & J. McBrine	for	Ireland	1986
10th	33 J.D. Monteith & P.M. O'Reilly	for	Ireland	1984

Best bowling performance in an innings for Scotland 5 for 48 C.R. Hogan v MCC 1963
Best bowling performance in an innings against Scotland 4 for 113 S.C. Corlett for Ireland 1986
Best bowling performance in a match for Scotland 7 for 117 D.G. Moir v Ireland 1986
Best bowling performance in a match against Scotland 5 for 98 S.C. Corlett for Ireland 1984
Largest crowd 3,000 v Ireland 1986

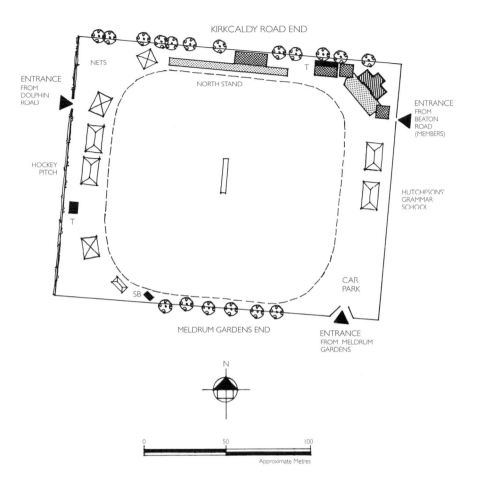

KIRKCALDY ROAD END

NETS

ENTRANCE
FROM
DOLPHIN
ROAD

NORTH STAND

ENTRANCE
FROM
BEATON
ROAD
(MEMBERS)

HOCKEY
PITCH

T

HUTCHESONS'
GRAMMAR
SCHOOL

SB

CAR
PARK

MELDRUM GARDENS END

ENTRANCE
FROM MELDRUM
GARDENS

N

0   50   100
Approximate Metres

LIMITED-OVERS MATCHES

Highest innings total for Scotland 208 for 6 v Nottinghamshire (B&H) 1990
Highest innings total against Scotland 259 for 5 by Northamptonshire (B&H) 1982
Lowest innings total for Scotland 174 v Derbyshire (B&H) 1995
Lowest innings total against Scotland 211 for 6 by Nottinghamshire (B&H) 1990
Highest individual innings for Scotland 73* A.B. Russell v Nottinghamshire (B&H) 1990
Highest individual innings against Scotland 130* C.E.B. Rice for Nottinghamshire (B&H) 1982
Highest wicket partnerships for Scotland

1st	30 T.B. Racionzer & H.K. More	v	Leicestershire	(B&H)	1980
2nd	63 W.A. Donald & R.G. Swan	v	Nottinghamshire	(B&H)	1985
3rd	44 W.A. Donald & O. Henry	v	Nottinghamshire	(B&H)	1985
4th	50 C.J. Warner & A. Brown	v	Warwickshire	(B&H)	1981
5th	90 R.G. Swan & O. Henry	v	Nottinghamshire	(B&H)	1990
6th	53 O. Henry & D.П. Drown	v	Nottlnghamshire	(B&H)	1990
7th	65 A. Brown & A.B. Russell	v	Nottinghamshire	(B&H)	1985
8th	22 D.L. Snodgrass & J.E. Ker	v	Worcestershire	(B&H)	1986
9th	42 J.E. Ker & G.F. Goddard	v	Warwickshire	(B&H)	1981
10th	20* A.B. Russell & J. Thomson	v	Nottinghamshire	(B&H)	1985

Highest wicket partnerships against Scotland

1st	121* J.G. Wright & A.J. Borrington	for	Derbyshire	(B&H)	1980
2nd	36 B. Dudleston & J.C. Balderstone	for	Leicestershire	(B&H)	1980
3rd	161 P.A. Todd & C.E.B. Rice	for	Nottinghamshire	(B&H)	1982
4th	72 D.J. Cullinan & T.J.G. O'Gorman	for	Derbyshire	(B&H)	1995
5th	52 A.I. Kallicharran & Asif Din	for	Warwickshire	(B&H)	1981
6th	40 R.T. Robinson & B.N. French	for	Nottinghamshire	(B&H)	1990
7th	85 R.T. Robinson & E.E. Hemmings	for	Nottinghamshire	(B&H)	1985
8th	19 R.T. Robinson & K. Saxelby	for	Nottinghamshire	(B&H)	1985
9th	39* T.S. Curtis & R.K. Illingworth	for	Worcestershire	(B&H)	1986
10th	– still to be established				

Best bowling performance in a match for Scotland 4 for 16 C.L. Parfitt v Nottinghamshire (B&H) 1990
Best bowling performance in a match against Scotland 4 for 21 Sarfraz Nawaz for Northamptonshire (B&H) 1982
Largest crowd 3,500 v Indians (Tour) 1990

HOW TO GET THERE

Crossmyloof station 100m; Maxwell Park station 100m, both reached from Glasgow Central
☎ 08457 550033.

Various Buses from City Centre to Shawlands Cross, thence 5 minute walk to Crossmyloof for Titwood Athletic Grounds.

From north: A81, A879, A803 or A80 follow signs Glasgow city centre, then follow signs Pollokshields for Titwood Athletic Ground in Kirkcaldy Road. **From south:** M74, M73 then M8 junction 20 then follow signs Pollokshields for Titwood Athletic Ground or A8, A89, A74 or A724 to Glasgow city centre then as north or A749, A724 or A77 to Glasgow city centre then as north. **From east:** M8 junction 20 then follow signs Pollokshield for Titwood Athletic Grond or A8, A89, A74 or A724 to Glasgow city centre then as north. **From west:** M8 junction 20 then as east or A737, A736, A8, A814 or A77 to Glasgow city centre, then as north.

Glasgow Airport ☎ 0141 887 1111

WHERE TO STAY

Glasgow Guesthouse (☎ 0141 427 0129), Guesthouse (☎ 0141 427 1006). For details of other places to stay contact Glasgow Tourist Board ☎ 0141 204 4400 or visit www.smoothhound.co.uk.

LOCAL RADIO STATIONS BBC Radio Scotland (92.5 MHz FM/810 KHz MW), Radio Clyde (102.5 MHz FM/1152 KHz MW)

LOCAL NEWSPAPERS *Glasgow Herald, The Scotsman, Scotland on Sunday, Daily Record*

Ireland

Dublin – Clontarf

IRISH CRICKET UNION, THE DIAMOND, MALAHIDE, DUBLIN, REPUBLIC OF IRELAND

Telephone 00 353 1 845 0710 **fax** 00 353 1 845 5545
Email typetext@eircom.net
Web www.theicu.org, www.cricketeurope.org/ICU

Founded 1859
Colours green
Crest shamrock
President S.C. Corlett
Chairman D. Brennan
Hon Secretary J. Wright
Hon Treasurer I. Gourley
Membership Secretaries M. Power (North), M. Ryan (South)
National Coach Adrian Birrell

Director of Coaching B.A. O'Brien
Cricket Development Officers B. O'Rourke (Leinster CU), B. Walsh (Northern Ireland CA)
Captain J.A.M. Molins
Scorer E.M. Power
Statistician G.N.J. Byrne

ACHIEVEMENTS

Gillette Cup 1st Round 1980
NatWest Trophy 1st Round 1981 to 1999
Cheltenham & Gloucester Trophy 3rd Round 2002

GROUNDS

Clontarf CC, Castle Avenue, Dublin (☎ 00 353 1 833 2621, 00 353 1 833 4427)
Eglinton CC, Londonderry (☎ 027 81 810250)
Civil Service CC, Belfast (☎ 02890 763325)

DUBLIN – Clontarf

Address Clontarf Cricket Club, The Pavilion, Castle Avenue, Clontarf, Dublin 3, Ireland
Prospects of Play ☎ 00 353 1 833 2621

HISTORY OF GROUND AND FACILITIES

CASTLE AVENUE, DUBLIN, is the home of Clontarf Cricket Club. The club field five adult XIs throughout the season, as well as two women's XIs and nine schoolboys/schoolgirls teams. Clontarf play within the Leinster Union and stage league matches against fourteen other teams including: Leinster, North County Pembroke, Phoenix, Malahide, Merrion and Dublin University.

Irish Cricket Union matches are generally shared between Northern Ireland and the Republic. The Castle Avenue ground is the main venue for Irish Cricket Union matches south of the border. It has been used for NatWest Trophy, Cheltenham & Gloucester Trophy and Benson and Hedges Cup games and matches against touring Test teams. In 1999 the World Cup match between Bangladesh and West Indies was played here.

One of Ireland's best results was in a Benson and Hedges match at Clontarf in 1997 when the home side achieved what is so far their only competitive victory over a county. Middlesex were the visitors and Ireland won by 46 runs. The Irish team that day included the late Hansie Cronje as the overseas player; he scored 94*. The Irish total was 281–4 and Middlesex were bowled out for 235 (Cronje 3–38) to the accompaniment of great celebrations by a substantial crowd.

The only permanent buildings on the ground are the pavilion, changing rooms, members' bar/lounge and the press room, which is at right angles to the wicket. The groundsman's store is north of the pavilion. There is also an electronic scoreboard at the northern end of the ground. There is no special members' enclosure for matches and the entire ground is open to all spectators. The playing area, measuring 122 metres by 118 metres, is smooth and flat and is defined by a rope and some advertising boards. If a match is televised the TV camera and commentary box are positioned at the Castle End directly above the sightscreen.

GROUND RECORDS AND SCORES

FIRST-CLASS MATCHES

Highest innings total for Ireland 331 for 9 dec v Scotland 1981
Highest innings total against Ireland 261 by Scotland 1989
Lowest innings total for Ireland 39 v Scotland 1977
Lowest innings total against Ireland 67 by MCC 1996
Highest individual innings for Ireland 144* S.J.S. Warke v Scotland 1985
Highest individual innings against Ireland 113 R.A. Gale for MCC 1968
Highest wicket partnerships for Ireland

1st	69 S.J.S. Warke & M.F. Cohen	v	Scotland	1989
2nd	109 S.J.S. Warke & M.P. Rea	v	Scotland	1985
3rd	58 H.C. McCall & I.J. Anderson	v	MCC	1966
4th	66 J.N. Rhodes & A.R. Dunlop	v	South Africa Academy XI	1999
5th	92 I.J. Anderson & R.T. Wills	v	Scotland	1981
6th	57 A.R. Dunlop & W.K. McCallan	v	South Africa Academy XI	1999
7th	62 P.J. Dineen & L.P. Hughes	v	Scotland	1969
8th	43 A. McBrine & P.B. Jackson	v	Scotland	1985
9th	21* M. Halliday & A.N. Nelson	v	Scotland	1989
10th	45 M. Halliday & J.W.G. Elder	v	Scotland	1985

Highest wicket partnerships against Ireland

1st	157 Q.R. Still & A. Amla	for	South Africa Academy XI	1999
2nd	105 R.A. Gale & D. Bennett	for	MCC	1963
3rd	79 D.L. Bell & R.G. Swan	for	Scotland	1981
4th	88 A.B. Russell & A. Brown	for	Scotland	1985
5th	50 B.M.W. Patterson & A.L. Goram	for	Scotland	1989
6th	70 J.D.C. Bryant & T. Tsolekile	for	South Africa Academy XI	1999
7th	53 J.M. Allan & J. Brown	for	Scotland	1969
8th	47 B.M.W. Patterson & D.J. Haggo	for	Scotland	1989
9th	33 B.M.W. Patterson & D.R. Brown	for	Scotland	1989
10th	48 D.R. Brown & J.D. Moir	for	Scotland	1989

Best bowling performance in an innings for Ireland 6 for 35 A.J. O'Riordan v MCC 1966
Best bowling performance in an innings against Ireland 8 for 24 J.A. Bailey for MCC 1966
Best bowling performance in a match for Ireland 8 for 97 J.D. Monteith v Scotland 1977
Best bowling performance in a match against Ireland 13 for 57 J.A. Bailey for MCC 1966
Largest crowd 3,000 v MCC 1966

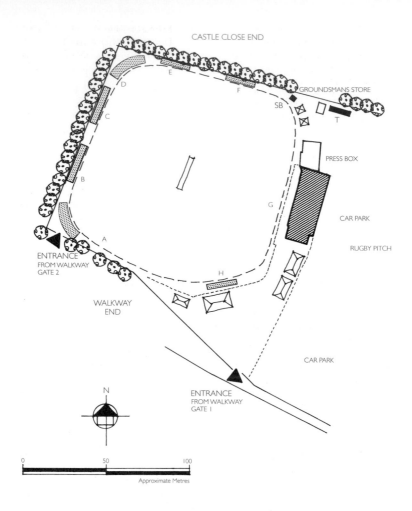

CASTLE CLOSE END

GROUNDSMANS STORE

PRESS BOX

CAR PARK

RUGBY PITCH

CAR PARK

ENTRANCE
FROM WALKWAY
GATE 2

WALKWAY
END

ENTRANCE
FROM WALKWAY
GATE 1

N

0   50   100

Approximate Metres

LIMITED-OVERS MATCHES

Highest innings total for Ireland 281 for 4 v Middlesex (B&H) 1997
Highest innings total against Ireland 308 for 3 by Gloucestershire (B&H) 1996
Lowest innings total for Ireland 75 v Gloucestershire (NWT) 1981
Lowest innings total against Ireland 235 by Middlesex (B&H) 1997
Highest individual innings for Ireland 94* W.J. Cronje v Middlesex (B&H) 1997
Highest individual innings against Ireland 123 A.J. Wright for Gloucestershire (B&H) 1996
Highest wicket partnerships for Ireland

1st	72 J.D. Curry & W.K. McCallan	v	Middlesex	(B&H)	1997
2nd	45 J.D. Curry & D.A. Lewis	v	Middlesex	(B&H)	1997
3rd	52 M.F. Cohen & D.A. Lewis	v	Middlesex	(NWT)	1991
4th	69 W.J. Cronje & J.D.R. Benson	v	Middlesex	(B&H)	1997
5th	54 E.C. Joyce & A.R. Dunlop	v	Glamorgan	(B&H)	1998
6th	64 W.K. McCallan & D. Heasley	v	Nottinghamshire	(C&G)	2002

7th	32 W.K. McCallan & P.J.K. Mooney	v	Nottinghamshire	(C&G)	2002
8th	42 C. McCrum & C.J. Hoey	v	Durham	(NWT)	1992
9th	47 P. McCrum & C.J. Hoey	v	Middlesex	(NWT)	1991
10th	16 A.R. Dunlop & M.D. Dwyer	v	Shropshire	(NWT)	2000

Highest wicket partnerships against Ireland

1st	48 S.P. James & R.D.B. Croft	for	Glamorgan	(B&H)	1998
2nd	221 A.J. Wright & R.J. Cunliffe	for	Gloucestershire	(B&H)	1996
3rd	78 M.W. Gatting & M.R. Ramprakash	for	Middlesex	(NWT)	1991
4th	65 D.L. Maddy & V.J. Wells	for	Leicestershire	(NWT)	1999
5th	86 Imran Khan & I.J. Gould	for	Sussex	(NWT)	1983
6th	74 A.W. Stovold & P. Bainbridge	for	Gloucestershire	(NWT)	1981
7th	75* M.P. Briers & S.M. McEwan	for	Durham	(NWT)	1992
8th	48 P.A. Cottey & Waqar Younis	for	Glamorgan	(B&H)	1998
9th	47 A.R.C. Fraser & P.C.R. Tufnell	for	Middlesex	(B&H)	1997
10th	10 J. Ormond & M.T. Brimson	for	Leicestershire	(NWT)	1999

Best bowling performance in a match for Ireland 4 for 47 D.A. Lewis v Middlesex (NWT) 1991
Best bowling performance in a match against Ireland 5 for 11 D.A. Graveney for Gloucestershire (NWT) 1981
Largest crowd 4,000 v Middlesex (NWT) 1991

ONE-DAY INTERNATIONALS (including Bangladesh v West Indies 1999 WC)

Highest innings total for Ireland 226 for 9 v South Africa 1998
Highest innings total against Ireland 289 for 5 by South Africa 1998
Lowest innings total for Ireland 121 v Zimbabwe 2000
Lowest innings total against Ireland 182 by Bangladesh v West Indies 1999
Highest individual innings for Ireland 101* A.R. Dunlop v South Africa 1998
Highest individual innings against Ireland 163 S.F.A.F. Bacchus for West Indies 1980
Highest wicket partnerships for Ireland

1st	48 M.S. Reith & J.F. Short	v	West Indies	1980
2nd	42 N.D. Carson & S.G. Smyth	v	Australia A	1998
3rd	59 S.G. Smyth & S.R. Waugh	v	Australia A	1998
4th	64 M.E. Waugh & A.R. Dunlop	v	Zimbabwe	2000
5th	80 A.R. Dunlop & B.J. Archer	v	South Africa Academy XI	1999
6th	57 A.R. Dunlop & D. Heasley	v	South Africa	1998
7th	13 P.J.K. Mooney & G. Cooke	v	Zimbabwe	2000
8th	75 A.R. Dunlop & J.O. Davy	v	South Africa	1998
9th	20 A.R. Dunlop & J.A. Bushe	v	South Africa	1998
10th	24* A.R. Dunlop & M.D. Dwyer	v	South Africa	1998

Highest wicket partnerships against Ireland/including (WC) 1999

1st	17 C.G. Greenidge & S.F.A.F. Bacchus	for	West Indies	1980
	67 S.L. Campbell & R.D. Jacobs	for	West Indies v Bangladesh (WC)	1999
2nd	85 S.F.A.F. Baccus & A.I. Kallicharran	for	West Indies	1980
3rd	58 J.L. Ontong & A. Jacobs	for	South Africa Academy XI	1999
4th	97 A.D.R. Campbell & G.W. Flower	for	Zimbabwe	2000
5th	142 D.J. Cullinan & W.J. Cronje	for	South Africa	1998
6th	67 S.F.A.F. Baccus & D.R. Parry	for	West Indies	1980
7th	28 D.R. Parry & A.M.E. Roberts	for	West Indies	1980
8th	20* D.R. Parry & J. Garner	for	West Indies	1980
9th	2 Enamul Haque & Hasibul Hossein	for	Bangladesh v West Indies	1999
10th	0 Hasibul Hossein & Manjural Islam	for	Bangladesh v West Indies	1999

Best bowling performance in a match for Ireland 4 for 24 P.J.K. Mooney v Zimbabwe 2000
Best bowling performance in a match against Ireland 4 for 27 T. Henderson for South Africa Academy XI 1999 (4 for 25 C.A. Walsh for West Indies v Bangladesh 1999 (WC))
Largest crowd 3,339 Bangladesh v West Indies (WC) 1999

GROUND INFORMATION

ENTRANCE Walkway from Castle Avenue (players, officials, members, public, vehicles).
MEMBERS' ENCLOSURE Pavilion and G enclosure.
PUBLIC ENCLOSURE Rest of the ground A to F and H enclosures.
COVERED STANDS Pavilion.
OPEN STANDS A to G enclosures.
NAME OF ENDS Castle Close End, Walkway End.
GROUND DIMENSIONS 122m x 118m.
CAR PARKING FACILITIEs Adjacent to ground on rugby field.
CAPACITY 4,500.

HOW TO GET THERE

 Dart service from Dublin City station to Killester station.

 Dublin Buses 32, 44A and 54A and 130 from Dublin city centre to Castle Avenue.

 There are cycle routes from surrounding areas of Dublin to this area.

 The Clontarf CC ground is situated off Castle Avenue close to the junction with Kincora Grove, to the east of the city centre. **From north:** from M1, N1, N2 or N3 follow signs Dublin and city centre, then Howth for Clontarf and cricket ground. **From south:** from N7 or N11 follow signs Dublin and city centre, then as north. **From west:** N4 or N7 follow signs Dublin and city centre, then as north.

 Dublin International Airport ☎ 00 353 1 814 111, customer.relations-dublin@aer.rianta.ie

WHERE TO STAY

Forte Crest Hotel, Dublin Airport (☎ 00 353 1 437 9211), Clontarf Castle Hotel (☎ 00 353 1 833 2321), Clontarf Court Hotel (☎ 00 353 1 833 2680)

LOCAL RADIO STATION Radio One, 2FM, NEAR FM (101.6FM), FM104, 98FM, Newstalk 106

LOCAL NEWSPAPERS *Irish Times, Irish Independent*

INDOOR POWER CRICKET

CARDIFF MILLENNIUM STADIUM

Address Millennium Stadium, Westgate Street, Cardiff
☎ 02920 822 228
Web www.cardiff-stadium.co.uk

HISTORY OF GROUND AND FACILITIES

THE MILLENNIUM STADIUM IN CARDIFF staged the first Power Cricket Raise the Roof cricket challenge on 4 and 5 October 2002 between The Brits and The Rest of the World. The two matches were staged under floodlights and indoors. More than 12,000 people attended.

Rain never stops play and players even have the chance to score 8, 10 or 12 runs by hitting the ball up on to the middle, top and roof levels of the stadium.

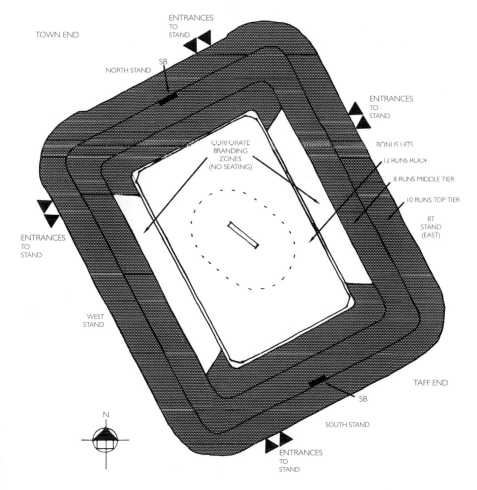

The cricket pitch is artificial and is laid out from south-east to north-west corner flag, diagonally across the centre of the stadium. The playing area is 126 metres by 79 metres and the two ends are the Town End (North Stand) and Taff End (South Stand).

Players who appeared in the competition in 2002 included for the Brits: Hussain (Captain), Jones, Maynard, Croft, Ealham, Crawley, Hollioake, Foster, Robin Smith, Irani, Fleming, Cork, Key, Fulton and Saggers. For the Rest of the World: Fleming (Captain), Walsh, Shahid Afridi, Wasim Akram, Azhar Mahmood, Muralitharan, Aravinda de Silva, Srinath, Mushtaq Ahmed, Mongia, Kaif, Andy Flower, Astle, Bond, Saqlain Mushtaq and Saeed Anwar.

Further competitions will be staged in 2003 in association with DP Cricket, Pertemps, the Millennium Stadium and BSkyB Sports.

The Millennium Stadium was built at a fixed-price contract of £99m by John Laing Construction plc and the first event staged here took place on 26 June 1999 when 29,000 witnessed the Wales v South Africa rugby international match. The ground's capacity is 73,434 and it has 125 hospitality boxes and 17 bars. The pitch is made up of a jigsaw of some 7,400 pallets which can be moved in and out of the stadium within a couple of days.

The stadium is also used for concerts, speedway, tennis, exhibitions, shows and association football, including Wales matches, the FA Cup Final, Division 1, 2 and 3 play-offs and the Worthington Cup Final.

Tours of the stadium can be made daily and operate from the shop near entrance Gate 3 in Westgate Street. The stadium is approximately 5 minutes walk from Cardiff Central station, 15 minutes walk from Glamorgan County Cricket Club's Sophia Gardens and on the site of Cardiff Arms Park Stadium. It is bounded to the north by Cardiff Rugby Club Ground.

GROUND INFORMATION

STANDS North Stand, South Stand, BT Stand (East) and West Stand.
NAME OF ENDS Town End and Taff End.

WHERE TO STAY

For where to stay in Cardiff see details in Glamorgan CCC section.

WOMEN'S CRICKET

ECB

England and Wales Cricket Board, Lord's Cricket Ground, London NW8 8QZ ☎ 020 7432 1200, fax 020 7286 5583

Executive Director Gill McConway
England Head Coach John Harmer
Captain Clare Connor

GROUNDS

The following venues are used for women's cricket in England and Wales:

SUPER FOURS FIXTURES

Loughborough University – see Loughborough UCCE section for details
Kings College, Taunton, no ☎ on ground
Reading CC (Sonning Lane) – see Berkshire section for details

TEST MATCHES

Shenley – see Middlesex section for details
Taunton – see Somerset section for details

ONE-DAY INTERNATIONALS

Chelmsford – see Essex section for details
Bristol – see Gloucestershire section for details
Cardiff – see Glamorgan section for details

OTHER MATCHES

Cambridge (Fenner's University Ground) – see Cambridge UCCE section for details

OTHER ASSOCIATED ORGANISATIONS

COMBINED SERVICES CRICKET ASSOCIATION

Secretary S.S. Frost
Address Army Sport Control Board, Clayton Barracks, Aldershot, Hampshire GU11 2BG
☎ 01252 348570
Fax 01252 348525

CRICKET CONFERENCES - CLUB CRICKET CONFERENCE

CEO B. Stuart-King
Address 361 West Barnes Lane, Motspur Park, New Malden, Surrey KT3 6JF
☎ 020 8336 0586
Fax 020 8336 0537

LEAGUE CRICKET CONFERENCE

Secretary N. Edwards
Address 1 Longfield, Freshfield, Formby, Merseyside L37 3LD
☎ 01704 877103

MIDLANDS CLUB CRICKET CONFERENCE

Secretary D. Thomas
Address 4 Silverdale Gardens, Wordsley, Stourbridge, West Midlands DY8 5NY
☎ 01384 278107

THE CRICKET FOUNDATION

Director T.N. Bates
Address ECB Offices, Lord's Cricket Ground, London NW8 8QZ
☎ 020 7432 1200
Fax 020 7266 4022

DANISH CRICKET ASSOCIATION

Vice Chairman S. Nissen
Address Idraettens Hus, 2605 Brondby, Denmark
☎ 0045 43 26 21 60
Fax 0045 43 26 21 63

EUROPEAN CRICKET COUNCIL

Development Manager I. Stuart
Address Europe Office, Lord's Cricket Ground, London NW8 8QN
☎ 020 7432 1019
Fax 020 7432 1091

INTERNATIONAL CRICKET COUNCIL

CEO M. Speed
Address The Clock Tower, Lord's Cricket Ground, London NW8 8QN
☎ 020 7266 1818
Fax 020 7266 1777

KNCB

CEO A. de la Mar
Address Nieuwe Kalfjeslaan 21B, 1182 AA Amstelveen, The Netherlands
☎ 00 31 20 645 1705
Fax 00 31 20 645 1715

MINOR COUNTIES CRICKET ASSOCIATION

Secretary G.R. Evans
Address Details as per Devon CCC section of book

MINOR COUNTIES WEB

Minor Counties Web www.mcca.cricket.org
Grounds Luton Town CC (see Bedfordshire CCC section for details), The Boundary Organisation, Milton Keynes (see Buckinghamshire CCC section for details)

PROFESSIONAL CRICKETERS' ASSOCIATION

Managing Director R. Bevan
Address 3rd Floor, 338 Euston Road, London NW1 3BT
☎ 020 7544 8660
Fax 020 7544 8515

OTHER USEFUL TELEPHONE NUMBERS AND WEBSITES

WEATHER INFORMATION AA Weatherwatch 09003 401100, www.bbc.co.uk/weather, www.weather.co.uk

TRAVEL INFORMATION www.ukpti.org.uk – The UK Public Travel Information site, covers air, rail, bus services nationwide
AA Roadwatch (Traffic News) ☎ 0870 550 0600 (members), 09003 401100 (non-members) (calls charged at 60p per minute)
RAC Traffic Alert ☎ 0906 470 1740 (calls charged between 35p to 60p per minute)
Cycling Touring Club ☎ 0800 243 731, www.ctc.org.uk.

HOW TO GET THERE

Road directions have been included where possible, but it should be noted that there are permanent signs directing motorists to the Test and County grounds. Where matches are being played on local grounds, there are usually temporary AA signs to the ground.

BIBLIOGRAPHY

Hignell, A.K., *Rain Stops Play*, 2002
Meynell, L.W., *Famous Cricket Grounds*, 1951
Peebles, I., *The Watney Book of Test Match Grounds*, 1967
Plumtree, G., *Homes of Cricket*, 1987
Sampson, A., *Grounds of Appeal*, 1980
Wisden Book of County Cricket, The
Wisden Book of Cricket Records, The
Wisden Book of One-Day International Cricket 1971–1985, The
Wisden Book of Test Cricket 1877–2001, The
Wisden Cricketers' Almanack 1864–2002
Yardley, N. and J.M. Kilburn, *Homes of Sport: Cricket*, 1952

PERIODICALS

Cricket Weekly Record
Cricket World and *The Club Cricketer*
Minor Counties Cricket Quarterly
Playfair Cricket Monthly
The Cricketer and *The Cricketer Quarterly*
Wisden Cricket Monthly

ABOUT THE AUTHOR

BORN IN LAHORE in 1964, William Powell is the acknowledged expert on cricket grounds in the United Kingdom. He is an avid club player and has represented The Cricket Society, Gentlemen of Hertfordshire, Vic Lewis, King's Langley, Watford Town, Budleigh Salterton and Rye CCs. He was a committee member of King's Langley CC aged 15 and is now a Vice President. He acted as Official Scorer to the Pakistan and Sri Lankan touring teams in England in 1987 and 1988. He has also played and watched cricket widely in Australia, Pakistan, South Africa, West Indies and USA.

A project management consultant, he is a fellow of the Chartered Institute of Building and a fellow of the Royal Society of Arts and is presently completing post-graduate studies in Information Technology.

He is a member of MCC, Middlesex, Surrey and Hertfordshire CCCs, The Cricket Society, The Cricket Writers' Club, The Cricketers' Club of London, The Primary Club, The Cricket Memorabilia Society and The Association of Cricket Statisticians and Historians.

A regular visitor to all the grounds included in this book, he has expanded and updated his previous ground guides to include all venues used for ECB matches in 2003. This is his nineteenth book and his fifth on cricket grounds to have been published since 1989.